CONQUISTADORS
WITHOUT SWORDS

*An account
with original narratives*

CONQUISTADORS WITHOUT SWORDS

ARCHAEOLOGISTS IN THE AMERICAS

LEO DEUEL

SCHOCKEN BOOKS • NEW YORK

First SCHOCKEN PAPERBACK edition 1974

Copyright © 1967 by Leo Deuel
Library of Congress Catalog Card No. 74–10153

Manufactured in the United States of America

To my mother and sister

Acknowledgments

In preparing this book I have enjoyed the assistance of a number of people and institutions, several of whom are named in the textual and pictorial acknowledgments. Mrs. Madeleine Edmondson offered sound advice on the entire manuscript. A special word of mention should be said of the expert editorial services rendered by Miss Ellie Kurtz. The few graces in style and presentation owe much to her sensitive skill. The typescript was examined by Professor Muriel Noé Porter of Hunter College, who made several invaluable suggestions. Needless to say, any shortcomings are my full responsibility.

L. D.
New York City

Foreword

Six years ago a book of mine appeared on the contribution of archaeology to our knowledge of the ancient Near East. In it I joined original narratives by pioneer explorers with my own interpretive text. One American critic expressed the hope that I would repeat "this trick" for other areas of the world. One field that had always tempted me was the pre-history of the Americas. Little realizing the tremendous scope of the subject, I began sleuthing through an endless bulk of literature and sought to gain insights into the problems connected with the recovery of the pre-Columbian past. As in the earlier volume, I set myself the goal of placing specific discoveries within a general framework of cumulative research.

The Western Hemisphere offers particular attractions, challenges, and rewards to the study of archaeology. Sealed off physically and intellectually from the mainstream of mankind, the twin continents seem to have run through the ages and phases of cultural evolution like a separate planet bound on an independent course. Unaccounted by the Old World, American aboriginals themselves lacked comprehensive written records with which to recapitulate their past from the dimmest beginnings to official "discovery" in 1492. They had only the vaguest notions of their forefathers, let alone of their origins and career in the vast lands. Traces of even the most recent achievements were wantonly wiped out by pale-faced conquerors from across the eastern seas. Never before had entire civilizations been so suddenly cut off and so thoroughly destroyed. By the sixteenth century the days of Indian America were not only over; to the few who cared, they were largely beyond recall.

Material remains—buried or on the surface—have been the source of almost everything we know about the ancient peoples of the Americas. Hence archaeology's unique role. American archaeology, in contrast to that of the Old World, from its start was total archaeology, and not just ancillary to classical studies or a supplementary technique of historiographic and philological investigations. The history of the Americas before the Spanish Conquest had to be written mainly with the spade.

Though in close association with anthropology—of which it is sometimes considered a branch—archaeology alone staged the recovery of pre-Columbian yesterdays, digging up unnamed cultures and cities, tracing the footsteps, filling out gaps, piecing together fragments and artifacts; but only in its fairly recent phases coming to draw upon many other disciplines from geology and botany to atomic physics, palaeontology, climatology, and linguistics (glottochronology, lexicostatistics). Where Cortés and Pizarro conquered with the sword, despoiled for gold, and, in the name of the Cross, suppressed the religious cults, arts, and societies of highly advanced peoples, archaeologists proceeded on no less imperial a road. Theirs is the triumph of the peaceful reconquest of the Americas before Columbus. They are the New Conquistadors.

The search for human pre-history in the Americas has occupied men since Columbus landed in the Bahamas. The New World and its inhabitants—ancient and modern—have been the subject of a great debate. Men of reckless, speculative bent eagerly advanced grandiose theories, while other men went down to earth and began the patient examination of physical evidence. Even though responsible archaeological analysis has lately gained the upper hand, controversies over ancient America persist, and continue to stimulate research. American archaeology, therefore, is not just toil and dust, tombs and potsherds, but an adventure of ideas.

It is the purpose of my book to recount the story of these archaeological recoveries and adventures, with a stress on modern advances and the lively discussions they never cease to arouse. Excavations, particularly in the last fifty years—accelerated after World War II by radiocarbon dating methods and other technological aids—have come up with successful answers to such hotly argued questions as the origin and racial affinities of the Indians, their relative antiquity and migration routes, their contemporaneity with Pleistocene mammoths, mastodons, and other beasts which they hunted, their transition from food gatherers and hunters to sedentary farmers, and the foci of their earliest civilizations. Peoples in some respects more creative than the Aztecs, Mayas, and Incas, whom they preceded, have been rescued from limbo, among them the "Olmecs" of Mexico and the Chavín and Moche of the Andean region of South America.

However, epochal discoveries have made American archaeology anything but a closed science. While the evidence is mounting for contacts by sea between the two culturally parallel centers of "Nuclear America"— roughly greater Mexico ("Mesoamerica") and Peru ("Central Andes")— opposing partisanship still marks views of the relation between them and the priority of one or the other in the introduction of agriculture, pottery, certain religious cults, and art styles.

When it comes to perhaps the most crucial problem of all—the first impulse to civilization, be it in Middle or South America—controversy increases in proportion to the inconclusiveness or incompleteness of new evidence. "Diffusionists" or "interventionists," who believe in Old World seeds carried somehow across the Pacific (few favor the Atlantic), battle with the "isolationists," who fervently maintain that Americans did it all by themselves without the slightest outside influence. In recent years, the pendulum has swung toward the diffusionists, and excavations in Ecuador (foremost those of the husband-and-wife team of Betty J. Meggers and Clifford Evans, Jr.) indicate the landing of East Asiatic parties as early as the second millennium B.C. Whatever the eventual verdict, the originality, inventiveness, and uniqueness of native American civilizations will continue to provoke archaeological warfare.

We are still far from certain where maize was first cultivated. Was the domestication of plants begun separately and simultaneously at several places? Do some of the crude choppers or pebble tools (Alex D. Krieger's "pre-projectile points") come from Palaeolithic men who trod the American soil ten thousands of years before the now fully recognized makers of the fine jasper spear points like Sandia, Clovis, and Folsom of a mere twenty-five to ten thousand years ago? Did Neanderthal ever reach America? What was the cultural baggage of the various waves of "Indians" coming across Bering Strait into the New World? Could the skill of making cord-marked pottery have entered the Western Hemisphere both via the Bering route and across the Pacific on ships from Japan? Despite the decipherment of Maya time counts and Mixtec annals and the invention of several sophisticated dating methods, American chronology remains almost as elusive as the concepts of time in an esoteric modern novel.

"The hour of the archaeologist," as a French scholar has observed, "has hardly begun in South America." The same can be said for the entire hemisphere. All the present findings may well be corrected some day, if not reversed. A survey of American archaeology—from American man's primitive ancestors to the glittering civilizations on the eve of the Spanish Conquest—must point out the fluidity and poverty of our knowledge as much as its richness, novelty, and growth; it should aim at anything but an illusory completeness. I have selected what appeared to me to be salient problems and key discoveries. A sense of participation and authenticity is the reward of reading original narratives: techniques, temperament, and approach of individual excavators become comprehensible as in no other way. The range in pre-Columbian time and in geographic space—from the Arctic to Patagonia—is of course enormous. It made drastic selectivity as mandatory as it was agonizing. Selection always amounts to a compromise, if not a prejudice. Regretfully I have had to leave out such three-star places on the archaeological map of America as Tikal or Bonampak of the Maya, Huaca Prieta or Sacsahuamán in Peru, San Agustín in Colombia, La Perra Cave in Tamaulipas, Mexico, and the Gallina towers or the Kuaua murals of the U.S. Southwest—to name just a few at random.

This then is a book of conquest and of conquerors. Though voices of austere scientists are presently being raised against a misplaced stress on human interest and on individual discoveries, and though oddball explorers' hackneyed adventures and thrills may frequently be overdone in the popular literature, it must be realized that much of American archaeology belonged to a pre-scientific age and was developed by dedicated individuals rather than squads from university departments or research institutions. Besides, archaeology not only reconquers history, but has a history of its own, the varied phases of which deserve to be recorded. My selections were not chosen for romantic entertainment or bizarre sensationalism, but rather for their intrinsic importance—as well as their readability. This compilation confines itself to actual accounts of original research. Despite inevitable lacunae, I strove to make the roster of investigators extensive and representative, though for the lack of suitable material or because of duplication—not to speak of limits of space—a host of leading savants had to be omitted: Eduard Seler, Antonio León y Gama, Antonio Peñafiel, A. F. Bandelier, Luis E. Valcárcel, Julio Tello, A. P. Maudslay, Max Uhle, Wendell C. Bennett, J. Eric S. Thompson, J. L. Giddings, Jr., and others.

One of the inherent difficulties beyond any anticipated when I started out on my documentary research, was that quite a few of the men mainly responsible for the great advances in our knowledge of the pre-Columbian past simply lack the broad humanistic and literary background so conspicuous among Old World archaeologists. First-hand narratives are actually few and far between. A majority of important discoveries are reported only in the dullest of technical papers, or are rendered in such a generalized manner that they lose all concreteness for the average reader. However, in one area—the study of the Mayas—the tradition of "writing up" popular accounts has been well established since Stephens in the mid-nineteenth century; several of my Maya selections are widely known and have been reprinted before. The preponderance of the Mayas, both in archaeological investigation and in popular imagination, simply could not be slighted, but I made an effort to include unpublished and less familiar records. With all selections, original style, spellings, and punctuation have been retained insofar as comprehension would permit.

Apart from projecting a sense of the excitement and wonder of restoring Indian America, still another basic concern was to emphasize continuity. The texts were chosen to tell a coherent story and they add up to an outline history, no matter how incomplete, of American archaeology. They are grouped along simultaneously regional, historical, and chronological lines. Both in time and in place, a beginning had to be made somewhere. Somewhat arbitrarily perhaps, I decided to start with Peru and the arrival of Alexander von Humboldt, the "new Columbus," on the scene at the end of the eighteenth century. Geographically this enables us to move northward into the Isthmus, the Mexican plateau, Mayaland, and, finally, into North America proper. Within each regional focus, selections follow more or less chronologically the order of investigations. In the sixth section, the strictly regional pattern is abandoned to permit hemispheric glimpses of researches concerning migration and origin of the earliest Americans. Such probing leads us into the archaeology of the Greenland and American Eskimo and their circumpolar affinities with Eurasia, and finally to the Viking footholds in the Western Hemisphere.

No mere collection of narrative excerpts can encompass both the immediacy of fieldwork and the place of isolated discoveries in the larger body of scientific knowledge. To give depth to the original material—as I did in *The Treasures of Time*—I have prefaced each selection with an essay devoted to background and interpretation. It is my hope that in this highly selective summary of what we have come to know about American antiquities, the reader will find a fresh view of the New World—a world virtually of the Stone Age, which in 1492 might have been closer to ancient Egypt or Babylon than to Renaissance Europe, but which archaeology is increasingly making a vital part of our common heritage.

Contents

Figures

Maps and Plans

Plates*

*All plates follow page 314; some captions refer to a grouping of plates.

PART I

ANDEAN SOUTH AMERICA

Archaeological sites and regions of Peru (Central Andes)

1

In March 1799 a young German baron appeared before the Spanish king Charles IV at Aranjuez. Barely thirty, but already renowned for his researches in natural history and for several works on botany, physiology, and geology, Alexander von Humboldt charmed the sovereign into granting him unlimited access to the Spanish colonies in the New World in order to carry out scientific investigations. He was given that rarest of privileges, a passport issued by the Spanish crown, without any qualification but for the pledge to provide the royal collections with scientific specimens.

Notoriously suspicious and wary of foreign ideologies, the monarchs of Spain had for a long time maintained a *cordon sanitaire* around their overseas possessions. As a result, first-hand knowledge of the vast American lands was hard to obtain. Sound descriptions of their fauna, flora, and topography were in short supply, and what had filtered down about their antiquities was a hodgepodge of hearsay, speculations, and misconceptions. No wonder European savants of the Enlightenment had come to discount almost categorically the reports of Conquistadores and missionaries, with their fanciful descriptions of indigenous cities and monuments. The fashion was to dismiss all pre-Columbian natives as barbarians, to deny their ability to advance beyond such lowly state.

Alexander von Humboldt's stay in the Americas was a turning point. His aristocratic background and multiple connections helped his undertaking. He himself acknowledged his debt to the Saxonian minister at Madrid. But what made his five-year trek across South America, Cuba, Mexico, and part of the United States so productive were his unusual talents. It has been said that he was the last man to have a grasp of all the sciences down to every detail and recent discovery. His contemporaries considered him the only equal of Goethe. Indeed Goethe, a worshipful friend of the younger man, said once that "the extraordinary men of the sixteenth and seventeenth centuries were academies in themselves, as Humboldt is in our time."

Prussian-born Humboldt's scientific career began with mineralogical and geological studies, and his first appointment was as an inspector of mines. But a restless temperament and a boundless curiosity made him give up a promising future in state service, and soon he was ranging over Europe, exploring rocks, plant life, air pressure, galvanism, and astronomical and other natural phenomena. Already there unfolded before him the vision of a great synthesis—laid down decades later in his summa physica, the *Kosmos,* in which he traced the relationships, if not the harmonies, that exist on Earth between plants and animals, climate, and physical environment. During a residence in Paris, he cast about for a faraway country in which to take the pulse of nature. A project to go to Egypt and India fell through because of Napoleonic schemes in that part of the world. Soon, however, the idea of American travels had taken possession of Humboldt, and he knew he had found his true element.

America—north, south, and center—was attuned to Humboldt as he was to the Western Hemisphere. Humboldt himself felt it from the very beginning when the Spanish corvette *Pizarro* out from Coruña dropped anchor off the coast of New Andalusia (part of modern Venezuela) and he spotted his first Indian—a tall, bronzed, muscular statue of a man, without any of the "extreme feebleness" he had been led to expect in that race. Even before he presented his papers to the Spanish governor, as the ship's captain urged him to do, he followed the native to his settlement at the fringe of the primeval forest, where he inhaled the aroma of exotic flowers. The American tropics fascinated him. To cross for months on end the torrid zone of jungles replete with jaguars, mosquitoes, morbid miasmas, savages, and extreme heat came to him as naturally as to hike in the fir-clad hills of Thuringia. Indeed, he declared, he never felt better, never as alive and stimulated. And he reacted likewise to the chill *páramos* and *punas* of the uplands: he was the first to climb Chimborazo in Ecuador, then believed to be the world's highest peak. All the time he collected, observed, measured, sketched, and took notes. Spanish viceroys, Creole noblemen, Hispano-American scholars, and men of kindred universality such as Thomas Jefferson sought his company. Wherever he went he was welcomed, and his prodigious labors to add to the knowledge of Western lands were immediately appreciated. In later years he loved to refer to himself as half-American. Americans from the Pacific Northwest to Patagonia have paid him tribute by naming mountains, lakes, rivers, counties, and an ocean current after him. Not only did Humboldt's studies—which took some twenty years to be published in authoritative volumes—open the Americas to American and European scientists, but his researches had immense practical consequences, from exploitation of mines and natural fertilizers to political and social reforms. His liberal and humanitarian ideals inspired independence movements in Latin America. The finest tribute to Humboldt *Americanus* came from the Liberator Simón Bolívar, who said, "the New World owes more to him than all the Conquistadores put together."

Humboldt's ardor for all things American led him to probe yet another field which was hardly within his original ken. This was the pre-Columbian past. It is a token of the man's versatility that from his initial contacts with natives he was alerted to the riddles of Indian origins and achievements. Though the subject had aroused the interest of a few foreign and American-born savants, it was Humboldt who awakened the learned world to the study of transatlantic civilizations and who wrote the first systematic treatise on American antiquities, *Vues de Cordillères et Monuments des Peuples Indigènes de l'Amérique* (1814), to which were appended splendid illustrations of landscapes, pyramids, statues, and picture codices—most of them based on his own drawings. Written in French, the work was translated into several languages, and lit a spark in many a young man: William H. Prescott, the Boston historian of the conquests of Mexico and Peru, John Lloyd Stephens, the rediscoverer of the Maya ruins, and such pioneers as France's Abbé Brasseur de Bourbourg and Germany's Eduard Seler.

According to Humboldt's own testimony, the discovery of pictographs deep in the jungle of the Rio Negro, a tributary of the Amazon, decisively turned his mind to ancient America. From then on the track led him to calendrical notations on stone slabs in the Colombian highlands, and to a sixteenth-century account, in an Indian language but Latin script, of native glories before the Conquest. The aboriginal languages themselves absorbed him; their ability to express subtle concepts and abstractions was to him ample proof of the high level of intelligence and cultural progress among the Indians. Could these idioms also offer a clue to the roots of the native populations and their possible affinities with eastern Asia? In posing such questions Humboldt often saw far ahead of later generations of archaeologists. And particularly in Mexico, where he carried out his most extensive researches, he was to anticipate discoveries of a later phase of scholarship such as the finding of a substratum of "archaic" farmers or the recognition that the building of the Teotihuacán pyramids preceded the accession of the Toltecs in central Mexico. He even suspected Australoid characteristics among certain Indian tribes.

Humboldt's active archaeological investigations—though they played second fiddle to his observations in the natural sciences—began in the Andean region once ruled by the vast Inca empire that shortly before the Spanish conquest had extended for more than two thousand miles from the southern reaches of modern Colombia into northern Argentina and

Chile. When Humboldt arrived in Quito from Colombia he had been in the New World for more than two years. During his six-month stay in this second capital of the Incas, he observed at a convent architectural remains of massive edifices characteristic of those pre-Columbian builders, and thereupon set up his easel to make a drawing which has been hailed as "the first really architecturally accurate plan of an Inca structure." On the inland road from Ecuador to Peru, evidences of Inca power cropped up again and again—several never described before. Humboldt's sketches of imposing fortresses have become a valuable record.

Penetrating into the Inca heartland, the young German scholar came to feel fully the omnipresence of the vanquished master race of the Andes. Once Humboldt and his party emerged from a seventeen-day detour into the Amazon Valley, they could see for themselves the stupendous Inca road system and the proliferation of buildings connected with it.

Capture of Atahualpa, after an early colonial manuscript by Poma de Ayala

Everything the sixteenth-century conquerors had said about the highways
—superior in some respects to those of the Romans—was true. For Humboldt the highways evoked the might of the Inca militarists. They also
marked the direction to Cajamarca, the melancholy site of the last ruling
Inca's humiliation and execution at the hands of bearded invaders. Here
Humboldt met a youth, an alleged descendant of the Incas, who was to
initiate him into the local traditions of buried Inca treasure.

ON TO CAJAMARCA

Alexander von Humboldt

After having sojourned for a whole year on the ridge of the Andes,
between 4° north and 4° south latitude, amidst the tablelands of New
Granada, Pastos, and Quito, and consequently at an elevation varying
between 8,500 and 13,000 feet above the level of the sea, it is delightful to
descend gradually through the more genial climate of the Cinchona or
Quina Woods of Loxa [Loja] into the plains of the Upper Amazon. There
an unknown world unfolds itself, rich in magnificent vegetation. . . .

Descending from the mountain node of Loxa, south-southeast into the
hot valley of the Amazon River, the traveller passes over the *páramos* of
Chulucanas, Guamani, and Yamoca. These *páramos* are the mountainous
deserts, which . . . in the southern parts of the Andes are known by the
name of *puna*, a word belonging to the Quechua language. In most places,
their elevation is about 10,125 feet. They are stormy, frequently enveloped for several successive days in thick fogs, or visited by terrific hailstorms; the hailstones being not only of different forms, generally much
flattened by rotation, but also run together into thin floating plates of ice
called *papa-cara*, which cut the face and hands in their fall. During this
meteoric process, I have sometimes known the thermometer to sink to 48°
and even 43° Fahrenheit, and the electric tension of the atmosphere,
measured by the voltaic electrometer, has changed, in the space of a few

From *Views of Nature or contemplation on the sublime phenomena of creation with scientific illustrations*, translated from the German by E. C. Otté and Henry G. Bohn. London: Henry G. Bohn, 1850, pp. 392-414 *passim*.

minutes, from positive to negative. When the temperature is below 43° Fahrenheit, snow falls in large flakes, scattered widely apart; but it disappears after the lapse of a few hours. The short thin branches of the small leaved myrtle-like shrubs, the large size and luxuriance of the blossoms, and the perpetual freshness caused by the absorption of the moist atmosphere—all impart a peculiar aspect and character to the treeless vegetation of the *páramos*. No zone of alpine vegetation, whether in temperate or cold climates, can be compared with that of the *páramos* in the tropical Andes.

The solemn impression which is felt on beholding the deserts of the Cordilleras, is increased in a remarkable and unexpected manner by the circumstance that in these very regions there still exist wonderful remains of the great road of the Incas, that stupendous work by means of which communication was maintained among all the provinces of the empire along an extent of upwards of 1,000 geographical miles. On the sides of this road, and nearly at equal distances apart, there are small houses, built of well-cut freestone. These buildings, which answered the purpose of stations, or caravanseries, are called *tambos,* and also Inca-Pilca (from Pirca, the wall). Some are surrounded by a sort of fortification; others were destined for baths, and had arrangements for the conveyance of warm water: the larger ones were intended exclusively for the family of the sovereign. At the foot of the volcano Cotopaxi, near Callo, I had previously seen buildings of the same kind in a good state of preservation. These I accurately measured, and made drawings from them. Pedro de Cieza [de León], who wrote in the sixteenth century, calls these structures *aposentos de mulalo.*

The pass of the Andes, lying between Alausi and Loxa, called the Páramo del Assuay, a much frequented route across the Ladera de Cadlud, is at the elevation of 15,526 feet above the level of the sea, and consequently almost at the height of Mont Blanc. As we were proceeding through this pass, we experienced considerable difficulty in guiding our heavily laden mules over the marshy ground on the level height of the Pullal; but whilst we journeyed onward for the distance of about four miles, our eyes were continually rivetted on the grand remains of the Inca road, upwards of 20 feet in breadth. This road had a deep under-structure, and was paved with well-hewn blocks of black trap porphyry. None of the Roman roads which I have seen in Italy, in the south of France and in Spain, appeared to me more imposing than this work of the ancient Peruvians; and the Inca road is the more extraordinary since, according to my barometrical calculations, it is situated at an elevation of 13,258 feet above the level of the sea, a height exceeding that of the summit of the Peak of Teneriffe by upwards of 1,000 feet. At an equal elevation, are the ruins said to be those of the palace of the Inca Tupac Yupanqui, and known by the name of the Paredones del Inca, situated on the Assuay. From these ruins the Inca road, running southward in the direction of Cuenca, leads to the small but well-preserved fortress of the Cañar, probably belonging to the same period, viz.: the reign of Tupac Yupanqui, or that of his warlike son Huayna Capac.

"House of the Inca" at Callo (Ecuador), after a drawing by Alexander von Humboldt

We saw still grander remains of the ancient Peruvian Inca road, on our way between Loxa and the Amazon, near the baths of the Incas on the Páramo of Chulucanas, not far from Guancabamba, and also in the vicinity of Ingatambo, near Pomahuaca. The ruins at the latter place are situated so low, that I found the difference of level between the Inca road at Pomahuaca, and that in the Páramo del Assuay, to be upwards of 9,700 feet. The distance in a direct line, as determined by astronomical latitudes, is precisely 184 miles; and the ascent of the road is about 3,730 feet greater than the elevation of the Pass of Mont Cenis, above the Lake of Como. There are two great causeways, paved with flat stones, and in some places covered with cemented gravel on Macadam's plan. One of these lines of road runs through the broad and barren plain lying between the sea-coast and the chain of the Andes, whilst the other passes along the ridge of the Cordilleras. Stones, marking the distances at equal intervals, are frequently seen. The rivulets and ravines were crossed by bridges of three kinds; some being of stone, some of wood, and others of rope. These bridges were called by the Peruvians, *puentes de hamaca* or *puentes de maroma.* There were also aqueducts for conveying water to the *tambos* and fortresses. Both lines of road were directed to Cuzco, the central point and capital of the great Peruvian empire, situated in 13° 31' south lat., and according to Pentland's Map of Bolivia, at the elevation of 11,378 feet above the level of the sea. As the Peruvians had no wheeled carriages, these roads were constructed for the march of troops, for the conveyance of burthens borne by men, and for flocks of lightly laden llamas; consequently, long flights of steps, with resting places, were formed at intervals in the steep parts of the mountains. Francisco Pizarro and Diego Almagro, in their expeditions to remote parts of the country, availed themselves with much advantage of the military roads of the Incas; but the steps just mentioned were formidable impediments in the way of the Spanish cavalry, especially as in the early period of the Conquista, the Spaniards rode horses only, and did not make use of the sure-footed mule, which, in mountainous precipices, seems to reflect on every step he takes. It was only at a later period that the Spanish troops were mounted on mules.

Sarmiento, who saw the Inca roads whilst they were in a perfect state of preservation, mentions them in a *Relación* which he wrote, and which long lay buried in the Library of the Escorial. "How," he asks, "could a people, unacquainted with the use of iron, have constructed such great and magnificent roads (*caminos tan grandes, y tan sovervios*), and in regions so elevated as the countries between Cuzco and Quito, and between Cuzco and the coast of Chili? The Emperor Charles," he adds, "with all his power, could not have accomplished even a part of what was done by the well-directed Government of the Incas, and the obedient race of people under its rule." Hernando Pizarro, the most educated of the three brothers, who expiated his misdeeds by twenty years of captivity in Medina del Campo, and who died at 100 years of age, in the odour of sanctity (*en olor de Santidad*), observes, alluding to the Inca roads: "Throughout the whole of Christendom, no such roads are to be seen as those which we here admire." Cuzco and Quito, the two principal capitals of the Incas, are situated in a direct line south-southeast, north-northwest in reference the one to the other. Their distance apart, without calculating the many windings of the road, is 1,000 miles; including the windings of the road, the distance is stated by Garcilaso de la Vega, and other Conquistadores, to be "500 Spanish *leguas*." Notwithstanding this vast distance, we are informed, on the unquestionable testimony of the Licentiate Polo de Ondegardo, that Huayna Capac, whose father conquered Quito, caused certain materials to be conveyed thither from Cuzco, for the erection of the royal buildings (the Inca dwellings). In Quito, I found this tradition still current among the natives.

When, in the form of the earth, nature presents to man formidable difficulties to contend against, those very difficulties serve to stimulate the energy and courage of enterprising races of people. Under the despotic centralizing system of the Inca Government, security and rapidity of communication, especially in relation to the movement of troops, were matters of urgent state necessity. Hence the construction of great roads, and the establishment of very excellent postal arrangements by the Peruvians. Among nations in the most various degrees of civilization, national energy is frequently observed to manifest itself, as it were by preference, in some special direction; but the advancement consequent on this sort of partial exertion, however strikingly exhibited, by no means affords a criterion of the general cultivation of a people. Egyptians, Greeks, Etruscans, and Romans, Chinese, Japanese, and Indians present examples of these contrasts. It would be difficult to determine what space of time may have been occupied in the execution of the Peruvian roads. Those great works, in the northern part of the Inca Empire, on the tableland of Quito, must certainly have been completed in less than thirty or thirty-five years; that is to say, in the short interval between the defeat of the ruler of Quito and the death of the Inca Huayna Capac. With respect to the southern, or those specially styled the Peruvian roads, the period of their formation is involved in complete obscurity. . . .

The early Spanish Conquistadores were filled with admiration on first beholding the roads and aqueducts of the Peruvians; yet not only did they neglect the preservation of those great works, but they even wantonly destroyed them. As a natural consequence of the destruction of the aqueducts, the soil was rendered unfertile by the want of irrigation. Nevertheless, those works, as well as the roads, were demolished for the sake of obtaining stones ready hewn for the erection of new buildings; and the traces of this devastation are more observable near the sea-coast than on the ridges of the Andes or in the deeply cleft valleys with which that mountain-chain is intersected. During our long day's journey from the syenitic rocks of Zaulac to the valley of San Felipe (rich in fossil remains and situated at the foot of the icy Páramo of Yamoca), we had no less than twenty-seven times to ford the Río de Guancabamba, which falls into the Amazon. We were compelled to do this on account of the numerous sinuosities of the stream, whilst on the brow of a steep precipice near us, we had continually within our sight the vestiges of the rectilinear Inca road with its *tambos.* The little mountain stream, the Río de Guancabamba, is not more than from 120 to 150 feet broad; yet so strong is the current, that our heavily laden mules were in continual danger of being swept away by it. The mules carried our manuscripts, our dried plants, and all the other objects which we had been a whole year engaged in collecting; therefore, every time that we crossed the stream, we stood on one of the banks in a state of anxious suspense until the long train of our beasts of burthen, eighteen or twenty in number, were fairly out of danger. . . .

Having at length reached the last of these mountain wildernesses, the

Páramo de Yanaguanga, the traveller joyfully looks down into the fertile valley of Caxamarca [Cajamarca]. It presents a charming prospect, for the valley, through which winds a little serpentine rivulet, is an elevated plain of an oval form, in extent from 96 to 112 square miles. The plain bears a resemblance to that of Bogotá, and like it is probably the bed of an ancient lake; but in Caxamarca there is wanting the myth of the miracle-working Botchia, or Idacanzas, the High Priest of Iraca, who opened a passage for the waters through the rocks of Tequendama. Caxamarca lies 640 feet higher than Santa Fé de Bogotá, and consequently its elevation is equal to that of the city of Quito; but being sheltered by surrounding mountains, its climate is much more mild and agreeable. The soil of Caxamarca is extraordinarily fertile. . . .

Overseer of the Inca highways, with way stations and storehouses, Poma de Ayala

Small mounds, or hillocks, of porphyry (once perhaps islands in the ancient lake) are studded over the northern part of the plain, and break the wide expanse of smooth sandstone. From the summit of one of these porphyry hillocks, we enjoyed a most beautiful prospect of the Cerro de Santa Polonia. The ancient residence of Atahuallpa is on this side, surrounded by fruit gardens, and irrigated fields of lucern (*Medicago sativa*), called by the people here *campos de alfalfa*. In the distance are seen columns of smoke, rising from the warm baths of Pultamarca, which still bear the name of Baños del Inca. I found the temperature of these sulphuric springs to be 156.2° F. Atahuallpa was accustomed to spend a portion of each year at these baths, where some slight remains of his palace have survived the ravages of the Conquistadores. The large deep basin or reservoir (*el tragadero*) for supplying these baths with water appeared to me, judging from its regular circular form, to have been artificially cut in the sandstone rock, over one of the fissures whence the spring flows. Tradition records that one of the Inca's sedan-chairs, made of gold, was sunk in this basin, and that all endeavours to recover it have proved vain.

Of the fortress and palace of Atahuallpa, there also remain but a few vestiges in the town, which now contains some beautiful churches. Even before the close of the sixteenth century, the thirst for gold accelerated the work of destruction, for, with the view of discovering hidden treasures, walls were demolished and the foundations of buildings recklessly undermined. The Inca's palace is situated on a hill of porphyry, which was originally cut and hollowed out from the surface, completely through the rock, so that the latter surrounds the main building like a wall. Portions of the ruins have been converted to the purposes of a town jail and a Municipal Hall (Casa del Cabildo). The most curious parts of these ruins, which however are not more than between 13 and 16 feet in height, are those opposite to the monastery of San Francisco. These vestiges, like the remains of the dwelling of the Caciques, consist of finely-hewn blocks of freestone, two or three feet long, laid one upon another without cement, as in the Inca-Pilca, or fortress of the Cañar, in the high plain of Quito.

In the porphyritic rock there is a shaft which once led to subterraneous chambers and into a gallery (by miners called a stoll) from which, it is alleged, there was a communication with the other porphyritic rocks already mentioned—those situated at Santa Polonia. These arrangements bear evidence of having been made as precautions against the events of war, and for the security of flight. The burying of treasure was a custom very generally practised among the Peruvians in former times; and subterraneous chambers still exist beneath many private dwellings in Caxamarca.

We were shown some steps cut in the rock, and the foot-bath used by the Inca (*el lavatorio de los pies*). The operation of washing the sovereign's feet was performed amidst tedious court ceremonies. Several lateral structures, which, according to tradition, were allotted to the attendants of the Inca, are built some of freestone with gable roofs, and others of regularly shaped bricks, alternating with layers of siliceous cement. The building constructed in this last-mentioned style, to which the Peruvians give the name of *muros y obra de tapia*, have little arched niches or recesses. Of their antiquity I was for a long time doubtful, though I am now convinced that my doubts were not well-grounded.

In the principal building, the room is still shown in which the unfortunate Atahuallpa was confined for the space of nine months, from the date of November 1532. The notice of the traveller is still directed to the wall, on which he made a mark to denote to what height he would fill the room with gold, on condition of his being set free. . . .

Descendants of the Inca still dwell in Caxamarca, amidst the dreary architectural ruins of departed splendour. These descendants are the family of the Indian Cacique, or, as he is called in the Quechua language, the Curaca Astorpilca. They live in great poverty, but nevertheless contented and resigned to their hard and unmerited fate. Their descent from Atahuallpa, through the female line, has never been a doubtful question in Caxamarca; but traces of beard would seem to indicate some admixture of Spanish blood. . . .

The son of the Cacique Astorpilca, an interesting and amiable youth of seventeen, conducted us over the ruins of the ancient palace. Though living in the utmost poverty, his imagination was filled with images of the subterranean splendour and the golden treasures which, he assured us, lay hidden beneath the heaps of rubbish over which we were treading. He told us that one of his ancestors once blindfolded the eyes of his wife, and then, through many intricate passages cut in the rock, led her down into the subterranean gardens of the Inca. There the lady beheld, skilfully imitated in the purest gold, trees laden with leaves and fruit, with birds perched on their branches. Among other things, she saw Atahuallpa's gold sedan-chair (*una de las andas*) which had been so long searched for in vain, and which is alleged to have sunk in the basin at the Baths of Pultamarca. The husband commanded his wife not to touch any of these enchanted treasures, reminding her that the period fixed for the restoration of the Inca empire had not yet arrived, and that whosoever should touch any of the treasures would perish that same night. These golden dreams and fancies of the youth were founded on recollections and traditions transmitted from remote times. Golden gardens, such as those alluded to (*jardines o huertas de oro*), have been described by various writers who allege that they actually saw them; viz., by Cieza de León, Parmento, Garcilaso, and other early historians of the Conquista. They are said to have existed beneath the Temple of the Sun at Cuzco, at Caxamarca, and in the lovely valley of Yucay, which was a favourite seat of the sovereign family. In places in which the golden huertas were not under ground, but in the open air, living plants were mingled with the artificial ones. Among the latter, particular mention is always made of the high shoots of maize and the maize-cobs (*mazorcas*) as having been most successfully imitated.

The son of Astorpilca assured me that underground, a little to the right of the spot on which I then stood, there was a large datura tree, or *guanto,* in full flower, exquisitely made of gold wire and plates of gold, and that its branches overspread the Inca's chair. The morbid faith with which the youth asserted his belief in this fabulous story, made a profound and melancholy impression on me. These illusions are cherished among the people here, as affording them consolation amidst great privation and earthly suffering. I said to the lad, "Since you and your parents so firmly believe in the existence of these gardens, do you not, in your poverty, sometimes feel a wish to dig for the treasures that lie so near you?" The young Peruvian's answer was so simple and so expressive of the quiet resignation peculiar to the aboriginal inhabitants of the country, that I noted it down in Spanish in my Journal. "Such a desire (*tal antojo*)," said he, "never comes to us. My father says that it would be sinful (*que fuese pecado*). If we had the golden branches, with all their golden fruits, our white neighbours would hate us and injure us. We have a little field and good wheat (*buen trigo*)." Few of my readers will I trust be displeased that I have recalled here the words of the young Astorpilca and his golden dreams. . . .

2

What had brought Pizarro and his band to Peru were rumors heard in Panama of a southern kingdom wallowing in gold. Between rumor and fulfillment lay a tortuous road of ten years. But the bold coup at Cajamarca extinguished at one stroke all effective Inca rule. The intricate administrative organization of the semi-socialist native realm melted away, and power and riches passed to the alien ruffians who thereupon fell upon each other. Though some of the conquerors were astonished by the sites of prosperous cities and awesome shrines, few responded with anything but passing comments. The handful of Spaniards who first entered Cuzco, an aboriginal Rome of colossal stone edifices, apparently had nothing to report.

In little time highways fell into disrepair and were left to be swept away by the elements. Native shrines were mercilessly rifled by treasure-seekers. Whole cities turned to rubble or were built over by the conquerors. A new religion and governmental system took full control. Yet, long after the death of their civilization, the name of the Inca continued to cast a spell.

A few years after the Pizarro brothers there came to Peru a stout Spanish soldier, Pedro de Cieza de León, who wrote faithfully of what he saw. After him we have the accounts by half-breeds such as that by the famous Garcilaso de la Vega, who spent most of his adult life in Spain, and the bulky work by Felipe Guamán Poma de Ayala, illustrated by himself, which remained unpublished until discovered in the Royal Danish Library at Copenhagen early in our century. Common to all these witnesses is an almost slavish reverence for the Incas. So deeply ingrained has become the conviction that culture in the South American Andes was a creation of the Incas, that up to the present day the non-specialist finds it hard to conceive of any other people in ancient Peru. As the Aztecs overshadowed all in Mexico, the Incas seem to loom everywhere in Peru.

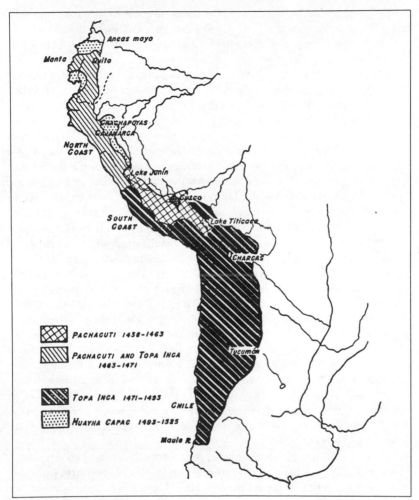

Expansion of the Inca Empire, compiled by John H. Rowe

The ubiquity of the Incas is largely the work of the Incas themselves. Ruthless empire builders in their own right, they not only fabricated a pious myth of their divine origin and mission, but consciously stamped out the traditions of their predecessors. Not without parallels in other continents and ages, they were adept manipulators of Clio in order to further their imperial image. Their small elite of the blood royal hammered into the masses that before their coming there had reigned unmitigated savagery. The Incas had even invented agriculture.

Despite such ambitious claims, the Incas, like the Aztecs, had appeared very late on the scene: all in all, little more than three hundred years before Pizarro. Their major conquests only got under way with the great Pachacutec in 1438. The Peruvian south coast, northern Chile, and Argentina were added within two decades prior to Columbus' first sailing. Nevertheless, in that little time the very names of the vanquished races had been virtually obliterated. While memories may have lingered on, nobody during the colonial age probed the mystery of who the builders of the Tiahuanaco megalithic structures of Lake Titicaca had been. Today, though the "Inca deceit" has been thoroughly deflated, we don't know the identities of the successive civilizations in the Andes and along the coast which can be traced to the first millennium B.C. We are equally in the dark about the languages they spoke. Instead we have to label them after present place names. Hence such a roster of pre-Inca phases of Andean culture as Chavín (probably the oldest), Tiahuanaco (which, it is believed, both spiritually and militaristically subdued most of Peru and part of Bolivia by the tenth century A.D.), the Moche or Mochica ("pre-Chimú") of the north coast, and Paracas and Nazca of the south coast. Only with the Chimú (which may not have been their name either) we stand on somewhat firmer ground. These pleasure-loving people, who ruled over a kingdom stretching for some six hundred miles along the Pacific, had been subdued too recently to be committed entirely to limbo. The Incas fought long to overcome them. And there is little doubt that the cultural graces and highly developed artisanship of the Chimú did not remain without influence on the more austere mountain people. Chances are that empire building and the construction of roads (with their relay messengers) were to some extent a Chimú legacy. Inca gold, plundered by the Spanish, was, at least in part, previously looted by the Incas when they vanquished their rivals.

That we can now discuss Peruvian pre-history in terms of thousands of years and that we have a fairly comprehensive idea of its course from the humble beginnings of early hunters and farmers, we owe entirely to archaeology. Though slow in getting started, the effort to uncover this history has enlisted men from many countries, of whom not the least was a Peruvian Indian, Dr. Julio C. Tello. In the 1940's at the Virú Valley, a kind of Tennessee Valley project of archaeology and anthropology unfolded a continuous story of 5,000 years of human activity.

On the threshold of the reconquest of pre-Inca Peru stands E. George Squier (1821–88). With some justice he is sometimes referred to as the first American "dirt" archaeologist deserving of the name. A native of northern New York state, Squier had spent his youth in poverty. Largely self-educated, he entered civil engineering and journalism. At the age of

27, with Dr. Edwin H. Davis, he produced a pioneering work on the moundbuilders of the Mississippi Valley. This book, based on thorough fieldwork, was to become a classic as the opening volume of the memoirs published annually since 1848 by the Smithsonian Institution.

While Squier was engaged in an additional study of the aboriginal monuments of New York state, his work had come to the attention of William H. Prescott. Through the historian's influence he obtained in 1849 an appointment as U.S. chargé d'affaires in Central America. Thus began his fruitful exploration of a then little known region, whose antiquities, ethnology, and linguistics he illumined.

A desire to carry out archaeological investigations in Peru, Squier confessed, had been originally instilled by an observation in Prescott's *History:* "The hand of the conquerors fell heavily on the vulnerable monuments of Peru; and in their blind and superstitious search for hidden treasure, they caused infinitely more ruin than time and earthquake. Yet enough of the monuments of the Incas remain to invite the researches of antiquity. . . ." A hoped-for visit to the land of the "Children of the Sun" was delayed by commitments connected with the projected Isthmian canal in Central America, and by Squier's deteriorating health. The "leading passion" in Squier's life was realized in 1862, however, when President Lincoln appointed him Commissioner of the United States at Lima, charged with the settlement of economic and legal disputes with Peru. The claims settled, Squier at once set off, at his own expense, on explorations of Peru which took him all over from Lima and the north coast to Cajamarca, Lake Titicaca, Cuzco, and deep into the Cordilleras. He was on the move for eighteen months. At various centers of antiquity he stayed for weeks in order to survey, dig, and photograph.

Among Squier's notable campaigns was that in the Moche and Chicama valleys near Trujillo where he drew up an exemplary plan of the old Chimú capital of Chan-Chan, one of the largest of pre-Columbian cities with an area of eleven square miles and sometimes estimated to have had a population close to 250,000. Squier not only threw light on the building style, the gardens, palaces, reservoirs, and artifacts of this metropolis, but proposed the now generally accepted view that the walled subdivisions of the city formed separate quarters of "clans." The extraordinarily realistic pottery of the desert people, which gives a veritable catalogue of human types and mores, he recognized as an articulate idiom, a kind of library of pictographic documentation. At a nearby village he collected evidence of the survival of an autochthonous Moche language. And on the basis of his materials he reached the firm conviction not only that "there were originally several detached and distinct civilizations in Peru, but that some of them antedated the Incas."

On his return to the United States, Squier was plagued by great personal difficulties and intermittent nervous disorders. He was unable to complete his book on Peru, and a brother of his eventually saw it into print in 1877. The result was, nonetheless, a singularly attractive work, long the most reliable and wide-ranging volume on the antiquities of the entire Central Andean area. The following selection from this book recounts Squier's preliminary visit to the Chimú capital of Chan-Chan and to the commanding adobe pyramids of the Sun and Moon nearby, which are now known to belong to the Mochica civilization that preceded the Chimú by several centuries.

Pictorial design from a Peruvian vase

CHIMÚ AND MOCHE

E. George Squier

Truxillo [Trujillo] stands in a little more than eight degrees of south latitude, on a level space, at a slight elevation above the sea, and on ground so flat that the *azequias* by which it is supplied with water have a scarcely perceptible current, and are consequently offensively charged with filth. It was founded, in 1535, by Francisco Pizarro, who named it after his native town in Spain, intending it for one of the great capitals of Peru. It is regularly laid out, the streets crossing each other at right angles, leaving here and there small open plazas or squares, on which the various churches usually face. In 1686 it was encircled by a wall of adobes, a regular oval in outline, and, with the exception of Lima, is the only walled city in Peru. Its present population is about fifteen thousand, made up largely of *hacendados,* or owners of estates in the surrounding valleys, and *comerciantes,* or traders, with the usual proportion of the lower orders and mixed breeds. It is, on the whole, well built; many of the houses being of two stories, with spacious and well-furnished interiors, indicative of wealth and a certain amount of taste. It has still some importance, but insignificant, compared with what it possessed under the viceroys, when it was the centre of an extensive jurisdiction, with high officers, a royal mint, and numbered families of high and historic titles among its inhabitants. It was also the seat of a bishop, and had five convents for men and two for women. The former have all been suppressed; but the latter, largely endowed, are still in existence, covering large areas within the city walls. The richest, Santa Clara, had, at the time of our visit, only thirteen inmates. There are thirteen churches within the walls, besides the cathedral. They are generally well built, and some of them, with their flying buttresses thrown out to support them against earthquakes, are both quaint and picturesque. The other public buildings are simply mean, neglected, and in decay.

Nearly all the leading inhabitants to whom we had introductions were absent on their estates at the sea-side; but we were fortunate in finding the gentleman whom we were most interested in meeting, and to whom I bore special letters from Lima—Colonel La Rosa, the most experienced, enthusiastic, and persistent treasure-hunter of Truxillo, where rummaging for *tapadas,* or treasures, has been a passion, I had almost said the main

From *Peru Illustrated. Incidents of travel and exploration in the land of the Incas.* New York: Hurst & Co., 1877, pp. 116–33 *passim.*

business, of the people since Juan Gutiérrez de Toledo commenced the practice nearly three hundred years ago. Years before, I had seen in London a large collection of articles, both curious and valuable, obtained by him from the ruins of Chimú, Moche, and Virú, and which he had confided to a person calling himself "Dr. Ferris" to dispose of, but who claimed to have discovered them himself, and sold them on his own account. A part went to the British Museum, and another portion was bought by the late Mr. George Folsom, and is now deposited with the Historical Society of New York. I had also seen a considerable collection of the colonel's in Lima, and had purchased some of the more remarkable articles in the precious metals.

Chimú silver cup

The colonel was neither an archaeologist nor an antiquary, and had little care for the relics he obtained in his excavations, except in a mercantile sense. He had rather a contempt for pottery, and for implements or utensils in bronze. His interest in Chimú architecture was mainly in the way of finding hidden vaults and chambers; he cared nothing for arabesques or paintings; and his knowledge of the ancient modes of sepulture was limited to ascertaining where the rich and powerful were buried, and where ornaments of gold and silver were most likely to abound. In these directions he had become proverbially expert. Of course, he did not sympathize greatly with my plans of surveying, measuring, and mapping the monuments, and evidently thought my declaration of such a purpose was merely a shallow pretext for diverting attention from my real object—that of finding the *peje grande*, or "great fish," as the yet undiscovered, legendary treasure of the Chimú has been called from immemorial days, and in trying to discover which millions of dollars had been expended. The colonel did not exactly tell me that he was confident I had got hold of some ancient itinerary, map, or guide, drawn up perhaps by the same Indian, Cazique Tello, who had confided to Gutiérrez de Toledo the secret of the *peje chica,* or "little fish," and which had been kept hitherto concealed. His manner implied that he was not at all deceived in the matter. He hardly waited for me to suggest that we should take a ride over the ruins next morning, but warmly seconded the proposition. It would be difficult for the possessor of the great secret to wholly retain that composure, when standing over the *peje grande,* which a quick eye and a ready wit could not penetrate! Thus, possibly, speculated Colonel La Rosa. But be that as it may, he reported himself early next morning at the hotel; and leaving P—— behind to prepare his photographic chemicals and apparatus, we set out in company with Mr. C—— for a reconnoissance of the ruins of Chimú.

We left the city by the Portada de Miraflores, one of the northern gates, past the Panteon, or cemetery, through a rich, well-cultivated district, till we reached the hamlet of Miraflores, a league or more from the city, at the foot of the hills that slope down to the plain in that direction. Here we came upon the remains of a great *azequia,* or aqueduct, which had tapped the Río Moche many miles up towards its source among the mountains for the supply of the ancient city, and which was here carried across the valley on a lofty embankment. This is still more than sixty feet high, built of stones and earth, with a channel on top, originally lined with stones, and of the dimensions of our ordinary canals. We followed this to the point on the slope overlooking the old city, where the water was distributed, through minor *azequias,* over the plain below.

All around us, on the arid slope, were remains of rude stone edifices, suggesting that here, perhaps, had been a suburb of the city, occupied by the poorer class of inhabitants. Below, however, stretching away in a broad sweep from the foot of the declivity to the sea in front, and from the base of the rocky pinnacle of Monte Campana on the north, to Huaman and the Río Moche on the south, over an area hardly less than from twelve to fifteen miles long by from five to six miles broad, was the plain of Chimú itself, thickly covered over with the ruins of the ancient city. They consist of a wilderness of walls, forming great inclosures, each containing a labyrinth of ruined dwellings and other edifices, relieved here and there by gigantic *huacas,* most conspicuous among which were those of El Obispo, Conchas, and Toledo—great masses, which the visitor finds it difficult to believe to be artificial.

On the side from which we approached the ruins, the city seems to have been protected by a heavy wall, several miles of which are still standing. From this wall, extending inwards at right angles, are other lines of walls of scarcely inferior elevation, inclosing great areas which have never been built upon, and which fall off in low terraces, carefully cleared of stones, each with its *azequia* for irrigation. These were evidently the gardens and pleasure-grounds of the ancient inhabitants.

Descending the slope, we encountered, outside of the great wall, two rectangular inclosures, situated about a quarter of a mile apart, each containing a truncated pyramid, or *huaca*. The first of these inclosures is 252 feet long by 222 feet at the ends. The wall is still 14 feet high by 6 feet thick at the base. The *huaca* is 162 feet square by 50 feet in height, and stands nearer one end of the area inclosed than the other. It is built, as are the walls, of compact rubble; that is to say, of tenacious clay mixed with broken stones, so as to form an indurated mass, almost as hard as mortar. Notwithstanding this, however, it has been much excavated and defaced, revealing that, towards its summit at least, it was made up of sepulchral chambers, from which great quantities of bones have been taken, which now lie strewed about in every direction. These were all slight, and appeared to have been of females, ranging from five to fifteen years old. I had occasion to observe afterwards that a custom of burying the dead of certain ages and sexes together, in certain places, existed among the builders of Chimú.

The other structure referred to corresponds very closely with this. It is 240 feet long by 210 feet wide, the outer walls 20 feet high by 8 thick, and the interior *huaca*, or mound, 172 feet long by 152 wide, and 40 feet high. No human remains were found here, but the summit of the mound showed that it had been divided into sections, or chambers, from five to six feet square, by walls of rubble eighteen inches thick. I could not resist the conviction that this structure, like the other, had been built for sepulchral purposes, but had not been used.

We entered the ruined city through a break in the outer wall, and I was at once struck with the care with which the open areas, which I have called gardens, had been cleared and prepared for culture. The principal *azequias* had been built close along the walls, and carefully lined with stones; while the smaller distributing channels had been carried in zigzags from terrace to terrace, so as to insure an equal and efficient distribution of water. All were dry now, as they had been for centuries, and a nitrous efflorescence covered the once fertile areas that they had made to bloom and blossom in past ages.

Directing our course towards the great *huaca*, Obispo, we passed a number of broad and deep rectangular excavations, their sides terraced and faced with rough but well-laid stones, and with zigzag slopes, or pathways, leading to the bottom. These, Colonel La Rosa insisted, were ancient granaries; but it did not require much intelligence to discern that they had been reservoirs of water. The vast size of the *huaca* became more obvious as we approached it, and the great excavation which had been carried into it from its north side, a century or more ago, made it appear like the crater of some extinct volcano.

The materials—stones, rubble, and adobes—that had been taken out of the excavation were heaped up in a high, irregular mass on the plain, literally covering acres; and close beside it were the ruins of an abandoned village, with a little church, in the plaza of which a cross was still kept up by pious hands. This village was built for the workmen, Indians (*encomendados*) and others, who had been employed, so runs the tradition, for twenty years in penetrating the *huaca*. Presuming that they conducted the work as similar work is still conducted in Peru—in other words, that the materials were loosened by little picks, gathered up by hand, and carried out in baskets on the head, or in improvised sacks made of *ponchos*—I see nothing improbable in the story. But, however accomplished, the undertaking was a gigantic one; yet how insignificant as compared with that of building the structure in the first instance!

I could not learn that treasure, or indeed anything else, was found in the *huaca* to compensate for the great labor and cost of its excavation. And while I could not help regretting the defacement and ruin of this fine monument, yet I was gratified in being able to discover how it was built. Its construction was similar to that of the Castillo at Pachacamac, of nearly equal parts of stones and rough adobes, the whole cast over with a kind of breccia or rubble-work. The excavation had been carried below the level of the surrounding ground, and revealed the natural strata. So the notion of subterranean chambers beneath the mass, evidently once entertained, was not supported by experiment.

We ascended to the top of the *huaca*, from which a distinct view of the whole plain and its monuments is commanded. Turning over an adobe for a seat, I discovered a little scorpion, the first and the only one I saw in Peru. Why he was at the summit of El Obispo, that scorched and arid heap in a scorched and arid plain, I did not stop to inquire, but inveigled him into an empty letter-envelope, and pickled him duly on my return to the city. Whether he belonged to any variety new or rare, I do not know; albeit I sent him, with an earnest solicitation, to a scientific friend, who affects scorpions, but from whom I have never heard a word in reference to the unique and virulent little reprobate.

Subsequently I made a visit to El Obispo, and measured it, with its surroundings, as well as its dilapidation would permit; in doing which, both C—— and myself were overhauled and somewhat roughly questioned by a body of mounted rural police in search of certain *ladrones* who had committed robbery and arson in the neighboring valley of Chicama, and, it was supposed, had taken refuge among the ruins. I shall never forget the blank look of the commander of the squad when he was assured that we were merely making surveys of the monuments. If he did not arrest us, I am sure it was because he doubted if taking charge of idiots and madmen fell within his line of duty.

El Obispo is about 150 feet high, and covers an area 580 feet square, equal to about eight acres; and as its sides are so abrupt, where unbroken, as to prohibit ascent, its contents may be roughly calculated at about fifty millions of cubic feet. Its summit was probably reached by zigzag inclines or a stairway on its northern face.

From the top of El Obispo, Colonel La Rosa pointed out to me the locality of his latest and most extensive excavations, to which we made our way through an ancient avenue or street, lined on both sides by monuments. The excavations were in what appeared to be a shapeless mound of debris, with very slight external evidence of having been, what it probably was, the palace of the princes of Chimú. The surface was rough and irregular, and we had some difficulty in riding over it. Suddenly, the colonel, turning abruptly around a huge pile of rubbish, reined up on the edge of a great pit, in which were exposed the lower walls, passages, courts and apartments of a part of some great structure long ago buried from the day. A single glance satisfied me that, thanks to Colonel La Rosa's passion for *tapadas,* we had before us a revelation of an entirely unique and very beautiful style of aboriginal American architecture. My eye ran with mingled surprise and delight over long walls covered with intricate arabesques in relief, and here and there glowing with brilliant colors, such as I had never seen in all my previous explorations on this continent. The colonel seemed to attach no importance to them, but eagerly directed my attention to the spot where he had found a concealed chamber or closet, piled full of vessels of silver and gold. . . .

From the palace the colonel led us to another mound, where excavation had revealed what there is good reason to believe were the royal tombs. Hence we took a long sweep past La Legua to an eminence near the sea, on which stands an extensive work with a *huaca* and other monuments inclosed, called, from its position and assumed purpose, El Castillo. The sandy soil in front of its principal entrance, over an area of several acres, is stuffed with skeletons, buried irregularly, as if after a great battle; a supposition supported by the fact that the bones which had been exposed by excavation or laid bare by the winds were all of adult men, and that a large part of the skulls bore marks of violence. Some were cloven as if by the stroke of a battle-axe or sabre; others battered in as if by blows from clubs or the primitive hammer to which the French have given the appropriate name of *cassetête*; and still others were pierced as if by lances or arrows. I picked up a piece of a skull showing a small square hole, precisely such as would be occasioned by the bronze arrow-heads found here and there among the ruins.

I could not resist thinking, in spite of tradition, that perhaps on this very spot had been fought the last decisive battle between the Inca Yupanqui and the Prince of Chimú, and that here were mingled the bones of

Mythical combat depicted on a vase from coastal Peru

the slain of both armies: a notion supported by finding mixed together the square, posteriorly compressed skulls of the peoples of the coast, the elongated skulls of the Aymaras, and the regular, normal heads of the Quechuas of the Sierra.

Inside the Castillo we found a terraced cemetery, containing, however, only the skeletons of young women, carefully enveloped in fine cotton cloth. These skeletons were apparently of persons that had died at between fifteen and eighteen years of age.

Returning from the Castillo through a wilderness of excavations and gigantic water-reservoirs, we rode in succession to a series of vast enclosures, themselves containing lesser ones, crowded with buildings, which are strangely called "palaces." One of the most interesting enclosures contained, besides a number of open squares of differing sizes, a great reservoir, and, in one corner, fenced off by massive walls, what we subsequently ascertained to be a prison. We visited also the *huaca* of Toledo, whence Don García Gutiérrez de Toledo had extracted his enormous treasures. It has been so worked upon and into, in the course of three centuries, as to have lost all shapeliness; and it now stands, a great uncouth mass, honeycombed, and pierced in every direction by shafts, passages, and adits, some quite recent, that must have cost hundreds of thousands of dollars to excavate.

At four o'clock in the afternoon, with my head in a whirl of surprise and excitement over the wide and unexpected revelations of the day, I was not loath to second the suggestion of my guide to ride along the sea-beach to the little watering-place and projected new port of Truxillo, Huaman. The sand-dunes, at a short distance back from the shore, like almost all vacant and desert spots around Chimú, are vast cemeteries. Skulls and bones projected everywhere above the surface, and were crushed under our horses' hoofs. The whole shore for miles is a veritable Golgotha. . . .

[On the next day] we resolved to utilize our time by visiting the Indian town of Moche and the remains in its vicinity, concerning which we had heard much.

Starting early in the morning, we cantered over a level road through rich green meadows of alfalfa, and fields of cotton, rice, and the nopal. . . .

About a league from Truxillo, we reached the river Moche, a considerable stream, flowing in a shallow, sandy bed, shut in by alders, acacias, and other trees and bushes. We forded it without difficulty, and, reaching the opposite bank, our ears were saluted by a confused noise of a drum and a *quina*, or Indian flute, accompanied by shouts and laughter, and in a few moments we came upon an extraordinary scene. A party of Indians and mestizos were excavating an *azequia*, or, rather, clearing out an old and abandoned one, while another party, acting as a relay, all half drunk, sat under the trees near by, around some jars of *chicha* and dishes of *picante*, eating, drinking, drumming, and cheering the men in the trench. Among them were several gaudily dressed women, with dishevelled hair, who formed a fitting adjunct to the bacchanalian scene. They shouted to us to dismount and join them; but as we did not seem inclined to do so, some of them seized our horses by their bridles, and led us into the centre of the throng, where they besieged us with bowls of *chicha* and little gourds of *picante*. We made the best of our situation; that is to say, ate and drank as little as possible. One of the dusky damsels made me the object of her special attentions, calling me familiarly *El Blanquito*. Observing my disposition to shirk the *aji*, she picked out choice bits from her own dish, which she took between her thumb and forefinger, and held them up to my mouth with a ludicrously tender leer, insisting that I should take them "for her own dear sake." I had great difficulty in avoiding the proffered morsels, thereby giving her much offence.

We escaped from our inebriated friends with some difficulty; and a ride of another league, over a flat country and a dusty road, brought us to the Indian pueblo, a considerable town, regularly laid out, of low cane huts, their roofs of reed-matting supported by crooked algarroba posts, and covered with a thin layer of mud to keep them from blowing away. There were a few houses of crude adobes, roofed in like manner, the whole presenting an aspect of squalid monotony. We rode directly to the house of the *gobernador,* a full-blooded Indian. His dwelling was merely an immense shed, with some compartments fenced off with adobes or canes, for such of the occupants as affected privacy. The bare earthen floor was strewed with the *aparejo* of mules and rude implements of husbandry, for the *gobernador* was both muleteer and husbandman. In front of the house, and partly in its shade, a sheep-driver from Virú had halted a flock of sheep, which he was taking to Truxillo. I noticed among them a very large proportion with three, four, five, and six horns.

The *gobernador* was not at home; the females were taciturn, and kept silently and impassibly at their work of spinning cotton, with perhaps the most primitive apparatus ever devised for the purpose. It was composed of a thin stem of the quinoa, as a spindle, stuck through half of a small green lime, for a whirl, or bob. Having vainly interrogated these industrious ladies about *huacas,* we resolved to consult the *cura,* who, we understood, was an intelligent man. We rode through the silent streets, fetlock-deep in dust, to the plaza, one side of which was occupied by the church, a quaint, old, tumble-down edifice, its bell-tower reached by a flight of stone steps outside the building. We paused a moment before it, when we were startled by a stentorian command of *"Quiten sus sombreros!"* ("Take off your hats!"), proceeding from a stern-visaged, gray-haired man reclining on a mud-bench under the corridor of a building close by, which we at once took to be the residence of the *cura.*

We did as we were ordered, and then rode to the house itself, where we were saluted with a torrent of invective, kept up by the *cura,* without stopping to take breath, until he was purple in the face. "None but Jews and infidels would pass in front of a church without taking off their hats. Even the ignorant Indian brutes of Moche know better; or, if they didn't, I would teach them! Holy Mother of God! I would teach them!" Here the *cura* shook his stout cane savagely in our very faces. We endeavored to explain, but he went on. When he broke down again, we once more sought to excuse ourselves, but could get no hearing, for the reason explained by the *cura* himself a little later: "It is of no use talking to me; I have been stone-deaf these ten years; you might fire a battery of artillery in the plaza, and I couldn't hear it. If you have got anything to say, come in here, where there is ink and paper."

He then led the way into his sitting-room, hung around with dusky pictures of saints and martyrs. Helping us with courtesy to seats, he thumped violently on the table with his stick. A meek Indian boy entered on the instant, and received the peremptory order, "Beast! coffee and cigars! Quick! Holy Mother!" One would have supposed the worthy *cura* overcome by rage; but the moment he was seated, his really fine face assumed a benignant expression, and he motioned with a smile to the writing materials, saying, "*Caballeros,* I welcome you to my poor house; it will be my pleasure to serve you. I seldom see white faces, except those of the scoundrel politicians who come down here to corrupt my poor Indians with their lies and their bribes. It was a woeful day, gentlemen, when the idiots in Lima gave these simple, innocent people the vote. You should have seen my Moche children forty years ago, when I first came here. They were industrious, sober, devout, and happy. You see what they are now: idlers, liars, drunkards, and thieves! Then, if a stranger or a traveller were to approach the town, the first man in authority would have sent to me a *chasqui* (fleet messenger) to say, 'Our good father, a traveller has come; he is dusty and weary: we will conduct him to you; we will bring alfalfa for his horses; we have eggs and fish, and bread of wheat, which we will bring to you for him. Good father, give us your blessing!' I would have died rather than witness the change that has taken place since. It has all come of the ballot, and the political villains of Truxillo. I have not put my foot within its accursed walls these many years. These poor people are mere children; they must be governed by a father. The Incas were right, after all. This voting is their ruin."

The good *cura* went on for a long time much in this strain, lamenting the part he took in his youth against the viceroys and in behalf of the republic. There was no longer public or private virtue; the duties of hospitality even were neglected, and religion had become a sham and a pretence.

We were not altogether sorry when the *cura*'s lamentations were finished, as they were with the entry of the coffee and cigars, and we were enabled to write out a few questions about the *huacas*. The *cura*, I found, regarded them all with aversion; they kept up unholy memories and traditions among the Indians, and he would like to see them levelled to the earth. But they were very strange things, nevertheless, very rich in gold and silver; and that, of course, was the matter in which we were most interested. We had not then entirely ceased to protest against being considered searchers after *tapadas*; but the *cura* would not be convinced that we could have any object except to dig for gold. He advised us to visit Virú, where, he said, the posts and beams of many of the old buildings were still standing, and where there were vast numbers of monuments. The most interesting objects around Moche, he said, were the Temple of the Sun, at the foot of the conical peak called Cerro Blanco, which he pointed out to us from his corridor, and a pyramid *muy disforme* (monstrous), surpassing El

Obispo in size. When we inquired for a guide, he volunteered to go with us himself, if we would ride slowly. This he did, mounted on a meek *burro*, his long robe almost trailing on the ground, and carrying over his broad sombrero a bright pink umbrella. One Indian servant led the *burro*, and another, the youth whom the *cura* had denominated "a beast" an hour before, trotted by his side, carrying the *cura*'s ominous cane and a flask of *chicha*. As we passed through the streets, the Indian women and children hurried to the doors of their houses, and, kneeling with uplifted palms, received the padre's blessing. It was rare, he said, of late years, that he ventured out of the town; it was twenty since he had visited the *huacas*.

We rode for some distance through cultivated fields, striped with lines of verdure following the courses of *azequias*, until we reached the flank of the hills above the reach of irrigation, where the desert commences. Here we fell into a path in the sand skirting the hills, the gray waste relieved here and there by a white human skull bleaching in the bright sunlight— for here, as everywhere amidst Chimú, were scattered mementoes of death.

As we approached the Cerro Blanco, the *cura* pointed out, as the Temple of the Sun, a mass of adobe walls, standing on a bold, rocky projection, or shelf, of the mountain at an elevation of a hundred feet or more. He declined to ascend; so, leaving him below, we clambered up to the structure, which, in position and style, more resembles a fortress than a temple. We entered by an inclined plane, through a massive gate-way, into a broad court, from which passages led off right and left, from one stage or terrace to another, until we reached the last and highest, from which we looked over the whole green valley of the Río Moche, past the low towers of

The great pyramid of Moche

Truxillo, to the *huacas* of Chimú, El Obispo rising boldly in the distance. The most conspicuous object which met our view was the great pyramid of which the *cura* had spoken, and which, in its magnitude, justified his description. It stands on the edge of the desert slope, at the base of Cerro Blanco, just where irrigation begins—a kind of gigantic landmark between luxuriant verdure and arid sands, between life and death. Viewed from this position, it was the most impressive monument we had yet seen in Peru.

We descended to the *cura,* and rode past the pyramid to a deep *azequia,* which was carried along its base on the side towards the valleys, and was fringed with graceful canes. Crossing it on a shaky bridge of poles, covered with weeds and earth, we entered a grove of fruit-trees, flanking a field of Chili peppers, in one corner of which, and under the shadow of the pyramid, stood a rude Indian cane hut. The occupants welcomed the padre, and treated us to *chicha.* The padre and his attendants soon started back for Moche, while we took a more direct road to the city.

We subsequently returned, and carefully measured and photographed the pyramid, which is sometimes itself called *El Templo del Sol* (the Temple of the Sun). We found it to be a rectangular structure, which the plan

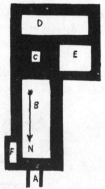

Plan of Moche pyramid

alone can make intelligible, having a greatest length of a little more than 800 feet, and a greatest width of 470, covering a trifle more than seven acres. Its greatest height, at the summit of the terraced structure, is upwards of 200 feet. It is constructed throughout of large adobes, which appear to have been built around a central core, or nucleus, having sides inclining inwards at an angle to the horizon of seventy-seven degrees. The bricks, however, were not laid in a continuous series around this core, but built up in blocks, like pilasters, one beside another, unconnected, and supported by common inclination around the centre. The whole seems to have been surrounded by a casing of the thickness of between thirty and forty adobes, interlocking, so that originally its faces were smooth and regular.

To comprehend the structure, we will ascend it from the side on which, if there were any facilities for ascent, they must have existed; namely, from the causeway [at] A. This extends from the base of the pyramid 1,120 feet to rocky hill, around which are some almost obliterated ruins, and is about 50 feet wide. From it there was probably a stairway, leading up to B, which is a level area, elevated nearly 100 feet above the plain, and is about 400 feet long by 350 wide. It may have been, and probably was, level: possibly it supported buildings; but it is now covered all over with heaps of rubbish from modern excavations or from demolished buildings. At the southern extremity of this lofty platform, or terrace, rises another, thirty or forty feet higher, on which stands a terraced pyramid, about 200 feet square. Seven stages are still distinct, but there are traces of nine. On its summit, as on most of the more important monuments of the *infieles,* stands a wooden cross, its elevation being, by computation, as already said, about 200 feet. The platform on which this stands was probably ascended by steps; but the ascent to the summit of the crowning pyramid itself seems to have been from the west, and by a graded way. The long platform [at] D is eighty feet below that on which rests the terraced pyramid, and E is still lower.

Here I may explain that if my measurements, estimates, and descriptions are not more specific and exact, it is due to the devastation which time and the elements—but, above all, the ruthless hands of men—have wrought in this grand old monument.

Passages and chambers are said to exist in the structure, the entrances to which are only known to the Indians, and kept carefully concealed beneath masses of rubbish. One of these passages, says common report, descends from the work on the mountain slope that I have already described, and extends beneath ground to the very sanctuary of the pyramid, the vault that contains the body of the mightiest prince of Chimú, and where, perhaps, the *peje grande* lies concealed.

We found neither passages nor chambers, but we did find an adit, or drift, driven in on a level with the natural soil, from the eastern side of the great mass, under the centre of the terraced pyramid [at] C. This had been dug by treasure-seekers, and the debris from the excavation formed a real hillock at the mouth of the passage. Having brought candles with us, we followed the passage to its extremity. It was fetid and slippery with the excrement of bats, which whirred past us when disturbed, dashing out our lights, as if they were the sinister guardians of the treasures of the Chimú kings. The survey showed us nothing beyond the constant layers

of adobes, with no signs of chambers or passages, nor the slightest variation from the system of construction I have described.

It is hardly possible to assign any other than a religious purpose to this
structure, which, with the *huacas* of Obispo, Toledo, etc., in common with
the *teocallis* of Mexico and Central America, may have supported buildings
sacred to various divinities, or a single *naos* dedicated to the Supreme
Essence.

3

Had it not been for tales of buried Inca treasure, Hiram Bingham (1875–1956) might never have found his lost city in the clouds.

Ever since the Spaniards seized Atahualpa and extracted a fabulous ransom from him—which did not save his skin—rumors had persisted that only a fraction of all the Inca gold had been handed over. The story went that a train of 7,000 llamas loaded with gold was on its way to Cajamarca when news of the ruler's murder was received. The transport was immediately halted and the hoard was unloaded in a secret place. None of this were the invaders able to recover. Likewise, once the Spaniards' ravenous appetite for the glittering metal—which to the natives had a religious rather than material value—became widely known, gold and silver objects of all kinds were quickly put away. Torture and ransacking helped little. And while the Spanish fury grew, some of the accounts of the buried caches undoubtedly reached legendary dimensions. What Humboldt heard in Cajamarca may have been a case in point. One such story was connected with a hoard Manco Capac II, the erstwhile Inca puppet ruler, took along when he rebelled against the Spanish and hid out with his followers in a remote valley of the eastern Andes, where he set up court and from whence he preyed on the Spanish. The Inca hideaways had remained secret for nearly four hundred years.

Hiram Bingham was a young Yale historian, who had made a specialty of following the roads taken by Simón Bolívar during his military campaigns, when in February 1909, after attending an international congress in Santiago de Chile, his track along the colonial trade route between Buenos Aires and Lima brought him to the Andean highlands. It was "the rainiest month of the rainiest season [and] an unfortunate introduction to exploration in Inca land." But a local official—prefect of the Department of Apurimac—coaxed him into searching out a far-away site called Choqquequirau, which in Quechua means "Cradle of Gold" and which he was certain *was* Manco's retreat: Vilcapampa (or Vilcabamba), lost capital of the last four Incas. The name seemed to imply buried treasure. Several previous visits to it had been abortive. Bingham was anything but enthusiastic. His own studies had been confined to the colonial era of Latin America and the wars of independence and their aftermath. Archaeology was a complete blank to him. Furthermore, conditions of weather and physical difficulties in climbing up to Choqquequirau were not in the least inviting. But the Peruvian prefect entertained no doubt that a holder of a doctor's degree and the great northern republic's delegate to an international scientific conference was just the man for the job. Bingham's pleading of archaeological innocence was put down as mere modesty. At last Bingham gave in, mindful of the advice Elihu Root, the U.S. Secretary of State, had given him when he appointed him a delegate to the congress: to be sure to generate international good will and to cooperate with the officials he met during his travels. Thus, inadvertently, Bingham drifted into the mysteries of aboriginal America.

Golden "zodiac" from Cuzco

As it happened, Choqquequirau, difficult of access as it was, was a disappointment. Unnamed treasureseekers had ransacked it, even using dynamite. If it had ever harbored riches, they had most certainly been carried away. Yet, the mountain-perched place with its clustered pre-Columbian ruins above the Apurimac—"The Great Speaker"—cast a spell. And it posed a riddle more intriguing to a scholar than all the buried Inca gold. Was Choqquequirau really Manco's Vilcapampa? Several authorities thought so.

On his return to Lima, Bingham discussed the question with Dr. Carlos Romero, an illustrious Peruvian historian. Señor Romero knew the Spanish chronicles well. The evidence presented there, particularly in the writings of Padre de la Cacancha, made the identification unlikely. Romero thought that the lost Inca ruins were in all probability located in another range of the high Cordilleras between the Urubamba and Apurimac rivers. Bingham from then on was obsessed with the ambition to renew his search for Vilcapampa. Back in the United States, Rudyard Kipling's words kept ringing in his ear: "Something hidden! Go and find it! Go and look behind the ranges—Something lost behind the Ranges. Lost and waiting for you. Go!"

His opportunity came in 1911 when he led a joint expedition of the National Geographic Society and Yale University. In July of that year he descended northward from the cool plateau around the ancient Inca capital of Cuzco into the narrow gorge of the Urubamba. The valley reminded him of the startling beauty of the interior of his native Hawaiian islands. Here the winding river had torn its bed through an escarpment which had been impassable until two decades earlier when the government had blasted a mule track alongside. Without this access the quest might have been doomed to failure.

Following up various hints and cross-examining the few people he encountered, Bingham at last was told by a local muleteer of major ruins above the precipices. Intelligence of that kind was not unusual and more often than not turned out to be a false lead. Bingham's travel companions were so doubtful of the man's promise to guide the party to a dead city that they stayed behind, one in order to collect insects ("there were more butterflies near the river"), the other to wash his shirt in the Urubamba. The discovery they missed was not just topographically a peak in American archaeology. The site itself, overlooking the white snake of the Urubamba deep in the abyss below, was located in the saddle between the Machu ("Old") and the higher Huayna ("New") Picchu. The aerie in turn was silhouetted against the icy majesty of the 20,000-foot Salcantay. Despite the altitude of some 8,000 feet, vegetation was so luxuriant that only gradually did Bingham perceive the enormous dimensions of human handiwork.

What he saw before him was a matted green carpet suspended in the sky. Compared to such a panorama even the celebrated ruins of Pompeii and rock-hewn Petra had to pale. In years since, the site has inspired more than one travel writer to ecstatic passages. The impressions of a seasoned globetrotter and sensitive aesthete like Sacheverell Sitwell may stand for them all: ". . . At every twisting of the road the view grew more terrific until it reached a pitch of magnificent wildness never known before. There

was no mist that morning and the huge mountains rose unencumbered
to their full height to which, I say, none but the greatest of Chinese landscape painters of nearly a thousand years ago could have done justice. . . .
It is the most stupendous approach there has ever been, to something
which in its own right is perhaps the most startlingly dramatic archaeological site in either the Old or the New World. For the setting is enough,
is almost too much in itself. It is nearly too good to be believed that there
should be something more to see here. . . ."

Hiram Bingham named the site Machu Picchu for the adjacent peak,
and thus it remains known to the world. Once the area had been cleared,
the city turned out to be virtually intact. It thus offers an exceptional
field of study for pre-Columbian, and particularly Inca, urban life and
planning. Whereas Cuzco had been repeatedly levelled by earthquakes
and built over by the Spanish, Machu Picchu has not suffered such harassments. To a surprising degree its architecture mirrors that of the ancient
capital. As in Cuzco, stone buildings and walls are massively constructed
on a cyclopean scale. Unlike Maya and Aztec edifices, or the high reliefs
and painted walls of the Chimú adobe temples, the Inca structures lack
ornamentation and impress by the simplicity of style and balanced solidity
of their bulk. Characteristic are the trapeziform windows and doors. As at
other Inca sites, some Machu Picchu buildings were erected from finely
cut rectangular stones of white granite that were put together in the manner
of bricks with such precision that, as has so often been remarked, no blade
could be passed between them. For the sake of proportion large blocks of
granite were often laid at the bottom and succeeded by stones gradually
smaller and narrower, thus giving an impression of perfect harmony and
grace. Another building style, also prominent in Cuzco, was that of var-
iously shaped enormous polygonal stones that were ingeniously fitted into
each other like a giant jigsaw puzzle without leaving any gaps whatsoever.
One such block at Machu Picchu, weighing several tons, had even more
edges (32 in all) than the famous 12-cornered block of a Cuzco wall. In
addition there were lesser buildings and walls put together more haphazardly from rubble (*pirca*) bound together by clay.

From its layout Machu Picchu seems to have served as a military outpost and refuge as well as a religious shrine, functions mirrored in its
diverse buildings. Within the walled compound there were a great many
palaces, sacred plazas, humble residences, "homes of the clans," the so-
called Temple of the Three Windows, the Palace of the Chosen Women,
and the Torreón, a combined natural cave and tower, which Bingham
thought was the burial place of the Inca lords. As noteworthy was the
Inti-huatana ("sun-dial" or "hitching post of the sun"), a structure chiseled
from the rock, which is believed to have served for the observation of the

summer and winter solstices. Such posts are found in all major Inca sites, and since the Spaniards considered them central to the Incas' idolatrous sun worship, they smashed them everywhere. But the one at Machu Picchu was fully preserved, a persuasive proof that the Spanish never got there. All over Machu Picchu, connecting a roller-coaster surface of changing levels and sections, there were steps cut into the rocks or added in flagstones. The city, apparently laid out to be self-sufficient, was ringed by a complex series of "hanging" agricultural terraces (*andenes*) to be reached by narrow staircases. A large aqueduct brought the town water, which was distributed by means of sixteen or seventeen cascading conduits or "fountains."

Machu Picchu—together with a smaller settlement higher up on Huayna Picchu—has now been identified as one of the last and probably most imposing of a whole belt of mountain-nestling cities which reached from Sacsahuaman above Cuzco down along the Vilcanota-Urubamba River and were linked by an ancient paved road. Among them are Pisac, Ollantaytambo, Huamanmarca, Patallajta, Loyamarca, Phuynpatamarca, and Sayacmarca. Peru's Dr. Tello discovered there in 1942 the extensive ruins of Wina y Waina. Peruvians now refer to the entire area as "Sacred Valley." All of these *pucarás*, built atop precipitous crags, are laid out in a maze of walls, tunnels, staircases, soil-banked terraces, sun temples, plazas, and adobe houses. Whether they were actual fortresses or a group of semi-military settlements guarding and pushing the frontier against hostile Amazon tribes is still a matter of debate. The outline of this vast system, paralleled by those of other valleys, was traced some thirty years after Bingham's discovery by Paul Fejos under the aegis of the Viking Fund (1940–42). Like some of these places, Machu Picchu may go back to pre-Inca days, having perhaps been founded as a village by primitive tribes from the Amazon. There is no doubt that other non-Inca peoples of the Andes have built stone cities atop the mountains such as the town of the Yarovilcas which Bertrand Flornoy located in 1955 near the Marañón River in northern Peru.

Bingham and several generations of Peruvianists firmly believed that the megalithic structures at Cuzco and elsewhere were the work of some ancient race—perhaps linked with the mysterious builders of Tiahuanaco—but this view is no longer held. By and large Machu Picchu is late Inca and was probably built during the reign of Pachacutec in the fifteenth century. Inca architecture comprised a variety of styles which reflect not so much successive occupants as different functions. During his extensive excavations at Machu Picchu, Bingham never found any objects older than the Inca era. He never dug up any golden treasures either; but he did come across a small piece of tin foil, obviously used in

Peruvian metal workers

the making of bronze, which has caused considerable interest among students of pre-Columbian metallurgy.

Despite the tentative tone in which Bingham interpreted his discovery
in his first printed account, which follows, his belief in the uniqueness of
Machu Picchu remained unshaken. If anything it grew over the years when
he published a number of books on the subject. Such a failing he shared
with a number of pioneer archaeologists, notably Heinrich Schliemann.
As Schliemann had uncovered dead Agamemnon's mask at Mycenae, so
Bingham had recovered Manco's mansion. Not content with that, he insisted that Machu Picchu linked Manco II with Manco I, legendary founder
of the Inca dynasty, and that it was from here that the Incas set out on
their road to the promised land at Cuzco and future empire. While his
fanciful theory on Inca origins has fallen into disregard, more credence
can be given to Bingham's claim that Machu Picchu *is* Vilcapampa.
But the thesis remains unproven. True, the Spaniards seem never to have
reached this "University of Idolatry." (European-made beads, which were
dug up, may have drifted there through indirect trade channels.) However, a number of other sites, uncovered since Bingham's days, could
equally qualify. In fact, in 1964 the Peruvian explorer Antonio Santander
Cascelli and an American, Gene Savoy, penetrated farther to the Urubamba headwaters, where they came across a series of ruins on successive
plateaus that exceed Machu Picchu in size if not in splendor, and tally
even better with the old Spanish accounts.

Whatever its identity or functions, Machu Picchu has made archaeological history. Its importance for the study of the Inca past was further

revealed by Bingham's three consecutive expeditions (1912–16). These rank as the first large-scale scientific campaigns ever carried out in Peru. They turned world-wide attention to the promise of Peruvian archaeology and inaugurated an era of intensive excavation by Peruvian and foreign archaeologists. Bingham also brought with him a number of young scientists who were to make significant contributions to Americanist studies in their own right, among them Isaiah Bowman, the geographer and later president of Johns Hopkins University; Philip Ainsworth Means, who came to record Inca history; and O. F. Cook, who examined the spread and cultivation of plants as archaeological evidence for ancient civilizations. Apart from making many archaeological finds—in pottery, metal tools, and human skeletons and trepanned skulls (the great majority those of women)—the Yale-National Geographic Society expeditions surveyed an unknown zone of the glaciated Andes, 1,500 square miles in area, the very existence of which had not dawned on anybody before 1911. And this *terra incognita* was little more than fifty miles removed from Cuzco! More than 12,000 photographs were taken during the course of the expeditions.

The son and grandson of American missionaries in Hawaii, Hiram Bingham had found his way from the delightful world of Polynesia to the great Indian civilizations of South America. But his active participation in American archaeology came to an end in World War I, when he saw distinguished service as a flier and came to head the largest Allied flying school in France. He served as a professor of Latin American history at Yale until 1924, only to embark on another career in U.S. politics, which put him into the governor's chair of the state of Connecticut and later into the U.S. Senate. He then had the misfortune to become one of the few members of that august chamber ever to be censured by his colleagues.

Six-foot-four, with what has been described as a "gorgeous head of silver," he looked like the Hollywood dream of a senior legislator. Yet after his failure in politics he had to admit that "Senators I understand not at all. I understand so much better the ethics and morals of explorers." However, shortly before Bingham's death in 1956, President Truman appointed the Republican ex-Senator chairman of the Loyalty Review Board of the Civil Service Commission. By then Peruvians had made Machu Picchu a part of their national heritage. In 1934 the site had been once more cleared of its underbrush under the direction of the Peruvian archaeologist Luis E. Valcárcel. Thenceforth it was developed as a major tourist attraction, a Peruvian combination of the Acropolis, Niagara Falls, and Shangri-la. A railroad was built from Cuzco to the foot of the mountain. When the connecting motor road farther up to the ruins was opened in 1948 Hiram Bingham was at hand as guest of honor. Fittingly, it was named *Carretera Hiram Bingham*.

THE DISCOVERY OF MACHU PICCHU

Hiram Bingham

One of the chief problems that faced the Yale Peruvian Expedition of 1911 was the question as to whether the young Inca Manco, fleeing from Pizarro's armies and establishing himself in the wilds of Vilcabamba, had left any traces in the shape of ruined palaces and temples. So we went about asking every one if they knew of any such.

It was known to a few people in Cuzco, chiefly residents of the province of Convención, that there were ruins, still undescribed, in the valley of the Urubamba. One friend told us that a muleteer had told him of some ruins near the bridge of San Miguel. Knowing the propensity of his countrymen to exaggerate, he placed little confidence in the report, and had passed by the place a score of times without taking the trouble to look into the matter. Another friend, who owned a sugar plantation on the river Vilcabamba itself, said he also had heard vague rumors of ruins. He was quite sure there were some near Pucyura, although he had been there and had never seen any. At length a talkative old peddler said there were ruins "finer than Choqquequirau" down the valley somewhere. But as he had never been to Choqquequirau, and no one placed any confidence in his word, anyhow, we could only hope there was some cause for his enthusiasm. Finally, there was the story in Wiener's picturesque but unreliable *Pérou et Bolivie,* that when he was in Ollantaytambo in 1875, or thereabouts, he was told there were interesting ruins down the Urubamba Valley at "Huaina-Picchu, or Matcho-Picchu" (*sic*). Wiener decided to go down the valley and look for them, but, owing to one reason or another, he failed to find them. Should we be any more successful?

We left Cuzco about the middle of July. The second day out brought us to the romantic valley of Ollantaytambo. Squier described it in glowing terms years ago, and it has lost none of its charm. The wonderful megaliths of the ancient fortress, the curious gabled buildings perched here and there on almost inaccessible crags, the magnificent *andenes* (terraces), where abundant crops are still harvested, will stand for ages to come as monuments to the energy and skill of a bygone race. It is now quite generally believed that the smaller buildings, crowded with niches, and made of small stones laid in clay and covered with a kind of stucco, were the work of the Incas and their subjects. On the other hand, the gigantic rocks so

Inca fortress (Sacsahuamán)

carefully fitted together to form the defenses of the fortress itself probably antedated the Incas, and, like the cyclopean walls of the Sacsahuaman fortress near Cuzco, were put in position by a pre-Inca or megalithic folk who may have built Tiahuanaco in Bolivia.

At all events, both Cuzco and Ollantaytambo have the advantage of
being the sites of a very ancient civilization, now shrouded in romance
and mystery. The climate and altitude (11,000 feet) of Cuzco deprive it
of lovely surroundings, but here at Tambo, as the natives call it, there is
everything to please the eye, from highly cultivated green fields, flower-
gardens, and brooks shaded by willows and poplars, to magnificent precipices, crowned by glaciers and snow-capped peaks. Surely this deserves
to be a place of pilgrimage.

After a day or two of rest and hard scrambles over the cliffs to the
various groups of ruins, we went down the Urubamba Valley to the northwest. A league from the fortress the road forks. The right branch ascends
a steep valley and crosses a snow-covered pass near the little-known and
relatively unimportant ruins of Havaspampa and Panticalla. Two leagues
beyond the fork, the Urubamba River has cut its way through precipitous
cliffs. This is the natural gateway to the ancient province of Vilcabamba.
For centuries it was virtually closed by the combined efforts of Nature

and man. The dangerous rapids of the river were impassable, but the precipices on the north side might with considerable effort be scaled. In fact,
the old road into the province apparently lay over their dizzy heights.
Accordingly man had built at the foot of the precipices a small but powerful fortress, Salapunco, fashioned after Sacsahuaman, but with only five
salients and re-entrant angles. The cliff itself was strengthened defensively
by walls, skilfully built on narrow ledges.

Salapunco has long been unoccupied. My first impression was that it
was placed here to defend the Ollantaytambo Valley from enemies coming
up from the Amazon valleys. Later I came to the conclusion that it was
intended to defend against enemies coming down the valley from Ollantaytambo. As a monolithic work of this kind could not in the nature of
things have been built by the Inca Manco when fleeing from the Spaniards,
and as its whole style and character seem to place it alongside the well-
known monolithic structures of the region about Cuzco and Ollantaytambo,
it seemed all the more extraordinary that it should have been placed as
a defense against that very region. Could it be that it was built by the
megalithic folk in order to defend a possible retreat in Vilcabamba? Hitherto no one had found or reported any megalithic remains farther down
the valley than this spot. In fact, Squier, whose *Peru* has for a generation
been the standard work on Inca architecture, does not appear to have
heard even of Salapunco, and Markham makes no mention of it. It never
occurred to us that in hunting for the remains of such palaces as Manco
Inca had the strength and time to build we were about to find remains
of a far more remote past, ruins that would explain why the fortress of
Salapunco was placed to defend Vilcabamba against the south, and not
the south against Vilcabamba and the savages of the Amazon jungles.

Passing Salapunco, we skirted the precipices and entered a most
interesting region, where we were continually charmed by the extent of
the ancient terraces, the length of the great *andenes*, the grandeur of the
snow-clad mountains, and the beauty of the deep, narrow valleys.

The next day we continued down the valley for another twenty miles.
And such a valley! While neither so grand as the Apurimac, near Choqquequirau, nor so exquisite as the more highly cultivated valleys of the
Alps, the grand cañon of the Urubamba from Torontoy to Colpani, a
distance of about thirty miles, has few equals in the world. It lacks the
rugged, massive severity of the Canadian Rockies and the romantic associations of the Rhine, but I know of no place that can compare with it
in the variety and extent of its charm. Not only has it snow-capped peaks,
gigantic precipices of solid granite rising abruptly thousands of feet from
its roaring stream, and the usual great beauty of a deep cañon winding
through mountains of almost incredible height, but there is added to this

the mystery of the dense tropical jungle and the romance of the ever-present remains of a bygone race.

It would make a dull story, full of repetition and superlatives, were I to try to describe the countless terraces, the towering cliffs, the constantly changing panorama, with the jungle in the foreground and glaciers in the lofty background. Even the so-called road got a bit monotonous, although it ran recklessly up and down rock stairways, sometimes cut out of the side of the precipice, at others running on frail bridges propped on brackets against the granite cliffs overhanging the swirling rapids. We made slow progress, but we lived in wonderland.

With what exquisite pains did the Incas, or their predecessors, rescue narrow strips of arable land from the river! Here the prehistoric people built a retaining wall of great stones along the very edge of the rapids. There they piled terrace on *anden* until stopped by a solid wall of rock. On this sightly bend in the river, where there is a particularly fine view up and down the valley, they placed a temple flanked by a great stone stairway. On that apparently insurmountable cliff they built unscalable walls, so that it should be actually, as well as seemingly, impregnable. They planted the lower levels with bananas and coca, and also yucca, that strange little tree whose roots make such a succulent vegetable. On the more lofty terraces they grew maize and potatoes.

In the afternoon we passed a hut called La Maquina, where travelers frequently stop for the night. There is some fodder here, but the density of the tropical forest, the steepness of the mountains, and the scarcity of anything like level land make living very precarious. We arrived at Mandorpampa, another grass-thatched hut, about five o'clock. The scenery and the road were more interesting than anything we had seen so far, or were likely to see again. Our camp was pitched in a secluded spot on the edge of the river. Carrasco, the sergeant sent with me from Cuzco, talked with a muleteer who lives near by, a fellow named Melchor Arteaga, who leases the land where we were camping. He said there were ruins in the vicinity, and some excellent ones at a place called Machu Picchu on top of the precipice near by, and that there were also ruins at Huayna Picchu, still more inaccessible, on top of a peak not far distant from our camp.

The next day, although it was drizzling, the promise of a *sol* (fifty cents gold) to be paid to him on our return from the ruins, encouraged Arteaga to guide me up to Machu Picchu. I left camp at about ten o'clock, and went from his house some distance up-stream. The valley is very narrow, with almost sheet precipices of solid granite on each side. On the road we passed a snake that had recently been killed. Arteaga was unable to give any other name for it than *"vivora,"* which means venomous, in distinction from *"culebra,"* or harmless snake.

Our naturalist spent the day in the bottom of the valley, collecting insects; the surgeon busied himself in and about camp; and I was accompanied on this excursion only by Carrasco and the guide, Arteaga. At ten forty-five, after having left the road and plunged down through the jungle to the river-bank, we came to a primitive bridge, made of four logs bound together with vines, and stretching across the stream a few inches above the roaring rapids. On the other side we had a fearfully hard climb for an hour and twenty minutes. A good part of the distance I went on all-fours. The path was in many places a primitive stairway, or crude step-ladder, at first through a jungle, and later up a very steep, grass-covered slope. The heat was excessive, but the view was magnificent after we got above the jungle. Shortly after noon we reached a hut where several good-natured Indians welcomed us and gave us gourds full of cool, delicious water, and a few cooked sweet-potatoes. All that we could see was a couple of grass huts and a few terraces, faced with stone walls. The pleasant Indian family had chosen this eagle's nest for a home. They told us there were better ruins a little farther along.

One can never tell, in this country, whether such a report is worthy of credence. "He may have been lying" is a good footnote to affix to all hearsay evidence. Accordingly we were not unduly excited. Nor was I in a great hurry to move. The water was cool, the wooden bench, covered with a woolen poncho, seemed most comfortable, and the view was marvelous. On both sides tremendous precipices fell away to the white rapids of the Urubamba River below. In front was the solitary peak of Huayna Picchu, seemingly inaccessible on all sides. Behind us were rocky heights and impassable cliffs. Down the face of one precipice the Indians had made a perilous path, which was their only means of egress in the wet season, when the bridge over which we had come would be washed away. Of the other precipice we had already had a taste. We were not surprised to hear the Indians say they only went away from home about once a month.

Leaving the huts, we climbed still farther up the ridge. Around a slight promontory the character of the stone-faced *andenes* began to improve, and suddenly we found ourselves in the midst of a jungle-covered maze of small and large walls, the ruins of buildings made of blocks of white granite, most carefully cut and beautifully fitted together without cement. Surprise followed surprise until there came the realization that we were in the midst of as wonderful ruins as any ever found in Peru. It seemed almost incredible that this city, only five days' journey from Cuzco, should have remained so long undescribed and comparatively unknown. Yet so far as I have been able to discover, there is no reference in the Spanish chronicles to Machu Picchu. It is possible that not even the conquistadors ever saw this wonderful place. From some rude scrawls on the stones of a temple we learned that it was visited in 1902 by one Lizarraga, a local muleteer. It must have been known long before that, because, as we said above, Wiener, who was in Ollantaytambo in the 70's, speaks of having heard of ruins at a place named "Matcho-Picchu," which he did not find.

The Indians living here say that they have been here four years. They have planted corn and vegetables among the ruins and on some of the terraces. One or two families live in ancient buildings on which they have built roofs. There are also three huts of recent construction. The climate seems to be excellent. We noticed growing sweet and white potatoes, maize, sugar-cane, beans, peppers, tomatoes, and a kind of gooseberry.

Travelers like the great Castelnau, the flowery Wiener, and the picturesque Marcou, who have gone north from Cuzco to the Urubamba River and beyond, had to avoid this region, where they would have found most of interest. The Urubamba is not navigable, even for canoes, at this point, and is flanked by such steep walls that travel along its banks was impossible until a few years ago. Even intrepid explorers like Castelnau were obliged to make a long detour and to follow a trail that led over snowy passes into the parallel valleys of the Occobamba and the Yanatili. Thus it happened that the Urubamba Valley from Ollantaytambo to the sugar plantation of Huadquiña offered us a virgin field, and by the same token it was in this very region that the Incas and their predecessors found it easy to live in safety. Not only did they find here every variety of climate, valleys so deep as to produce the precious coca, yucca, and plantain of the tropics, and slopes high enough to be suitable for maize and potatoes, with nights cold enough to freeze the latter in the approved aboriginal fashion, but also a practically impregnable place of refuge.

About twenty years ago the Peruvian government, recognizing the needs of the enterprising planters who were opening up the lower valley of the Urubamba, decided to construct a mule trail along the banks of the river. The road was expensive, but it has enabled the much-desired coca and aguardiente to be shipped far more quickly and cheaply than from the Santa Ana Valley to Cuzco, and it avoids the necessity of climbing over the dangerous snowy passes so vividly described by Marcou and others. This new road enabled us to discover that the Incas—or their predecessors— had left here, in the beautiful fastnesses of Vilcabamba, stone witnesses of their ancient civilization more interesting and extensive than any found since the days of the conquistadors.

It is difficult to describe Machu Picchu. The ruins are located on a ridge which ends in a magnificent peak, on top of which are said to be the ruins of Huayna Picchu. There are precipices on both sides, and a large number of terraces, evidently intended for agricultural purposes.

There are also *azequias* (stone-lined watercourses), although it is at present somewhat difficult to see whence the water was brought. There are three small springs here, but the Indians do not know of any running water. As it must have taken a considerable water supply to furnish water to the inhabitants of such a large place as Machu Picchu, it may be that an irrigating ditch was carried back into the mountains for many miles to some point from which an unfailing supply of water could be secured.

There is a very nicely made bath-house, a fountain with some niches, and an adjoining retiring-room with a seat. The water was conducted into the bath-house through a stone channel, over a nicely cut stone block. On top of a gigantic granite boulder near the bath-house is a semicircular building, made of nearly rectangular blocks, and containing nicely finished niches on the inside. Underneath the boulder is a cave lined with carefully worked stone and containing very large niches, the best and tallest that I have ever seen. There are many stairways made of blocks of granite. One stairway is divided so as to permit the insertion of a catch-basin for water. This stairway leads to a point farther up the ridge, where there is a place which I have called the Sacred Plaza.

On the south side of this plaza there are terraces lined with large blocks, after the fashion of Sacsahuaman, and also a kind of bastion, semicircular, with carefully cut, nearly rectangular stones, somewhat like those in the well-known semicircular Temple of the Sun, now the Dominican Monastery, at Cuzco. On the east side of the Sacred Plaza are the walls of a rectangular building, twenty-nine feet long by thirty-seven wide, containing niches and projecting cylinders resembling in many ways the buildings at Choqquequirau. It has two doors on the side toward the plaza, but no windows.

On the west side is a remarkable structure, truly megalithic, entirely open on the side facing the plaza, and entirely closed on the other three sides. The interior measurements of this building are 25.9 x 21 feet. As in the case of all the other buildings, its roof is missing. It is made of blocks of white granite, arranged in tiers. The stones in the lower tier are very much larger than those in any of the others. . . The upper tiers are of nearly rectangular blocks, very much smaller, but cut with indescribable accuracy, and fitted together as a glass stopper is fitted to a bottle. The distinguishing characteristic of this building is that the ends of the walls are not vertical, but project in an obtuse angle. At the point of the angle the stone was cut away, apparently to admit a large wooden beam, which probably extended across in front of the structure to the point of the angle at the other end of the wall. This may have been used to support the roof, or to bring it down part way, like a mansard roof. This building is lined with small niches, high up above reach, and made with great care and precision. In the center of the back wall, and near the ground, is the largest stone of all, which measures 14.1 feet in length, and appears to have been either a high seat or an altar.

From the Sacred Plaza there is a magnificent view on both sides; to the north a tumbled mass of gigantic forest-clad mountains, rising to snow-capped peaks, and to the south the widening Urubamba Valley, with the river winding through its bottom, protected on both sides by precipitous mountains. On the highest part of the ridge is a small structure, carefully built of rectangular blocks, with nicely made niches. Near it is a large boulder, carved into what is known as an *intihuatana* stone, supposed by some to have been a sun-dial. It has steps carved in it, and is in a fine state of preservation.

Directly below the Sacred Plaza the terraces run down to a large horseshoe-shaped plaza, evidently an ancient playground, or possibly an agricultural field. On the other side of this are a great many houses of lesser importance, although well built and huddled closely together. Many of the houses are simple in construction. Some have gabled ends. Nearly all have niches. A few are of remarkably fine workmanship, as fine as anything in Cuzco. The material used is nearly uniformly white granite. The finish is exquisite, and the blocks are fitted together with a nicety that surpasses description. The work is of the same character as that which so aroused the marvel of the Spanish conquerors. Some of the structures are nicely squared, like the palaces at Cuzco. Others have niches which resemble the best at Ollantaytambo. Cylindrical stone blocks, projecting from the walls, are common, both inside and outside the structure. In general they are larger and very much better fashioned than those at Choqquequirau. In places the ruins are almost labyrinthian. The plan gives a better idea than can be expressed in words of the extent and character of Machu Picchu.

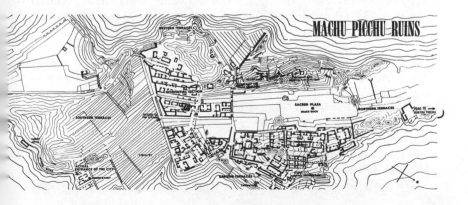

On the north side of the Sacred Plaza is another structure, somewhat resembling that described as being on the west side, in that the side facing the plaza is entirely open. Outside of the building are cylindrical stones projecting from the wall. Huge stones were employed in the lower tier, as in the similar building on the west side of the plaza, and their ends— that is to say, the ends of the side walls—are followed out in an obtuse angle, as in the other structure. Similarly, the point of the angle contains a hole cut into the stone, evidently intended to permit the admission of a large wooden beam. In order to support this beam, which extended across from one end of the building to the other, a single block was erected, half-way between the ends, and notched at the top, so as to permit the beam, or the ends of two beams if such were used, to rest upon it. This structure has an internal measurement of 14.9 x 33.7 feet. Its most striking feature is its row of remarkable windows. Three large windows, 3.1 feet wide and nearly 4 feet high, are let into the back wall, and look out upon a magnificent prospect over the jungle-clad mountains. Nowhere else in Peru have I seen an ancient building whose most noticeable characteristic is the presence of three large windows. Can it be that this unique feature will help us solve the riddle of this wonderful city of white granite?

Sir Clements Markham, in his recent and valuable book on the Incas of Peru, devotes a chapter to a myth which was told to all the Spanish chroniclers by their native informants, which he believes is the fabulous version of a distant historical event. The end of the early megalithic civilization is stated to have been caused by a great invasion from the south, possibly by barbarians from the Argentine pampas. The whole country broke up into anarchy, and savagery returned, ushering in a period of medieval barbarism. A remnant of the highly civilized folk took refuge in a district called Tamputocco, where some remnants of the old civilization were protected from the invaders by the inaccessible character of the country. Here the fugitives multiplied. Their descendants were more civilized and more powerful than their neighbors, and in time became crowded, and started out to acquire a better and more extensive territory. The legend relates that out of a hill with three openings or windows there came three tribes. These tribes eventually settled at Cuzco and founded the Inca empire. *Tampu* means "tavern," and *toco* a "window." The Spaniards were told that Tamputocco was not far from Cuzco, at a place called Paccaritampu, but the exact locality of Tamputocco is uncertain. So far no place answering to its description has been located. It seems to me that there is a possibility that the refuge of this pre-Inca fugitive tribe was here in the Vilcabamba mountains, and that Machu Picchu is the original Tamputocco, although this is contrary to the accepted location.

Certainly this region was well fitted by nature to be such a refuge;

unquestionably here we have evidences of megalithic occupation; and here at Machu Picchu is a "tavern" with three windows. A view taken from this Temple of the Three Windows from below makes it easy to suggest that this was the hill with the three openings or windows referred to in the myth of the origin of the Inca empire. I may be wholly mistaken in this, and I shall await with interest the discovery of any other place that fits so well the description of Tamputocco, whence came the Incas.

In the mean time it seems probable that Machu Picchu, discovered while on a search for the *last* Inca capital, was the *first*, the capital from which the Incas started on that glorious career of empire that eventually embraced a large part of South America.

Inca builders, Poma de Ayala

4

Robbing the dead has been a flourishing industry in Peru since the Conquest. Hence the conspicuous *huaquero*—a Quechua derivation meaning the man who digs *huacas,* sanctuaries or burial places, and retrieves *huacos,* sacred objects. Before archaeological investigation ever got under way, knowledge of buried Peruvian antiquities was entirely due to the reckless trade in which whole villages might engage full time. *Huaqueros* transmitted the first reports of startling ceramics and textiles. Of course, precious metal was their prime objective, and the exquisite silver and gold objects and jewelry they found rarely survived their cupidity. They wrought destruction beyond remedy. Yet today museum collections all over the world owe most of their treasures from the Chavín, Moche, Chimú, and Nazca civilizations to disreputable pothunters. In almost every instance that scholars became aware of hitherto unknown cultures, they had initially been alerted by the ware thrown on the market by the professional grave robbers.

Whatever their dismay, it is only the priggish among the archaeologists who would deny their debt. And then, before it became fully and self-consciously scientific, archaeology itself differed rather in intention than method from the practices of those irreverent rascals. Every archaeologist sooner or later realizes that all the talk about "stratification," "in situ," and "carbon-14" cannot hide the ugly fact that he too is engaged in disturbing the peace of the dead. The dividing line between him and the grave robber is uncomfortably thin. No honest account of antiquarian pursuits can gloss this over.

A. Hyatt Verrill, who was an explorer-adventurer first, and only on occasion an archaeologist (and then little concerned with technique), exemplifies the role of the amateur, who will often be blessed with discoveries where the expert draws blank after blank. Lady Luck shone on Verrill many times during his unconventional digs, as he freely notes with a dose of self-directed irony in the following account.

But what made his successes possible were the conditions peculiar to Peru. This South American country has along its thousand miles of Pacific coast one of the globe's driest deserts. The nitrate-rich soil is hence an excellent preserver of delicate articles, including mortal man himself. Here is one of the reasons why ancient Peruvian textiles—among the world's great artistic creations—are so important: even though cloth of equal

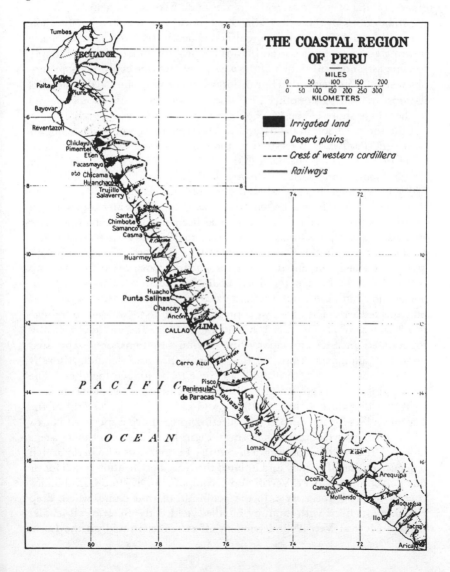

quality may have been produced in the more humid Andean inlands and in other American regions from Mexico to Ecuador, little of it has survived.

This desert belt is crossed by some thirty rivers bringing down water from the Andes and affording, with the aid of irrigation, intensive cultivation. The small streams were regular little Niles. They provided the setting for a great number of desert cultures, some concentrated in one valley, others spilling over into several adjacent ones. Like the ancient Egyptians, the inhabitants of the valley kingdoms would lay out their towns, their pyramids and shrines in the non-cultivated desert, thereby unintentionally insuring greater staying power. In time the proliferation of the dead simply became astronomical. Much of the area grew into one continuous necropolis where, as in Belzoni's Theban forays, every step one took "crushed a mummy in some part or other." E. George Squier, as we have seen, referred to the whole shore of the Moche valley as "a veritable Golgotha."

Still another boon to the despoilers—be they *huaqueros* or archaeologists —was the Peruvians' piety toward the dead coupled with the universal belief in an afterlife. The dead had to be well equipped on their further travels. Some were buried with a golden disk in the mouth—like the Chinese—apparently to be able to offer an "obolus" for their passage to the netherworld. There is no reason to read into all this an obsession with death, of which the Egyptians have also been wrongly accused. Ancient Peruvians nevertheless—and this is characteristic of the various civilizations on the coast and in the Andes—maintained a strange intimacy with their own dead, which amounted to ancestor worship. Corpses were buried and reburied. We know that the dried bodies of the Inca rulers were taken out of their burial chambers and, dressed in gorgeous finery, paraded at religious festivals. They then were presented with food and left to indulge in solemn conversation. Even in colonial days an Indian would have a mummified ancestor accompany him in vital situations. Some appeared in such a manner at court, so that a Spanish witness could write: "It appears that the living and the dead come to be judged together." The kidnapping of a corpse could be used in blackmailing its offspring.

Verrill dug during the late 1920's and early 1930's in several of the coastal valleys for the purpose of collecting museum specimens. At Nazca and Pachacamac (southern and central Peru) he followed in the footsteps of Max Uhle, the dean of twentieth-century Peruvianists who inaugurated sequence dating of pottery and isolated the Nazca civilization noted for its fine polychrome pottery. Verrill also accompanied Dr. Julio C. Tello, discoverer of the Paracas style, to the peninsula of that name, where deep burial crypts filled with mummy bundles yielded the finest of all textiles known. Most of Verrill's independent efforts concentrated on the Lurín

Valley near Lima. There, in the shadow of the great pyramid shrine of Pachacamac, a mecca of Peruvians during pre-Inca and Inca days, burials crowded in even more than elsewhere, because of the desire to be near Pachacamac-Viracocha, the supreme creator.

A. Hyatt Verrill was in his long life (1871–1954) extraordinarily prolific as author of 105 books, illustrator, naturalist, and explorer. Born in New Haven, the son of a Yale professor, he attended the Yale School of Fine Arts, and studied zoology under his father. He then illustrated the natural history sections of Webster's International Dictionary. Meanwhile, he had already begun exploring in Bermuda, the West Indies, the Guianas, and Central America. In the Dominican Republic he discovered in 1907 a supposedly extinct animal, the *Solenodon paradoxus,* an insectivorous mammal. He took out patents in color photography as early as 1902. For years on end he resided consecutively in the British West Indies and British Guiana. During a visit to Panama in 1924 he excavated a hitherto unknown pre-Columbian culture, which is his one great archaeological contribution. Peru and Bolivia, where he had traveled previously, became his territory from 1928 to 1932. In later years Verrill was engaged in salvaging Spanish galleons. He settled permanently in Florida in 1940, launching a business in shells and continuing his writing career. His discussions of pre-Columbian civilizations revived some of the more fantastic nineteenth-century theories of Old World (Egyptian, Sumerian, etc.) connections, with their inevitable apparatus of sunken continents, bearded strangers, and white (preferably Aryan) culture bearers.

Exhibiting mummy of dead Inca, Poma de Ayala

MINING FOR INCA MUMMIES

A. Hyatt Verrill

One might think that the people of Lurín, who dwell at the very edge of the ruins of Pachacamak, might be afraid of ghosts, for as a rule the Latin-Americans, and more especially the humbler folk, are exceedingly superstitious. And surely, if spirits ever walk, then Pachacamak should be the most thoroughly haunted. But apparently the people who dwell in the shadows of the ruins have not the slightest dread of ghosts or spirits. Perhaps, to their way of thinking, only Christians have ghosts, or it may be that they feel that the ghosts of Pachacamak have enough and to spare to attend to within the confines of the ruined city and will not wander far afield. Whatever the reason, the close proximity of the city with its thousands of dead, and which at night is a most uncanny and spectral spot, does not seem to trouble the living in the least. Indeed, those who dwell upon the borders of the ruins have had no small part in the desecration of the Pachacamak graves, and human bones and grinning skulls lie scattered about their dooryards.

Pachacamac ruins

Even those who have business abroad do not hesitate to ride at dead of night through the ruins, passing the cemeteries with their countless graves as casually as though the bleached bones were so many rocks, and trampling many a skull under their horses' feet.

But in these respects the inhabitants of Lurín differ not at all from all the other inhabitants of Peru—both natives and foreigners. In fact were the dwellers in and about Lima at all nervous for fear of ghosts or did they respect the dead, there would be no Lima, or for that matter any other cities or towns in most parts of Peru, for the country is one vast cemetery.

From Ecuador to Chile and from the coast to the Andes there is scarcely a square mile without its cemeteries, its mounds or its ruins filled with dead. No one would dare estimate the number of bodies that were interred or that yet remain even in a small area of the country.

Many cemeteries cover hundreds of acres; many burial-mounds are stupendous, and in many ruined cities every available bit of ground is filled with mummies. The Huaca Juliana just outside of Lima—nearly half a mile in length, nearly a quarter of a mile wide, and over one hundred feet in height—is composed of countless brick cubicles containing mummies, and this is but one of dozens of almost equally large burial-mounds in the vicinity of Lima alone.

The Avenida Progreso that connects Lima with Callao, is cut through another immense mound and for months after the highway was completed the roadsides were littered with human skulls—many with the dried skin and hair still attached—human bones, mummy wrappings, broken pottery, wooden implements, and other artifacts ruthlessly torn from the tombs and dumped aside by the steam-shovels. Even today, bones, wrappings, and skulls may be seen protruding from the sides of the mound where it was cut through to form the road. Many of the hazards on the Lima Country Club Golf Course are ancient graves and mounds, and in the new urbanization developments about Lima the homes of the suburbanites are erected over ancient graveyards. It is not at all unusual to see a modern residence with scattered skulls, scalps, mummy wrappings and bones within a few feet of the front door, and in cultivating their flower gardens the residents are as likely to turn up skulls as stones.

I doubt if there is another country on earth where the inhabitants dwell happily and contentedly in the midst of countless dead; but as I said before, no one gives the matter a thought and the people do not appear to regard bodies and bones of men a thousand or more years old in the same way as they regard cadavers of persons who have died and been buried recently.

Ever since the days of the Spanish conquest, mining for mummies has been a more or less lucrative industry in Peru. Not that the mummies were desirable or valuable, but because the Incans and pre-Incans interred ornaments, weapons, utensils, and implements with their dead, and some of these were of silver or gold. How many tens of thousands of mummies have thus been disinterred and destroyed no one can guess. And in addition to the countless numbers thus dug up by the professional mummy miners, or *huaqueros* as they are called, thousands more have been disinterred by archaeologists, curio seekers and others, while many thousands more have been destroyed in the course of constructing railways and roads, digging irrigation ditches, cultivating land and carrying on various public and private works.

One would suppose that, years ago, the supply of mummies would have been exhausted. But so vast was the number of dead buried in Peru that despite all that have been disinterred practically no impression has been made, and what is more, scientists are constantly finding mummies and remains of hitherto unknown races and cultures.

Strictly speaking, the mummies are not mummies. That is, aside from those in one or two districts, the bodies were not embalmed nor purposely preserved. They merely were buried in the dry desert sand, in adobe brick tombs, or in cylindrical rock-lined graves where, owing to the dry climate and a certain amount of nitrates in the earth, they become desiccated and are indefinitely preserved. And the same conditions also preserve the innumerable articles interred with the bodies. The finest textiles, the most delicate laces, the most gorgeous of feather robes and headdresses are as fresh, as bright and as perfect as on the day they were made, and from these various objects it is possible to reconstruct and revisualize much of the life, the customs and the habits of these Peruvians who lived from one to perhaps five thousand years ago.

Obviously the majority of bodies are those of poor and humble peasants, of farmers, fishermen, and their ilk whose mummy-bundles contain very little of interest or of scientific or intrinsic value. Stone, shell or clay ornaments, an occasional stone implement, gourds filled with maize, peanuts, or other food; baskets containing needles, thread and weaving implements, pouches filled with cotton seeds; llama-hair slings and cotton spindles are the usual objects found, together with pieces of pottery and various kinds of woolen and cotton cloth. But one never knows beforehand what may be found when mining for mummies in Peru. There is no means of distinguishing the burial place of a peasant from that of a prince, a priest, a chief, or a medicine-man, and oftentimes a wonderful collection of archaeological treasures may be revealed.

From one grave I obtained a magnificent bronze battle-axe with handle complete, a most beautiful and effective weapon still capable of slicing a man's head from his shoulders or cleaving his skull. From another grave— in a small, insignificant mound on the outskirts of Lima, a mound so small and unpromising I had never bothered digging into it, I disinterred the mummy of an old medicine-man. Upon his head was a crown of black feathers, he was dressed in elaborate robes, and tucked into the folds of these were numbers of small woven pouches containing his stock of medicines, his "herbs and simples," and his instruments. About his neck was a silver collar and a string of lapis lazuli beads from which was suspended a carved wooden llama and a silver pin in the form of a heron's head. Evidently he belonged to the heron clan, for the pottery found with him bore designs embodying herons while a carved wooden spoon—possibly used in dispensing his medicines—also bore the figure of the heron.

Peruvian mummy

There were also several stoppered bottles made from gourds, each containing remains of dried-up medicinal preparations, a curved bronze surgical knife, a number of bronze pincers—used for extracting hairs—a feather wand, a bundle of knotted *quipos* or message strings and a peculiar wooden knife-like implement. Altogether the old doctor's mummy-bundle contained over one hundred different specimens—a veritable miniature museum in itself. In another grave I found the mummy of a woman who judging from her garments, must have been high in the social whirl of her day; a woman of wealth and station and a leader of fashion. No doubt when she walked Peruvian soil and queened it over her less fortunate sisters, she was regarded as the best dressed woman of Peru, as she deserved to be. Her gown, which might well have been the model from which present day evening gowns are copied, was of the finest lace, the upper portion of rich brown, the lower portion of old ivory, while over this was a drapery of pale gray-blue lace, the whole so perfectly preserved that it might be worn by any woman today. About her head was a fillet of chased silver; she wore a necklace of polished carnelian and turquoise beads as large as pigeons' eggs; about her wrists were bracelets of silver, pearl shell, and semi-precious stones, and her long hair was confined in a net of loosely woven human hair and was fastened at the back by means of a fibre band decorated with delightfully carved figures cut from mother-of-pearl.

And instead of being wrapped in coarse textiles, this Peruvian lady of over two thousand years ago was wrapped in a shroud of thirty-five yards of the most beautiful white lace! Talk about old lace! Here was really old lace, moreover, lace made of wool as well as cotton, and as perfect as on that far distant day when sorrowing friends and bereaved relatives wrapped the dead woman's body in the filmy material she loved so well in life.

But even more interesting were the other objects buried with this Moujik [Moche] woman. There was a hand loom with a strip of cloth half finished upon it, and there was a work basket filled with needles, woolen and cotton thread, yarn and a leather thimble, showing quite clearly that even if she were a leader of fashion she was no drone, no idle rich, but an industrious young lady. Still she must have been as vain as any woman of today and as careful of her personal appearance, for two beautifully woven and decorated pouches or "vanity bags" contained her toilet accessories and her cosmetics—practically exact counterparts of those carried by every girl and woman today. There was a mirror of polished marcasite set in a carved and painted wooden frame, a comb made from palm wood, a powder box formed from a gourd and a powder puff of soft feathers; there were bronze pincers for removing superfluous hair, a bronze knife for paring her finger nails, a little gourd phial containing cinnabar paste with a silver spatula for applying it to the lips, several pins, a cuticle stick much like the modern ones of orange wood; a dainty spoon—perhaps the owner was squeamish and preferred an individual spoon when taking her maté tea. There were also various other articles that may be found in almost any woman's purse, ancient or modern.

The discovery of such interesting and scientifically valuable mummies is, however, a matter of luck and nothing more. To be sure, certain localities contain a larger proportion of richly clad, richly decorated mummies than others, yet as a whole I should say that not one in five hundred mummy-bundles contains gold, silver, or other valuables, and that not one in fifty contains anything other than the commonest textiles, the most ordinary utensils and the plainest pottery. Luck may have no standing in the realm of science, it may be impossible to prove—either by logic or by any known scientific formula—that such a thing or condition exists, yet it enters very largely into all or nearly all scientific discoveries and achievements. Especially is this the case with such branches of science as archaeology and ethnology. I have known competent, trained archaeologists to delve and dig for months without notable results, and then along comes some amateur at the game and, at the first spadeful of earth, he turns up priceless archaeological treasures. In the many years I have devoted to ethnology and archaeology in South and Central America, luck has ever been my strongest ally and it proved faithful to me in Peru.

Unfinished cloth found at Pachacamac

For nearly six years I had delved in prehistoric ruins that were teeming cities a thousand or more years before Christ was born. I had resurrected pottery, weapons, tools, and textiles from tombs that had been sealed in the days when Ur was at its zenith. I had mined mummies in the desert sands, had burrowed into immense burial-mounds, and had dug into strange, bottle-shaped graves on rock-strewn *punos*.

Scores of mummies had been brought to light. I had been very lucky. I had secured feather robes and ornate headdresses from the shrivelled, desiccated bodies of long-dead Moujik chieftains; marvellous ceramics from the immense mummy-bundles of the mysterious Nascans; beautiful pottery from the cell-like niches wherein the Chimus placed their dead; copper, bronze, and silver ornaments with here and there a bit of gold. I had obtained carved woodwork and objects rich with mosaics; beads of lapis, of turquoise, of semi-precious stones; I had found the mummy of an ancient medicine-man, the lace-wrapped mummy of a prehistoric debutante—in fact nearly every object known to or used by the Incan and pre-Incan races.

But never had I discovered the mummy of an Inca. By that I do not mean the mummy of one of the Incan people. On the contrary, having been the most recent of Peruvian aboriginal cultures—barely six hundred years of age—that of the Incans left the most abundant of all remains. And as the Incan people as a whole were woefully lacking in worldly goods, as they were a most efficiently utilitarian race who rather neglected the arts for art's sake only, and who considered neither gold, silver, nor precious stones intrinsically valuable, and as practically every museum in the world possesses large collections of Incan culture artifacts, I had, as a rule, passed by their mounds and burials and had confined my work to more promising and less known graves and tombs of the Incans' predecessors. So when I say I had never found the mummy of an Inca I mean the mummy of a person of royal blood—a reigning Inca, a noble, a prince, a governor of a province; and for that matter I never dreamed of finding one.

Mining for mummies is an expensive business—or pastime—and I had found by experience that mining Incan mummies was a waste of time and money.

Neither is mining for mummies pleasant work. It is a hot, tiresome, and exceedingly dirty occupation. The light dust of ages; the mingled sand, disintegrated animal matter, decayed outer textiles of the mummy-bundles, and portions of bodies which have failed to dry up, surrounds one in a cloud, and one literally breathes mummies. It is bad enough digging under such conditions where the chances are even if not in favor of finding something scientifically worth while. But it is heartbreaking labor thrown away when the chances are all on the side of finding little or nothing.

Still, somewhere, buried in some tomb, or grave, or mound, there must be mummies of Incan nobility—even the bodies of the supreme reigning Incas themselves. And as the Incan nobility—which included the priests, the lawmakers, the provincial rulers, the generals, and practically all Incan officials, were gloriously arrayed and adorned with the finest products of Incan looms, with ceremonial paraphernalia, with insignia, and with ornaments of precious metals, their mummies must, I knew, be veritable archaeological treasure-troves.

No one, as far as known, had ever found one of them, however, and hence there was little real first-hand knowledge of just how the Incas and their nobles were attired, for the reports of the old Spanish conquerors do not agree on these matters. Why no one had ever found a royal mummy was something of a mystery. Perhaps, I thought, they were most carefully secreted to insure that they would never be disturbed. Perhaps the old Dons tortured those who knew of their burial-places until the unfortunates revealed where the royal mummies might be found and stripped of their valuables by the conquerors. Or again there was the rather remote possibility that the Incas were not interred with their riches but were buried in ordinary clothes and wrappings like those of their subjects.

At all events it would have been a hopeless task to have dug all or even a small portion of Incan graves in the faint hopes of finding the body of an Inca. And I did not trust sufficiently to my proverbial good luck to cause me to feel that I might dig at random in any one spot and be rewarded by coming upon the mummy of one of those "golden ears" as the Spaniards called the Incan nobles, because of the gold shells or ear-coverings worn by them.

This custom, by the way, according to tradition, had a most curious and interesting origin. One of the sons of the Inca, Pacha-Kutik [Pachacutec or Pachacuti], lost an ear in battle, and to hide the mutilation he wore oval golden coverings over his ears. Then, in order that he might not be conspicuous—as well as to commemorate his bravery—the Incan princes all followed his example and wore the *huancos* which in time became the recognized insignia of royalty.

But that I should ever find a mummy with the golden ears never entered my head. And then "Lady Luck" stepped in and played her little joke.

I had long intended to try digging in a very small, very inconspicuous mound which, somehow, seemed different from the others in the vicinity. I had taken my medicine-man with his hundred odd implements and articles from another small mound, and I had begun to have a "hunch" that small mounds might prove richer fields for excavations than the larger ones. At any rate they were easier to dig and could be excavated more thoroughly. Moreover, this particular mound contained very little adobe brickwork but was mainly composed of loose gravel and earth. So at last, selecting a spot that appeared to be promising, I started work. Dust flew in clouds, under the blazing sun perspiration ran in streams, but presently a human skull was unearthed. There was no sign of a mummy or even a wrapping; evidently the cranium had fallen from some body that had been buried near the surface and had weathered out in the course of centuries. Then a bed of sticks and leaves was disclosed—sure indications of a burial beneath. Carefully this was removed, revealing a few fragments of animals' skeletons, some bits of textiles, and two or three pottery jars. Then two more skulls—one a woman's, the other an infant's—and a few bones. I was, as the children say in Hunt the Thimble, "getting warm." Somewhere below that thick layer of tightly packed leaves and trash was a mummy; but whether that of some humble farmer or a man or woman of high station was impossible to guess.

To go farther with the pick and shovel would have been to court disaster, so on hands and knees I commenced digging carefully with a trowel. Presently I came upon a small, tightly wrapped bundle of basketry containing the mummified body of a little Incan dog. The next moment my trowel struck wood, and most carefully scraping away the sand and dust I discovered four upright stakes. They were lashed together with fibre ropes to form a quadrangle and the intervening space was packed with fine dry fibres.

My interest and excitement now ran high. Never had I found a burial of this sort, and with the utmost care I lifted the fibre. A cry of amazement and delight came from my lips. Brilliant yellow and scarlet feathers were revealed, and very gently I lifted a gorgeous crown from the mass of brownish hair that covered the skull beneath. It was a regal affair and in a

Mummy bundles

perfect state of preservation. But more surprises were in store. Beside one of the upright posts was a wooden shield; beside another a bronze-headed spear with palm-wood staff, and a magnificent bronze axe was beside the third stake. Little by little I withdrew the masses of fibre that filled the grave, until at last the mummy could be seen, a shapeless bundle wrapped in heavy striped cloth. But it scarcely could be called a mummy. Little of the body remained except the bones. Scarcely a trace of skin adhered to the skeleton, and though every care was used the bones dropped apart when the bundle was lifted from the grave. But the wrappings were intact and as I commenced unwrapping the bundle I scarcely could believe my own eyes. Never had I seen such a mummy. There were textiles of the rarest and finest weaves and patterns; ornate pouches, bundles of *quipos,* woven sashes and belts. And as each strip of cloth or each garment was removed more and finer objects were disclosed. There were implements of bronze and wood, charms or amulets, a carved wooden sceptre or staff tipped and ornamented with gold. About the bony wrists were golden bands with raised figures of birds and the Sun-god. Below the knees were golden bands from which hung little metal ornaments tipped with scarlet feathers. Upon the skeleton's chest were three golden disks each embossed with the tiger-head image of Inti. And at the front of the headdress, above the exquisite *llautu* or head-band about the painted wooden false face, was the golden symbol of the rainbow—the royal Incan standard—topped by a pompom of scarlet and black feathers with a little gold sun hanging over the forehead. All or any of these alone would have proved the mummy that of a royal personage, for only Incan nobility was permitted to wear the rainbow symbol and the golden Sun-gods. But best of all, there were the golden *huancos* that in life had covered the ears of the deceased. Their presence left no doubt of my tremendous luck. I had unearthed the mummy of an Inca!

5

After World War I Peru was no longer, archaeologically speaking, a no man's land. Travelers and surveyors on the lookout for any evidence of ruins had crossed it again and again from the parched coast to the high Andes. Their narratives, beginning in the early nineteenth century, swelled the literature on ancient sites, which in both number and grandeur could vie with those of the Near East. A few surprises might still have been hidden in the forest vastness where the Andes sloped down to the Amazon, yet here, too, it was widely believed, Hiram Bingham had rounded off the record when he at last located the one missing Inca city. Undoubtedly, the desert continued to cover untold burials, which *huaqueros* would sooner or later sniff out. From such tombs quantities of objects could be expected to flow, though it was held unlikely that they would add much to the knowledge of pre-Columbian Peru. Yet new developments were afoot.

Around the turn of the century, a German archaeologist had brought to the Peruvian work the stratigraphic techniques of Flinders Petrie. Soon Tello's excavations at the Paracas peninsula did actually add new and quite unanticipated elements to the pre-Inca picture. However, perhaps the greatest stimulus to the archaeology of all of Peru came neither from excavation of underground crypts nor from exploration along jungle trails. It was brought about by aviation and air photography. In Peru that new phase was initiated by the Shippee-Johnson Peruvian Expedition of 1931. Its members were a group of young men from New Jersey led by twenty-year-old Robert Shippee, son of a Red Bank broker, who acted as pilot and historian to the air-borne mission. Co-leader George R. Johnson had already been engaged in aerial photography for the Peruvian Naval Air Service.

That the airplane should give the archaeologist one of the most exacting instruments of discovery is not without paradox. Instead of burrowing in the soil and extracting objects—the traditional task of the "dirt" archaeologist—distance rather than proximity is the great boon of this twentieth-century approach. The farther up you go—to a point—the more tangible may become the handiwork of the ancients—the overall principle being that observation from a high altitude offers perspective not visible from the ground. From the air, changes in the soil and its vegetation, due to partly or completely effaced human occupation, will show up in precise patterns under photographic exposure or even to the naked eye. Conditions of light, optic angles, or humidity of the soil may help. In this manner it has been possible to sight long-abandoned irrigation canals, fortifications, roads, and whole settlements over which men have trod for generations without having any suspicion of their existence. Air photography can also furnish maps which, in a split second, may perform the tedious work of months of ground surveys, besides being of a far higher degree of exactitude.

It was largely with the purpose of recording by camera the best known ruined sites of Peru that the Shippee-Johnson Expedition had been launched. One of its principal objectives had been the study of Chan-Chan. Nevertheless, the young fliers were blessed with spectacular discoveries, most valuable of which was that of a great wall running for some fifty miles from the coast through the Santa Valley into the highlands. It showed up like a long cicatrice across desert ridges. The wall was constructed from stones and adobe. Originally it rose to a height of about fifteen feet from a base of equal breadth.

Peruvian warriors, from a coastal vase

The new "Chinese Wall of Peru," as it was immediately dubbed by the press, had never been reported in the literature. Julio Tello, who knew the terrain better than anybody else, stated flatly that he had no inkling of it. Like Sir Aurel Stein's *limes* in Central Asia, the discovery was momentous. But while Stein was able to elucidate the origin and purpose of his *limes*, the Peruvian wall remains something of a riddle. This points up one of the difficulties of archaeology in South America, where the reconstruction of antiquity has to proceed almost wholly from excavated evidence. When the leading Peruvianists were consulted, the majority thought the wall was built to protect the Chimú empire. Perhaps it was meant to ward off Inca invasions.

Or did it just mark a boundary? That it was part of a defense system, there could be little doubt because of the nearness of a number of round and square fortresses—on both sides—which the Shippee-Johnson Expedition sighted during a second flight. These bastions (some fifty have been pinpointed so far) are not, however, immediately adjoining. They could conceivably be of a later date. Shippee himself was puzzled by the fact that the wall was far inland from what was known to have been the southern border of Chimú territory at Paramonga. He thought it was likely to have been a second or last line of defense. However, it also might have marked an earlier stage of Chimú expansion and then served, as Victor von Hagen suggests, both defensive and aggressive purposes.

Three years after Shippee, in 1934, Cornelius Van S. Roosevelt, the son of Theodore Jr. and grandson of Theodore Sr., came to Peru to further investigate the wall. When he learned that Dr. Tello was about to leave on a field trip to Chavín de Huántar, he agreed to accompany the Peruvian scholar as cameraman. Tello promised to lead off the trip with a visit to the wall.

After examining burials under the wall and others apparently of a date later than its construction, Tello reached the conclusion that the wall was of pre-Chimú origin. This view seems to be supported by the findings of another American explorer, Gene Savoy, who visited the wall in later years and traced it to its terminus at an elevation of 1,500 feet in the Andean foothills. However, the authoritative *Handbook of South American Indians* considers cultural association and date uncertain.

When the members of the Shippee-Johnson Peruvian Expedition returned to the United States eight months, one air crash, a Peruvian revolution, 3,000 first-rate aerial photographs, and thousands of feet of motion film later, they were hailed almost in Lindbergh style. *The New York Times* greeted them in an editorial ("the greatest value is in· the fresh proof that such expeditions give of the undying spirit of quest and conquest in man"). More even than by the "Chinese Wall," the public had been thrilled by news of aerial discovery of the virtually forgotten Colca Valley with its fourteen "lost" settlements, a virgin territory of three hundred square miles north of Arequipa in the southern Peruvian Andes.

But most important of all, the worth of the airplane in archaeological investigation had been amply demonstrated. The flat and dry coastland between the Andes and the Pacific, physically comparable to Mesopotamia, lent itself particularly well to the air method. Aerial photography was continued in Peru by the Servicio Aerofotográfico Nacional, whose aerial mosaic maps in turn were to guide the Virú Valley project and other expeditions, which after World War II made the enigmatic desert civilizations the target of their research.

THE GREAT WALL OF PERU

Robert Shippee

While we were still operating from the base that we had established at Trujillo for the mapping of the well-known ruins of Chan-Chan, we made a flight with the photographic plane inland as far as the Marañón River and, on the return, circled southward around Mt. Huascarán and then followed the valley of the Santa River to the coast. Our course was over the edge of the foothills bordering the narrow upper valley of the river on the north. Johnson, co-leader and photographer of the expedition, watching for photographic subjects, noticed what appeared to be a wall flowing up and down over the ridges beneath the plane, wondered for a moment as to the purpose of such a structure, decided that it was worth recording, and made a number of photographs of it. We hoped to be able to return later to make a more complete record of the wall but were not certain that we should have time to do so. The photographs, printed a few weeks later in our Lima laboratory, led to so much discussion, however, that just before our departure we arranged to make a special trip to re-locate and examine the wall from both the air and the ground.

Johnson and I with our Peruvian observer, Captain Ceballos, flew to Chimbote in the photographic ship and established a temporary base there. Chimbote lies on one of the largest bays of the Peruvian coast, a few miles south of the Santa Valley, of which it is now the principal port. The little town in the lee of three tall, barren sand hills can boast of two things only—a natural harbor that would make the most ideal naval,

From "The Great Wall of Peru and other aerial photographic studies by the Shippee-Johnson Expedition," *The Geographical Review*, XXII:1 (Jan. 1932), pp. 1–14.

aviation, or submarine base imaginable and a level, hard landing field
that is used by the Peruvian commercial air lines.

The natives of Chimbote assured us that they knew about the wall,
that they had heard of it from their ancestors, and that it was pre-Incaic.
They could tell nothing, however, of its purpose or its history and, indeed,
gave little real evidence that they had ever even heard of it.

From Chimbote the flight to the mouth of the Santa River was a
matter of a few minutes only. Turning inland from there we picked up the
wall about five or six miles from the coast at the ruins of a small village.
At that end the wall divides into two sections for a short distance. . . .

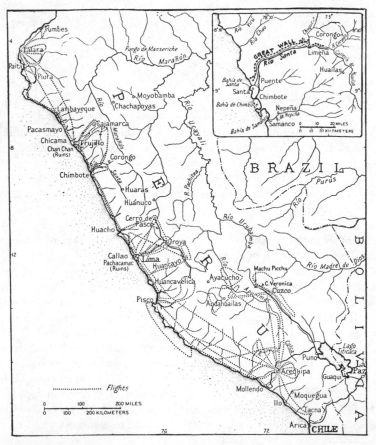

Flights of Shippee-Johnson Peruvian Expedition, with insert of the
"Great Wall" in Santa River valley

It may have once extended to the shore line; but, if it did, it has been broken down, and the stones have either been removed for other building purposes or covered by the drifting sand.

From the ruined village, itself all but lost under the sand, the wall leads away up the north side of the river, first across the level, sandy plain of the river delta and then, as the valley narrows, over the edge of the foothills bordering the valley. As the foothill ridges become sharper and steeper, the wall rises and dips and in places is turned slightly from its generally straight course. Its distance from the river is in general about a mile and a half, although in one place at least it dips down close to the edge of the river bed. In places it blends so well with the background as to be almost indistinguishable.

It was impossible to make an accurate check on the distance we followed the wall, for the air was so unusually rough that, as we approached the Andes, we had to circle and climb for more and more altitude; but we followed it for at least forty miles and possibly more. Then we lost it. We had already passed over several short breaks, but this time we failed to pick it up again. The light, which was poor when we started—for the flight was made in August, a winter month when the coastal valleys are nearly always overcast and often filled solid with fog—was getting rapidly worse; so we headed back for Chimbote taking only a few minutes out to get more close-ups of the forts on both sides of the wall.

It so happened that none of our first photographs showed any of these forts. But, on this second flight we noticed at irregular intervals on both sides of the wall, but at short distances from it, a series of small forts—some circular and some rectangular—most of which were more or less inset in the top of small hills so as to be quite invisible from the valley floor. Those on the south side, and they were the larger, were located in the hills on the south side of the Santa River opposite the wall. We believe that we located and photographed all of these forts—a total of fourteen. The largest one appeared to be about 300 feet by 200 feet, with walls about fifteen feet high and perhaps five feet thick, and was of piled stone construction. A few of the others were of the same construction, but most of them appeared to be of adobe.

At Chimbote we at once began preparation for a trip to the wall overland. From a rough sketch made while in the air we figured that we could reach at least the western end of the wall by automobile. There is a bridge over the Santa near its mouth, and, once on the other side, it would be simply a question of how far the car could plow through the sand. The next morning we loaded our equipment into an old Ford and started off on a trip that was to take five hours of bumping over crude roads, slithering down muddy cow paths, and pushing through deep sand. Steering our course by a method of "dead reckoning" especially devised for the occasion, we at last reached the sand-covered ruins of the little village at the end of the wall. It was just by chance that we did not miss them entirely. From the air we had been able to make out the plan of the streets and the walls of the separate houses. From the ground we saw nothing but a few sand-covered ridges.

Just beyond these ridges, which were crumbled adobe walls buried beneath centuries of drifted sand, we saw the wall stretching away to the horizon. We followed along it for several miles. Then the valley began to narrow and the cross ridges to dip more sharply down to it. The Ford could go no farther. We struggled on afoot for another mile, lugging the cameras and stopping at intervals for still and motion pictures showing construction details and the character of the terrain on which the wall stands.

The wall, as far as we followed it, now averages about seven feet in height. It is built of broken rocks set together with adobe cement, and, where it has not been greatly disturbed, its outer surface is so well chinked with small rocks that it would be practically impossible to scale it without ladders. In occasional places, as seen from the air, the wall must still be twenty or thirty feet high where it crosses gullies. We found it impossible to make anything like accurate measurements. The rocks that have slipped from the top with the beating of the winds and the occasional rains spread away for a considerable distance on either side of the wall and aid the drifted sand in obscuring its base. We estimated that, in its original state, it was about twelve or fifteen feet thick at the base and was built to taper upward to an average height of twelve or fifteen feet.

We were unable to come to any conclusion concerning the origin of the wall. As Dr. A. L. Kroeber remarks, that will require careful examination by an archeologist familiar with different types of construction and able to interpret potsherds or other fragments that may be found in association with the wall. If we had had time to carry our ground explorations farther and to investigate the forts we might have found more definite indications as to its history; but we had already spent eight and a half months in Peru instead of the five months originally planned.

Further exploration to determine how far the wall extends into the Andes would be especially worth while. We estimate that when we finally lost sight of the wall we were in the neighborhood of Corongo. Wiener mentions strongly fortified hills in the Corongo region. We have, therefore, the possibility of a defensive wall joining the fortifications of the Corongo region with those at the mouth of the Santa River.

Clearly the wall with its double line of forts was erected as a defensive barrier. If it is true that the fortified hilltops at Paramonga, some fifty miles farther south, mark the southern limits of the domain of the Great Chimú, there are many guesses that can be made as to the origin and purpose of the wall. It may be an inter-tribal defense that antedates the consolidation of the Chimú kingdom. Or it may be a secondary line of defense erected by the Chimú against the Inca invader. If the latter is the case it may explain why, as tradition says, the Inca abandoned his invasions of the Chimú kingdom from the south along the coast and finally conquered it by advancing his armies through the Andes and laying direct siege to Chan-Chan, the Chimú capital.

Moche battle scene

The suggestion has been advanced by Dr. R. L. Olson of the University of California that the wall may represent one of a series of defense structures built by the Chimú as they extended their territory to the north and south. While engaged in field work in this part of Peru two years ago Dr. Olson noted a number of walls in the Chao Valley, about twenty miles north of the Santa Valley, mostly fragmentary and running for short distances only. He describes a larger wall cutting across the pampa between Trujillo and Chicama that was built presumably for the defense of Chan-Chan.

Professor Marshall H. Saville suggests that the wall may have been erected by the Chimú or pre-Chimú occupants of the Santa Valley to prevent the neighboring tribes on the north or possible invaders from the north from gaining access to the river where by damming or otherwise diverting the stream they could cut off the water supply from the great aqueducts, still largely in fairly good repair, that irrigated the densely-peopled Santa delta. In connection with this suggestion may be cited Montesinos' account that the Inca finally conquered the Great Chimú by cutting off his water supply. It may have been the supply to the Santa Valley that was cut off by the Inca, since Montesinos does not state which valley it was in which the Chimú finally capitulated, while Garcilaso de la Vega says that it was the Santa Valley, although he makes no mention of the cutting off of the water supply.

Dr. Julio C. Tello, Director of the Archeological Museum of the University of San Marcos and a leading authority on the Inca and pre-Inca civilizations, states in reply to a letter addressed to him by the American Geographical Society that not only had he never heard of the wall until it was reported by the Shippee-Johnson Expedition but that he has been unable to find anyone among the owners of the large haciendas in the Santa Valley who knows anything of it. Dr. Tello reports that he has discovered several walls similar to the Great Wall of the Santa Valley in valleys south of Lima, although none of them are more than a few kilometers in length. He also mentions the wall between Trujillo and Chicama described by Dr. Olson, but offers no suggestion as to the possible purpose of this or others of what he describes as the "mysterious walls of Peru."

It is still hard for us to believe that we have actually made a new discovery of such evident importance in a region whose ruins have been for more than seventy-five years the subject of frequent and careful explorations by a long list of noted archeologists, many of whom have made their reputations there. From the air the wall and its forts are so striking a feature of the landscape that it is difficult to understand how they could have so long escaped notice from the ground. That this is the case seems less astonishing, however, when one considers that, even though the wall were noticed at its western end where it crosses the delta of the Santa River, it would appear only as one more wall in a region filled not only with the ruins of elaborate fortifications—fortified hills and defensive walls of various sorts—but also with the remains of cities, towns, and extensive irrigation works. Only when one looks down upon the wall from the air and thus is able to see long sections of it can one realize that it is a feature quite distinct from the short sections of wall characteristic of the Santa delta. This broad view presented to an observer and camera is what makes the airplane so important an instrument in modern exploration. The aerial observer is afforded, and the aerial camera records frequently in a single exposure, a synthesis of details whose relationships might otherwise never be discovered.

6

A few people flying across the desolate hills and plateau adjacent to the Nazca Valley in southern Peru had from time to time noticed a strange jumble of geometric figures crisscrossing the surface. Were they an optical illusion of the desert? Some lines looked unmistakably like roads, but they began and ended in the middle of nowhere. Were they perhaps irrigation canals? But where was the water to feed them? And why should some of them run uphill? Were they perhaps furrows of long-abandoned fields? Or did they represent symbols left by an expired race?

Those men who bothered to give them a second thought jokingly referred to the prominent trapezoid patterns as "prehistoric landing fields." Others likened the whole network to the canals of Mars, which were equally perplexing. One fantastic theory saw in them guidelines to hidden Nazca treasures. Natives, if at all aware of them, labeled them "Inca Roads." Aside from such passing comments, quickly forgotten, nobody had paid the desert puzzle any serious attention until 1941. In that year it aroused the curiosity of a New York history professor who had begun a study of the irrigation system of pre-Columbian Peru. To him irrigation was a universal agent in the rise of ancient civilizations all over the globe. Hence his particular interest in the pre-Inca desert cultures of the Pacific coastlands. He wondered whether the strange markings near Nazca could shed further light on his subject. Thus it came about that Dr. Paul Kosok embarked on a systematic study of the phenomenon. In the course of his investigation he took several hundred photographs. His pictures, which began to reach the illustrated magazines, caused quite a sensation. To American archaeologists they revealed a mystery which even today awaits complete solution.

Dr. Kosok had good reason to assume that the figures were connected with the Nazcas who had preceded the rise of the Incas. But next to nothing was known of these people, who had only entered archaeological consciousness in 1901 when Max Uhle identified their lost culture. Prior to that just five exceptionally fine ceramic pieces from the area had reached collections, though their origin was then unknown. The Paracas burials, discovered a quarter of a century later at a peninsula a hundred miles northwest of Nazca, were to show definite affinities in style. But since the Nazcas, unlike Moche and Chimú, rarely painted realistic scenes or shaped their vases into human figures, relatively little about their way of life can be deduced. Excavations of Nazca sites undertaken since 1952 have added some light, particularly in matters concerning material skills and religious cults. It was then found that several of their buildings appear to have an astronomical orientation. This feature ties in precisely with the hypothesis Kosok advanced for the desert "roads" some ten years earlier.

Huge geometric figures on the Nazca desert. Drawn by Dr. Maria Reiche

The astronomical interpretation had come to Kosok in a flash of insight, undoubtedly prompted by his familiarity with the calendrical preoccupations of all higher American civilizations. Their knowledge of the stars and seasonal changes, while raised to a complex ritual and developed with scientific thoroughness, was, as in ancient Egypt and Mesopotamia, rooted in the needs of a farming people for reliable data on such vital matters as the onset of harvest time or the rise of river floods.

To help him in the limited time available to him, Dr. Kosok was able to enlist Maria Reiche, a German-born scientist from Lima, in further testing his hypothesis and accumulating data. For years since, even after Kosok's death, she has been surveying the lines with measuring tape, compass, and theodolite. While the results of her labors have so far been released only in preliminary publications, she has been able to prove conclusively that several Nazca lines coincide in their direction with the solstices. Others may well point to the stars and the rising and setting of the sun. She also tested the ingenious idea that celestial deviations since the time the desert designs were laid out could offer a clue to their age. An approximate age determined by her from a reading of the Pleiades was verified in 1957 by a carbon-14 test of wooden artifacts. Both sources independently gave a date of about A.D. 500.

However, Kosok at an early stage of his research allowed for the possibility that not all the radiating and crossing lines, the spirals (coiled snakes?) and animal figures, were of immediate calendrical significance. Rituals, beliefs, and folklore, and perhaps even a bit of free-wheeling artistic delight, must have intruded. The larger fields could have been set aside for worship, maybe by separate clans. Scattered here and there are various piles of stones, which look like altars. Or were they observation posts? Astronomical features notwithstanding, the overall pattern may have entailed a magic message to the gods or at least had a part in religious processions and ceremonies.

Aside from meaning and purpose, there remains the riddle of how exacting designs of such enormous dimensions could have been laid out, considering that they are barely visible from ground level and could never be seen as a whole. The Incas, by the way, seem to have been oblivious of the entire canvas when they built their highway to the coast smack across it.

Since Kosok's first reconnaissance, attention has been drawn to comparable desert designs in areas far beyond the immediate vicinity of the Nazca Valley. The Paracas peninsula has the gigantic Tres Cruces, carved into sand cliffs above the sea, like a sign for navigators. Other such patterns have been reported from northern Peru, Chile, and even California. Are they in some way connected with the effigy mounds of the Ohio Valley?

Paul Kosok, head of the history department and director of music at Long Island University, New York, had come late to Peruvian archaeology via his lifelong interest in the early stages and transitions of Old World civilizations. One learned society called him a "palaeo-hydrologist" —a new term coined for a student of the role of water in pre-historic times. Most of his publications dealt with the political history of modern Germany, though Kosok was equally at home in the exact sciences, and in fact wrote a number of mathematical treatises on the side. As a tribute to the South American countries he composed an "Andean Rhapsody," which was performed by the National Symphony Orchestra of Peru in 1958, one year before his death. Kosok's own account of his explorations in coastal Peru, *Life, Land and Water in Ancient Peru,* was published posthumously in 1965.

NAZCA MARKINGS IN THE SAND

Paul Kosok

Near Nazca in southern Peru the land rolls back from the coast in waves of barren plains crested by ranges of equally barren low hills. Aerial views of this region . . . show the land crisscrossed by an intricate network of ghostlike lines, some of which connect with vast geometric figures.

These markings are understood in part now, but they still contain one of the most intriguing science riddles of the Americas.

They extend for 40 miles or more across desert so devoid of life that it takes the visitor back to pre-man time on earth. Yet man does exist not far distant, along the narrow irrigated banks of slight streams that in wet seasons rush from the hills to form Peru's Río Grande River. Man has existed along these streams for probably some 2,000 years. Here was produced the Nazcan culture that flourished long before the golden era of the Incas.

Viewed from the ground, the markings are difficult to distinguish from the motley desert cover. Most of them, actually double parallel lines, look like roads with slightly elevated edges. Some are many miles long. They all seem to have been made by the simple process of removing the surface dirt and pebbles, darkened by exposure to the air, from the lighter-colored soil below and piling them in a uniform way along both sides.

Soon after my wife and I began an investigation of these puzzling markings, we suspected that they had served the Nazcans in making astronomical observations, and might prove similar to remains left by other early peoples in different parts of the world.

"Desert Puzzle of Peru," by Paul Kosok. Copyright © 1947. *Science Illustrated,* II:9 (Sept. 1947), pp. 60–61.

When we made our first attempt to analyze these markings, a fortunate series of coincidences gave us the clue to solving the mystery.

We had followed one of the strange "roads" to the top of a plateau. From here we could see that it was the largest and most impressive of several roads, which, together with a number of single lines, radiated from a kind of "observation center."

Roaming around the plateau, we found not only many more lines, but also two huge rectangles or trapezoids and, most amazing of all, the faint remains of a pebble-and-dirt drawing over 150 feet long, which was suggestive of similar designs found on early Nazca pottery.

Our minds whirling with endless questions about these fantastic remains, we stayed to watch the desert sunset. And we suddenly noticed that the sun was setting almost exactly over the end of one of the single lines.

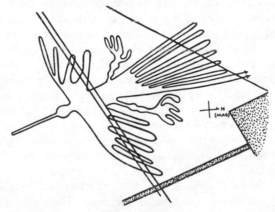

Stylized bird, about 400 feet in length; parallel to the wings runs a solstice line. Drawn by Dr. Maria Reiche

A moment later we recalled that it was June 22, the day of the winter solstice in the Southern Hemisphere—the shortest day of the year, the date when the sun sets farthest north of due west.

With a great thrill we realized at once that perhaps we had found the key to the riddle. For very likely the ancient Nazcans had constructed this line to mark the winter solstice. And if this were so, the other markings were probably tied up with astronomical activities.

The "largest astronomy book in the world" seemed spread out before us. The next step was to learn to read it.

I first made a general survey of the whole region, taking compass readings of as many lines as possible. These confirmed our theory that the Nazca markings were astronomical in nature. Unable to continue these observations, we gave this information to Miss Maria Reiche of Lima, a graduate engineer trained in astronomy, who continued the field work.

By watching the sunrise and sunset at solstice time, just as the ancient Peruvians had probably done, Miss Reiche has been able to confirm 12 solsticial lines. She has also discovered 18 drawings in addition to the one my wife and I found on that June 22. Some of them are several hundred feet long and appear to belong to the early Nazca period—sometime before 1000 A.D.

The narrowest lines were apparently used as sight lines to mark the periodic appearance of various astronomical bodies. The double lines that appear like roads may have been processional roads, following certain sacred alignments determined by the position of heavenly bodies. The huge geometric figures possibly were ceremonial enclosures. The drawings may well have been constellation or totemic figures, or both.

If, as suspected, many of the markings in the desert astronomy book were oriented so that the rising and setting points of stars (other than the sun) could be sighted, invaluable archeological discoveries may result. For the heliacal rising and setting points of such stars move appreciably along the horizon in the course of centuries. And so a competent scientist, by studying the desert markings in relation to star history, might be able to tell fairly definitely when the Nazcans built what appears to be antiquity's most extensive astronomical monument.

That is exactly what is happening. Miss Reiche is now trying to identify possible star lines in the maze of markings and establish dates of their construction.

The major problem still remains. It is to understand the great maze of lines that do not refer to solstices or equinoxes. These may fall into one of five separate categories:

1. They may be markings of the place of sunrise or sunset on days other than the equinoxes or solstices.

2. They may have marked the risings and settings of the moon, since moon worship was an important part of the ancient Peruvian culture.

3. They may mark the risings and settings of various planets.

4. Or the risings and settings of important stars. We know, for example, that the Pleiades provided a time marker for Peruvians of the coast. And, since the rising points of the Pleiades and the sun at solstice coincide in Nazca, the solstice lines may also have been Pleiades lines.

5. Some of the lines may not have been sight lines at all, but connecting roads and markers leading to related figures.

It appears that the ancient Nazcans considered earthly events to be reflections or replicas of the organization and motion of the heavenly bodies. And so there developed an extensive priesthood that attempted to foretell or control events on earth by studying the heavens.

When more of this ancient desert astronomy book is deciphered, we shall have more than new light on the complexities of the astronomical knowledge of over 10 centuries ago. We shall also have a better understanding of the social life and customs of the ancient Nazcans, for apparently the whole fabric of their society was intertwined with astronomy.

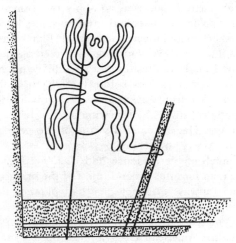

Spider figure, crossed by astronomical line. Drawn by Dr. Maria Reiche

7

What better approach could there be to the history of the Incas, their rise from one remote Andean valley, their aggressions, military expansion, and sudden collapse, than to chart their life artery, the stupendous Inca road system? Here all the phases of this pre-Columbian empire were carved into the Peruvian earth. If one were to apply the elements of history, of geography, anthropology, archaeology, and, to some degree, engineering, such a reconnaissance should throw considerable light on ancient America. The idea occurred to Victor W. von Hagen, a veteran American explorer, who for years had made Latin America's wildlife and surviving native tribes, as well as the civilizations before the advent of the Spanish, his province. He took a leaf from Alexander von Humboldt, to whom he had devoted a biographical study, by renewing interest in the Inca roads. By the same token Von Hagen made a virtue of the peripatetic approach long prevalent in American archaeology.

To be sure, much of the evidence had been swept away. Landslides had covered the road for miles on end; most of the bridges had collapsed; motor roads and railways of a new age had plowed through the Inca roads or had simply incorporated long stretches. But it was precisely one of the aims of Von Hagen's Inca Highway Expedition (undertaken in cooperation with the American Geographical Society) to discover those lost portions, in particular the vital lateral links between the coastal and highland parallels.

Starting out in the winter of 1952 at Lake Titicaca near the Bolivian border, the expedition was on the move for two years. In the footsteps of the Incas it plodded its way amid arctic cold and snow at altitudes higher than the highest Alpine peaks. At points it penetrated the rain-drenched *montaña* fringes of the Amazon basin. Along the Pacific desert belt it was exposed to relentless tropical sun. Besides the standard transportation of motor trucks, the explorer and his young wife, Silvia (who acted as staff artist and co-leader of the campaign), together with an archaeologist, topographer, and cameraman, frequently took to mules or simply climbed across narrow precipices. From time to time an airplane was enlisted to pick up loose ends of the road. The photographs of the Shippee-Johnson Expedition were of great help. Prior to setting out, basic information had been culled from Spanish colonial documents. In fact, one student had been occupied for a whole year in extracting the pertinent material from old sources.

There was, for instance, a description given in 1547 by the soldier-chronicler Pedro Cieza de León of "the grandest road there was in the world as well as the longest." He stated his belief that "since the history of man has been recorded there has been no account of such grandeur as is to be seen in this road, which passes over deep valleys and lofty mountains by snowy heights, over falls of water, through living rocks and edges of tortuous currents. In all these places it is level and paved, along mountain slopes well excavated, by the mountains well terraced, through the living rock cut, along the river bank supported by walls, in the snowy heights with steps and resting places, in all parts swept clean, clear of debris, with post and store houses and Temples of the Sun at appointed intervals. O! what greater things can be said of Alexander, or of any of the powerful kings who have ruled in the world than that they had made such a road as this and conceived the works which were required for it."

So far, the evidence of men like Cieza de León had been insufficiently tested by archaeological surveys. To a much greater extent than Humboldt, who had never even been to Cuzco, Von Hagen was to show that the facts reported by Cieza de León were on the whole sound. But there were a number of details that had never been properly investigated. In the main these pertained—apart from the actual course and location of the various branches of the road net—to building technique. Was it true that the roads were surfaced in their entirety and were, in part, "macadamized," as Humboldt had suggested? Did they have a standard width? At what intervals were relay stations built for the *chasqui* courier service? How widely spaced were the *tampus* or so-called Inca inns which not only served as hostelries for rulers and officials, but provided food for an army on the march and functioned as storehouses in case the neighboring area needed relief? How far did the Incas use pre-Inca roads, and in what way were they different from the Incas' own? Was there any truth to the report that runners via a special road from the coast rushed fresh fish to the Inca's dining table at Cuzco, hundreds of miles away and thousands of feet above? Could lost cities be tracked down on the way, while one gained insights into the rationale of Inca rule and administration?

To some of these questions Von Hagen could give concrete answers—even though he was able to cover but 2,000 miles of a transportation system that must have measured close to 10,000 miles. Yet the basic characteristics of the whole road net were clear. The Inca highways were royal roads in the manner of those of the great empires of the ancient Near East. Von Hagen calls them outright "roads of conquest." As such they were of little use to the common people, who, not being prone to travel anyhow, were in fact barred from them. Via the road marched the armies, chased the messengers, and flowed royal taxes in kind. Along it was borne the Living Sun, hoisted in his ornate majesty on a litter. Actual test runs staged by Von Hagen were to confirm the accounts of early chroniclers that a message could be conveyed by relay couriers in five days from Cuzco to Quito and in two days from Cuzco to the coast.

All roads led to Cuzco, or rather radiated from it. There, from the central square of the metropolis, branched out the four main roads into the four quarters of the world: *Tawantin-suyu*, the Incas' name for their empire. Most important were the two longitudinal highways, one following the spine of the Andes, the other near the Pacific coast. The former, actually called the Royal Road (*Capac-nan*), came to reach a length of some 3,200 miles from 1° latitude above the equator to 35° south, traversing present-day Ecuador, Peru, and Bolivia and bifurcating into Argentina and Chile. The coastal road began at Tumbes in the extreme Peruvian north, where Pizarro first landed in 1534. It also went down to central Chile where it connected with the Andean highway. The number of laterals has not been ascertained. Von Hagen explored eleven of them. He also established a standard width for the coastal road of twenty-four feet, and he is of the opinion that this gauge as well as its adobe side walls (mainly to keep out drifting sand) mark it as Inca-built rather than pre-Inca.

The major engineering feat was the Andean route. Because of the difficulty of the terrain, no uniform width could be maintained, though the average was between fifteen and eighteen feet. Often it trickled down to a path five feet wide or less. It was paved intermittently with closely fitting flagstones, but most of it was left without artificial covering just like the coastal road. The dry, hard soil of the *puna* vouchsafed permanence and compactness sufficient to withstand the foot traffic and relatively light-weight llamas.

Physical conditions of the terrain required variety in the manner of construction of the "royal road." To such challenges the Inca engineers, without dynamite, iron instruments, or mathematical calculation, rose magnificently. Where the road could climb slowly to Andean heights, it was traced in moderate grade through zigzags and sinuous twinings. As a rule, a rise in the road was overcome by widely spaced steps. If need be, the road—or ladder—was carved out of the rock. Whole intervening crags were pierced by tunnels. Across marshlands, the Incas—like the Mayas—built formidable causeways from blocks of rock or adobe. However, the authentic masterpieces of aboriginal engineering were the bridges. They were of several types. Lake inlets were crossed on pontoons laid out on a succession of tortora reed boats. If a chasm was too deep to be filled with stonework, or if it was cut by a wide turbulent river, the Incas erected their famous suspension bridges from thick fiber ropes, which from their anchorage in massive pylons on both sides swung delicately above ravines. The maintenance of each bridge was the task of the local people of the area, who had to renew the cables at regular intervals. Some of these bridges lasted into the nineteenth century. Best known of all, the bridge across the Apurimac (220 feet long, 118 feet above the river) was photographed and later engraved by Squier before its replacement in 1880. It was immortalized in Thornton Wilder's *The Bridge of San Luis Rey*.

Inca suspension bridge

Wilder's allegory is just one of the many tales the Inca roads can tell. Von Hagen came across many more, and lived through some of his own. But easily the most ironic was written by the white conquerors in Inca blood. Shortly after their landfall, they galloped swiftly over the Inca road to Cajamarca, then on to Cuzco, and beyond toward the Araucanian domain of Chile—everywhere putting an end to the native civilization. The system that had tied a vast empire together, also helped to tear it apart. Unintentionally, but not without logic, Von Hagen's Inca Highway Expedition ended in December 1954 at Cajamarca.

Victor von Hagen's zestful narrative of his expedition, *Highway of the Sun* (1955), though not devoid of flamboyant touches, enjoys well-deserved popularity in the recent literature of American archaeology. It deals with his most ambitious enterprise in American exploration, begun in 1931 (when he was 23) with research in Mexico on aboriginal paper making. Since then, Von Hagen has achieved repute as naturalist, ethnographer, and prolific author. His first book dealt with Ecuador and the Galápagos Islands. Biological studies in the latter were inspired by Darwin, to whom he erected a monument in the archipelago.

In Ecuador, in 1934, he first saw a section of the Inca road, followed it for a few miles to the edge of a canyon, and wondered whether it really led to Cuzco, 1,500 miles away, and then on to Argentina, 2,000 miles in all. The thought of the Inca road never quite left him. Later he came to recognize that all his earlier expeditions were only a preparation for his rediscovery of the ancient highway.

For several months in 1936 Von Hagen lived among the headhunters of the Amazon. On his fourth expedition he set himself the task of locating and capturing the legendary Quetzal, sacred bird of ancient Middle America. So well did he succeed that he was able to supply the zoos of The Bronx and London with live specimens. Julian Huxley called this "the outstanding zoological feat in two decades." Von Hagen then concentrated on writing about other men who had been excited by the same world his explorations had opened up for him. Foremost was his *South America Called Them* (1945), which includes perceptive essays on Humboldt and Darwin. There followed biographical works on the Maya explorers John Lloyd Stephens and Frederick Catherwood. But his promised biography of E. George Squier, like some of his other previously announced projects, has so far not been forthcoming. In the 1960's he launched a new expedition, this time to investigate the Incas' Old World counterparts, the Romans, and their road net around the Mediterranean. In 1965 he published a survey of the ancient desert kingdoms of Peru.

THE HIGHWAY OF THE SUN

Victor W. von Hagen

The Mantaro River is shaped something like a fishhook. Unlike other rivers which slowly emerge from out of inoffensive trickling rills and in descending become a fury of rushing waters, this one leaps into being fullborn where it comes out of the ice-fringed Chinchay (Junín) Lake. Drawing the run-off of rain from the plenteous *punas* through which it flows, the Mantaro becomes, within fifty miles, less a river than a gargantuan earth-moving force which has gouged out a canyon so deep that it does not allow man to harness it for his benefit. It is useless alike to nature and man. So the Mantaro must, like unreasonable weather, be endured. Yet the Incas refused to endure it—they avoided it. Since they did not have the wheel and their means of travel were not those of the modern world, they laid their communication system above it and out of harm's way.

We however could not escape it. At this point in our journey, we were —alas—bound to the modern highway which here has been cut alongside of the canyon-edge of the Mantaro, making it the most dangerous in all Peru. One hundred and fifty miles out of Chinchay Lake the river makes a fishhook turn to race east to join with another turbulent river and so form the Upper Amazon. Just at the point where the hook makes the twist and becomes the sharpened barb on which it pinions nature and man, there were we, hung quite literally for a few dreadful moments on the edge of Mantaro. Suspended between safety and disaster, one half of the Power Wagon dangled over the canyon while the other half still rested on the so-called road. Almost everything in the way of Expedition gear we had was in the truck. Charts, maps, notes, plans, photographs, equipment—and our hopes; all the months of climbing and searching recorded in our written reports—all this now hung there on the edge of the abyss. . . .

At first there had been no portent in the sky other than the sun. But we had scarcely passed the guard check-point, where because of the narrow road traffic is regulated, when the sky darkened and it began to rain. Within two hours, so heavy was the downpour that we traveled a road streaming water. Above us were sheer walls of mud and stone rising two thousand feet; below us, two hundred feet down, was the rampaging Man-

From *Highway of the Sun.* New York: Duell, Sloan & Pearce; Boston: Little, Brown & Co.; London: Victor Gollancz, Ltd., 1955, pp. 161–85 *passim.*

taro. Had an Inca engineer proposed the building of such a road, his life would have been forfeit. Inca roads were built so as to exclude all water. Water was the determining factor in their every move and knowing that a road along the canyon-edge of the Mantaro could not be maintained, the Incas had split their road at Mayoc, where once hung a suspended bridge, and had flung their step road up the opposite sides to the high *puna*. From that point they had built it across the rolling mountains.

Overseer of bridges, Poma de Ayala

Any idea of drainage on the part of those who cut this modern vehicular road was totally lacking. Water poured down from the towering cliffs onto it, washing immense chunks of it into the river, while wooden bridges that spanned the larger rills were left hanging on hope and air. It was a diurnal nightmare. . . .

A whole lifetime passed . . . as slowly the truck was pulled forward until all four wheels rested on firm ground. As soon as I was breathing again, I reached into the forward chamber of the truck and took out a bottle of rum. . . .

We arrived, days later, at Izcu-chaca, having traveled a distance of but forty-five miles. Where a graceful colonial Spanish bridge curves over the Mantaro gorge, a second river, the Angoyaco, joins it; and here, over a writhing, twisting torrent just below the Spanish bridge, the Inca had once hung another suspension bridge. Here too we found ourselves at last on the Highway of the Sun, the main road of the Inca system.

So we traveled on day after day, our caravan keeping to the modern dirt road until we could find a place to leave the trucks, then we would double back by foot until we found the Inca road again. It was a laborious business—this incessant climbing, this following of and photographing the road. . . .

The high marching cliffs of the Mantaro dissolved into a valley and we came to the little village of Marcavalle. This was the first village in the Jauja-Huancayo valley area, and it was here that the two Inca roads which had split one hundred miles southward at Mayoc, to take to the *puna* above the Mantaro Canyon, joined and became the wide Highway of the Sun.

We stopped at a wayside inn where Indians came to slake their thirst with *chicha,* a grayish fermented-corn drink. I had hoped that about this time we should have some word of our young Peruvian who was still somewhere in the hills tracing out the east wing of the Inca road, but there was no sign of him. So, after leaving instructions with an old Indian woman who smilingly showed us her single tooth, we again took to the road and in an enveloping gray dust we bore down upon Huancayo.

That night, too exhausted to eat, I fell asleep betimes under the portrait of Andrew Carnegie which hangs in the rooms of the old Carnegie Research Station.

Huancayo is one of the largest cities in Peru. Every Sunday the largest and most colorful markets in all the Andes are held there, strung along the Inca road which here stretches to three times its original width. In this present-day Andean market the Indians, as they had in other times, put up their stalls where the things of their earth are sold. We followed the Indians to the market early one Sunday morning shortly after our arrival, walking along the modern highway which rests on the King's Highway [the Spanish *Camino Real*], which in turn stands on the road of the Incas. There is no telling how many come to Huancayo on fair days but at such times the Royal Road of the Incas literally swarms with people.

The Jauja-Huancayo Valley, fifty miles long, is approximately the geographical center of Peru. It is now and always has been an important self-contained valley and a strategic one. On a direct line with Jauja, and scarcely one hundred miles away, lies Pachacamac on the shore of the Pacific. The mecca for most of ancient Peru and the site of the oracle of the creator-god Pacha-camac, it was one hour's journey from the valley as the condor flies, three days as the Indian walked.

To the east of the valley and relatively close were the montaña and the jungles. The valley, controlled by the Huanca tribes, was once defended on all sides by towering hills topped with fortresses. "Even now," wrote Cieza in 1548, "they appear, to one seeing them from a distance, like towers of Spain."

We reached Jauja within an hour's dusty ride from Huancayo, traveling over the route of the Inca road. Where the Mantaro River leaves the valley to begin its passage through its gorge, there, surrounded by hills covered with moldering ruins, lies old Jauja. The ancient fortresses had once belonged to the Wankas, a fierce little people whose houses, built as "rounded fortresses of stone, were like small castles."

It was this tribe, "field guardians" the Incas called them, that for a time effectively blocked the Incas' northern conquest. Although the Inca sought through his ambassadors to induce them to "embrace his friendship . . . without his having to get it by making war," the Wankas, faced with an offer of absorption or extinction, chose extinction. And in the great battle which followed, the Incas conquered and forthwith adopted the survivors into their kingdom, imposing upon them Inca religion and techniques but permitting them to keep their own customs and language. And so Jauja became the Inca capital of Chinchay-suyu, one of the quarters of the Inca world.

Even though today a modern highway runs through the town and there is a railroad station on the outskirts, the outlines of the original town are still visible. In the rubble is part of an Inca wall and an old church stands on the site of the Sun Temple, once a structure three tiers high of worked stone with stairways and thick straw roofs. Near to it was the Temple of the Virgins.

We walked among the walls, gathering potsherds and trying to reconstruct the ancient city from the piles of amorphous stones. Nowhere was there any sign of the onetime grandeur of this, the first capital of Peru. All we know of it is in the records. On Francisco Pizarro's march southward to Cuzco in November 1534, we found the following notation: "In the city of Santa de Hatun Jauja, this twentieth and ninth day of November, 1534, the very noble lords found the city . . ."

In the valley north of Jauja where the eroded limestone hills command the view, we again found the Royal Road. Built across the flat *puna,* twenty-four feet wide and bound by crumbling walls, it was a joy to follow. For the first time in five hundred miles we were able to make a leisurely tour of the highway without being subjected to an exhausting scaling of the heights. It was only when the road mounted an obstructing hill in broad low-stepped treads—it was always the Incas' way to mount obstacles rather than avoid them—that we had to make a detour in the trucks over the vehicular dirt road until we could take to the ancient road again.

Since the modern road turned and twisted to provide the same gradient which the Inca provided by steps, when we came upon it next we were on a higher pampa. My first sight of it from a little distance away showed that the direction had changed radically—the road now ran northeast rather than northwest as it had when we had left it. This puzzled us for, generally speaking, the Incas built their roads with directional straightness. It was Silvia who gave us the first indication of the truth. When we reached the road, we found it going over a rise in a series of large steps. There was something unusual about this section of the road.

"Look," said Silvia, who was pacing the width in long strides, "this road is forty-five feet wide."

"But how . . ."

"Either the Royal Road became much wider after we last were on it or this is another road. Do you suppose we have found their military road?"

From the top of a hill we had full view of the valley stretched out northward. At the base of the hill was one road and this, since it was the regulation twenty-four feet in width, was without doubt the Royal Road. Following it through our binoculars, we saw that it went along the valley floor frequently passing over bare stone, its rock-balustrades fully marked, its plainly visible steps conforming to the rise and fall of the escarpment until it appeared on the continuing pampa. There we could see the remains of a building and there the road divided. Forming a V junction, the Royal Road kept to its directional straightness while the second road veered a full fifteen degrees to the east. From this distance it seemed twice as wide as the other. We stared fascinated at what we saw. Could this be . . . ?

I thumbed through the sheaf of notes we had along until I found a copy of a report on the Inca roads, dated 1543, entitled *The Ordering of the Halting Stations (Tampus): The distance of one to the other, the methods of the native carriers and the obligation of the respective Spanish overlords of said tambos: done in Cuzco the 31st of May, 1543.* This was the first Spanish report on the Inca highway and the *first* road regulations ever made in all the Americas. "Due," it read, "to the serious depopulation of natives at said halting-stations called tambos, and the empty untraveled roads both in the mountains and the plains and the excessive cargoes the Indians are forced to carry and the large journeys that are forced on them and the bad state of repair into which the highway had fallen . . ." and so on for some fifty pages. A commission sometime earlier had been formed to look into the state of the road and this, its official report, described the direction of the road and mentioned many of the halting places. Then we read: "Now make note that from the tambo of Jauja, there are two roads the one parting here for Huánuco and the city of the frontier, Chachapoyas . . ."

The large maps of the American Geographical Society were unfolded. We traced the Inca road to Huánuco, a hundred miles to the north, then on to the right bank of the Río Marañón, one of the longest tributaries of the Amazon. Far, far beyond, in the high mountains on its right bank, at the very edge of the deep green of the Upper Amazon jungle and more than four hundred miles away, lay Chachapoyas. Was that where this road led? There was nothing in our records about *this* radial or why the Incas had built a road into this region. What mystery lay here?

This road, if that Spanish report written in 1543 was true, ran east of the Royal Road for a distance of some four hundred miles. Why so great a road? We knew from history that when the Lord Inca was bent on conquest he would hurry as many as one hundred thousand troops over his roads in a single movement and that accompanying the troops were burden-bearers and thousands of llamas serving as dray animals. This army was primarily a land army which moved only over roads, and with the rise of this Andean Empire, new formulae were injected into warfare. The Inca wars were no ritualistic military promenades nor elaborate panoplies to overawe an enemy; they had but a single object—victory! . . .

Was it possible that we were now looking at the very road over which these great Inca armies had passed on their campaign of conquest? Northward lay our route. At the top of a high pass, close to 14,000 feet, at a spot referred to as Inka-Katana (seat of the Inca) by a little old man whose house we came upon at the side of the road, we reached the wide road. Ahead of us it stretched out for miles across the naked plain, while to the south there was a cascade of stone-tread steps. We calculated that we were seeing at least thirty miles of continuous, wonderfully preserved road, precisely what we had been hoping to find: a stretch of road long enough to permit us to study techniques of road construction, determine the Inca concept of topography, and details, if such could be found, of their extraordinary system of communications, and . . .

. . . What I wanted to see was just how these roads were built, and when the turf was removed and the dislodged stones replaced I would then have a chance to examine the equivalent of an original section of the mountain highway. The day was only a thin solution of the fog-bound night. In this voiceless region without a tree or a bush to break the monotony of the flatness, it seemed as if we were on another planet. We had dressed as we should for the arctic, for the winds were sharp and snow still covered the *puna*. Yet by the time the men had started their task of cleaning the turf and the sun commanded the temperature, it was warm enough to melt the snow.

A cleansed section of the ancient road revealed the first surprise. It was not, as we had supposed, paved. The hard *puna* had offered a natural surface for such wayfarers who had only to worry about the scuff of the foot and the tread of llamas. While there were, we found, many sections of paved roads in the ancient system, they were not all stone-laid. Construction changed with the terrain and circumstances. If the road passed over a marsh, it was raised on a causeway; if it traversed a region of constant rainfall, it was paved. But generally on the hard *puna*—and we were to find this true also on the coastal pampa—the road surface was the earth. But no matter what material the surface, the mark of the Inca road was always to be found in the stone boundary walls. Here the wall of dry masonry stood two and a half feet high, its purpose to mark the boundaries of the road, to contain it, and to keep soldiers and llamas to a defined path. Wherever the road ascended a gradient, it was laid with stone steps at intervals of twenty feet, and between each ran a stone-laid drainage which effectively drained water off the earth-surfaced roads. That it had served its purpose could be easily seen, for where the stones had been dislodged the road was cicatrized with a small eroded gully. . . .

In lifting the turf off a road built more than five hundred years ago in this inhospitable land, where in four days we had been subjected to hail, snow and freezing winds at an altitude higher than that of most European peaks, and in examining the revealed techniques of road construction, we found an index to the marvels wrought by the Inca civilization before it was destroyed centuries ago.

While the work of excavation went on, Silvia and I decided to walk out over the highway to see what we could discover of its other features. We started off down the great road early one morning while the fog still hung over the *puna,* armed with cameras, compass and measuring tape. For a while we shared the wide highway with a herd of llamas being driven out by two small girls to graze in the distant hills.

In the weeks past we had not had much time for leisurely talk together of the death of kings and ruins of empire. As often as not in our search for the road, we had had to climb breathlessly to a road-bed which was most accurately described in literal terms as the "highway"—and on arrival we were at once involved in making measurements, or else in worrying about each step we took on the perilous hanging road, to be given the luxury of speculation. Now it was different. Although we were thousands of feet high, we were walking along a flat *puna.* This road, we had decided after studying it and our too brief notes on its history, had been built fairly late, probably about the year 1470. Why had it been built? If it was a military road, against whom or what was it directed? At that time the Inca was concerned with his conquest to the north where he planned to overwhelm his rival, the fabulous Kingdom of Chimor [Chimú], on the coast. At the same time a second column of conquest pushed slowly on toward Quito. The main highway, the Royal Road, swarmed with workers laboring like an endless stream of ants to project that overwhelming road across the sterile land. Then why *this* road?

The Chancas again! In the lives of people as well as in the lives of nations there is often a single, a traditional, enemy. Time and the alchemy of time changes that enemy, makes him less real; the physical threat is gone, the enmity has lost its potency, yet remembrance of the hated one remains. The Incas had such a traditional enemy in the Chancas. We had met the ghosts of this tribe, of which only Cieza de León has written, many times along our way. At the site of the Plain of Blood battlefield, we had seen where they had been defeated and where the Inca erected his macabre museum of stuffed Chanca warriors. We had met them again at Andahuaylas, their traditional tribal home before they were forced out of it by their conquerors. And now along this road. After the defeat inflicted upon them by the Incas, the tribal survivors, under Hanco-huallu, the Chanca leader, had successfully resisted the usual process of absorption into the new order and had escaped to the eastern Andes. This the Incas never forgot. This road, so we now believed, had been built to make a final conquest of the hated tribe.

Within an hour's walking time we came upon two *chasqui* stations.

It was not the first time we had seen ruins of these courier stations, way stops for the native runners who carried the Inca's messages throughout the Inca Empire, but this was the first time that we found them in succeeding order. These raised platforms lying close to the road on which were circular houses, each large enough for two Indians, have often been described by the early Spaniards, who thought the *chasqui* system one of the marvels of the "newe founde worlde."

With the discovery of two such ruined stations we proceeded more carefully, setting our pedometers so as to have a relative idea of the distance between the stations. On the top of a hill near Mesapata we found

A royal messenger (*chasqui*), Poma de Ayala

our third *chasqui* station, an even more elaborate one with raised platforms on either side of the road and large night quarters for the runners. That day we found seven such stations at intervals of a little less than two miles apart. We decided to give an empirical twist to our explorations by actually making test runs between the stations. . . .

Late November found us traveling through the snowbound antiplano. Silvia maintained she could no longer remember a time when she had been really warm. Only at rare moments did the sun give respite from the unrelenting cold and rain, hail and snow, swept down in succession and with no pattern.

Through it all we followed that continuing road, stretching endless miles across the flat snow-swept plains, climbing the rock mass of mountains, crossing on stone causeways over some bottomless bog. But all this was no longer a cause for wonder on our part. We had reached a point where the best we could do was to record the unusual, make out our reports, film some remarkable engineering features, set our compass and move on. Once Silvia was sure she was suffering from the *surumpi* (snowblindness) or that she had the beginnings of hallucinations, for as she stood on the road stamping circulation into her frozen feet, she thought she saw a line of black-winged flamingos walking in front of her. . . . It was no illusion. Flamingos *had* walked by. We had come by way of the Inca road to Lake Junín.

All the rest of that day we kept to the east side of what is Peru's second largest lake. It was high and cold—and deserted. The little villages at the edge of its thirty-six-mile shore lie at an altitude of 13,000 feet with no protecting hill to break the blast of the ice-laden winds. Junín was once called Chinchay-cocha (Lake of the Lynx). The original inhabitants, famed for their warlike spirit, when attacked would take to island-fortresses in the lake's center and to conquer them the Lord Inca had to send to the coast for balsa-reed boats with which to assault their island strongholds. Once they were subdued, however, they became loyal vassals of the Inca, and the region of such importance that it became "one of the directions of empire." The northern route of the highway itself was called the Chinchay Road.

Our caravan continued on along the Inca road stopping only long enough to take compass bearings and mark the route down on an overlay of the Peruvian military map. At the northern end of the lake, the land became an immense bog and we lost our way constantly in the thick fog and, to make matters more complicated, it began to snow heavily. By the end of the second day's travel we had no idea where we were. Mud dwellings had appeared here and there but when we approached them the people were too frightened to answer our questions. We were looking for

Bonbón, where, according to our research, lay a large Inca site and where three roads were said to have met. By nightfall we could only inch along literally feeling our way. About us was a horrid desolation. It was so cold now that we had to take turns riding in the Power Wagon which alone of our cars had a heating system. It was impossible to prepare food outside, so we munched on the last of our chocolate and found some consolation in drinking coffee. A primitive bridge which we crossed in darkness indicated that we had gone over the only river which drains this lake. We were puzzled to see that this flowed due north, while our maps showed that the river we sought flowed south.

Should we stop and make camp in the snow or empty out the Power Wagon and sleep in it? Should we keep on searching for that illusive Inca site or should we drive on? We were considering these alternatives when, above the throb of the motors, we heard the roar of falling water. It grew louder as we went slowly on, until it was deafening. Then, as the road turned, we saw the twinkling of electric lights. Soon we had pulled up in front of a wooden house. Almost at once we were around a pot-bellied iron stove which gave out a wonderful glowing heat. After so many days and nights on the antiplano, we were now to have heat and the comfort of a bed. Gratefully we allowed ourselves to be provided with hot food before we dropped into oblivion.

In the morning we could hardly believe our eyes. The Inca site of Bonbón, which for a century had thwarted historians' attempts to pin-point it on the map, lay before us. This was a somewhat embarrassing situation for an explorer! The whereabouts of this town—the hub site of three radial roads, so it was reported by the early chroniclers—was actually no mystery at all. Close by was a modern dam which held back the Mantaro River as it flowed out of Lake Junín. This had been built by the Cerro de Pasco Mining Corporation, whose engineers had torn down much of the ancient village to get the stones for the dam. But there was no doubt about its origin. On the banks in the backed-up waters we could see the remains of an Inca suspension bridge. A causeway led from the bridge up to a wide stone staircase and entered northwest along the walls of what once were large stone buildings and extended toward the immense plaza. We had seen nothing like it in size since we had explored Vilcas-huaman ["Sanctuary of the Hawk," an Inca center, some 150 miles north-northwest of Cuzco]. The trapezoidal-shaped plaza proved, when accurately measured, to be over a thousand feet long. In the center stood a Sun Temple, and from its approximate sides went radial roads—one to the coast which an Indian could reach in three days of walking on the Inca road, another to the north which went over the *puna* to the highways of the snow-capped mountains of the white cordillera, and yet another, the Royal Road, which led to the northeast and the stone city of Huánuco the Old. There must have been five hundred stone structures within Bonbón and those which had not been entirely denuded still revealed their original form.

Eager to learn something more of the history of this place, we began to gather such potsherds as we came across. Silvia found a large cache of broken pottery on the stone-terraced banks of the river, and soon we were scrounging in the debris of centuries. In a few hours we had a large collection of fragments of broken pottery, spindles, spindle whorls, pieces of figurines and ax clubheads. They were, as we could see by the design, shape and structure, all Inča artifacts and the type of polychromic ware used when the Incas had reached their peak. Therefore, since these fragments were many and lay close to the surface of the earth, we felt we could safely assume that the Incas had built Bonbón. It is well known that the history of preliterate people is mainly written in such artifacts. There was little doubt that this was the same Bonbón to which Hernando Pizarro had come on March 11, 1533, "when he marched into Pompo where he stayed for the day he arrived and one day more." The scrivener's description of it fits the place exactly; he wrote that the river (the Mantaro) which originated in the lake flowed by Bonbón "very clear and deep" and that it "connected with the Royal Road" as it did by means of the bridge. We found the remains of three cable stone towers which by some miracle had survived time, weather, and immersion in the Mantaro when its watercourse was high. It was this bridge or fragment of bridge which Poma de

Inca and his wife carried on a litter, Poma de Ayala

Ayala, chronicler of Inca events, in his guide to the roads and tambos on the road, mentions cryptically: *bonbon tambo rreal puente de crisnexas del inga topa ynga yupanqui.* Translated this indicated that Bonbón, a royal way station with a suspension bridge, had been built by the Lord Topa Inca. That placed it close to A.D. 1450.

It was well that we had not delayed in our examination of the ruins of Bonbón, for two days later, the sky grew dark, snow began to fall, and soon the ruins were blotted out of sight.

8

On cliffs lining the Cassiquiare River in tropical South America Alexander von Humboldt had sighted rock drawings which started him wondering about ancient man in the New World. Subsequently he found the strange iconography widely scattered in the Amazon lowlands. Quite a few examples of it, though widely separated, resembled each other. A majority represented animal figures, but there were also a number of apparently formalized symbols which he did not hesitate to call hieroglyphic characters, though he doubted that they were alphabetic. Yet, their abstract style, he thought, pointed to their association with an advanced culture and a once large population in these virtually empty lands. Frequently the figures were placed high above the water levels. It seemed unlikely that they could have been painted without elaborate scaffolds. A group of natives, who held them in awe, told Humboldt that they dated from the time of the Great Flood when all but one human couple perished and their ancient progenitor, floating on the swollen waters, had painted them.

Rock paintings are in evidence all over the Western Hemisphere from Alaska to the West Indies to Patagonia. They have caused others besides Humboldt to wonder. E. George Squier took stock of them in Nicaragua. Since early colonial times men have read into them inscriptions left by Phoenicians, Hebrews, Greeks, or some other enterprising white men. In Peru, a nineteenth-century traveler was certain that they represented nothing less than the historical records of the Incas. But, apart from such haphazard speculations, the glyphs have received scant attention. Between those who declared them a mysterious script, the key to which they were about to disclose, and others who dismissed them as infantile scribblings, the sober middle ground of sound analysis found little scope. The handful of scholarly works devoted to them rarely went beyond mere description. While the Magdalenian cave paintings of western Europe, the Bushman drawings of South Africa, or the remarkable rock pictures of the Sahara desert at Tassili drew world-wide attention, these antiquities in the Americas have been neglected, and this despite their great profusion. Several major new sites have been reported in our own day, and a good many more undoubtedly remain to be discovered.

Dr. Disselhoff, a German Americanist, is one of the few long fascinated by these conspicuous artifacts, and he considers them worthy of concentrated study. During his first Peruvian archaeological campaign in 1938 he was able to examine rock paintings in northern Peru, particularly in the Chicama Valley. He was even then startled by their considerable spread in the central Andean country, an area where, because of the preponderant view that actual writing was unknown in pre-Columbian South America, all kinds of pictorial renderings assume a heightened importance. He—and others—consider it possible that standardized signs contained rudiments of a hieroglyphic system. (In a sense, of course, all pictograms contain a message and are predecessors of writing.)

To Disselhoff, not the least interesting aspect of rock paintings is that there exist affinities among them all over the globe. Particularly in the Americas, similarities are remarkably evident throughout. One common all-American image is the human hand—met on occasion also in the Old World. Of course specific local features abound in each area. However, the absence of literary or oral traditions is a formidable obstacle to the derivation of meaning from exotic signs. In addition, painted or engraved boulders and rock walls may have been decorated by successive generations so that the task of disentangling different periods and styles verges on the impossible, though cautious comparison of isolated specimens from different areas may conceivably bring some clarity or order into the jumble. Disselhoff also made it a practice to relate characteristic designs to artifacts—such as ceramics or textiles—from a cultural horizon that had already been studied.

At Toro Muerto in southern Peru, Disselhoff found for instance the

Rock engraving from northern coastal Peru showing Chavinoid characteristics

picture of an anthropoid creature with jaguar features, his ribs bared as on an X-ray, who was somehow related to the carved figures from Cerro Sechín, an ancient Chavinoid site in the north. Masks and faces recalled the weeping gods of Tiahuanaco and perhaps even the effigies of the Mexican rain god Tlaloc. Disselhoff has also been able to propose persuasive hypotheses concerning the purposes and origins of the rock art in Peru, as will become clear from the first-hand account of his visit to a giant "picture book" in rocks to which he had been alerted by a young Peruvian colleague.

Hans-Dietrich Disselhoff, since 1954 director of the Berlin Museum of Ethnology, embarked on his second archaeological field trip to Peru in 1953 when he was invited to join Victor von Hagen's Peruvian Highway Expedition. However, the pace of that itinerant enterprise offered him little chance for the spade work he had hoped to carry out. Nor was he attuned to the volatile publicity with which the expedition was conducted. Hence he was happy to continue on his own, aided by funds from the Wenner-Gren (Viking) Foundation for Anthropological Research in New York. Once more he pursued his studies of rock paintings and of the connections between coast and highlands in the rise of Peru's oldest civilizations.

PICTURE BOOK IN STONE: TORO MUERTO

Hans-Dietrich Disselhoff

I pricked up my ears when the junior archaeologist of the University of Arequipa, Don Eloy Linares Málaga, an enthusiastic champion of Indianism, told me of rock drawings. This was a subject which I had first looked into in the Peruvian north. Here was a chance to pursue it further and to make good use of the little time left to me. No great funds, which I lacked anyhow, were needed.

It was by pure accident that Linares had noticed one day some large stones being unloaded from a truck at an Arequipa building lot. At first

From *Gott Muss Peruaner Sein. Archaeologische Abenteuer zwischen Stillem Ozean und Titicacasee.* Wiesbaden: F. A. Brockhaus, 1956, pp. 136–59 *passim.* Translated by Leo Deuel.

he took an interest only in the geological nature of the stones. They were of the same white volcanic rock from which the churches and houses in the white city were built. But then Don Eloy moved closer, while shielding his eyes against the glaring sun. Yes, he was right. There were dark lines scratched into the light stones: figures, circles, and an animal head—its eyes and ears clearly marked.

"Where do the rocks come from?"

"But, why, Caballero, from the Maje Valley, a day's journey away. There they lie around by the hundreds, yours for the picking."

Linares then enquired more about the area.

This incident happened several years ago; Linares was quite young, easily enthused, and not in the least afraid of hardships. Soon after, he had the opportunity to hitch a ride on a truck. He told me that after half a day's journey by car and a short walk he came upon rocks covered with scrawls. The name of the place was Pitis. He plunged into the maze of scratched signs and images. The same evening he ventured to the other side of the river. The day, however, was running short. The car could not wait. The driver was hungry and thirsty.

This was just three years ago. Linares had always wanted to return so that he could thoroughly examine the other side of the river. Would I care to join him? He assured me that I could not have any idea of the quantity of pictures there were to see: hundreds, no, thousands! Not even he had seen half of them. The place across the river was called "Toro Muerto." The land there belonged to the hacienda of an Englishman.

And how I itched to go! If the account was true, this was exactly what I had been looking for. I had Linares show me the place on a map. Unfortunately the maps lacked sufficient detail. Best of all was the Esso automobile map. An auto road led to the hacienda. . . .

A few days later we were moving along an arid plateau, without any vegetation in sight. We descended to cross the Vitor River which had cut a deep canyon into the volcanic terrain. Lava and ashes were piled hundreds of feet high. One had the impression that the whole world consisted of nothing but lava and ashes. Down in the valley gleamed the green hue of cane fields. The yellow cotton bushes were in bloom; a few blossoms had a reddish tinge. Large-leaved vines spread their dark foliage in dense arbors. The river banks were seeded with big rocks.

And then up again! Nothing but winding roads and the abyss. At last, after seven hours of driving, we stopped high above an even more precipitous gorge, the valley of the torrential Maje. Yet more downhill turns of winding roads were to follow. The sight of steep defiles towering over heaps of loose rubble made us dizzy. Afterwards our eyes could rest on cliffs close to both sides of the river. At that moment Linares pulled my sleeve: "*Pinturas rupestres!*" Just on the right, along the curb of the road, rock pictures began to appear—animal sketches, probably of llamas. A barbaric advertisement for the Callao brewery was splashed over it.

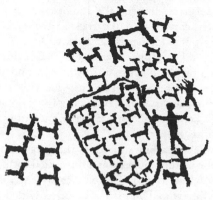

Rock drawing of llamas and herdsmen, Maja (Majes) Valley

The road left the hollow. To our right was a group of huts. We got out of the car and climbed the slope on the left. At the top we soon came upon the decorated blocks which Linares had seen three years before. Many animals were engraved into their flat surfaces: deer and foxes, lizards and snakes. Most common were pictures of jaguars, easy to recognize by their spots. Pictures of men were rare but for a stone slab with a faded drawing of a jaguar man, his chest laid open. That large picture was more stylized than all the other sketches. It faintly recalled the style of the celebrated reliefs of jaguar men at the temple of Sechín, which Dr. Tello uncovered seventeen years ago in a northern Peruvian coastal valley near the country town of Casma. Just off-hand I would put it down as the oldest of the rock pictures of Pitis. It is also the most weathered. But any chronological attribution would be premature. Tello placed the Sechín reliefs he discovered in the Chavín age. Here, atop the steep escarpment of the Maje Valley the stone slab with the jaguar man lies horizontally in the sand. This sets it apart from the other rock pictures which had been engraved, frequently one above the other, on sloping planes of large boulders. One may suspect that several of the deeper engraved images among them are perhaps older. . . .

Deer and serpents, foxes and jaguars, as well as a quantity of pictures of other animals, made us think of a zoological textbook of Stone Age men. Was it possible that the children of hunters had sharpened their wits on them? Far below us, white like milk, foamed the Maje. Its roaring could not be heard at this height. Our eyes wandered over a primeval landscape which, by dint of sheer human will power and toil, had been illuminated with spots and stripes of greenery: fields of corn, vineyards, and sugar cane plantations. At some places, however, there prevailed the blackish verdure of the jungle, which in the days when animal images were carved into the rocks, perhaps covered the entire valley. Even now, it is said, herds of delicate Andean deer, known for their long antlers, take refuge there below. Conceivably, prehistoric hunters, who rested on the heights during their wanderings, worshipped at the rock pictures before descending into the valley to hunt. But unmistakably magic scenes, present in such profusion among the stone drawings of other continents, cannot be pinned down with sufficient authority on the Pitis blocks.

We continued to climb along the rim of the gorge. Only a few hundred yards away from the picture blocks was a ransacked Indian cemetery. Near multicolored shards decorated in Tiahuanaco style there were lying a few oval pebbles from the river. Their surfaces were divided by diagonals into four sections of opposing reds and whites. I had seen amulet stones of a similar pattern a year before at the Hamburg Museum of Ethnology, and when consulted was at a loss to give out any information on their source. Now I found them in association with Tiahuanaco potsherds. Since the cemetery was so close, I could not help thinking that at least some of the Pitis animal pictures may have had their origin in the same age. With the exception of the decayed anthropomorphous figure with the open chest they are not likely to be older; otherwise, considering their soft stone, they would be more weather-worn. . . .

At dawn the next day I drove with Linares downhill to the San Vicente estancia. There we had a drink of delicious grape liqueur (which is not on sale and is served only to select guests), while discussing our projected trip to Toro Muerto. None of the men of San Vicente had so much as heard of the place and its rock pictures. However, a subordinate from one of the plants was reported to be familiar with the entire region. He was summoned. Indeed, he knew the rocks, though by no means the whole lot of them. He would gladly guide us. The young Peruvian agricultural engineers of the estancia were curious and promised to accompany us. Once all the chores connected with saddles and harnesses had been taken care of, we finally rode away with six horses. After such a long time, the clanking of spurs and creaking of saddle leather was music to my ears.

On the way, our first surprise was a recently dug-up prehistoric cemetery. Tattered shrouds were strewn among colored pieces of pottery. We gathered whatever seemed to us of interest such as two fully preserved corn cobs—food for the dead, who apparently had disdained them. If the yellow kernels could only be made to sprout!

Much more saddening was the fact that we found evidence of fire. The old man who showed us around declared that treasureseekers had simply burnt all the ancient textiles and had taken away only bowls and plates and earthenware figures. Where these objects had eventually wound up, he did not know. Where could it be that Don Antonio and Don Fernando and Doña Carmencita—or whoever the illegal diggers and their accomplices were—had dragged the motley ware to? Too many people had been involved. What shocked us most of all was that *quipus* (records of knotted strings to register supplies of goods and population censuses), which on account of their rarity are of the greatest value to science, had also been burnt. What incredible misfortune! I could not help thinking of the difficulties put in the way of professional archaeologists, who must have all kinds of legal papers for their operation. While official *permisos* are so hard to obtain, nobody gives a hoot when treasureseekers and pothunters are at large. They can go on a rampage without interference, loot tombs, mutilate and set fires. The few knot records kept in museums come from graves, but in no instance are the places where they were found—a knowledge of which is so important for their interpretation—properly identified. During the Conquest a great many quipus were still extant until fanatic Spanish clerics, perhaps aided by suspicious government functionaries who distrusted such means of communication, destroyed them wholesale as "recipes of the devil." Now we stood around and fingered sadly actual

Peruvian *quipu* (knot record)

fragments of precious quipus, which had been burnt only the day before yesterday. Linares, the young Peruvian archaeologist, glanced at me with noticeable embarrassment.

We mounted our horses again and trotted in silence. The hoofs buried themselves deep in the loose sand. The old man led the way up a continuously rising incline. The white of the sand was blinding. "This is the way to Chuquibamba in the mountains," said the old man. "Indians of the sierra use the road to get to the coast. They carry wool and sometimes corn. On their return they load dried fish and fruit. It may have been the same way in ancient times."

The old man was probably right. We found llama bones along the road, also a human jaw-bone, bleached white by the strong sun. Immaculate teeth rattled in their sockets. Who could determine their age? The sand which must have covered them for decades, if not centuries, had been blown away by the wind.

There was not much time for such meditations. Suddenly I jumped from my horse. From a distance I had already seen the first pictures on one of the white stone blocks, which lie around as if they had been sown for miles on the glittering sandy plain by the hands of a giant. Some volcano must have spewed them up, if, as I hope, my assumption is geologically correct and sound.

We found ourselves in the midst of an enormous picture book, whose pages we could not turn, because they are heavy stones. It included stone blocks of various sizes. Several were twelve to fifteen feet wide and some ten feet high. Sometimes all sides of a block were scrawled with pictures and signs. Many are probably buried three or more feet in the sand. One would have to dig them out in order to get hold of every single picture. Such an operation might well double the number of pictures. But there remain more than enough to see and decipher above the surface. Everywhere pictures and signs, signs and pictures. New pictures were cropping up all the time.

The gentlemen from the hacienda, who had come along, were trained agronomists from various parts of Peru. Our enthusiasm infected them. They pointed out one pictured stone here, another there. We jumped from block to block, everybody turning in a different direction. A man would run back toward us shouting from a distance: "Did you see this picture here, and that one there, or the other one over yonder?" Thus it went for hours on end. Nobody tired. Nobody noticed how the time passed, probably not even our old guide.

Alas, the sun was already low. Entire pages of the rocky picture book were blotted out by black shadows. Only at the sunny side could one take photographs. My Rolleiflex camera clicked at brief intervals. Again I had to change the film in the shade of a large boulder. I knelt in the sand. Meanwhile Linares was fully absorbed in sketching and measuring.

What a shame that so many, many pictures had been previously chopped up, had been immured in road beds, or were forever destroyed! Halved and quartered blocks were left lying around. The enormous picture book of at least six square kilometers has been used for years as a quarry. Whole pages have been torn out and erased. We made up our minds to ask the authorities to put a stop to such barbaric destruction of cultural remains. Legislation existed, it is true; but few paid any attention to it. Many more were ignorant of it. Later on we followed up our resolution and intervened on the way back with the sub-prefect. Linares was of the hopeful opinion that my foreign name might help to bring about effective steps. The prefect, on his part, promised to do everything within his power. I trust that he kept his word.

Meanwhile we were still roaming among the scattered rocks on the sandy pampa of Toro Muerto. We were overpowered by the countless images of animals and men and undeciphered geometric signs. We tramped from rock to rock through the rippling sand—photographing, measuring, and sketching. Somewhere our horses were tied to posts and sadly drooped their heads. . . .

Nowhere else in Peru where I had formerly examined rock pictures, had I seen so much movement. On the other hand, in the pampa of Toro Muerto one rarely came across the static and abstractly shortened images of men so common elsewhere in Peru and other South American countries.

The next day, on a second visit to Toro Muerto, I looked around me to appraise the entire panorama of sand and stone with the steep river bank on the other side as backdrop. The sun beat down mercilessly. It was the ancient Indian deity in the cloudless firmament. My horse had run away. That did not bother me much, but I called my companions. They were too far away. My voice could not reach them in this open wilderness. Suddenly I saw next to me in the sand what seemed fresh tracks of a puma. What could the big beast of prey be looking for in this sandy desert? Even during the most radiant sunshine, in the middle of the day, one can become superstitious. Imagination jumps in leaps and curves and searches for mystical connections between rock paintings and the fresh animal imprints. Reason informs one of the stupidity of all this. But imagination continues to jump.

Puma and jaguar turn up again and again in the rock pictures. The jaguar can always be recognized by its spots. Its image has often little but the dots in common with the living model. There is one that has six instead of five claws. Its muzzle is much too long. The tail ends in a serpent's head. (Here as everywhere in ancient America the serpent!) A forked tongue protrudes from the mouth. Around it whirl smaller animals. A few birds squat clumsily in between. Could it be that the puma or jaguar is the master of all these animals? Frequently, various kinds of animals swarm about on the same stone. In several instances, large beasts carry a human head with long strands of hair or a complete body in their mouths.

Entire herds of animals are schematically grouped on other stones. They are undoubtedly llamas. These animals are similarly outlined on the textiles of the Inca period. The human figures which accompany them—presumably their herdsmen—are much more awkwardly drawn than the impressionistic dancers of related scenes. An encircling line on one of the pictures apparently represents some kind of pen filled with a herd, with other animals waiting outside. Nearly all their heads turn in one direction. Such abstractly drawn herd animals also occur in the immediate vicinity of scenes with dancers. I hesitate to decide whether they belong together. I do not think so. . . .

A large mask is carved into still another stone block. Its cheeks show traces of tears shaped like lightning symbols. Such tears are typical of the Tiahuanaco deities. Shortened animal figures are tied in with the mask. From the upper edge of the mask starts an irregularly winding line which comes to an end in a meandering hook. Who can venture to say whether it represents a symbol for irrigation which the god of the mask has the power to grant? It is true that the ancient irrigation ditches actually terminate in meanders. More than once we encountered them clearly outlined in formerly cultivated desert valleys.

It has become customary to interpret the majority of the rock pictures of the Old World as magic or as representations of magic activities. The mask, which I also found in the rock art of other Peruvian regions, allows us to draw similar conclusions. By the same token one may well explain the dancers from Toro Muerto as performers of cultic rites. What else could the man who kneels before a herd in a conjuring gesture be up to? . . .

Quite often numerous scenes and pictures will border on each other so that it becomes difficult to isolate individual subjects, particularly since one cannot tell whether all these pictures were drawn at the same time. Occasionally, however, an animal stands all by itself, such as a long-legged, dotted quadruped. But is it a deer or just a flayed skin? The curved club in front of it could be a boomerang. Years ago we found a similarly shaped throwing stick made of pure copper in a grave of the northern coastal region.

And what could be the meaning of other signs? Some that return constantly—also on rock pictures of other areas—I mentioned before: meander symbols, which appear either horizontally or vertically on stone surfaces.

At times, broadly carved straight lines run below the meanders. I am inclined to interpret the meanders as irrigation ditches. The straight lines would then be furrows to conduct the water to them. Simple small crosses seem to be stars, while a circle with rays may be seen as the sun. Next to lines one often notices rows of points in varying multiples. Inescapably their sight evokes numerical symbols. In any case, it is rather unlikely that they were carved into the block out of mere playfulness.

There are single stones which bear nothing but such symbols apart from the occasional presence of little men. But it is quite debatable whether these men belong with these signs or are later additions. Among other patterns are winding lines which are remindful of the river courses on maps. Zigzag lines sometimes ending in heads of serpents bring to mind symbols for lightning. Quadrangles that frequently recur are subdivided by diagonal lines into four equal parts. Into them are scratched varying numbers of dots. Just like the "lightning symbols" I found these same figures in other parts of Peru. No other sign illustrates so clearly the transition from a more or less realistic picture to the beginning of written symbols.

No onlooker will doubt that the different pictures belong to various styles. . . . To arrange them into a definite system would, however, be premature. What is needed is a thorough sifting of the several hundred Peruvian rock pictures I recorded. This will require lengthy and patient desk work—comparisons with other South American stone drawings, which I have not been able to see myself, as well as with the styles and subjects from the artistic manifestations of all of ancient America, in addition to an examination of the vast literature in that field. . . .

In sum: We came across representations of animals, men, and distinct signs, perhaps also symbols. Wherever I saw such drawings in Peru they were scratched into blocks of stone or into living rock; and in open country, never in caves as in the Old World. Possibly the scratched lines were occasionally filled with pigment which time has washed away. Yet, I have never found incontrovertible evidence of paint. In the sandy wastes of Toro Muerto and on the heights above the right bank of the trench of the Maje we saw pictures only on big boulders. The stones were of relatively soft volcanic rock. Had it not been for the permanent aridity of that zone, the pictures would undoubtedly have been much more weathered during the course of centuries. Nevertheless, the rock is far too soft to allow us, for this reason alone, to assume any excessive time span since the creation of the pictures. It is evident that various periods of style have been responsible for them. The earliest may well point to the Tiahuanaco age, which can be dated from the twelfth century A.D. Other scenes, such as the figures of llamas, show affinities with the Inca period. Only the almost faded figure from across the river in the vicinity of the hamlet of Pitis can with some certainty be attributed to a considerably earlier date. Chronologically, however, much of the material overlaps.

In a lecture which I delivered at the University of Arequipa, I outlined a hypothesis, final conclusions of which have yet to be tested. It seems to me that the majority of the pictured stones lie along the migration routes of ancient Indians. Those at Toro Muerto are situated astride the road to Chuquibamba which even today is used by natives. This section of the road links the coast with the mountainous interior. The same observation can be made about the Jequetepeque Valley in the Peruvian north. The rock pictures there are near the ancient road to Cajamarca, the last place of residence of the ill-fated Inca Atahualpa. The stone drawings from Alto de la Guitarra, which stylistically range from the Chavín era to the peak of the Mochica civilization, mark a mountain pass on the route joining the valley of the Moche with that of the Virú. . . .

Perhaps one is mistaken if one looks everywhere for magic. There is at least a possibility that recollections of an incident during the trip were captured in a picture. Peruvian scholars have hinted at certain road signs or road maps so to speak. All this can, of course, not be proven, it remains conjecture. . . .

In terms of human developments, pictures are the oldest writing on the globe. The cave or rock paintings of the Old World have been shown to be of considerable antiquity. That the rock drawings of America can boast of a comparable age, as distinguished scientists have maintained, I seriously doubt. Despite the astronomical and mathematical knowledge of Maya priests, all America belonged to the Stone Age when proselytizing Spaniards visited the continent for the first time. As to the ancient Peruvians, unlike the Mayas and the Mexicans, they did not know how to manufacture paper. Until very recent times they inscribed stones and rocks.

Our task is to determine parallels in style and subject matter with representations on old Peruvian ceramics and tapestry which were, in fact, a kind of picture writing. In a majority of cases these wares can be dated. In addition, it will be necessary to systematically sort and compare the abstract signs and symbols in order to probe the riddle of their meaning. There is still a long road ahead of us.

Serpent symbol from a Moche vase

9

"The persons buried here did not die a natural death, but were victims of strangulation. Proofs of this statement are to be seen in . . . the unnatural thinness of the neck, which seems drawn in to two inches in diameter. It may also be observed that the scalp in its dried state covers the lower opening of the skull, which is only possible when the neck has been dislocated before death. Again, in other cases, several vertebrae were found in a distorted position beneath the back of the lower jaw-bone, and the skin below was highly drawn in. . . . The manner of strangulation which we can here trace with the assurance of a coroner was the cause of death of all the persons buried in this cemetery."

This grisly post mortem was written down by Dr. Max Uhle when he excavated in 1897 the cemetery on a terrace of the Sun Temple of Pachacamac, the focal shrine near Lima. All the persons buried in this sacred ground were women. Judging by their age, the type of burial, and funerary equipment, they must have been Inca maidens dedicated to the service of the Sun. There was little doubt—they had been sacrificed to the divinity and upon the order of the Inca.

Here, at last, was physical proof that the Incas indulged in human sacrifice as did virtually all the peoples of ancient America. The Inca historian Garcilaso de la Vega, partial to his mother's people, had categorically denied that such offerings were made. But he stood overruled by the majority of other early chroniclers. If not to the monstrous degree of the Mexicans and some of the races they conquered in South America, the Incas practiced the slaughter of humans for the glory of their gods with at least the same readiness as had the ancient peoples of the Near East and China thousands of years earlier. As at the royal graves of Ur in Sumeria, a host of servants and concubines were, on occasion, made to accompany a great man on his last journey. Cieza de León reports that when one of the last Inca rulers died some four thousand were killed. In a great variety of instances bloody tribute of this kind was exacted. Illness of a ruler or of other exalted persons, a battle, or any religious festival were considered opportune for animal or human sacrifice. Indeed, sacred virgins such as those buried at Pachacamac were especially picked for glorious extinction. Often the Inca would officiate himself. And, it seems, all human sacrifice became the prerogative of the Lord Inca. Infant sacrifices, mainly of children of nobles at around the age of eight, are known to have been considered most pleasing. Still another aspect of human sacrifice was reported to be connected with the worship of mountains where at high sanctuaries, like the one atop the Huanacauri, the Inca would schedule massacre of the innocent by divine sanction.

A chance find, made more than half a century after Uhle's campaign at Pachacamac, was to add much new evidence to our knowledge of these appalling Inca customs. When it was announced in 1954, the object of the find as well as the manner of its discovery stirred the press of several continents. It did not involve the desiccated, eviscerated, or decomposed mummies of pre-Columbian Indians, but the almost lifelike frozen body of a handsome boy (not of a beautiful princess as first announced), who had been abandoned to the gods of a high peak of the Andes some five hundred years before. The Indian boy was not only fully dressed but adorned with jewelry. He wore the typical Inca head band (*llautu*), and had been buried with trinkets, various pouches, and effigies wrought from silver and gold, all of which bore vivid testimony to Indian customs and artisanship, and to the spread of Inca culture far south into present-day Chile.

That we should ever look upon the actual face—hardly touched by time—of an inhabitant of the New World before the arrival of the white man was beyond anyone's expectations. Once when they had opened a sarcophagus, Renaissance men had been able to look for a few brief moments at the seemingly flawless features of a Roman girl, but then suddenly the ancient beauty had disintegrated to dust. In 1950 in a peat bog of Jutland, Danish scientists had come across the well-preserved body of "Tollund man." He too had met death by execution or sacrifice. Now treasureseekers at an Indian shrine high up on an Andean peak had made possible what is one of the rarest of archaeological opportunities.

To Dr. Grete Mostny, an Austrian-born scholar and head of the anthropology division of Chile's National Museum of Natural History at Santiago, fell the good fortune to receive the first news of the discovery. Eventually she assisted in its acquisition—apparently not without some battling over the body with a rival institution, if we are to believe the somewhat contradictory accounts then issuing from Chilean and North American newspapers and magazines. Dr. Mostny gave the first official report in a paper delivered at the 31st International Congress of Americanists in São Paulo in 1954. Three years later, after the body and its trappings had been thoroughly examined by a number of anthropologists, archaeologists, chemists, and anatomists, and had come to rest in her Museum, she published an authoritative monograph on "The Mummy of El Plomo."

THE LITTLE PRINCE FROM EL PLOMO

Grete Mostny

On the sixteenth of February [1954] there came to my office at the National Museum of Natural History in Santiago de Chile two men, who told me of an archaeological find they had made high up in the Andean cordillera. They brought along a silver figurine attired in cloth and plumes and described additional objects of their discovery, foremost the dressed "mummy of a little Indian girl," which, according to them, was vastly different from the mummies [desiccated bodies from Chile's nitrate desert] preserved in the Museum. With this mummy they had also found various bags and two statuettes of llamas. I assured them that the National Museum of Natural History would be interested in acquiring the entire cache. The men then informed me that they had come across the mummy in a grave at an altitude of over 5,400 meters. Because winter was approaching, they had considered it best to bring it to a much lower place until they had decided on its future. I then proposed that they should bring the mummy down to Santiago and notify the Museum. On the fifteenth of March, the two men returned. Once again they had with them the silver statuette and another one made of shell. They told the director of the Museum, Don Humberto Fuenzalida, and me that the mummy was now in their house at Puente Alto, a village quite close to the capital. On the following day I went there to see the "mummy." It turned out to be the frozen body of a young child, clothed in Inca style.

"El Niño del Cerro 'El Plomo,'" *Thirty First International Congress of Americanists.* São Paulo: Editorial Anhembi, 1955, Vol. II, pp. 847–62 *passim.* Translated by Leo Deuel.

So remarkable was its state of preservation that it looked like a child who had fallen asleep. Aware of the importance of the find, I rushed back to the Museum, where I left a note for the director advising him to acquire the collection immediately. In fact, that very afternoon Señor Fuenzalida made his way to Puente Alto and managed to reach an agreement on the purchase price—45,000 Chilean pesos—a sum advanced from funds at the disposal of the Department of Anthropology of the University of Chile under the direction of Dr. [Richard] Schaedel. That sum was returned to the anthropology department a few weeks later, except for 10,000 pesos which the University contributed towards the purchase.

Immediately afterwards the corpse was taken by the director of the Museum to the Institute of Legal Medicine to have it stored there overnight in a freezer. We considered this a necessary precaution because we were dealing with a frozen body. After a few hours, it became clear that the cold but humid environment might prove to be harmful, and the doctors of the Institute thought it would be better to keep the body in a dry atmosphere of normal temperature. As a consequence, we decided next morning to take the body away and to store it in the Museum itself, where it belonged and where it is now. . . .

Silver statuette of llama

From various meetings with the discoverers, who are prospectors, we learned that the find was made near the peak of "El Plomo" [Lead Mountain], province of Santiago, at 5,400-meter altitude. In that area there were three structures named by the mountaineers "pircas de los Indios" [walls of Indian masonry]. In one of them, below the ground level, was the tomb which contained the child and its belongings.

It so happened that on the first of February of that year a group of mountaineers were in the vicinity of this place when they saw two men descending with a heavy sack loaded on their shoulders. It later came out that the child's body was hidden inside.

In the second week of April, an expedition sponsored by the National

Museum of Natural History climbed El Plomo in order to check at the site the details given by the prospectors. The expedition was carried out by members of the Andean Mountaineering Club of Chile under the direction of Señor Louis Krahl. Several students from the Department of Anthropology of the University of Chile joined it. Krahl and two of his companions succeeded in getting to their destination and later brought back an account of the observations they made. According to them there are two groups of structures on the mountain, one at an altitude of 5,200 meters consisting of an elliptical enclosure, which the mountaineers call the "altar." It seems to be, indeed, a pre-Columbian place of worship. The deviation of the main axis of the building is 22° toward northeast. The second group, at 5,400 meters, is very close to the summit and consists of three rectangular structures, the largest one with an annex at one corner. It is noteworthy that the main axis of this precinct has the same direction of 22° to northeast as the shrine farther down. The dimensions of the building are 7 meters long and 3.5 meters wide (about 22 feet by 11 feet). Its walls still stood some 0.7 to 0.8 meters high, while the interior was filled with earth and stones. In the center of it was the tomb. The frozen soil underneath had been excavated to a depth of 0.7 meters and was covered with a stone slab. The observations made by Señor Krahl and his mountaineers corroborated the information given by the prospectors who had discovered the body. The latter also told us that the cadaver was surrounded by its belongings and that it had been soft and flexible when they found it; it hardened only later. In fact, when it reached the Museum it was still moderately soft after having been exposed to air for six weeks.

From the data reported by Señor Krahl we can deduce that the structures on El Plomo formed a ceremonial compound of a pre-Columbian people. According to archaeological evidence these were the Incas and their contemporaries, though, naturally, this does not rule out previous visits to the site by other people.

The body was encountered in a seated position, its knees flexed toward the chest, the legs crossed. The right forearm rested on the knees and the left hand was holding the right hand. The last two phalanges of the three middle fingers of the left hand displayed the aspect and coloring typical of a human body frozen to death within 24 to 48 hours. It was once again Señor Krahl who drew attention to this phenomenon well known to mountaineers of the Andes.

During the medical examination performed by doctors from the Institute of Legal Medicine, it could be seen that the cadaver belonged to a child of the male sex. X-ray tests yielded the following results: (1) The age appeared to be eight to nine years. Ossification was not yet complete and growth cartilage was in evidence, just as permanent dentification had not fully replaced temporary teeth; (2) The first metatarsal was much shorter than the rest and was abnormally thickened, amounting to an atavistic bone development; (3) It was possible to establish the presence of such internal organs as brain, heart, diaphragm, and a not too clearly differentiated mass in the abdomen, perhaps the liver; (4) As to the rest, the skeleton had a normal appearance, although one should draw attention to the size of feet and hands which were small in proportion to the body in general; (5) It has not been possible to observe further details due to the excessive thickness of the soft garments, a thickness probably caused by having been partly congealed and by incipient mummification.

The report by physical anthropologists stated that the head had a cephalic index of 81.8, which points to a brachycephalic type. The hair was smooth, thick, black, and somewhat curled, and the hair follicles were perfectly preserved. The face was wide, with a very high index of facial width. The nasal index of the low and wide nose was exaggerated by postmortem damage. All these characteristics indicate that the child belonged to the Mongolian race, as was to be expected. . . .

The child's body was dressed in a tunic (*uncu*) of black wool with stripes of white fur, a shawl (*yancolla*) of gray wool with a red fringe, a black head band (*llautu*) and a headdress of black wool with a crest of condor feathers in front. On the feet it wore moccasins (*hisscu*) of leather with a woolen border. On the right forearm it had a silver bracelet. An ornament of the same metal shaped like half moons hung over the chest.

The hair, which reached much below the shoulders, was plaited in countless fine braids. The face was brightened by red paint over which diagonal yellow stripes had been drawn. A pouch (*chuspa*) for coca leaves was slung across the shoulders. Apart from these trappings, the child was accompanied by various accouterments consisting of a purse of woven material covered with feathers, inside which there were coca leaves; a total of five little bags made from animal intestines with small balls of fallen or cut hair, milk teeth and nail parings inside; and finally a silver idol, dressed in the manner of Inca women, which was buried apart from the two figurines of llamas, one made from a silver-gold alloy, the other from a piece of shell.

The find of the El Plomo child permits us to draw a number of conclusions. The child was about eight to nine years old and was an Inca subject. It is impossible to say to which of the many ethnic entities subjugated by the Inca empire it belonged. The headdress could perhaps give the clue, since the chroniclers never tire of repeating that the various parts of the kingdom were distinguished by the different headdresses they used, and which they were forbidden under severe penalty to change. Thus says

Folded and unfolded Peruvian purse

Pedro de Cieza, and Garcilaso bears him out. But no one has described the kind of headdress the child wore. Nor did Guamán Poma draw it.

Nevertheless, certain signs indicate that the child belonged to a people of the altiplano of the southern Andes. It also appears that in these highlands of the south, moccasins as well as sandals were in use. The pectoral is identical with one found on an island of Lake Titicaca by Bandelier and with a drawing of a cacique from Collasuyu by Guamán Poma. The same cacique wore also a bracelet like that of the child and according to the author of the *Relaciones Geográficas* the rich people of La Paz had the habit of wearing bracelets of gold and silver. Likewise the pouch of condor feathers suggests perhaps that we are faced with an inhabitant of the altiplano, because in the lower left corner of the picture of a cacique from Collasuyu by Guamán Poma a condor is shown on a shield.

The *llautu* of the child is black. According to Garcilaso, the first privilege which the Inca granted to a subject nation was the right to wear a black *llautu*. In the ceremonies of the Capac Raymi the selected youths wore black *llautus*. But our child from El Plomo mountain was too young for this ceremony. There were, however, some tribes, as for instance the people of Jauja, who always wore the black *llautu*.

The tunic and the shawl were made from rather coarse and ordinary cloth. I would like to draw attention to the dimensions of the tunic which was very short and which barely covered the child's trunk, though it was a general rule that the *uncu* should reach to the middle of the thigh. But one must remember that we are dealing with a child and very little is known about the particular ways in which children were dressed. The son of the Inca Roca, who was represented as a child by Guamán Poma, also sports a black *uncu* with two B-shaped designs. These are missing from the El Plomo child's tunic, but he has instead four stripes of white silky fur sewn on it. Surely he was not a son of the Inca, but probably of a provincial nobleman or at least of a rich man.

The tender age of the child is also conspicuous in the lack of trousers and of holes in his ears. According to Inca custom, a young Indian received his first trousers at the age of fourteen or fifteen in a ceremony called Huarachikuy (Waracikoy) which was performed during the festival for Capac Raymi. On that occasion, a youth of noble blood had to pass certain tests for physical aptitude. Afterwards his ears were pierced, he was given weapons and trousers, and his hair was cut. At that time he also received his definite name. The child from El Plomo had not yet undergone those ceremonies.

In his brief life he had only passed one ceremony which was performed when he was between one and two years old. At that time his eldest uncle cut the hair and nails of the child and gave him the name which he was to use until puberty. It was the custom to guard the hair and nails carefully. In fact, we found them together with his milk teeth in the little bags made from animal intestines.

At the time of his death, the child's hair had once more grown and had been arranged in fine plaits reaching far below his shoulders. We do not know the significance of this hairdo. Cieza de León mentioned that the Indians of Riobamba wore their hair in many plaits. Also the pre-Inca inhabitants of northern Chile and Argentina and of the Bolivian altiplano used to braid their hair in many fine tresses, which were combined into one large plait at each side of the head. The child lacks the latter detail. However, his may have been a hairdo special for the occasion, because it had certainly been done shortly before his death.

The child's face was painted with red color and yellow stripes which descended slantwise across the cheekbones. Red color seems [according to tradition] to have been a favorite; warriors painted themselves in red and other colors in order to frighten the enemy. Color was also used at festivals and dances. This is one of the most interesting aspects of the El Plomo discovery, because for the first time it permits us to observe the application of facial paint to a subject of the Inca empire.

Finally, there remains for us to discuss how the child came to be buried on the summit of the mountain. It is known that the Incas, like other Andean people, attributed supernatural powers to mountains. The higher and more prominent a mountain was, the greater its power. Mountains covered by eternal snow were especially singled out for worship. Among these was El Plomo as borne out by the structures encountered on and about its peak and the remains of a road leading up to it. The locale of the "pircas de los Indios" has long been known to prospectors and muleteers visiting the region. Years earlier the discoverer of the child had found in one of the buildings seven or perhaps nine statuettes of gold and silver, which he sold "opportunely." (It has been impossible to trace the people who acquired them.) In one of the *pircas,* the aforementioned mountaineers chanced to notice a fairly large excavation, which looked as if it had been made a long time ago, and it is quite likely that this one, too, once contained the body of a sacrificed child. For I have no doubt whatever that the child whose body is now at the National Museum of Natural History was sacrificed.

The majority of the chroniclers of ancient Peru were in agreement that human sacrifices existed in the age of the Incas. . . . Men, women, and children were sacrificed on certain occasions, and provinces of the realm had to render an obligatory tribute in human beings. Sacrifices were staged when a new Inca ruler ascended the throne, after victories in battle, when the Inca was sick, and during calamities. There were four methods of dispatching the victims: strangulation, tearing their hearts out, breaking their necks with a stone, and, finally, burying them alive. It seems that the custom of sacrificing children was particularly widespread among the inhabitants of the Andean regions. According to some colonial sources, such sacrifices were made in pairs—a boy and a girl. This practice was called Capacocha, which refers to the victims' approximate age of ten years. The victims put on their best things and among the objects

Scene of "Great Feast of the Sun" (Capac Inti-Raymi) during which the Incas buried some five hundred children alive, Poma de Ayala

which accompanied them small silver and gold figures of llamas are especially mentioned. Certainly the bag of feathers with coca leaves belonged to the ritual equipment, whereas the *chuspa* and the small bags of skin with hair, nails, and teeth formed part of the victim's personal possessions.

As to the manner of killing, the only possible one in our case was death by live burial. X-ray examination established beyond any argument the absence of the slightest lesion or shock. It was the practice to intoxicate victims with a strong brew of *chicha* [liquor] before immolating them; and this must surely have been the case with the child from El Plomo. He was made drunk and was then carried to the tomb. Before this alcoholic stupor could have passed, the child was frozen, suffering a peaceful death as seems to be attested by the quiet expression on his face.

10

Trying to solve the question of Polynesian settlement of the island specks of the Pacific Ocean, Thor Heyerdahl inadvertently ventured into the thorny debate over American origins—and into popular fame. All of a sudden, in 1947, the name of the Norwegian explorer and that of his venturesome vessel became household words associated with one of the most colorful modern seafaring exploits. For a world-wide audience—the narrative of the voyage was translated into 53 languages—*Kon-Tiki* was an open sesame to the mysterious past of the Western Hemisphere which they found as persuasive and satisfying as the sibyllene accounts of Atlantis. Scholars, on the whole, resisted the spell, often without giving it the benefit of detached scrutiny. However, there is no doubt that since Heyerdahl's bold thesis hit the scene, American archaeologists have been forced to deal with what appears to be undeniable evidence of trans-Pacific contacts between the Old World and the New.

Students of American antiquities had of course long been aware of similarities in artifacts, customs, and institutions between the Americas and Southeast Asia, particularly, as well as Polynesia and Melanesia. The Mexican game of patolli can be considered an almost exact replica of the parchesi of Hindu India. The pan pipes in use all over the Andes and into Brazil are virtually indistinguishable from those known to Burma and the Solomon Islands. Star-shaped mace heads from Melanesia resemble those from Peru. The people of Easter Island built masonry of polygonal blocks fitted into each other just as the Incas did. The native sweet potato of South America not only was cultivated in Polynesia before the white man landed there, but bore the same name, *kumara,* a Quechua word. The Swedish ethnologist Baron Erland Nordenskiöld listed forty-nine such parallels between Oceania and South America. Recently scholars have added still more to them. But how was one to explain these phenomena?

For a while, the pat answer was "diffusion," or rather, sunken continents like Mu; wayward Hebrews; or Egypt, the mother of us all. Yet, so unscientific and fantastic were these theories in their elaboration that they discredited diffusion altogether. As a consequence few serious Americanists would even examine the problem. Outside the lunatic fringe, the opinion prevailed that resemblances, if at all relevant, were due to coincidence or some "psychic unity," inherent in all races of man, rather than external influences. From agriculture to weaving and metallurgy the American Indian had invented everything himself. Ethnologists declared their own Monroe doctrine for the Americas, and those who had made the cultural achievements of the Indians their cause, displayed a somewhat irrational pride in what they judged to be the wholly autochthonous cultures of the New World.

It was such a climate of opinion that Heyerdahl invaded with his ideas, which, had it not been for their sweep and intercontinental claims, should have actually pleased American ethnocentrists. As everybody knows, Heyerdahl made the ancient Peruvians the original settlers of the far-flung archipelago of the Pacific Ocean, who were in turn succeeded by another wave of migrants radiating from the American Northwest coast. Until Heyerdahl there had been general agreement that the Pacific islanders had come from the Asiatic mainland, probably via the Malay land bridge. Asiatic affinities in race, culture, and language seemed fairly conclusive. However, it should be noted that the American origin of Polynesians had been proposed from time to time since the early nineteenth century.

Thor Heyerdahl did not just formulate his doctrine in general terms, but set out to prove, if not its veracity, at least its feasibility. A first concern was to establish proof that the ancient Peruvians, possibly the builders of Tiahuanaco, had indeed been "Polynesian" colonizers. Then there was the great stumbling block of how these pre-Columbian people could ever have crossed vast bodies of water, considering their allegedly rudimentary skill at navigation. It is to this very problem that Heyerdahl devoted the following essay (based on two papers read by him at the International Congress of Americanists at Cambridge, England, in 1952), which establishes the theoretical basis for his celebrated trip on the raft *Kon-Tiki*. In it Heyerdahl reviews his researches into pre-Columbian seafaring, which convinced him that Inca and pre-Inca people were no mean mariners and had in fact embarked on major voyages. Equally important were his inquiries into the manner in which the Peruvians constructed seaworthy balsa rafts and how the vessels managed to keep afloat for many months despite the known tendency of balsa wood to soak up water and sink. Archaeology itself furnished models from tombs, which, Heyerdahl thought, settled moot points of construction.

And then, on April 28, 1947, the Norwegian flag was hoisted on a rather preposterous sailing "ship" at the Callao Yacht Club. Six men on a raft—not to forget a parrot—sailed with the Humboldt Current westward into the Pacific blue. A hundred and one days afterward, and 4,300 miles from the coast of South America, the raft landed on a reef in the Tuamotus of French Oceania. Heyerdahl had made his point.

Archaeologists, like other scientists, are in the habit of finding what they have been looking for all along. For Heyerdahl the quest had begun ten years earlier when as a young zoologist, recently graduated from the University of Oslo, he went on a field trip to a small island of the Marquesas group, far out in the Pacific. The problem he had set out to study was: how did animals get to these remote islands that had risen from the ocean without ever having been linked to any of the large land masses? But soon the riddle of human settlement was to absorb all his interest. On his return to Norway he handed over his "glass jars of beetles and fish from Fatu Hiva to the University Zoological Museum." From now on he was going to "tackle primitive people." The zoologist became an anthropologist.

The magic name of Tiki had cast its spell over Heyerdahl when an aged native, last survivor of an extinct tribe on the Marquesas, had, in reference to a giant statue, spoken one night of that god and chief who had brought his ancestors to these islands from the east across the sea. By what seemed to him a flash of intuition, the young zoologist was reminded of the great monoliths of the South American Andes. Even then he thought he was near a solution of the South Sea migration puzzle. Tiki was to be his key. And soon enough the legendary hero materialized when Heyerdahl read of the sun god Con-Ticci Viracocha, who, according to Inca tradition, had left Peru and sailed out into the Pacific with his followers.

The outbreak of the Second World War, during which he served in the Free Norwegian forces, interrupted Heyerdahl's studies. When peace came he did further research in museums and libraries and thereby rounded off and documented his theory. South American Indians, he was now convinced, had peopled the Pacific. The only way they could have reached the islands was on balsa rafts. And, against all objections raised by skeptics, he was going to prove it.

A full account of Heyerdahl's thesis was issued in 1952 under the title *American Indians in the Pacific*; it ran to more than 600 pages. There followed in 1954 an archaeological expedition to the Galápagos Islands, where Heyerdahl was in fact able to dig up unmistakably pre-Columbian pottery. During his next expedition to Easter Island (1955–56) Heyerdahl and his co-workers carried out what are often considered the first major excavations in Polynesia. These proved that the islands had been occupied much earlier than the date generally accepted for the first Polynesian colonization anywhere in the Pacific. Carbon-14 tests established a date of about A.D. 380—a thousand years prior to what it should have been if Easter Island lay last in line of the Asiatic east-to-west migration. Once again Heyerdahl was certain he had identified Peruvian characteristics in the two culture strata that preceded the present "native" population.

Suffice it to say that Heyerdahl's Kon-Tiki fixation has met with harsh criticism, as have his interpretations of Polynesian-Peruvian resemblances and relationships. More recent research rather tends to stress the Asiatic roots of Polynesia, reaffirmed by a decipherment of the Easter Island script. But thanks to Heyerdahl the likelihood of pre-Columbian voyages westward into the Pacific is no longer ruled out and occasional contacts and cultural exchanges between Polynesians and New World aboriginals are widely accepted.

However, the spread of cultural traits, the give and take, turns out to be a far more tangled web than the explanatory frame of a single grandiose hypothesis. Just as Peruvians landed on Pacific isles, Polynesians may well have reached the American coast on several occasions. Far Eastern cultural elements—the way they traveled, their chronology, extent of impact, and precise foci in the Western Hemisphere—remain among the most mystifying riddles of American archaeology, even though reputable scientists have now traced some of them and have persuaded many of their colleagues that these elements are far too close to their counterparts and too complex in their manifestations and associations to have been independently evolved in the New World.

KON-TIKI'S ANCESTORS

Thor Heyerdahl

Aboriginal navigation in Peru and adjoining sections of north-western South America was based on boat-building principles entirely different from those on which our own civilization based its maritime evolution. To the European mind the only seaworthy vessel is one made buoyant by a watertight, air-filled hull big enough to be beyond reach of the waves. To the ancient Peruvians the only seaworthy craft was one which could never be filled with water because its open construction gave no space in

"Kon-Tiki's Ancestors," *Geographical Magazine* (London), XXV (1952), pp. 421–26.

which to retain the invading seas, which washed through. Their object was thus achieved by building exceedingly buoyant, raft-like vessels of balsa or other very light wood, or of bundles of reeds or canes lashed together in boat fashion, or by making pontoons of inflated seal-skins carrying a soft deck. Such craft tend to appear primitive, incommodious and unsafe to anyone who is unfamiliar with their qualities at sea, and this may be the reason for the widespread assumption that the peoples of ancient Peru were without seagoing craft or capable sailors, in spite of their 2,000-mile coastline and their outstanding cultural level in nearly all other respects.

When Francisco Pizarro left the Panama Isthmus in 1526 on his second voyage of discovery down the Pacific coast of South America, his expedition encountered Peruvian merchant sailors at sea long before he discovered their country. His pilot, Bartolomeo Ruiz, was sailing ahead to explore the coast southwards near the equator, when off northern Ecuador his ship suddenly met another sailing vessel of almost equal size, coming in the opposite direction. The northbound vessel proved to be a large raft, and its crew were the first Peruvians ever seen by Europeans. Immediately afterwards a report was sent to Charles V by Juan de Sáamanos, and the episode was recorded even before Peru itself had been visited. The event was also narrated in 1534 by Pizarro's own secretary, Francisco de Xeres. From both sources we learn that the large balsa raft was captured by the

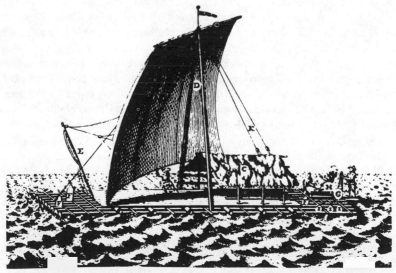

An eighteenth-century drawing of a balsa raft from Guayaquil

Spaniards, who found a crew of twenty Indian men and women aboard. Eleven were thrown overboard, four were left with the raft, and two men and three women were retained aboard the caravel to be trained as interpreters for the later voyages.

The balsa raft was a merchant vessel heavily laden with cargo. The Spaniards estimated its capacity at thirty *toneles,* or about thirty-six tons, as compared with the forty tons of their own caravel, which carried only half as many persons as did the balsa raft. The cargo was carefully listed by the Spaniards, and included some items which could only have come from Peru proper.

The craft was described by Sáamanos as a flat raft, composed of an underbody of logs covered by a deck of slender canes raised so that crew and cargo remained dry while the main logs were awash. The logs as well as the canes were lashed securely together with henequen rope. Sáamanos says of the sail and rigging of the raft:

> It carried masts and yards of very fine wood, and cotton sails in the same shape and manner as on our own ships. It had very good rigging of the said henequen, which is like hemp, and some mooring stones for anchors formed like grindstones.

Ruiz now returned to Pizarro with his prisoners and booty, and a few months later a new expedition, led by Pizarro, pushed southwards to the northern coasts of the Inca Empire. On the way to Santa Clara Island in the open Gulf of Guayaquil, Pizarro overhauled five sailing balsas in two days, and opened favourable negotiations with their crews. Then he crossed the Gulf to the Peruvian port of Tumbez, the home of some of his captives. When approaching the coast the Spaniards saw a whole flotilla of balsa rafts standing towards them, carrying armed Inca troops. Running alongside the fleet Pizarro invited some of the Inca captains aboard his vessel, and by establishing friendly relations through his interpreters—those captured from the first raft encountered—he learnt that the whole flotilla was bound for Puna Island which was then under Peruvian rule.

Other balsa rafts came out of the bay with gifts and provisions for the Spaniards, and we learn from Francisco Pizarro's cousin, Pedro, that a little further down the Peruvian coast the Spaniards overtook some balsa rafts, aboard which they found precious metals and some of the clothes of the country, all of which they kept, so that they might take them to Spain to show to the King.

But even before Ruiz captured the first merchant balsa off Ecuador, the Spaniards had already heard rumours about Peruvian navigation from the natives of Panama. The chronicler Las Casas, son of Columbus' companion, who himself went to settle in the New World, stated that the aborigines in Peru possessed balsa rafts in which they navigated with sails and paddles, and that this fact was also known in pre-Conquest times to the oldest son of Comogre, a great chief in Panama, who spoke to Balboa of a rich coastal empire to the south where people navigated the Pacific Ocean with ships a little smaller than those of the Spaniards, propelled by sails and paddles.

Several of Pizarro's contemporaries recorded details of the craft navigated by the coastal natives of Ecuador and northern Peru: Oviedo (1535), Andagoya (1541) and Zarate, who came to Peru as Royal Treasurer in 1543. Their similar accounts describe rafts made of "long and light logs," an odd number—five, seven, nine or eleven—tied together with crossbeams; the navigation with sails and paddles; the ability of the large ones to carry up to fifty men and three horses. Andagoya, who took part in the earliest expeditions of discovery northwards and southwards along the Pacific Coast, was particularly impressed by the quality of the native henequen rope ("stronger than that of Spain") and the excellent cotton canvas.

The Italian traveller Girolamo Benzoni, who came to Peru about 1540, even included a very primitive drawing of a small sized balsa raft of seven logs and carrying eight Indians. In his text he states that there were rafts for navigating which were much greater, made up of nine or even eleven logs, and carrying sails which varied according to the size of the raft.

Garcilasso de la Vega, who was of Inca descent and left Peru for Spain in 1560, devotes most of his attention to the wash-through fishing craft of reeds or rushes which were numerous and by far the dominant vessel along the Peruvian coast; he says they usually went from four to six leagues off the coast (fifteen to twenty-four English miles) and more if necessary. He adds that when the natives wanted to convey large cargoes they used the rafts of wood on which they hoisted sails when they navigated the open sea.

Father Cabello de Balboa, who came to Peru in 1566, learnt from the Inca historians that some two or three generations before the arrival of Pizarro, Inca Tupac Yupanqui had descended to the coast, and, selecting some of the best local pilots, had embarked with a whole army upon a vast number of rafts and sailed away from the coast. He was absent for about a year. On the return of the flotilla to Peru, the Inca and his captains claimed to have visited two inhabited islands far out in the ocean. It is well known that it was the rumours of Peruvian merchant sailors with balsa rafts and the account of Inca Tupac's voyage of discovery which prompted the famous navigator Sarmiento de Gamboa to urge the Peruvian viceroy to organize the Mendaña expedition in search of these islands, an enterprise which resulted in the discovery of Melanesia, and subsequently also of Polynesia.

The prominent early historian of Peru, Bernabé Cobo, goes into considerable detail in describing the remarkable qualities of the balsa timber used for the ocean-going rafts, and also the native ability to navigate and swim. He wrote:

> The largest rafts used by the Peruvian Indians living near the forests, like those of the harbours of Payta, Manta, and Guayaquil, are composed of seven, nine, or more logs of balsa timber, in the following manner: The logs are lashed one to the other lengthwise by means of lianas or ropes tied over other logs which lie as cross-beams; the log in the middle is longer than the others at the bow, and one by one they are shorter the closer they are placed to the sides, in such a way that, at the bow, they get the same form and proportions as seen on the fingers of an extended hand, although the stern is even. On the top of this they place a platform, so that the people and the clothing on board shall not get wet from the water which comes up in the cracks between the large timbers. These rafts navigate on the ocean by means of sail and paddles, and some are so large that they are easily able to carry fifty men.

A peculiar drawing of a balsa raft in Paita harbour, 120 miles south of Tumbez, was done by Spilbergen on his voyage around the world between 1614 and 1617. The interesting feature of this otherwise crude drawing is that it shows a crew of five men, three of whom are navigating the raft by means of centre-boards, an art which was completely unknown in Europe until about 1870. Spilbergen states that this balsa raft had been away fishing for two months and came back with enough provisions to distribute to his whole fleet.

The first unsuccessful attempt to introduce centre-board navigation to Europe was in 1736, after the Spanish naval officers Juan and Ulloa had made a very excellent survey of balsa raft navigation in Guayaquil Bay. They claimed that a native crew with sufficient skill in manipulating the centre-boards could sail as well in any wind as a regular ship.

The principal Peruvian ports for the wooden rafts in Inca times were Paita and Tumbez and other villages on the northern coast near the great balsa forests, but from there balsa logs for building rafts were transported by sea and even overland to the desert areas of southern Peru. Valverde has recorded how the Spaniards under Hernando Pizarro, when they advanced to the south shore of Lake Titicaca, found great quantities of large balsa timber transported there on the backs of labourers to build wooden balsa rafts on this southern lake for the Inca Huayna Capac.

Only one practical detail remained unrecorded by the early chroniclers or observers, namely, how the lashings were secured to the slippery logs, and how the individual logs were shaped in the bow and stern; but this information may be gained from the tiny model rafts—or more properly the one-man spirit-rafts—which have been found in the Arica desert graves. They, among other objects, were left there more than a thousand years before the arrival of Pizarro, and show that the lashings were fastened in grooves cut around the logs. They also show that to decrease the water resistance each log was pointed boat-fashion fore and aft.

By combining historical and archaeological information, we thus possess a fairly accurate knowledge of the construction of the principal craft which permitted aboriginal navigation in Peru and adjacent Pacific waters, and in 1947 I constructed a balsa raft based on this information. It was of average size, and quite small as compared to the specimens described by Sáamanos, and later drawn by Ulloa, Humboldt, and Paris. It was composed of nine 2-foot-thick balsa logs, ranging in length from thirty to forty-five feet, the longest in the middle, and lashed to cross-beams supporting a bamboo deck and an open bamboo hut. A bipod mast, carrying a square sail, five centre-boards, and a steering-oar completed the construction. This was the *Kon-Tiki,* which we launched off Callao harbour in Peru on April 28 with a crew of six men; ninety-three days later the first inhabited Polynesian island was sighted and passed. After a total journey of 4,300 miles in 101 days, *Kon-Tiki* grounded on the reef of Raroia Atoll in the Tuamotu Islands, with crew and nearly all the cargo safe.

The object of the expedition had been to test and study the true qualities and abilities of the balsa raft, and what was more, to get an answer to the old and disputed question whether or not the Polynesian islands were within feasible reach of the raftsmen of ancient Peru.

It proved to be an exceedingly seaworthy craft, perfectly adapted for carrying heavy cargoes in the open and unsheltered ocean. Of all the valuable qualities none surprised and impressed us more than its outstanding safety and seaworthiness in all weather conditions at sea. Next to its unique ability to ride the waves came perhaps its carrying capacity, which, however, was no surprise, since balsa rafts capable of carrying up to thirty tons were described by the early Spaniards.

The theoretical judgments of the balsa raft had deemed it not seaworthy because of the water-absorbent nature of the balsa wood, which would make it sink if not regularly dismantled and dried; also because it was thought that the rope lashings which kept the logs and the whole craft together would be worn through by friction when the great logs began to move at sea. The light and porous wood was also considered to be too fragile should high ocean seas lift the bow and stern up while crew and cargo were weighing upon the central part. Finally, it was considered that a one-and-a-half-foot freeboard on the flat and open raft would leave crew and cargo entirely exposed to the ocean seas.

Our experience provided the answer to these problems, and showed that the ancient culture-peoples of Peru and Ecuador had their good reasons for evolving—and abiding by—this very type of deep-sea-going craft.

Dry balsa wood, as commercially distributed and generally known today, is exceedingly water-absorbent and unsuitable for raft construction, but green balsa wood, put into the sea when freshly cut and still filled with sap, is very water-resistant, and although the water gradually penetrates the sun-dried outer section, the sap inside prevents further absorption. *Kon-Tiki* was still capable of holding tons of cargo when it was finally pulled ashore for preservation more than a year after the expedition.

The balsa logs did not chafe off the rope lashings. The reason was that the surface of the logs became soft and spongy, and the ropes were left unharmed as if pressed between cork. The two-feet-thick balsa logs proved to be tough enough to resist the assault of two storms with towering seas, and even an emergency landfall on an unsheltered reef in Polynesia.

The secret of the safety and seaworthiness of the unprotected balsa raft, in spite of its negligible freeboard, was primarily its unique ability to rise with any threatening sea, thus riding over the dangerous water-masses which would have broken aboard most other small craft. Secondly it was the ingenious wash-through construction which allowed all water to disappear as through a sieve. Neither towering swells nor breaking wind-waves had any chance of getting a grip on the vessel, and the result was a feeling of complete security which no other open or small craft could have offered. Moreover the shallow construction of the raft, and the flexibility allowed by all the independent lashings, made it possible even to land directly on an exposed reef on the windward side of the dangerous Tuamotu archipelago.

During the voyage a few experiments were carried out with the centre-boards. It was found that five centre-boards, six feet deep and two feet wide, when securely attached, were enough to permit the raft to sail almost at right angles to the wind. It was also ascertained that by raising or lowering centre-boards fore or aft, the raft could be steered without using the steering oar. The raft's crew was quite inexperienced in the use of centre-boards and raft navigation, and an attempt to tack into the wind failed completely, although several of the early chroniclers, and also such accurate observers as Juan and Ulloa 200 years ago, clearly record having seen aboriginal Peruvian raftsmen sailing into the wind by a correlation of sail and centre-boards.

Some of the rafts seen by early Europeans carried merchants with their women and tons of cargo; others were used for army transportation, and still others for fishing expeditions of long duration in the Humboldt Current. Most of these would be well equipped with food and water, because of the barren nature of the Peruvian coast; all would at least have an initial water supply. Our experience showed that sufficient rainwater could be collected *en route* to sustain life; and what was more, a constant supply of fish kept near the raft and provided not only all the food necessary for mere survival, but also a thirst-quenching liquid which could be chewed or pressed from their lymphs.

These observations made it possible to establish the fact that, for the aboriginal Peruvians of high culture, there was no practical barrier between the west coast of South America and Polynesia.

PART **II**

CENTRAL AMERICA
(Panama and Nicaragua)

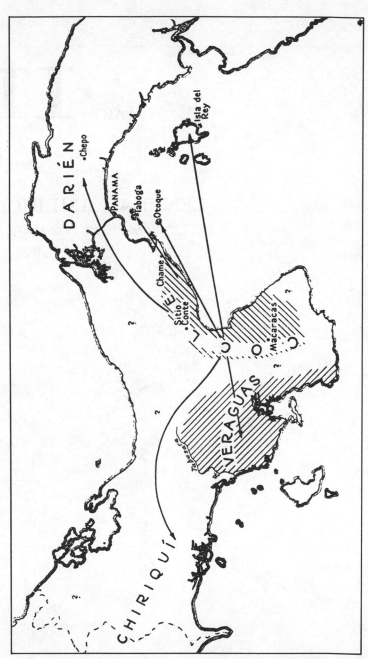

Principal archaeological regions and culture zones of Panama at the time of the Spanish Conquest

11

Two culture zones of ancient America have achieved a pre-eminence unequaled anywhere else in the Western continents, those of Peru (Central Andes) and Mexico (Mesoamerica). All experts concur in the opinion that these were the twin peaks to which aboriginal civilization rose in the New World. Modern scholars have come to call them Nuclear America, because of their advancement in the arts and government, and the influence that emanated from them. Mexico and Peru loom so large in the literature of American antiquities that we are often likely to forget the achievements of "marginal" areas. The gold works of the Quimbaya Valley in western Colombia compare favorably with those of Lambayeque or Batan Grande (Moche) in Peru. A system of highways in difficult terrain was also built by the Taironas, a people isolated in the Santa Marta range of the Caribbean coast of South America. Chibchas domiciled around modern Bogotá had evolved a kingdom which exacted the admiration of the white invaders. Natives of the American Southwest invented a process of etching that apparently antedated similar techniques in European metallurgical and graphic arts. As to the richly decorated and almost baroque pottery from the Amazon basin, in particular from Santarem and from the island of Marajó in the great river's mouth, it is well-nigh unique.

Part of the reason for the towering role of Peru and Mexico is no doubt the fact that they were the most populous areas, ruled by powerful princes, which the Conquistadores encountered. Quite naturally, archaeological attention has almost invariably concentrated on them. However, such concentration, though it may have resulted in an unbalanced picture, was also a reflection of their cultural richness and the archaeological prizes to be expected. If we conceive of Mexico and Peru in their widest sense—which would include part of Central America on the one hand, and Ecuador and Bolivia on the other—we will have to admit that only in these focal lands did the Indians build on a monumental and architecturally sophisticated scale. Only here do we find major urban complexes. Here were devised advanced methods of keeping records. There is some likelihood that it was in Nuclear America that aboriginal hunters made the first transitions to farming societies and developed such crops as maize, squash, manioc, potatoes, beans, cocoa, and cotton.

Yet, by singling out these two central areas, we are at once faced with a number of excruciating problems. Why was it in greater Peru and Mexico rather than in California or Rio Grande do Sul that ancient Americans made the greatest progress? And why, indeed, in two separate regions? Did they develop apart and without any mutual stimuli? Where was maize cultivated first? How can we account for the close resemblance between the "stirrup" vases of Tlatilco in the Valley of Mexico and those of Chavín and coastal Peru? Were the jaguar cult and unmistakably Olmec features introduced from Mexico into ancient Peru? Did human sacrifice originate in South America? If cultural exchange occurred, did its manifestations travel overland or by sea? Were there intermediaries?

Students of American antiquity have discussed such questions for many decades without arriving at any satisfactory conclusions. As the titles of addresses at any international congress of Americanists will bear out, the parallel evolution and affinities between the two foci of Nuclear America have been judged of basic importance; in fact, so much so that consideration of the specter of trans-Pacific contacts was repeatedly set aside, at least as long as these more immediate points of debate could not be settled. Whether such a restriction may have been wise, will not be argued. But there is at least the possibility that direct trans-Pacific intrusions—at specific points in time and space—may help to account for some of the singular aspects of the "nuclear" zones, setting them apart from the rest of the Americas which in turn continued, to a remarkable degree, to mirror common cultural features from Canada to Argentina.

However, even when narrowing the inquiry to relations within Nuclear America, "diffusion" was bound to raise its head again, and the arguments pro and con sounded much the same. "The breadth of the topic is so oppressive!" declared Alfred Louis Kroeber, a leading Peruvianist from the United States, when observing in 1928 that next to nothing was known about actual links in early times between the Central Andean and Middle American regions. Since Kroeber made this statement, much new evidence has accumulated. In Peru itself whole new (very ancient!) "horizons" were just then being revealed, while in Mexico the "Olmecs" began to emerge. Metal objects of apparently South American origin turned up at Mesoamerican sites from Yucatán to Oaxaca. Even before Heyerdahl, archaeologists re-examined testimony for coastal navigation between the Peru-Ecuador coast and Central America, in particular Panama.

At least equally important, in the late 1920's and during the 1930's several archaeological campaigns were to concentrate on the intervening zones. Significantly enough, it was in the present republic of Panama, which occupies the natural land bridge between Middle and South America, that spectacular finds were made. While they were a long way from establishing a "missing link" between Mesoamerica and the Central Andes, they highlighted the relative continuum that existed between the two culture peaks. At the same time it became clear that inter-American connections during the pre-Columbian age were of such great intricacy as to challenge the combined efforts of archaeologists, ethnologists, and linguists.

Panama, a former province of the South American nation of Colombia, is geographically part of Central America. Together with neighboring Costa Rica and Nicaragua at its northwest, it joins the American land masses in more than a physical sense. When the early Conquistadores chose it as a jumping board (as well as a source of information) to the rumored Inca kingdom in the far south, they followed a precedent undoubtedly going back to the first hordes of hunters who filtered into the southern continent some 10,000 and more years ago. In pre-Columbian times Chibcha-speaking tribes from Colombia penetrated deep into Central America and met there with others coming from the north. A few scholars even allowed for the possibility that the Maya themselves, allegedly kinsmen of Caribs and Arawaks, had migrated from northern South America.

Despite its preordained role in American population movements and its status since colonial times as a pothunters' paradise, the Central American land bridge south of Honduras has received comparatively scant attention from archaeologists. Columbus, on his fourth voyage, had noticed the large golden ornaments worn by local chiefs. Other Conquistadores in 1515 had been witnesses of the opulent burial of a great chief in the Darien area, replete with jewelry and sacrificed slaves. They did not fail to act upon such intelligence, and promptly named the land *Castilla del Oro* ("Golden Castile"), just as the adjoining country became *Costa Rica* ("Rich Coast"). Starting with the Spanish invaders, an enormous amount of gold has been extracted, and this even before Aztec and Inca treasures had become known. Rumor has it that the fortunes of some of the leading families of Panama were founded on looted graves. Francisco Morazán, the tragic Central American statesman, tried to recoup his fortunes in the 1830's by launching one of the first organized "excavations" of Panamanian graves. In 1859 the western province of Chiriquí was visited by a veritable gold fever when images adding up to hundreds of pounds in weight of precious metal were dug up within a fortnight. Few of these fine animal and human idols reached collections. It was left to campaigns of a later day to convey an authentic picture of the artistic wealth and resourcefulness of pre-Columbian Panama, and to establish the area as a center of several independent cultures rather than a mere stopover for migrant styles and tribes. It was then that other provinces than Chiriquí—foremost, Veraguas and Coclé—achieved archaeological prominence.

Golden figurine from a Chiriquí (western Panama) treasure trove found in the mid-nineteenth century

In 1924 when A. Hyatt Verrill was in Panama collecting ethnological specimens for the Museum of the American Indian (Heye Foundation) in New York, natives brought him prehistoric vases strikingly different from any hitherto found in Panama. He was directed to Coclé province, near the Pacific coast. There he came across monuments hitherto unreported, which he cleared in part and excavated. The site appeared to be a vast place of worship, covered by rows on rows of monolithic idols and phallic columns. While he did not find any gold objects to speak of, or burials, he recovered a number of multicolored ceramic pieces of far greater refinement than the stone sculptures. Several effigy vessels of humans and animals reminded him of the vases of coastal Peru.

Even before Verrill, at the beginning of the century, a river southeast of the Panama Canal had changed its course and shining objects were sighted by natives at its new eastern bank. At last the Peabody Museum of Harvard University, which had acquired some objects through trade channels, got wind of this site and launched three consecutive campaigns from 1930 onward. In 1933–34, Dr. Samuel Kirkland Lothrop was in charge when the most substantial discoveries were made. He was assisted by his second wife, Eleanor Bachman. Aside from the amusing, if not irreverent, tone, her intimate version of life as a helpmate is above all an engrossing account of what was—certainly materially —one of the great bonanzas in the annals of American archaeology.

Lothrop's excavations at Sitio Conte along the Río Grande de Coclé on the Pacific watershed of Coclé province brought Panama into focus as the site of flourishing, though probably not very ancient, American cultures. A series of superimposed graves pointed to a stratified sequence. Yet the largest and some of the most recent burials could also be the deepest. One sumptuous grave contained as many as twenty bodies of women and retainers laid out flat around their seated master. Implements exhibited high craftsmanship and luster. They included golden breastplates, helmets, nose rings, and greaves. Archaeologically and artistically as intriguing was the polychrome ceramic ware "painted in black, red, orange, grey, blue, and purple upon a cream base." Apart from highly original abstract patterns, its zoomorphic designs showed Peruvian and other South American motifs, while the technique of painting seemed to be indebted to the Chorotega of Nicaragua. An ethnologically interesting detail was the fact that some of the Panamanian skeletons belonged to men who, quite unusually for aboriginal Americans, must have attained in life a height of six feet and more.

Samuel Kirkland Lothrop was at the time of his death in 1965 one of the few men who had a sovereign first-hand command of the whole range of American archaeology, equaled perhaps only by John Alden Mason, who in 1940 continued excavations at Sitio Conte for the University Museum of the University of Pennsylvania, with similar success. The Harvard-trained New Englander had begun his active fieldwork at Pecos in New Mexico. Puerto Rico, Guatemala, Yucatán, Chile, and Tierra del Fuego in southernmost South America were way stations in his productive career. In 1925, passing through Peru from excavations in Argentina, he made the acquaintance of Dr. Julio Tello and proposed to him that they use his remaining funds on an archaeological junket of the latter's choosing. Tello opted for a place south of Lima on an isolated peninsula, which, because of its inaccessibility, had been little disturbed by *huaqueros*. The brief visit led to the discovery in subterranean crypts of the all-important Paracas culture. Central American ceramics and South Americal metallurgy received Lothrop's special attention, interests happily joined in his various Panamanian campaigns. In his later years Lothrop turned to writing comprehensive studies of American art. It was to this subject that he devoted his last work, *Treasures of Ancient America* (1964).

COCLÉ—PANAMA

Eleanor Lothrop

Most people's ideas of archaeology, if they have any, are romantic and farfetched. Like mine used to be. To the uninitiated, archaeology means digging a hole and pulling out gold and precious stones. This is about as unlikely an event as for a high school girl to visit Hollywood and be invited to dance with Clark Gable. Sam warned me from the start. "You have got to get over the notion," he insisted, "that all an archaeologist has to do is sink a pit into the ground and, presto, out pop gold and emeralds. It just doesn't happen that way." But that was just the way it did happen.

Panama was the kind of experience I've always dreamed about. It was the kind of experience Sam might have dreamed about too. A good archaeologist is chiefly concerned in making a discovery of scientific value, and if at the same time that discovery happens to be something hitherto unknown, he will do handsprings. An amateur like myself, on the other hand, goes for loot. In Panama we found both rolled into one. We didn't even have to hunt for the place; it was sitting there, just waiting to be plucked. And all as a result of pure accident.

In the early part of the 1900's, the Río Grande de Coclé in Panama changed its course, probably due to log jams during the flood season. The new channel was some distance from the old one, and the river, in digging it out, chanced to cut through the edge of an ancient Indian graveyard. This act of God went unnoticed until many years later, when a group of natives, poling their way upstream in a canoe, spotted something shiny sticking out of the riverbank. They went right for it, of course, and when they saw several objects that looked like gold, they frenziedly dug them out with their hands, throwing hunks of earth, pottery and bone into the water in their rush. I don't suppose they had the slightest notion of the value of their find or why it was there, but those glittering pieces probably looked good for at least a few drinks at the nearest bar. Actually, the bartender, who must have recognized a good thing when he saw one, was more generous than the men had hoped, and the local firewater which he gave them in exchange kept them unconscious and happy for weeks.

The gold ornaments eventually reached the antique stores in Panama

---

From *Throw Me a Bone. What Happens When You Marry an Archaeologist.* New York: Whittlesey House—McGraw-Hill Book Company, Inc., 1948, pp. 136–214 *passim.* Copyright © 1948 by Eleanor Lothrop. Included by permission of the author's agent Margot Johnson Agency, 405 E. 54 Street, New York, N.Y. 10022.

City. Here they were bought for Harvard University, which, after checking the story back of the treasure, decided to organize an expedition to explore the site. Sam Lothrop was put in charge of the work, and with wife as self-appointed assistant, got ready to set out for Panama. . . .

Nothing I had ever experienced or read or been told about archaeology prepared me for the dig at the Sitio Conte. It was like a circus. There was almost too much going on. It used to make me miserable not to be able to be in three places at the same time. I'd be flipping earth off a skeleton or getting ready to remove the contents of a grave, when I'd hear an exclamation from Sam or from one of the workmen and I'd know that something exciting had turned up somewhere else. The first few times this happened I dropped what I was doing and rushed over to join the fun. But when it got to the point where I was spending all my time hopping out of one grave and into another, I had to give that up.

Luckily you develop a very special feeling about what you yourself are doing, no matter what it is. "Did you see *my* pot, or *my* plate?" you are apt to ask about something you have merely cleaned or lifted out of the ground. "It's not as good as *mine,*" is the answer you'll undoubtedly get. I don't know what makes the amateur digger so proprietary about the pieces he works on. After all, they're not his and he knows he may never see them again, but that doesn't seem to matter. Fortunately.

Excavating started even before our camp was finished. Sam picked out the spot for the men to start a large trench, and they attacked the hard earth with pick and shovel, throwing the dirt to leeward. When a great mound had accumulated, some of them would climb on top and throw it further off so that the wind, which never let up, would not blow it back into the pit.

The digging was always divided into trenches, and these were large enough for all the men to work in at the same time and usually contained numbers of graves. As soon as there was any evidence of a burial an attempt was made to outline it, and the men removed the top earth down to a little above grave level. Sometimes the outline was easy to find, as the earth in the grave shaft was often softer and of a different color from that around it. Otherwise it was necessary to dig along the outer edge of the exposed objects until the contour showed up clearly. The procedure at all times was to make a sort of ditch in the surrounding earth so that the entire grave would be brought up like a table or platform. That way you didn't have to stand on your head when you worked.

When this point was reached the men were switched to another spot and started all over again with picks and shovels, searching for further remains. They were perfectly amiable about what must have been frustrating work and they were completely without superstition. In fact they joked about the burials, and though their humor was anything but sophisticated and rarely varied, it seemed to amuse them.

"Aha," José Casada would say to Bernabel as a skeleton came to light. "Here is Tio Fernando, that uncle of your father, the one you told us ran off and was never heard from again."

"Nonsense," Bernabel would retort. "This must be one of *your* relatives. He's round-shouldered like all the Ramos family."

Or José Casada, going into rapturous contortions at the sight of a bunch of bones, "Now *that* is a girl I could really go for." . . .

Polychrome plate from Sitio Grande (Coclé, Panama)

The Sitio Conte was obviously the burial ground of a very high-class group of people. There must have been a lot of them, too, for it teemed with graves. Not only did you strike one wherever you dug, but there were so many that they were often on top of each other and came out in layers. It took a good deal of digging to get at them, for although the top graves were only three or four feet below the surface, the deepest ones were as far as twelve feet below. How the Indians had managed with primitive tools to push their ancestors down so far is a mystery. The largest graves were usually the deepest, and they were the richest, too. As they got nearer to the surface they got poorer. Economic times must have changed, and the men in the upper layer, who rarely had even a woman buried with them and very little jewelry, must have gone through something equivalent to the 1930 depression.

Those in the intermediate-sized graves usually did have a woman with them, but only one. This didn't mean that it was all they had had when they were alive, for monogamy in pre-Spanish days was still a thing of the future. However, these men had probably only been sub-chiefs and when buried didn't rate anything more than one bride, about forty pieces of pottery and a mere snitch of jewelry.

We found six really large graves and they were fantastic. Some contained three bodies and some more than twenty, with the chief occupant always placed in the center—usually on a stone slab—and surrounded by his wives and followers. In addition to the skeletons, these graves had an average of two hundred pieces of pottery, as well as a raft of tools, weapons, food, jewelry, fabrics and ornamental objects. Here, obviously, were buried supreme chiefs of their day.

It is fun to try to reconstruct from some old bones and what's buried with them the character and mode of life of people who lived hundreds of years ago. At least it is fun for an amateur—for an archaeologist it is a serious matter and the basic reason for his having taken up this science in the first place.

Like any good archaeologist, Sam is disinclined to commit himself on the significance of any discovery until he has had a chance to study the appropriate historical accounts, comparative work of fellow scientists, chemical analyses of metals or clay, and a lot of other things which to me seem dry as dust. By that time I'd have lost interest. It would happen time and again, two, three years after a dig was completed, that Sam would come home, passion in his eye, and say something like "Remember the skeleton in Grave No. 18 that was lying with his arms crossed under him and a broken tibia—the one who had the incense burners buried with him?" "Of course," I'd answer. "And what did you find out about Him or Her?" Naturally I didn't have the slightest idea what he was referring to, but I was brought up to believe that a wife should encourage her husband.

At the time, though, it is different. At the time you dig him up, you can't help having a proprietary interest in your skeleton. You're inclined to indulge in flights of fancy (in case you're not a scientist), and I find that if you give your ancient remains a name, he assumes a definite personality and you digest your archaeological education more easily.

The skeleton I called Oscar Wilde, for instance, gave me the first inkling that queer things had gone on in prehistoric times, too. Oscar was one of the big chiefs—we found him placed in the center of the grave, laden with gold—and there were three bodies buried with him, all male. Nor could this be explained away by just calling him a misogynist, for, heaped on and around the bodies, were women's ornaments and women's utensils—such as stone metates for grinding corn. And grinding corn is definitely not a man's job.

Then there was the girl I named Pavlova. Pavlova turned up lying on her face with her shins doubled over her thighs so that her feet rested on top of her buttocks—a position not even a double-jointed ballet dancer could have assumed while alive. Poison had obviously been her lot. As a matter of fact, we'd already found out that the custom at the Sitio Conte had been to kill the chief's retainers and his women before they were buried. Their bodies were always so neatly arranged (except for Pavlova who was probably an afterthought) that they must have been dead before being deposited in the ground. Pavlova only confirmed what we already knew. But she made it easy for me to remember.

Golden pendant of curly-tailed monkey from Sitio Grande

Just once did we find evidence of a different system of burial. That was when we dug up Romeo and Juliet—two skeletons lying side by side, one with its arm around the other's neck. There could be no doubt but that they had been buried alive and had shared death throes in the grave itself, clutched in each other's arms. Unfortunately the bones and teeth of the lovers were in such bad condition that no one was able to determine their sex, but they did add a romantic touch to our excavations.

Sam, as might be expected, ignored the names I gave my ancient friends. He always took full descriptive notes on the skeletons and just a glance at these was enough to refresh his memory. I'd look at his little book and find listed: "Skel. No. 10: age adult, sex female, body extended, chest down, face south, arms straight, legs flexed." Or "Skel. No. 24: age adolescent, sex male, body flexed, chest up, face north, arms bent, legs straight."

This might have meant something to Sam, but to me it sounded like nothing more than setting-up exercises on the radio, and no matter how hard I tried I wouldn't be able to conjure up any kind of picture of skeletons 10 or 24. If they'd just had names attached like "Old Mrs. Tuttle" or "Baby Carlos," it would have been a cinch.

Lots of the time, of course, it was impossible to draw any conclusions from what we found. The graves were unbelievably complicated to start with. Then the dampness of the earth had played such havoc with the skeletons that often the bones had completely disintegrated. And many of the funeral objects had been deliberately broken.

This is what in archaeology is termed "killing" an object. The belief was general among prehistoric peoples that the spirits of inanimate things accompanied the spirits of the dead with whom they were buried. Just to be sure there would be no mistake, however, certain skeptics "killed" the objects before they put them in the ground, so that their souls would surely be released. The "killing," as a rule, took the form of making a hole in the bottom or sides of a piece of pottery, but those of the ancient inhabitants of the Sitio Conte who believed in this custom had apparently not been satisfied with such minor destruction. They'd gone ahead and trampled the pottery and sometimes even twisted the metal. It was as if you were to spread out your best dinner set and then jump up and down on it. At least that's what it looked like.

"This," said Sam, "will be known as Grave Number 26!" I was shocked. It was as if you tried to give a true picture of the Colossus of Rhodes by describing it as a statue 105 feet high. Or the Pyramids of Egypt as a group of geometrical buildings. All correct as far as it went. Grave No. 26 had followed the discovery of Grave No. 25 and would precede that of Grave No. 27. But it might better have been called "The Grave of Graves" or "Locus Lothrop" or "Harvard's Happy Hunting Ground."

Grave No. 26 was the first grave to come to light after our return to camp from Veraguas. One grave! One grave measuring twelve feet by ten. And what came out of that one grave could have stocked a good-sized store. It took more than two weeks, all of us working like mad, before Grave No. 26 was fully excavated and its contents removed After which Sam, Teck and I collapsed in a weary heap with just enough energy left to count up the score.

There were mirror backs of stone, stone axes and arrow points, metal, agate and bone pendants, agate and bone beads, quartz crystals, pierced sharks' teeth and dog teeth for necklaces, a carved whale's tooth, the carved rib of a sea cow, incense burners and sting ray spines, these last for use as spear points. There were nearly two hundred and fifty pieces of pottery—some painted in lovely colors and in perfect condition, some badly broken and incomplete. Almost all, however, had been brand new when buried, showing that they had been specially made for use in the next world.

The gold alone included three necklaces of large beads, twenty-nine disks or plaques, quantities of ear rods, round cuffs for arms and legs, finger rings, boar tusks set in gold, jaguar teeth, carved whale's teeth encrusted with gold, chisels, pendants—one in the shape of twin crocodiles, another a doubleheaded bat—and, finally, two large emeralds in gold settings.

The excitement around camp was terrific. We hardly slept nights, waiting to see what the next day would bring forth. Breakfast and lunch were necessary evils which took us away from the other world in which we were living. We each had our own section to work in, and we each kept crying *"look"* as more things came to light, and nobody paid any attention as they were much too busy with their own discoveries. Except the workmen, who left what they were doing (they'd been banished to another trench) and ran over every few minutes to see what was new.

Sam kept murmuring "but this is *different*. I've never seen anything like this before." Teck indulged in a running conversation with himself about the pieces of carved bone, each of which put him in a state of rapture. As for me, for once I couldn't talk. I just gaped with delight.

Almost right from the beginning it looked as if we were in for a big haul. Although the grave itself was comparatively small, we found, surrounded by their treasures, what had once been twenty-two bodies, crammed so close together that it was often impossible to tell whose bones belonged to whom. There was no question, though, as to which skeleton represented the head man. What was left of him—for convenience I'll call him Caesar—reposed on a large stone slab set in the center of the grave. His body had been placed sitting up, whereas his cohorts had been laid out in rows about him. His belongings were not only the cream of this grave but were much more elaborate than anything found in any other grave.

Some of the riches had probably been looted from other burials, for there was evidence that in originally digging the shaft of Grave No. 26 an earlier burial had been cut through and almost entirely destroyed, while, underneath, another one had been mangled and robbed of some of its spoils. Even so, Grave No. 26 must have been extraordinarily rich to start with and Caesar an extremely important man.

On the earth which covered his body were strange little cabalistic signs which looked just as if some rodent had been buried by mistake and had scrabbled around trying to get out for a breath of fresh air.

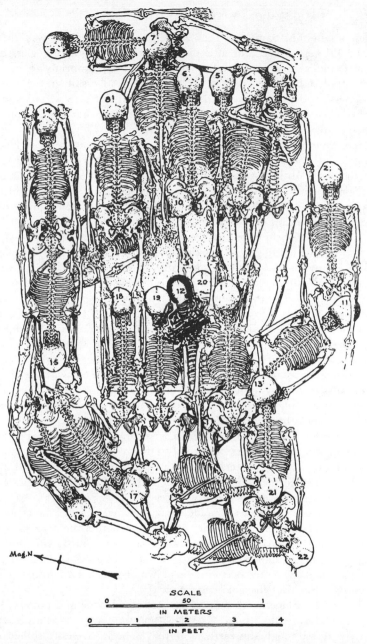

Coclé grave No. 26: The owner (skeleton 12) had been placed sitting in the center with his 21 companions spread around him.

When I said this, Sam and Teck looked at me in such a way that I wished I'd kept quiet, and after bringing out a magnifying glass and other technical instruments, they pronounced the imprints to be designs of what had once been a textile which had disintegrated due to dampness. And heaped on top of what I'm still not sure weren't mouse tracks but which I suppose I'll have to accept as what-had-once-been-a-textile, were Caesar's treasures.

Here we found all twenty-nine plaques, the three gold-bead necklaces, the gold leg and arm cuffs, six pairs of ear rods, four gold finger rings and the larger of the two emeralds. And, interspersed with them, smaller gold ornaments, ornaments of stone and bone, and a great pile of weapons and pots and pans. Caesar had obviously been equipped to face almost anything anywhere.

As I've noted before, one of the first rules of archaeology is that, in excavating, the entire grave is neatened up and everything in it exposed before so much as a splinter is taken out of the ground. However when we struck Caesar's gold all rules were off. The ornaments were so obviously valuable that it seemed like tempting fate (and the Panamanians) to leave them exposed, and Sam, Teck and I worked by lamplight until late hours, taking notes, drawing pictures and, finally, pulling out our treasure.

And what treasure it was! The large plaques were slightly bigger than the ordinary dessert plate and were of beaten gold with designs in relief, always portraying a crocodile in some form or other. They were so handsome that any self-respecting crocodile should have been flattered at the way he'd been glorified.

The twenty-five smaller gold disks were of a variety of shapes and, although undecorated, were extremely effective. Like the big plaques, they had tiny holes along their edges, through which, Sam deduced, they had been sewn to their owner's shirt or shirts. Of the shirts themselves, of course, there was no longer any trace.

The ear rods, which were made to be inserted through holes in the ears, were of different types and varied in length from two to seven inches. Some were of hollow gold and had been filled with gum to strengthen them. Others were made of stone tipped with gold, and one pair had evidently been made of wood which had rotted away, leaving nothing but the gold ends. . . .

The gold ornaments, as well as the stone and bone and pottery, had been spread over and around Caesar without any attempt at order. And scattered all through the earth as if they'd been carelessly spilled out of a hat, were hundreds of immense gold beads which, when matched, made up three necklaces. The most spectacular one consisted of a hun-

dred and twenty hollow ping-pong balls—this was literally the size—
and when strung was so long that it could be looped double to the
waist.

When Eulogio saw these he said, rather sourly, "When I was a
child we used to play marbles with those."

"You *what?*" asked Sam.

"We used to play marbles," he repeated. "You know, marbles. The
other boys and I would fill them with clay to make them heavy and
then we'd roll them. This way." He threw back his arm as if he were
in a bowling alley and demonstrated.

"But where did you find them?" asked Sam.

"There were hundreds and hundreds of them," Eulogio said. "When
I was about eight, the river changed its course and cut new banks, and
these things turned up all around. We thought they were some form of
tin."

"Whatever happened to them?" I asked, always the practical one.

"Oh, eventually we lost them all." He sighed reminiscently. "It was
a good game, though."

In my mind's eye I could see the gold beads rolling over the ground,
sliding down the bank into the river, burying themselves in the muddy
bottom. In fact I was so fascinated by the picture of a group of little
black boys shooting marbles with prehistoric ping-pong balls that I
paid but little attention to the work I was doing. AND THAT WAS
WHEN I FOUND CAESAR'S EMERALD!

I must admit I didn't have the slightest idea what it was; all I saw
was a dull and dirty green hunk. "What's this funny stone?" I asked
Sam. He took a look and said, "Probably a piece of jade," which seemed
pretty thrilling at the time, and he picked it up and dipped it into a
bucket of water which was conveniently sitting nearby. Just then the
midday sun happened to hit it full force and green lights shot out
and nearly blinded us.

I yelled like any amateur, while Sam, giving me a warning look,
quickly slipped the stone out of sight and smiled vaguely at the workmen who had rushed over to see what the excitement was about. They
may have thought I'd seen a snake. They may even have suspected the
truth. At any rate, no explanations were ever given.

That afternoon, after everyone had gone home, we took out our
prize and just looked at it. It was decided to dirty it up again, as we
were afraid what might happen if word got around that we had found
an emerald. With a little plastic, earth and water, Sam performed such
a workmanlike job that our jewel looked like nothing so much as a
piece of rubble, and then he began to worry that someone might find

it and throw it away as a useless hunk of rock. In fact it was obvious that whatever we did the stone was going to be a headache until we got it out of the country. I was sorry I hadn't just grabbed it in the first place and kept quiet.

My reasons for this were not entirely unselfish. The emerald was truly spectacular. It not only looked gigantic to us, it was gigantic—actually weighing 189 carats and measuring an inch by an inch and a half. It was something you might conceivably imagine in Tiffany's window but certainly not in the wilds of Panama.

The stone was magnificent in spite of being in anything but perfect condition. Interior light, which nowadays you get by cutting facets on the outside surface, had been produced by drilling eight small holes into it. Someone had tried, too, to cut a hole right through the center, probably to enable it to be worn on a chain, but this had apparently proved too difficult and the idea had been abandoned halfway through. As a result, the stone was chipped and slightly cracked, but it was still green and sparkling and beautiful.

The emerald must have had quite a history, too. According to Sam, Panama produces no emeralds and this one was therefore a trade piece. "From Ecuador," he finally pronounced, after squinting at it carefully. "This is the type drilling they used down there. Yes, it all fits in," he went on, as if he were Hercule Poirot or some other famous detective. "The ancient Panamanians used to send ships as far south as the coast of the Inca Empire. They probably made the trade down there."

I decided to give his little gray cells a bit more exercise. "What did they trade it for, Hercule—I mean Sam?"

"God knows," he disappointed me by saying. "Of course a lot of sea shells native to Panama and Central America have been found both in Ecuador and in Peru. . . ."

"A fine detective you are," I broke in. "You're not trying to tell me the Ecuadoreans would let the Panamanians palm off some old shells for a magnificent emerald?"

"You've got a false sense of values," said Sam witheringly. "There are other things in the world as important as emeralds." But I knew he didn't mean it. He was just as excited about our mammoth jewel as I was.

Near the emerald was buried its setting. Or, rather, a rough casting for the setting. This was a massive hunk of gold weighing the equivalent of five old-time twenty dollar gold pieces and designed to portray a mythological monster. Although it hadn't been finished and the socket was not worked smooth, it had obviously been created for the emerald to fit into it and, together, to make a pendant. Though the emerald had come from far away the setting, because of its similarity in style to the rest of the gold in Grave No. 26, must have been the result of home talent.

Sam refused to make any definite statement as to why the pendant had been deposited in the earth unfinished. "However," said he, "it looks—and don't quote me please—as if the pendant had been specially made for this burial and the work took so long that the burial couldn't wait. So they put it in as was."

This didn't satisfy me. "I should think it would have been an insult to Caesar to bury something with him that wasn't even finished."

"Not at all," said Sam. "The Indians, naturally, would expect it to be finished in the other world. They may even have buried the artisan who did the preliminary work along with it so that he could complete the job later on. An important leader, naturally, would rate that kind of service."

I saw nothing natural in any of this, but people who work like mad to create beautiful things and then put them in the ground and jump on them are apt to do almost anything. Fortunately the emerald was one trophy they hadn't been able to hurt.

Coclé polychrome plate

The dig at the Sitio Conte turned out to be one of the most spectacular digs ever undertaken in the New World. From the point of view of what might be described either as loot or as archaeological artifacts, depending on who was doing the describing, it was enough to make the most blasé individual's eyes pop. But what was even more important was that, in Coclé, an unknown civilization had come to life. It wasn't Aztec or Maya or Inca, as people invariably assume—

those being the only Latin American civilizations to get any publicity—it was absolutely new.

Sam was as surprised at this discovery as Sir Isaac Newton must have been when the apple hit him. "But what is so strange about that?" I asked him. "It's exciting, yes, but exciting things do sometimes happen."

"I didn't expect anything like this in Panama," said Sam. "Panama is the gateway to South America and, as such, should show evidence of the great migrations to that continent which must have taken place thousands of years ago."

"And doesn't it?"

"Not a sign," mourned Sam. "Archaeologists have been unable to discover any remains or temporary camp sites dating back to those days. Instead we find a settled and complex community showing permanent occupation for some centuries before the Conquest."

Golden pendant from Chiriquí

"But aren't you pleased to have found something new and wonderful? Columbus didn't discover what he expected to, either, but nobody complained."

Sam acknowledged my comparison with a deep bow. "Of course I'm pleased," he admitted. "It's just that this upsets all previous theories. Panama is a place you would expect people to have passed through, not settled in."

"Why?" I asked, probably for the hundred thousandth time since I married an archaeologist.

"The culture of South America is as highly developed as any known in the New World," Sam explained patiently, "and the people must have arrived there from somewhere. And how else except through Panama?"

"Why not by boat?" I cried triumphantly.

But Sam demolished that theory in no time at all. "And how did the prehistoric horses and animals of the camel family, such as llamas and alpacas, get south? Do you by any chance think the Indians could have squeezed a horse into one of their tiny boats?"

"You win," I admitted. "But where does that leave us?"

"With a permanent population that shouldn't have existed and no sign of the transitory one that did exist."

"What a science!" I said admiringly. "You find some ancient pots and pans and make a liar out of history."

12

The archaeological discoveries in Panama failed in one vital respect to fulfill the more sanguine hopes of Lothrop and his colleagues—and that was age. On various grounds the princely burials could barely antedate the landing of the Spanish by more than two centuries. Even though we do not know the name of the people or of any of their royal masters, they and their customs and equipment undoubtedly differed little from what the first Conquistadores saw. That Panama, which must have played a key role in the peopling of ancient America, has but for primitive pottery little authentic evidence to offer on the human dawn in the Americas, can only be judged a disappointment. Panama may well have been a crucible in the cultural and ethnic connections between the Western continents, but again the record, save for the most recent pre-Columbian phase, remains extremely fragmentary.

In the rest of Central America, east of the Maya sphere of Mexico, Guatemala, and Honduras, the archaeological picture is only slightly more revealing. Primitive celts (chisels) have been reported from time to time. Imprints of human feet on lava, said to be associated with some footprints of extinct bison, were first described a century ago and have drawn considerable attention. But in either case, the age is uncertain. All this simply means that in most of Central America systematic excavation is still in its infancy, stratification studies of its artifacts have rarely been attempted (notable exceptions are the work of Lothrop on ceramics in Costa Rica and Nicaragua), and reliable data on the identity, sequence, and chronology of cultures are sorely missing.

From the scarcity of research we might expect a commensurate poverty of material. But this is not the case. While non-Maya Central America apparently produced few temples and palaces in stone, its pottery and metal goods vie with the finest in the hemisphere. Some of these people too, like Mexicans and Maya, kept pictographic records. However, among all the remains of the area, none are more impressive than the stone statues of the islands of the Nicaraguan lakes. Strongly naturalistic, they are quite different from anything the Maya and the people of central and southern Mexico carved. On account of their location and style they are in a way as stunning as the stone faces of Easter Island. They have been known for some time. The man who can truly be called their discoverer is E. George Squier. In 1850 and 1851 when he was in Nicaragua as U.S. chargé d'affaires, he even arranged for several of the monoliths to be shipped to the United States.

Squier's appointment to the Central American republics was by no means apolitical. During his service he had his hands full with power politics connected with the inter-oceanic Canal project. He then missed no chance to counteract every British move, often with such combativeness that he overstepped his authority and embarrassed his own government. Yet he seems to have been convinced that the interests of the great republic he represented were completely at one with those of Central America. The United States acted only as natural leader of the American family of nations. Squier's anti-British passions nevertheless endeared him to most of the people of Central America and he had free run of the land when carrying out his mission. Apart from concluding treaties and sending voluminous reports to Washington, he found the time to survey the area thoroughly and to produce a two-volume study of Nicaragua which incorporates geographic, topographic, economic, historical, and ethnographic data. Several lengthy digressions (previously published as magazine articles) are devoted to antiquities, marking his propitious entrance into the field of Middle American archaeology and linguistics.

Characteristically, few of the educated local elite Squier consulted had any knowledge of native monuments. "In all our inquiries," wrote he, "concerning antiquities, of the padres or licenciados, indeed of the best-informed citizens of Granada, we had not heard of the existence of these monuments. . . . But experience has taught me that more information upon these matters was to be gathered from the bare-footed *mozos,* than from the black-robed priests." More so even than John Lloyd Stephens at the Mayan site of Copán a few years earlier, Squier trod, archaeologically speaking, virgin land on the islands of Lakes Managua and Nicaragua. Obviously influenced by Stephens' fine narratives, he does not lag far behind the graces of his model.

Squier was immediately struck by the boldness and freedom of the sculptures he saw on the various islands—foremost those on Zapatero (Zapatera)—and declared them unique among the statuary works of American aborigines. For one thing, they were nude, but not asexual in the Mesoamerican tradition. The majority of the figures rested on columns and were as a rule enclosed by an animal—the "alter ego" motif of man and his guardian spirit. Since the days of Squier a number of statues, related in subject but differing in their more abstract low-relief columnar style, have been described from the Nicaraguan highlands. Among these are human statues with duck bills suggestive of the famous jadeite Tuxtla statuette from the Mexican Gulf.

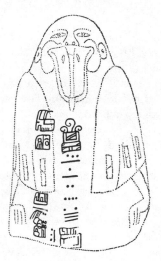

Tuxtla statuette

The age and affinities of these statues have caused considerable discussion but no agreement. Squier himself tended to believe that they but little antedated the Conquest and had been tumbled and mutilated by the first white invaders. However, the Nicaraguan statues show also, as we have seen, an evolution in style and hence are not likely to be all of the same age. The first investigator after Squier to turn a more than passing attention to the statues was C. Bovallius, a Swede, who devoted a monograph to them in the 1880's but failed to improve on previous assumptions. It fell to S. K. Lothrop to attribute them to the Chorotega, an apparently northern people resident in Central America long before the Chibchas entered from the south and Nahuatl-speaking people from Mexico settled in their midst. Lothrop was also convinced of the monuments' considerable antiquity. He argued that certain statues at Copán were related to those in Nicaragua and anteceded the Maya epoch. Copán itself was originally Chorotega as were a few enclaves in Mexico. Lothrop's thesis is strengthened by the ancient date inscription of the non-Maya Tuxtla figurine. This argument provokes intriguing speculations on the roots of Mesoamerican civilization in general. However, others have challenged Lothrop's claims and denied all resemblance between Copán and Nicaragua sculptures, though they are puzzled by the duck-bill motif which is undoubtedly old.

As to the relationship of Nicaraguan sculptures to those of other parts of the Americas, the consensus is that, while they have little in common with Maya and Mexican art, they have counterparts in other Central American countries and are intimately connected with the monumental effigies of San Agustín in western Colombia and the South American monoliths of Chavín and Tiahuanaco. Certain vases of coastal Peru come close to being replicas of "alter ego" statues from Zapatero Island. Once more we are faced with the phenomenon of South American intrusion into the northern continent without being able fully to account for it.

ZAPATERO ISLAND, LAKE NICARAGUA

E. George Squier

A broad bay stretched dimly inwards towards the city of Nicaragua; and directly before us, at the distance of twenty-five or thirty miles, rose the high, irregular island of Zapatero; beyond which a stationary mass of silvery clouds showed the position of the majestic volcanic cones of the great island of Ometepec. The wind was still strong and the waves high, and the boat tumbled about with that unsteady motion so painful to landsmen. Amidst a great deal of confusion the sails were raised— sails large enough for an Indiaman, for the marineros of Lake Nicaragua consider that everything depends on the size of the canvas. The *Grenada* was schooner-rigged, and no sooner was she brought to the wind, than her sails filled, and she literally bounded forward like a race-horse. She keeled over until her guards touched the water. . . . The lull, if it can

---

"Ancient Monuments in the Islands of Lake Nicaragua, Central America," *The Literary World,* VI:11, suppl. to No. 163 (New York, March 16, 1850), pp. 269–70, 304–5.

so be called, under which we had started, was only temporary. Before we had accomplished a tenth of the distance we had to go, the wind came on to blow with all of its original violence. The waters fairly boiled around us, and hissed and foamed beneath our stern. I cried to Juan, who was struggling at the rudder, to take in sail, for the canvas almost touched the water, and seemed fairly bursting with the strain, but he responded "too late," and braced himself with his shoulder against the tiller, holding with both hands to the guards. I expected every moment that we would go over,—but on, onward, we seemed fairly to fly. The outlines of Zapatero grew every moment more distinct, and little islands before undistinguished came into view. As we neared them the wind lulled again, and we breathed freer, as we dashed under the lee of the little island of Chancha, and threw out our anchor close to the shore. . . .

The sun was up; we were close to a little patch of cleared land, upon one side of which, half-hidden among the trees, was a single hut. The owner, his wife, his children, and his dogs, were down on the shores, and all seemed equally curious to know the object of our sudden visit. Juan frightened them with an account of a terrible revolution, how he was flying from the dangers of the shore, and advised the islander to keep a sharp look-out for his safety. M——[James McDonough, a fellow American who acted as draughtsman] however delivered the poor man from his rising fears, and ordered Juan to put on his shirt and pull across the channel to Zapatero. An inviting calm harbor was before us, but we were separated from it by a channel five hundred yards broad, through which the compressed wind forced the waters of the lake with the utmost violence. It seemed as if a great and angry river was rushing with irresistible fury past us. A high, rocky, projecting point of Zapatero, in part intercepted the current below us, against which the water dashed with a force like that of the ocean, throwing the spray many feet up its rocky sides. The men hesitated in starting, but finally braced themselves in their seats, and pulled into the stream. The first shock swept us resistlessly before it, but the men pulled with all their force, under a volley of shouts from Juan, who threw up his arms and stamped on his little quarter-deck like a madman. It was his way of giving encouragement. The struggle was long and severe, and we were once so near the rocks that the recoiling spray fell on our heads; but we finally succeeded in reaching the little sheltered bay of which I have spoken, and, amidst the screams of the thousand waterfowl which we disturbed, glided into a snug little harbor, beneath a spreading tree, the bow of our boat resting on the sandy shore. "Here at last," cried M——, and bounded ashore. I seized a pistol and sword, and followed, and leaving the Doctor and the men to prepare coffee and breakfast, started in company with Manuel to see the *"freyles."* Manuel was armed with a double-barrelled gun, for this island has no inhabitants, and is proverbial for the number of its wild animals, which find a fit home in its lonely fastnesses. I carried a first-class Colt in one hand, and a short, heavy, two-edged Roman sword in the other, as well for defence as for cutting away the limbs, vines, and bushes which impede every step in a tropical forest. Manuel said it was but a few squares to the *"freyles,"* but we walked on and on, through patches of forest and over narrow savannahs, covered with coarse, high, and tangled grass, until I got tired. Manuel looked puzzled; he did not seem to recognize the landmarks. When he was there before, it was in the midst of the dry season, and the withered grass and underbrush stripped of leaves, afforded no obstruction to the view. Still he kept on, but my enthusiasm, betwixt an empty stomach and a long walk, was fast giving place to violent wrath towards Manuel, when suddenly that worthy dropped his gun, and uttering a scream, leaped high in the air, and turning, dashed past me with the speed of an antelope. I cocked my pistol, raised my sword, and stood on my guard, expecting that nothing less than a tiger would confront me. But I was spared the excitement of an adventure, and nothing making its appearance, I turned to look for Manuel. He was rolling in the grass like one possessed, and rubbing his feet and bare legs with a most rueful expression of face. He had trodden on a bees' nest, and as he had taken off his breeches, to avoid soiling them, before starting, I "improved" the occasion to lecture him on the impropriety of such practices on the part of a christian, a householder, and the father of a family. I was astonished, I said, that he, a gentleman past the middle age of life, the owner of two islands, should make such a heathen of himself as to go without his breeches. And as I have heard the special interposition of Providence urged on no more important occasions than this at home, I felt authorized in assuring him that it was clearly a signal mark of divine displeasure. Manuel appeared to be much edified, and as I was better protected than himself, he prevailed upon me to recover his gun, whereupon, taking another path, we pushed ahead.

After toiling for a long time we came suddenly upon the edge of an ancient crater of great depth, at the bottom of which was a lake of a yellowish green, or *sulphurous* color, the water of which Manuel assured me was salt. This is probably the fact, but I question much if any human being ever ventured down the rocky and precipitous sides. Manuel now seemed to recognise his position, and turning sharp to the left, we soon came to a broad level area, covered with immense trees, and with a thick undergrowth of grass and bushes. There were here some large, regular mounds composed of stones, which I soon discovered were artificial. Around these Manuel said the *freyles* were scattered, and he commenced cutting right and left with his machete. I followed his example, and had not proceeded more than five steps, when I came upon an elaborately sculptured statue, still standing erect. It was about the size of the smaller one discovered at Pensacola, but was less injured, and the face had a mild and benignant aspect. It seemed to smile on me as I tore aside the bushes which covered it, and appeared almost ready to speak. In clearing further I found another fallen figure, but a few feet distant. From Manuel's shouts I knew that he had discovered others, and I felt assured that many more would reward a systematic investigation—and such I meant to make.

I was now anxious to return to the boat, so as to bring my entire force on the ground; and so calling Manuel, I started. Either Manuel took me a shorter path than we came, or else I was a trifle excited and didn't mind distances; at any rate, we were there before I expected. The sailors listened curiously to our story, and Juan, like Pedro before him, whispered that *"los Americanos son diabolos."* He had lived, man and boy, for more than forty years within sight of the island, and had many a time been blockaded by bad weather in the very harbor where we now were, and yet he had never seen, nor ever so much as heard that there were *"freyles"* there!

During our absence a weather-bound canoe, with Indians from Ometepec, discovering our boat, had put in beside us. They were loaded with fruit for Grenada, and "walked into" our good graces by liberal donations of *papayas, marignons, oranges, pomegranates, zapotes,* &c. They were small but well-built fellows, much lighter colored than the Indians near León, and with a marked difference of features. All have their heads closely shaved, with the exception of a narrow fringe of hair around the forehead extending from one ear to the other; a practice which has become very general among the people. I admired their well-formed limbs, and thought how serviceable half-a-dozen such stout fellows would be among the monuments, and incontinently invited them to accompany us, which invitation they accepted, much to my satisfaction.

Leaving a couple of men to watch the boats, I marshalled my forces, and set out for the *"freyles."* We mustered twenty-four strong, a force which I assured myself was sufficient to set up once more the fallen divinities, and possibly to remove some of them. As we went along we cleared a good path, which, before we left, began to have the appearance of a highway.

While M. commenced drawing the monument which still stood erect, I proceeded with the men to clear away the bushes and set up the others. I knew well that the only way to accomplish anything was to keep up the first excitement, which I did—and I have no doubt my tee-total friends will be horrified at the confession,—by liberal dispensations of agua ardiente. But the necessity of the case admitted of no alternative. The first monument which claimed our attention was a well-cut figure, seated crouching on the top of a high ornamental pedestal. The hands

Zapatero Island (Nicaragua) statue

were crossed below the knees, the head bent forward, and the eyes widely opened as if gazing upon some object upon the ground before it. A conical mass of stone rose from between the shoulders, having the appearance of a conical cap when viewed from the front. It was cut with great boldness and freedom, from a block of basalt, and had suffered very little from the lapse of time.

A hole was dug to receive the lower end, ropes were fastened around it, our whole force was disposed to the best advantage, and at a given signal, I had the satisfaction to see the figure rise slowly and safely to its original position. No sooner was it secured in place than our sailors gave a great shout, and forming a double ring around it, commenced an outrageous dance, in the pauses of which they made the old woods ring again with their favorite *"hoo-pah!"* I did not like to have my *ardiente* effervesce in this manner, for I knew the excitement, once cooled, could not be revived; so I broke into the circle and dragging out Juan by main force, led him to the next monument, which Manuel called the *cannon*. It was a massive cylindrical block of stone, about as long and twice as thick as the twin brother of the famous "peacemaker" now in the Brooklyn navy yard. It was encircled by raised bands, elaborately ornamented; and upon the top was the lower half of a small and neatly cut figure. In the front of the pedestal were two niches, deeply sunk and regular in form, connected by a groove. They were evidently symbolical. Notwithstanding the excitement of the men, they looked dubiously upon this heavy mass of sculpture; but I opened another bottle of the ardiente, and taking one of the levers myself, told them to lay hold. A hole was dug as in the former case, but we could only raise the stone by degrees, by means of thick pries. After much labor, by alternate prying and blocking, we got it at an angle of forty-five degrees, and there it appeared determined to stay. We passed ropes around the adjacent trees, and placed *falls* above it, and when all was ready, and every man at his post, I gave the signal for a *coup de main*. The ropes creaked and tightened, every muscle swelled, but the figure did not move. It was a critical moment, the men wavered; I leaped to the ropes and shouted at the top of my voice, *"Arriba! arriba!! viva Centro America!"* The men seemed to catch new spirit; there was another and simultaneous effort,—the mass yielded; *"poco mas, muchachos!"* "a little more, boys!" and up it went, slowly, but up, up, until, tottering dangerously for a moment, it settled into its place and was secured. The men were silent for a moment as if astonished at their own success, and then broke out in another paroxysm of ardiente and excitement. But this time each man danced on his own account, and strove to outdo his neighbor in wild gesticulation. I interfered, but they surrounded me, instead of the figure, and danced more madly than before, amidst "vivas" for North America and *"muerte á los Ingleses!"* uttered in a tone half-demoniac, and which showed the intensity of their hatred. But the dance ended with my patience,—luckily not before. By a judicious use of the ardiente, I managed to keep up their spirits, and by four o'clock in the afternoon, we had all the monuments we could find, ten in number, securely raised and ready for the draughtsman. Besides these we afterwards succeeded in discovering a number of others,—amounting in all to fifteen perfect ones or nearly so, besides some fragments.

The men, exhausted with fatigue, disposed themselves in groups around the statues, or stretched themselves at length amongst the bushes. Wearied myself, but with the complacency of a father contemplating his children, and without yet venturing to speculate upon our singular discoveries, I seated myself upon a broad, flat stone, artificially hollowed in the centre, and gave rein to fancy. The bushes were cleared away, and I could easily make out the positions of the ruined *teocalli,* and take in the whole plan of the great aboriginal temple. Over all now towered immense trees, swathed in long robes of grey moss, which hung in masses from every limb, and swayed solemnly in the wind. I almost fancied them in mourning for the departed glories of the place. In fact a kind of superstitious feeling, little in consonance with the severity of philosophical investigation, began to creep over me. Upon one side were steep cliffs, against which the waters of the lake chafed with a subdued roar, and upon the other was the deep extinct crater, with its black sides and sulphurous lake; it was in truth a weird place, not unfittingly chosen by the aboriginal priesthood as the site of their strange and gloomy rites. While engaging in these fanciful reveries, I stretched myself, almost unconsciously, upon the stone where I was sitting. My limbs fell into place as if the same had been made to receive them—my head was thrown back, and my breast raised a second, and the thought aroused my mind with startling force—*"the stone of sacrifice!"* Was it the scene, the current of my thoughts—but I leaped up with a feeling half of alarm. I observed the stone more closely; it was a rude block altered by art, and had beyond question been used as a stone of sacrifice. I afterwards found two others, clearly designed for the same purpose, but they had been broken by the devotees of a rival superstition.

We spent three days here, coming early and returning late. The weather was delightful; and each night when we returned to the boat, it was with an increased attachment to the island. We had now a broad well-marked path from the shore to the ruins, and the idols were

Zapatero Island statues

becoming familiar acquaintances. The men had given them names; one they called *"Joro bado,"* "the Humpbacked"; another, *"Ojos Grandes,"* "Big Eyes."

At night, the picturesque groups of swarthy, half-naked men preparing their suppers around fires, beneath the trees, in the twilight gloom, or gathered together in busy conversation in the midst of the boat, after we had anchored off for the night,—the changing effects of the sun and moonlight on the water, and the striking scenery around us,—the silence and primeval wilderness,—all contributed, apart from the strange monuments buried in the forest, to excite thoughts and leave impressions which cannot be effaced. Our stay passed like a dream, and when we departed, it was with a feeling akin to that which we experience in leaving old acquaintances and friends.

PART

CENTRAL AND SOUTHERN MEXICO

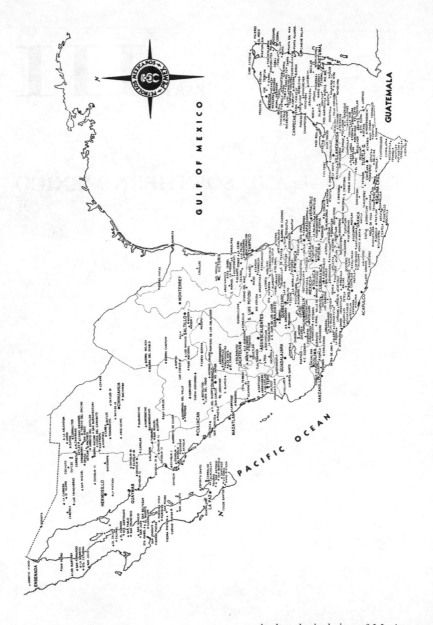

Archaeological sites of Mexico

13

After he had landed at the Gulf Coast on Good Friday 1519, burnt his ships behind him, and founded Veracruz, Cortés resolved to march into the interior with his band of four hundred warriors. The plan was buoyed by gifts from Moctezuma, which, instead of bribing the foreign invaders to leave Mexico, only helped to confirm their belief in a mighty native empire of untold riches. To reach that empire's nerve center, Tenochtitlán, now became their goal. Seven months later, from a high point above the Valley of Mexico, they beheld the metropolis shimmering on the horizon above a large inland lake. There was a city as fair as any of them had ever seen, and some, as early chroniclers remind us, had been to Venice, and Rome, and Constantinople. A kaleidoscope of islands, canals, gardens, temples, palaces, and pyramids met their eyes. Recapturing the impression in his old age, one of Cortés' companions, Bernal Díaz del Castillo, wrote: "We were astonished and declared this was like the wonders related in the Book of Amadis, on account of the huge towers, pyramids and other buildings, all of stone, that arose above the waters. Some of us soldiers even asked ourselves whether all we saw might not be just a dream."

Within a few years after the coming of the Spanish, every vestige of Tenochtitlán had been systematically destroyed. Unlike Cuzco in Peru, not one structure was allowed to stand. Only bits and pieces lie buried under modern Mexico City. To reconstruct the splendor of what was the most populous city of the hemisphere and probably the equal of any in the Old World, we have only unreliable colonial documents and maps to go by. For any adequate archaeological survey one would have to demolish first of all the stately Spanish buildings around the Zócalo, the modern city center (as it was in pre-Columbian times), and dig underneath. Such an undertaking is clearly impossible at present. Yet hopes of catching a glimpse of the Aztec capital have been unexpectedly rewarded by excavations carried out from time to time in connection with repair work on the cathedral and other buildings and sanitation projects in the vicinity. One such dig in 1790 came up with some of the best-known of all Mexican monuments.

The finds were made south of the cathedral and included aboriginal sculptures extraordinary in their bulk, execution, and subject matter. We owe it to the relative enlightenment of the age that such testimonies of idolatry were not hacked up into building stones, but were, if grudgingly, preserved. Foremost among them was the Aztec Calendar Stone or Piedra del Sol, a circular block thirteen feet in diameter and weighing some twenty tons. What was carved into it was not so much the sacred calendar of the Aztecs but their synthesis of the universe—the sun in the center—with its five ages of the world. It illustrated the passage of time through astronomical, calendrical, and related imagery. Since its discovery the giant dial has become a national emblem of Mexico.

Even more powerful in its bas-relief sculpture is a circular stone drum, usually called Stone of Tizoc or Sacrificial Stone, the center trough of which was probably used for the burning of hearts from

Relief, circular Stone of Tizoc, Tenochtitlán (Mexico City)

human sacrifice. The greatest strain on Western sensibilities, however, was caused by an enormous sculpture of the goddess Coatlicue, whose savagery might well have shocked the worshippers of Baal and his abominations in Biblical times. Coatlicue, reputedly the mother of the gods in the Nahua (central Mexican) pantheon, stands erect as a block of eight feet six inches adorned with a full catalogue of her loathsome accouterments. Her dress is made of plaited serpents. As her necklace she wears a string of chopped-off hands and hearts along with a skull as pendant. She is crowned by two snake heads, while claws protrude from her feet. Despite all the hideous details of the monstrous creature, the statue has an overwhelming compactness and strength, which the twentieth-century onlooker can appreciate. But rather than as a work of art, its validity is first of all as a ruthless statement of Mexican religious beliefs, of which the mass slaughter of human beings was an article of faith.

Some twelve years after the discovery of these monumental Aztec sculptures, Alexander von Humboldt, reversing the route of the Spanish conquerors, reached Acapulco in 1803. Once he had made his way to the capital his passion for American antiquities came into its own, and grew into a constant preoccupation and wonderment. No longer satisfied with accidental brushes, he now went out of his way to seek remains of the pre-Columbian past, inquired among local savants, visited collections, and acquired various items. Out of these researches, later continued in Europe, developed his design for a separate treatment of aboriginal cultures and their monuments.

Humboldt had not been long in Mexico City before he heard of the ancient works of sculpture dug up near the cathedral. Immediately he set out to investigate. However, he encountered some difficulties when trying to pay his respects to Coatlicue, who had been reinterred by outraged Dominican priests. Humboldt's experience was to be duplicated two decades later by an Englishman, William Bullock.

Bullock was one of a number of travelers who came to Mexico in the wake of the German baron. Not only had they avidly read Humboldt's tome on American antiquities, but they were eager to find out for themselves. Since they had an insatiable curiosity and also wrote attractively, their accounts reached a wider audience than Humboldt's learned and formidably priced discourse, besides covering more Mexican ground. Though now undeservedly forgotten, they did in a sense for the Mexico of the Aztecs, Toltecs, and Teotihuacán what Stephens was later to do for the Maya. Indeed some, like William Latrobe, friend of Washington Irving and later British governor of Victoria in Australia, knew—and discussed in their writings—Maya temple cities before Stephens appeared on the archaeological scene. Like Stephens and Catherwood these men practiced ambulatory rather than "dirt" archaeology. On the heels of vague rumors they would visit the wholly neglected sites of great pyramids and temples. Occasionally they did a little bit of digging on the side.

William Bullock ranks with the earliest of this crew. He was an erstwhile Liverpool jeweler and amateur naturalist of antiquarian tastes. In 1822 he left Portsmouth in the company of his son and stayed in Mexico for six months. Since he found the few sources then accessible to him contradictory in their accounts of ancient remains, Bullock made it a point to mention nothing in his book that had not come under his own observation. During his ramblings in the Valley of Mexico he explored the decayed palace of Texcoco—"the Athens of America"; the pyramids of Teotihuacán, of which he made models; and the so-called Baño de Montezuma, hollowed out of a conical mountain thirty miles from Mexico and to his knowledge never reported before. In addition he ascended the pyramid of Cholula and dug into an adjacent pile of unburnt bricks, from which he extricated human bones, pottery, and primitive weapons. During these exploits he not only became a mine owner but assembled an impressive collection of Mexican objects and plaster replicas—he even made a cast of Coatlicue—which he exhibited in 1824 with great showmanship at London's Egyptian Hall in Piccadilly. For the first time a wide public in Europe was thus made aware of the exotic glamour of pre-Columbian cultures.

Bullock, about whom otherwise little is known, returned in 1827 to Mexico via the United States. Later he settled in Cincinnati. With him began a long line of British Americanists including the unfortunate Lord Kingsborough, A. P. Maudslay, Sir Clements R. Markham, J. A. Joyce, and J. Eric S. Thompson. His book on Mexico went through several editions and was translated into German.

IDOLS OF TENOCHTITLÁN

William Bullock

The only works of art of the inhabitants of the city of Mexico before the conquest, then called Tenochtitlán, now publicly seen, are the great Calendar stone, popularly called Montezuma's Watch, and the Sacrificial stone, or the grand altar, once standing in the great temple before the principal idol. The former measures twelve feet in diameter,

From *Six Months Residence and Travels in Mexico.* London: John Murray, 1824, pp. 333–42.

and is cut from one large block of porous basaltic stone. It is supposed to have been placed in the roof of the great temple in the same manner as the Zodiac was in the temple of Tentyra in Upper Egypt. It now stands against the north-west wall of the cathedral, and is an attractive object of antiquarian research, and a striking proof of the perfection the nation to which it belonged had attained in some of the sciences:— few persons, even in the most enlightened cities of Europe, and at the present day, would be capable of executing such a work.

From the first moment I beheld it, I determined, if possible, to convey to Europe a fac-simile of this fine specimen of Aztec skill. Through the influence of Don Lucas Alaman, the prime minister, I obtained permission of the clergy to erect a scaffold against the cathedral, and took an impression of it in plaster, which was afterwards carefully packed up, and with some difficulty conveyed to Vera Cruz. It has fortunately arrived safe in England, and now forms one of the subjects of the Exhibition of Ancient Mexico to be seen in the Egyptian Hall.

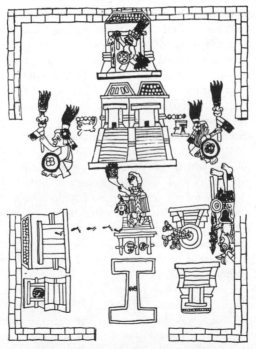

Sketch of main (double) temple of Tenochtitlán, dedicated to the gods Tlaloc and Huitzilopochtli. Other temples and a ballcourt are in front. From early colonial Codex Madrid

The Sacrificial stone, or altar, is buried in the square of the cathedral, within a hundred yards of the Calendar stone. The upper surface only is exposed to view, which seems to have been done designedly, to impress upon the populace an abhorrence of the horrible and sanguinary rites that had once been performed on this very altàr. It is said by writers that 30,000 human victims were sacrificed at the coronation of Montezuma. Kirwan, in the preface to his Metaphysics, states the annual number of human victims immolated in Mexico to be 2,500. I have seen the Indians themselves, as they pass, throw stones at it; and I once saw a boy jump upon it, clench his fist, stamp with his foot, and use other gesticulations of the greatest abhorrence. As I had been informed that the sides were covered with historical sculpture, I applied to the clergy for the further permission of having the earth removed from around it, which they not only granted, but moreover had it performed at their own expense. I took casts of the whole.—It is twenty-five feet in circumference, and consists of fifteen various groups of figures, representing the conquests of the warriors of Mexico over different cities, the names of which are written over them. More information is to be acquired from these figures, respecting the gaudy costumes of the ancient warriors, than can be obtained elsewhere. During the time (and it occupied several days) the operation of taking the casts was going on, the populace surrounded the place, and, although they behaved with great order and civility, would frequently express their surprise as to the motives that could induce me to take so much pains in copying these stones; and several wished to be informed whether the English, whom they considered to be non-Christians, worshipped the same gods as the Mexicans did before their conversion. I availed myself of the publicity which this operation gave to my pursuits, to offer to purchase any articles of curiosity from the Indians, or to reward those who could procure me intelligence of such. The consequence was, that various articles which had been carefully concealed were brought to light. Such as were portable I purchased, and of others I took casts and drawings, to enable me to make fac-similes on my return to England.

The largest and most celebrated of the Mexican deities was known to be buried under the gallery of the University. With some difficulty the spot was ascertained. Application was made to the heads of the College through the politeness of Señor Del Río, Professor of Mineralogy, and the great goddess was disinterred at the expense of the University. It was the labour of a few hours only, and I had the pleasure of seeing the resurrection of this horrible deity, before whom tens of thousands of human victims had been sacrificed, in the religious and sanguinary fervour of its infatuated worshippers.

Those who have read (and who have not?) the relation of Cortez of the transactions of the siege of Mexico must have shuddered at the horrid recital of the enormities committed on those who were unfortunately made captives by the natives. The heart, still panting with life, was taken by the priest from the breast, and deemed the more acceptable to the deity if it smoked with life: and the mangled limbs of the victim were then divided amongst the crowd as a feast worthy of the goddess. . . .

Statue found in Mexico City depicting a priest or god clad in skin of a sacrificed human

Some writers have accused the Spanish authors of exaggeration in their accounts of the religious ceremonies of this, in other respects, enlightened people; but a view of the idol under consideration will of itself be sufficient to dispel any doubt on the subject. It is scarcely possible for the most ingenious artist to have conceived a statue better adapted to the intended purpose; and the united talents and imagination of Brughel and Fuseli would in vain have attempted to improve it.

This colossal and horrible monster is hewn out of one solid block of basalt, nine feet high, its outlines giving an idea of a deformed human figure, uniting all that is horrible in the tiger and rattle-snake: instead of arms it is supplied with two large serpents, and its drapery is composed of wreathed snakes, interwoven in the most disgusting manner, and the sides terminating in the wings of a vulture. Its feet are those of the tiger, with claws extended in the act of seizing its prey, and between them lies the head of another rattle-snake, which seems descending from the body of the idol. Its decorations accord with its horrid form, having a large necklace composed of human hearts, hands, and skulls, and fastened together by the entrails,—the deformed breasts of the idol only remaining uncovered. It has evidently been painted in natural colours, which must have added greatly to the terrible effect it was intended to inspire in its votaries.

During the time it was exposed, the court of the University was crowded with people, most of whom expressed the most decided anger and contempt. Not so however all the Indians:—I attentively marked their countenances; not a smile escaped them, or even a word—all was silence and attention. In reply to a joke of one of the students, an old Indian remarked, "It is true we have three very good Spanish gods, but we might still have been allowed to keep a few of those of our ancestors!" and I was informed that chaplets of flowers had been placed on the figure by natives who had stolen thither, unseen in the evening for that purpose; a proof that, notwithstanding the extreme diligence of the Spanish clergy for three hundred years, there still remains some taint of heathen superstition among the descendants of the original inhabitants. In a week the cast was finished, and the goddess again committed to her place of interment, hid from the profane gaze of the vulgar.

Sketch of top of Stone of Tizoc, which may have been used for human sacrifice

14

Tenochtitlán was at its height when it fell. Little did it then betray its humble beginnings as hovels on marshy islets where barely two centuries earlier a small tribe of miserable and despised nomads from the north were allowed to make their homes while relegated to semi-servitude. The Aztecs (or Tenochcas) had arrived in the Valley of Mexico only around A.D. 1215. Appearances to the contrary, they were never quite able to shake off their recent escape from savagery. What they possessed in cultural polish they took over from a long line of predecessors in central Mexico, who had built cities and cultivated the land for many centuries before them. Thanks to the discoveries of recent years we can now fathom the antiquity of human occupation in this area. The successive stages from hunters and primitive farmers to the "classic" age of Teotihuacán and the "post-classic" flowering of the Toltecs—paralleling to a considerable degree the evolution of civilization in the Central Andes of South America—are at last emerging. Needless to say, the Aztecs had but the vaguest ideas of central Mexico's past. In a spirit not unlike that of the rulers of Cuzco, an Aztec king of the fifteenth century ordered the destruction of all chronicles that may have slighted the historical role of his people. Yet, the Aztecs were on the whole quite liberal in acknowledging the role of one former imperial people, the Toltecs, with whom they claimed the closest ties of kinship and who appeared to them a protean race of builders and conquerors issuing from a semi-legendary capital, Tollan (Tula).

Throughout the nineteenth century, in the works of Humboldt, Prescott, and others, the "magnificent Toltecs" rule almost supreme. To these writers, the pre-history of central Mexico amounts to little more than an extension of the Toltec record. A Frenchman, Désiré Charnay, who explored Mexican and Mayan ruins in the 1850's and 1860's, quite naturally reflects similar views in his writings. Charnay, a pioneer excavator, however, contributed tangible new evidence of the Toltecs' ascendancy in the Valley of Mexico, and beyond. Though modern archaeologists are wont to consider his writings somewhat "extravagant," they have been forced to tacitly accept some of his deductions, foremost his identification of Tula in the state of Hidalgo with the Tula of the Toltecs. It was there that Charnay excavated one of the then unknown Atlantean figures, which have come to be recognized as characteristic of Toltec architecture. Charnay likewise was probably

Atlantid column, Tula, state of Hidalgo (central Mexico)

the first to observe the close resemblance between Tula and Chichen Itzá in the Maya territory of Yucatán, nearly a thousand miles away. While scholars of far greater repute, as for instance his countryman and contemporary the Abbé Bourbourg de Brasseur, proposed fantastic theories on the origins of pre-Columbian civilization and its priority over the Near East, Charnay remained a pillar of common sense. He cogently argued that our admiration for the American Indian achievement need not entice us into assuming a hoary antiquity. "Why then," he asked the mythmakers, "should the people who raised the American monuments be less deserving of our regard, because they built them ten centuries sooner or later? Does it alter the character of the monuments, or destroy an art unknown to us hitherto?" But his plea met with little response.

Charnay's most important archaeological coup did not fare much better with his fellow Americanists. Since it did not fit at all into preconceptions about New World cultures, it too was rarely accepted as trustworthy—until many decades later additional finds amply bore out its strange testimony. The discovery concerned wheeled "toys" from a central Mexican cemetery at an altitude of some 13,000 feet on a slope of snow-capped, fuming Popocatepetl. Even today, a hundred years later, the general public is convinced that the principle of the wheel was not known anywhere in pre-Columbian America.

The very site of Charnay's excavations was re-examined in the 1930's by George C. Vaillant, who laid the foundation for a systematic stratigraphy of central Mexico. Vaillant was able to show that its artifacts placed it squarely with the Toltecs, just as Charnay had anticipated. In the modern ceramic classification it belonged to the Mazapán I-Toltec horizon, i.e., the period between the eclipse of Teotihuacán and the rise of the Aztecs.

As to the occurrence of the wheel in pre-Columbian America, there is no longer the slightest doubt that it was widely known all over Mexico—and for a long time. Wheeled clay animal figures have been dug up at the Gulf Coast (Pánuco, Tres Zapotes) as well as in the highlands of central (Culhuacán) and southern Mexico (Monte Albán). Some of these are of greater antiquity than Charnay's from Tenenepango (Tenenepanco) and may be coëval with Teotihuacán, about A.D. 300–900. However, Charnay's suggestion that American aboriginals made any practical use of the wheel in transportation has so far found little if any support. Why ancient Americans should apply the wheel only to toys—or perhaps ritual objects (in the opinion of Gordon F. Ekholm, foremost modern student of pre-Columbian knowledge of the wheel)— without discovering its technological potential has been as frequently debated as the question of whether the invention could have been made independently in the New World. Such issues touch on fundamental problems of American civilizations. They are also grist for the mill of the neo-diffusionists who can point to wheeled clay "toys" from the Old World—ancient Syria, Mesopotamia, India, and China—that closely resemble those from Mexico.

Désiré Charnay would, no doubt, have sided with the diffusionists. He was a firm believer in American affinities with the extreme East and clearly stated that these resemblances are "something better than fortuitous analogies." He sounded a prophetic note when he added that they "point to a vast and novel field for the investigation of archaeologists."

Such opinions had been strengthened by Charnay's visit to Java years after he had taken up his American explorations. Born in 1828 near Lyon, Charnay had started out as a seventeen-year-old teacher of French in New Orleans. He had first come to Mexico in 1857. To Popocatepetl he was then attracted by the scenery, and made the ascent to Tenenepango for the purpose of taking photographs. But while his men were busy setting up the formidable nineteenth-century photographic machinery, he amused himself with poking the ground with a stick. To his surprise he scratched the surface of some pottery. He then used his dagger and promptly dug up whole vases and human bones. But at the time photography claimed most of his interest. As yet he was at a loss as to what to make of ancient objects. Twenty-three years later, by then a seasoned archaeologist, he was back at the same spot to follow up his previous find. It was then that he made the unique discovery of wheeled figurines.

Charnay's later campaigns were largely undertaken under combined American and French auspices and with the financial support of the Franco-American magnate Paul P. Lorillard, after whom he named a newly found Maya city. His archaeological finds were collected at the National Museum of Mexico City and at the Trocadero in Paris. However, his "wheeled toys" have since dropped from sight.

WHEELED "TOYS"

Désiré Charnay

With a good horse and a comfortable saddle, the ascent of Popocatepetl is a delightful ride. The road rises so rapidly that the view, which was confined to the charming valley of Amecameca, becomes finer and more extensive at every turn of the road, embracing at last the entire plateau.

From *The Ancient Cities of the New World,* translated from the French by J. Gonino and Helen S. Conant. New York: Harper & Brothers, 1887, pp. 163–82.

The air is crisp, the sun, though hot, is bearable, and when, after three hours' march, we reach the high mountain ridge, we pause to admire in silence the finest panorama in the world: the two great volcanoes to our right and left, the plain of Puebla on our rear, whilst before us stretches the marvellous plain of Mexico, every detail of which is distinctly visible in this clear atmosphere.

We are so lost in contemplation that the guide has at last to remind us that, unless we resume our march, we shall be late for luncheon, which awaits us at Tlamacas; but when we did reach it we found that the only accommodation to be had was a shed, open to rain, wind, and cold. There was fortunately a table and a chimney, and with our camp-beds we managed pretty well.

As soon as we had seen to our luggage we sallied forth in search of the cemetery under the escort of the chief guide, and began the ascent of Monte del Fraile, 782 feet high, over a distance of three miles. This may appear a small matter—but a short walk; yet a climb performed at an altitude of 13,000 feet on moving sand, every step of which is painful, is no joke: the head aches, the pulse throbs, every breath drawn is a gasp, the throat is dry, every attempt to stoop makes one dizzy, rest becomes necessary every few minutes; and on reaching the crest of Tenenepanco rock we were thoroughly exhausted.

My impatience to find the cemetery was so great, that I could not stop long to contemplate the fine view to be seen here; we immediately began our search. But though I seemed to recognise the plateau, it looked somewhat different—strewn with flat stones I had not observed before—consequently I climbed higher, followed by an old Indian who had been with me in my first expedition, and who opened the ground in several places. It was found very hard, compact, gravelly, without any appearance of ever having been disturbed; so after many fruitless attempts, I returned to the first place, when the old Indian, who had not breathed a word hitherto, said:

"Señor, this is the place where you found some vases the last time you were here."

"But how do these flags come here?"

"Oh, from subsequent excavations."

"Then I am sold, robbed, done out of my find," I cried in my disappointment, as though the cemetery were my property.

"But," objected the old volcanero softly, "only a few loads of detritus were taken away; there must be more to come out."

Acting on advice which seemed so reasonable, I soon discovered numerous *tepalcates*, fragments of vases, cups, and various potteries; we had lost so much time, however, in looking about, that we were soon

Toltec burial ground at Tenenepango, central Mexico, after a photograph by Charnay

obliged to abandon the mountain, trusting in what the morrow would bring forth.

A few words about our encampment may not be out of place here. The men occupied an open shed, with a huge chimney in the centre, where twice a day they prepared their own food, consisting of a small quantity of meat and the indispensable tortilla, the whole washed down with a good drop of mezcal. They slept on trusses of dry grass and mats. We were not better housed than the men, whilst our cooking was a great deal worse; if our shed was not quite so open, it was sufficiently so to admit the bitter night cold; the wind came in at all the windows unprotected by any shutters, through the thousand cracks of the ill-jointed enclosure, searing our faces and causing incessant sneezing. Although whole trees were burnt in the huge chimney, it made no appreciable difference in the atmosphere of the room, and as there was no tunnel we were nearly suffocated by the smoke, which, hovering about us, only escaped through the roof. At this altitude, with six or seven degrees below zero (Centigrade) at night, our bed of gutta-percha felt like icicles, and every time I came in direct contact with it, I instantly awoke. . . .

The chill nights were certainly trying, but they were made up to us by the glorious mornings; we rose with the first light of day; the sun, still invisible to us, was already greeting the summit of the great volcano, from which rose a light vapour. We watched the snow changing from a delicate pink to dazzling white; the crest of El Fraile, as yet wrapped in nocturnal mists, showed gray against a transparent blue sky, whilst its base, shrouded by a deep fringe of funeral pines, gradually emerged from their gloom at the sun's magic touch. To the east the plain of Puebla, and far away on the horizon the imposing cone of Orizaba, whilst in the middle distance the severe outline of Malinche seemed to divide the sky. The city de los Angeles [Puebla], with her square massive buildings, her steeples, cupolas, the towers of the cathedral, the stately pyramid of Cholula rose at our feet bathed in a flood of morning light.

The old Indian proved a true prophet; my predecessors had not removed everything; trenches branching off in every direction so as to embrace the whole plateau were at once made and brought to light wholly undisturbed tombs. The first was that of a woman whose head I was able to preserve intact: the bones of all the rest were unfortunately reduced to a gelatinous paste. The dead were buried at a depth varying from some two feet to four feet eight inches; the bodies doubled up, both chin and arms resting on their knees; hands and feet were gone. Within the tomb, over the head, was a *sebile,* or hollow terra-cotta plate, two small black earthen horns, besides several vases. The whole was damp and moist, the vases filled with earth and water, and the utmost care was required in taking up such fragile objects. They soon, however, hardened by exposure, when they could be easily and safely cleaned and packed. As far as could be judged from the bones and pottery, one of the tombs contained the bodies of a man and a woman. Another, probably that of a chief, had no human remains left, but I found a great variety of precious objects, made of *chalchihuitl,* a hard green stone, which takes a fine polish, a kind of jade or serpentine, much valued by the Indians; besides these were numerous arrows of obsidian, beads for necklaces, some of hard stone, some of terra-cotta, and a few small figures. A singular circumstance marked this tomb; not a single bead, not a single ornament but was broken, presumably at the time of burial, as a token of grief. It is at least the only plausible solution which can be given for so many hard and resisting objects having been systematically destroyed.

Moreover, by far the largest proportion of these granite or porphyry beads, whether owing to their great antiquity or their having lain in a very destructive soil, crumbled away at our touch. Broadly speaking, the tombs which had not been disturbed were two to one; the dead had been buried without any regard to their position.

We are not yet inured to our life at an altitude of 13,000 feet, and our daily ascensions are painful in the extreme; our faces literally peel in this sharp wind and hot sun, whilst our hands are frightfully chapped and almost paralysed. It would be difficult to bear up long against our hardships were it not for the stupendous result of our excavations: kitchen utensils, every variety of vases representing the Toltec god Tlaloc, fruit cups, jewel cups, with feet shaped like a duck's bill or a boar's head; chocolate cups with porpoise-like handles; beads, jewels, a whole civilisation emerges from these tombs, and carries us back to the life of this long-forgotten people. Here we have caricatures of ancient warriors; further on a water-carrier bearing his jars like the modern "aguadores"; next are toys and tiny terra-cotta chariots, some are broken, some still preserve their four wheels; they were, presumably, a fond mother's memento who, ages gone by, buried them with her beloved child. These chariots are shaped like a flattened *cayote* (a kind of long-bodied fox) with its straight ears and pointed face, and the wheels fit into four terra-cotta stumps; on my renewing the wood axle-tree, which had been destroyed long since, the chariots began to move.

Many more objects were brought to light from these tombs—richly ornamented "fusaïoles," marbles, necklaces, baby-tables, which, like the toy chariots, represented some quadruped—resembling Greek toys. This coincidence between people so different and so far removed from each other is not surprising, for elementary ideas generally find a common expression. It should also be observed that these toys, however rude, do not necessarily mark a very ancient epoch. Early manifestations live on through ages and are found side by side with the highest civilisations, and are still to be met among people long after the well-to-do possess objects of art.

The 9th of July was one of our best days. Out of ten tombs five were found intact and yielded sixty remarkable pieces, one of which is unique and of peculiar interest. It is a three-footed terra-cotta cup some six inches by three by one and a half at the bottom inside; wonderful to relate, it emerged without a blot from its gloomy abode. Both the inside and outside are covered with pretty devices painted white, yellow, blue, green, and red, fused into a harmonious whole. The colours are in relief and like enamels. Next, one almost as beautiful but smaller, and covered with dirt, was found. These two lovely cups were put out to dry in the sun, when, to my horror, I saw that one was fast scaling off, whilst the brilliant colours of the other were fading visibly. To remove them into the shade was the work of an instant, but, alas! it did not arrest the work of destruction, which continued at an alarming pace. A photograph of the finest cup, as well as the colours of the paintings, was immediately obtained, but it only gives a faint idea of the beauty of this charming work of art.

Vases from Tenenepango

From these tombs were likewise unearthed a number of diminutive brass bells, which were used both as ornaments and currency; besides large fat vases with a hand painted red over a black ground. This was a Toltec memento, either symbolic of Hueman or of Quetzalcoatl, so often seen on the walls of Yucatec palaces, and likewise on the monuments of some North American tribes. But our most curious "find" was a perfectly well-preserved human brain, the skull of which was gone. This cerebral mass had been protected from the pressure of its surroundings by a stout cup into which it was wedged. No doubt was possible: the two lobes, the circumvolution of the brain to the minute red lines of the blood-vessels, all was there.

The fact that a human brain could have been found in good preservation when the skull had disappeared, was received with Homeric laughter; all I can say is that it is so, that the finding of it was witnessed by my associates; that in every tomb where the skull should have been, was invariably observed a whitish substance, which at first was mistaken for lime, but which subsequently whenever it was met with, the men instantly cried out: "*Aqui esta uno—here is one*" (body), and near it vases and fragments clearly indicating the presence of a tomb. These brains, however, not having been protected like the first, were all flattened into a white cake of some five inches by two in thickness. The only explanation I can offer is that at an elevation of 13,000 feet, close to the volcanic cone of Popocatepetl, in a soil saturated with sulphureous vapours (a film of sulphide always extended over my nitrate of silver washes), the same chemical combinations which destroyed the bones, may have acted as a preservative on cerebral matter. But it will be asked, why not have borne away that wonderful brain? I ought to have done so, no doubt, but without alcohol the thing was impossible; besides, had I done so, should I have a better chance of convincing people at a distance?

The toy chariots found no better favour with the public. Our illustrations, however, will settle once for all this vexed question. As must appear to the most inexperienced eye, the character of these toys is exceedingly archaic, nor am I aware that any museum or private collection has anything to show at all approaching them. This was conceded, but it was denied that they were chariots at all—the wheels were only "malacates," *i.e.* "fusaïoles"! Numerous spindles were indeed found by us in the cemetery. Profuse collections may be seen and compared in every museum, when the most ignorant must see that these wheels are quite different to "fusaïoles" or whorls. It will be said that this toy was but the copy of a chariot brought in by the Spaniards; but a glance at the drawing will show how absurd is the assumption, and carry conviction to the most incredulous.

Granted that is so, what inference do you draw from it? That the Mexicans had chariots? Hardly, since all authorities are silent on the subject, and when we know that the only means of transportation was afforded by carriers. But if such chariots were not available in distant expeditions across rivers, over mountain paths, through immense forests, it was not so within the radius of a city having good roads; and what is there against the possibility of a hand-cart corresponding with ours having been in use?

I am far from affirming that it was so, although certain expressions and quotations might be adduced which would show the supposition to be not so far-fetched as it looks on the face of it. We read in the Ramirez manuscript, for instance, that Montezuma II. set out for his Huaxateca expedition with a numerous army and *carruages*. Why should the Indian writer have used an ambiguous word meaning both *chariot* and *transport*, when the former must already have been extant when he wrote— that is, after the Conquest? Farther, Padre Durán relates how this same Montezuma, wishing to erect a temalacatl, had a huge block quarried at Aculco, near Amecameca; and [his illustration] shows this block raised

Wheeled "toys" from Tenenepango

by means of a rude chariot having clog-wheels, drawn by a multitude of Indians. The text, it is true, does not specify a chariot; but if they were unknown, how do they come in his drawing? It is unaccountable, too, that no mention is made of the stone having been brought on rollers or wheels, seeing that it could not have come so great a distance by any other means. It is altogether a mystery.

Lastly, Juarros, in describing the battle at Pinar, fought against Alvarado, mentions war-engines, or what would now be called ammunition carts, moving on *rodadillos,* which were drawn by armed men wherever they were required. These carts were loaded with arrows, spears, shields, stones, slings, etc., and men, chosen for the service, distributed them as they were wanted. Does "rodadillo" mean here a clog-wheel or a roller? If these carts carried arms to combatants in different parts of the field of battle, does it not follow that they moved on wheels, since rollers would have made the diminutive "forts" immovable, contrary to the end proposed?

Should, however, both quotations and arguments seem valueless, it might be added that the toy chariots were perhaps of primeval Toltec invention, the use of which had been lost after their expulsion from the plateaux.

But to return to the cemetery. Whether it be considered Toltec or otherwise, whether ancient or comparatively modern, we hold to its antiquity, to its being essentially Nahua, dedicated to Tlaloc, the god of rain and plenty, the fertiliser of the earth, the Lord of Paradise, the protector of green harvests. We are in his dominions, for he was believed to reside where the clouds gather, on the highest mountain-tops.

We reached the plain at last, and a few minutes brought us to Amecameca.

Our excavations on the high plateau are over; we leave for the warm region, to follow the Toltecs in their great migration at the beginning of the eleventh century.

15

The Valley of Mexico, or Anahuac, which was the scene of the three consecutive civilizations of Teotihuacán, the Toltecs, and the Aztecs, is an extensive oval basin in central Mexico situated at an altitude of about 7,500 feet and measuring some fifty to seventy miles in length and forty miles in width. With Mexico City in its southern section it is today a rich farming and manufacturing region, the most populous of the nation, just as it was before the advent of the Spanish. High mountain chains rim it on virtually all sides, while the eternally snow-capped Popocatepetl ("Smoking Mountain") and its sleeping consort Ixtacihuatl ("White Woman") guard its southeastern flank. During the time of the Aztecs a series of interconnected lakes, bridged by wide causeways, covered part of the area. Most of these have now been drained, with rather ill effect on the climate and on the buildings of Mexico City, which are gradually sinking into the porous subsoil. Cortés, who entered it through a pass at the foot of Popocatepetl, only followed in the footsteps of Indians to whom the valley has been a desirable goal since times primordial.

Again and again waves of nomadic tribes from the north swept into the Valley of Mexico, replaced earlier settlers, acquired some of the amenities and cruelties of civilization, and were conquered in turn. Hence its rather chequered and turbulent history, which makes it so challenging an area for the student of Mexican antiquities. The area itself is saturated with ruins and mounds. But archaeologists met with immense difficulties when trying to penetrate the buried past in this all-important center of pre-Columbian evolution. Above all they needed to know the sequence and age of the various cultures. While the history immediately before the Aztecs was as much confused as lit up by colonial documents, further Indian antecedents, apparently unrecorded by written or oral traditions, seemed beyond any strain of memory. However, there were slowly accumulating diverse materials that served as hints of human occupation in the valley by more primitive cultures prior to the Toltecs or even Teotihuacán.

When in the second half of the nineteenth century a few small, rather whimsical, clay figurines were encountered by French explorers attached to Napoleon III's mission and by a Mexican bishop of antiquarian bent, only passing attention was paid to them. Though they appeared to be quite distinct from the formidable ceremonial style of known religious representations, students of Mexican antiquity were not yet mentally prepared to conceive of people more ancient than Toltecs and Aztecs, albeit Humboldt had had premonitions of them. However, in 1907 a distinguished American-born archaeologist, Miss Zelia Nuttall, acquired similar artifacts taken from a large lava field—the Pedregal—on the southern outskirts of Mexico City near the present University campus. They had been dug up by workers quarrying the lava for building stone. It was Miss Nuttall who recognized the figurines' "archaic" character.

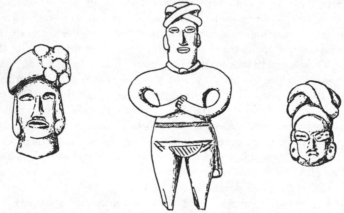

"Archaic" figurines from central Mexico

A few years later, in 1910, American anthropologist Franz Boas together with a Mexican colleague, Manuel Gamio, launched the first stratigraphic excavation in the Valley of Mexico and was able to show that such "archaic" figurines preceded known Aztec and Toltec horizons. This signalled the emergence of an "archaic age" in Mexican pre-history, now usually referred to as formative or pre-classic. (To the confusion of many students, the term "archaic" is often used today to refer to a still earlier pre-ceramic age.)

In 1917, Herbert J. Spinden, a U.S. scholar chiefly known for his Maya studies, extended the concept of an "archaic age" beyond the

Valley of Mexico by suggesting that the same horizon prevailed over most of Mexico, Central America, and South America. All the civilizations later to rise in those regions showed a common matrix. Though Spinden's thesis found no endorsement at the time, it has been partly rehabilitated in later years since the close parallels between the formative cultures of Mesoamerica and the Central Andes became evident.

Meanwhile, also in 1917, Manuel Gamio continued probing archaic layers underneath a lava field at Copilco. In April 1922, Dr. Byron Cummings from the University of Arizona visited the Pedregal with Dr. Gamio, who was by then Mexico's director of anthropology. Just off the road from Mexico City to Cuernavaca, the two scholars noticed a large overgrown hill, Cuicuilco, enveloped by prehistoric lava streams. There was at least a suspicion that the hill may have been artificial. If such were the case, Dr. Cummings thought, an extraordinary opportunity presented itself to throw light on the archaic age of the Valley of Mexico. He quickly gained Dr. Gamio's permission to excavate.

Cummings also obtained the cooperation of the Mexican government and the University of Arizona. Thereupon he spent nine months in removing the lava cover, occasionally with the aid of dynamite. The campaign was renewed in July 1924 and continued till September 1925, this time with the additional sponsorship of the National Geographic Society of Washington. The hill turned out to be nothing less than an enormous pyramid or rather a truncated cone with four galleries, a central staircase, and a horseshoe altar on top. True to the Mesoamerican tradition, new structures had been superimposed at successive stages. It clearly mirrored a primitive phase of Mexican pyramid building. Construction methods from coarse lava boulders, pebbles, adobe, and sand and clay filling were crude, leaving no doubt of the structure's relative antiquity. Indeed, the cyclopean cone is generally regarded as Mexico's oldest large structure in stone. Its importance as a prototype of Mesoamerican architecture may well be compared to the step pyramid of Zoser in early dynastic Egypt.

But what about the temple mound's actual age? When Cummings did his work Mexican stratigraphy was still rudimentary. Far too little ceramic material had been assembled to place Cuicuilco in a continuous and datable sequence. Even today, estimates for the construction of the cone (600 B.C.–A.D. 200) and the subsequent, though probably much later, eruption of Xitle [Xictli] (200 B.C.–A.D. 300), which buried it, vary by some centuries. In Cummings' day, a New Zealand geologist placed the deposit of the Pedregal lava field between 2,000 and 7,000 years ago—the difference of a split second in geological time, but in terms of the human past, of course, an enormous span. Cummings preferred to accept a maximum age, for reasons never convincingly stated, but possibly inspired by the unconscious urge of Americanists to establish for New World civilizations an antiquity at least as great as that of the Old World. By the same token, a Polish scholar gave Tiahuanaco ("the cradle of mankind") an astronomical age counted in hundred-thousands of years, and A. Hyatt Verrill and the Abbé Brasseur de Bourbourg put forward only slightly more modest claims for Central American ruins. "Eight thousand years," Cummings declared, "is a very conservative estimate of the time that has elapsed since the primitive people toiled up the slope of Cuicuilco and reared a mighty temple to their gods." He argued that a local Indian tradition would have survived, if Xitle had visited devastation a mere two thousand years ago. Besides, the Pedregal lava indicates "a long period of weathering." Yet, what the exact criteria and degrees of "weathering" are and how they can be translated into a time count, he fails to say.

Ancient Mexican fire god (Huehueteotl)

Since Cummings' excavations at the Pedregal, our notions of Mexican pre-history and antiquity have been completely altered. While man may indeed have roamed Mexico ten thousand and more years ago, the "formative" culture of farmers, potters, and builders made a much later appearance—at about 4,000 to 3,500 years ago. Only since the initiation of Vaillant's extensive stratigraphic surveys in the Valley of Mexico has it been possible to assign reasonably plausible dates to pre-classic and even classic horizons. Vaillant's studies also made it clear that Mexican farming cultures of refreshing artistic naïveté preceded Cuicuilco and the related Copilco which already mark a considerable development toward a hierarchical society under the thumb of organized religion and an elite of priests and princes. Cummings himself found among the archaic ceramics an image of the Mexican fire god familiar from later sites. However, the title of the Cuicuilco mound to the status of oldest truly monumental religious building in the Americas is rarely disputed, even if the far less imposing Mound I at Tlapacoya may have been erected somewhat earlier. Excavations by the University of Southern California in 1957 disclosed four additional pyramids within the Cuicuilco mound. Otherwise, little progress has yet been registered in freeing the surrounding Pedregal area which is believed to cover an extensive settlement connected with the ceremonial pyramid.

Byron Cummings, born in New York state in 1861, played a notable role in the study of the American Southwest. For many years professor of archaeology and museum director of the University of Arizona, he had taught Greek and Latin, first in Eastern high schools and then at the University of Utah, before his fascination with nature and natives of the American deserts redirected his interests. Cummings led many expeditions to cliff-dwelling ruins in southern Utah and northern Arizona, and helped to restore a prehistoric Pueblo village. He is also credited with the discovery of natural bridges in the American mesas.

CUICUILCO—THE OLDEST TEMPLE IN NORTH AMERICA

Byron Cummings

South of Mexico City some thirty miles stands old Ajusco. It is one of the natural landmarks on the rim of surrounding mountains and guards the pass leading from the Valley of Mexico to that surrounding Cuernavaca. From its cones stretch out great ridges of dark flinty lava that embrace the slopes and valleys below like the tentacles of some mighty octopus. To the north from a rounded cone lying some distance below the crest and known as Xichtli, emerged a stream that poured down around hills and knolls of yellow tufa and hard blue lava that had been poured out from Ajusco in some former age. This great

"Cuicuilco, the Oldest Temple in North America," *Art and Archaeology*, XVI, Nos. 1 & 2 (July–Aug. 1923), pp. 51–58.

northerly stream extends off across the plains and is known as the "Pedregal."

Beneath this lava near San Angel have been uncovered human skeletons, pottery and stone implements of a crude type and classed as archaic. Beneath the remains of the Aztec and the still older Teotihuacán cultures at Atzcapotzalco and in the sacred city of Teotihuacán are encountered similar articles of similar manufacture. In the state of Morelos and all through the plateau country of Mexico are found objects evidently belonging to the same cultural stage. But in none of these locations have been found structures that could be classed as the work of these early people. Their homes were probably crude huts of perishable material and it had been thought that they had not learned to build walls and rear temples and pyramids. But the facts now brought to light demonstrate quite the contrary.

Near Tlalpam this great Pedregal spread out toward the east past Chontongo and Sacatepec, two hills now crowned with ruined pyramids, and surrounded a hill that seemingly had been used as a sacred gathering place for ages. Years had multiplied into centuries and centuries into millenniums since the feet of men kept time to the music of the drum on its wide-spreading platform. The black scorching stream, burning everything in its wake, crowded up against this low hill until it had hemmed it in on every side. The flinty stream spread over the valley, charring to a blackened mass the quite dense vegetation then growing there, and covering the homes and other evidences of human culture with a capping that has sealed their record so effectively and so long that not even tradition seems to have the vaguest suggestion of the people or their time.

This hill, called by the natives San Cuicuilco, raised its crest above the deadly fumes and dark tentacles settling around its base threatening to destroy it like some mighty fire-breathing dragon of old. This was not the first time it evidently had stood in silent defiance of the terrible forces of the fire god. From Ajusco or some other near-by point in some long forgotten age this mighty spirit had shot forth quantities of lava shells that rolled down its slopes and lay heaped around its base. Great showers of mud and ashes and pumice had covered the entire region. Strong winds had whirled these about the slopes of the pyramid and piled them over its crest. Did man occupy these valleys then? We have always supposed that the sub-Pedregal period—the culture immediately underlying the Pedregal lava flow—was the earliest in this valley: but at Cuicuilco this culture lies on top of the thick stratum of volcanic ashes and mud that covers the structure, and ex-

Artifacts found below the lava field (Pedregal) in the outskirts of Mexico City

tends out under the Pedregal lava. Thus a much older population must have occupied this part of Mexico at some earlier period, for beneath some ten feet of volcanic material are encountered the walls of a large truncated cone whose base lies 25 feet below the surface of the present base of the hill.

The building is circular in form, some 450 feet in diameter at the base and its latest construction on the top platform attained an elevation of about 100 feet. The sides rise in sloping walls that have an inclination of 45°. These walls are broken by three terraces respectively 13, 38, and 68 feet wide, while the top platform has a diameter of 130 feet. The sloping wall to the first terrace measures 46 feet, that to the second 24, while that to the third seems to rise only 4 feet. The top platform or fourth terrace rises 5 feet higher. This top platform and the terrace below (68 feet wide) are covered with volcanic material to the depth of 7 feet on the platform and 12 feet on the terrace. On the south-western side of the platform made by leveling off this volcanic material was a mound of earth and ashes mingled with chunks of lava and water-worn boulders that rose some 20 feet higher. On the lower terraces wherever there was lodging space and about the base of the structure is found volcanic material similar to that encountered covering the two top terraces. At one place on the eastern side it had accumulated to a depth of $17\frac{1}{2}$ feet and held the lava back 33 feet from the pyramid. At another point the ruins of a lofty platform extend out from the pyramid 29 feet, and 11 feet of this lies under the lava of the Pedregal. Whenever we have excavated to the pavement surrounding the temple, the story is the same: first a mass of lava shells, then a thick stratum of volcanic material consisting of yellowish clay, ashes and fine pumice, above that the blackened stratum caused by the great heat at the time of the Pedregal lava flow and resting upon that a thick accumulation of recent soil. Where the volcanic material had slid down off the slopes and accumulated at the base of the cone, the lava flowed in over it, burying the base far beneath the enveloping mass.

On top in the center eight feet below the surface is a platform made by bedding large chunks of lava and water-worn boulders in the volcanic soil. Upon this was constructed another platform of similar materials, oval in form and about one foot high. The eastern half of this is raised three feet higher with a wall of water-worn boulders laid in clay. The interior of this is raised to within a foot of the top with water-worn boulders and clay soil. The outer wall thus forms a horseshoe-shaped altar made of water-worn boulders and clay.

Beneath the platform upon which this altar rests is encountered a clay pavement and that portion of the pavement lying beneath the altar has been painted red. Thus the original building seems to have

Reconstruction of Cuicuilco circular temple pyramid with Xitle in eruption

been constructed of lava rock laid up in walls several feet thick and filled in the center with soil. This structure was covered completely with volcanic material which later was leveled off into a broad platform on top and narrow irregular terraces on the side. These terraces are sustained by walls of lava rock and smoothed boulders, plainly of a later period of construction than that of the original pyramid. Their faces are made by selecting chunks of lava with fairly flat surfaces and placing these surfaces on the outside, giving a smoother face to the wall than found in the original. The higher terrace walls are more carelessly constructed and together with the mound on the top of the highest platform seem to be the latest structures of the temple. Thus there are at least three periods of building manifest in these structures, all of which antedate the eruption of Xichtli that produced the Pedregal lava.

The walls of this great cone are constructed of chunks and shells of lava of a flow occurring before the volcanic showers which produced the materials that envelop it. The interior for several feet from the surface is a mass of lava rock while the surface walls are made of large chunks of hard bluish lava of the forms known as andasite and basalt. Many of them are a meter or more in length with the larger ends roughly fitted together to form the surface, while the smaller ends extend inwards at right angles to the surface and are bedded in small stone. No hewn stones are encountered in the entire structure. No filling material such as cement, plaster, or even clay was employed. It is crude cyclopean masonry; and yet such large boulders are used at the base and the rock packed so securely in the sloping walls, that they stand today seemingly about as strong as when first constructed.

Not a bit of lava of the Pedregal type is found in the entire structure. The rock from the older lava flows, together with some water-worn boulders, constitute the materials employed. These water-worn boulders must have come from some stream now forcing its channel beneath the Pedregal. No such river bed can be found anywhere in the region.

When we consider that this building must have been constructed before some great eruption in the vicinity sent forth its deluging showers of ashes, mud and pumice, and that this calamity occurred long before the Pedregal flow which geologists estimate occurred from two to seven thousand years ago and that the stone implements are grinding and polishing stones, flaked knives, borers and scrapers, that the pottery even near the surface is crude and archaic, that the entire structure contains no hewn stone and no cement or plaster of any form, we realize that architecture had its beginning in Mexico long before the Christian era, and that the early populations of this land had undoubtedly commenced the mastery of the material universe about them probably quite as soon as the primitive peoples surrounding the Mediterranean. Dr. Gamio has proved with reasonable satisfaction that the great structures of Teotihuacán and the period of the highest culture of its skillful people were developed about the first century of our era, or some 2,000 years ago. Cuicuilco is an illustration of one of the first great structures reared by the ancestors of those tribes who later adorned Mexico not only with mighty pyramids but also with richly decorated temples and palaces. This crude structure, unembellished and unadorned yet massive and solid, stands as mute evidence that the native American developed his masterful architecture here on American soil. As in old Pompeii the mighty forces of nature covered and sealed the handiwork of man that it might speak to future generations, so here in the Valley of Mexico those same forces have preserved a chapter of human history, more primitive yet no less interesting than the worn pavements and marble peristyles of the ancient city of the Italian coast.

How long were the people of Cuicuilco in developing the ability to rear this massive pyramid? Through how many centuries had this American branch of the human family struggled before they gained sufficient mastery of material things and sufficient social and political co-operation and organization to produce such results? How many centuries elapsed between the building of Cuicuilco and the ornate pyramid of Quetzalcoatl and those of the Sun and the Moon at Teotihuacán? Human progress under primitive conditions has always been slow, and early American progress was no exception to the natural course of events. This great temple then pushes the horizon of human history in North America back many centuries and opens up a chapter of human progress on this side of the Atlantic of which men have dreamed but which has never been recorded in authentic annals.

16

Mexican archaeologists never struck it so rich as when, in January 1932, Alfonso Caso opened the now famous Tomb 7 at Monte Albán, some 200 miles south of Mexico City in the state of Oaxaca. All at once 'this fertile part of southern Mexico became one of the country's most important archaeological zones. Caso's explorations helped to focus attention on two little known ancient people, the Zapotecs and Mixtecs, and revealed unsuspected dimensions of the Mesoamerican scene. There unfolded at Monte Albán a record of more than two thousand years of continuous human occupation from the archaic beginnings to the Spanish Conquest.

It was with the hope of finding links here to the central valley cultures on the one hand and to the Mayas on the other that the Mexican scholar had embarked on his Monte Albán campaign. As it turned out he accomplished much more. Besides bringing forth treasures of the greatest material and aesthetic value, and substantiating southern Mexico's close connections with the pre-classic, Teotihuacán, and Toltec and Aztec phases, he opened new vistas on early civilization in Mesoamerica and on the decisive Mixtec contribution to the vigorous art, the calendar, and the pictographic script of the Aztecs. Monte Albán showed clearly that in the late post-classic age the Mixtec (Vaillant called it Mixtec-Puebla) style exerted a profound influence over all of Mesoamerica, even Mayaland and as far south as Nicaragua.

Monte Albán (Spanish for "White Mountain," a distortion of the Zapotec *Danib'aan*, "Sacred Mountain") lies some seven miles from the state capital of Oaxaca on a series of promontories rising to 1,300 feet at the junction of three subtropical valleys and with the jagged silhouette of the Sierra Madre del Sur in the background. The site, 6,500 feet above the sea, was levelled by prehistoric men to enormous terraces of living rock on which were laid out large squares, stelae, an observatory, a ballcourt, staircases, pyramids, temples, and burial vaults. Though only

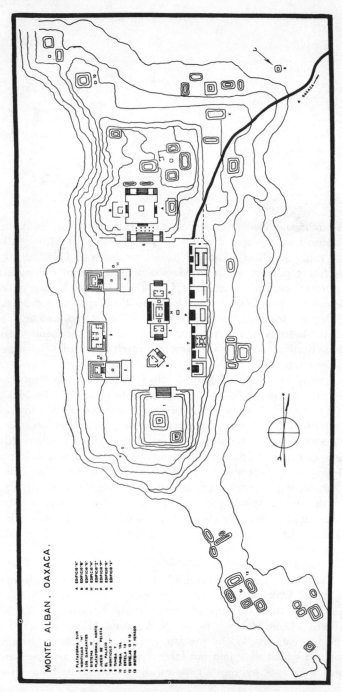

MONTE ALBAN. OAXACA.

1 PLATAFORMA SUR
2 MONTICULO "M"
3 LOS DANZANTES
4 SISTEMA IV
5 PLATAFORMA NORTE
6 JUEGO DE PELOTA
7 EL PALACIO
8 MONTICULO "J"
9 TUMBA
10 TUMBA 104
11 ESTELA 18
12 SISTEMA 13 Y 19
13 SISTEMA 7 VENADO

A EDIFICIO "A"
B EDIFICIO "B"
G EDIFICIO "G"
H EDIFICIO "H"
I EDIFICIO "I"
P EDIFICIO "P"
Q EDIFICIO "Q"
X EDIFICIO "X"

Plan of Monte Albán. Tomb 7 is at lower right, off the Oaxaca highway.

parts have been cleared, the complex is estimated to cover more than twenty square miles. Despite its easily defensible, fortress-like topography, Monte Albán presumably never served any military purposes—no weapons to speak of have been found in the burials—but was one of those vast religious shrines and places of pilgrimage raised by American men to their demanding gods. Unlike Teotihuacán in the Valley of Mexico or Chan-Chan in coastal Peru, it does not seem to have been a true urban center, though aerial observation has reported possible traces of humble settlements on the mountainsides. But since there is no water nearby, one may well doubt whether the area could ever have attracted any sizable number of inhabitants.

So commanding a site as Monte Albán, close to the colonial metropolis of Oaxaca, has, of course, always been known. Caso found evidence that local Indians had made offerings to the old gods as recently as fifty years before his time. Together with nearby Mitla, another Zapotec center, travelers and savants came to visit Monte Albán throughout the nineteenth century. Still earlier arrived the treasureseekers, who rifled the tombs and edifices. That they had been able to extract many precious objects was no secret. The greater was the surprise that there were any undisturbed mounds left. While the government here as elsewhere did little to curb such utterly destructive plundering, it nevertheless raised absurd obstacles to any scientific excavation. The British Maya explorer A. P. Maudslay, at the turn of the century, intrigued by the Zapotecs, cooled his heels for years waiting to obtain permission to dig at Monte Albán, but finally had to give up in disgust. Luckily Alfonso Caso, a Mexican—and a director of the National Museum— thirty years later had fewer chicaneries or prejudices to put up with. Even superstitious natives, who tended to believe that the digging of ancient graves would bring the vengeful spirits of the dead on the ransacker, came around with picturesque tales improvised to account for Dr. Caso's blissful state after he had excavated Tomb 7 without suffering any ill effect.

However, tombs had not been Caso's immediate objective. Only toward the end of the first year's campaign did he turn to adjacent burial mounds, situated below the summit just off the road to Oaxaca. His initial goal had been to clear the main plaza—some 1,000 by 650 feet—and the surrounding structures. When removing overgrowth from shapeless ruins to the north he freed a wide stairway which is regarded as the widest on the continent. Of far greater interest were a number of stone slabs with relief sculptures he freed at the northern platform. They had evidently been torn from an older edifice in the west to be used as building material. The figures were quite unusual. They showed male bodies, most of which were in contorted positions or were physically deformed. None bore the slightest resemblance to known Zapotec carvings. Equally unfamiliar were the hieroglyphic signs inscribed on several of the slabs. To Caso, who had made a special study of Zapotec writing before excavating Monte Albán, this was one of the campaign's exciting finds. Here was an unknown script, the cultural affinities of which were quite perplexing.

In time to come, these sculptures and hieroglyphics were to occasion much speculation. Caso himself was at a loss to account for the quaint, if not pathological, figures. Some showed bearded old men. Several of the faces appeared to be of a negroid cast. It occurred to him that they might depict enemies of the people of Monte Albán who were held up to ridicule. Or could they represent a procession of the sick seeking a miraculous cure at what may have been a pre-Columbian Lourdes? Though the meaning and origin of these reliefs—among which the so-called *Danzantes* are the best known—have not been fully resolved, Caso soon learned to associate them with the earliest epoch of Monte Albán. Apparently they preceded the Zapotecs and were attributable to the original builders of the great temple city. This was the first notable insight into the evolution of Monte Albán. Inevitably it introduced new riddles.

How Caso entered Tomb 7 and found in an antechamber objects presumably untouched since their deposit; how this initial probe fanned his hope for an unopened grave; how a flashlight inserted through a hole below brought further confirmation; and how the delighted screams of an assistant, who had squeezed through a narrow breach, quickened his pulse—all belong to one of the spectacular adventures of archaeology. It was a curious counterpart to Carter's discovery of the tomb of Tut-enkhamon.

But while the enormous funerary hoard of the Eighteenth-Dynasty boy pharaoh added very little to our knowledge of Egyptian civilization, at Monte Albán the case was the reverse.

Before the opening of Tomb 7 next to nothing had been known to verify the descriptions by the early Spanish of the skill of Mexican goldsmiths and jewelers. There was the often quoted entry in the journal of Albrecht Dürer, the German Renaissance artist, himself the son and grandson of Nuremberg goldsmiths. In August 1520 he had visited Brussels in the Spanish Netherlands, where golden loot from Mexico, shipped by Cortés to Emperor Charles V, had recently arrived. Dürer wrote: "I have also seen objects brought to the King from the new Land of Gold: a sun all in gold, as much as six feet in diameter, and a moon all in silver, likewise of considerable size; there were two chambers full of armour used by those people, and all kinds of weapons, cuirasses, wondrous shields, strange clothing, bed-clothes, and all manner of curious objects for various purposes, more exquisite than any marvels. All these things were so costly that they are estimated at 100,000 guilders in value. And all my life long I have never seen anything that gave me such delight as did these objects. For among them I have seen wondrous and artistic things, and was amazed at the great ingenuity of this people in foreign lands. And I cannot describe all the things that have been displayed before me there."

One of the *Danzantes* relief figures from the first epoch of Monte Albán

Alas, all of these marvels were melted down. The few pieces that showed up from time to time could convey only a shadowy picture of the artistry that had astonished a Dürer or a Peter Martyr (Anghiera) and enraptured some of the more sensitive Conquistadores like Bernal Díaz del Castillo. In fact such enthusiastic descriptions were frequently discounted in a later age. Hence Caso could now declare: "Not until to-day, with the discovery of Tomb 7, have we been able to form an idea of the great opulence that dazzled the conquerors, and we can affirm that their accounts, which at times seemed exaggerated, conform to, if they are not inferior to, reality." What added further significance to the Monte Albán treasures was the fact that they had been fashioned by the same people whose craftsmen were in the employ of the Aztec rulers and who were probably responsible for the precious articles admired by Dürer.

The variety of the materials worked with such consummate skill—from jade, turquoise, and rock crystal to amber, onyx, alabaster and jet (the latter two never before reported from Mexico)—excited admiration. Yet, as Dr. Caso emphasizes, Monte Albán's riches go far beyond their artistic value. They are of supreme scientific interest. For one thing, they identified the people responsible for the burial as intruders into an already extant Zapotec grave. Caso had no difficulty recognizing them by their style, and particularly the glyphs, as Mixtecs—Nahua-speaking "Cloud People," who for many centuries contested the hegemony of the Zapotecs in southern Mexico. Caso was at first puzzled by their presence in traditionally Zapotec territory. However, his later researches were to make it clear that the Mixtecs gained control over Monte Albán by the early fifteenth century and were in turn subdued by the Aztecs shortly before the arrival of Cortés.

Thus, Monte Albán rewarded Caso with epigraphic material far in excess of the calendrical and numerical notation on Zapotec stelae. With newly discovered pre-Zapotec glyphs, which may have been as old as, if not older than, any Maya initial series, in his grasp and with an unexpected cache of what could well be ancient pre-Columbian documents, he must have felt like Keats's hero "when a new planet swims into his ken." It was the Mixtec epigraphic testimony from Tomb 7 which stimulated his interest in the few surviving pre-Columbian picture manuscripts, the majority of which he now could identify as also of Mixtec origin. From here Caso went on to furnish a decipherment of a group of Mixtec codices. These bewildering picture books yielded unexpected historic details and made of the Mixtec, once one of the most elusive of Mexican races, the best documented of them all. As Caso came to read them they contained a consecutive record of some thousand years going back to A.D. 692.

The discovery of Tomb 7 aroused world-wide attention and produced a flood of popular articles. Wonderstruck throngs milled around the recovered objects when a few months later they were put on exhibit in Mexico City and a number of cities in the United States. There followed a cantankerous episode during which the state of Oaxaca sued the National Museum for absconding with the treasures and forced their extradition to its local museum at Oaxaca City.

The first Monte Albán campaign led to further explorations guided for many years by Dr. Caso. These helped bring order to the 2,000-year-long cultural sequence of the site, which came to be divided into five periods. Of these, Monte Albán III and IV, roughly contemporary with the classical period of Teotihuacán in the Valley of Mexico, are associated with the Zapotecs, while Monte Albán V designates the Mixtec occupation. In the course of the work about 150 tombs—some decorated with fine murals—were excavated by Caso and his assistants. A vast amount of material was collected and interpreted in meticulous publications so that, in the words of Miguel Covarrubias, Monte Albán is today "the most carefully and thoroughly explored and studied site in all of Mexico."

THE TREASURES OF MONTE ALBÁN

Alfonso Caso

The majority of people interested in Mexico know much about the Aztecs and Mayas but very little of the Mixtecs and Zapotecs whose civilizations were in some respects superior and who constituted the link between the peoples of the central plateau and those of Yucatán and Central America.

Three years ago I began to study the Zapotec hieroglyphs and published *Las Esteles Zapotecas* (The Zapotec Stelae). I noted then that there were many elements lacking to reach a definite conclusion on this subject. Hence, with the object of carrying out large-scale investigations, we organized, with the consent of the Department of Monuments of the Mexican Ministry of Education, the first campaign at Monte Albán, which ended in the month of February of this year [1932].

Monte Albán, the archaeological city, is situated on a chain of mountains that borders on the Valley of Oaxaca and rises to 400 meters. An excellent road, constructed by the state government, takes the traveller from Oaxaca City to Monte Albán in 25 minutes.

"Los Hallazgos de Monte Albán—The Finds of Monte Albán," *Mexican Folklore,* VII:3 (July–Sept. 1932), pp. 114–28.

The principal plaza of Monte Albán is a great rectangle, 300 meters long and 200 meters wide, completely surrounded by platforms from which rise pyramids.

The entire mountain was transformed by the ancient Indians and one can clearly see the terraces, walls, and mounds constructed above the tombs.

The first season of our work consisted of exploration of the northern platform and the tombs. After uncovering the great stairway of this platform, we found architectural fragments of great archaeological interest. We explored several tombs, among which No. 7, where the jewels were found, deserves special mention.

We began exploring this tomb on January 6, 1932, and discovered in its upper part the foundations of some small rooms whose floor was formed by a thick layer of stucco. We also found a sort of canal or ditch, about 30 centimeters wide, a feature very characteristic of Zapotec tombs. Days later we picked up a marine shell in an outer room of the tomb, which had been cut at the end to form a mouthpiece and to convert it into a trumpet. Near it were two most handsome strings of jade and two small earrings of the same material. There were no human remains accompanying these treasures.

Inside the tombs of Oaxaca, one frequently finds near the principal burial the bones of a man or a dog in association with various objects. The ancient Mexicans believed that on the journey which the soul had to undertake to reach the kingdom of the dead, it came to a wide river difficult to cross. For that reason they killed a dog to accompany his master on his last journey, believing that its spirit would reach the other side of the river first and that, when the master presented himself, it would throw itself into the water to help him make the shore. The human remains usually encountered near Zapotec burial chambers probably have a similar explanation; they are perhaps of slaves who were killed to accompany their chiefs to the kingdom beyond the grave. When we found the sea shell and jade ornaments, we realized that the tomb below most likely would turn out to be very rich.

Three days later we lifted one of the stones that formed the arch of the crypt and through the narrow opening, lighted by an electric lantern, we saw a human skull. Near it were two vessels, one of which seemed to be of black clay extraordinarily polished. It was a cup of crystal rock, which looked black because of the dirt it contained.

My assistant and I squeezed through the narrow hole with much difficulty. Lighting the area with the electric lamp, we were able to discern splendid treasures. In the middle of the second chamber, we found a white transparent vessel of a sort of marble or *tecali*. On the threshold separating the two chambers and amidst a heap of bones

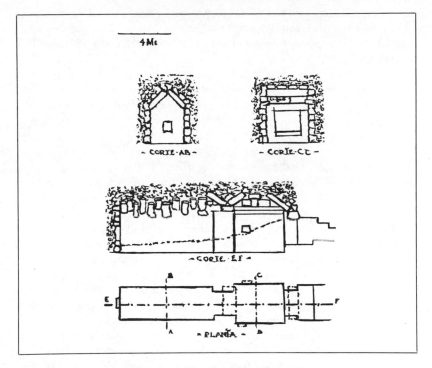

Plan and cross-section of Tomb 7

were bells and other shining objects of gold. Around the arm bones of one of the corpses glittered ten bracelets, six of gold and four of silver.

We also found on the same threshold a massive gold object, probably a belt buckle, which was decorated with the figure of a spider.

Near the door was a golden diadem and close to it a feather which at one time was attached to it. Later we came upon a human skull ornamented with turquoise.

Mixed with the earth were pearls, gold and jade beads, and innumerable little turquoise plaques that once formed mosaics now impossible to reconstruct.

My wife, my two assistants, Martin Bazán and Juan Valenzuela, and some workers and I worked during the whole night and continued discovering real treasures of artistic and scientific value such as had never before been discovered in the Americas.

We worked fourteen hours a day for another week, exploring the tomb, collecting and cataloguing the objects.

Due to the humidity of the tomb and probably to the fact that the dead were buried in a sitting posture, or that these might have been secondary burials, we found heaps of decayed bones. Nothing of wood, cloth, or any other soft material was conserved, so that the beautiful masks and breastplates decorated with turquoise mosaics were invariably ruined.

It is notable that among the articles were only five clay *malacates* (ancient spindle whorls); the rest were all of precious metals.

We counted in all more than 300 objects extracted (and catalogued) from Tomb 7. However, a single item may have included a necklace of gold, pearls, or turquoise, each of which contained hundreds of beads. To be sure, these were restrung by us. We gathered the beads that were found in one pile, washed and strung them. Otherwise, no object has been restored or polished, only freed from the dirt that covered it. In a very few cases we found the beads on their strings. Sometimes the beads were laid out as if they were still forming a necklace.

The vessels are for the most part of *tecali*, a kind of marble from the mountains south of Puebla and north of Oaxaca. There is also a rock crystal goblet and a cup of a natural alloy of silver and gold in the form of a pumpkin, which contained moist earth and a jaguar tooth. The *tecali* vessels were so beautifully polished that their walls were transparent. One of the vessels is formed like a section of a pumpkin and, in spite of its hard material, looks as if it were made of clay, for it appears as if the potter's fingers had molded a dent in the center. Another has ten heads of a sacred animal carved around the base. Still another small one has three legs that end in serpents' heads. The fact that these legs were perforated with drills to make them transparent shows how exquisite the work is.

The rock crystal goblet is perhaps one of the most extraordinary objects to appear in the tomb. It is 14 centimeters high, measures 8 centimeters in diameter, and has walls which are one centimeter thick. Yet, rock crystal is one of the hardest and most difficult materials to work.

So far it has not been possible to determine what the vessels contained, for it would be necessary to make a microscopic analysis of the dirt found in them. Nevertheless, one can surmise [the nature of the original contents] since the first Spaniards who wrote on Indian subjects say that it was the custom to bury the dead with food and drink which were to sustain them on their journey beyond the grave.

The Mixtecs worked other hard stones besides rock crystal. In Tomb 7 we discovered objects made of obsidian, a volcanic glass, which is exceedingly difficult to fashion.

The earrings from the tomb are of a round type similar to spools, with wide outer edges. The Indians inserted these in their ear lobes.

Holes were made in childhood so that they might gradually be widened until pieces up to five or six centimeters in diameter could be inserted. The lobe around such pieces turned into just a strip of flesh. Earrings made of obsidian were shaped in such a way that they were as thin as paper and completely transparent.

The small obsidian knives found in the tomb were used by the priests for the auto-sacrifices they practiced to extract blood from their bodies, which they afterwards offered to the gods. Some engraved bone points, also present in Tomb 7, were used for the same purpose.

Strange as it may seem, among all the objects taken from this tomb, a copper axe was the only one that might qualify as a weapon, which would indicate that the personages buried there were kings and priests rather than warriors.

Jade pieces were numerous and varied. They included a fan handle in the form of a serpent, three rings, a beautiful bird's head with golden eyes, an eagle's head with a gold plaque on its back which served as a lip adornment, several pendants (one of them in the form of a turtle shell), earrings, and a great many beads that made up several necklaces, among which stood out an admirable, almost white, string of jade, formed by three large rectangular beads that alternated with globular ones.

Metal objects we excavated were of gold, silver, and copper—the only metals the ancient Mexican Indians knew. In working them they employed such varied processes as casting, filigree, hammering "in the cold," and polishing.

A gold pectoral made to represent a Jaguar Knight deserves special mention. It shows a human head, which wears a jaguar helmet adorned with feathers of golden threads. Over the mouth is a mask in the form of a fleshless jaw; the cords that hold it in place can be clearly seen passing below the nose. In the ears are disks ending in projecting serpents and on the chest rests a necklace with a little bird as pendant. If the artistic merit of this object is noteworthy, its scientific value is no less so, the reason being that in the plaques below the god's image there appear two dates. These are expressed by a symbol resembling the interlaced letters A and O, which is the Mixtec year sign. There are two distinct hieroglyphs to the right and two to the left. They are joined with the year symbol and a series of numerical dots: ten in the right plaque and eleven in the left, with still another small symbol to which are added two dots.

The complete reading of this inscription on the breastplate would be the following: "Year 10-wind, day 8-flint-knife. Year 11-house." In my opinion this means that the year which the Mixtecs called 11-house was the same as the one the Zapotecs named 10-wind. The golden pectoral thus helps to prove that the jewels of the tomb were Mixtec, for the Zapotecs and Mexicans never used the symbol A–O to represent the year. . . .

One of the most beautiful of the golden articles is a tiny mask, 8 centimeters high, depicting the head of the god Xipe Totec, "Our Lord, the Skinned One" [who was worshipped in the image of a human sacrifice].

In one of the bloody rites to make the earth yield fruit, one of the sacrificed slaves was skinned and a priest then dressed in the skin. The little mask shows the skin of the flayed slave as well as the open eyes and half-open mouth [of the god] and cords at both sides of the head to hold up the skin.

Xipe Totec was the god of vegetation, of corn, and of the jewelers who worked in turquoise mosaics, because the corn cob is a natural mosaic. He was also a god of the goldsmiths, who plated diverse objects with gold foil, just as the priest covered himself with the skin of a sacrificed slave.

One of the gold objects that attracted most attention was a diadem, decorated with a large feather of the same metal. Common warriors used red leather bands to hold up their hair and adorned them with eagle feathers; but the nobleman buried in Tomb 7 of Monte Albán, due to his high rank, used instead a diadem with golden feathers. . . .

The only mosaic conserved, although greatly damaged, is the one that was done on a human skull. The skull probably belonged to a warrior captured and sacrificed by the Mixtecs. It was thus used as a macabre war trophy, with its top perforated and painted red inside. The turquoise mosaic was afterwards stuck on with a paste made principally from copal and plant seeds. A "flint knife" of shell was inserted in the nose of the skull.

The carved bones will be of vital importance to the study of the history, the writing, and the mythology of the Mixtec people. These bones are probably of a large animal, perhaps a jaguar or deer, and their use is still a mystery to me. They are carved in high relief and the work is so exquisite that it is not surpassed by the best Chinese and Hindu productions in ivory. Many of them had their background encrusted with turquoise, which made the design stand out strongly. Some may have served as picks for the auto-sacrifices of the priests.

Two of these bones represent the first thirteenth part of the calendar. The symbols of the days are exactly like those that appear in the Mixtec manuscripts that have come down to us and are entirely different from the signs used by the Zapotecs and Mayas in their writings. Once again this proves that the objects found in Tomb 7 belonged to the Mixtec civilization.

Another bone represents the birth of a child, probably a very important personage. On it is seen a boy who descends from the thirteenth heaven via the sacred tree. In front of him are seated various persons, each with his hand on the shoulder of the one in front, thus indicating their genealogical line. The bone is dated, and in subsequent investigations I hope to determine the date.

In addition to the objects recovered from the surface of the soil which covered the main tomb, there appeared in the same layer, but deeper, little vessels and the fragment of a clay urn, all characteristically Zapotec. . . . I believe, therefore, that Tomb 7 was made use of on two occasions: first by the Zapotecs who constructed it and later by the Mixtecs who removed the corpses and most of the objects that were in the tomb. After completely covering the entrance, they left through the roof, while closing the exit by means of a stone with Zapotec inscriptions, which had been used in the first burial to seal the entrance.

It will now be our task to find out why the Mixtecs buried their lords in this Zapotec tomb, and to determine who the dead were. The very precious jewels with which they were adorned are a sign of their rank.

Its monuments and tombs clearly establish Monte Albán as a Zapotec metropolis. Thus a burial of Mixtec nobles in this city presents a real puzzle. Were they perhaps Mixtec princes whom the Zapotecs ambushed or killed in battle?

When opening in October my second season of explorations at Monte Albán, I hope to gather further evidence. I may well discover other tombs as rich in precious objects as No. 7.

Mixtec glyphs indicating place names, from the carved bones of Tomb 7

17

As in the Old World, archaeology in the Americas pushes backward into the past while it peels off layer after layer of human manifestations. At the outset it all seemed very simple. In Mexico there were the Aztecs (no one had heard of the Mayas at the beginning of the nineteenth century) and Chichimecs and the half-mythical Toltecs, to whom one could ascribe most of the monuments or relics above and below the ground. After them one was bound to hit rock bottom. Yet in the process of exhuming the artifacts of known peoples, invariably older, hitherto unknown civilizations made their appearance. Further divisions of historic and prehistoric time became necessary. Antecedents had their antecedents. Thus the builders of Teotihuacán in the Valley of Mexico and of Tajín on the Gulf Coast, and the Mixtecs and Zapotecs in southern Mexico, came into their own. Each in turn, for a brief moment in scholarship, might enjoy the reputation of having evolved the arts of civilization all on their own in this part of the globe, only to have their exalted position just as quickly challenged. Some like the Maya or Zapotecs may retain their diehard champions even today, but the majority of archaeologists prefer to look upon all of them as creative participants in a common Mesoamerican heritage rather than as the individual inventors of writing, the calendar, or the priestly state with its magnificent ceremonial cities.

At the ancient temple center of Monte Albán, Alfonso Caso, as we have seen, learned to distinguish glyphs and sculptures which deviated from the familiar style of the Zapotecs and could be attributed to previous settlers of a remote age. But who were this mysterious race? Had they chiseled the floating and misshapen bodies of the negroid *Danzantes* in their own image? Had they left traces elsewhere in Mexico? Where had they come from? Had they been the first to use a hiero-glyphic script and to record dates?

It so happened that an interesting hypothesis based on varied and up till then unclassifiable materials was proposed only a few years after Caso had begun his explorations at Monte Albán. Originally inspired by a small jadeite statuette in the collection of the American Museum of Natural History, it took in a vast territory of scattered Mexican cultural phenomena, including pre-Zapotec Monte Albán, and grew into an all-embracing theory of the origin of the great Mesoamerican civilizations. It meant the sudden emergence of the so-called "Olmecs," a most shadowy people of uncertain name, race, language or domicile, who were conjured up from limbo and became Sumerians of the Americas.

The resurrection of the "Olmecs"—though perhaps an inevitable phase in Mexicanist research—was initiated by George Clapp Vaillant (1901–45) in an ingenious piece of what one may term speculative archaeology. That is to say it depended for its insight on the analysis and synthesis of existing evidence followed by bold conclusions rather than on actual sifting of the soil. As such it is a notable example of how archaeology may be advanced by other avenues than the dirt road.

Significantly the man who made this contribution was not one to spin idle theories in an academic vacuum. He had been chiefly responsible for putting the stratigraphy of central Mexico on a sound basis through his painstaking excavations (1928–36) at such sites as Zacatenco, Ticomán, and El Arbolillo in the Valley of Mexico. As a result of his pioneer work he was able to replace the crude scheme of Aztec-Toltec-Archaic with a detailed, concrete scale which outlined sixteen centuries of civilization in central Mexico and laid the basis for the chronological sequences and cultural horizons now recognized in the pre-Columbian pre-history of Mexico. By the same token, Vaillant's crossdating of the ceramics of Cuicuilco with those he had excavated at Ticomán put once and for all an end to the claims for Cuicuilco's fantastic age. Though the systematic stratigraphy of central Mexico was his most notable achievement, Vaillant, who had begun his active career in Mesoamerica on expeditions to Chichen Itzá in Yucatán (he served his archaeological apprenticeship in Egypt and Carthage), also concerned himself with similar problems in Maya antiquity. His associates were particularly impressed by his unerring "flair" for appreciating and relating styles of art from many epochs. No doubt his identification of the "Olmecs" owes much to such sensibilities.

When Vaillant died by his own hand at the age of forty-five, he was at the peak of his career, with an international reputation as a scholar. He was equally effective as university teacher and museum administrator. The United States government selected him to be its Cultural Relations officer in Peru in 1943. Shortly before his death he was appointed to the same office in Madrid.

In addition to monographs on his stratigraphic field studies, Vaillant contributed articles on various aspects of American archaeology written with the breadth and literary grace of a true humanist. One of his essays, "A Bearded Mystery" (1931), is another example of archaeological detective work; it anticipated some of the deductions made a year later in an article on the "Olmecs." In "Hidden History" (1933) he elucidated the Mexican occupation of Chichen Itzá. His *Aztecs of Mexico* (1941), which earned him an honorary professorship from the National Museum of Mexico, has become a classic, even though advances—often inspired by his researches—have made his equation of Teotihuacán with the Toltecs obsolete. The book has been updated in a 1962 edition by Vaillant's widow, Suzannah Beck Vaillant, who had assisted him on many campaigns.

A RIDDLE IN JADE

George C. Vaillant

The little jade tiger or ocelot now among the treasures of the Mexican Hall in the American Museum [of Natural History] fulfills two great imaginative requirements, charm and mystery. Although perhaps not beautiful from the point of view of the European aesthetic, its minute grandeur and the consummate excellence of its sculptural technique prove to the most untrained eye that the tiger is a masterpiece of the jade worker's art. To the curious who ponder on its origin and on the identity of its makers there opens through the unmapped jungles of Mexican prehistory a tortuous path toward an unknown destination. There is drama, too, in the details of the jade's discovery, since the rôle Chance plays in archaeological discovery is thrust forward so prominently.

The tiger was found in 1909 during the construction of a dam for the great power plant at Necaxa in the mountains of northeastern Puebla.

"A Pre-Columbian Jade," *Natural History*, XXXII:6 (Nov.–Dec. 1932), pp. 512–20, 557–58.

An American engineer engaged in destroying a mound by hydraulic pressure noticed something shining in the mud sluiced out by the powerful stream. On investigation this object turned out to be the tiger, but the engineer had no time to search further, for the water behind the dam was rising fast. Sixty feet of it now cover the site of the discovery.

The engineer returned to San Antonio the next year and took the tiger with him. Except for a newspaper article in a San Antonio paper and the comments of those who had seen it, nothing further was known of the jade until 1932, when the owner died and his widow offered it for sale. There was great danger that the piece might fall into private hands and perhaps be lost to archaeology, particularly as the specimen was thought to be Chinese. But with generous foresight Mrs. Payne Whitney, Mrs. Charles S. Payson, and Mr. John Hay Whitney acquired the tiger and presented it to the American Museum, thereby preserving it forever, accessible to layman and student alike.

Head with typical Olmec "tiger" features, from Morelos, central Mexico

Although a glance at the photographs or at the specimen itself will show the figure's artistic worth, a brief analytical description will be necessary to show its historical importance.

The tiger, properly speaking ocelot or jaguar, is of sea-green jade and measures three and one quarter inches high by two inches basal diameter. The jade is of the New World variety, quite distinct from the Asiatic, and the cutting was achieved by the rude abrasives of the pre-Columbian Americans, who had no metal tools suitable for the task. Three holes at the base and one at the top suggest that the tiger was attached vertically to a headdress or a sceptre, and not suspended as a pendant. The presentation is theological rather than zoological for, although the posture and the teeth are naturalistic, the arms and face are humanized, and such details of adornment are shown as a sash, headdress, wristlets, and a necklace. The back of the head, moreover, is divided by a groove which might be the parting of the hair, or else may have ceremonial significance. Faces engraved in profile on either cheek may represent tattooing, but other designs inscribed on the chest indicate perhaps a gorget. On the back of the figure a small glyph is drawn that although possibly decorative, might also be its name.

If the tiger represents a divinity as all these human attributes suggest, it should be possible to identify it. The grave difficulty obtrudes, however, that although we have considerable data on the nature of the Maya, Zapotec, and Nahua gods, we have no such information for the Vera Cruz region where this object was found. Such great authorities as Madame Zelia Nuttall and Professor Saville incline to place the tiger in Aztec theology as a representation or aspect of the god Tezcatlipoca, the "Flaming Mirror," one of the chief divinities in that religion. Professor Seler, however, in his commentary on the Codex Fejervary-Mayer, describes the Mixtec god Tepeyollotli, God of the Mountains, as having sometimes the guise of the tiger or ocelot and at other times the attributes of Tezcatlipoca. Since the Mixtec region borders on central Vera Cruz and since tiger gods are quite often shown in Mixtec codices, such an identification has much to commend it. In the adjacent Zapotec region, moreover, funerary urns in the shape of tigers are commonly found. However, to assign the name of a divinity to this jade tiger, when we are by no means sure from which of the Mexican civilizations it emanated, can only be defended by the thesis of the homogeneity of Mexican religion, and that thesis is a controversial one. Let us therefore examine the stylistic evidence for the origin of this specimen.

Plastically the tiger belongs to a group of sculptures which all exhibit the same features, a snarling tiger mouth surmounted by a flat pugnose and oblique eyes. Often the back of the head is notched like our specimen. The great jade axe, on exhibition in the Mexican Hall and one of the largest from the New World, is a notable representative of the type. Professor Saville in his paper "Votive Axes from Ancient Mexico" divides these "tiger-face" sculptures into two classes, votive axes like our great jade, and statues and reliefs like the tiger. The geographical distribution of these carvings centers around southern Vera Cruz, southern Puebla, and northern Oaxaca.

This "tiger-face" class tends to merge with a group of carvings which, although having infantile features, retain the contorted mouth of the tiger sculptures. One of these "baby-faces," a jade bead from Chiapas, makes a definite link, for on its cheeks are inscribed the same designs as on those of the Necaxa specimen, a "tiger-face" in profile. The "baby-faces" cover the same geographical range as the tiger but in addition several examples emanate from Chiapas and Guerrero. In the excavations carried on by the Museum last winter at Cuernavaca, Morelos, a clay "baby-face" was found under early circumstances, which might well be a prototype of the two groups just discussed.

So far we have dealt with art styles but now we must consider representations of a racial group, characterized by flat noses, oblique eyes, low foreheads, and often beards. I have described a number of such examples in "A Bearded Mystery." The relation of this physical type to the "tiger-face" sculpture is dramatically shown by the gold pectoral from Tajín near Papantla in Central Vera Cruz. This place is only two days on horseback from Necaxa, the source of the jade tiger.

When a physical type can be linked to an art style there is strong likelihood that we are dealing with the makers of that style. It sometimes happens that people take as national symbols those animals most resembling them in appearance or psychology, as for example the British and their bull dog. The sculptures listed in the article on bearded men might be taken as internal evidence of their existence, but strengthening this idea are two paintings that show them in contact with other peoples. One of these is the painting on the celebrated Chamá vase where a number of Mayas are shown receiving a flat-nosed bearded ambassador.

Chamá vase, from a grave in Chamá, Guatemala

The other is one of the murals at the Temple of the Warriors at Chichen Itzá, where the Mexican inhabitants of Chichen are shown giving a resounding beating to a group of flat-nosed tribesmen, some of whom have whiskers. Reused stones in Zapotec buildings in Monte Albán depict the flat-nosed type with and without beards, and indicate that before the arrival of the Zapotecs, these people had established themselves there. The area within which bearded figures occur is so much greater than that occupied by the "tiger-face" and "baby-face" sculptures, that it seems possible the bearded flat-nosed people may have been driven back through the rise of the Nahua and Maya tribes in early times and later achieved their artistic evolution in the Vera Cruz-Oaxaca-Puebla region.

However, not all bearded figures have flat noses. A leptorrhine type of bearded figures is shown on sculptures at Santa Lucia Cosumalhuapa in southern Guatemala, others appear on stelae at Seibal and Yaxchilán, and ceremonial vases of lustrous plumbate ware, which was traded from Salvador throughout Guatemala and Mexico, often depict the Old God and the Rain God as bearded. High-nosed bearded figures occur in carvings in the Mexican buildings at Chichen Itzá and on some of the Zapotec stelae at Monte Albán. Perhaps in these cases divinities are represented, for in the Mixtec group of codices, Quetzalcoatl, and Ehecatl, the wind god who often doubles for the former, are shown with beards. Moreover, Tepeyollotli, the God of the Mountains, when not in tiger form, is usually bearded. It is very curious that according to Nahua mythology these gods are associated with the east and south, the directions from the Valley of Mexico where lie the Vera Cruz-Oaxaca-Puebla areas.

Fragment of an Olmecoid "baby-faced" figurine

Now it sometimes happens that bygone peoples are transmuted by folk-lore into mythological beings, even as Andrew Lang suggested that the dwarfs and giants of Europe may have had their origin in the wild folk driven back into the mountains with the growth of civilization. Moreover, in Mexico we find the Toltecs, who preceded the Aztecs in the Valley of Mexico, endowed by their successors with almost super-natural skills in the arts. Perhaps in the same way the bearded people were thus considered, and certain of their chieftains or even mayhap their gods were absorbed into the Nahua pantheon.

Supposing that this condition were true, we might examine the list of peoples given in the semi-mythical histories of the Nahua tribes, and by the process of elimination decide which of these is not linked to a defined material civilization. We know the art styles of the Aztec, the Toltec, the Zapotec, perhaps the Totonac, and certainly the Maya. But there is often described in the traditions a highly civilized people called the Olmec, who lived anciently as far north as Tlaxcala, but were later dispersed to southern Vera Cruz, Chiapas, southern Puebla, and eastern Oaxaca. They were famed for their work in jade and turquoise, and were credited with being the chief users of rubber in Central America.

The geographical position of these people roughly coincides with the distribution of the "tiger-face" and "baby-face" sculptures and they could have been in contact with Nahua tribes to the north, Zapotec to the west, the central Maya to the southwest, and the Maya and Mexican populations of Yucatán to the southeast. However, no material culture has been assigned to these Olmec.

Thus in view of an art style which is foreign to the defined civilizations, a geographical situation roughly conterminous with the centers of distribution of the art styles, and a historical position which is relatively early, it would seem that the Olmec fulfill very well the requirements for the peculiar art styles we have been discussing. Moreover, Professor Saville in his paper on "Votive Axes" lends his authority to the suggestion.

No formal excavation has been undertaken in the Olmec area and we know nothing of their beginnings nor of their relations to other cultures. The Olmecs move like shadows across the pages of Mexican history; a few notices that there were such people, a few delineations of a physical type foreign to the racial features of the known peoples like the Maya, and a handful of sculptures out of the known artistic traditions comprise the testimony of their existence. Perhaps investigation in the Olmec area would clarify the much discussed relationship between the Mexicans and the Mayas, or even reveal the origin of the great theocracies that gave Central America its civilization.

The little tiger of jade, therefore, well deserves its place of honor. Its artistic excellence can be seen by comparing it with . . . more famous jades . . .; its historical implications are sketched in the preceding pages; and its romance lies in the circumstances of its discovery and the mystery surrounding its makers.

18

Grotesque relief sculptures in rhythmic poses from the oldest phase of Monte Albán; beautifully carved jadeite celts and axes representing half-jaguar and half-human monsters occurring from the Valley of Mexico to as far as Guatemala and Costa Rica; sexless, baby-faced clay figurines and bearded snub-nosed masks from central and southern Mexico; a tiny effigy of a duck-billed sage carrying a date older than any Maya count and originating from a non-Maya site—these were typical of the strange artifacts that were increasingly coming to scholars' attention. They did not seem to fit into any known pre-Columbian tradition. Despite their astounding artistic finish and considerable subtlety they pointed to great antiquity. All of them also shared, as George Vaillant was the first to perceive clearly, a basic kinship of style.

When Vaillant traced the craftsmen of these powerful pieces to "type sites" in the lowlands of the Gulf of Mexico in the state of Veracruz and northwest of the territories occupied by the Mayas, no systematic excavation had ever been carried out in the tropical jungles. However, giant heads and other colossal sculptures scattered at several coastal sites had been occasionally reported. A Mexican engineer had been startled in the late 1860's by their "Ethiopian" features. Around the turn of the century, a German savant, Eduard Seler, and his wife went down to the Veracruz region on an archaeological junket to examine the rumored remains. The celebrated Tuxtla statuette of a man in duck disguise was found in 1902 at Hueyapán near Tres Zapotes and was shortly after acquired by the U.S. National Museum (Smithsonian Institution) in Washington. It caused much comment. But it was a Tulane University expedition in 1925, led by Frans Blom and Oliver La Farge, that gave the first reliable account of a major temple city at La Venta (already mentioned by Charnay in 1887), an island in the coastal swamps of western Tabasco. Though the Tulane scholars spent only a single day there and had no time to excavate, they took photographs of mounds and stelae.

Beginning in 1938 at Tres Zapotes and followed by campaigns at La Venta, Cerro de las Mesas, and San Lorenzo, Matthew W. Stirling truly inaugurated the archaeological history of the Gulf area. Tres Zapotes alone yielded four of the enormous sculptured faces of young men, weighing some fifteen and more tons each and exhibiting an unusual racial type with thick lips, broad noses, and Mongoloid eyes, wearing head bands which looked like helmets. They bore an uncanny resemblance to twentieth-century American football players. Their realism was as surprising as their bulk and masterly execution. Stelae and altars of equally huge dimensions in low and high relief helped to confirm the opinion that one dealt here with some of the outstanding sculptures of the continent which could be ranked with anything produced by Old World antiquity.

Giant "Ethiopian" granite head from Gulf of Mexico,
after a nineteenth-century engraving

Stirling at first took these monuments as signs that Maya civilization had reached much farther into the central coastland of Mexico than previously assumed. The date column he found on a broken Tres Zapotes stone slab, then by far the most ancient inscribed date in the Americas (21 B.C. according to the most reliable scale), was to him a further extension of the Maya record. But as time passed associations with "Olmec" characteristics became ever more obvious. The stelae displayed a profusion of sexless figures with the same pudgy, high-domed baby faces with snarling trapezoid jaguar mouths, low broad noses, and swollen eyelids known from jadeite effigies. Indeed, diminutive figures in hard greenish and blueish stone, such as those familiar from other parts of Mexico, were to turn up in increasing number. Just as the bearded type and smooth babyish faces had been previously observed at central Mexican sites, so these facial characteristics of the "Olmec" tradition were now found to be prominently represented at the Gulf locations. On occasion, the bearded type lost all resemblance to the customary bulgy-eyed chubby look remindful of Greek satyrs, but were distinguished by beaked Armenoid noses, profuse mustaches, and flowing beards that gave them an entirely non-Indian appearance. One such figure looked to the expedition staff like the spitting image of Mephistopheles in a slick operatic production. Needless to say, the Caucasoid type rekindled the worn-out twaddle about pre-Columbian landings of white men, or, at least, tales of a superior group of light-skinned bearded rulers and conquerors. Unfortunately most such fantasies are oblivious of the racial heterogeneity of the American aboriginals among whom, as with the Ainus of Japan, the hirsute stock may be even older than the Mongolian. Spaniards landing in Panama noted that the natives sported finer beards than they had themselves. Pure-breed bearded Indians were met by explorers among the Taironas in northern Colombia. Nordenskiöld described them in the southern Andes of Bolivia.

Stirling's discoveries stirred mightily the minds of Mexicanists. In the face of such impressive testimonies, the "Olmec Problem" became pivotal to all discussions of Mesoamerican archaeology. It was especially disturbing to Maya scholars, some of whom had fervently maintained that all the higher achievements were the original creations of these supremely gifted "Greeks of the New World." What was one to make of the fact that the oldest temple at Uaxactún in the Maya "Old Empire" was decorated in unmistakably "Olmec" style, or that the oldest date inscription then known was carved in the bar and dot system on a monument outside Maya territory? One way out was to challenge Stirling's reading of the date since the stela was broken. Also, the date could conceivably have been carved retroactively to commemorate an earlier event. And then there was the possibility that the "Olmecs" themselves were of Maya language and race. But how was one to explain the dissemination and distinctiveness of the "Olmec" style? Did it not appear before the efflorescence of the great ceremonial centers of the classical age at Teotihuacán and Tikal? Could not the temples, altars, stelae, and pyramids of La Venta or Tres Zapotes have served as models of the former? And what part did the "Olmec" intrusions into the more primitive pre-classical cultures of central Mexico play? Were there any primary sources for the extraordinary techniques and artistic finesse of these people? Who indeed *were* the "Olmecs," and where did they originate? Were they the one great founding civilization of Mesoamerica? What were the actual meanings of such strange features as snarling jaguar men, baby faces, human freaks, and bearded strangers?

In the train of Stirling's discoveries, the Mexican Society of Anthropology organized two round table conferences dedicated to the *Enigma de los Olmecas*. They found the very term "Olmec" misleading and proposed the adoption of "La Venta" for the mysterious culture. But they

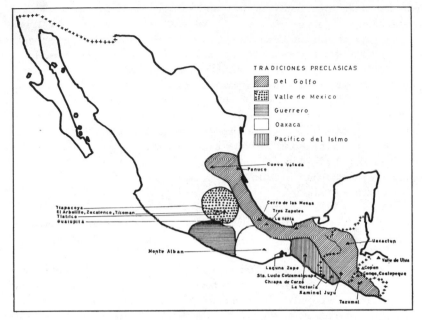

TRADICIONES PRECLASICAS

Del Golfo
Valle de Mexico
Guerrero
Oaxaca
Pacifico del Istmo

Distribution of Olmec "infantile" sculpture in pre-classic Mesoamerica

made little headway apart from outlining crucial problems. Presented with so many disturbing questions and hopelessly inadequate material, Miguel Covarrubias commented that the riddle of "Olmec" archaeology had "grown so complex that it is just short of incomprehensible even to most archeologists, who handle it with the repugnance with which they would handle a rattlesnake." *Mutatis mutandis,* the observation still stands.

Meanwhile, even before excavation of "Olmec" type sites at the Gulf Coast had gotten under way, Covarrubias, a noted Mexican caricaturist, connoisseur, and collector, had been pursuing traces of the "Olmec" style on his own. His attention and that of fellow artists had been drawn for some time to brickyards at Tlatilco outside Mexico City. There the workers had come up with unusually fine pottery and figurines as well as occasional pieces of jade. Covarrubias and his friends made a habit of visiting the place regularly and acquiring exquisite specimens for a song. Most of the objects were of pure Zacatenco peasant style—according to Vaillant the oldest of the valley. But among the more or less common run of "archaic" ceramics were strewn artifacts of considerably greater refinement. They were of the same "Olmec" characteristics as the objects singled out by Vaillant.

The contemporaneity of two such divergent elements—Zacatenco and "Olmec"—in very ancient layers set Covarrubias on edge. When Tres Zapotes and La Venta emerged, he hastened to study the evidence there. The visit led him into a thorough investigation, summarized in the following selection. It also helped to turn him into an active archaeologist, who was to carry out systematic excavations at Tlatilco in 1942 and from 1947 to 1949. In the course of these campaigns he uncovered more than two hundred burials. Out of the work, in turn, grew Covarrubias' re-examination of the pre-classical stratigraphy of the Valley of Mexico. With the aid of carbon-14 dating methods, he was able to suggest for Tlatilco and its Zacatenco-"Olmec" elements an antiquity reaching into the second millennium B.C. and going far beyond Vaillant's conservative estimates.

In an age in which archaeology has become increasingly the precinct of university-educated specialists, Covarrubias was that *rara avis,* an amateur who became a recognized expert and who by his brilliant insights left a lasting influence.

There could not have been a greater difference in background and training than between Vaillant, the Harvard-educated scientist, and Covarrubias, a popular Mexican artist of little schooling who in his early twenties became overnight a New York celebrity when he appeared as the elegant caricaturist for *Vanity Fair.* Yet the two men had much the same unfailing grasp of style, just as their archaeological interests covered surprisingly similar ground. Like Vaillant's, Covarrubias' understanding of American antiquity ranged over most of the hemisphere and was nourished by a profound anthropological knowledge. His life too was cut short before he could complete his three-volume survey of pre-Columbian art from Alaska to Patagonia.

Covarrubias' absorption in archaeology may have had its beginnings in his enthusiasm for folk art, which he pursued even after his caricatures, set designs, and paintings brought him fame and success in the United States. In New York he delighted in sketching the Negroes of Harlem. His first serious book was on the *Islands of Bali* (1937) and combined ethnology with sympathetic reporting and the author's own illustrations. In a mural for the San Francisco Golden Gate International Exposition (1939–40) depicting the achievements of the various peoples of the Pacific, he showed his encyclopedic command of anthropological and geographical subjects of many lands. This project and his stay in Bali converted him to belief in trans-Pacific contacts and the overall importance of cultural exchange in the pre-Columbian world. The trans-Pacific problem is dealt with at length in his later writings, which include some of the most incisive expositions of the controversial issue, even though a friendly critic commented that he "talked too much, knew too much, and felt too deeply" about it.

With regard to the "Olmecs," Covarrubias felt as intensely. Where other scholars feared to tread, he marched boldly through the jungle and recruited friends to join him in the pursuit of the subject. While North American scholars held out for a late classical date of "Olmec" civilization, Covarrubias was in the forefront of those who insisted that La Venta was pre-classic, i.e., about 800 to 400 B.C. Later testimony from carbon dates fully bore him out. On the survival of "Olmec" style into consecutive ages, such as his suggestion that the classical iconography of the rain god Tlaloc originated in "Olmec" baby-faces, his observations were novel and acute. His view that the great ceremonial sites of La Venta and Tres Zapotes were probably later developments and adaptations of traits already current much earlier at Tlatilco won only limited acceptance, however. "Olmec" culture, he held, may well have spread from the Pacific area in the state of Guerrero in western Mexico, where the primitive art of Mezcala (first described by Covarrubias) shows surprising affinities with the "Olmecs." He also thought it likely that the original "Olmecs" were associated with the Mixtecs rather than the Mayas. Covarrubias bequeathed his own unsurpassed collection of Olmec art to the Mexican nation.

Since the death of Covarrubias in 1957 we have not come any closer to a solution of the "Olmec Puzzle." While some scholars have now embraced the dogma that the "Olmecs" contributed all the main ingredients of Mesoamerican civilization and that they are, indeed, autochthonous to the Gulf Coast, others are less certain. The "Olmecs" after all are an archaeological abstraction of recent times: Whether there ever existed one such cohesive group of a clearcut racial and linguistic, if not political, identity may well be argued, even if the ubiquity, forcefulness, and impact (from Peru to the Ohio) of the "Olmec" style seems beyond dispute.

COLOSSAL HEADS AND JAGUAR GODS

Miguel Covarrubias

Even today the Indians regard the jaguar with superstitious awe; subconsciously they refer to it as The Jaguar, not as one of a species, but as a sort of supernatural, fearsome spirit. Immediately after the Conquest of Mexico, Friar Sahagun wrote of the jaguar with the naïveté and candor of his Indian informants, describing it as a pleasure-loving, lazy animal endowed with supernatural powers and an almost human cunning. The jaguar was believed to hypnotize his victims with "hiccups (hipo), the air of which rendered the prey's heart faint"—paralyzed with fear. Sahagun wrote that the Indian hunter upon meeting a jaguar in the forest knew he could shoot no more than four arrows at the animal, which the jaguar would catch in the air and break with his teeth. Should the Indian miss a fourth time, he knew he was beaten; the jaguar would then stretch leisurely, lick his chops, snarl viciously and take a gigantic leap, killing the helpless Indian. Friar Las Casas relates that meeting a jaguar in the forest, the Indians of Vera Paz, Guatemala, fell to their knees, began confessing their sins and were naturally devoured.

In those days the ancient jaguar cult prevailed throughout Southern Mexico and in Central America, superimposed upon the formal, official Indian religion. After the Conquest it took the form of politic-religious secret societies called *Nahualistas,* from *nawal,* totem. The word *nawal* or *nahual* is today the name of a sort of werewolf, a weretiger, to frighten children who won't go to sleep. The *Nahualistas* were much like the criminal secret societies of the African Tiger-men, to quote Sahagun again: "people like assassins, daring and accustomed to kill, they carried on their persons pieces of jaguar skin, of the forehead, chest and the tips of the tail, the claws, the canines and the lips to make them powerful, brave and fearsome. . . ." Chieftains who wanted to be courageous ate jaguar flesh roasted or boiled. It was a cure for insanity, for fevers and "to cool off the temptations of the flesh."

In ancient times the jaguar was an earth god, symbol of the interior of the earth and of the night, of darkness, because jaguars were believed to swallow the sun and cause eclipses. He was the god of caves, the dark interior of mountains, the "Atlantean god of earthquakes who

From *Mexico South, the Isthmus of Tehuantepec,* by Miguel Covarrubias, pp. 7–101. Copyright © 1946 by Alfred A. Knopf, Inc. Reprinted by permission of the publisher. [Originally published as "Colossal Heads and Jaguar Gods," *Dyn,* No. 6 (1944), pp. 24–33.]

supported the world upon his shoulders." As such, he was worshipped throughout Southern Mexico and particularly around Tehuantepec. The Mayas of Chiapas called him Uotan, "Heart," "Innermost"; the Mexicans knew him as *Tepeyollotl,* "Heart of the mountain," "Heart of the land," and worshipped him second-hand, having acquired him from the tropical south, along with the religious magic calendar, where he ruled over the third week as an ominous, unlucky sign.

The "Heart of the Land" had a sanctuary inside a great cave on the small wooded island of Monopoxtiac on the Tehuantepec lagoons, and such was the fearful reverence with which the Indians regarded the Jaguar God, that the Zapotec King brought him secret offerings, even after he was converted to Catholicism.

Jaguar, after Dresden Codex

The Heart-Jaguar had other important national cave-sanctuaries. Of the cave of Achiotlán, Friar Burgoa tells a remarkable tale. "There was," he writes, "among other altars, one of an idol they called 'Heart of the Land' which received great honor. The material was of marvelous value, for it was an emerald (clear green jade) the size of a thick pepper pod upon which were engraved with greatest skill a small bird and a little serpent ready to strike. The stone was so transparent it shone from within with the brightness of a flame. . . . The first missionary of Achiotlán, Fray Benito, afterwards visited the sanctuary and succeeded in persuading the Indians to surrender the idol to him. He had it ground to powder, although a Spaniard had offered him 3,000 ducats for it, and he poured the dust on the earth and trod upon it to destroy the heathen abomination and to show in the sight of all the impotence of the idol. . . ."

A great and mysterious race of artists seems to have lived since early times on the Isthmus, particularly around Los Tuxtlas and the Coatzacoalcos River Basin. Everywhere there are archeological treasures that lie hidden in the jungles and under the rich soil of southern Veracruz—

burial mounds and pyramids, masterfully carved colossal monuments of basalt, splendid statuettes of precious jade, and sensitively modelled figurines of clay—all of an unprecedented high artistic quality. The tantalizing presence of a great and remote past in what is now uninhabited, impenetrable jungle, is all the more puzzling since most archeologists now agree that many of these artistic masterpieces date back to the beginnings of the Christian era. Appearing suddenly out of nowhere in a state of full development, they constitute a culture that seems to have been the root, the mother culture from which the later and better known (Maya, Totonac, Zapotec, etc.) cultures sprang.

This oldest of native American high cultures is also the newest, since it was "discovered" only a few years ago and still awaits exhaustive scientific study. Our interest in this culture began back in the days before motor roads and tourists, when we used to explore the countryside in search of pre-Spanish antiquities that the peasants dug up in their fields. On one occasion, in Iguala, State of Guerrero, we acquired an intriguing statuette in shiny black serpentine: a monstrous baby or dwarf born without a lower jaw, his head thrown back in an expression of tortured anguish, showing a realistic windpipe that emerged between the collar-bones and terminated in a puckered mouth, between two puffed, squirrel cheeks. The two fragments forming the statuette were found at places and times far apart, and the fractures were ancient, the head more eroded than the body. A hole drilled in the stump of the missing leg showed that an effort had been made to repair it.

Later we found more such figurines, in various parts of southern Mexico, hunchbacked or clubfooted, and one with a hand to his ear as if he were deaf. There were many other objects in museums and private collections, in blue-green jade, serpentine, and common stone, all so Oriental in appearance and so beautifully carved and polished that it was difficult not to believe they had come from China. These unusual objects, then regarded as unclassifiable freaks of Mexican archeology, were all so similar in style and technique it was obvious they were the product of a definite and important artistic school. Eventually some sensational monuments of this style were discovered and a new archeological complex was recognized, which was labelled, for lack of a better name, "Olmec," after the legendary aborigines of the southern Gulf Coast, where so many such objects were found. We became more and more fascinated by the mysterious new culture and "Olmec" art and archeology became our most passionate hobby.

The term "Olmec" (from *olli*, "rubber") has proven so confusing, even to archeologists, that an explanation of its implications becomes imperative here. *Olmec* means "Citizen of Olman." The rubber country, the tropical lowlands in general, and more specifically the southern Gulf Coast, from where the best rubber came. We knew about the Olmec, supposedly the oldest civilized inhabitants of Mexico, from the chronicles of sixteenth-century writers who quoted from contemporary Indian histories and legends. Our knowledge of pre-Spanish history does not go beyond the ninth century A.D., but the beginnings of high Indian culture in southern Mexico can now be traced back at least two thousand years, with at least five cultural horizons within this long period of time. It is clear that the so-called "Olmec" style dates back to one of the earliest of these cultural horizons, and, to avoid the misleading denomination, archeologists have rebaptized it as "Culture of La Venta" —after its most important site. However, the new name is clumsy and impractical; habit has branded it "Olmec" and Olmec it will probably remain despite their efforts. Consequently, as a concession to habit, and since there seems to be a continuity of style in the various cultures of the Gulf Coast, we have adopted the terms of "Early Olmec" for the still unidentified archeological complex which is the main subject of this chapter, the culture of La Venta; we shall use "Middle Olmec" for the subsequent Classic Epoch; and "Late Olmec" for the historical peoples that held sway from about the tenth century to the sixteenth, those whom the Spaniards found when they landed in Veracruz.

The Early Olmec lapidaries excelled at making statuettes, masks and great votive axes, generally representing squat, fat men with elongated, pear-shaped heads, small perforated noses, fat necks, heavy jowls and stubborn chins. Their eyes are decidedly Mongoloid—almond-shaped or narrow slits between puffed eyelids. But their most characteristic feature is a large despondent mouth, with the corners drawn downwards and a thick, flaring upperlip, like a snarling jaguar's. It is evident that these artists meant to represent a definite, traditional concept—a plump character with short but well-made arms and legs and with small hands and feet, either standing or seated crosslegged, Oriental fashion. They are generally shown nude and sexless, or wearing a simple loincloth or a short skirt with an ornamental buckle in front. There is always a strong feline feeling, coupled with a haunting infantile character and expression about their faces, as if they were meant to represent a totemic prototype, half-jaguar, half-baby, so characteristic and powerful that it is short of being an obsession. In fact, many of these sculptures are actually jaguars or rather a jaguar deity, perhaps a jaguar cub-ancestor, since so often their snarling mouths show toothless gums.

Nothing is known about the makers of these objects. Procedence alone is not more enlightening since they come from widely scattered places—all over Southern Mexico, Guatemala, and even from Costa

Rica, where one exceptionally fine winged dwarf of jade was found. From an artistic point of view they are often among the finest works of art ever found on this continent; technically they are unsurpassed, and archeologically they are a deep mystery since they present the dilemma of a most sophisticated art and a highly advanced technique as belonging to the earliest known cultural horizon of the Mexican Indians.

Primitive method of drilling employed in the working of pre-Columbian jade, after a Mexican codex

At first all the known Early Olmec-style objects were found accidentally by peasants or grave robbers and there was no scientific data as to the conditions under which they were buried. Eventually they began to appear in archeological explorations—they turned up in the earliest levels at Oaxaca, as well as in "Archaic" tombs in Michoacán and Morelos. But the climax came when Matthew W. Stirling, of the Smithsonian Institution, began digging in the practically unexplored soil of Veracruz. At a place called Tres Zapotes, in Los Tuxtlas, he uncovered a colossal head of basalt, seven feet high, powerfully carved in the likeness of a flat-nosed, thick-lipped, rather Negroid man's head, wearing a headdress reminiscent of a football player's helmet. There were other exciting sculptures at Tres Zapotes, but the prize find was a broken stone slab carved with a jaguar mask panel on one side, and on the back, if correctly interpreted, no less than what would be the earliest recorded date yet found in the Americas—B.C. 31—over two thousand years ago, written in bars and dots in the classic Maya manner. The find raised a storm of debate. The invention of the calendar and the use of a system of bars and dots as numerals for recording dates is generally recognized as a Maya achievement; but the slab was definitely non-Maya and Tres Zapotes lies far from the Maya area, furthermore, all the known Maya dated stones bear later dates than those found up to now outside the Maya area. While the debate raged unabated as to the interpretation of these dates, Stirling pitched camp at La Venta, on the jungles of the Veracruz-Tabasco border. His finds were artistically so important that we hastened to La Venta to see the exciting new discoveries.

La Venta used to be just a name in the trackless swamps that border the Tonalá River, directly on the Isthmus of Tehuantepec. It was known there were ruins on the spot and the archeologist Frans Blom had visited the lonely, jungle-covered swamp many years before, but no one suspected the spectacular and artistic importance of the monuments and the buried treasures until Stirling cleared the jungle around them and dug them out of the soft alluvial soil.

La Venta is an island of high ground covered with tall jungle, clearly standing out of the mangrove swamp, formed by the accumulation of soil washed down from the Isthmian Divide. From aerial photographs we saw at the petroleum office, it seemed possible that the island once stood in the middle of a great lagoon that opened into the Gulf. We thought we saw traces of another river, now clogged and turned into swamp, on the opposite side of the island. The ruins are reached from the oil camp by a narrow and slippery border half a mile long, built of piled up mud across the treacherous black ooze of the swamp. On a grassy clearing stand eight or ten thatched huts, the Ranchería of La Venta, with about 30 inhabitants, Nahua-speaking Indians, all descendants and relatives of an 80-year-old patriarch named Sebastián Torres.

The ruins are located in the thick of the jungle, which is traversed by amazingly well-kept roads, "well-swept" they say there, in places wide enough for automobiles. Along these roads and on the rivers the Indians travel great distances by foot, horse, and dugout canoe. During our stay old Sebastián found that he had to go to Huimanguillo "on business." With all his 80 years he undertook the 50-mile trip alone, there and back in a week's time.

At La Venta there are four colossal heads like the ones at Tres Zapotes, besides carved altars, statues and stelae of stone. Over twenty carved monuments have been discovered thus far and many of these are among the largest, most thrilling examples of early Indian art. The carving on the monoliths is sensitive and realistic, with a unique mastery of technique and creative expression. These sculptures are free of many of the vices that contaminate much of the later Indian art: stilted stylization, stifling overloading of ritualistic detail, and a purely decorative flamboyancy.

The first monument we saw was the seven-foot-high colossal head, the masterpiece of La Venta. It represents a chubby youth with a flat nose, heavy lids and a full and sensual mouth. He wears a sort of football helmet, with strange grooves and holes on top, probably made in later times, perhaps to sharpen an instrument. The other three heads ("B," "C," "D") are a good distance away and two of them bear a subtle smile, showing a row of small rounded teeth. They all wear helmets, side-burns, and large earplugs. There are also six enormous stone altars, one of which (altar "A") measures ten feet in length, six feet in width and five feet in height. Altar "B," nicknamed "the Quintuplet altar," because it has five infants or dwarfs carved on its sides, shows in front a magnificently carved personage, sitting crosslegged, emerging from a cave-like niche, and holding in his arms the limp body of a baby. He wears a tall cap bound by a headband with an ornament in front representing a jaguar mask. On the right and left sides of this altar are carved in low relief four characters, two on each side, wearing unique capes and hats, each holding in his arms a mischievous, naked baby or dwarf in the attitude of resisting or trying to escape. One of these dwarfs has the deeply split head characteristic of this art.

Like the Mayas, the people of La Venta erected stelae, carved upright stone slabs to commemorate an event, and two of these show distinguished personages wearing tall Ziegfeldian headdresses. On stela "C" two impressive chieftains stand face-to-face, surrounded by lesser men suspended in space. The face of the man on the left is smashed, but the other is untouched and represents a stern, fully bearded man, with an enormous aquiline nose, totally different from the flat-nosed people of La Venta. It is, in fact, unlike anything ever found in Mexico before, a personage with surprisingly pronounced Semitic features. Stela "A" has as central motif an overdressed character, wearing a headdress as tall as himself, holding a mace in his hands. He is also surrounded by six flying gnomes with grotesque jaguar faces and maces in their hands. Elsewhere is a great block of stone (stela "B"), hollowed out like a box, the cavity shaped like a simplified jaguar mouth containing a standing feminine figure. Beyond is a whimsical statue of a dwarf, locally known as "The Little Grandmother," holding in his hands a small stone box. A curious monument is the badly damaged Altar "E," shaped like a jaguar god's head, with a great hole that goes in on one side, turns at a right angle and comes out at the mouth, which Stirling suspects was used in some ceremony to make the altar talk. These are among the many monuments thus far discovered at La Venta, each an almost impenetrable puzzle, and there may be many more, hidden in the jungle or that have sunk out of sight in the soft alluvial soil.

Hardly discernible in the forest is a great pyramid of packed earth, completely overgrown with large trees, with a sort of wide apron, also of clay, on its western side.

The entire complex runs directly in a north-south direction, with all sorts of mounds—large and small, round and long ones—neatly aligned to form extensive plazas. When cleared of jungle and excavated, the great plaza to the north of the central pyramid turned out to contain a strange enclosure 54 by 68 yards square, formed by rows of naturally-shaped hexagonal pillars of basalt, placed side by side like a picket fence and forming a solid wall. The heavy columns, weighing in some cases over two tons each, were set standing on a thick base or foundation of clay, forming a sort of sunken court, the original floor of which is still undetermined. This court has a gate flanked by two smaller enclosures or bastions, 21 by 27 feet square, made of the same basalt pillars.

Stirling proceeded to excavate the eastern bastion and found it to be filled with great sun-dried bricks of clay for a depth of many feet. At the bottom of the fill of bricks was a cache of 37 axes of serpentine carefully arranged in the form of a cross. From then the pit was filled with simple earth that covered—not a tomb as the archeologists had expected, but a beautifully fitted and polished floor of green serpentine slabs closely fitted together in a gigantic mosaic of rather abstract design vaguely reminiscent of a jaguar mask. The open spaces within the mosaic that stood for the jaguar's eyes, eyebrows, nose and mouth, were filled with blue clay, while a border of yellow ochre framed the green mosaic, setting it off against the reddish soil of La Venta. The mosaic was set in a layer of asphalt over a foundation of crushed stones. The floor lay at the bottom of a pit 23 feet deep, and no clues were found that would indicate its significance or purpose. There was another, although incomplete, mosaic floor in front of the great mound, and there is little doubt that a third such floor lies at the bottom of the western bastion. However, the difficulties involved in bringing the necessary man-power and machinery to the remote jungle swamp to explore further, will preclude for some time the finding of a satisfactory answer to the mystery of the beautiful floor, fitted and polished with such a loving care, laid at the bottom of a deep pit, only to be buried with clay and rubble, then sealed to the surface with bricks.

To the north of the enclosure there was a low mound that contained more artistic treasures as well as new headaches for the archeologists. The mound concealed a great rectangular sarcophagus of stone, carved in low relief like a crouching jaguar, and was covered by a flat stone lid. It contained a fine statuette of stone, a seven-inch spatula of jade, a pair of jade earplugs and two jade pendants shaped like jaguar's teeth. These objects were in place, that is, the corpse they once adorned had disintegrated, but the earplugs were on each side of where the head had been, while the spatula and the figurine were on the place of the thighs, probably held originally in the corpse's hands.

In front of the sarcophagus was a unique tomb 24 feet long, made of heavy upright basalt pillars placed close together like a picket enclosure. It was roofed with the same sort of columns placed horizontally and the door consisted of five more columns that leaned over the structure like a ramp. Only some simple pots were found in the front of the clay-filled chamber, but in the back was a raised platform floored with flagstones, where three or four corpses had been laid many centuries ago, under a six-inch layer of bright red cinnabar. No bones remained, but there were many figurines and other objects of jade, as bright and shiny as the day in which they were buried. There were two beautiful statuettes of translucent blue jade, four and five inches long, one realistic and in the round, the other flat and stylized. There was a splendid three-inch figurine of a nude, seated man with an extreme head-deformation, carved out of green jade, a masterpiece of solid, monumental sculpture. There was still another figurine in gray jade, covered with a coat of red cinnabar and with a glimmering little disk of crystalline hematite stuck on its chest. It represents a plump girl wearing a short skirt, with her hair hanging loose in the back and with bangs in front. Her face resembles the colossal heads and bears the same wistful smile that distinguishes two of them. Also of the finest jade were a pair of green, square earplugs engraved with eagle's heads, a realistic replica in jade of a large clam shell, a bulb-shaped object with a stem, a delicate copy of a stingaree's tail in clear blue jade, a paper-thin little mask of a duck's head, and a number of emerald-green jade beads shaped like sections of bamboo. In the tomb were also found large disks of hematite undoubtedly to be worn on the chest as in the statue of the girl, a necklace of stingaree's tails inlaid with minute squares of hematite, and a great tooth of a fossil shark. Hundreds of jade axes, generally in groups of thirty-seven, were found buried at various places, undoubtedly offerings, carefully arranged in rows and groups, apparently with a magic purpose in mind. One of these was carved with the everpresent jaguar mask, and three others showed abstract incised designs.

La Venta is an inexhaustible mine of precious archeological objects. In this 1943 season of excavation Stirling found more "Olmec" figurines, this time with eyes inlaid with hematite, more axes and endless objects of jade, many made out of the priceless, emerald green clear variety called in China "jewel jade," known to come only from Burma and now found in America for the first time. Nothing like the discoveries at La

Venta have ever been found before, and the identity and cultural connections of its inhabitants remain shrouded in the deepest mystery.

It is as difficult to explain the significance of the findings at La Venta as it is to arrive at any definite conclusions regarding the tantalizing new culture. One of its mysteries lies in the extravagant use of the enormous blocks and the hundreds of pillars of basalt in which its

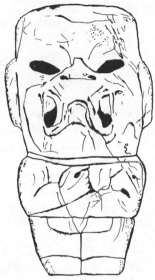

Olmec votive axe of jade, from Vera Cruz

sculptors lavished their greatest skill, taste and inconceivable material effort. In some unexplainable manner, the people of La Venta quarried, carved and transported great stones, weighing many tons each, to a stoneless island, through rivers and swamps, most likely by sea, from the Zone of Los Tuxtlas, the nearest source of basalt, approximately a hundred miles away. Only the sheer man-power of a flourishing community, possessing unlimited resources of labor, engineering ingenuity, and capable artists could have accomplished the great task of erecting such imposing monuments.

Thus far it is not possible to accurately date La Venta by the most reliable method in use—the identification of various superimposed layers of remains that can be related to other known cultures or epochs by means of the broken pottery found. At La Venta there is yet no evidence of more than one occupation of the site, but the great heads there are nearly identical to the one found at Tres Zapotes, where basalt is abundant. Here there are signs of long human occupation and the ceramic styles vary so that they can be divided into three epochs: Lower, Middle, and Upper-Tres Zapotes. The clay figurines found at La Venta are similar to those of the Middle Tres Zapotes epoch, consequently it is safe to assume that the great heads and in general the complex of La Venta was created by the people responsible for the Middle epoch of Tres Zapotes, sometime during the first centuries of our era. It was perhaps that the elite of an ancient and proud Jaguar-people was gradually pushed out from Los Tuxtlas into the isolation of La Venta, by waves of new arrivals in the region, people of a new race and religion, worshippers of serpents, whom the People of the Jaguar could not tolerate.

The little clay heads and figurines found at La Venta and Tres Zapotes show two different racial types: one is the infantile, fleshy, flat-nosed Mongoloid type of the "Jaguar-Baby" sculptures, but there are also representations of bearded people with large aquiline noses. The strangely Semitic chief carved on the great stela faces a personage whose face has been deliberately smashed, while his own face is intact. We venture to guess that the smashed face was that of a typical "jaguar-baby" type, and that the scene represented the visit of a bearded, long-nosed foreign chief to La Venta. Perhaps La Venta was the last stronghold of this ancient culture, having probably survived well into the classic period, remote and isolated, although maintaining relations with other peoples. Its sudden death may have come when a religious or political conflict arose between these peoples—the Serpent-People against the Jaguar-People, the basic, legendary feud that haunts Mexican mythology. Most of the monuments are battered beyond recognition and this would explain the deliberate mutilation, done at the expense of great physical effort before they became slowly engulfed by the jungle after the place was abandoned; only the most fanatical will of religious reformists could be responsible for such destruction of works of art.

It is equally difficult to explain the significance of the monuments; the colossal heads were meant to be simply heads without bodies to rest upon the ground, which is in itself a rather unique idea. These heads face directly north-south and they could have been astronomical sights or simply memorial monuments. The central motif of the "Quintuplet" altar seems to represent a birth scene, or perhaps a ceremony in which babies or dwarfs took part. These jaguar-like babies or dwarfs seem to have obsessed the artists of La Venta to the point where this embryonic character with headband, chin straps, and a deeply notched head, became their most important art motif. Everything about these "jaguar-babies" is hard to grasp—their deformed bodies, their rudimentary arms and legs, their despondent, toothless mouths, their stern, hollow eyes, deep-set under elaborate supercilliary ridges and knitted brows, with a deep, V-shaped cleft on top of their heads. Does this cleft refer to a form of sacrifice, an ax-blow? or does it represent the soft, half-closed skull of a newly born baby, symbol of the connection between man and the divinity through the occiput? The idea of the top of the head as the "seat" of the divinity is common to many lands and has a contemporary equivalent among Catholics in the tonsure and the split mitres of bishops. This cleft is often so extreme that their split heads look like the claws of hammers, used to extract nails.

The little monsters could also represent spirits of the jungle, rather like the mischievous *chanekes* that supposedly still infest the Veracruz Coast. The *chaneke* is a dwarf, only two feet high, who passes the time playing unpleasant tricks on human beings and falling in love [with] (and even kidnapping) good-looking girls. They seem to originate in the belief, common among modern Indians of the most ancient lineage, in little spirits of the wilderness, "very old dwarfs with baby faces," masters of the game and fish, who live in caves or behind waterfalls, where they hide the best corn and other treasures. They are wilful and dangerous to human beings, but they will provide rain if properly propitiated.

The almost exclusive use of the jaguar in the art of La Venta is another clue as to its antiquity since jaguar gods (of the earth, rain and thunderbolts) were among the oldest gods. Today, however, more than 400 years after the Spanish Conquest and 2,000 probable years since its origin, the were-jaguar, the *nawal*, is still invoked to frighten children who will not go to sleep. The modern Indians of Oaxaca and Guerrero still perform jaguar dances of long-lost significance.

Besides jaguars these artists carved statuettes and masks of men, perhaps an ancestral archetype that followed a well-established esthetic pattern. Although generally nude, these figurines are modestly and deliberately sexless, with long shaven heads and fine features—extremely Mongoloid, puffy eyes, droopy mouths and heavy jowls. A strong feline character permeates these figurines, but the human element is dominant and there is an emphasis on a definite physical type, radically opposed to the bony and aquiline type we are accustomed to regard as Indian. However, the type occurs frequently today among the older Indian groups of southern Mexico (Mazateca, Chinanteca, Popolacas, Totonacas, Zapoteca, Mixteca, and so forth) and the distribution of the living type coincides with the general distribution of the art style of La Venta. It is likely that this type represented at one time a distinct ethnic element; perhaps the dominant type of Archaic times since it appears frequently in Archaic figurines. It is a fact that bony narrow faces and aquiline noses make their first appearance in post-Archaic art, which is another argument in favor of their antiquity.

The art of La Venta is unique; it is by no means primitive, nor is it a local style. It is rather the climax of a noble and sensual art, product of a direct but sophisticated esthetic spirit, an accomplished technique, and a sober dignified taste. The sculptors of La Venta delighted in massive and squat forms, realistic and sensitive, quite in accord with the Indian physique of southern Mexico. Arguments in favor of its great antiquity can be seen in certain characteristics of a style, for instance, the lack of elaborate symbolism, its archaism of conception, in contrast with the baroque flamboyancy of the later arts of the Lowlands, or the stilted and purely decorative stylization of the Mexican Highlands. Furthermore, while a trace of the jaguar-mask complex persists in the transitional forms of the classic arts, no influences from these arts are to be found in the culture of La Venta; the two most characteristic features of these later arts, the use of great fans of *quetzal* bird feathers, and the combination of spiral motifs, are totally absent in the style of La Venta. No one in the Americas ever carved jade like the La Venta lapidaries, in such a free and apparently easy manner, quite in contrast with the later Oaxacan (Mixtec) and the so-called "Maya" jades, where the hardness, the shape and color of the material, as well as the mechanical means in use, dictated the style and even the nature of the carved object.

Olmec jadeite figurine, from Guerrero, western Mexico

PART IV

MAYA LANDS

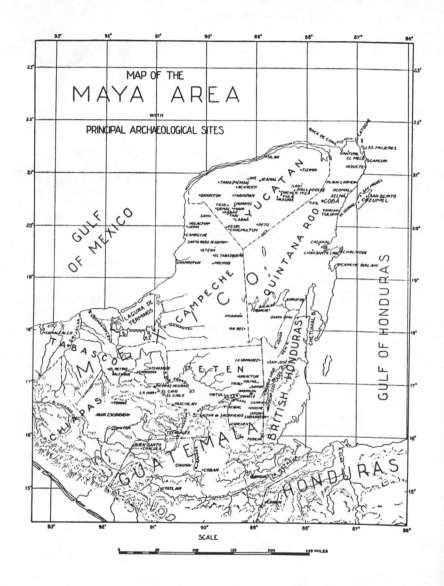

MAP OF THE

MAYA AREA

WITH

PRINCIPAL ARCHAEOLOGICAL SITES

SCALE

19

So superbly did a young New York lawyer write in the early 1840's of his explorations in tropical forests that he awakened readers everywhere to the romance of lost cities in Central America. In the public mind the young lawyer's name became fixed as the discoverer of the Mayas—*el padre del Mayismo*—if not the founder of American archaeology itself. John Lloyd Stephens was the first to insist that from Central America the New World could reclaim a heritage that might well vie with the glories of ancient Greece and the Near East. At a time when no one had yet grasped the brilliance of this buried civilization, and opinion about the dismal cultural level of American aboriginals still prevailed despite Humboldt's writings, Stephens could justly proclaim at the sight of the ruins of Copán: "I am entering abruptly upon new ground." Faced with the impressive vestiges of such highly accomplished builders and artists, his own doubts, nourished by European savants, vanished. "America, say historians, was peopled by savages; but savages never reared these structures, savages never carved these stones . . . all the arts which embellish life, had flourished in this overgrown forest; . . . beauty, ambition, and glory, had lived and passed away, and none knew that such things had been, or could tell of their past existence."

Barely a hundred years ago the Mayas were virtually unknown. Neither Humboldt nor Prescott ever mentioned them. In fact, Stephens himself had only a vague notion that the jungle-covered ruins he tracked down belonged to a civilization quite distinct from, and possibly older than, that of the Aztecs or Toltecs. Who the builders were he could not say. For some time after him, people would refer to the great temple mounds as "Mexican"; the "Mayas" were slow in coming into their own.

About no other pre-Columbians has so much been written, none has occasioned so many scientific and pseudo-scientific speculations. How the imagination was stirred by enormous white temple cities, by glyph-covered stelae, by the intricate Mayan calendar more precise than the Gregorian time count of contemporary Europe, by the advanced Mayan numerical system that used the number zero before Arabs and Hindus. The Mayas, it came to be known, had developed—presumably alone among pre-Columbians—a true and standardized form of writing, an unequivocal sign of higher civilization, and their astronomical knowledge had been vast. Before long, Mayaland more than any other part of the Americas lured archaeologists. By the mid-twentieth century the region has become archaeologically almost as crowded as Mesopotamia and Egypt.

Stephens, of course, was preceded by others—as all pioneers are. A Spanish officer, Diego García de Palacio, as early as 1576 wrote a letter to Philip II about the ruins of Copán, the first city Stephens was to seek out. But like so many colonial documents the letter was committed to limbo in Spanish archives. A later report on Palenque in Chiapas prompted archaeologically minded Carlos IV to send out a Captain Antonio del Río in 1786. Even before the belated (1822) publication of Del Río's paper, a retired army officer, Guillelmo Dupaix, went in 1807 on an expedition to various sites in southern Mexico. His writings, too, together with illustrations by Luciano Castañeda, were left to moulder for thirty years, even though Mexican antiquarians were cognizant of his explorations.

Humboldt and several early nineteenth-century writers who visited Mexico also knew by hearsay of Palenque and perhaps a few other sites in farthest southeastern Mexico. In the 1820's there appeared on the scene Count Jean-Frédéric Waldeck, an eccentric Franco-German adventurer of somewhat uncertain title, whose second mission, in 1830, was subsidized by the famous Viscount Kingsborough, a compulsive apostle of the age-old theory that the American Indians had descended from the Lost Tribes of Israel.

The Waldeck-Kingsborough cooperative enterprise aroused little confidence. Could the skeptics be right after all? Were there really any temples and altars in the jungle? Stephens avidly studied the scant literature on alleged Central American antiquities. Eventually he hit upon a brief narrative (just published in 1835) by "Juan Galindo," an Irish soldier of fortune, on the "Ruins of Copán in Central America." This settled his mind: he must seek out Copán and for himself separate fact from fiction. Yet it was "with the hope, rather than expectation, of finding wonders" that John Lloyd Stephens embarked, in the fall of 1839, from New York for the Caribbean port of Belize in British Honduras.

Stephens was accompanied by an English artist, Frederick Catherwood, a man as gifted in recording antiquities with pencil and brush as Stephens was with the writing pen. The two had met in London in 1836, drawn together by their kindred interest in Greece and the Near East, which both had previously visited. Their unique partnership was to be as significant in American archaeology as that of Lewis and Clark in the opening of the great West of the northern continent. Archaeologists today marvel at the precision of Catherwood's draughtsmanship, which struggled heroically against his own deep-rooted romanticism—nurtured on Piranesi —and managed to capture the very details and spirit of an alien sensibility. Maya hieroglyphs, entirely inscrutable to him, can be recognized in his sketches.

From Belize the two friends penetrated the lush interior of a country torn by a three-cornered civil war. They proceeded first by steamer and then scaled ranges on precipitous muletracks. During the hazardous trip they were thrown into jail by a drunken officer and almost met disaster. When they reached the small village of Copán in northern Honduras, just across the Guatemala border, no one at first could tell them of ruins. But wonders they did find. Here, indeed, in the jungle wilderness of Central America was a majestic city of monumental buildings and sculptures of artistry beyond question.

After buying the Copán ruins for fifty dollars, Stephens and Catherwood toiled for two weeks to hack away the jungle's tentacles and reveal the city's layout and artistic wealth. There were surprises without end: they located eleven stone stelae with sculptured figures and unmistakable hieroglyphic inscriptions; carved heads of jaguars pierced through the brush; shrines, terraces, courts and pyramids were everywhere. The edifices were joined by flights of stairs—one of them decorated with some 2,500 glyphs, which Stephens hoped would some day reveal the "entire history of the city." Experienced antiquarians or no, Stephens and Catherwood were startled, because everything at Copán was literally beyond compare. Here was archaeologically virgin soil, "there were no guide-books." But the very novelty created in the explorers an enduring interest never before experienced by them when visiting the celebrated and more familiar ruins of the Mediterranean world. All was enhanced by "dark, impenetrable mystery."

They could not help pondering over their discoveries. Who were the creators of such stupendous works? How and with what instruments did they achieve such mastery over stone? What feats of engineering erected the colossal structures? What was their meaning? And what happened to these gifted people? Where had they gone?

For Stephens and Catherwood, Copán was only a beginning. While Stephens had to rush to Guatemala City on political business, Catherwood completed his sketches at Copán and then discovered the neighboring site of Quirigua. Later the two friends went on to Palenque about 300 miles northwest in Chiapas, Mexico, and then farther on into Yucatán to Uxmal, where Stephens fell seriously ill and was forced to return to the United States.

The two men returned to Uxmal for a second trip from 1841 to 1842. Afterwards they concentrated in the main on Chichen Itzá, in northern Yucatán, today probably the best known among Maya cities. Altogether they were to explore forty-four cities, many never reported before. In the meantime *Incidents of Travel in Central America, Chiapas and Yucatan,* with Catherwood's drawings, had been published in September 1841 in three volumes. Despite its great length, the book was immediately popular, running quickly through several editions in the United States and England, as well as German and Spanish translations. Stephens' work served as a guide to future generations of scholars. His eloquent prose conjured up the achievements of the forgotten Mayas, and set a standard of excellence for writing on Central American antiquities. The Mayas were to become the one topic in New World archaeology amply covered by popular literature.

Stephens' explorations had their beginning when at twenty he toured the Illinois prairies and sailed down the Mississippi to New Orleans. Back in New York, a sedentary legal career was not to his liking for long. In 1835 he embarked on a two-year trip across Europe, Egypt, Syria, and Arabia, recording his observations as *Incidents of Travel in Egypt and Arabia Petraea* (1837). In a long review Edgar Allan Poe praised this book for its "freshness of manner" and "manliness of feeling." Poe hoped to "take other journeys" with such a perceptive and entertaining writer. Stephens, whom Van Wyck Brooks has called "the greatest of American travel writers," was fortunate in possessing literary talents commensurate with the magnitude of his subject; he is never pompous or moralistic in the manner of so many nineteenth-century traveling antiquarians. The promising young author soon found new, even more challenging, territories for his pen.

His New World expeditions owed some of their success to Stephens' foresight in having had himself appointed diplomatic agent in Central America by President Martin Van Buren, for whose election he had previously campaigned. Apart from his literary and antiquarian pursuits, Stephens was active in steamship and railroad promotion. Anticipating the building of the Panama Canal, he secured the right to lay a railroad across the Isthmus in 1848, and was made president of the Panama Railway in 1850.

World traveler, archaeologist, writer, businessman, lawyer, and "admirer of the ladies in Casanova's fashion," Stephens, still young, died in New York City in 1852. In a piece of pious field archaeology, his forgotten tomb in the Marble Cemetery on New York's Second Street was located in 1941 after a long search by a member of the New Jersey Historical Society. An authoritative biography of "the discoverer of the Mayas" by Victor von Hagen was published in 1947. Stephens' own narratives of exploration are at long last being reissued by American presses.

Some of the questions Stephens posed have been answered during a century of archaeological research in the jungles and savannahs of Guatemala, Honduras, Yucatán, Chiapas, and Quintana Roo. Modern scholars have established that Copán was settled about the fifth century A.D. and occupied for about five hundred years. It is the southernmost of the great Maya centers as well as one of the most extensive of them all. The preponderantly religious significance of the city, surmised by Stephens, has been confirmed. Hints have been found in the reliefs that Copán may have been the meeting place for Maya priest-astronomers in a kind of scientific congress to settle discrepancies in their calendar. Here perhaps the Mayas refined their theories about the tropical year, the moon, and eclipses. Herbert J. Spinden, who strongly endorsed this thesis, also believed that two stelae within a distance of four and a half miles served as parts of a "giant sun-dial." Stephens' own supposition has also been borne out that the carved stelae carried dates and were set up at regular intervals of time.

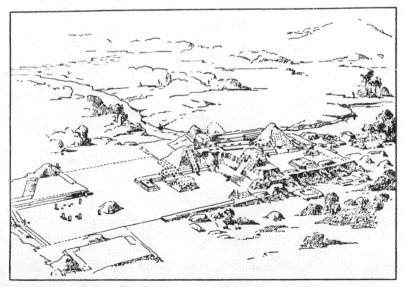

The ruins of Copán, Honduras, as viewed by a modern archaeologist-artist, Tatiana Proskouriakoff

At the end of the nineteenth century, decades after Stephens and Catherwood, Copán was systematically surveyed by Alfred P. Maudslay, a British explorer who had come to Central America just as a traveler but stayed on to become the first scientific investigator of Mayadom. He freed several structures, excavated, made casts, and took photographs. His task was the more formidable because Copán had been torn asunder by vegetation, and repeatedly suffered from earthquakes. (A particularly destructive one occurred in 1934.) Not only that, but the nearby Copán River had washed away part of the "acropolis." At long last, in 1935, the Republic of Honduras joined with the Carnegie Institution of Washington to initiate the reconstruction of the badly damaged city.

Since the days of Stephens, the world has come to recognize in the fierce exoticism of the Mayas an art that must rank among mankind's supreme creations, though it may lack the simplicity, grace, and traditional standards of beauty Westerners associate with the classical age of Greece. For all their artistic genius, however, the Mayas most likely were grouped in militaristic, mutually aggressive theocracies, and indulged in bloodthirsty ceremonials on the scale of the other Mesoamericans. There is even suspicious evidence that some of them collected and wore shrunken heads like the Jívaros of the Amazon or the Nazcas of ancient Peru. Foremost, the discovery in 1946 of the Bonampak Maya murals helped to destroy forever the early sentimental picture of mild, meditative, and moderate Mayas.

COPÁN—LOST CITY IN THE JUNGLE

John Lloyd Stephens

Almost immediately from the hacienda we entered a thick wood, dense as that of the Mico Mountain, and almost as muddy. The ascent was toilsome, but the top was open, and so covered with that beautiful plant that we called it the Mountain of Aloes. Some were just peeping out of

From *Incidents of Travel in Central America, Chiapas and Yucatan.* New York: Harper & Brothers, 1841, Vol. I, pp. 90–160 *passim.*

the ground, others were twenty or thirty feet high, and some gigantic stalks were dead; flowers which would have kindled rapture in the breast of beauty had bloomed and died on this desolate mountain, unseen except by a passing Indian.

In descending we lost the path, and wandered for some time before we recovered it. Almost immediately we commenced ascending another mountain, and from its top looked completely over a third, and, at a great distance, saw a large hacienda. Our road lay directly along the edge of a precipice, from which we looked down upon the tops of gigantic pines at a great distance beneath us. Very soon the path became so broken, and ran so near the edge of a precipice, that I called to Mr. Catherwood to dismount. The precipice was on the left side, and I had advanced so far that, on the back of a perverse mule, I did not venture to make any irregular movement, and rode for some moments in great anxiety. Somewhere on this road, but unmarked by any visible sign, we crossed the boundary-line of the state of Guatemala and entered Honduras.

At two o'clock we reached the village of Copán, which consisted of half a dozen miserable huts thatched with corn. Our appearance created a great sensation. All the men and women gathered around us to gaze. We inquired immediately for the ruins, but none of the villagers could direct us to them, and all advised us to go to the hacienda of Don Gregorio. We had no wish to stop at a village, and told the muleteer to go on, but he refused, and said that his engagement was to conduct us to Copán. After a long wrangle we prevailed, and, riding through a piece of woods, forded once more the Copán River, and came out upon a clearing, on one side of which was a hacienda, with a tile roof, and having cosina and other outbuildings, evidently the residence of a rich proprietor. We were greeted by a pack of barking dogs, and all the doorways were filled with women and children, who seemed in no small degree surprised at our appearance. There was not a man in sight; but the women received us kindly, and told us that Don Gregorio would return soon, and would conduct us to the ruins. Immediately the fire was rekindled in the cosina, the sound of the patting of hands gave notice of the making of tortillas, and in half an hour dinner was ready. It was served up on a massive silver plate, with water in a silver tankard, but without knife, fork, or spoon; soup or caldo was served in cups to be drunk. Nevertheless, we congratulated ourselves upon having fallen into such good quarters.

In a short time a young man arrived on horseback, gayly dressed, with an embroidered shirt, and accompanied by several men driving a herd of cattle. An ox was selected, a rope thrown around its horns, and the animal was drawn up to the side of the house, and, by another rope around its legs, thrown down. Its feet were tied together, its head drawn back by a rope tied from its horns to its tail, and with one thrust of the machete the artery of life was severed. The pack of hungry dogs stood ready, and, with a horrible clicking, lapped up the blood with their tongues. All the women were looking on, and a young girl took a puppy dog and rubbed its nose in the crimson stream, to give it early a taste for blood. The ox was skinned, the meat separated from the bones, and, to the entire destruction of steaks, sirloins, and roasting-pieces, in an hour the whole animal was hanging in long strings on a line before the door.

During this operation Don Gregorio arrived. He was about fifty, had large black whiskers, and a beard of several days' growth; and, from the behaviour of all around, it was easy to see that he was a domestic tyrant. The glance which he threw at us before dismounting seemed to say, "Who are *you*?" but, without a word, he entered the house. We waited until he had finished his dinner, when, supposing that to be the favourable moment, I entered the house. In my intercourse with the world I have more than once found my overtures to an acquaintance received coldly, but I never experienced anything quite so cool as the don's reception of me. I told him that we had come into that neighbourhood to visit the ruins of Copán, and his manner said, What's that to me? but he answered that they were on the other side of the river. I asked him whether we could procure a guide, and again he said that the only man who knew anything about them lived on the other side of the river. As yet we did not make sufficient allowance for the distracted state of the country, nor the circumstance that a man might incur danger to himself by giving shelter to suspected persons; but, relying on the reputation of the country for hospitality, and the proof of it which we had already met with, I was rather slow in coming to the disagreeable conclusion that we were not welcome. This conclusion, however, was irresistible. The don was not pleased with our looks. I ordered the muleteer to saddle the mules; but the rascal enjoyed our confusion, and positively refused to saddle his beasts again that day. We applied to Don Gregorio himself, offering to pay him; and, as Augustin said, in the hope of getting rid of us, he lent us two, on which to ride back to the village. Unfortunately, the guide we sought was away; a brisk cock-fight was then pending, and we received no encouragement, either from the appearance of the people, or from invitation, to bring back our luggage to that place. And we learned, what was very provoking, that Don Gregorio was the great man of Copán; the richest man, and the petty tyrant; and that it would be most unfortunate to have a rupture with him, or even to let it be known at the village that we were not well received at his house. Reluctantly, but in the hope of making a more favourable impression, we returned to the hacienda. Mr. C. dismounted on the steps, and took a seat on the piazza. I happened to dismount outside; and, before moving, took a survey of the party. The don sat on a chair, with our detestable muleteer by his side, and a half-concealed smile of derision on his face, talking of "idols," and looking at me. By this time eight or ten men, sons, servants, and labourers, had come in from their day's work, but not one offered to take my mule, or made any of those demonstrations of civility which are always shown to a welcome guest. The women turned away their heads, as if they had been reproved for receiving us; and all the men, taking their cue from the don, looked so insulting, that I told Mr. Catherwood we would tumble our luggage into the road, and curse him for an inhospitable churl; but Mr. Catherwood warned me against it, urging that, if we had an open quarrel with him, after all our trouble we would be prevented seeing the ruins. The don probably suspected something of what passed; and, fearing that he might push things too far, and bring a stain upon his name, pointed to a chair, and asked me to take a seat. With a great effort, I resolved to smother my indignation until I could pour it out with safety. Augustin was very indignant at the treatment we received; on the road he had sometimes swelled his own importance by telling of the flags hoisted and cannon fired when we left Belize; and here he hoisted more flags and fired more guns than usual, beginning with forty guns, and afterward going on to a cannonade; but it would not do. The don did not like us, and probably was willing to hoist flags, and fire cannons too, as at Belize, when we should go away.

Toward evening the skin of an ox was spread upon the piazza, corn in ears thrown upon it, and all the men, with the don at their head, sat down to shell it. The cobs were carried to the kitchen to burn, the corn taken up in baskets, and three pet hogs, which had been grunting outside in expectation of the feast, were let in to pick up the scattered grains. During the evening no notice was taken of us, except that the wife of the don sent a message by Augustin that supper was preparing; and our wounded pride was relieved, and our discontent somewhat removed, by an additional message that they had an oven and flour, and would bake us some bread if we wished to buy it.

After supper all prepared for sleep. The don's house had two sides, an inside and an out. The don and his family occupied the former, and we the latter; but we had not even this to ourselves. All along the wall were frames made of sticks about an inch thick, tied together with bark strings, over which the workmen spread an untanned oxhide for a bed. There were three hammocks besides ours, and I had so little room for mine that my body described an inverted parabola, with my heels as high as my head. It was vexatious and ridiculous; or, in the words of the English tourist in Fra Diavolo, it was "shocking! positively shocking!"

In the morning Don Gregorio was in the same humour. We took no notice of him, but made our toilet under the shed with as much respect as possible to the presence of the female members of the family, who were constantly passing and repassing. We had made up our minds to hold on and see the ruins; and, fortunately, early in the morning, one of the crusty don's sons, a civil young man, brought over from the village José, the guide of whom we stood in need.

By reason of many vexatious delays, growing out of difficulties between José and the muleteer, we did not get away until nine o'clock. Very soon we left the path or road, and entered a large field, partially cultivated with corn, belonging to Don Gregorio. Riding some distance through this, we reached a hut, thatched with corn-leaves, on the edge of the woods, at which some workmen were preparing their breakfast. Here we dismounted, and, tying our mules to trees near by, entered the woods, José clearing a path before us with a machete; soon we came to the bank of a river, and saw directly opposite a stone wall, perhaps a hundred feet high, with furze growing out of the top, running north and south along the river, in some places fallen, but in others entire. It had more the character of a structure than any we had ever seen, ascribed to the aborigines of America, and formed part of the wall of Copán, an ancient city, on whose history books throw but little light.

I am entering abruptly upon new ground. . . . With regard to Copán, mention is made by the early Spanish historians of a place of that name, situated in the same region of country in which these ruins are found, which then existed as an inhabited city, and offered a formidable resistance to the Spanish arms, though there are circumstances which seem to indicate that the city referred to was inferior in strength and solidity of construction, and of more modern origin. . . .

The wall was of cut stone, well laid, and in a good state of preservation. We ascended by large stone steps, in some places perfect, and in others thrown down by trees which had grown up between the crevices, and reached a terrace, the form of which it was impossible to make out, from the density of the forest in which it was enveloped. Our guide cleared a way with his machete, and we passed, as it lay half buried in the earth, a large fragment of stone elaborately sculptured, and came to the angle of a structure with steps on the sides, in form and appearance, so far as the trees would enable us to make it out, like the sides of a pyramid. Diverging from the base, and working our way through the thick woods, we came upon a square stone column, about fourteen feet high and three feet on each side, sculptured in very bold relief, and on all four of the

Hieroglyphic staircase at Copán, drawn by Tatiana Proskouriakoff

sides, from the base to the top. The front was the figure of a man curiously and richly dressed, and the face, evidently a portrait, solemn, stern, and well fitted to excite terror. The back was of a different design, unlike anything we had ever seen before, and the sides were covered with hieroglyphics. This our guide called an "Idol"; and before it, at a distance of three feet, was a large block of stone, also sculptured with figures and emblematical devices, which he called an altar. The sight of this unexpected monument put at rest at once and forever, in our minds, all uncertainty in regard to the character of American antiquities, and gave us the assurance that the objects we were in search of were interesting, not only as the remains of an unknown people, but as works of art, proving, like newly-discovered historical records, that the people who once occupied the Continent of America were not savages. With an interest perhaps stronger than we had ever felt in wandering among the ruins of

Egypt, we followed our guide, who, sometimes missing his way, with a constant and vigorous use of his machete, conducted us through the thick forest, among half-buried fragments, to fourteen monuments of the same character and appearance, some with more elegant designs, and some in workmanship equal to the finest monuments of the Egyptians; one displaced from its pedestal by enormous roots; another locked in the close embrace of branches of trees, and almost lifted out of the earth; another hurled to the ground, and bound down by huge vines and creepers; and one standing, with its altar before it, in a grove of trees which grew around it, seemingly to shade and shroud it as a sacred thing; in the solemn stillness of the woods, it seemed a divinity mourning over a fallen people. The only sounds that disturbed the quiet of this buried city were the noise of monkeys moving among the tops of the trees, and the cracking of dry branches broken by their weight. They moved over our heads in long and swift processions, forty or fifty at a time, some with little ones wound in their long arms, walking out to the end of boughs, and holding on with their hind feet or a curl of the tail, sprang to a branch of the next tree, and, with a noise like a current of wind, passed on into the depths of the forest. It was the first time we had seen these mockeries of humanity, and, with the strange monuments around us, they seemed like wandering spirits of the departed race guarding the ruins of their former habitations.

We returned to the base of the pyramidal structure, and ascended by regular stone steps, in some places forced apart by bushes and saplings, and in others thrown down by the growth of large trees, while some remained entire. In parts they were ornamented with sculptured figures and rows of death's heads. Climbing over the ruined top, we reached a terrace overgrown with trees, and, crossing it, descended by stone steps into an area so covered with trees that at first we could not make out its form, but which, on clearing the way with the machete, we ascertained to be a square, and with steps on all the sides almost as perfect as those of the Roman amphitheatre. The steps were ornamented with sculpture, and on the south side, about half way up, forced out of its place by roots, was a colossal head, evidently a portrait. We ascended these steps, and reached a broad terrace a hundred feet high, overlooking the river, and supported by the wall which we had seen from the opposite bank. The whole terrace was covered with trees, and even at this height from the ground were two gigantic Ceibas, or wild cotton-trees of India, above twenty feet in circumference, extending their half-naked roots fifty or a hundred feet around, binding down the ruins, and shading them with their wide-spreading branches. We sat down on the very edge of the wall, and strove in vain to penetrate the mystery by which we were surrounded. Who were the people that built this city? In the ruined cities of Egypt, even in the long-lost Petra, the stranger knows the story of the people whose vestiges are around him. America, say historians, was peopled by savages; but savages never reared these structures, savages never carved these stones. We asked the Indians who made them, and their dull answer was "Quién sabe?" "who knows?"

There were no associations connected with the place; none of those stirring recollections which hallow Rome, Athens, and "The world's great mistress on the Egyptian plain"; but architecture, sculpture, and painting, all the arts which embellish life, had flourished in this overgrown forest; orators, warriors, and statesmen, beauty, ambition, and glory, had lived and passed away, and none knew that such things had been, or could tell of their past existence. Books, the records of knowledge, are silent on this theme. The city was desolate. No remnant of this race hangs round the ruins, with traditions handed down from father to son, and from generation to generation. It lay before us like a shattered bark in the midst of the ocean, her masts gone, her name effaced, her crew perished, and none to tell whence she came, to whom she belonged, how long on her voyage, or what caused her destruction; her lost people to be traced only by some fancied resemblance in the construction of the vessel, and, perhaps, never to be known at all. The place where we sat, was it a citadel from which an unknown people had sounded the trumpet of war? or a temple for the worship of the God of peace? or did the inhabitants worship the idols made with their own hands, and offer sacrifices on the stones before them? All was mystery, dark, impenetrable mystery, and every circumstance increased it. In Egypt the colossal skeletons of gigantic temples stand in the unwatered sands in all the nakedness of desolation; here an immense forest shrouded the ruins, hiding them from sight, heightening the impression and moral effect, and giving an intensity and almost wildness to the interest.

Late in the afternoon we worked our way back to the mules, bathed in the clear river at the foot of the wall, and returned to the hacienda. . . . In the morning we continued to astonish the people by our strange ways, particularly by brushing our teeth, an operation which, probably, they saw then for the first time. While engaged in this, the door of the house opened, and Don Gregorio appeared, turning his head away to avoid giving us a buenos días. We resolved not to sleep another night under his shed, but to take our hammocks to the ruins, and, if there was no building to shelter us, to hang them up under a tree. My contract with the muleteer was to stop three days at Copán; but there was no bargain for the use of the mules during that time, and he hoped that the vexations we met with would make us go on immediately. When he found us bent on remaining, he swore he would not carry the hammocks, and would not remain one day over, but at length consented to hire the mules for that day.

Before we started a new party, who had been conversing some time with Don Gregorio, stepped forward, and said that he was the owner of "the idols"; that no one could go on the land without his permission; and handed me his title papers. This was a new difficulty. I was not disposed to dispute his title, but read his papers as attentively as if I meditated an action in ejectment; and he seemed relieved when I told him his title was good, and that, if not disturbed, I would make him a compliment at parting. Fortunately, he had a favour to ask. Our fame as physicians had reached the village, and he wished remedios for a sick wife. It was important to make him our friend; and, after some conversation, it was arranged that Mr. C., with several workmen whom we had hired, should go on to the ruins, as we intended, to make a lodgment there, while I would go to the village and visit his wife.

Our new acquaintance, Don José María Asebedo, was about fifty, tall, and well dressed; that is, his cotton shirt and pantaloons were clean; inoffensive, though ignorant; and one of the most respectable inhabitants of Copán. He lived in one of the best huts of the village, made of poles thatched with corn-leaves, with a wooden frame on one side for a bed, and furnished with a few pieces of pottery for cooking. A heavy rain had fallen during the night, and the ground inside the hut was wet. His wife seemed as old as he, and, fortunately, was suffering from a rheumatism of several years' standing. I say fortunately, but I speak only in reference to ourselves as medical men, and the honour of the profession accidentally confided to our hands. I told her that if it had been a recent affection, it would be more within the reach of art; but, as it was a case of old standing, it required time, skill, watching of symptoms, and the effect of medicine from day to day; and, for the present, I advised her to take her feet out of a puddle of water in which she was standing, and promised to consult Mr. Catherwood, who was even a better medico than I, and to send her a liniment with which to bathe her neck.

This over, Don José María accompanied me to the ruins, where I found Mr. Catherwood with the Indian workmen. Again we wandered over the whole ground in search of some ruined building in which we could take up our abode, but there was none. To hang up our hammocks under the trees was madness; the branches were still wet, the ground muddy, and again there was a prospect of early rain; but we were determined not to go back to Don Gregorio's. Don Mariano said that there was a hut near by, and conducted me to it. As we approached, we heard the screams of a woman inside, and, entering, saw her rolling and tossing on a bull's-hide bed, wild with fever and pain; and, starting to her knees at the sight of me, with her hands pressed against her temples, and tears bursting from her eyes, she begged me, for the love of God, to give her some remedios. Her skin was hot, her pulse very high; she had a violent intermitting fever. While inquiring into her symptoms, her husband entered the hut, a white man, about forty, dressed in a pair of dirty cotton drawers, with a nether garment hanging outside, a handkerchief tied around his head, and barefooted; and his name was *Don* Miguel. I told him that we wished to pass a few days among the ruins, and asked permission to stop at his hut. The woman, most happy at having a skilful physician near her, answered for him, and I returned to relieve Mr. Catherwood, and add another to his list of patients. The whole party escorted us to the hut, bringing along only the mule that carried the hammocks; and by the addition of Mr. C. to the medical corps, and a mysterious display of drawing materials and measuring rods, the poor woman's fever seemed frightened away. . . .

All day I had been brooding over the title-deeds of Don José María, and, drawing my blanket around me, suggested to Mr. Catherwood "an operation." (Hide your heads, ye speculators in up-town lots!) To buy Copán! remove the monuments of a by-gone people from the desolate region in which they were buried, set them up in the "great commercial emporium," and found an institution to be the nucleus of a great national museum of American antiquities! But quere, Could the "idols" be removed? They were on the banks of a river that emptied into the same ocean by which the docks of New-York are washed, but there were rapids below; and, in answer to my inquiry, Don Miguel said these were impassable. Nevertheless, I should have been unworthy of having passed through the times "that tried men's souls" if I had not had an alternative; and this was to exhibit by sample: to cut one up and remove it in pieces, and make casts of the others. The casts of the Parthenon are regarded as precious memorials in the British Museum, and casts of Copán would be the same in New-York. Other ruins might be discovered even more interesting and more accessible. Very soon their existence would become known and their value appreciated, and the friends of science and the arts in Europe would get possession of them. They belonged of right to us, and, though we did not know how soon we might be kicked out ourselves, I resolved that ours they should be; with visions of glory and indistinct fancies of receiving the thanks of the corporation flitting before my eyes, I drew my blanket around me, and fell asleep.

At daylight the clouds still hung over the forest; as the sun rose they cleared away; our workmen made their appearance, and at nine o'clock we left the hut. The branches of the trees were dripping wet, and the ground very muddy. Trudging once more over the district which contained the principal monuments, we were startled by the immensity of the work before us, and very soon we concluded that to explore the whole extent would be impossible. Our guides knew only of this district; but having seen columns beyond the village, a league distant, we had reason to believe that others were strewed in different directions, completely buried in the woods, and entirely unknown. The woods were so dense that it was almost hopeless to think of penetrating them. The only way to make a thorough exploration would be to cut down the whole forest and burn the trees. This was incompatible with our immediate purposes, might be considered taking liberties, and could only be done in the dry season. After deliberation, we resolved first to obtain drawings of the sculptured columns. Even in this there was great difficulty. The designs were very complicated, and so different from anything Mr. Catherwood had ever seen before as to be perfectly unintelligible. The cutting was in very high relief, and required a strong body of light to bring up the figures; and the foliage was so thick, and the shade so deep, that drawing was impossible.

After much consultation, we selected one of the "idols," and determined to cut down the trees around it, and thus lay it open to the rays of the sun. Here again was difficulty. There was no axe; and the only instrument which the Indians possessed was the machete, or chopping-knife, which varies in form in different sections of the country; wielded with one hand, it was useful in clearing away shrubs and branches, but almost harmless upon large trees; and the Indians, as in the days when the Spaniards discovered them, applied to work without ardour, carried it on with little activity, and, like children, were easily diverted from it. One hacked into a tree, and, when tired, which happened very soon, sat down to rest, and another relieved him. While one worked there were always several looking on. I remembered the ring of the woodman's axe in the forests at home, and wished for a few long-sided Green Mountain boys. But we had been buffeted into patience, and watched the Indians while they hacked with their machetes, and even wondered that they succeeded so well. At length the trees were felled and dragged aside, a space cleared around the base, Mr. C.'s frame set up, and he set to work. I took two mestizos, Bruno and Francisco, and, offering them a reward for every new discovery, with a compass in my hand set out on a tour of exploration. Neither had seen "the idols" until the morning of our first visit, when they followed in our train to laugh at los Ingleses; but very soon they exhibited such an interest that I hired them. Bruno attracted my attention by his admiration, as I supposed, of my person; but I found it was of my coat, which was a long shooting-frock, with many pockets; and he said that he could make one just like it except the skirts. He was a tailor by profession, and in the intervals of a great job upon a roundabout jacket, worked with his machete. But he had an inborn taste for the arts. As we passed through the woods, nothing escaped his eye, and he was professionally curious touching the costumes of the sculptured figures. I was struck with the first development of their antiquarian taste. Francisco found the feet and legs of a statue, and Bruno a part of the body to match, and the effect was electric upon both. They searched and raked up the ground with their machetes till they found the shoulders, and set it up entire except for the head; and they were both eager for the possession of instruments with which to dig and find this remaining fragment.

It is impossible to describe the interest with which I explored these ruins. The ground was entirely new; there were no guide-books or guides; the whole was a virgin soil. We could not see ten yards before us, and never knew what we should stumble upon next. At one time we stopped to cut away branches and vines which concealed the face of a monument, and then to dig around and bring to light a fragment, a sculptured corner of which protruded from the earth. I leaned over with breathless anxiety while the Indians worked, and an eye, an ear, a foot, or a hand was disentombed; and when the machete rang against the chiselled stone, I pushed the Indians away, and cleared out the loose earth with my hands. The beauty of the sculpture, the solemn stillness of the woods, disturbed only by the scrambling of monkeys and the chattering of parrots, the desolation of the city, and the mystery that hung over it, all created an interest higher, if possible, than I had ever felt among the ruins of the Old World. After several hours' absence I returned to Mr. Catherwood, and reported upward of fifty objects to be copied.

I found him not so well pleased as I expected with my report. He was standing with his feet in the mud, and was drawing with his gloves on, to protect his hands from the mosquitoes. As we feared, the designs were so intricate and complicated, the subjects so entirely new and unintelligible, that he had great difficulty in drawing. He had made several attempts, both with the camera lucida and without, but failed to satisfy himself or even me, who was less severe in criticism. The "idol" seemed to defy his art; two monkeys on a tree on one side appeared to be laughing at him, and I felt discouraged and despondent. In fact, I made up my mind, with a pang of regret, that we must abandon the idea of carrying away any materials for antiquarian speculation, and must be content with having seen them ourselves. Of that satisfaction nothing could deprive us. We returned to the hut with our interest undiminished, but sadly out of heart as to the results of our labours.

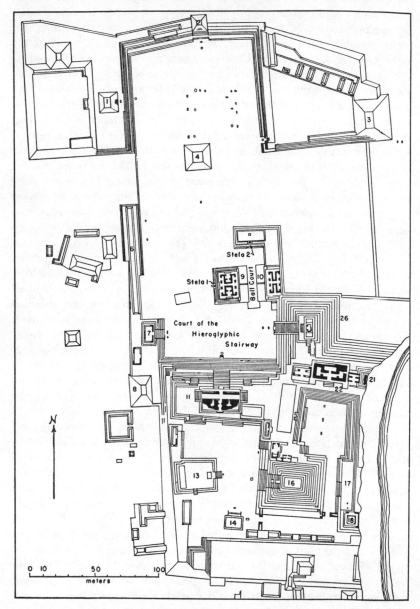

Plan of the main ruins of Copán

Our luggage had not been able to cross the river, but the blue bag which had caused me so many troubles was recovered. I had offered a dollar reward, and Bartolo, the heir-apparent of the lesseeship of our hut, had passed the day in the river, and found it entangled in a bush upon the bank. His naked body seemed glad of its accidental washing, and the bag, which we supposed to contain some of Mr. C.'s drawing materials, being shaken, gave out a pair of old boots, which, however, were at that time worth their weight in gold, being water-proof, and cheered Mr. Catherwood's drooping spirits, who was ill with a prospective attack of fever and ague or rheumatism, from standing all day in the mud. Our men went home, and Frederico had orders, before coming to work in the morning, to go to Don Gregorio's and buy bread, milk, candles, lard, and a few yards of beef. The door of the hut looked toward the west, and the sun set over the dark forest in front with a gorgeousness I have never seen surpassed. Again, during the night, we had rain, with thunder and lightning, but not so violent as the night before, and in the morning it was again clear.

That day Mr. Catherwood was much more successful in his drawings; indeed, at the beginning the light fell exactly as he wished, and he mastered the difficulty. His preparations, too, were much more comfortable, as he had his water-proofs, and stood on a piece of oiled canvas, used for covering luggage on the road. I passed the morning in selecting another monument, clearing away the trees, and preparing it for him to copy. At one o'clock Augustin came to call us to dinner. Don Miguel had a patch of beans, from which Augustin gathered as many as he pleased, and, with the fruits of a standing order for all the eggs in the village, being three or four a day, strings of beef, and bread and milk from the hacienda, we did very well. In the afternoon we were again called off by Augustin, with a message that the alcalde had come to pay us a visit. As it was growing late, we broke up for the day, and went back to the hut. We shook hands with the alcalde, and gave him and his attendants cigars, and were disposed to be sociable; but the dignitary was so tipsy he could hardly speak. His attendants sat crouching on the ground, swinging themselves on their knee joints, and, though the positions were different, reminding us of the Arabs. In a few minutes the alcalde started up suddenly, made a staggering bow, and left us, and they all followed, Don Miguel with them. While we were at supper he returned, and it was easy to see that he, and his wife, and Bartolo were in trouble, and, as we feared, the matter concerned us.

While we were busy with our own affairs, we had but little idea what a sensation we were creating in the village. Not satisfied with getting us out of his house, Don Gregorio wanted to get us out of the neighbourhood. Unluckily, besides his instinctive dislike, we had offended him in drawing off some of his workmen by the high prices which, as strangers, we were obliged to pay, and he began to look upon us as rivals, and said everywhere that we were suspicious characters; that we should be the cause of disturbing the peace of Copán, and introducing soldiers and war into the neighbourhood. In confirmation of this, two Indians passed through the village, who reported that we had escaped from imprisonment, had been chased to the borders of Honduras by a detachment of twenty-five soldiers under Landaveri, the officer who arrested us, and that, if we had been taken, we would have been shot. The alcalde, who had been drunk ever since our arrival, resolved to visit us, to solve the doubts of the village, and take those measures which the presence of such dangerous persons and the safety of the country might require. But this doughty purpose was frustrated by a ludicrous circumstance. We made it a rule to carry our arms with us to the ruins, and when we returned to the hut to receive his visit, as usual, each of us had a brace of pistols in his belt and a gun in hand; and our appearance was so formidable that the alcalde was frightened at his own audacity in having thought of catechising us, and fairly sneaked off. As soon as he reached the woods, his attendants reproached him for not executing his purpose, and he said, doggedly, that he was not going to have anything to say to men armed as we were. Roused at the idea of our terrible appearance, we told Don Miguel to advise the alcalde and the people of the village that they had better keep out of our way and let us alone. Don Miguel gave a ghastly smile; but all was not finished. He said that he had no doubt himself of our being good men, but we were suspected; the country was in a state of excitement; and he was warned that he ought not to harbour us, and would get into difficulty by doing so. The poor woman could not conceal her distress. Her head was full of assassinations and murders, and though alarmed for their safety, she was not unmindful of ours; she said that, if any soldiers came into the village, we would be murdered, and begged us to go away.

We were exceedingly vexed and disturbed by these communications, but we had too much at stake to consent to be driven away by apprehensions. We assured Don Miguel that no harm could happen to him; that it was all false and a mistake, and that we were above suspicion. At the same time, in order to convince him, I opened my trunk, and showed him a large bundle of papers, sealed credentials to the government and private letters of introduction in Spanish to prominent men in Guatemala, describing me as "Encargado de los Negocios de los Estados Unidos del Norte," and one very special from Don Antonio Aycinena, now in this city, formerly colonel in the Central army, and banished by Morazán,

Glyph-covered Copán Stela 3, after Catherwood's drawing

to his brother the Marquis Aycinena, the leader of the Central party, which was dominant in that district in the civil war then raging, recommending me very highly, and stating my purpose of travelling through the country. This last letter was more important than anything else; and if it had been directed to one of the opposite party in politics, it would have been against us, as confirming the suspicion of our being "enemigos." Never was greatness so much under a shade. Though vexatious, it was almost amusing to be obliged to clear up our character to such a miserable party as Don Miguel, his wife, and Bartolo; but it was indispensable to relieve them from doubts and anxieties, enabling us to remain quietly in their wretched hut; and the relief they experienced, and the joy of the woman in learning that we were tolerably respectable people, not enemies, and not in danger of being put up and shot at, were most grateful to us.

Nevertheless, Don Miguel advised us to go to Guatemala or to General Cascara, procure an order to visit the ruins, and then return. We had made a false step in one particular; we should have gone direct to Guatemala, and returned with a passport and letters from the government; but, as we had no time to spare, and did not know what there was at Copán, probably if we had not taken it on the way we should have missed it altogether. And we did not know that the country was so completely secluded; the people are less accustomed to the sight of strangers than the Arabs about Mount Sinai, and they are much more suspicious. Colonel Galindo was the only stranger who had been there before us, and he could hardly be called a stranger, for he was a colonel in the Central American service, and visited the ruins under a commission from the government. Our visit has perhaps had some influence upon the feelings of the people; it has, at all events, taught Don Gregorio that strangers are not easily got rid of; but I advise any one who wishes to visit these ruins in peace, to go to Guatemala first, and apply to the government for all the protection it can give. As to us, it was too late to think of this, and all we had to do was to maintain our ground as quietly as we could. We had no apprehension of soldiers coming from any other place merely to molest us. Don Miguel told us, what we had before observed, that there was not a musket in the village; the quality and excellence of our arms were well known; the muleteer had reported that we were outrageous fellows, and had threatened to shoot him; and the alcalde was an excessive coward. We formed an alliance, offensive and defensive, with Don Miguel, his wife, and Bartolo, and went to sleep. Don Miguel and his wife, by-the-way, were curious people; they slept with their heads at different ends of the bed, so that, in the unavoidable accompaniment of smoking, they could clear each other.

In the morning we were relieved from our difficulty, and put in a position to hurl defiance at the traducers of our character. While the workmen were gathering outside the hut, an Indian courier came trotting through the cornfield up to the door, who inquired for Señor Ministro; and pulling off his petate, took out of the crown a letter, which he said he was ordered by General Cascara to deliver into the right hands. It was directed to "Señor Catherwood, a Comotán o donde se halle," conveying the expression of General Cascara's regret for the arrest at Comotán, ascribing it to the ignorance or mistake of the alcalde and soldiers, and enclosing, besides, a separate passport for Mr. Catherwood. I have great satisfaction in acknowledging the receipt of this letter; and the promptness with which General Cascara despatched it to "Comotán, or wherever he may be found," was no less than I expected from his character and station. I requested Don Miguel to read it aloud, told the Indian to deliver our compliments to General Cascara, and sent him to the village to breakfast, with a donation which I knew would make him publish the story with right emphasis and discretion. Don Miguel smiled, his wife laughed, and a few spots of white flashed along Bartolo's dirty skin. Stocks rose, and I resolved to ride to the village, strengthen the cords of friendship with Don José María, visit our patients, defy Don Gregorio, and get up a party in Copán.

Mr. Catherwood went to the ruins to continue his drawings, and I to the village, taking Augustin with me to fire the Belize guns, and buy up eatables for a little more than they were worth. My first visit was to Don José María. After clearing up our character, I broached the subject of a purchase of the ruins; told him that, on account of my public business, I could not remain as long as I desired, but wished to return with spades, pickaxes, ladders, crowbars, and men, build a hut to live in, and make a thorough exploration; that I could not incur the expense at the risk of being refused permission to do so; and in short, in plain English, asked him, What will you take for the ruins? I think he was not more surprised than if I had asked to buy his poor old wife, our rheumatic patient, to practice medicine upon. He seemed to doubt which of us was out of his senses. The property was so utterly worthless that my wanting to buy it seemed very suspicious. On examining the paper, I found that he did not own the fee, but held under a lease from Don Bernardo de Aguila, of which three years were unexpired. The tract consisted of about six thousand acres, for which he paid eighty dollars a year; he was at a loss what to do, but told me that he would reflect upon it, consult his wife, and give me an answer at the hut the next day. I then visited the alcalde, but he was too tipsy to be susceptible of any impression; prescribed for several patients; and instead of going to Don Gregorio's, sent him a polite request by Don José María to mind his own business and let us alone; returned, and passed the rest of the day among the ruins. It rained during the night, but again cleared off in the morning, and we were on the ground early. My business was to go around with workmen to clear away trees and bushes, dig, and excavate, and prepare monuments for Mr. Catherwood to copy. While so engaged, I was called off by a visit from Don José María, who was still undecided what to do; and not wishing to appear too anxious, told him to take more time, and come again the next morning.

Copán altar: two sides. Reliefs perhaps depict a congregation of priest-astronomers.

The next morning he came, and his condition was truly pitiable. He was anxious to convert unproductive property into money, but afraid, and said that I was a stranger, and it might bring him into difficulty with the government. I again went into proof of character, and engaged to save him harmless with the government or release him. Don Miguel read my letters of recommendation, and re-read the letter of General Cascara. He was convinced, but these papers did not give him a right to sell me his land; the shade of suspicion still lingered; for a finale, I opened my trunk, and put on a diplomatic coat, with a profusion of large eagle buttons. I had on a Panama hat, soaked with rain and spotted with mud, a check shirt, white pantaloons, yellow up to the knees with mud, and was about as outré as the negro king who received a company of British officers on the coast of Africa in a cocked hat and military coat, without any inexpressibles; but Don José María could not withstand the buttons on my coat; the cloth was the finest he had ever seen; and Don Miguel, and his wife, and Bartolo realized fully that they had in their hut an illustrious incognito. The only question was who should find paper on which to draw the contract. I did not stand upon trifles, and gave Don Miguel some paper, who took our mutual instructions, and appointed the next day for the execution of the deed.

The reader is perhaps curious to know how old cities sell in Central America. Like other articles of trade, they are regulated by the quantity in market, and the demand; but, not being staple articles, like cotton and indigo, they were held at fancy prices, and at that time were dull of sale. I paid fifty dollars for Copán. There was never any difficulty about price. I offered that sum, for which Don José María thought me only a fool; if I had offered more, he would probably have considered me something worse.

We had regular communications with the hacienda by means of Francisco, who brought thence every morning a large guacal of milk, carrying it a distance of three miles, and fording the river twice. The ladies of the hacienda had sent us word that they intended paying us a visit, and this morning Don Gregorio's wife appeared, leading a procession of all the women of the house, servants, and children, with two of her sons. We received them among the ruins, seated them as well as we could, and, as the first act of civility, gave them cigars all around. It can hardly be believed, but not one of them, not even Don Gregorio's sons, had ever seen the "idols" before, and now they were much more curious to see Mr. C.'s drawings. In fact, I believe it was the fame of these drawings that procured us the honour of their visit. In his heart Mr. C. was not much happier to see them than the old don was to see us, as his work was stopped, and every day was precious. As I considered myself in a manner the proprietor of the city, I was bound to do the honours; and, having cleared paths, led them around, showing off all the lions as the cicerone does in the Vatican or the Pitti Palace; but I could not keep them away, and, to the distress of Mr. C., brought them all back upon him. . . .

Of the moral effect of the monuments themselves, standing as they do in the depths of a tropical forest, silent and solemn, strange in design, excellent in sculpture, rich in ornament, different from the works of any other people, their uses and purposes, their whole history so entirely unknown, with hieroglyphics explaining all, but perfectly unintelligible, I shall not pretend to convey any idea. Often the imagination was pained in gazing at them. The tone which pervades the ruins is that of deep solemnity. An imaginative mind might be infected with superstitious feelings. From constantly calling them by that name in our intercourse with the Indians, we regarded these solemn memorials as "idols"—deified kings and heroes—objects of adoration and ceremonial worship. We did not find on either of the monuments or sculptured fragments any delineations of human, or, in fact, any other kind of sacrifice, but had no doubt that the large sculptured stone invariably found before each "idol" was employed as a sacrificial altar. The form of sculpture most frequently met with was a death's head, sometimes the principal ornament, and sometimes only accessory; whole rows of them on the outer wall, adding gloom to the mystery of the place, keeping before the eyes of the living death and the grave, presenting the idea of a holy city—the Mecca or Jerusalem of an unknown people.

Broken Copán sculpture

In regard to the age of this desolate city I shall not at present offer any conjecture. Some idea might perhaps be formed from the accumulations of earth and the gigantic trees growing on the top of the ruined structures, but it would be uncertain and unsatisfactory. Nor shall I at this moment offer any conjecture in regard to the people who built it, or to the time when or the means by which it was depopulated, and became a desolation and ruin; whether it fell by the sword, or famine, or pestilence. The trees which shroud it may have sprung from the blood of its slaughtered inhabitants; they may have perished howling with hunger; or pestilence, like the cholera, may have piled its streets with dead, and driven forever the feeble remnants from their homes; of which dire calamities to other cities we have authentic accounts, in eras both prior and subsequent to the discovery of the country by the Spaniards. One thing I believe, that its history is graven on its monuments. No Champollion has yet brought to them the energies of his inquiring mind. Who shall read them?

> Chaos of ruins! who shall trace the void,
> O'er the dim fragments cast a lunar light,
> And say "here *was* or is," where all is doubly night?

20

The reading of Stephens' books made a Maya enthusiast of a New England boy, Edward Herbert Thompson (1860–1935), whose hobby was the collection of Indian relics. As a result of his untamed *Mayismo,* he contributed to the *Popular Science Monthly* in 1879 a fanciful article, "Atlantis Not a Myth," wherein he warmed up the tedious claptrap that the magnificent Mayas were really a branch of the lost Atlantis civilization. Such a fantasy may not have held out great promise for its youthful author's future reputation in scholarship, but the roads to archaeology are of infinite variety and varying respectability. Flinders Petrie, who became the most exacting of Egyptologists, started out with an absurd theory on the magic proportions of the great Pyramids of Gizeh.

However, Thompson, whose archaeological discoveries were to be manifold and substantial, always retained the traits of a dreamer and adventurer. He belongs with such nineteenth-century explorers of Old World antiquities as Botta, Layard, and Schliemann. Professional archaeologists rarely take kindly to his work, and disapprove of his failure to properly organize his findings. In all his campaigns he worked alone, employing only untrained natives, or, in the case of the Sacred Well, a few Greek sponge fishers. He trusted implicitly traditions, folk memories, or the hints dropped by ancient authors; once they had fired his romantic imagination, he would cling tenaciously. And in the end some of his hunches were borne out by archaeological conquests.

Thompson settled at the ancient Maya city of Chichen Itzá, in northern Yucatán about seventy miles east of Mérida, in the early 1890's. This was the site explored by Stephens in his later travels. A highly ornate, rich metropolis with a great number of impressive buildings—including the typical Mesoamerican cluster of pyramids, temples, ballparks and observatory, in addition to a colonnaded market place—Chichen Itzá is culturally and artistically one of the most vital centers of pre-Columbian America. It was undoubtedly a celebrated shrine for religious pilgrimages, visited by the faithful who offered their gifts and received guidance. Chichen Itzá apparently was abandoned around A.D. 1480, but it was known to the early Spanish invaders, who fought an engagement from the steps of one of the pyramids.

Thompson's attention was turned to the so-called Well of Sacrifice (*chen ku* in Maya) through his study of the *Relación de las Cosas de Yucatán* by a sixteenth-century Spanish bishop of Yucatán, Diego de Landa, whose manuscript had only been rediscovered and published by the Abbé Brasseur de Bourbourg in the 1860's (hence its printed version could not have been quite as "musty" and "old" as Thompson declares).

The well was a caved-in subterranean lake or limestone cavern, a jurassic formation not at all rare in Yucatán, called by the Spanish *cenote* (a corruption of the Maya *dz'onot*). Dzibilchaltún, north of Mérida, had as many as fourteen of these, and twenty-eight have been reported on Cozumel Island. Chichen Itzá—the name means literally "mouths of the wells of the Itzá"—had actually two large wells. One was used as a water reservoir. Latter-day archaeologists enjoyed it as a swimming pool. The other, less attractive one, in the city's north, was a sacred ritual and devotional center. A wide causeway from the "Castillo" or Pyramid of Kukulcan led to it and an adjoining small temple where priests must have offered sacrifices. Bishop Landa says that the Maya held the well at Chichen "in the same veneration as we have for pilgrimages to Jerusalem and Rome; and so they used to go to these places and offer presents. . . . They threw into it [the well] many other things like precious stones and things which they prized. And so, if they had possessed gold, it would be this well that would have the greater part of it, so great was the devotion which the Indians showed for it."

Later on, Thompson came across still another early Spanish account, indicating that offerings included sacrifices of beautiful maidens, who were cast into the watery pit in order to propitiate the great Rain God living at the bottom of the well. Survivors of the ordeal were supposed to transmit messages from the god.

The grisly *cenote* of dark, stagnant waters, which attracted Thompson's curiosity, is an uninviting oval water hole about 165 by 200 feet, with a depth of some 35 feet of water and an underlying layer of mud and silt approximately as deep. It is surrounded by vertical limestone cliffs rising another seventy feet above the water surface. Thompson's defeat of the "grim old pit," the terror of the natives, and the doubts of scholars is one of the ever-popular yarns of archaeological adventure. His brave underwater explorations anticipated the submarine researches of Jacques-Yves Cousteau, Philippe Diolé, and their followers. Repeated divings, mostly from 1904 to 1907, produced a number of fairly precious objects:

pottery, gems and carved jades (some dated), besides copper bells, exquisitely chased golden bowls, pieces of fabrics, spear throwers (*atlatls*), balls of copal incense, sacrificial knives, and human skeletal remains. Objects had been deliberately broken—"killed"—to let their spirits escape. Most of Thompson's findings were handed over to the Peabody Museum in Cambridge, Massachusetts.

During the Carranza regime at the beginning of World War I, rumors of fabulous gold treasures from the *cenote* reached the Mexican government, which accused Thompson of illegally exporting antiquities and sued him for a fantastic amount. Joining several political opponents of Carranza, Thompson boarded an unfinished schooner. In a hair-raising escape, without naval instruments or sufficient provisions, they reached Havana in thirteen days. Thompson was never again to see Mexico, where he had spent some thirty years.

At the age of twenty-five Thompson had come, in 1885, to Yucatán as American consul. The foreign appointment served him as a convenient base for archaeological exploration. Later, when with the aid of wealthy American friends (the Armours of Chicago) he was able to buy virtually the entire site of the Chichen Itzá ruins—a former cattle ranch of roughly three square miles—he devoted himself largely to excavation on his unique estate. His discoveries at Chichen Itzá and nearby, recorded with great gusto in his autobiographical *People of the Serpent* (1932), include a "Maya Venus"; the grave of a high priest, remindful of Ruz Lhuillier's later excavations at Palenque; the Temple of the Painted Columns; the Chichen Itzá date stone; and the hidden city of Xkichmook.

For many years Thompson planned the Well of Sacrifice campaign, which he hoped would be the "culminating achievement" of his career. This, indeed, it proved to be, though it required enormous labors and risks, impaired his health, and in the end drove him from the land he had loved, the land where he had gained the friendship of the native inhabitants (he was initiated into their secret Sh' Tol society and attended Maya ceremonies never seen by another white man).

Returning to the United States, Thompson settled in New England. There he lectured and wrote on his chosen subject. In addition, he explored ancient Indian sites in Oklahoma. In his last years he could say: "I have spent my substance in riotous exploration and I am altogether satisfied."

During the civil disturbances of the Mexican Revolution, Thompson's hacienda with his priceless collection was burned down. Soon after, the Mexican government confiscated the Chichen Itzá estate. Later, however, the buildings were leased to the Carnegie Institution of Washington.

New campaigns to recover sacrificial objects and treasures from the

Chichen Itzá well were undertaken successfully in years to come. But first Alfred M. Tozzer and Samuel K. Lothrop re-examined and described the various objects Thompson had sent to the Peabody Museum of Archaeology and Ethnology, Harvard University. The well section determined so ingeniously by Thompson as being the one most likely to be the site of submerged offerings proved to be by no means the only one rich in treasures of all kinds. Skeletal examinations also poured cold water on the eerie picture—so dear to the popular literature—of beautiful flower-decked young maidens diving to their doom in the murky well. The majority of the bones belonged to men and, true to sacrificial practices all over the Americas, to children—at least half of them less than six years old. Of eight women, seven were of mature age. Most likely, human sacrifices took place at the *cenote* even after the arrival of the Spaniards, until as late as 1580.

THE CHICHEN ITZÁ CENOTE

Edward Herbert Thompson

I have referred before to an article, "Atlantis Not a Myth," written during my college days, and of the important bearing it had on determining my future course. It was while hunting up material for this article that I first came upon an old volume written by Diego de Landa, one of the earliest Spanish missionaries to Yucatán and later bishop of that diocese. Among other things recounted in quaint old Spanish in this book was a description of Chichen Itzá, the capital and sacred city of the Mayas. The wise priest laid a special emphasis upon the traditions concerning the Sacred Well that lay within the confines of the city.

According to these traditions, as told to De Landa by his native converts, in times of drought, pestilence, or disaster, solemn processions of priests, devotees with rich offerings, and victims for the sacrifice wound down the steep stairway of the Temple of Kukil Can, the Sacred Serpent, and along the Sacred Way to the Well of Sacrifice. There, amid the

Reprinted by permission of G. P. Putnam's Sons from *People of the Serpent*, by Edward Herbert Thompson (Boston: Houghton Mifflin Co., 1932, pp. 268–89). Copyright © 1930 by Edward Herbert Thompson.

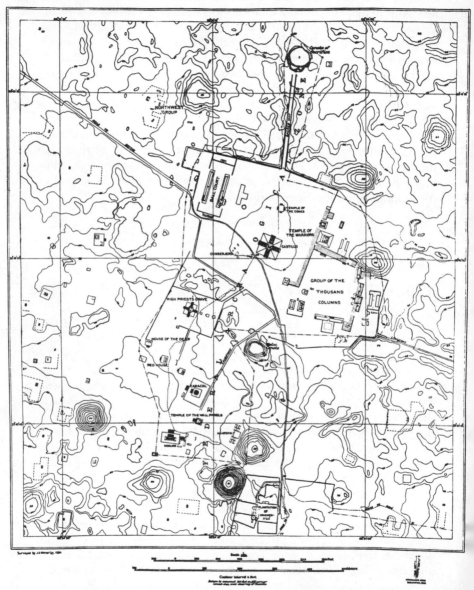

Principal ruins of Chichen Itzá. The modern highway runs across; the Well of
Sacrifice lies at the top.

droning boom of the *tunkul,* the shrill pipings of the whistle and the plaintive notes of the flute, beautiful maidens and captive warriors of renown, as well as rich treasures, were thrown into the dark waters of the Sacred Well to propitiate the angry god who, it was believed, lived in the deeps of the pool.

From the moment I read the musty old volume, the thought of that grim old water pit and the wonderful objects that lay concealed within its depths became an obsession with me. Then, long years after, by what seemed to me almost an interposition of Providence, I became the sole owner of the great Chichen plantation, within whose confines the City of the Sacred Well and the Sacred Well itself lay.

For days and weeks after I purchased the plantation, I was a frequent worshiper at the little shrine on the brink of the Sacred Well. I pondered, mused, and calculated. I made measurements and numberless soundings, until, not satisfied but patiently expectant, I put my notebook aside and awaited the accepted time. It came when I was called to the United States for a scientific conference. After the session was over, at an informal gathering I told of the tradition concerning this Sacred Well of Chichen Itzá, of my belief in its authenticity, and the methods by which I proposed to prove it.

My statements brought forth a storm of protests from my friends.

"No person," they said, "can go down into the unknown depths of that great water pit and expect to come out alive. If you want to commit suicide, why not seek a less shocking way of doing it?"

But I had already weighed the chances and made up my mind. My next step was to go to Boston and take lessons in deep-sea diving. My tutor was Captain Ephraim Nickerson of Long Wharf, who passed to his reward a score of years ago. Under his expert and patient teaching, I became in time a fairly good diver, but by no means a perfect one, as I was to learn some time later. My next move was to adapt to my purpose an "orange-peel bucket" dredge with the winch, tackles, steel cables, and ropes of a stiff-legged derrick and a thirty-foot swinging boom. All this material was crated and ready for immediate shipment when ordered by either letter or wire.

Then, and not until then, did I appear before the Honorable Stephen Salisbury of Worcester, Massachusetts, and Charles P. Bowditch of Boston, both officers of the American Antiquarian Society and of Harvard University of which the Peabody Museum is a part. To them I explained the project and asked the moral and financial aid of the two organizations they represented. Although I had headed several important and successful expeditions under the auspices of these institutions, I found both of these gentlemen very reluctant to put the seal of their approval upon what they clearly believed to be a most audacious undertaking. They were willing to finance the scheme, but hesitated to take upon themselves the responsibility for my life.

I finally argued them out of their fears, and all other obstacles having been overcome, the dredge and its equipment were duly installed on the platform to the right of the shrine, and close to the edge of the great water pit, the Sacred Well.

During my preliminary investigations I had established what I called the "fertile zone" by throwing in wooden logs shaped like human beings and having the weight of the average native. By measuring the rope after these manikins were hauled ashore, I learned the extreme distance to which sacrificial victims could have been thrown. In this way I fixed the spot where the human remains would probably be found. Regulating my operations by these calculations, I found them to respond with gratifying accuracy.

I doubt if anybody can realize the thrill I felt when, with four men at the winch handles and one at the brake, the dredge, with its steel jaw agape, swung from the platform, hung poised for a brief moment in mid-air over the dark pit and then, with a long swift glide downward, entered the still, dark waters and sank smoothly on its quest. A few moments of waiting to allow the sharp-pointed teeth to bite into the deposit, and then the forms of the workmen bent over the winch handles and muscles under the dark brown skin began to play like quicksilver as the steel cables tautened under the strain of the upcoming burden.

The water, until then still as an obsidian mirror, began to surge and boil around the cable and continued to do so long after the bucket, its tightly closed jaws dripping clear water, had risen, slowly but steadily, up to the rim of the pit. Swinging around by the boom, the dredge deposited on the planked receiving platform a cartload of dark brown material, wood punk, dead leaves, broken branches, and other debris; then it swung back and hung, poised, ready to seek another load.

For days the dredge went up and down, up and down, interminably, bringing up muck and rocks, muck, more muck. Once it brought up, gripped lightly in its jaws, the trunk of a tree apparently as sound as if toppled into the pit by a storm of yesterday. This was on a Saturday. By Monday the tree had vanished and on the pile of rocks where the dredge had deposited it only a few lines of wood fibre remained, surrounded by a dark stain of a pyroligneous character. Another time the dredge brought up the bones of a jaguar and those of a deer, mute evidence of a forest tragedy. And so the work went on for days.

I began to get nervous by day and sleepless at night.

"Is it possible," I asked myself, "that I have let my friends into all this expense and exposed myself to a world of ridicule only to prove, what many have contended, that these traditions are simply old tales, tales without any foundation in fact?"

At times, as if to tantalize me, the dredge recovered portions of earthen vessels undeniably ancient. I resolutely threw aside the thought that these might be the proofs I sought. Potsherds, I argued, were likely to be found anywhere on the site of this old city, washed from the surface deposits by rains. Boys are boys, whether in Yucatán or Massachusetts, and have been for some thousands of years. The instinct of a boy is to "skitter" any smooth hard object, stone or potsherd, across smooth waters like those of the deep water pit and then it rests amid the mud and rocks at the bottom until brought up by the dredge. I could not accept these chance potsherds as the proofs that I required.

One day—I remember it as if it were but yesterday—I rose in the morning from a sleepless night. The day was gray as my thoughts and the thick mist dropped from the leaves of the trees as quiet tears drop from half-closed eyes. I plodded through the dampness down to where the staccato clicks of the dredge brake called me and, crouching under the palm leaf lean-to, watched the monotonous motions of the brown-skinned natives as they worked at the winches. The bucket slowly emerged from the heaving water that boiled around it and, as I looked listlessly down into it, I saw two yellow-white, globular masses lying on the surface of the chocolate-colored muck that filled the basin. As the mass swung over the brink and up to the platform, I took from it the two objects and closely examined them.

They were hard, formed evidently by human hands from some substance unknown to me. They resembled somewhat the balls of "bog butter" from the lacustrine deposits of Switzerland and Austria. There, ancient dwellings were built on piles in the midst of the lake to protect them against raiding enemies. The crocks of butter were suspended by cords let down between the piles and immersed in the ice-cold water for preservation. Despite all their precaution, raids did occur and the dwellings were destroyed by casual fires as well as by raids; so the crocks of butter fell unobserved from the charred piles down through the icy waters to rest unheeded in the increasing deposit until ages of time changed them into the almost fossilized material known to archaeologists as "bog butter."

But these two nodules could not be bog butter, for unless the known data are strangely wrong, the ancient Mayas kept no domestic animals of any kind, much less cows or goats. They seemed to be made of some resinous substance. I tasted one. It was resin. I put a piece into a mass of lighted embers and immediately a wonderful fragrance permeated the atmosphere. Like a ray of bright sunlight breaking through a dense fog came to me the words of the old *H'Men,* the Wise Man of Ebtun: "In ancient times our fathers burned the sacred resin—*pom*—and by the fragrant smoke their prayers were wafted to their God whose home was in the Sun."

These yellow balls of resin were masses of the sacred incense *pom,* and had been thrown in as part of the rich offerings mentioned in the traditions. That night for the first time in weeks I slept soundly and long.

For a long time the belief had been growing in my mind that the scientific exploration of this Sacred Well of Chichen Itzá was to be the crowning event of my life-work, and that to do it as it should be done, I must give it all my time and attention. With the finding of these two nodules and realization of what they indicated, this belief became a certainty. After much reflection I resigned my position as consul and devoted myself entirely to the work.

Chichen Itzá, *cenote* in foreground, drawn by Tatiana Proskouriakoff

From that time on for months there was seldom a day when the dredge failed to yield objects of great scientific interest, earthen vessels, temple vases and incense burners, arrow-heads, lance-points finely shaped and chipped with wonderful skill, axes and hammer stones of flint and calcite. There were copper chisels, too, and disks of beaten copper covered with symbolical emblems and the conventionalized figures of the Maya deities, bells, disks, and pendent figures of low-grade gold, beads, pendants, and fragments of jade. Among the finds were the skeletons of young women, of thick-skulled, low-browed men. In every detail the old traditions were corroborated.

And now we come to the weirdest part of the weird undertaking, but, in order to put each thing in its proper place and make all matters clear, I must speak once more of the details of the sacrifices at this Sacred Well as reported in the ancient accounts.

The legend regarding the Sacred Well and the sacrificial rites performed therein was so clearly and yet so quaintly stated by the Alcalde of Valladolid, Don Diego Sarmiento de Figueroa, in 1579, that I am going to give his account here. Valladolid is the shire town of the *partido,* or county, in which Chichen is situated, and the *Alcalde* corresponds as nearly as possible to the office we call mayor. This account is the official and authentic report rendered by the *Alcalde* to his sovereign, Carlos V of Spain. He writes of the Sacred Well, called by him the *Cenote,* as follows:

The lords and principal personages of the land had the custom, after sixty days of abstinence and fasting, of arriving by daybreak at the mouth of the *Cenote* and throwing into it Indian women belonging to each of these lords and personages, at the same time telling these women to ask for their masters a year favorable to his particular needs and desires.

The women, being thrown in unbound, fell into the water with great force and noise. At high noon those that could cried out loudly and ropes were let down to them. After the women came up, half dead, fires were built around them and copal incense was burned before them. When they recovered their senses, they said that below there were many people of their nation, men and women, and that they received them. When they tried to raise their heads to look at them, heavy blows were given them on the head, and when their heads were inclined downward beneath the water they seemed to see many deeps and hollows, and they, the people, responded to their queries concerning the good or the bad year that was in store for their masters.

I had some time before caused to be built a large, flat scow to serve me in the diving operations which I planned to carry on later and had lowered it by means of the derrick down to the surface of the well. There, moored to a rock shelf, it floated on the still water, awaiting the time for its use. One day I sat in it writing my notes and waiting for repairs that were being made on the dredge. The scow was moored ten feet under the overhang of the cliff-like wall and directly under the site of the derrick, sixty feet or more above. Looking casually over the gunwale, I saw that which gave me a thrill. It was the key to the story of the woman messengers in the old tradition.

The waters of the two great *cenotes* around which the ancient city was built are totally unlike. The water of one, called by the natives *Toloc*, and used by me as a bathing-pool, is dark blue by reason of depth, but is actually as clear and transparent, if not as cool, as the waters of a mountain lake. The water of the other, *Chen Ku*, or Well of the Sacrifices, is, on the contrary, dark colored and turbid, changing in hue at times from brown to jade green and even to a blood-red, as I shall later describe, but it is always so turbid that it reflects the light like a mirror rather than deflecting it like a crystal.

Looking over the gunwale of the pontoon and downward to the water surface, I could see, as if looking down through great depths, "many deeps and hollows." They were in reality the reflections of the cavities and hollow places in the side of the cliff directly above me.

When they recovered their senses, the women had said: "Below, there were many people of their nation and they . . . responded to our queries." As I continued to gaze into those deeps and hollows, I saw below many people of their nation and they, too, responded. They were the heads and parts of the bodies of my workmen, leaning over the brink of the well to catch a glimpse of the pontoon. Meanwhile they conversed in low tones and the sound of their voices, directed downward, struck the water surface and was deflected upwards to my ears in words softly sounding in native accent, yet intelligible. The whole episode gave me an explanation of the old tradition that developed as clearly as the details of a photographic negative.

The natives of the region have long asserted that at times the waters of the Sacred Well turn to blood. We found out that the green color the water sometimes shows was caused by the growth of a microscopic algae; its occasional brown hue was caused by decaying leaves; and certain flowers and seed capsules, blood-red in color, at times gave the surface of the water an appearance like that of clotted blood.

I mention these discoveries to show why I have come to believe that all authentic traditions have a basis of fact and can always be explained by a sufficiently close observation of the conditions.

The time finally came when the dredge no longer brought up valuable material from the bottom of the well. For weeks and months it had ceaselessly chewed its way through the thick deposit on the bottom within the area of the "fertile zone." For some time past the material that collected in the basin of the dredge was mostly a thin, watery mud, with only an occasional object of scientific value embedded in it. For a while the dredge doubled its trips and lessened the time of making them by dumping the load into the waiting scow, where the contents were carefully examined and the tailings dumped on the shore of the Little Beach.

On the western side of the Sacred Well and nearly on a level with its waters, a rock shelf stands out from the cliff-like walls far enough to form a narrow beach and strong enough to support a thick clump of balsawood trees called by the natives *mash*. The interlacing roots of these strange trees, half-buried in the black mold about them and half-showing, darkly smooth and shining, seem like the writhing bodies of antediluvian reptiles. In the moist and darkly shadowed places beneath them can be seen the glistening eyes of giant toads, turtles, and lizards. This little beach is like a scene from the time when the world was young.

As each afternoon the tailings were thrown from the scow to the beach, the big lizards, their serrated backs bristling, would slink silently deeper into their holes, and the giant toads, their eyes blazing like diamond points in the darkness of their sheltered crannies, would cry out in deeptoned chorus: "Don't! Don't!"

At least so it seemed to me as, wet to the skin and plastered with sticky, black mud, I kept on throwing out the tailings.

When the dredge at the Sacred Well came up holding in its basin only the mud and sticks that had fallen into it from the loose material above; when the sharp-pointed steel teeth came up gritting with slivers of the rock bottom between them, we decided that our work with the dredge was finished. From now on human fingers must search in the crevices and the crannies of the bottom for the objects that the dredge could not reach to grasp. Nicolas, a Greek diver with whom I had previously made arrangements, arrived from the Bahamas where he had been gathering sponges. He brought an assistant, also a Greek, and we prepared at once for under-water exploration.

We first rigged the air pump in the boat, no longer a scow but once more a dignified pontoon, and then the two Greeks, turned instructors, taught a chosen gang of natives how to manage the pumps and send through the tube in a steady current the air upon which our lives depended and how to read and answer signals sent up from below. When they considered that the men were letter perfect, we were ready to dive.

We rode down to the pontoon in the basin of the dredge, and while the assistant took his place by the men at the pump to direct them, we put on our suits, outfits of waterproof canvas with big copper helmets weighing more than thirty pounds and equipped with plate-glass goggle eyes and air valves near the ears, lead necklaces nearly half as heavy as the helmets and canvas shoes with thick wrought-iron soles. With the speaking-tube, air hose, and life-line carefully adjusted, I toddled, aided by the assistant, to where a short, wide ladder fastened to the gunwale led down into the water.

As I stepped on the first rung of the ladder, each of the pumping gang, my faithful native boys, left his place in turn and with a very solemn face shook hands with me and then went back again to wait for the signal. It was not hard to read their thoughts. They were bidding me a last farewell, never expecting to see me again. Then, releasing my hold on the ladder, I sank like a bag of lead, leaving behind me a silvery chain of bubbles.

During the first ten feet of descent, the light rays changed from yellow to green and then to a purplish black. After that I was in utter darkness. Sharp pains shot through my ears, because of the increasing air pressure. When I gulped and opened the air valves in my helmet a sound like "pht! pht!" came from each ear and then the pain ceased. Several times this process had to be repeated before I stood on the bottom. I noted another curious sensation on my way down. I felt as if I were rapidly losing weight until, as I stood on the flat end of a big stone column that had fallen from the old ruined shrine above, I seemed to have almost no weight at all. I fancied that I was more like a bubble than a man clogged by heavy weights.

But I felt as well a strange thrill when I realized that I was the only living being who had ever reached this place alive and expected to leave it again still living. Then the Greek diver came down beside me and we shook hands.

I had brought with me a submarine flashlight and a submarine telephone, both of which I discarded after the first descent. The submarine flashlight was serviceable in clear water or water merely turbid. The medium in which we had to work was neither water nor mud, but a combination of both, stirred up by the working of the dredge. It was a thick mixture like gruel and no ray so feeble as that of a flashlight could even penetrate it. So we had to work in utter darkness; yet, after a short time, we hardly felt the fact to be a serious inconvenience; for the palpic whorls of our finger-ends seemed not only to distinguish objects by the sense of touch, but actually to aid in distinguishing color.

The submarine telephone was of very little use and was soon laid aside. Communication by the speaking-tube and life-line was easier and even quicker than by telephone. There was another strange thing that I have never heard mentioned by other divers. Nicolas and I found that at the depth we were working, from sixty to eighty feet, we could sit down and put our noses together—the noses of our helmets, be it understood—and could then talk to each other quite intelligibly. Our voices sounded flat and lifeless as if coming from a great distance, but I could give him my instructions and I could hear his replies quite clearly.

The curious loss of weight under water led me into several ludicrous mishaps before I became accustomed to it. In order to go from place to place on the bottom, I had only to stand up and push with my foot on the rock bottom. At once I would rise like a rocket, sail majestically through the mud gruel and often land several feet beyond where I wanted to go.

The well itself is, roughly speaking, an oval with one hundred and eighty-seven feet as its longer diameter. From the jungle surface about it to the water surface varied from sixty-seven to eighty feet. Where the water surface commenced could be ascertained easily, but where it left off and the mud of the bottom began was not so easy to determine, for the lines of demarcation did not exist. However, I can roughly estimate that of the total depth of mud and water, about sixty-five feet, thirty feet was a mud deposit sufficiently consistent to sustain tree-branches and even tree-roots of considerable size. About eighteen feet of this deposit was so compact that it held large rocks, fallen columns, and wall stones. Into this mud and silt deposit the dredge had bitten until it had left what I called the "fertile zone" with a vertical wall of mud almost as hard as rock at the bottom and fully eighteen feet high. In this were embedded rocks of varied shapes and sizes, as raisins are embedded in plum puddings.

Imagine us, then, searching in the darkness, with these mud walls all about us, exploring the cracks and the crevices of the rough limestone bottom for the objects that the dredge had failed to bring up to the light of day. Imagine also that every little while one of the stone blocks, loosened from its place in the wall by the infiltration of the water, would come plunging down upon us in the worse than Stygian darkness that was all about us. After all, it was not so bad as it sounds. It is true that the big blocks fell when and where they would and we were powerless to direct or even to see them, but so long as we kept our speaking-tubes, air hose, and life-line and ourselves well away from the wall surface we were in no special danger. As the rock masses fell, the push of the water before and around them reached us before the rock did and even if we did not get away of our own accord, it struck us like a huge soft cushion and sent us caroming, often head down and feet upward, balancing and tremulous like the white of an egg in a glassful of water, until the commotion subsided and we could get on our feet again. Had we incautiously been standing with our backs to the wall, we should have been sheared in two as cleanly as if by a pair of gigantic shears and two more victims would have been sacrificed to the Rain God.

Before the dredge had even been installed and months before it brought up the first load, I had been told by a *H'Men*, pointing to a certain spot: "There is where the Palace of the Rain God lies, as our fathers told us."

That spot was out of the "fertile zone," and considerably to the right of it, but I determined to examine it. I found a deep natural depression in the floor of the pool that, so far as my observation could show, existed in no other place; and around the edge of that depression I found the outstretched skeletons of three poor women. Around the neck of one of them there were several jade beads as pendants. Portions of the garments worn by these victims preserved from decay in some strange way were secured for examination and study.

By what mode of reasoning did the *H'Men* or his predecessors select that special spot as the place where the Rain God dwelt? Its depth, if nothing else, made it physically impossible for a native diver to reach the place, spy it out, and return to the surface alive to tell of it. Who knows?

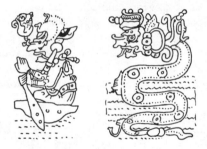

Images of Maya water god, after Dresden Codex

The natives for ages have believed that somewhere in those unknown depths the powerful God of the Waters had his home and that his anger caused the droughts, the pestilences, and the plagues of insects that from time to time descended upon the land. It was this belief that caused them to send messengers with supplications and rich gifts to propitiate the God. It can safely be inferred that the messengers were neither old women nor ill-favored.

The present natives of the region believe that big snakes and strange monsters live in the dark depths of the Sacred Well. Whether this belief is due to some faint remembrance of the old serpent worship, or is based upon something seen by some of the natives, can only be guessed at. I have seen big snakes and lizards swimming in these waters, but they were only snakes and lizards that in chasing their prey through the trees above had fallen into the pool and were trying to get out. We saw no traces of any reptiles or monsters of unusual size anywhere in the pool.

No strange reptile ever got me in its clutches, but I had one experience that is worth repeating. Both of us, the Greek diver and I, were busily

digging with our fingers in a narrow crevice of the floor and it was yielding such rich returns that we neglected some of our usual precautions.
Suddenly I felt something over me, an enormous something that with a
stealthy, gliding movement was pressing down on me. Something smooth
and slimy was pushing me irresistibly into the mud. For a moment my
blood ran cold. Then I felt the Greek beside me pushing at the object
and I aided him until we had worked ourselves free. It was the decaying
trunk of a tree that had drifted off the bank of mud and in sinking had
encountered my stooping body.

One day I was seated on a rock gloating over a remarkable find, a
moulded bell of metal, and I quite forgot to open the air valves as I
should have done. I put the find in my pouch and rose to change my
position, when suddenly I began to float upward like an inflated bladder.
It was ludicrous, but also dangerous, for at this depth the blood is charged
with bubbles like champagne and unless one rises slowly and gives the
blood time to become normal, a terrible disease called the "bends" results, from which one can die in terrible agony. Luckily I had enough
presence of mind to open the valves before going up very far and so escaped the extreme penalty, but I suffer the effects of my carelessness today in a pair of injured ear drums and greatly impaired hearing.

Even after I had opened the valves and was rising more and more
slowly, I struck the bottom of the pontoon topsy-turvy, half-dazed by
the concussion. Then, realizing what had happened and laughing at the
thought of the fright my boys must have had when they heard me thump
on the bottom of the boat, I scrambled from under it and threw my arm
over the gunwale. As my helmet appeared over the side I felt a pair of
arms thrown around my neck and startled eyes looked into the plate-
glass goggles of my helmet. As they took off my diving-suit and I rested on
a seat, getting back into normal condition and enjoying a cup of hot
black coffee and the sunlight, the young Greek told me the story.

"The men," he said, "turned a pale yellow with terror when they
heard the knock on the bottom that announced your unexpected arrival. When I told them what it was, they shook their heads mournfully
and one of them, faithful old Juan Mis, said, 'It's no use, El Amo the
master is dead. He was swallowed by the Serpent God and spewed up
again. We shall never hear him speak to us again'; and his eyes filled
with tears. When your helmet came over the gunwale and he looked into
its window, he raised both arms high above his head and said with great
thankfulness, 'Thank God, he is still alive, and laughing.' "

As for the results of our dredging and diving into the great water
pit, the first and most important is that we proved that in all essential
details the traditions about the Sacred Well are true. Then we found a
great store of symbolical figures carved on jade stone and beaten on

gold and copper disks, copal masses and nodules of resin incense, many skeletal remains, a number of *hul chés,* or dart-throwers, and many darts with finely worked points of flint, calcite, and obsidian; and some bits of ancient fabric. All these had real archaeological value. Objects of nearly pure gold were encountered, both cast, beaten, and engraved in *repoussé,* but they were few in number and relatively unimportant. Most of the so-called gold objects were of low-grade alloy, with more copper than gold in them. That which gave them their chief value were the symbolical and other figures cast or carved upon them.

Golden repoussé disc from the Well of Sacrifice

Most of the objects brought up were in fragments. Probably they were votive offerings broken before being thrown into the well, as a ritualistic act performed by the priests. The breaking was always in such a way that the head and features of the personages represented on jade plaque or gold disk were left intact. We have reason to believe that these jade pendants, gold disks, and other ornaments of metal or stone when broken were considered to have been killed. It is known that these ancient civilized races of America believed, as did their still more ancient forbears of northern Asia and as the Mongols to this day believe, that jade and other sacred objects have life. Accordingly these ornaments were broken or "killed" that their spirits might serve as ornaments to the messenger, whose spirit would be appropriately adorned when it finally appeared before the *Hunal Ku,* the One Supreme God in the Heavens.

That this belief has come down through the ages to the present day is shown by this curious fact: A Maya noted for his knowledge of herbs and native medicines, not quite a *H'Men,* but respected among his people, lost his wife in childbirth and, as a particularly esteemed friend of the family, I was invited to the death feast, a ceremony much resembling the Celtic "wake." I was the only white man present.

The body of the beloved was dressed in new garments of white cotton cloth finely embroidered in the native fashion and handsome new shoes. I noticed first that the soles of the shoes had been cut in several places until the white stockings were to be seen between the slashes and then I saw that the new white garments had been similarly treated. I asked the husband the reason for this, and he answered:

"It is so that her soul shall appear before God dressed as the soul of my wife should be. If we had not done this, the spirits of the garments she wore would have remained in the coffin until the things rotted. Meantime the soul of my wife would remain without clothing, and that ought not to be."

The value in money of the objects recovered from the Sacred Well with so much labor and at such expense is, to be sure, insignificant. But the value of all things is relative. The historian delves into the past as the engineer digs into the ground, and for the same reason, to make the future secure. It is conceivable that some of these objects have graved upon their surfaces, embodied in symbols, ideas and beliefs that reach back through the ages to the primal home of these peoples in that land beyond the seas. To help prove that is well worth the labor of a lifetime.

21

"With consideration for the limitations of their facilities, the Maya were the greatest race that ever lived on this earth," wrote Sylvanus Griswold Morley (1883–1948), who in his lifetime became something of a high priest of *Mayismo*. On lecture tours and in articles he tirelessly reiterated his faith that prehistoric American Indian culture culminated in the Mayas. To him they were simply "the Greeks of the New World." The calendar and astronomy of the Dresden Codex—one of three surviving Maya manuscripts—were to him "the highest intellectual achievement" of pre-Columbian America. Not content with that, he proclaimed the Maya glories as "100% American."

Morley's hyperbole may now strike us as dated. But it must be seen against a pioneer's forty-year career in American archaeology, which had begun when next to nothing was known about the multiplicity and complexity of the Mesoamerican culture scene. It reflects not only the emergence of the Mayas as a prime target for research but the impact their extraordinary accomplishments made upon their impressionable resurrectors. If Morley's estimate may have overshot its mark, it is understandable in a man who dedicated all his studies to one people alone. Invariably, the deeper he probed, the more tangible evidence he found of the antiquity and superiority of his chosen people. And, allowing for modern adjustments, his high opinion of the Mayas has still much to recommend it.

If the magnificent Mayas triumphed over an unhealthy climate in the tropics—against the pronouncements of geographical determinists— the reconquest of their lost civilization, staged under just such adversities, assumes similar heroic proportions. Morley's explorations into the Central American jungle were of that cast. Year after year he ventured into the moist, dark interior, struggled with heat, rain, insects, and vegetation to copy Maya inscriptions from fallen, overgrown stelae. To bring back the "epigraphic bacon" was his declared purpose. Nothing could hold him back whenever the slightest rumor of Maya inscriptions reached him. Morley's explorations immensely increased the corpus of hieroglyphic texts and "Initial Series" (calendrical notation counted from a fixed date and placed at the opening of a carved inscription). He collected the data in masterly studies, chiefly *The Inscriptions of Petén,* which alone ran to more than 2,000 pages. To add ever new material he enlisted the help of native hunters and ubiquitous chicleros—the Indian or half-caste collectors of chicle gum from the sap of the sapodilla tree. He posted notices ("veinte-cinco pesos para una ciudad real") in the camps of chicle gatherers for any information that would lead him to a new site. Thanks to his many friendships the system worked exceedingly well. In the vital Petén area of northern Guatemala he was thus led to seven unknown cities. One of these proved to be a site of utmost importance: Uaxactún, about fifteen miles northeast of Tikal. The place had been first sighted by chicleros three years earlier.

It was at Uaxactún in 1916 that Morley found what was for a long time the oldest known date inscribed on a Maya stela (Stela 9), corresponding to April 9, A.D. 328. In time Uaxactún became recognized as perhaps the most ancient of Maya cities. As such it was a magnet for archaeologists. Under Morley's aegis Uaxactún was selected in 1924, together with Chichen Itzá, as a choice objective for systematic investigation by the Carnegie Institution of Washington. In time Uaxactún yielded a continuous series of pottery which made it possible to establish a complete overall Maya stratigraphy and periodization. No less valuable was the unromantically named Pyramid E-VII sub, excavated (1938), as its name implies, from underneath another temple mound. The beautiful low stone structure, covered with white plaster, was ascended by staircases on four sides, between which were rows of jaguar masks in stucco. According to Morley "the oldest Maya stone construction that has come down to us," it belonged to the formative or pre-classic epoch. The jaguar masks, in particular, bore the markings of "Olmec" style. But such relationships never disturbed Morley much. One year before his death, in the volume *Ancient Maya,* he once more described the Mayas as "practically free from alien influences." He recognized antecedents of the Maya civilization in the Uaxactún area, but even in those he saw Maya characteristics.

The following extract was selected from Morley's unpublished diary, which Alfred V. Kidder, a longtime friend and colleague, deposited with the American Philosophical Society in Philadelphia. The diary's thirty-nine volumes cover Morley's active years in Central American research from 1905 to 1947. They add up to a lively memoir of considerable historical value both to Maya scholarship and to an understanding of Central American social and political conditions in general. Unfortunately, Morley died before he was able to polish and edit his day-to-day jottings. His original notebooks have been lost; the typewritten copy extant in Philadelphia was evidently made by a Latin American clerk whose command of English was as deficient as his or her skill in deciphering the writer's reputedly small and cramped pencil notes made under difficult circumstances in the field. However, this selection is presented with a minimum of "corrections."

The diary entries refer to Morley's explorations at Uaxactún (May 4–10, 1916), which he always regarded as the most important of his entire career. Carried out under the sponsorship of the Carnegie Institution, the campaign was led by Morley as field director. Arthur Carpenter of the Peabody Museum (Harvard University) was the second in command. The only other American was Dr. Moise Lafleur from Louisiana, who acted as the expedition's surgeon. Morley hired two native "camp boys," Andrew and Marius Silas, and local chicleros and muleteers.

A deep shadow was cast on the brief campaign's remarkable success when, on the trip back from Uaxactún, Morley and his men were ambushed by trigger-happy Guatemalan government troops. Taking the harmless small group for revolutionaries, the soldiers killed without warning Dr. Lafleur and several of the natives. The tragic incident may be pondered by those who think that all popular accounts of the dangers besetting archaeological expeditions are hopelessly romanticized. It stands as an authentic reminder of the harassments met by explorers into the Central American jungle barely half a century ago.

The experience at Uaxactún, no matter how shattering, did not keep Morley from taking similar chances on his "hieroglyphic hunts." He suffered innumerable bouts of malaria. Previously, at Copán in 1912, copying an inscription, he almost died of fever. Earl Morris, who was with him then, took him on a three-day ride out of the jungle by lashing him to a mule so he would not fall off during his delirium. On another occasion he came close to death from amoebic dysentery. Far from physically strong, he made up for it by his agility. Oddly enough it was nearsightedness that kept him from riding ahead of his men and thus saved him, in 1916, from Guatemalan bullets.

Morley was one of the rare "characters" in American archaeology— lovable, exasperating, and the subject of many anecdotes. He could never conceive of anybody being bored by the smallest piece of trivia from his adored Mayas. To enunciate the very name "Maya" became with him an almost sensuous delight. The affectionate recollections of his many friends in the United States, Mexico, Guatemala, and Britain were posthumously published as *Morleyana* (1950).

Despite his long residence in Yucatán, Morley never fully mastered Spanish. Alfonso Caso once concluded a bilingual session at which scientific papers had been delivered (Morley had chosen to read his in "Spanish") by saying that it had been "a most memorable occasion with speeches in English, in Spanish, and in Morley." A genuine love of comfort did not keep this researcher from going into the wilderness. To bring back more drawings of Maya inscriptions was ample reward. Yet he would discount any sentimental attachment to such hardships. "Only liars and damn fools like the jungle," he once told a young colleague.

Substructure of Pyramid E-VII with its Olmecoid stucco masks

HIEROGLYPHIC HUNT AT UAXACTÚN

Sylvanus G. Morley

May 4th—Thursday [1916]. It rained in the night and tried hard to do so in the day. José [the local guide] was very triste indeed, said he felt too ill to look up the ruins. It created an awkward situation. . . . L. [Dr. Moise Lafleur] doped him up, a little strychnia, a little whiskey, a little

From *The Diary of Sylvanus Griswold Morley,* unpublished typescript at The American Philosophical Society, Philadelphia, Vol. VIII, 1916, n.p.

camphor mono-bromate, etc. Under these and my moral suasion we finally got him off. L. accompanied him, to keep him "in condition," and Alfonso who was to show the way to the champas [camps of chicleros] of San Leandro near which the ruins are said to be located.

They had scarcely gone before a shot was heard, and José came back bringing a cojolito [*conejolito,* "little rabbit"?], which Alfonso had killed.

Arthur [Carpenter] had found some honey, and went out to get it. The camp settled down to quiet. I plotted up our dead reckoning, on my two available maps, and found out the startling fact that we are west of the Flores meridian, and not too far from Chuntuqui. I feel this may be an exaggeration of the distance we have covered and in my final map shall consider two miles an hour—in the straight line toward our final destination—about as much as we have done. In this way the morning slipped away. . . .

At about four or thereabouts L. returned with most heartening news. They had found the ruins, and three stelae, two sculptured and one plain. For a while he said it had looked as though José would cave in, but he nursed him along, and they finally "brought home the bacon." It was very encouraging news to all, and put spirits into everyone.

That night, probably because he had overdone at my insistence, José turned up with a hot fever and was delirious; at least I felt responsible. He groaned and cried, and felt sure he was going to die in the bush. L. worked over him like a Trojan. Hot compresses, morphine. We put him on Marius's bed and by ten he was quiet, after which L. retired.

View of Uaxactún, sketch by Tatiana Proskouriakoff

May 5th—Friday. A remarkable day, all things considered. At about eight o'clock six of us, L., A[rthur] and myself, Andrew, Marius and Alfonso left for the ruins. An hour and a half in a southerly direction brought us to the champas of San Leandro, where we left our horses and proceeded the rest of the way on foot.

We filled our canvas buckets at the aguada [water hole], and started off in a westerly direction, Alfonso in the lead. He only lost the picada [trail] once or twice, and in half an hour we were skirting the right hand edge of a small ravine, on the edge of which the ruin stands.

José was truthful enough. He had seen a stela with a figure on it. The figure was in an excellent state of preservation, but oh what a bitter disappointment, after all these weary leagues, the glyphs, the only three on the front, were almost entirely effaced, and those on the sides so far gone as to be almost doubtful!

The stela next to this one was broken off, and the top missing. The figure was badly gone, and I could find no glyphs at all. I was indeed downcast and it looked as though all our efforts had been in vain. L. showed me the plain stela, a good example of its kind, but what was such to offer to one starving for dates in the "desert"? Arthur had in the meantime disappeared, but a shout soon advised that he had found something: "Here are some glyphs!" The cry brought me to his side quickly, and to my great delight I found he had discovered a stela with an I.S. [Initial Series] on one side. Although somewhat effaced I could read its date very clearly as 9.16.0.0.0   2 Ahua   13 Tzec. Black disappointment instanter gave way to complete satisfaction. All those weary leagues, those heated arguments, those "multitudinous humbugs" had not counted for naught.

Between the plain stela and the one A. had found was another large stone prostrate, which had apparently fallen face up and had nothing on it. While I was deciphering this date Arthur had continued around the sides of this plaza, and found several more stones. Three of these appeared to be altars, and the fourth a broken stela. This had glyphs on its sides, but was in very bad condition. The altar in front of this stela was six feet in diameter and had nine plain circles on top around the edge. Again Arthur disappeared and again a shout, this time from both Alfonso and Arthur. They had discovered another stela, with glyphs on it, but broken and fallen. I turned toward their shouts. The new find was a large monument with an I.S. on one side. Its katun coefficient is surely 1, 2 or 3, its tuns 11, 12 or 13; its uinals and kins 0, and the day 2 Ahua and the month 13? I had not brought the tables with me and did not have time to work this out in my head. When I returned to camp, however, found it was 9.3.13.0.0   2 Ahua   13 Ceh.

Alfonso again made off. Here indeed was ample recompense, two dated stelae, one of them the third oldest monument ever reported. It was a splendid find. We looked around for other monuments, but, barring two plain ones that Arthur found, nothing more turned up. About 12:30 we were planning to return to the champas and eat when Alfonso came in with a wonderful story. He had cruised around in the bush, and had found another group. . . . Five stones, two carved standing stones, one 15 feet high with a double row of letters on its back. We hurried back to the champas to eat lunch. Tea, sardines, crackers and fruit. How good it tasted with the magic sauce of anticipation!

Without wasting much time over the repast however we sallied forth in the same direction as in the morning. Only now we climbed the left bank of the same little ravine. . . . As it was getting on we did not tarry long, but scattered to look for the stelae. I followed Alfonso, but Arthur found one of the sculptured stelae first.

This had an I.S., each glyph thereof being presented in a circular cartouche. I was unable to decipher it off hand, but it is either in katun 6 or katun 7, 8 or 9.

Polychrome vessel, from Uaxactún

A shout from Alfonso, albeit a faint one, summoned us to another stela, his 15-footer. This is a tallish stone, 9½ feet above ground by actual measurement, and now leaning some 2 to 3 feet out of the perpendicular.

The front leans downward and has a human figure. The sides are plain.

The back of this leaning stela makes it the most important monument in the Maya area, for it undoubtedly presents a Cycle 8 Initial Series. Careful examination of the cycle coefficient established that it could only be 8. The katun coefficient is surely above 10 and under 16; the tun 5 or 10; the uinal 11, 12 or 13; the kin, 15 or 16; and the day over 5 and under 11. It was getting too late to linger, but I feel sure that I will be able to decipher this date when I come to examine it closely. After seeing one or two more plain stelae we returned to the champas, and saddled our horses for the two-league ride back to Bejucal. By pushing our mounts we got in by half past five, thoroughly tired out but well satisfied with the day's work. Poor Alfonso found no one had cut his ramoneo [branches for fodder] until three o'clock, and in consequence ten of our seventeen mules have strayed. . . .

May 8th—Monday. Shortly after we got up Chon came in with an ocellated turkey and a kambul. The former was indeed a perfect specimen, and promised delectable eating. If I dwell on eating so much it is not because we are gourmands but because our fare is really getting pitifully slender. A. and L. skinned the turkey before we left for the ruins.

The plan this morning was to raise the katun 3 stela which seemed as though it might have fallen face downward. All save José assembled for the turning, which made nine [of us]. We got the stone, which weighs all of two tons, up on one edge, until it must have been 50° with the ground, enough to see that it had a sculptured face. The figure there presented is in excellent condition. I made out the head of the god which stands for the number 7.

I have passed over the work which raising this monolith entailed. But my silence should not be taken as indicating that no labor was expended. The sweat, the curses, the directions in Spanish and English, the straining of muscles and tempers to the point of exhaustion, were enough to have moved the Pyramid of Cheops if applied at one time, and even then we failed of getting it upright. It became apparent finally that we were too exhausted to work efficiently on it further, so called it off for a final try to-morrow.

My "drawing hand" was ruined for the morning, so A., L., Marius and I went to see Arthur's new site, Site C, which lies about half a mile east or northeast of the champas amongst some ramoneos [bushes]. There are two sculptured and six plain stelae. I saw all except two of the latter. One of the sculptured stelae had two columns of intaglio relief carved on the back. Unfortunately, the detail is quite gone and I was unable to decipher a single glyph. After making a sketch map of the plaza where these monuments were located, we returned to the champas for lunch.

In the afternoon I took Juan and with L. went back to Group A to finish up there. Juan wanted to leave in the morning but I persuaded him to stay over to-morrow and help in the last attempt to turn over the big stela at Group A. He consented to do this for a consideration of one dollar.

May 9th—Tuesday. Got my cuadrilla of hearties together early for the attempt on the half-turned stela. We tried a new plan—namely to tie a strong pole to the monument and another smaller one on the other side so the first would not slip, and then, by pulling with a rope and raising with a pole at the same time, we hoped to raise it upright. It was the last shot in our quiver, and if it failed I knew we would have to abandon the attempt. It was an anxious moment therefore when we finally got the rope and poles adjusted, and began to pull. Slowly the heavy stone swung upright, and as our strength was exhausted we rested while the rope held what we had gained. Thus, "poco a poco," we pulled the stela upright. There are no glyphs on the front but the relief is in pretty good condition. The figure holds the ceremonial bar horizontal across his breast, the left hand head appears to be that of the Sun God.

After getting the stone upright we disbanded, Andrew, Chon, Alfonso and Galileo returning to camp, A[rthur] and Marius remaining to clean and photograph the stone. L., Juan and I went over to Site B to begin my work there. While I was drawing the stela with the glyphs in single cartouches, L. went to look up the tall leaning stela. . . .

May 10th—Wednesday. We were all up early. . . . José, L. and I went to Group B by ourselves. I finished drawing the I.S. on the beautiful stela found yesterday. After this I began to copy the leaning stela in the center. I have already touched upon this important inscription, which presents the earliest date yet deciphered. This date I was unable to decipher the first day I saw this monument, but a careful examination of each bar and dot coefficient—while I stood on a scaffold which L. and José had built against the monument—established the original reading to have been: 8.14.10.13.15   8 Men   8 Kayab. In the correlation of Maya and Christian chronology which I am advocating, this corresponds to 50 A.D. [computed as A.D. 328 by a more modern system]. The style of the monument is sufficiently archaic to warrant this date. The glyph blocks are irregular in outline, and archaic in form. It was difficult to draw because of this irregularity and it was nearly one o'clock when I finished. . . .

L. and I set off for the ruins again a little after two. At the fork of the trail I left him to go on to Group B, while I went back to Group A for a few minutes to see the big stela we turned. A. had cleaned it up, but in some places the relief, which is low, is badly weathered. Unfortunately one of the places which has suffered most has been the head and face. I took a few final notes on the intaglio I.S. of Stela 5, and then went back to the fork and took the trail to Group B. As I climbed up the ravine I heard monkeys roaring in the tree-tops. This noise increased in violence as I approached the Great Plaza of Group B, and just as I entered the plaza it reached its climax in a final roar succeeded by a heavy thud. I felt L. had at last landed his heart's desire—a big baboon. This was indeed the case. He and A. between them had brought down a big black male monkey, a baboon. They hit it four times, and even in spite of the sixty-odd-foot fall, there seemed to be a last spark of life in the poor creature after it reached the ground. It was literally alive with beef-worms, and smelled unto high heaven. L. on the spot decided to take all parts of it not subject to immediate putrefaction to Cayo. But for the present we had other things to do. A. and Marius left for camp and Group A, while L. and I set to work taking the necessary notes for a sketch map of the plaza of Group B, sufficient to locate the monuments. This took us until five o'clock, when we had finished. A rain was coming on, and a good mile separated us from the champas. L. strung the baboon on a pole and carrying this on our shoulders we set out, the baboon bobbing between us, an ugly hairy blob.

In leaving the ruins to their majestic solitude again, I could not help but wonder when and under what circumstances it would be broken again. For centuries, for a thousand years and then centuries, they have been left alone, and now we come and in a few hurried hectic days turn over their sculptured masterpieces and with pencil, tape, note-book and camera violate their peace. Well, we are leaving them. Our trails will soon be overgrown, and traces of our brief sojourn effaced. They will be as before with this one exception—their secret, or better a fraction of it, will have been given up to the outside world.

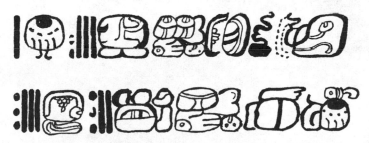

Maya inscription on capstone

We set off for camp at a good rate as the rain was rapidly approach-ing. It had suddenly grown quite dark, and our time was limited. As we came out of the ravine we struck a more rapid pace and when the rain finally caught us, a short distance from the champas, we were fairly running through the bush with our ugly burden lurching between us.

A. and Marius were already at the hut; the rain was coming down in torrents. After it cleared, A. had to take a few final photographs, and by the time the animals were saddled it was 5:45. The ride back took us close on to two hours, and the last half hour was done in the pitch dark.

Several mishaps occurred. L.'s horse stumbled, turned a somersault and fell, L. himself clearing the plunging animal by a happy jump. My animal fell to his knees but made a quick recovery. Marius's mule shied, and by a sideways jump unseated Marius, who came to Mother Earth promptly. A. contracted an escoba spine in his belly in an unsuccessful encounter with a tree of that family, and all told we were more or less bunged up. The greatest danger was from the horses stepping on and being pierced by sharp sticks, and from hitting our heads against low trees and bejucos [a kind of Spanish moss]. I was glad enough to see the lights of camp and hear the voices of the boys. This is the second time I have been caught in the bush after dark, and I do not like it. The going is too perilous. Andrew had a good dinner ready for us and against the hard day ahead of us to-morrow we all turned in more or less early.

22

Cobá in the Mexican territory of Quintana Roo on the northeastern Yucatán Peninsula is one of the major Maya cities left to be discovered until the twentieth century. John Lloyd Stephens, on reaching the frontier town of Chemax in 1841, picked up little but the name; he was dissuaded from venturing to try to find Cobá. Its existence in an area long under the control of hostile Indians had been rumored from time to time. However, no one seemed to know its precise location. Then the translation of a Maya document into Spanish focused attention on the half-forgotten site. And suddenly, in 1926, the name of the lost city loomed very large. A crotchety Britisher, Dr. Thomas Gann, after reading of Cobá in a recently published edition of the *Chilam Balam of Chumayel,* had succeeded in his ambition to visit the place. Within only a few months of Gann's discovery (later it came out that Teobert Maler had been there once in the 1890's), the Carnegie Institution sent out four expeditions from Chichen Itzá. J. Eric S. Thompson, who participated in all of them—and several thereafter—even took his bride there on a honeymoon. When S. G. Morley, enticed by reputedly old stelae, saw Cobá, he told his companion Thompson: "This can't be a Yucatán site. We must have traveled south for ten days and landed up in the middle of the Petén [the lowlands of northern Guatemala, hitherto considered the cradle of Maya civilization]."

Cobá simply did not fit into any preconceptions of Maya history. Its appearance acted as a real shocker, forced re-examination of all materials, and gave Maya studies a new orientation. Luckily it turned up just when the great Carnegie project at Chichen Itzá was getting under way. Thus the evidence from both Yucatán sites, one in the north, the other in the northeast, could be compared and related. Cobá itself became an extension of the Carnegie scientific onslaught on the Yucatecan Mayas.

Until 1926 it had been virtual dogma that Yucatán had no part in the great classical age of the Mayas, but was only colonized around A.D.

900 after the collapse of the magnificent thearchic centers of Copán, Tikal, Palenque, Quirigua, and others to the south of it. It was thought that refugees on the peninsula inaugurated another flowering of Maya civilization and founded eventually a "New Empire," a somewhat eclectic and short-lived rehash of the "Old Empire" lacking almost entirely in some of the more ancient refinements such as the "Initial Series" on date stones or stelae.

Historical generalizations—no matter how elegant and plausible—if based on insufficient evidence are always suspect. The entire scheme of Maya Old and New Empire, though still current in the popular literature, simply does not hold water. Whether the Mayas ever enjoyed the dubious benefits of an empire in the manner of the Incas, or even the Aztecs, is rather debatable. Even more questionable is the sequence of two phases and the concept that Yucatán was a later and secondary site of Maya settlement. Actually, Cobá belongs largely to the first half of the classical age. Its architecture is stylistically linked with that of the Petén. Even Chichen Itzá, though apparently not quite as old, includes buildings that belong to the "Old Empire." Dzibilchaltún, perhaps the most extensive Maya city, which is ten miles north of Mérida, probably goes back as far as 1500 B.C. People identifiable as Maya have been in Yucatán as long as in Guatemala, Chiapas, and Honduras.

The sensation caused by Gann's discovery was in a large measure due to Cobá's unexpected antiquity. Its considerable age was mirrored unmistakably in a profusion of inscribed stelae unearthed and deciphered by consecutive expeditions. All of a sudden they more than doubled the number of Yucatán stelae. News of these markers brought Morley to the scene. He identified the so far earliest known Cobá stela, which, according to the now accepted correlation, bears the date A.D. 621. Added to such antiquity was the likelihood that the enormous ruined site of Cobá had been continuously occupied for some 800 years and unlike Copán or Tikal was not abandoned centuries before the advent of the Spanish. Ballcourts at Cobá were the first to be discovered in a purely Maya city of Yucatán. Formerly it was believed that the game and its peculiar playgrounds had been introduced much later by invaders from central Mexico.

Another attraction of Cobá was its picturesque situation on five lagoons, quite unusual for the otherwise arid Yucatán limestone flats. Due to the humid climate of eastern Yucatán near the Caribbean coast, huge trees have pierced through the buildings. The large temple plaza is domed by a dense forest through which beams of sunshine rarely penetrate.

However, what stimulated greatest interest was an extensive system of causeways radiating from Cobá. Most of these roads were built on raised platforms of varying heights. Some crossed the arms of lakes and were as wide as sixty feet. The longest reached more than sixty miles westward. It ended, as J. Eric S. Thompson was to establish, not at Chichen Itzá, which at the time of the road's construction was an insignificant place, but at another old ceremonial center south of Chichen, Yaxuná. Though Bishop Landa and other early colonial writers had reported native highways, and though causeways within the large temple cities were well known, before the exploration of the Cobá area information on Maya roadbuilding was hard to come by. Now a whole new subject was added to Mesoamerican studies. Various expeditions were exclusively devoted to the tracing of the Cobá roads, of which sixteen are now known to radiate from the city. Since several of these connected with nearby suburbs and towns, the roads, contrary to former opinion, may have served regular traffic and commerce rather than exclusively ceremonial purposes as Gann suggested. Even if the roads cannot stand comparison with Inca highways—certainly not in mileage—their construction from boulders, cement, and stucco was quite remarkable. Our knowledge of Maya roads remains fragmentary, but there are indications that a whole network may once have covered the land. During air reconnaissance, an oil company found traces of an extensive causeway in the northern Petén. Possibly, like the Incas, the Mayas marked distances at regular intervals and maintained way stations.

It was left to one Cobá road expedition to come up with perhaps the most startling surprise of all, found near Ekal on the way to Yaxuná: a giant five-ton limestone drum. Now broken in two, its length was some thirteen feet. It measured two feet in diameter. It looked for all the world like a formidable roller made to compress the gravel surface of the road. Though quite a few scholars decline to commit themselves as to its use, it may well indicate the only known practical application of the wheel principle in the New World!

Thomas Gann became a full-time student of the Maya when he retired in 1923 as principal medical officer of British Honduras, only three years before his epochal visit to Cobá. However, he had been carrying out intensive antiquarian researches from the time he landed at Belize in 1894. Gann's medical missions to outlying districts offered him rare chances to explore regions barely touched by archaeologists. In northern British Honduras, at Santa Rita, he discovered what were then unique mural paintings. He was also the first to report on the so-called "eccentric flints," bizarre stones chipped by Maya craftsmen. In time he became an avid decipherer of Maya inscriptions, and used his skill to good purpose on the Cobá stelae.

Besides Cobá, several major Maya sites in Quintana Roo and British

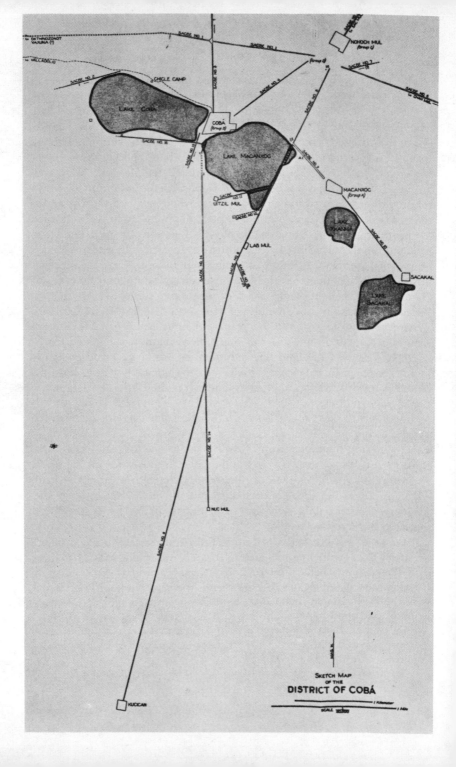

SKETCH MAP
OF THE
DISTRICT OF COBÁ

Honduras such as Lubaantún, Ichpaatún, and Tzibanche owe their archaeological rebirth to him. The University of Liverpool appointed him lecturer in Central American archaeology. Gann's papers in learned journals were highly thought of by ethnologists and archaeologists. But it was only with a series of semi-popular, somewhat testy, travel books appearing after World War I that he gained a wider audience. At the same time, his articles in the *Illustrated London News* and radio talks over the BBC did much to stimulate public interest in the Mayas.

COBÁ AND ITS ROADS

Thomas W. F. Gann

After a few days' rest at Chichen Itzá, where more than all the usual comforts of home are provided by the Carnegie Institution, I left Dzitas for Valladolid, the former capital of Yucatán, but now a sleepy agricultural provincial town, gradually slipping towards a painless extinction along the *mañana* route.

No one ever hurries here, and no one worries about anything as long as they possess enough to eat, plenty to drink, and a cotton shirt and trousers. And though they may not even have got all of these, well, why worry anyhow?

From Chichen Itzá we had engaged what is known as a *volan coche* to carry ourselves and our luggage, which consisted mostly of photographic outfit, hammocks, and food, from Valladolid to Chemax, the nearest Indian village to the ruins of Cobá, reported to be situated somewhere between Valladolid and the ruined city of Tuluum, on the east coast of Yucatán.

Within the last few months there has been done into Spanish by Dr. Solis Alcala the "U Kali Katunob" of Chumayel, an ancient, aboriginal, Maya historic document, never before translated from the original. In it occurs the passage, *"Cuando empezo la miseria en Chichen-Itza, se fue al Oriente y llegó al casa del Sacerdote Cobá,"* meaning, "When the plague at-

From *Mystery Cities*. London: Gerald Duckworth & Co., 1925, pp. 103–27 *passim.*

tacked the people of Chichen Itzá, they migrated to the east and arrived at the settlement of the priest Cobá." This appears to have been their earliest migration, and to have occurred some time before the middle of the seventh century.

The American explorer, Stephens, in 1842, heard from an Indian of ruins existing at a place named Cobá, to the east of Chemax, where he had seen painted figures upon the walls of the temple.

So far as is known, these were the only two references to this deserted city, which had never before been visited by Europeans. Having ascertained from Indians that ruins did actually exist on a lagoon in this situation, we determined to visit them at all costs.

We found the owner of the *volan coche* awaiting us on our arrival in Valladolid, but no *volan*. He informed us that *volans* were not allowed within the *barrios*, or limits, of the town, so we would be compelled to hire a disreputable old Ford truck, which awaited us at the station, and took ourselves and baggage to the *barrios*.

Before this, however, as we were making for the little hotel of the place to get some lunch, he steered us off to a friend of his own, where he said we should get much better food. We did not. On joining him at the *volan*, he asked us how much we had paid, and, adding insult to injury, told us we had been robbed. To this I replied that we had quite expected it, as it had become a but too familiar experience. This, as it turned out, was an injudicious remark on my part, and I could see him pondering it carefully. The brain-wave resulted in the announcement that the *volan* was incapable of carrying both ourselves and our baggage, and that he had provided a *carreta*, or cart, and five more mules to draw it, while we occupied the *volan*.

I did not credit either statement, as the *volan* was perfectly capable of carrying twice the burden, while the *carreta*, which we were told was not yet ready, was obviously an after-thought; but I merely asked "How much?" as we were completely at his mercy, and argument was, I knew, simply wasting breath and temper.

After half an hour's wait the *carreta* turned up, with our little pinch of baggage, covered with a tarpaulin, looking like a pea on a threshing-floor upon its vast expanse. . . .

The road between Valladolid and Chemax was not, strictly speaking, a road at all, but rather a wide swathe, cut through the virgin scrub, between the two places. The road-bed consisted of the barren limestone outcrop of the peninsula, ridges from 5 to 15 ft. high, covered with ripples and projections of limestone and great irregular boulders, interspersed between little depressions of muddy *chacluum*, the red earth of the country.

Who shall describe the misery of that journey! Crandall, the photographer who accompanied me, is short and fat, and his little legs got cramp because there was nothing to which to fix them; I am long and thin, and my legs got cramp because I could not stretch them out. The mattress kept slipping towards the centre of the cart, leaving one half of our sterns resting on the painful meshes of the netting bottom.

We had to grab on for dear life when crossing the ridges at a gallop, and then were sometimes hurled up against the roof, against each other, or painfully against the tail-board or side of the cart.

Our driver was an extraordinarily dirty and disreputable mestizo, dressed in short cotton pants, and the sketchy remains of an old *camisa*, or cotton shirt. He had a long, thin, mournful face, and Crandall christened him Ali Baba, as he resembled his childhood's conception of that hero. Later in the expedition he was known to the other men as "Abuelo," or grandpa, and became their constant butt.

He was the only one who did not bathe in the lagoon at Cobá, and when asked why, said it was very dangerous to bathe in cold water. "But," I said, "how do you get a hot bath when you are always on the road?" "Well, Señor," he said, "we poor people have many things to put up with, and the want of a bath is the least of them."

He smelt strongly of *anisado*, or anise flavoured rum, every day, and was usually maudlin drunk before midday throughout the whole trip, though where he managed to secrete his supply I was unable to ascertain, as beyond the drawers, and shirt on his back, he did not carry a single article of food, bedding, or clothing.

The journey only occupied seven hours, but I would sooner spend seven days crossing the north Atlantic in a hurricane than undergo it again. . . .

On arrival at Chemax we found a fiesta in progress, to celebrate the last day of carnival. Home-made rockets were going up at short intervals, a *mestisada* was being danced in front of the church, and the braying music, added to the howls and yells of drunken Indians, promised anything but a quiet night.

The Alcalde, a stout, important-looking Indian, greeted us, and offered a large house in a strategic position, just in front of the dance-platform, but we modestly chose a small mud-floored leaf hut on the outskirts of the village, where Crandall in his hammock, and I in my cot, passed a very uneasy night, made hideous by the band, which as the night wore on, and the musicians got more and more drunk, produced sounds less and less like music. The howling of the half-starved dogs, and the night-long quarrel between a Maya couple in a hut opposite, both man and woman suffering from too much fiesta, while the children bawled in chorus, all added to the racket.

On Sunday morning we arose early, and in the dark Crandall upset our only precious half-pound of tea on the mud floor; on scooping it up we found we had well over the half-pound, the surplus being chiefly mud.

I expected Isauro, our Chichen Itzá Indian servant, to appear with five horses and an Indian guide who knew the way well—that he had been told to hire for the trip to Cobá. He did not turn up till 8 a.m., bringing the news that only two horses were available in the village, the owner of which wanted thirty pesos each to hire them for the trip to the ruins, and that furthermore, being pack animals, he possessed no saddles, which would have to be hired separately from another man.

He had also obtained estimates of the distance, which varied from 6 to 16 leagues—15 to 40 miles—and discovered that the only man in the town who had ever actually been there was an Indian chicle-bleeder, at present absent in the bush.

This was, however, the usual thing to expect in Yucatán, where no one will do any work or hire anything to a stranger, if he can possibly avoid it, and if so pressed that he is compelled to yield to superior will-power, soothes his conscience for having assisted the "Sassenach" by putting every obstacle in his way, and charging 500 per cent. above the usual price.

While waiting we walked round the village, which contains some 2,000 souls. It is a miserably poor and squalid settlement of Indians, situated outside the henequen belt, and subsisting on such poor crops as a neg-lected system of agriculture, combined with a poor soil, afford. . . .

Everything being at last ready, we set out from Chemax just before midday, the cavalcade consisting of two horses for ourselves, two cargo-mules, and four men.

As we passed down the long main street of the village, everybody came out to see us off. The women and children evidently considered us a great joke, shouting from hut to hut. . . . "Come and see them, they are off for Cobá. . . . They are going to make it in a day."

I did not see the joke at the time, but later when we found the road beyond Chemax all grown up in bush, which had to be cleared, and blocked with fallen trees, round which a pass had to be cut, we began to realise where it lay.

We made the four and a half leagues to a little Indian settlement, named San Juan del Chen, just before dusk and found a single hut with three women and innumerable children and dogs, the men not having as yet returned from their corn plantations.

On asking if they could give us a lodging for the night, one of the women, pointing to a small hut in the clearing, told us we could sleep in the house of the *Santos Idolos,* or Holy Idols.

We found that it contained, on one side, a store of corn in the ear, and on the other, an altar, upon which stood two crucifixes, decorated with cotton garments, nicely embroidered in coloured devices, like the women's *huipils,* or chemises. On the altar were sprays of habin, the ancient Maya sacred herb, so we concluded the owners were taking no chances, and honoured both the old and new gods.

We got our water from the *chen,* or well, after which the place is named—a small round hole, leading down to an immense subterranean pool of water, similar to the *cenote* at Chichen, except that it was completely roofed in by a natural covering of limestone.

We made an early start for Cobá in the morning, along a limestone track, very much grown over with bush, and, about two leagues from San Juan del Chen, struck what the guide had told us about, though we had entirely disbelieved his statement—a great elevated road, or causeway, 32 ft. wide, and varying, according to the configuration of the ground, from 2 to 8 ft. in height.

We followed this road for about four leagues to within a mile of the ruins, turning aside only when we reached the lake margin, to put up for the night near a good water supply.

This was probably one of the most remarkable roads ever constructed, as the sides were built of great blocks of cut stone, many weighing hundreds of pounds; the central part was filled in with unhewn blocks of limestone, and the top covered with rubble, which, as is indicated by the traces of it which remain here and there, was once cemented over.

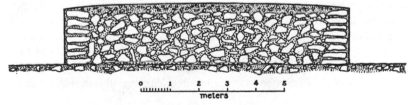

Cross-section of Maya road or *sacbe*

It was convex, being higher in the centre than at either side, and ran, as far as we followed it, straight as an arrow, and almost flat as a rule.

The guide told us that it extended for fifty miles direct to Chichen Itzá, passing near the village of Tixcacal, and missing Chemax and Valladolid entirely; and furthermore that it ended at the great mound, two kilometres to the north of the Nohku, or main temple, in a great ruined building, which we saw from the top of the former.

Along its course we noticed numerous openings into *chultunes,* or underground chambers, but had not time to explore any of these, as we were anxious to reach the ruins before night.

We also passed several *sartenejas,* or rock basins, no doubt scooped out to afford a water supply to the great body of labourers which must have been employed on the road, and for whom, in this arid region, drinking-water would have been a serious problem.

At one of these holes the men drank water, but as it was full of insects and leaves, and inhabited by a number of immense black tadpoles two inches long, we, though consumed by thirst, decided to await our arrival at the lagoon.

On each side of the road were great quarries from which the stone used in its construction had been taken. Some of them showed the method of quarrying very clearly. Holes were apparently sunk round the great blocks, in which they built fires, and then, pouring water into the red-hot holes, caused the rock to split, so that slabs of it could be easily dug out.

By far the most interesting discovery, however, was made about half-way between San Juan and Cobá; here by the side of the road, and placed about a kilometre apart, we came across three small stelae, or monoliths. Unfortunately they had lain with their sculptured sides up, and were so badly weathered that it was almost impossible to make out the hieroglyphics with which they had been covered.

The first numerical coefficient on the first slab was undoubtedly 8, written with a bar and three dots, and that on the right of it was almost as certainly 10, written with two bars, but neither the glyphs themselves, nor their numerical coefficients, could be made out in any of the other glyph spaces. . . .

Immediately after passing the sculptured stones, there got up almost from under my horse's hoofs an immense cock *pavo del monte,* or wild turkey, his great body hurtling off through the bush with a tremendous racket, and his gorgeous coppery plumage gleaming like burnished gold in the sun.

To find this magnificent bird so tame here was a sure indication of the remoteness of the spot, for they are unfortunately getting to be one of the rarest species in Yucatán. They are sought by the Indian hunters for the flesh, which is far superior to that of their tame cousin, and for their plumage by collectors, as the skins and tails always find a ready market, the former as museum specimens and for feather ornaments, the latter for fans.

To what use this great causeway could have been put by the builders it is impossible to imagine. It probably links up two of the most important ruined cities in Yucatán; for I think that Cobá will be found to rank very close after Chichen Itzá in importance. It was built long before the Toltec invasion, and represents an enormous expenditure of time and labour, involving the quarrying, transport, facing, and building in, of nearly a million tons of stone, and is unique throughout the whole of the Maya area, for though cement-covered roads exist in and around many of the ruined cities, no such elevated causeway as this has been found elsewhere.

Roman roads, proverbial for their permanence, have disappeared, and can be traced to-day only with difficulty, or not at all. Our modern roads will, if left to the forces of nature, have completely disappeared, without leaving a trace, in 500 years, but this great Maya road has withstood the passage of the centuries, in a country of heavy rainfall and luxuriant vegetation, and with the exception of its cement facing, is almost the same now as it was upon the day when the last Maya trod its smooth level surface.

And yet, so far as one can see, it was absolutely useless, for the Maya had neither wheeled vehicles, nor beasts of burden to draw them, and for walking purposes it was impossible to get a better surface than the natural limestone outcrop, when smoothed off and cleared of stones.

We must then, I think, accept the only possible explanation, namely, that it was used purely as a ceremonial road, or *via sacra*, leading from the principal city of the east to the great city of the Plumed Serpent, the civil and religious capital of Yucatán, and in later days the Mecca of Mayadom.

One can visualise the gorgeously arrayed procession of priests and nobles setting out from Cobá, their jewels, bright-coloured garments, and magnificent feather head-dresses glittering in the sun, preceded by singers and players on the flute and drum, and followed by white-robed priests, bearing grotesque censers, scattering the sweet-scented smoke of burning copal incense.

Probably if the occasion were an important one, they bore with them, in addition to offerings of jewels and precious stones, the most beautiful of their youths and maidens, marching along joyously to their sacrifice in the great *cenote* at Chichen Itzá, for were they not about to attain eternal bliss in the actual presence of the god, at the price of one brief plunge into the deep, still, mysterious waters, and a moment's short, choking struggle?

Then, three days' march along the great elevated causeway, white and gleaming like porcelain in the rays of the tropic sun, the inhabitants of all the cities and villages along the road turning out to do them honour: the halt in the cool of the evening, at one of the many temples found, now in ruins, adjoining the road, till at last they reached their destination, the foot of the great castillo at Chichen, where they were met by a procession of priests of the great Plumed Serpent, and could look down the straight, sloping road, towards the dead, gloomy waters of the sacred *cenote* where their offerings would be either accepted or rejected by the god.

Scenes such as these must have been enacted along this causeway over a period of many centuries, and as one trod its vast appalling loneliness, one could not but reflect on the impermanence of all human institutions and faiths, for temples and palaces are in ruins, gods and religions have perished, men and women, with their loves and hates, ambitions and struggles—all, all are gone—only the road remains.

We camped for the night in a bush hut left by some chicleros, the only people who had ever penetrated to this remote spot, drawn by the precious latex of the sapote tree, the basis of chewing-gum, which, with rubber, has drawn men to remoter fastnesses of the Central and South American bush than even the lure of gold, and has incidentally uncovered secrets of the ancient Maya, which might otherwise have lain buried for centuries in the heart of this almost impenetrable tropical jungle.

Ali Baba built a roaring fire of sticks by the side of the door, or rather hole in the wall, for no door existed, and entry was free for tigers, peccari, snakes, and other possible objectionable nocturnal visitors. It was also hoped that the smoke might keep off at least the less venturesome of the army of mosquitoes, whose skirmishers began to appear soon after our arrival.

My section of floor space was within a few feet of this furnace, and I was nearly roasted alive, but Ali, who slept nearly on top of it, was entirely unaffected by the heat.

During the night something nearly stampeded the horses and mules, but fortunately they were securely tied, and Ali arose and soon succeeded in quieting them. We could not see what had caused the disturbance, but it was probably a wandering jaguar, prospecting for food.

Next morning at daybreak we set out along the shore of the lagoon towards a great bush-covered mound on its eastern side, which the guide told us marked the highest building. The lagoon, a beautiful little stretch of clear blue water, about half a mile long by a quarter broad, was heavily wooded right down to the shore. A dim mist covered it, and great flocks of water-fowl flew in all directions, calling weirdly through the fog, as they went about their day's work of foraging for food.

The only fish in the lake were tiny little fellows, less than two inches long, but enormous quantities of *hooties,* great fresh-water snails, were to be picked up along the shore.

This lagoon, and its twin to the north, had a sentimental interest for us, for we were probably the first Europeans whose eyes had ever seen them, and whose mouths had ever drunk of their waters; no craft can have navigated the surface of either since the last of the Mayas left the last dug-out on its banks some five centuries ago.

The very snakes seemed tame in this remote place, for I passed within a step of a 3-ft. "coral," and he never even moved. Possibly an hereditary trust in man had come down from those of his ancestors whom the Maya worshipped as living images of their great Feathered Serpent god, and zealously protected. If so, he was vastly mistaken, for I cut a switch and slew him incontinently, lest one of the men following might tread on his tail.

We first passed a great pyramid, now a mere mass of ruins, at the base of which I perceived from a distance, with feelings of intense excitement, two monoliths, still standing upright.

On rushing up to them, however, in the full expectation of being able to date the city, I was woefully disappointed, for the stone was so weathered that very little but the outline of the glyph block could be made out on the first monolith, and nothing whatever on the second but the deep-sunk line which had enclosed the inscription.

Upon the first stone eight glyph spaces could be traced on each side of a human figure, sculptured in low relief, of which very little but the sandalled feet now remained.

This stone was 4 ft. long by 3 ft. broad, but the top had been broken off, probably by the fall of a large tree centuries ago, and was lying on the ground in front of the stela, inscribed side down.

In nearly every case where this had happened, the hieroglyphics beneath were well preserved, as they had been protected from the weather, but in this case the limestone was so poor in quality that it had flaked away from contact with the earth, leaving nothing but the outline of the glyph blocks, and no trace whatever of the glyphs themselves.

Immediately south of this mound, and almost touching it, we came upon a vast edifice standing on a terrace, approached by a flight of steps from the water side of the western lake. It consisted of a great stone-faced, terraced pyramid, corresponding to the castillo at Chichen Itzá, and the house of the dwarf at Uxmal, but probably higher than either of these structures, standing nearly 150 ft. above the lake level, though as I had no means of taking the altitude with me beyond an aneroid, this needs verification.

On each side of the courtyard were ranges of buildings, now in a very ruinous condition, and at the base of the pyramid a broken stela, still standing upright. This measured 56 ins. high by 40 ins. broad, and showed divisions into over sixty glyph blocks, all of which were so badly weathered as to be entirely undecipherable.

In the first row, occupying blocks five and six from the top, were two numerical coefficients, 5 and 10 respectively, but even these were extremely doubtful.

In front of all the three stelae encountered, small altars had been constructed of flat stones; upon these were the remains of many candles which had been burnt upon them, and on one lay a small metal receptacle, which had apparently served as an incense-burner.

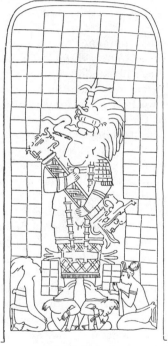

Cobá Stela 1

Servolo Canul, our chiclero guide, told us that Indian hunters, who passed here when out after game, with which the place swarmed, always burnt a candle in front of the *santos idolos,* to invoke their aid in the chase, as, though the Christian santos were helpful in most emergencies, the ancient gods still ruled the forest, the lagoons, and the *cenotes,* and for success in hunting they gave better returns to the candle than any of the santos of the Christianos.

Now a candle, even a one-cent dip, to a hunter in the bush, several days' march away from the nearest supply, was a very valuable asset, as it probably meant the difference between comfort and discomfort when he camped at night, and, if he offered it to any god, new or old, he did so only in the sure and certain hope of getting good value for his money.

It will be noticed that the same term, *santos idolos,* was used to describe the ancient gods as was used by the woman at San Juan del Chen to describe the crucifixes in her little sanctuary.

I christened this great structure the Nohku, or Great Temple, in Maya, as the Castillo seemed an inappropriate name for a building which, unlike that at Chichen, had never been occupied by the Spaniards. Upon its summit stood a small single-chambered temple, with a narrow courtyard in front. The interior of this little temple had been covered with stucco, painted bright red, now nearly all peeled off.

From its summit a perfectly magnificent view was obtained over the whole surrounding country, but as far as the eye could reach nothing was visible in all directions except the unbroken, green, flat expanse of immemorial bush.

So flat indeed was the land that at this elevation it should have been possible to see sailing vessels passing on the Caribbean, some thirty miles away, though along this barren, sparsely inhabited shore boats are of unfrequent occurrence.

About two kilometres to the north-east we saw a great group of ruins, covered with vegetation, standing up like gaunt sentinels in the forest, and the guide informed us that it was at the foot of this group that the great stone causeway ended.

Unfortunately neither time nor food permitted of our visiting it, as we had barely two days' provisions left, and the men had but one, and that only plain, dry corn-cake, which, with water alone, makes a nutritious but uninteresting dietary.

It is not improbable that here may be found a stela, bearing a readable Initial Series inscription, which will date the ruins beyond the shadow of a doubt, as the limestone we encountered along the road was of a tough, resistant character, better able to withstand weathering than the softer material used in the stelae found in the ruins.

The situation of the Nohku group of ruins was ideally delightful, filling up, as it did, almost the whole of a little isthmus, separating two beautiful, clear, blue lagoons, the one roughly 1,000 by 500 yds., the other 1,000 by 300 yds., the latter curving on itself, somewhat like a boomerang.

It seemed incredible that this ruined city, with the remarkable causeway, unlike anything found elsewhere throughout the Maya area, and the two beautiful little lakes, could have remained unexplored up to the present day, for it is probable that we were the first Europeans to visit them; but it must be remembered that they are situated in the least known and most sparsely populated region of Yucatán, and the nearest settlement, the Indian hut of San Juan del Chen, is twenty miles away, through an almost trackless wilderness, traversed only by chicleros and Indian hunters. . . .

Running due south from the Nohku was a great range of buildings, 240 ft. in length, and varying from 15 to 40 ft. in height. Maya arched rooms were found amongst the ruins of these at three different levels, indicating a height, at one time, of three stories.

From the southern extremity of this range a second series, 300 ft. long, ran due west. This was of a uniform height of 20 ft., and broken in the centre by a stairway leading to the summit, flattened along the whole extent of the range, and only 6 ft. broad. From the western extremity of this last range a steep mass of ruins extended for 100 ft. due north.

This briefly describes the frontage of the group on the western lagoon.

Our next survey started well to the north-east of the Nohku, where we discovered a great stone stairway, 120 ft. broad, with five rows of steps, the treaders being $4\frac{1}{2}$ ft. deep, with a rise of 12 ins. The steps were constructed of immense blocks of cut limestone, 4 to 5 ft. long, and were precisely similar to those we discovered at Lubaantún.

These are the only two places in the Maya area where stairways of this type have been encountered, and so similar are they in every respect that the conclusion is irresistible that there must have been at some time intimate communication between the two places.

This stairway led to a flat plaza, 60 ft. long, terminating in a second flight of stairs exactly like the first, leading to a second plaza, 90 ft. long, beyond which was a great mound of ruins. On each side of both plazas, completely shutting them in, were great masses of ruined buildings.

Immediately to the east of the larger plaza was one of the most remarkable structures in the whole group. It consisted of a two-storied, flat-roofed building, the floor of the upper and roof of the lower story of which had been formed by great flat flags of limestone, laid across beams, supported on pillars, both probably of sapote wood, as there were no traces whatever amongst the debris covering the floor of the former existence of stone columns.

The lower chamber still showed traces of an exceedingly hard red stucco, which originally had covered the interior of the entire building.

This type of building is known as Tuluum style, from the ruins of Tuluum, on the east coast of Yucatán, where it was extensively employed. . . .

Adjoining the building was a broad, sunk plaza, bounded on the north by another flat-topped mass of ruins abutting on the foreshore of the eastern lagoon.

At one place a flight of stone steps descended from a flat-topped mound to the lagoon-margin, and was continued as a pavement along the floor of the lake itself, forming a delightful bathing-place and wharf for canoes, for both of which purposes it was doubtless used by the ancient inhabitants.

At the north-west corner of the sunk plaza we came across a narrow Maya arch leading into an arched, stone-faced passage, about 120 ft. long and 4 ft. broad, which, passing in a south-easterly direction, opened into a second small sunk plaza, completely surrounded by a range of Maya arched rooms.

The doors of these rooms had for the most part been closed by the fall of masses of masonry, but access to many of them was to be obtained through openings in the top, where the roofs had caved in.

They contained many curious recesses, of all sizes and shapes, sunk in the masonry of both the sides and ends of the rooms. Some of these recesses were from 5 to 6 ft. in depth, and all were covered with stucco, which in many cases was painted red.

In more than one place we found the red imprint of the Maya hand, which was made by pressing the palm, dipped in red paint, against the smooth surface of the stone or stucco, and indicated, when used in this way in a building, as the signature, so to speak, of the architect, that the structure was completed.

In some cases the thumb and finger whorls could still be made out quite clearly in these red signatures of the ancient builders, made from five to fifteen centuries ago, so that, were the signatories to come to life again, they could be identified with as much certainty as if their finger-prints were preserved in the archives of Scotland Yard or Mulberry Street.

The ceilings were formed by the Maya arch, but, instead of the sloping variety usually found, they were constructed in the form of a double inverted stairway.

On several occasions we came across rude walls of rough stones, built without mortar, which had been erected across the chambers, evidently by later occupants. These may possibly have been intended to wall off sepulchral chambers, but the time at our disposal did not admit of our investigating any of them, so they had to be left for later explorers.

To the south of this plaza were the ruins of another two-storied, Tuluum-style building, and to the south of this the remains of one extremity of what had evidently been a curious oval room, most un-Maya in appearance, beyond which was another great mass of ruins leading to a large terrace overlooking the foreshore of the eastern lake.

Sculptured panel from Cobá ballcourt

Our stay at the ruins had been a delightful one, as the high bush all around the northern end of the lake, where our camp was situated, was almost free of undergrowth, and completely tickless, a blessing which only the resident in Yucatán during the dry season can appreciate, where, after the shortest walk, even in the well-cleared bush around a *hacienda,* one often comes in with a couple of dozen of these miserable pests cling- ing to one, necessitating constant gasolining, bathing, and changing of one's clothes.

The lagoons offered good bathing-places, so rare in the peninsula, where water, unless pumped up by windmill from the bowels of the earth, was practically unknown, and though we had to pay for the water supply by the presence of the ubiquitous mosquito, for which it pro- vided the only convenient breeding-place probably for many miles around, we had the comforting assurance that he was incapable of inoculating us with malaria, yellow fever, filariasis, or even the common or garden sep- tic micro-organisms, for the simple reason that no human being existed within twenty miles from whom he, or rather she, could obtain a supply of the necessary germs.

We left with great reluctance, for our food had almost entirely given out, and the nearest supply was two days' journey away, which meant four days before we could expect to get any in.

In one respect we were greatly disappointed, as our chiclero had told us that game came down to the lagoons for water in great numbers, and that tiger, wild hog, deer, curassow, gibnut, and wild turkey were to be obtained without any difficulty. With the exception, however, of a single wild turkey, we never saw a head of game. . . .

We had had a wonderful experience in discovering in the heart of the jungle of Yucatán this vast city of an ancient people, whose beginnings probably go back into the dim mists of the past, and whose civilisation must have endured right up to the Spanish Conquest, and it may be even for a century or so beyond that period.

One often hears people express wonder that the great ruined cities of Yucatán were so frequently overlooked by the Spanish conquerors, and the fact is usually ascribed to their lack of interest in the history and ethnology of the conquered races, whom they regarded, alive, solely as sources of wealth, which might be wrung by sweat out of their unfortunate bodies, and of spiritual kudos, which could be acquired after their death out of the salvation of their sinful souls.

But this was not the whole truth, as anyone who has visited the remoter outposts of Spanish colonial rule throughout the peninsula begins to realise. In all these settlements are found great, strong-walled, stone houses, with narrow openings—more fortresses than dwellings—from which with great difficulty, and in constant danger of their lives, the conquerors moved about the surrounding country, full of hosts of hostile Indians only awaiting an opportunity to revenge themselves for the persecution they had undergone upon any wandering Spaniard who might fall into their hands.

They were, in fact, bottled up in these settlements, and rarely came in contact with the Indians, except as slaves, and never went among the wilder tribes of the east, except in large punitive or foraging expeditions, so that it was really little to be wondered at that a ruined city, even of the size of Cobá, should have escaped them, even though it was not entirely deserted at the time they came into nominal possession of the country; for it was situated thirty miles from Chemax, their nearest settlement, and in the very centre of a country which has never been completely subdued to this day.

Then, after the War of the Castes, in 1847, the Spaniards were completely driven out of this part of Yucatán, which to this day is solely in possession of the Maya, so that till *chicleando,* as the Indians call chicle-bleeding, came in, probably no one but an occasional wandering Maya hunter has been near Cobá for close on a century.

Perhaps the most remarkable thing about this city was the fact that in it we found, brought together under one roof, as it were, three different types of Maya civilisation, supposed to be separate and distinct, though often found merging the one into the other at certain sites.

First, undoubtedly, in point of time, we have the Older Maya, represented by the Nohku, the stelae, and the various ranges of arched Maya rooms; second, the Tuluum, or East Coast type, represented by the flat-roofed, stucco-covered buildings; and finally the Lubaantún type, represented by the great stairways, found only here and at Lubaantún.

It was easy to understand the presence of the Tuluum style of architecture mixed with the Older Maya, for the former was but an offshoot of the latter, and Cobá was probably the nearest Maya city to Tuluum itself, distant not more than about thirty miles, so that communication between the two must have been frequent and free during probably two or three centuries. . . .

Another remarkable circumstance was that although Cobá must undoubtedly have flourished during the whole of the Toltec occupation of Chichen Itzá, and intercourse between the two cities must at one time, as indicated by the presence of the great causeway joining them, have been very close indeed, yet not a single Toltec feature was to be found throughout the whole city, not a Chacmool statue, a serpent column, an Atlantean figure, not, in fact, a single sculpture in the round, of which such innumerable specimens are to be found in every Toltec site as to lead one to conclude that sculpture in stone must have been one of the chief recreations of the populace, and not infrequently of such utter crudeness as to suggest the work of very young children, or imbeciles.

It is not improbable that the Toltec conquerors, who were more or less segregated in Chichen Itzá, were not strong enough to attack and subdue such a stronghold of the Maya as Cobá must have been, and one so remote from their own capital. They were indeed very likely in much the same position as the Spanish conquerors, some three centuries later, and while nominally in possession of the country, were actually afraid to move far from their own base, except in large, well-armed parties.

Mochica pyramid near Trujillo, northern Peru. The ancient coastal highway passes by, crossing the picture diagonally. *Courtesy Wenner-Gren Foundation for Anthropological Research, New York City*

Eroded walls of Chan-Chan, the pre-Inca coastal metropolis near Trujillo. *Courtesy Panagra—W. R. Grace, New York City*

View of Machu Picchu. *Courtesy Panagra—W. R. Grace, New York City*

The "Great Wall of Peru" stretching for some 40 miles along the Santa Valley into the Andean foothills. *Reprinted from* Life, Land and Water in Ancient Peru, *by Paul Kosok, Long Island University Press, Brooklyn, New York, 1965*

Web of mysterious geometric markings in the Nazca desert of central Peru. *Reprinted from* Life, Land and Water in Ancient Peru, *by Paul Kosok, Long Island University Press, Brooklyn, New York, 1965*

Rock drawings from Toro Muerto near Arequipa, southern Peru. *Permission granted by F. A. Brockhaus, Wiesbaden, Germany*

Statue of Coatlicue, mother of gods, which was found near the temple plaza of Tenochtitlán (Mexico City) at the end of the eighteenth century. It is now at Mexico City's Museum of Anthropology. *Courtesy Mexican National Tourist Council, New York City*

Side view of excavated circular pyramid of Cuicuilco near Mexico City. *Courtesy Instituto Nacional de Antropología e Historia, Mexico, D.F.*

A reconstruction (model) of the principal temples of Tenochtitlán. *Courtesy Instituto Nacional de Antropología e Historia, Mexico, D.F.*

Tomb 7, Monte Albán, during Alfonso Caso's excavation. *Courtesy Instituto Nacional de Antropología e Historia, Mexico, D.F.*

Golden Mixtec pectoral from Tomb 7 at Monte Albán. The plaques bear year symbols and date glyphs. *Courtesy Instituto Nacional de Antropología e Historia, Mexico, D.F.*

Panoramic view of temple platform of Monte Albán, Oaxaca, southern Mexico. *Courtesy Instituto Nacional de Antropología e Historia, Mexico, D.F.*

Giant Olmec head from La Venta, Tabasco. *Courtesy Instituto Nacional de Antropología e Historia, Mexico, D.F.*

Jade "tiger" from Necaxa, Puebla, now at the American Museum of Natural History, New York City. It led to George C. Vaillant's identification of a hitherto unknown Mexican civilization. *Courtesy American Museum of Natural History, New York City*

Group of monumental structures of Chichen Itzá, identified with "Toltec" occupation. In the foreground is the ballcourt (left) and the Citadel (right); the Temple of the Warriors is in the background. *Courtesy Mexican National Tourist Council, New York City*

Sacred well (*cenote*) with adjacent temple ruin, Chichen Itzá, Yucatán. *Courtesy Instituto Nacional de Antropología e Historia, Mexico, D.F.*

Bells recovered from the Chichen Itzá *cenote*. *Courtesy Instituto Nacional de Antropología e Historia, Mexico, D.F.*

The Temple of the Warriors, Chichen Itzá, upon completion of its reconstruction in 1927 by a team of archaeologists from the Carnegie Institution of Washington. *Courtesy Mexican National Tourist Council, New York City*

Aerial view of Cobá, Quintana Roo. Crossing lines in center mark old Maya roads. *Courtesy University Museum of the University of Pennsylvania, Philadelphia*

The Temple of Inscriptions, Palenque, Chiapas—(a) before and (b) after restoration. *Courtesy Mexican National Tourist Council, New York City*

Burial crypt of Temple of Inscriptions, Palenque. *Courtesy Instituto Nacional de Antropología e Historia, Mexico, D.F.*

Stucco mask from the Temple of Inscriptions. *Courtesy Instituto Nacional de Antropología e Historia, Mexico, D.F.*

Divers at Lake Amatitlán, Guatemala, a rich source of Maya artifacts. *Courtesy Milwaukee Public Museum, Milwaukee*

Maya clay vessels recovered from bottom of Lake Amatitlán. *Courtesy Milwaukee Public Museum, Milwaukee*

Lintel 3 and Stela 14 from Piedras Negras, Guatemala, which served as "keystones" in Tatiana Proskouriakoff's "dynastic hypothesis" and decipherment. *Courtesy University Museum of the University of Pennsylvania, Philadelphia*

Aerial photograph of the Serpent Mound, Adams County, southern Ohio. *Courtesy Smithsonian Institution, Washington, D.C.*

Cliff Palace, Mesa Verde, southwestern Colorado. *Courtesy American Museum of Natural History, New York City*

General view of the bison quarry near Folsom, New Mexico, where early American man was first identified. *Courtesy American Museum of Natural History, New York City*

Arroyo which laid bare fossil bisons with "Folsom" spear points. *Courtesy American Museum of Natural History, New York City*

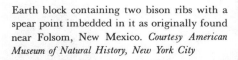

Earth block containing two bison ribs with a spear point imbedded in it as originally found near Folsom, New Mexico. *Courtesy American Museum of Natural History, New York City*

(a) Mouth of Gypsum Cave, Nevada, where Mark R. Harrington discovered important artifacts of early American hunters

(b) Skull with jawbone of ground sloth from Gypsum Cave

(c) Basket fragment from Gypsum Cave

(d) Wooden dart pieces from Gypsum Cave. *Courtesy Southwest Museum, Los Angeles*

Mural at Mexico City's Museum of Anthropology showing prehistoric fauna of the New World (giant sloth, mammoths, horse, cameloid, bison, saber-toothed tiger, etc.) contemporary with the earliest Americans. *Courtesy Mexican National Tourist Council, New York City*

Fluted projectile points found lodged in mammoths at the Naco elephant-kill site of southern Arizona. *Courtesy Arizona State Museum, University of Arizona, Tucson*

Tepexpan man, the "first Mexican" of perhaps some 10,000 years ago found by Helmut de Terra in the Valley of Mexico at the site shown in the picture (now a museum). *Courtesy Instituto Nacional de Antropología e Historia, Mexico, D.F.*

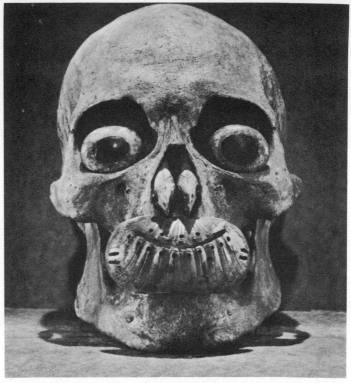

Inlaid skull from the prehistoric "Arctic metropolis" of Ipiutak in north-western Alaska. *Courtesy American Museum of Natural History, New York City*

Ruins of the Gardar cathedral, built by Norsemen in southern Greenland. *Courtesy Nationalmuseet, Copenhagen, Denmark*

Cape with hood taken in frozen state from a churchyard in southern Greenland. Viking settlers in a subarctic outpost of the Western Hemisphere had thus preserved an article of European fashion which we know as the typical four-teenth-century headgear of Dante and Petrarch. *Courtesy Nationalmuseet, Copenhagen, Denmark*

23

Chichen Itzá in northern Yucatán remains the best known of Maya sites. It is also the most accessible. Archaeological activities, particularly by scholars from the United States, have centered on it for generations. According to Stephens, who appeared there in 1841, the first modern visitor to precede him was an American engineer then employed in the Yucatán city of Valladolid. "In 1838," Stephens writes, "Mr. [John] Burke came from Valladolid to the village of Cawa, six leagues distant from Chichen. While making excursions in the neighborhood, one of the young men told him of old buildings on his hacienda, from one of which Valladolid was visible. Mr. Burke rode over, and on the fourth of July stood on the top of the Castillo, spyglass in hand, looking out for Valladolid."

For some time after the ferocious War of the Castes of 1847, when much of Yucatán including the Chichen Itzá hacienda was ransacked, foreign explorers shied away. In the 1860's the procession really started. One of the most notable visitors was Charnay who made acute observations on the varied style of the buildings. Augustus Le Plongeon, an argumentative crackpot, was the first to carry out excavations in the 1870's, most of them ruinous. However, he was the one to dig up the now famous statues of reclining figures, specimens of which were later found in other parts of Chichen Itzá and also in central Mexico and beyond Yucatán, in Central America. These pieces, vastly admired by modern sculptors like Henry Moore, probably represent a minor Toltec deity, though Le Plongeon baptized them fancifully, and for no good reason, *Chac Mool*, meaning Red Tiger. Le Plongeon was followed by a much more sober Austrian-born German, Teobert Maler, the great loner of Maya archaeology, who was long associated with U.S. institutions. With him, and the equally competent Englishman Alfred P. Maudslay, begins the scientific dawn. Maudslay stayed at Chichen for six months in 1889, making his home in one of the ancient ruins. He then produced an admirable record of structures and sculptures later incorporated in his monumental *Biologia Central-Americana.* Maudslay and his companion both fell sick with malaria during their stay. But since the cyclical disease attacked each on different days, one was able to nurse the other during his intermittent reprieve.

Chac Mool, Chichen Itzá

While Edward Thompson was still the proprietary lord of the unique archaeological garden, Chichen Itzá drew increased attention. Most intrigued by it was Sylvanus G. Morley, of all twentieth-century American archaeologists perhaps the most dedicated Maya scholar. He had conceived a plan to mount a large-scale campaign of excavation and repair at Chichen Itzá such as had never yet been undertaken in the Americas. To free an entire Maya city from the bondage of dust and time had long been his dream while crossing the forests in search of ancient inscriptions. Chichen Itzá intrigued him above all. In 1914, after the Mexican government had reclaimed the ruined site, he persuaded the Carnegie Institution of Washington to take over his cherished project. No Mexican could harbor doubts about that institution's selfless pursuit of scientific research or its capacity to carry it out effectively. The Carnegie people, while supplying brain power and finances, would seek no other aggrandizement than knowledge. All artifacts found during excavations were to be turned over to the Mexican authorities. Carnegie scholars pledged to retain only the privilege of excavating, restoring, and publishing the results. Such a generous proposal meant a revolution in international archaeological practices—a long way from Stephens' scheme to spirit the Copán monuments away to New York. It was bound to allay the suspicions even of notorious Yankee haters.

Yet scarcely had negotiations gotten under way, when Mexico herself was tossed from revolution to revolution. An agreement signed by one government was unlikely to be endorsed by its rebellious successor. Dr. Morley had to wait and continue on his own perilous jungle trail. At last, in 1923, the Carnegie Institution was granted a ten-year concession by the Mexican government, beginning on January 1, 1924. It was approved by the Dirección de Antropología which had jurisdiction over all archaeological monuments. This was the start of the Carnegie Institution's prolonged operations in the area (the concession was repeatedly renewed). Chichen Itzá became the Institution's Central American headquarters, while Uaxactún in Guatemala served as another center. Later on Carnegie expeditions went from Chichen to other Maya ruins on the Yucatán Peninsula. Virtually all leading United States *Mayistas* at one time or another were associated with the Chichen Itzá project. George C. Vaillant, Karl Ruppert (who was to lead the first Carnegie-sponsored expedition to Bonampak), J. Eric S. Thompson, British, but long connected with American museums, and Gustav Stromsvik, a Norwegian ex-sailor, here cut their archaeological teeth.

Awareness that archaeology implies not so much the digging up of random relics, but preservation and piecing together of what was part of the life of an ancient civilization, was what had persuaded the Carnegie Institution to launch Morley's program of restoration in the first place. From Carnegie campaigns emerged some of the magnificent buildings which today have become stock in trade of travel posters. ("Archaeology, like every other science," it has been said, "needs its show-windows.") No Carnegie effort was more ambitious than the excavation and reconstruction—without fake additions à la Sir Arthur Evans's "concrete Crete" —of the so-called Temple of the Warriors, an imposing example of Toltec impact on Mayan architecture.

Though Morley headed the overall Chichen Itzá project, excavations were directed by Earl H. Morris, who had already made a name for himself combining engineering skill with archaeology at the cliff dwellings and pueblos of his native U.S. Southwest. It was Morris who picked out a large, rugged, tree-topped mound strewn with broken blocks of worked stone. A small section of a wall protruded from it. Otherwise there was little to suggest that the shapeless mass some fifty feet high covered the tumbled remains of an architectural masterpiece which rested on a pyramidal foundation of four retreating terraces.

The mound, which belonged to a large complex in the northeastern part of the city, adjoined a court of about five acres. Through the underbrush one could see there a rare phenomenon among American ruins: rows of round columns made from regularly fitted cylinders of stone. Dubbed by the Carnegie people "the Court of the Thousand Columns," it was cleared first during the brief initial campaign of 1924. It later proved to be surrounded by roofed colonnades. The precise function of the extensive building complex is not known. But once the mound to the northwest of the court had lost its earthen cover and revealed glistening limestone façades, there was little doubt that it had been a temple, probably dedicated to the Toltec-Maya god Kukulcan, known in central Mexico as Quetzalcoatl.

It took Earl Morris and an army of native help four seasons to dig out and repair the sizable building. The task of rescuing a structure the bare outline of which could only be surmised from a heap of earth, debris, and pieces of scattered masonry was tremendous. It called for bold and untried methods. Morris rose to the challenge: the native workers addressed him respectfully as *Ingeniero*. His direction of this operation set a pattern for all the later reconstruction undertaken in Chichen Itzá and elsewhere in Mayaland. What makes Morris's description of his work so unusual in the literature is his lucid record of the interplay of technical problems with archaeological excitements.

The rebirth of one of the finest of ancient pre-Columbian edifices was, indeed, beset with excitements. Morris discusses in the opening chapter of *Temple of the Warriors* the encounter with giant columns of feathered rattlesnakes, their fanged jaws resting sideways on the floor, plumed tails and rattles fifteen feet above at the top. The fearsome beasts flanked the temple's entrance, which led into a spacious hall with the altar (or throne?) resting on Atlantean figures. The square columns of the interior were all sculptured to represent warriors in Toltec garb, members probably of the militaristic knighthoods of Jaguar and Eagle, whose divinely appointed task it was to bring the enemy back alive so that he could have his heart torn out for the greater glory of a bloodthirsty god. The columns still bore vivid colors, as did the walls. The latter retained paintings of a variety of religious, martial, and even domestic scenes. Morris's wife, Ann Axtell Morris, and the Franco-Mexican artist Jean Charlot were enlisted to copy this precious iconography. Also of considerable aesthetic merit were the sculptured friezes along the vertical walls of the pyramid foundation. They showed related scenes of warriors and of animals clutching human hearts. One frequently depicted furry creature of unknown biological identity, the Carnegie scholars referred to simply as "woolly."

In the 1925 season, deep below the Temple of the Warriors in the northeast corner of the pyramid, Morris came across another serpent column, which led him to assume that an older building had been used as foundation of the later one. Consecutive seasons proved this to be the case. During excavations a buried temple within a temple was laid free in its entirety, though it required ingenious constructions to carry on without endangering the Temple of the Warriors above. To the archaeologists' delight it was found that the painted walls and columns of the older temple had fully preserved their startling colors, none the worse for six hundred years of entombment. Such brilliant display of colors had never before been seen on Maya ruins.

Mural depicting Maya village scene, Temple of the Warriors

Before he began to clear this temple Morris had a premonition that there was a Chac Mool, a reclining sculpture, inside. To his own surprise, an unusually fine sculpture of that type came speedily to light, and thus supplied a name for the buried structure: Temple of Chac Mool.

Morris's empathic understanding of American antiquities contributed much to another thrilling recovery, described below with considerable narrative verve by Morris's wife. In time to come, the treasure trove from the old temple was to guide archaeologists to comparable finds at other sites. Not the least of these was a ceremonial deposit from an older temple within Chichen Itzá's Castillo or Temple of Kukulcan.

The Carnegie mission's most important result, however, was the elucidation of the architectural evolution of Chichen Itzá, which mirrored the city's perplexing ethnic and political history. It now became possible to distinguish and approximately date the Toltec periods and the eclipse of Chichen Itzá's leadership in northern Yucatán. There could no longer be the slightest doubt of the priority of purely Maya style and culture. The full extent of alien influences from central Mexico could at last be gauged, though the amazing parallel between the Temple of the Warriors and the main temple of Tula, in the central Mexican state of Hidalgo, was only conclusively established in the 1950's when the latter city was excavated.

The Itzá, who invaded the northern Maya city around A.D. 900, nevertheless remained a puzzle. One could not be certain whether they were Toltec conquerors or a Maya-speaking people from adjacent Tabasco who may previously have absorbed some central-Mexican traits, even though the main Toltec influx at Chichen Itzá took place after their arrival. Equally hazy is the role of Kukulcan—alias Quetzalcoatl—the semi-legendary fugitive Toltec ruler who, to make things worse, had many namesakes in ancient Mexico, including a deity with whom folklore chose to fuse him.

The age of the Temple of the Warriors is also in doubt, but it appears to belong to the last Toltec phase; in the opinion of J. Eric S. Thompson, it was built around A.D. 1100. The shrine was sacked a hundred years later; Chichen Itzá was virtually depopulated and sank into insignificance apart from continuing to draw pilgrims to its sacred *cenote*.

Earl Halsted Morris (1889–1956) owes his archaeological awakening to his childhood in the Indian country of New Mexico, to which his father had come as an early settler. He dug for pottery from the age of four. Barely out of his teens he took part in excavations in the Southwest and in Central America. The Pueblo culture and its Basket Maker antecedents have been his lifelong interest. Some of his notable discoveries were made at Arizona's "Canyon of Death." His restoration of the Great Kiva at the prehistoric Aztec Ruin in New Mexico earned him a reputation for ingenious field technique, later given full scope at Chichen Itzá. For his contributions to both Southwestern and Mesoamerican research Morris was given the Kidder Memorial Medal in 1953.

Morris's wife, Ann Axtell Morris, who died in 1945, did not come to archaeology just by accident or marriage. As a young graduate student she pursued prehistoric research in France. In 1923 she became Morris's active partner and later was co-author of the official report on the Temple of the Warriors. She made a special study of cave paintings and pictographs of the Southwest. Her two highly readable books, *Digging in Yucatan* (1931) and *Digging in the Southwest* (1933), though aimed primarily at a young audience, are among the best popular writing on American antiquities by a practicing archaeologist.

THE TEMPLE OF THE WARRIORS

Earl H. Morris

The first season of extensive exploration by Carnegie Institution of Washington among the ruins of the old Maya metropolis of Chichen Itzá was about to begin. Although we had come to Yucatán in May, 1924, at the close of the Mexican revolution, we had found opportunity for little more than to get the feel of the place before the advent of the rains made excavation among the fallen temples impracticable. Now [in early 1925] we were on the ground early in the dry season, and had in readiness foodstuffs, tools, and equipment for a long and, we hoped, a fruitful campaign.

As our first undertaking, we wished to open a building of a type not hitherto excavated, one which would not only yield important historical data, but which, when repaired, would stand as a monument to the architectural genius of the Maya. Moreover, Doctor John C. Merriam, President of Carnegie Institution, was to visit us only three weeks hence, and we greatly desired to have something of special interest laid bare by the time of his arrival. Whether or not we would succeed in this depended entirely upon our choice of a site. Certain it was that among the wreckage of a city once magnificent, nature had entombed many an object or structure which it would quicken the pulse to behold, but it was equally certain that between the spots where such lay buried there were stretches where our workmen might delve for weeks among nothing but barren debris. Thus far we had been unable to settle upon the spot where the spade should pry at the lock of time.

At dusk Pablo had halted before the *portal* of the Hacienda which served as field headquarters with the last load of our fifty tons of freight. Missing from it, lost upon the way, was the only rod of tool steel which in New Orleans, our distant base of supplies, I had included among the necessities for the season's work. I could see that rod made up into mason's chisels, bars for moving heavy stones, and put to half a dozen other uses for which only good tough steel would serve. As soon as the evening meal was over, Doctor Morley and I set out into the misty rain in search of it. As we bumped over the stony road it seemed as if a giant swell had molded the contour of its troughs and broken crests upon the floor of

---

the shallow sea before Yucatán had been pushed above the waves. We moved as upon the back of a great measuring worm, now up, now down across the alternate sequence of swales and hummocks. Legend ran that once upon a time the rented Ford had been kicked blind by a mule. Wedged between a fender and the hood sat Isauro, from his hand a gasoline lantern pendant before the radiator in lieu of headlamps. From the roadway the eyes of a night bird gleamed ruby red as it turned to face the glare, while just beyond twin orbs of green became a streak of phosphorescence as a wood cat abandoned quest of food to vanish into the sheltering haven of the bush. Gravel rattled against the hood, flung by the heels of a buck that crossed in front of us, racing in startled terror from this one-eyed monster of the night. Above, misshapen trees leaned inward to intertwine their branches, thus to hide the white scar that scored the jungle from the ruins to the railway at Dzitas.

While I held the rickety car to the road, scanning with peripheral vision the weeds that fringed the wheel tracks for a coveted gleam of metal, we reviewed once more the arguments for and against the several localities, one of which we soon must choose as a point of beginning. Under our contract with the Mexican Government, we had agreed to centre our activities upon the Court of the Thousand Columns, a huge cluster of ruined buildings flanking a five-acre open court in the northeastern quarter of the city. Towering above the northwest corner of the ranges of lower mounds stood a large and rugged pyramid, bush-clad and difficult to climb. We had worked our way upward through the tangle of vines upon the nearly vertical eastern slope to the stump of a fallen tree, clasped among the roots of which were wall stones bearing bits of a fresco done in vivid red and green. And on the western edge of the summit we had seen the huge capitals, each graven from a single block, that once had capped the serpent columns in the portal of a splendid temple. We knew that to free the temple and the pyramid upon which it stood of the debris of centuries, and properly to repair them, would constitute a task by no means easy. Nevertheless I recommended, since it appeared to me to offer the most striking possibilities of any ruin that lay within the limits defined by our concession, that we begin upon it at once.

"But, Earl," Doctor Morley asked, "have we had enough experience to tackle such a job?"

"I believe we can swing it," I replied.

"Well, old man, if you think so, go ahead," was the response.

And so, during our search for the lost rod of steel, was born, that rainy February night in 1925, the decision to explore the great architectural complex which was to be called The Temple of the Warriors.

The following Monday, as the white fog dissolved before the warmth of the rising sun, the heavy air muted the swash and clink of machetes as lithe blades sliced through vines and underbrush, or glanced off from hidden stones. A swarm of workmen, like white-coated ants, were slowly eating their way up the slope of the pyramid, while from the summit Old Juan, the Mayor Domo, perching like a battered eagle upon the stump of a wind-riven tree, watched and directed the brood below.

By sundown the hill was swept clear of all herbage except the larger trees, and the resultant rubbish had been dragged a safe distance away and piled in windrows, there to be burned some afternoon when the sap had dried and a wind was running. Now that it had been well barbered, one could form some notion of the actual size and contour of the knobby head that had grown so rank a thatch. Full fifty feet high it stood, and one hundred fifty feet broad in either direction at the base. The north and east faces rose in a steep unbroken slope from base to summit. The talus at the south side spread out upon the surface of the mound covering the north range of the Court of the Thousand Columns. Near the southwest corner of the pyramid this north range reached a junction with the long, ruined hall forming the western boundary of the same court. Thence the latter structure continued northward as a mound twelve feet in height and fifty broad, entirely across and somewhat beyond the north

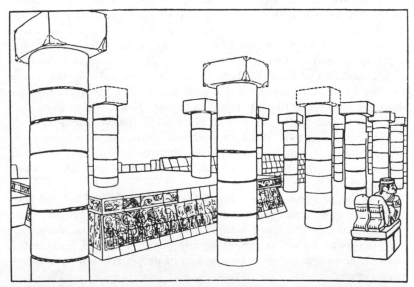

The North Colonnade, abutting the Temple of the Warriors, drawn by Tatiana Proskouriakoff

end of the western skirt of the pyramid. Up the centre of the western side was a ramp of lesser gradient than the slope on either hand. Cluttered about the foot of it were scores of finely hewn blocks tumbled down from the stair steps with which the ramp had once been faced. When the last workman had answered the call of the bell that clanged from the ruined church atop the knoll beside the Hacienda, I climbed that ramp. At three-fourths the height of the pyramid it gave upon a nearly flat terrace which I knew marked the level of the platform which had flanked the front of the temple. Upon it, half buried, lay the tail pieces of the serpent columns, and midway between them rested a more than life-size sculpture of a semireclining human figure, headless, battered, and pitted by the rains of centuries. Farther up the slope were strewn great blocks from the shafts of the columns, and near the summit protruded a single stone from each of the jambs, thus indicating the breadth of the tripartite doorway.

A turn or two back and forth across the irregular crest of the elevation gave me the form and approximate size of the temple. Here and there a stone with its smooth face in vertical position, depending upon the direction in which the tooled surface pointed, revealed the inner or outer line of a wall. Between such stones I stepped the distance from north to south and from east to west. The building was somewhat more than sixty feet square, and faced the west. A partition in the north and south axis divided it into two long chambers of practically the same size. In each of these a few top blocks of square columns stood just above the mould, and I could see that all four sides of these were carved. Apparently there were two rows of columns running from north to south in each chamber. Quick-falling darkness finally drove me from the temple top, but the stars had described a wide arc of their circle before sleep obscured the images that my mind cast upon the curtain of closed lids as I viewed that tumbled hill from every angle that imagination could devise, and sought to project my vision beneath the shroud of humus and fallen masonry. Ere dawn I had to know where each of the fifty workmen, who would emerge from the mist when again the church bell clanged, was to ply his spade.

If we were to have made appreciable headway on the .tangled heap within the three weeks' limit which was our immediate objective, speed was necessary, but to speed caution could not be sacrificed. Moreover, the attack was not unlike that of an army upon a fortress, and the first blow of the vanguard had to be struck in its proper relation to the whole campaign.

Across the northern two-thirds of the eastern slope, some six feet from the summit, a line of faced stones sloping outward showed that even the inner course of the rear wall had fallen to that height. Along this expanse I placed a row of workmen as close together as they could conveniently use their tools. They were to dig toward the west, thus slicing off the upper half of the debris that filled the eastern chamber. The stone and crumbled mortar removed was to be cast down the slope behind them. This was crude, rough work, for there was little chance of finding even a sculptured stone in the roof debris. The more intelligent appearing of the men I had separated from the rest. These were divided into two groups. One was placed at the southwest, the other at the northwest corner of the platform in front of the temple. The surface earth was the black humus of decayed vegetation. At a depth of about one foot it gave way to undisturbed masonry. This level was traced across the entire front and then inward toward the temple wall. As the depth of debris increased, root action had been less pronounced. Soon a film of white mortar began to appear as a coating over the surface of the rough masonry, and not long after a pick blade scraped upon a beautifully polished red-tinted floor. We had established our first definite point— the exact level of the platform which led toward the temple door. Inward the drift was run toward the ragged line where, at a higher level, the material from the fallen roof, with its intermingled network of stumps and roots, was being broken down and cast behind, thus bringing the vertical banks ever so slowly toward an eventual meeting.

Ere long a shout echoed from the lips of one of the diggers at the front of the temple. His pick had loosened a sculptured stone from the wreckage. Most of those about him dropped their tools and crowded close to view and to speculate what might be this bit of carving. Carefully I watched them to judge the relative keenness and interest of each of them as they gazed at the fanged jaw, which the finder was wiping clean of earth, for from that group I must gradually select the few to whom would be entrusted the difficult and meticulous bits of excavation that I knew would, sooner or later, be encountered. Pick and shovel are the tools of a lowly and misunderstood profession. Casually it would seem that any lump of animate matter with sufficient intelligence to guide food and drink to his lips could wield them with all the effectiveness lying within the possibilities of such gross implements. Never was a notion more erroneous. There are almost as many different kinds of picks and shovels as there are of artists' brushes, and each one is shaped for a definite and specific use to which it may be put with blundering stupidity or consummate skill. Sufficient mental alertness quickly to recognize the object which his pick point or shovel blade has laid bare, an ability to evaluate the mechanical relationship between the components of the mass to be moved, and good co-ordination between eye and hand, are, far more than size or strength, the essentials to the making of a master craftsman in the art of digging ditch or driving tunnel. And if ever the touch of the master is needed, it is in archaeological excavation. There even an additional qualification is almost prerequisite—that of interest in the work. A single careless blow can reduce an exquisite pottery vessel to a hundred frayed and tattered sherds; mar a plaque of jade beyond hope of restoration, or destroy utterly some feature of a priceless sculpture.

Before noon of the first day carved stones were coming from the debris all across the front of the temple. For the most part they were thin flat blocks graven in low relief, component elements of large mosaic panels which had adorned the upper reaches of the outer wall. Each one was carried directly forward from the spot at which it was found and added to a heap of its fellows. Karl Ruppert stood with paint pot in hand, ready to brand each stone in a way that would facilitate the task of fitting the mosaics together again when the time came for reassemblage.

The tail pieces of the serpent columns we left as they lay. As the breast of the excavation moved inward, the debris was taken out from beneath each of the heavy rectangular blocks of the toppled shafts, and the stone was let down upon the pavement of the platform, the same side up, and in exactly the same position relative to the others in which it had been found. Corners and flakes had been riven from some of the blocks by the heat of bush fires. Old Juan watched for these among the stones and crumbled mortar which caved down under the picks of the workmen. Much of his thirty years' residence at Chichen had been spent among the ruins, and in consequence he had developed what amounted almost to instinct for recognizing fragments of worked stone. Very often he stooped to recover some ragged spall that might help to fill out a splintered block, for as keenly as we did, he looked forward to the day when this pair of serpent columns would be re-erected in its entirety.

The serpent column, upon which the architects at Chichen specialized, is perhaps one of the most bizarre architectural concepts the world has ever seen. The head, with wide-flung jaws and protruding tongue, lies flat upon the floor plane of the building, jutting forward from the line of the front wall. From behind it the body rises vertically, functioning as the shaft of the column. At the height of the capital, it turns forward at a right angle and continues for a distance sufficient to reach beyond the jutting molding which occurs just above it, then bends vertically upward. This terminal portion is graven to represent the rattles of the rattlesnake, surmounted by a tuft of flowing plumes. No ordinary serpent this, but the Plumed Serpent, the patron deity of Chichen Itzá, combining the qualities, both mystic and mysterious, of the most subtly powerful of

Toltec serpent column

the creatures of the earth, and of the bird, master of the element wherein
man had no power or domain.

In front of several of the ruins scattered throughout the city lay fallen
serpent columns, battered and splintered by the vicissitudes of time. In
no known instance was the head of one of them complete. So deep was
the debris where we were digging that the heads which we knew should
there be present were completely buried, and being thus protected, we
hoped that they might be in nearly perfect condition. But there was no
predicting what fate they might have suffered before detritus from the
walls above had entombed them.

When, near the northwest corner, the temple wall was finally uncovered, findings there injected a new element into our calculations. Because of the height of the mound above the level we had been following, we fully expected to find a series of steps leading up from that level
to the entrance of the temple. The highest columns known to exist elsewhere in the city had an altitude of little more than nine feet, hence it
was to be expected that the ones in the building we had chosen to explore
would be of no greater height. The tops of those which showed above

the earth upon the summit were more than twelve feet above the frontal platform, hence our conclusion that the floor of the temple would be at a higher level. Since there were no steps the columns would have a height of between twelve and thirteen feet, and moreover, owing to its greater depth, the debris to be moved from the interior of the building would have a bulk one-fourth greater than that upon which we had calculated, which of course would lengthen the time of excavation.

The portion of the front wall which had been buried was in excellent condition. It rose to a height of more than four feet with a decided inward slant, at the top of which ran a bevelled molding course. Resting directly upon the molding at the northwest corner was the finely carved tooth-studded lower jaw of a grotesque mask, and southward from it spread other features of the mask. Midway between the corner and the north jamb of the door, above one tall course of plain-faced stones, were the basal stones of a mosaic panel, graven to represent the huge clawed feet of a bird. And adjacent to the jamb there remained in place a considerable part of a mask like that found at the corner, except that it was conformed to a flat surface, whereas the median line of the other formed the apex of the corner so that one-half of the mask faced west and the other half north. The half of the wall south of the doorway duplicated these conditions. As a result, we had the key for the rebuilding of these walls to a considerable height. It remained only to fit together the blocks of the mosaics which had been recovered from the debris, and to see that the masons put them back in their proper places in the walls. This sounds easy in the telling, but days, even weeks, of tedious labor had elapsed ere the task was done.

As the diggers drew in upon the area where the serpents' heads should be, Ruppert and I were as restless as dogs which watch at the mouth of a hole for a rabbit to be poked out. Manuel pried down a rough stone, and beyond it I saw a glint of red. "Wait," I ordered before another blow could be struck, and took the pick in my own hands. In an interval that seems devoid of duration as I look back upon it, I had loosened earth and stone from one entire side of the great head, and willing hands had scraped it away behind me. The masterly piece of carving, waist-high, and four feet long, stood before us unmoved and scarcely marred, in almost perfect condition. The upper jaw was flung far upward to reveal a wide-open mouth, painted a dark and brilliant red, and studded, contrary to anatomical veracity, with a huge pair of fangs in the lower as well as in the upper jaw. The eye was a deep-sunken cavity filled in with a black paste which outlined a yellow-white pupil, and above the socket was carved an inverted crescent painted a deep and pleasing blue. From the angle of the jaw a spiral whorl reached backward toward a collar of bright green feathers, beyond which long graceful plumes, also green, were carved to turn upward on the first vertical block of the shaft of the column. From the flat top of the head two short curving horns struck upward. One of them was broken off and missing, and one tooth or fang was gone from the lower jaw.

Sweat molded the flimsy white shirts of the workmen to every contour of their supple torsos as they clawed away the mass that impeded access to the other side of this sculpture, and to the second one that lay beyond. By quitting time both heads stood free, one as nearly perfect as the other. There was no difficulty now in visualizing exactly what had taken place. Slowly at first the topmost portion of the temple wall had crumbled. Plaster and mortar washed down by the rains, then later stones from face and hearting of the wall, had built up an accumulation around the heads, to a height sufficient slightly more than to cover them. Then the whole upper half of the front of the building had fallen outward *en masse*. The two columns swung forward as a severed tree might fall. The lower blocks, wedged by the massive heads, stood firm, but those above lay as we had found them, like sections sawed from a prostrate trunk. Not four inches of earth separated the upflung jaws from the blocks that rested directly above them, but that small layer had been enough to cushion the shock and to preserve these heads in the condition in which we dreamed of finding them.

To the inner line of the door jambs the drift was dug, and then the workmen were transferred elsewhere. The face of the cut was now twelve feet high. The surface beyond would serve as a platform from which to work during the replacement of the serpent columns, stronger and more effective than any that we could build. Also the trees that had been left standing on top of the mound would come handy as anchor posts for brace ropes and tackle lines. We set up an A made of two stout timbers, strongly lashed together a short distance below their tops, between one column and the bank of debris behind it. From somewhere in the bush Isauro, son of Juan, and his squad, brought a straight slender trunk of hard wood forty feet long. This we laid horizontally so that it rested in the crotch at the top of the A, the butt protruding beyond the forward face of the column some four feet above it, the tip reaching far back onto the mound. To the butt was lashed a powerful chain block. With this improvised hoist once erected, all was in readiness to begin the rebuilding of the column.

Those elements of the two shafts which had fallen farthest forward had been moved at some time since their collapse, to the extent that from position alone it was impossible to tell to which column a particular one belonged. So we aligned them upon the ground, matching the carving on each with the lines that crossed onto the block above, and the block below. Half of the top stone of the shaft of the south column was missing. Finally Old Juan found it at the foot of the pyramid. Certainly it had been pushed over the brink of the temple platform by human hands.

One by one the rectangles of stone were hoisted, swung into place, the corners plumbed, and the crack beneath wedged so that the block could not sag out of line when the tackle was loosened. Then the crack was sealed with mud, except for a short distance at its highest point. Here a metal pipe was inserted, and through it liquid cement was poured until the crack was completely full. Thus each unit that was added was firmly knit to the one beneath, so that when finished, the column was, in effect, monolithic. The individual blocks of the shaft varied in weight from four hundred to seven hundred pounds, hence were not difficult to raise. With the capital or tail piece the situation was not so simple. It weighed well over a ton, but that was not the chief obstacle. The block, when viewed from the side, was shaped much like a builder's square. When in position it stood as if with the short arm pointing vertically upward, and the free end of the blade resting upon the shaft of the column. As a result the centre of gravity lay forward of the face of the column, and the stone would not remain in position unless supported. Originally the lintels which spanned the door rested upon these tail pieces so that they were bound in place by the tremendous weight of the superstructure. But, as we had no idea of replacing the upper reaches of the building, some other plan of anchorage must be devised.

Upon a bed of wooden rollers the great tail piece was dragged into position beside the column. Ropes, soft but strong, were passed about it, and through these was slipped the hook of the chain block. To the rhythm of Old Juan's "Yo heave," the heavy stone rose till it swung clear of the shaft. The tip of the long horizontal pole, to the butt of which the tackle was attached, served as a sweep, free to move through an arc of more than forty-five degrees. By means of it the tail piece was swung over the capital, and the chains were slackened until it came to rest upon the stone beneath, just where it had originally been placed some centuries before. The tip of the sweep was tied to a stump, and weighted down with logs as an extra precaution, for the capital was poised, ready, if a rope gave, or any feature of the hoist weakened, to crash down upon and shatter the gorgeous head which lay directly beneath it.

Now there came a use for that rod of tool steel that no one had foreseen. We did not find it the night that we searched so long, but two days later it came to the Hacienda on the back of a native who had picked it up and hidden it, to bring it in when convenience dictated, with the hope of a piece of silver for reward. In the forge that we had set up be-

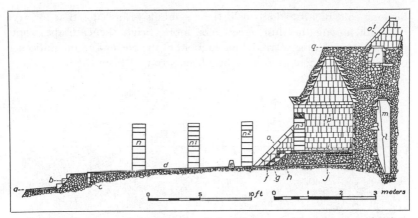

Cross-section of part of the Temple of the Warriors with stairway and colonnade; restored

neath a huge laurel tree I gave one end of it the shape and temper of a miner's drill. All the following day the clang of steel on stone pulsed through the bush as four workmen, led by Ruppert, who knew the handling of a churn drill, stood on a scaffolding above the poised capital and drove the rod deeper and deeper into the shaft beneath. At length the column was pierced from top to bottom and the bore extended well beyond into the foundation. Then a rod of soft iron three-fourths inch in diameter and of the proper length was threaded at one end and split at the other so that the tip of an iron wedge would fit into the slot. The rod was let down into the bore in the column and driven until the wedge had spread the lower end as wide apart as the diameter of the hole would permit. Then the space around the rod was poured full of liquid cement. When this had set, a recess was cut into the top of the capital surrounding the tip of the rod, a plate was fitted over the latter and drawn down tight with a heavy nut. When the countersunk area had been filled with cement not one trace remained visible of the fourteen-foot bolt which united column, capital, and even the foundation beneath into one unit of solid substance which could not fall, barring an earthquake or the actual breaking of stone.

The night after the tackle was removed from the second completed column I sat upon the brink of the terrace and gazed long at the weird and beautifully graven emblems that stood clear limned against the pale white sky, quite lost in the wilderness of my own imaginings. Ere the end I wondered if I were the only one who watched the portal of this ancient shrine. Perhaps in that limbo to which all old discarded gods are at length consigned, one among the host felt a glow of warmth in his long-cold breast as he beheld these symbols of his cult, that for ages had lain among the dust, erect once more, bright beneath the tropic moon, battered, time-scarred, but eloquent of the power and magnificence of the deity to whose glory they had been wrought from the living stone.

Sculptured band, south side of the Temple of the Warriors

THE HIDDEN TURQUOISE MOSAIC

Ann Axtell Morris

Dedication day was near at hand. The temple was just about ready to be turned over formally to the Mexican government. Various high officials were on their way from Mexico City to attend the ceremony, and Dr. Merriam and Dr. Kidder had come from Washington to officiate at the presentation. Mexico is very proud of its old monuments and devotes a deal of expense and attention to those found in its territory. In this respect she sets an excellent example to other nations for she contributes from her annual national budget more money for archeological exploration and preservation than any other country in the world.

The entire Chichen Itzá staff was busy as a swarm of bees in preparation for the event. Every nook and cranny was swept and garnished with the utmost care and solicitude. And in addition, since the end of the dry season was drawing nigh, we were hastening with our own individual work in order to catch up all the loose ends before it was necessary to return to the United States.

From *Digging in Yucatan*. New York: Junior Library Guild—Doubleday, 1931, pp. 253–71.

Old Angelino was burrowing his last tunnel through the Warriors' pyramid, the one which was to prove conclusively that yet other buildings had not been buried in its far corners. By this time he was an expert at the dangerous task, so Earl felt free for the first time to devote himself to checking up on a little private idea of his own. This particular hunch, by the way, was to produce such remarkable eleventh-hour results that people have often asked him just where and how the inspiration happened to strike him. In his own words, the story runs somewhat as follows:

"One evening last winter (1927) during the Annual Exhibition held in the Carnegie Institution at Washington, D.C., I was on duty to explain to the visitors the Chichen Itzá exhibit which had been installed. During a quiet interval my thoughts drifted away from the Maya city, back to the ancient ruins in New Mexico where I had spent my boyhood. For some reason I began thinking of the dedication offerings of turquoise and shell, which I had found built into the sacred rooms there. Then, like a bolt from the blue, it struck me that maybe the Maya had done the same thing." In so many instances have the peoples of old America given evidence of thinking and acting in similar manner, even when they were thousands of miles separated, that a parallel in the present case was just possible. "I remember thinking then that the altars would be the most logical places to bury such offerings, and I determined to test out the possibility when I returned to Yucatán."

However, when he did return, the press of immediate tasks demanded his attention, and in the difficult work involved by the roofing of the Buried Temple and tunneling around its base there was no time for the chase of a phantasy until close on the season's end. When Dr. Merriam arrived, Earl told him of his idea about the altars, and he was instantly and intensely interested.

The two of them set out together one morning, fairly exuding secretiveness, while brown-skinned Danyel, who was a most careful digger, was ordered to fall in behind. First they went to the sculptured altar in the Northwest Colonnade, and when the protective sand had been swept from its polished red surface a large white patch was seen to mar its beauty. Dr. Merriam looked at Earl, and Earl stared back in dismay.

"It looks as if someone had been here before us, but it also seems as if there might be something to the idea, doesn't it? Start in here, Danyel, and we'll see."

Beneath the white plaster coat, the altar body showed distinct evidence of having been stirred, for bits of the red floor were scattered throughout. Against the foot of the back wall a broken pottery urn was found, but nothing else. It was quite evident that the place had been looted of some objects of value; then the thieves, for some unknown reason, had neatly refilled the hole, plastered it over, but had not repainted it red. I never have figured out why they should have taken such pains to cover the traces of their crime and then neglected the most obvious step of all, unless it was that they were caught at the task. If that was true, the booty must have been hijacked, because it certainly was not restored to its rightful position.

Next, Earl and Dr. Merriam turned to the altar in the North Colonnade, this time very hopefully, because in spite of early bad luck the very fact that an offering had once been there was most encouraging. The center of the second altar was gouged into with no success, the trench carried to the back wall, but still nothing was found, and Danyel, who had become infected with the excitement of the chase, leaned dejectedly against his pick. Suddenly he brightened.

"Engineer, there is another altar of solid stone where you and I worked the first year. Maybe that one will not deceive us so."

"Bueno, Danyel, vamanos!" And the three treasure seekers, probably mindful of the old adage that the grass in the next field is always greener, moved on.

This time, the very first blow of the pick sounded against a flat slab that rang hollow. Trowels were used, and when the great stone was lifted a sizable cavity was revealed, but seemingly empty except for a little fine dust over the floor. Earl sifted the dust carefully between his fingers, and in the very last corner discovered a small pottery dish, two dishes of shell, and a few badly decayed bones of a small bird. Obviously the carefully constructed vault had been made to hold something of more value than these few wretched specimens. Doubtless the objects of real beauty had been wrought in some perishable substance—carved wood or richly woven tapestry—which had perished through decay.

"Well," said Earl, "we haven't contributed in a very startling fashion to Maya archeology so far. Let's go back and tackle that second altar again. It can't be absolutely bare. If there is anything there, we'll get it if we have to dig the whole heart out."

Danyel flew at the masonry like an ambitious gopher until Earl put a restraining hand on his shovel handle.

"Just a minute, my friend. You mustn't throw jade around the country like that." And to Danyel's intense chagrin he stooped and rescued from the pile of debris a brilliant green bead as large as a walnut.

They all combed with their fingers through the dirt that had been thrown out, but evidently that bit of jade was the only object which had been in danger of being lost. Then, carefully working the bottom of the pit, ten more small pieces of the green stone were found, a few bits of shell, and two large disks made of a soft yellow sandstone.

Affairs seemed to be improving, but the last solid altar had been tapped, and the finds had been admittedly scanty. Earl was disappointed, and he felt hardly toward the long-treasured hunch which seemed to have let him down so badly. Just then the noon bell rang and he and Danyel plodded dejectedly for the Buried Temple in order to lock up their tools, while Dr. Merriam returned to the hacienda.

Serpent from buried Temple of Chac Mool

In the Buried Temple, Earl looked speculatively at the spot where the altar had once stood. Since this one had not been of the solid masonry type, but had consisted of slabs supported by little stone human figures, any chance of offerings seemed remote. The only possible opportunity would lie in its burial beneath the floor. Earl took Danyel's pick and tapped over the entire area once covered by the altar in an effort to detect the tell-tale resonant ring betraying a hidden cavity. No spot sounded conclusively hollow, but one point seemed to echo a bit more than the rest. Beneath it Danyel dug, but he encountered nothing but stones laid in lime. The cavity was only a tiny hollow where the mortar had not completely filled the space beneath a stone chip.

"It's no good, Danyel. You go get your lunch, for you have worked well. My luck is bad, that's all."

Earl stood there alone for a space to adjust himself to the disappointment, for he found that he had hoped for far more than he had ever realized in his speculations on the idea. I believe then the spirit of the old Plumed Serpent must have fairly held its phantom breath in fear of this intrusive alien white man who at that very moment stood within a hand's breadth of the treasure it must have wished to guard for itself.

Just then Jean and Gustav came down into the temple to leave the tools of their various crafts over the noon hour. Earl told them about what he had been up to all morning, and how poorly it had turned out. "Well, sor," said the loyal Norwegian, "if you can't find anything, then there's nothing to find."

Maybe it was that remark that tipped the scale, possibly it was a characteristic dogged persistence that wouldn't admit defeat, or again, it might have been a certain brooding, intangible sense of old memories that hung over the spot which chimed in with the earnest seeker's tautly strung mind. At any rate, as the two boys tell it, Earl suddenly shook himself and said, "Wait a minute, fellows, I want to tap this floor once more." Carefully he sounded the area again and again while they all listened with rapt attentiveness. It was as if all the senses were for the moment paralyzed, while their several powers were concentrated in hearing alone.

Finally, between the hole that Danyel had dug and the back wall, a spot no larger than a saucer seemed to give forth a deeper rumble. One blow with the pick point, and the blade broke through to pass into a cavity below. Bare hands clawed at the bits of broken floor crust and, thrusting his fingers in the hole made by the pick, Earl raised a lid of stone. Three heads craned eagerly over the opening to peer down into a cylindrical recess of polished stone. From the bottom came a gleam of jade and something that even in the half light of the gloomy temple glinted as blue as a bit of tropical sky.

"Careful, boys." Earl's voice shook. "We'll have to go slowly here, for we've got something real at last."

They covered the opening with Jean's drawing board, and carefully tested the padlock on the barred temple door.

At their slightly belated lunch the three conspirators kept their eyes strictly on their plates and ate so little withal—an abstinence very contrary to custom—that their elaborately circumspect manner fairly shrieked of the extraordinary. Finally, Dr. Morley—I think it was he—couldn't bear it another minute.

"Look here, old man, the proverbial cat that ate the oft-mentioned canary must have had an expression precisely like yours. What *have* you found?"

Earl swallowed the greater part of a whole boiled potato at one gulp and replied, "If you want to learn something to your advantage, meet me at the Buried Temple at two o'clock."

On the dot of time the entire personnel of Chichen gathered before the door of the Temple and stared in at the familiar empty interior, which, now that the hole in the floor was covered by the big drawing board, seemed to offer no clue whatever as to where the mystery lay. When Earl came down the steps and teasingly displayed a flashlight, a teaspoon, and a camel's-hair brush, anticipation grew as keen as it was puzzled.

First he lengthened the hole that Danyel had dug earlier in the day in order that his working position might not be so awkward. Then the drawing board was carefully laid aside and a score or so of quickly drawn breaths, as we all crowded in, attested to everybody's startled interest.

At the center of the cavity lay a large spherical ball of dark jade polished as glass. This was one of the *zaz-tuns* or "light stones" which the old priests had used for prophecy, much as do the crystal gazers of the Orient to-day. Beside it was a piece of apple-green jade beautifully carved to represent a human face, and flanking it were two more jade beads and strings of shell. Near these were some bird bones.

These things could be detected by the glow of the flashlight but beneath them lay a film of dust which had filtered in during the long ages while the jar remained buried in the earth.

Then Earl reached for a long-handled camel's-hair brush which I recognized with some dismay as the last one in my possession from which the insects had not devoured the bristles. Delicately brushing toward one side, the fourth or fifth stroke left behind it a broad swath of blue so intense and beautiful that we cried out in astonishment.

Dr. Morley fetched Earl a whacking blow on the shoulders. "Old man, it's a turquoise mosaic. They are as rare as hen's teeth. Hurry up and see how big it is!"

He was right, but hurry was impossible, much as Earl's fingers itched to reveal the treasure immediately. The measure that differentiates archeology from the pell-mell joy of treasure seeking seems to lie chiefly in the science of delay, which brings acutest mental torture to its followers. Great age inevitably makes exceedingly fragile the majority of archeological finds, so that the utmost care has to be used in dealing with them. In addition to this, photographic records have to be made every step of the way when anything is being uncovered.

A camera was set up, and a hasty group calculation concerning the light in the sanctuary determined a three-minute exposure. When the first film was taken, it was rushed to the laboratory to be developed, and was found to be completely blank. The time was doubled, and still the film showed no record. Mirrors were rigged for reflecting purposes, and fifteen minutes were accorded the stubborn camera. Still not the slightest vestige of anything appeared upon the film. I began to wonder if the thing was real, for it seemed disconcertingly like one of those illusions which a cold-blooded camera's eye refuses to see. Finally, in exasperation, Earl opened the shutter, resolutely turned his back on it, and stared at the opposite wall for thirty-seven endless minutes. I don't know what dictated such an interval, except that possibly it was as long as he could bear the suspense. At its termination he snapped out the plate holder and handed it to the messenger, saying, "If this one isn't any good I'm going to resign and give the job to somebody without any nerves."

The last exposure proved to be timed to a second—for the picture was perfect. But not until then could he proceed to uncover further the precious turquoise mosaic. As he swept it clearer of the heavy dust film, which was scooped out with the teaspoon, he found that it covered the whole bottom of the container—indeed, it fitted so accurately that we later decided the heavy stone jar must have been made precisely for the purpose of holding it.

But now it began to be apparent that the problem of clearing the disk and of successfully getting it out of its deep snug bed was going to be terrifically difficult. The mosaic had been encrusted on a slab of wood which had rotted away into powder from behind it, and the only thing which held it together at all was a thin film of the adhesive which had originally fastened it to the wooden backing. Although most of the pattern was intact, nevertheless the slightest jar or a heavy breath would shatter it hopelessly into a meaningless chaos.

The situation was truly precarious. Earl says he felt like a dog that has found a porcupine. He didn't dare touch the mosaic and he couldn't leave it alone. Everybody went into executive session to determine what to do, and many were the schemes that were suggested and rejected as impracticable. You may imagine we kept at a safe distance from the treasure, and we tiptoed lest we jar the floor. Earl shivered at his strenuous soundings with the heavy pick in the morning, and was fairly appalled when he remembered the debris he had crashed to the ground when the temple was being cleared. The top of the jar was not more than three inches beneath the floor, where solid tons of stone and rubble had tumbled in their fall.

Finally it was determined to strengthen the disk as much as possible where it lay. A thin solution of Ambroid—a strong waterproof glue—was spread over the surface, a very little at a time lest the ether-like solvent soften the original adhesive before it evaporated. After half-a-dozen coats had been applied, the surface appeared considerably stronger.

By that time night had fallen, and as a thoughtless member of the party had remarked in Spanish to some natives that twenty thousand dollars in American gold would be small value for the mosaic, we were a bit apprehensive. Gustav and Rogers volunteered for all-night guard duty. They relieved each other during the dinner hour, then camped for the night inside the barred door, armed and ready for a defense which fortunately proved unnecessary.

The next morning the problem arose of removing the disk, jar, and all to safer keeping at the hacienda. First the jar had to be freed from the solid ground wherein it was snugly embedded without allowing a single grain to fall inside. In order to cover the aperture satisfactorily, two heavy wires were cut slightly larger than the diameter of the jar. These were bent until they could be admitted into the opening and then sprung so that their ends pressed firmly against the slightly rough stone. Upon these supporting crossbars, set at right angles to one another, was laid a disk of paper upturned at the edges. Then the crack between stone and paper was closed by the drip of a tallow candle, thus completely sealing the open top.

With the greatest possible care the earth was cleared from around the jar in such a manner that not the slightest vibration or shock would be transmitted to the container. Again a photograph was taken of jar and lid in position, then with painful solicitude the find was lifted from its age-old nest and set upon a short plank. About board and stone Gustav wove a mesh of heavy ropes, knotted as only a sailor knows how, and made a sling which passed over a stout pole. With Gustav at one end of the pole and Earl at the other, it was lifted slowly to their shoulders, and while Jean and Dr. Morley held it to prevent any side swing, the four proceeded with cautious slow steps to the top of the Warriors' pyramid, down the steep staircase to the ground, and over the long rough mile to the hacienda. Mr. and Mrs. Walter Trumbull, who were visiting Chichen at the time, took some moving pictures of the careful progress, and they said that they'd have to speed it up in the projector or people would think that they were giving them "slow-motion" pictures. When the paper cover was removed, as far as anybody could judge not a sliver of turquoise had been displaced.

Obviously, however, the disk could never be moved from Chichen, and it would perish if left in its original state. It had to be replaced upon a new base of strong wood without too much delay. Dr. Merriam cabled to New York, requisitioning the services of a phenomenally skillful Japanese artist preparator who was then working for the American Museum of Natural History.

Mr. Shiochi Ichikawa luckily caught an immediate boat and within a week's time he appeared at Chichen, vastly concerned because someone had told him we lived on lizards and snakes. For a day or two he haunted the kitchen before meal time, but finally he was reassured as to our diet of turkey and good American corned beef, which latter nourishment, by rights, ought to have bothered him more than it seemed to.

Under Mr. Ichikawa's deft hands the disk was rapidly glued to a smooth round wooden plaque backing. Some of it was solid enough to be moved in sections from the deep jar. Other bits had decayed so badly that they had to be transferred a stone at a time. When we found by actual count that more than three thousand separately cut mosaic turquoises had been utilized in its composition the magnitude of the task of repair seemed appalling. And even more than before, we felt respect for those ancient jewelers who so accurately shaped and ground to an almost paper thinness the infinity of tiny sections which made up their desired pattern.

The plaque was more than a simple jeweled studding which filled a round wooden surface. An intricate design in different shades of color had been worked out with the greatest care, using stones of varying sizes so shaped as to outline the patterns to be accented.

At the center of the plaque was a disk of soft pinkish sandstone about two and one-half inches in diameter. This was encrusted with mosaic plates of an iron oxide. The use of such an ugly low-grade rock in the very center of a priceless jewel is rather puzzling. Sandstone is soft and crumbly, would never have taken a high polish, and is of no intrinsic value whatsoever. However, for some reason the Mayas held it in high regard, and used it almost invariably in dedicatory offerings. The same material composed the two disks which were found in the North Colonnade altar and the two disks found beneath the front corner stones of the Temple of the Warriors. In the turquoise plaque the same custom held, and though this time the unsightly sandstone was hidden from view, nevertheless the offering was carefully endowed with its peculiar powers or properties. Perhaps it was derived from some sacred mountain far from Yucatán, or it may have been a part of a mother altar in an earlier home—but that is yet purely a matter for conjecture.

Encircling the sandstone center was a narrow ring of infinitesimally tiny brilliant blue turquoises. From this radiated strips of a yellow vegetable material which divided the main part of the plaque into eight wedge-shaped segments. Each alternate one of the eight was of plain turquoise mosaic, while the remaining four bore a pattern consisting of the head and claw and foreshortened body of the omnipresent Plumed Serpent. This decoration was worked out by the shaping of the stones, variation in their color, and by the use of pitchy black gum to accentuate important features, such as the gaping jaws and the long claws. A blood-red ball of gum was inserted in the eye socket. The outer rim of the disk consisted of sixteen petal-shaped blocks of mosaic outlined by brilliant red lacquer.

The plaque is complex to a degree, and beautiful beyond my powers of description. In itself it constitutes one of the most remarkable discoveries ever made in America. But, more than this, it is archeologically important because it was found in a definitely recognized and datable archeological horizon, while the circumstances of its discovery were under expert observation and control. Moreover, the exquisite quality of turquoise

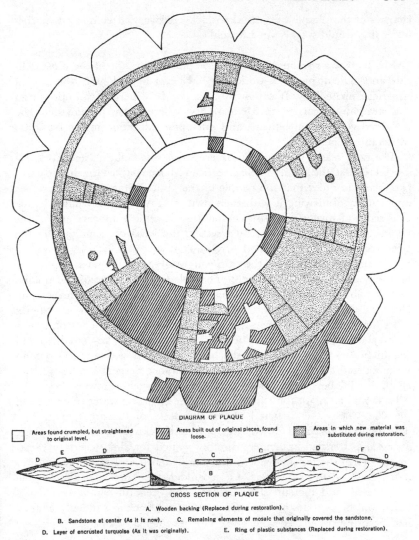

DIAGRAM OF PLAQUE

☐ Areas found crumpled, but straightened to original level.   ▨ Areas built out of original pieces, found loose.   ▦ Areas in which new material was substituted during restoration.

CROSS SECTION OF PLAQUE

A. Wooden backing (Replaced during restoration).

B. Sandstone at center (As it is now).   C. Remaining elements of mosaic that originally covered the sandstone.

D. Layer of encrusted turquoise (As it was originally).   E. Ring of plastic substances (Replaced during restoration).

Turquoise plaque from altar deposit

marks the raw material as of probable derivation from the mines of New Mexico, while the workmanship is that characteristic of the Valley of Mexico. After a trip across thousands of miles of desert and jungle it was laid away beneath a temple which was in its turn destined to be completely buried from view by the greater structure built on top of it. The chances of the plaque's eventual so lucky recovery, if computed mathematically, would stagger an Einstein.

Mr. Ichikawa's reconstruction of the plaque was one of the most delicate and difficult pieces of work that have ever been done in the field of American archeology. It came from his hands in perfect condition, and was straightway carried to Mexico City, where it was presented to the delighted government officials and put upon exhibition in the National Museum of that city.

The next year a Congress of Americanists was held in New York. By special request, the honored delegates from Mexico packed the disk to carry with them in order that the people of the United States might have the opportunity of viewing it with their own eyes. And thereby hangs a tale of a series of misfortunes so peculiar that it almost appears as if some malevolent power were bent on wresting the jewel once more from the hands of men.

Off the port of Progreso the ship caught fire, and the passengers were hastily transshipped to the shore. The delegate in charge of the plaque tells that he carried it "next to his heart" and never let it leave him. Nevertheless, the jewel was returned, for the moment, to the very shores of its homeland. Then, when the fire was brought under control, it was found that slight damage had been done, so everybody re-embarked and the anchor was weighed for further voyage. Hardly was land left behind when a dreadful storm broke. Did the old Plumed Serpent feel his treasure again slipping beyond his reach, and make one last effort toward recovery? All day and all night the wind increased in intensity; water poured from the skies and waves towered above the decks of the great liner. The hatches were battened down, the port holes closed, and in the close, airless ship terrified passengers dumbly waited for almost certain catastrophe. Then the lee shores of Cuba were reached and the boat slid into more quiet, protected waters. Of a sudden the hurricane abated, the rain ceased, and the sun shone again. The dreadful winds which had blown out of the skies of Yucatán were sucked back as suddenly as they had been unleashed. The old gods had been defeated of their prey.

24

Explorers such as Stephens in the early 1840's and a Frenchman, the Abbé Brasseur de Bourbourg, a few years later, were haunted by tales of a living Maya city hidden deep in the dark forests. Rumors cropped up every so often of ancient pageantry and rites still performed without interference from the white man. Considering that the Itzá tribe had been able to maintain its ancient way of life on the islands of Lake Petén until the late seventeenth century, when their centers were finally wiped out by the Spaniards, expectation of encountering such survivals was far from preposterous. Working in the jungle fastness of British Honduras, Thomas Gann had reason to believe that Maya-Itzá priests escaping the Petén massacre had perpetuated their cults well into the nineteenth century, still possessing knowledge of writing and continuing to erect date posts. Even after Gann, archaeologists were startled to find traces of recently burnt incense in forlorn decayed temples. On occasion, when they thought themselves out of range of any living soul, they suddenly sensed Indian eyes peering at them out of the foliage and carefully watching their every step until they had completed examining the shrines.

While a living Maya city has never been found, and the likelihood of its existence continuing into the closing decades of our millennium is slim indeed, some vestiges of Maya culture and customs, as evidenced by copal burning at the fallen temples, have nevertheless managed to withstand the alien onslaught for the past four hundred years. Surprisingly, these "artifacts of the mind" have long been slighted by most travelers and scholars, who have been more concerned with tracing buried monuments. Others, too sanguine about locating an entirely untouched community, rarely stopped to think that among the outwardly or partly assimilated full-blooded Indians of some colonial towns Maya "antiquities" might persist as a rich, though hidden, spiritual heritage. If any proof was needed that these Indians were the descendants of the people who built the great cities and accumulated stupendous astronomical knowledge, all doubts were dispelled once their jealously guarded traditions and magic rites were probed.

The difficulty was to penetrate the secrecy with which the Indians keep their native wisdom and practices from the white *ladinos.* The gaining of information about a tribe's ceremonials has been likened to the attempt to become familiar with the ritual of a Masonic lodge without becoming a Mason oneself. Compared to such a task, the tracking down of lost cities in the steaming bush was a challenge merely to physical prowess. The Indians' suspicions were to be overcome only by an unusual combination of patience, sympathy, ethnological understanding, and plain ruse. But there loomed ample rewards. Light might be thrown on ancient Maya ceremonies, partly described by early Spanish writers. Perchance, new clues could turn up to Maya hieroglyphics, the names and symbols of their gods, and on a whole gamut of pre-Columbian institutions.

Oliver La Farge came perhaps as close as anyone ever will to uncovering Maya survivals. In 1927, as leader of the Third Tulane University Expedition, he spent several months in the town of Jacaltenango in the Cuchumatán highlands of Guatemala near the Mexican border. There he found the sacred Maya calendar (*tzolkin*) still in use. In addition, he was able to compile day lists with their divinatory significance, and, above all, learn the secret lore centering on the so-called Year Bearers, current among some mountain people since olden days. To an unexpected degree, he was to realize, the ancient calendar continued to dominate the daily lives of the people. Typically, the esoteric power connected with knowledge of the calendar was wielded by only a few men, who evidently carried on the priestly tasks from pre-Conquest times. Among them were the Prayer Makers and a kind of head soothsayer. Modern conditions showed that, as it had four hundred years ago, religion lay "in the hands of a small group." The very manner of "crystal gazing," as well as the ceremonies for worshipping the Year Bearers, had their precise counterparts in the old Maya codices. La Farge's autobiography, *Raw Material,* describes this rare and exciting opportunity to catch archaeology alive.

Oliver (II) Hazard Perry La Farge (1901–1963) was a Pulitzer Prize-winning novelist who devoted his life to archaeology and ethnology as much as to literature. Most of his writing deals with Indian subjects. He inherited his love for America's ancient people from his father, a well-known architect. One of his grandfathers was the painter John La Farge, and the poet Christopher La Farge was his brother. He was also a direct descendant of Benjamin Franklin. Already as a boy he called himself an "Indian man." Yet, though he later made the cause of the Indians his own and presided for many years over the Association of American Indian Affairs, he fought any attempt to "Americanize" or sentimentalize the aboriginals just as he resented the U.S. government's patronizing policies.

Physically, the tall and lean New Yorker—sun tanned, black haired, with a finely chiseled face and a gangling gait—was often taken by Indians for one of themselves. He began his American-Indian studies as an undergraduate at Harvard and then participated in three expeditions sent to the Southwest by the Peabody Museum. In 1925 he served as assistant to Frans Blom on a memorable six-month expedition to southern Mexico and Guatemala which brought back valuable new information from marginal areas of Maya occupation, besides turning attention to vast temple centers on the Gulf of Mexico, later to be associated with the "Olmecs."

During this expedition, while sitting in the plaza of a little town in Chiapas, La Farge and Blom got into conversation with a local citizen who told them about strange Indian customs at the Guatemalan town of Jacaltenango. These related to the worship of Year Bearer gods. As of old, it seemed, the Indians sacrificed a turkey on the Year Bearer's Day and offered its blood to the god—one of four divinities who presided in turn over each year. The two explorers were much excited to learn that such rites, known to them from the ancient Dresden Codex and early Spanish reports, were still enacted in a remote mountain valley. The decision was made to send out an expedition exclusively devoted to a study of the Jacaltecans. It was the beginning of La Farge's concentration on Maya ethnology and linguistics. He was to head several further campaigns in the Cuchumatán sierra, during which he established the relationships between the Jacaltecan and Kanhobal Maya languages. Other studies of his dwelt on the extraordinary religious mélange created among the Indians of northwestern Guatemala when Christian elements were added to their pantheon of calendrical deities.

La Farge's finding of the continuation of Maya day counts and Year Bearer ceremonies was confirmed by S. K. Lothrop in 1928 at Momostenango and Frans Blom in the same year at Zapotal. At Jacaltenango, La Farge worked out a list of days with all their attributes, a system remarkable in that it not only was a device for magicians, but focused on the everyday needs of the people. It was part of the way of life in a small Indian town, as it had probably been in pre-Columbian times. For once, an archaeologist-ethnologist did not have to labor at a sterile reconstruction, but could report on "a living and functioning power." The complex magic calendar of the Mayas had been carried on at Jacaltenango faultlessly and continuously since the Conquest.

Facsimile, column of the Dresden Codex

ARCHAEOLOGY ON THE HOOF

Oliver La Farge

My second expedition outside the United States, in 1927, was to the Jacalteco Indians of the Cuchumatán Highlands in Guatemala. With me went Douglas Byers, now head of the Andover Museum. Byers had been with me in Arizona, he was an ideal companion for a long, difficult assignment, he seemed about to become a banker, and I was in hopes of seducing him back into anthropology.

Casual information which Frans Blom and I had picked up when we passed through Jacaltenango in 1925 proved to us that here in secret there was a rich and rare survival of the ancient Mayan religion. To learn about that I came back with Byers.

The Highland Maya of Guatemala live in what can best be called townships, using the word in a New England sense. The townships are areas with legally determined boundaries, often secured to the tribe by royal grants of considerable age. (Jacaltenango holds its territories from Ferdinand VII.) Within the township is a village which is the seat of government, with the Town Hall, jail, church, market and other institutions. Two *alcaldes* and a number of *regidores,* or councilmen, democratically elected at least in theory, form the local government under the supervision of one or more officials representing the federal government. The Jacalteco tribe numbers about seven thousand, of whom the greater part lives all year or for part of the year in the village of Jacaltenango, leaving it at intervals to cultivate their fields in the outlying sections. Within the township they enjoy a measure of self-government, freedom to follow their customs, free enterprise, freedom in the small things of everyday life, which has been extended only recently to our Indians. Here for the first time I came to know a tribe of Indians whose future was not inevitable, steadily approaching ruin and disaster. The native culture had changed, was changing, and would continue to change until at long last it merged with the general Latin-American pattern but there would be no destruction, only adaptation and absorption proceeding gently. Although the Guatemalan Indian was a conquered man, meek before his conquerors, socially despised, subject to a special and unequal justice, exploited in many ways, and full of hatred, I felt that were I a native of one of our own tribes I would sooner move down here and face all the difficulties and humiliations than remain to await the deadly

From *Raw Material.* Boston: Houghton Mifflin Co., 1945, pp. 166–76.

end prescribed for me. Here at least I could share in the American dream, that my son might become President. Here it had happened.

One descended upon the village from the high backbone of the Cuchumatanes, firs, pines, and tall cedars above on the crest, more great evergreens across the gorge a couple of miles away, alongside the trail manifold patches of corn and wheat on slopes so steep that falling would be a genuine hazard of farming. The houses, hundreds of them, sprawled over the delta-like hanging valley, straw-thatched huts scattered higgeldy-piggeldy with the big, white church and municipal buildings at the centre, here and there the deep green of coffee groves or the yellower colour of bananas. The valley was open to the west, falling off at the edge of the village in a cliff, then below the cliff the land dropped away, ridged and rugged, a thousand feet and another thousand and another, down to the Mexican border ten leagues away. Far beyond the Sierra Madre rose again, a jumbled, blue formation over which the red sunsets formed. Late afternoon light came yellow over the houses, in its bath the smoke seeped through the thatched roofs so that each house carried a trailing, sunshot nimbus. There were wild, white roses along the trail; in the village, hibiscus by the doorways.

Here were seven thousand people of whom I knew virtually nothing. I had done a little work among related tribes the other side of the border. I had heard tales that, pressed hard enough, the men of these tribes will kill to protect their gods. I knew what one could see in passing through. The men were slender, small, golden-skinned, neatly made. They wore a heavy, black wool tunic over white cotton shirts and trousers, kept their hair short, occasionally carried blowguns. The women were handsome, they too were slender, their long skirts of green cotton with an all-over blue and white design wrapped in a narrow sheath, showed that, unlike our Indians, they did not spread as they grew older. They wound their dark hair in a crown around their heads with wide ribbons of native weave, rich and lustrous in colour.

As one looked down over the steep edge of the trail one could see in front of the church the great cross, seventy-two feet high, slender, grey-weathered, skeletal. Its base I knew was a crude, square altar containing a number of fire pits. In the dusk I had seen a file of some six men go to that altar. Instead of the ordinary tunics they wore long ponchos of black wool, on their heads and also over their shoulders like stoles were kerchiefs with a striped design, predominantly dark red. They carried long staves. They had gone quickly and quietly to the base of the cross and prayed there while the clouds of *copal* incense billowed up from the fires they kindled. The dull flames of the pitchwood licked into the base of the rising smoke. Then they had risen and moved on to another part of the village, quiet, intense, oblivious.

These things I knew. We were riding down to face a strange personality and attempt the ridiculous task of persuading it that two young men, unknown to it, alien in race, should be accepted by it to the inner limits of confidence. This was my big chance, this if it succeeded would wipe out past failures, it would forestall the drudgery of getting a Ph.D. It would say something important to me about myself. The tales one had heard of that personality were strange and streaked with violence. The horses continued moving steadily, mechanically, down upon the village. I felt the gun under my leg and wondered if I should need it, I speculated upon failure.

The religion of Jacaltenango existed upon four levels. There was, first, formal Christianity, public and shared with the Ladinos—the small group of Spanish-speaking people who had settled in the village. Then there were Mayan practices so publicly carried on that it would be absurd to attempt to conceal them. These were *practices:* clearly observable, external performances and little more. Then there was that part of the old religion which was known to every Indian but jealously guarded from white men. This included the major myths and most of what a man had to know in ordinary times in order to ensure the well-being of himself and his family, but even in the course of an ordinary year a layman would not be able to fulfill all his religious needs unaided. Lastly, there was the completely esoteric part known only to the priests, without which no prayer could be offered for the community as a whole, no major ceremonies conducted, no serious personal crisis met. Penetration of this fourth sector was made more difficult by the fact that it was divided into specialties according to the divine gifts or the training of the practitioners, so that there was no one man who knew everything, although there were a few who understood the whole structure and had a general grasp of the specialties they themselves could not practice, as was necessary if the whole pattern of ritual and prayer was to be co-ordinated.

A few local white men had from time to time picked up scattered information concerning the fourth level. Many of them, from living side by side with the Indians, from daily contact and observation, and the casual talk of friends, had a sketchy, general idea of the layman's practices. But complete initiation of a white man was unthinkable. Items might leak out so that in the course of thirty or forty years one had learned a good deal, but no Indian would sit down and deliberately give a white man a coherent account of his beliefs. In fact, white men *were not capable* of receiving such knowledge, just as only certain Indians were capable, by innate gift, of induction into the esoteric part.

Further, the Indians did not like the Ladinos. And the Ladinos, with their sense of racial superiority, from time to time did things which violated the native religion, sometimes obliviously, sometimes out of mere curiosity or in a mood of idle, coarse humor. We rated, of course, as Ladinos, and the idea of telling us anything secret was so unheard of that it would be necessary to open new channels in the Indians' brains before such a thing could be contemplated.

I suppose ethnologists work in many different ways. I know, for instance, that most are in the habit of hiring informants. I have always suspected this method except where one finds, as among the Navajos, a positive desire to have the secret things recorded in books. Then it is fair enough to compensate a man for sitting down with you and working hard to achieve something you both desire.

I have very seldom paid an informant except for the making of linguistic lists. My method has been to hire men for normal, unsurprising work and then lead them into telling me what they know as a friendly matter undertaken almost without realizing it. This is not easy to do but the results are more trustworthy and in the end one gets much further. Of course one pays medicine-men the fees they would expect from other Indians, and even allows oneself to be grossly overcharged—ten cents for a service ordinarily worth a nickel.

The process is heartbreakingly slow; in other ways, too, it is close to heartbreaking, close to intolerable. First, to stick to this case which is typical, we had to establish ourselves in the minds of the Jacaltecos as something entirely outside of their previous experience and therefore of their established rules. We had to open their minds to the previously unthinkable. It was no use playing Indian. Byers was blond, tall, humourous—the last a characteristic to which they responded eagerly. I may be dark-haired and my skin tan deeply, but among these little Mongoloids there was no hope of my becoming an Indian. No, we had to be Ladinos. Then, we had to be a kind of Ladino they had never met before, we had to be utterly and totally new.

The main means of this is sincere democracy, a genuine belief in the brotherhood of man, and an unsurprised respect for all the tribe's customs, prejudices, and manners. Courtesy comes automatically out of this. If you really believe that these people are your full equals, after a long period of doubt, of suspicion, of watching for the fraud or the ulterior motive behind your attitude, will come a surprised, grateful, warm response and solid loyalty.

But it's a long period, during which your delicate tentatives meet nothing but rebuff—or, if you're skillful, the signs that if you pushed further you would meet rebuff. Nothing happens, nothing opens up, and all this time the secret, inner men, who are nobody's fools, are thinking and worrying about you and hardening their hearts against you.

He has asked questions of the young men. Yesterday Shuwan heard

Kash Pelip, who works for him, telling him part of the story of How the Sun Rose. What is he after? Why has he come all the way from New York, a country which they say is even further than Germany, to disturb us here? What evil does he portend? We see him look at us as we go to pray at the altars of the guardians, what is he trying to do with his looking? He is a strange, new kind of a man and we are afraid of him, and it might be well to send him a message that he must not try to enter the House of the Prayermakers, he must not ask questions of the Prayermakers. Let us pray about him, let us ask the gods a question what we should do about him.

The unease runs through the village. The Prayermakers, seeing you at a distance as they go on their rounds, turn to look at you, speak to each other, and then pass on. A Knower, seeing you on the road, turns aside and detours to avoid passing you.

You let another rumour go out. Not only did Kash tell the man about How the Sun Rose, but the man already knew the story, a little different, but he had heard of it. Perhaps he knows something, perhaps he has some power. He is not like other Ladinos at all. Perhaps he has knowledge.

Maya sun god

Week after week and nothing happening. In all this time you cannot be yourself. You cannot make enemies. You may know that a certain old man is a moocher and a fraud, but he has his position in the community and you cannot throw him out on his ear as you would wish. You are feeling in the dark along a blank wall, looking for a crevice, you may never stop feeling even for an instant, and you have no idea in what place, at what moment, the crevice will appear.

Therefore you can have no normal relation with anyone. This is irritating with casual acquaintances and people you dislike. The requirement to be everybody's friend, always a good fellow, a complete politician, builds up in you a deep longing to root an Indian, any Indian, violently in the tail. But it is much worse with your friends. You like these men and they have learned to like you. They are trusting you increasingly. Everything they say, their most casual remarks, their actions, must always be sifted in your mind. God only knows where the lead may be. You prostitute your friendships, and that is a nightmare. Throw in a touch or two of malaria, a few attacks of dysentery, but do not allow them to deflect your constant, steady attention to business. Why in God's name does anyone want to be an ethnologist?

When the pressure gets too heavy you have, in that country, the relief of saddling up and going to visit some small ruin you have been told of. The travel is refreshing, and no diplomacy is needed to clear away brush and draw a plan. A spell of skilled work with the inanimate is delightful. And then, of course, the men you have brought with you become more closely allied to you, you camp and eat together, sit over the fire, there is some legend about this place, and away from the village tongues are loosened. By golly, you have brought your torment right along with you.

Luck enters into every enterprise. What you are trying to do is to be ready for the break that must come sometime, but the waiting is dreadfully long. In the end, not through your skill but by an accident, you find the crevice. Then, to shift metaphors, the dam breaks. Then, if you have handled yourself rightly, you and a number of Indians become allied in the enterprise of putting the heart of their life down on paper. If your malaria gets bad at that time it's tough luck. Eat quinine till your ears ring, have a stiff drink, but don't let the process drop.

All of this is fairly directly contrary to escapism. You have made a major escape from the problems of your own world to those of an alien and somewhat simpler one, but now escape has been so perfected that it begins to become endowed with many of the drawbacks of reality. You have been robbed of sentimentalization; you have to make hard, accurate judgments of your men, you have to consider all factors, economy, relation to white men, good and ugly customs, stupidities, meannesses, nobilities, for just exactly what they are. You may bathe yourself in this Indian world, but you cannot go on pretending about it. Every factor which forms or malforms its character must be directly and fully faced.

In return you acquire a form of power as you achieve a fair degree of knowledge while retaining a perception which is impossible for the people themselves. For instance: one of the cornerstones of the esoteric religion is the process of divination or soothsaying, carried on by specialists called Knowers. The most important Knower is called The Shower of the Road. He is one of two or three key men in the entire hierarchy. He does not merely "answer questions," through his deep knowledge of ritual and communication with the gods he dictates major religious and, I believe, civic policies, prescribes prayers and rites, determines whether or not a man is fit to receive or retain priestly office. I had a natural desire to meet this man, and I discovered a Ladino who was on fairly friendly terms with him and to whom he had once let fall a few items of information—nothing much, for The Shower of the Road's knowledge is as esoteric as Hell.

I arranged to go to him to ask a question about a lost object, which gave me a chance to observe the process of soothsaying. It was thrilling to discover that what he was doing was the ancient, priestly process which the first Spanish conquerors had described in an incomplete way and which archaeologists had partly reconstructed, not entirely correctly. From what I saw and heard in those few minutes I knew that in fact there did exist here a survival of the ancient lore such as had never before been found. Here was antiquity still alive and functioning, archaeology on the hoof. I wanted more of this man.

He thought otherwise. After I left he became frightened and fled me. The door slammed shut again.

Putting together everything I had picked up from laymen, what I had seen, and what archaeology I knew, I had a fair idea of how a divination worked. I can't exactly reconstruct that incomplete idea now because later, in another village, I became a qualified Knower myself, but I can describe the general system as far as it relates to this story. There are twenty powerful gods who rule the days in turn, much as if on Monday we worshipped the moon and it ruled us, on Tuesday, Tue, on Wednesday, Wodin, and so forth. Archaeologists refer to these characters as "day-names"; they are not, they are gods. This gives us a "week" of twenty days. In addition, days are counted by numbers up to thirteen, the two systems revolving as do our weeks and days of the month only in reverse proportion. Thus if we start with a day ruled by Imish, god of the soil, it also has the number one. The numbers go on to thirteen then start at one again, so that when we come to the end of the list with Ahua ruling (he has too many powers to list here), the number is seven, then comes Imish with eight to start over again. At the end of two hundred and sixty days Imish will come in conjunction with one again.

Each of these gods has his own character, some good, some bad. The numbers also have their qualities. The soothsayer takes a number of seeds at random from a pile and throws them on a cloth. Then, starting with the god and number of the current day (that combination is the true day-name), he counts forward according to the number of seeds. Their arrangement will indicate that certain names and numbers reached on the way are important, others unimportant.

He may make one cast, one count, and give an answer, or he may

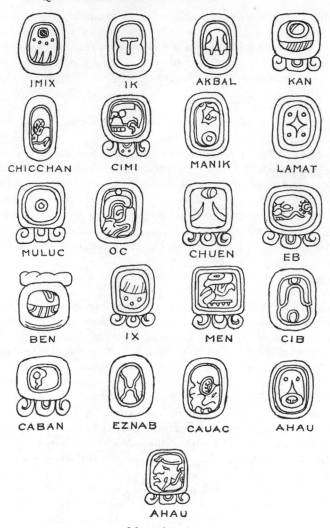

Maya day signs

cast over and over again, either because the answer is unclear or because he hopes for a pleasanter one.

I suspected then what I know now, that there was wide range for interpretation in this system. You seldom get a simple case of the ace of spades meaning death. You are more likely to get a bad god, say Chabin, who relates to death, with a pretty good number like four, and then have

Cheh of the animals turn up with a neutral number, which can mean death or sickness to an animal or death or accident because of an animal, or might be overbalanced by Watan, the farmer's friend and one of the strongest gods coming along with a very good number such as thirteen. The soothsayer's predisposition is most important.

For various reasons it became increasingly important for me to get through to The Shower of the Road. I had begun to acquire the reputation of being "one who knows something," which means someone initiated in some part of the esoteric knowledge, and hence "a man of clear heart," which is a person innately qualified to receive knowledge and therefore possessing some power. And fortunately the Ladino who was my link with The Shower had a deep belief in the reality of all forms of Indian magic, however little he might think of their religion. So I tried a gamble.

I told my Ladino friend in the most impressive way I could that he was to take a message to The Shower and to use my exact words. He was to tell The Shower to bring out his seeds, to make his prayer, and to ask his question of the gods. I, of my knowledge, would tell him in advance what the answer would be. I knew that the gods would not lie, I was perfectly confident of the gods. They would tell him to receive me and tell me what I wanted to know. They would tell him that I was a man of clear heart, and that I ought to know these things.

The Ladino was astounded. He believed me. It had been a good act. And it worked. Since then I've pulled the trick twice more, once in rather a serious crisis, and it's worked each time. I've done it with a little more confidence since I learned to use the native phrases and to have the message conveyed so that it sounded like one priest sending word to another; still, I hope I don't have to try it too often.

The old man received me with the Ladino interpreting. He was a nice, sincere old man with a fine, wrinkled face. He was deeply interested in his lore, he had an alert mind and had done some speculating about the mathematical laws governing the calendar and other such things. He was prepared to talk now, and his confidence increased as he saw that I was not entirely ignorant and that my attitude was reverent. Now we met a new obstacle. The Ladino was a hopelessly incompetent interpreter. Not only was his grasp of Jacalteca extremely limited, but he was one of those dummies whom no amount of explanation can cure of rendering five minutes of careful explanation as "He says, 'Yes.'" Also, his presence was a deterrent in itself, since I might be a man of clear heart, but he was just an amiable alien.

Antel, The Shower, had no Spanish. I had the kind of Jacalteca one might be expected to pick up in three months during which I had made some effort to learn. We were treating of serious matters which it was blasphemous to convey incorrectly, we both became interested. And between us this dope destroyed rather than aided communication.

I worded a rather long, careful question. I heard the interpreter render it in four words. I cut in and stated the question again, begging him to translate it in full. He pretty nearly did. The answer was nearly as long, and was returned to me as "No." We tried that again, and failed. The trouble was that the man didn't understand the full of what Antel had said. I think I understood as much as he did.

Digging into my brain for all the Jacalteca I could summon, I asked the next question for myself. Antel hesitated. Then a lovely look of relief came over his face in the candlelight, and he answered me *in halting Spanish*. The interpreter was astonished, so was I. It was a beautiful tribute, the laying aside of a shield, an advantage he had guarded for years. We worked together from there on, helping each other, piecing the two languages together in co-operation in order to deal with sacred things. Of all my work among Indians, this remains the highest moment.

25

In archaeology as in other fields of knowledge, dogmas die hard. For a long time it had been almost an article of faith that the great pyramidal structures of Mesoamerica served exclusively ceremonial purposes. They were, for all to see, solid mounds, truncated at the top and ascended by one or more broad staircases. On platforms stood squat temples where priests officiated, and, on occasion, made astronomical observations. This view was supported by known practices and general evidence, and had the advantage of distinguishing the American pyramids from their Egyptian counterparts, with which wild speculations had tried to link them though they were separated in time by some three thousand years. This distinction was yet another proof that New World civilization was *sui generis*. The similarities between the Pyramids of Gizeh and Teotihuacán were, if anything, superficial and coincidental.

However, Egypt was not the only Old World country which built pyramids. The ziggurats of ancient Mesopotamia and the Buddhist structures of Cambodia were certainly temple platforms and closely paralleled in form and function the Mesoamerican type—which is not to say that such analogies clinch the case for culture contacts. And were the facts really so unequivocal? Within the Americas, where a close kinship permeated the customs and institutions of all parts, the mounds scattered widely over the United States as well as the great pyramids of the Peruvian coastal valleys had already revealed sumptuous burials of notables. As to Mexico itself, Humboldt and Bullock had already noted an intricate system of passages in the great pyramid of Cholula and reported on a burial in a section severed from the main structure. A century later (1896), in one of his dramatic adventures, Edward H. Thompson at Chichen Itzá had lowered himself into an inner shaft of a pyramid where underneath, in a natural cave, he found the tomb of a "high priest." But professionals did not pay much attention to Thompson's discoveries. He was eccentric and so were his exploits. The dogma reigned supreme—until a turnabout was engineered at Palenque in 1954 by Dr. Alberto Ruz Lhuillier. His archaeological coup was the kind that keeps rotary presses and international wire services busy and invariably becomes enshrined in numerous popular retellings.

Palenque, in the jungle of the rain-drenched Usumacinta Valley in the Mexican state of Chiapas, is one of the westernmost Maya centers, halfway between the Gulf of Mexico and the Guatemala border. The architecture of this religious metropolis, though less imposing than that of the Petén, is of greater simplicity and grace. Its stucco sculptures and low-relief limestone tablets with their subtly traced figures and hieroglyphic characters rank among the world's masterpieces. The place has been a magnet for students of Maya glories since the eighteenth century.

Cortés on his march to Honduras in 1524 must have passed within thirty miles of Palenque. But there is little likelihood that he as much as heard of it. Palenque had been abandoned more than half a millennium before the Spaniards and was almost totally reclaimed by the jungle. The forest in the Chiapas foothills is so lush and aggressive that though an area had been cleared, another party of explorers arriving within a few years could only orient themselves by map and compass.

Palenque—Spanish for palisade—is named for the nearby Mexican village of Santo Domingo del Palenque. Its Maya name is uncertain. Indians of the area probably first drew attention to an agglomeration of carpeted hillocks and interspersed masonry in the mid-eighteenth century. News of the place reached a local padre. Much taken with what he saw there, in 1773 he wrote a memorandum to the *audiencia* of Guatemala. In his wake arrived others who dutifully reported to the royal authorities, but their notes were never published. However, Carlos IV heard of the fabulous ruins in Central America and due to his initiative Don Antonio del Río, an artillery captain in Spanish service, was entrusted with an archaeological reconnaissance in 1786.

Del Río's mission was carried out with military aplomb and brute force. The ruins still bear the battlescars of the assault techniques of the captain and his battalion of two hundred Indians. Del Río himself bluntly stated his conviction that "in order to form some idea of the first inhabitants and of the antiquities connected with their establishment, it would be indispensably necessary to make several excavations. . . . By dint of perseverance I effected all that was necessary to be done, so that ultimately there remained neither a window nor a doorway blocked up, a partition that was not torn down, nor a room, corridor, court, tower, nor a subterranean passage in which excavations were not effected from two to three yards in depth." Later visitors would wryly observe that it was not the least of Palenque's distinctions to have withstood exploratory operations so overwhelming as these.

The manuscript of Del Río's report gathered dust until it was finally published in an English edition in London in 1822 with engravings by Count Waldeck. This was the book brought to the attention of John Lloyd Stephens by Catherwood during the former's 1836 visit to England. For Stephens, until then with little knowledge of or curiosity about American antiquities, it meant a first awakening. Once his plan for an investigation of Central American ruins had fully matured, Palenque was one of his principal goals. From Guatemala City he and Catherwood went on the long trail northwest into Mexico. The sight of a Maya metropolis with several buildings virtually intact—unlike those of Copán— was worth all hardship:

> Through openings in the trees we saw the front of a large building richly ornamented with stuccoed figures on the pilasters, curious and elegant; trees growing close against it, and their branches entering the doors; in style and effect unique, extraordinary, and mournfully beautiful. We tied our mules to the trees, ascended a flight of stone steps forced apart and thrown down by trees, and entered the palace, ranged for a few moments along the corridor and into the courtyard, and after the first gaze of eager curiosity was over, went back to the entrance and, standing in the doorway, fired a *feu-de-joie* of four rounds each, being the last charge of our firearms.

Stephens went on to write of the excitement of entering for the first time a building erected by aboriginal inhabitants "before Europeans knew of the existence of this continent." The immense "palace" of many chambers and inner courtyards had the unexpected feature, quite rare in Maya edifices, of a large windowed stone tower with an inner stairway. The visitors were even more fascinated by the many sensitively executed stucco figures. Atop one of the pyramids, southwest of the *palacio* in the so-called Temple of Inscriptions, they noted what has remained one of the largest epigraphic panels of the Mayas. Under this roof, Stephens and Catherwood took up lodging while exploring the area.

The two friends were not the first after the Spanish captain Del Río to visit fabulous Palenque. But, as at Copán, it was Stephens who furnished a reliable and sound survey. Unlike the previous sketches of Count Waldeck, Catherwood's drawings did not try to twist exotic Maya architecture and decorations into Roman or Phoenician shapes to prove a preconceived theory. With the Stephens–Catherwood publication, as Victor W. von Hagen has said, "the history of the city has been set on a firm archaeological basis."

Since the 1920's the Mexican government has undertaken a systematic restoration of the finest buildings, while the whole area has been

Palenque ruin, after Catherwood

declared a national monument. The city's past, belonging to the classical Maya age, is being elucidated by continuous research, but the full extent of the vast city remains to be demarcated. Most of its date inscriptions, as well as the Palenque jade offering found at the Chichen Itzá *cenote,* belong to the seventh and eighth centuries.

Virtually all the foremost modern Maya scholars carried out studies at Palenque. After such competent and intensive research, few surprises were to be expected. No one could have anticipated that Palenque would become the scene of a spectacular find in Maya archaeology which, according to its discoverer, "changed our concept of Maya history."

When Dr. Alberto Ruz Lhuillier was appointed Director of Research at Palenque by the National Institute of Anthropology and History of Mexico in 1949, the main task assigned to him was to continue restoring the principal edifices. He had the good fortune to discover in the first year of his campaign a fallen wall which bore an undamaged hieroglyphic inscription of 262 signs. However, his interests, like those of Stephens and Catherwood, soon came to center around the Temple of Inscriptions, the highest structure at Palenque. This edifice, older than Thompson's Tomb of the High Priest at Chichen Itzá (of the Mexican-Toltec period), was a pyramid with a platform topped by a temple with a roof-comb. The temple primarily attracted him because of its unusually fine stucco decorations and extensive inscriptions. It cried for restoration.

Dr. Ruz knew that "the ancient inhabitants of Central America were in the habit of building on top of older constructions, more with the object of increasing their height and bringing them closer to the heavens in which the gods lived than for any practical purpose."

It is now archaeological history that instead of finding an older pyramid inside the Temple of Inscriptions, Ruz discovered a royal or priestly tomb. The pyramid itself was apparently constructed around the crypt and maybe after the burial. Now, suddenly, there was evidence that in at least one instance, a Central-American Maya pyramid closely paralleled in construction and function the "mountains of the pharaohs," which were giant mausoleums. Nevertheless, it is too soon to proclaim any new doctrines about Maya pyramids. Even though the chamber under the Temple of Inscriptions was of the funerary type, the majority of Maya pyramids seem to have served merely as temple bases.

The excavations from 1949 to 1953 at the Temple of Inscriptions revealed the extraordinary engineering skill of the Mayas in the construction of the pyramid's arched crypt, interior stairway, and air channel, as well as in the complexity of the overall plan. With the possible exception of the youthful Copán maize god, no finer stucco sculptures than the two buried in the Palenque tomb have ever been found. But there also came to the fore a rather shocking detail which, like the superb Bonampak murals, helped to complete the demolition of the almost discredited myth about the mildness and humanity of the classical Mayas. Outside the crypt were found the skeletons of six (noble?) youths—five males and one female—who evidently had been killed to serve as companions or attendants for the great man. This pointed indeed—though it may mean nothing but analogous developments—to another similarity with Old World funerary practices from the Sudan and Sumeria to China of the Shangs.

An additional element of surprise was introduced by Dr. Ruz's disclosure that the illustrious person buried at Palenque was considerably taller than the average Maya and therefore may have been an alien. Whether any other non-Maya or even non-Indian physical characteristics have been identified in these skeletal remains is doubtful. But the suggestion leaves unfortunate scope for mystification, darkly hinting that perhaps a white man from across the ocean brought light to the red man and ruled as revered king of Palenque.

Dr. Alberto Ruz Lhuillier was born in 1906 in Cuba and received his education in Paris and at the University of Havana. He then did graduate work in anthropology at the Universidad Nacional de Mexico. After several years of teaching in Cuban secondary schools, he returned to Mexico and became a naturalized citizen of that country. He has been a professor at the Escuela Nacional de Antropología since 1939, and from 1940 he has been associated with Mexico's Instituto Nacional de Antropología e Historia.

THE PYRAMID TOMB OF PALENQUE

Alberto Ruz Lhuillier

When in the spring of 1949 the National Institute of Anthropology and History of Mexico appointed me Director of Research at Palenque, I fully appreciated that this was the most important event in my professional life.

I knew that my predecessors had been explorers, artists, scientists, distinguished men, and that marvellous sculpture had been discovered there during the course of 150 years; but I was convinced that many other archaeological treasures still lay hidden in the rubble of the palaces, temples and pyramids, and beneath the dense and mysterious Chiapas jungle which had been their jealous guardian.

A feature of my working plan was one which should always be present in the plans of archaeologists working in Mexico and Central America: to seek for architectural structures of an earlier date and lying beneath the actually visible building. It has, in fact, been proved that the ancient inhabitants of Central America were in the habit of building on top of older constructions, more with the object of increasing their height and bringing them closer to the heavens in which the gods lived than for any practical purpose.

For various reasons I decided to make such a search in the Temple of the Inscriptions. First, because it was the tallest building in Palenque and therefore the most likely to have been built on top of something older; secondly, because of its importance and its containing some fine, large, sculptured panels and one of the largest Mayan hieroglyphic in-

---

"The Pyramid Tomb of a Prince of Palenque," *The Illustrated London News*, CCXXIII, No. 5967 (Aug. 29, 1953), pp. 321–23.

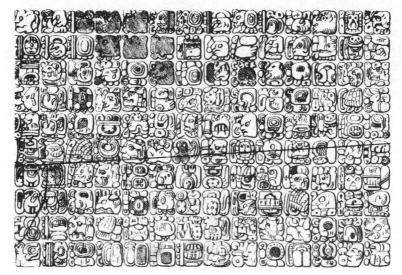

Hieroglyphic panel from Temple of Inscriptions, drawn by Catherwood

scriptions; and thirdly, because it had never been explored and its flooring was more or less intact—owing to its being made of great slabs instead of the more usual simple levelled plaster.

The temple is composed of a portico leading to a sanctuary and two lateral cells; and in the central room of the temple one of the slabs of the flooring caught my eye, as it had done with my predecessors on the site. This slab has round its edges two rows of holes provided with stone plugs. After thinking for some hours on its possible purpose, I came to the conclusion that the answer would be found underneath the stone; and accordingly I began to clear the floor beside it, in a place where the slabs had been already removed or broken by treasureseekers, who had been discouraged from going on by meeting with a heavy filling of large stones.

Quite soon after beginning to remove the rubble I noticed that the temple's walls were prolonged under the floor instead of stopping at its level—a sure sign that there was "something" to be found underneath. Elated by this prospect, I began excavating and on the next day—May 20, 1949—there appeared that stone which, in Mayan buildings, is always used to close up a vault. The Mayans did not build a true arch, their vaulting being simply the result of bringing walls closer together by means of inclined facings which converge until there remains only a very small space to be closed with a single flat stone. A few days later I found a step, and then more and more steps. What had been found was an interior staircase descending into the pyramid and which for a reason which we then did not know, had been made impracticable by a filling of large stones and clay.

Four spells of work—each two-and-a-half months long—were needed before we were able to clear the filling from this mysterious staircase. After a flight of 45 steps, we reached a landing with a u-turn. There followed another flight, of 21 steps, leading to a corridor, whose level is more or less the same as that on which the pyramid was built—*i.e.*, some 22 metres under the temple flooring. In the vaulting of the landing two narrow galleries open out and allow air and a little light to enter from a near-by courtyard.

Above one of the first steps we reached we found a box-shaped construction of masonry containing a modest offering: two ear-plugs of jade placed on a river stone painted red. On reaching the end of the flight we found another box of offerings, backing on to a wall which blocked the passage. This time it was a richer offering: three pottery dishes, two shells full of cinnabar, seven jade beads, a pair of circular ear-plugs also of jade, the plugs of which were shaped like a flower, and a beautiful tear-shaped pearl, with its *lustre* pretty well preserved. An offering of this kind, at such a depth, told us without any doubt that we were approaching the object of our search.

And, in fact, on July 13, 1952, after demolishing a solid obstruction some metres thick, made of stone and lime—this was very hard and the wet lime burnt the hands of the workmen—there appeared on one side of the corridor a triangular slab, 2 metres high, set vertically to block an entrance. At the foot of this slab, in a rudimentary stone cist, there lay, mixed together, the largely-destroyed skeletons of six young persons, of whom one at least was a female.

At noon on the 15th of the same month we opened the entrance, displacing the stone enough for a man to pass through sideways. It was a moment of indescribable emotion for me when I slipped behind the stone and found myself in an enormous crypt which seemed to have been cut out of the rock—or rather, out of the ice, thanks to the curtain of stalactites and the chalcite veiling deposited on the walls by the infiltration of rain-water during the centuries. This increased the marvelous quality of the spectacle and gave it a fairy-tale aspect. Great figures of priests modelled in stucco a little larger than life-size formed an impressive procession round the walls. The high vaulting was reinforced by great stone transoms, of dark colour with yellowish veins, giving an impression of polished wood.

Almost the whole crypt was occupied by a colossal monument, which we then supposed to be a ceremonial altar, composed of a stone of more than 8 square metres, resting on an enormous monolith of 6 cubic metres, supported in its turn by six great blocks of chiselled stone. All these elements carried beautiful reliefs.

Finest of all for its unsurpassable execution and perfect state of preservation was the great stone covering the whole and bearing on its four sides some hieroglyphic inscriptions with thirteen abbreviated dates corresponding to the beginning of the seventh century A.D., while its upper face shows a symbolic scene surrounded by astronomical signs.

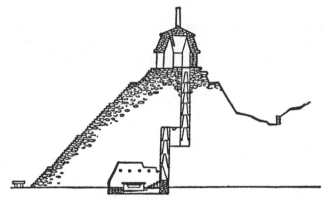

The Temple of Inscriptions in cross-section, with shafts and burial crypt

I believed that I had found a ceremonial crypt, but I did not wish to make any definite assertions before I had finished exploring the chamber and, above all, before I had found out whether the base of the supposed altar was solid or not. On account of the rains and the exhausting of the funds available for this phase of the exploration, we had to wait until November before returning to Palenque. I then had the base bored horizontally at two of the corners; and it was not long before one of the drills reached a hollow space. I introduced a wire through the narrow aperture and, on withdrawing it, I saw that some particles of red paint were adhering to it.

The presence of this colouring matter inside the monolith was of supreme importance. The offerings found at the beginning and the end of the secret staircase had borne red paint; and the sides of the great stone showed traces of having been painted red all over. This colour was associated in the Mayan and Aztec cosmogony with the East, but also it is nearly always found in tombs, on the walls or on objects accompanying the dead person or on his bones. The presence of red in tombs came, therefore, to indicate resurrection and a hope of immortality. The particles of cinnabar adhering to the wire inserted into the centre of the enormous stone block [were] therefore unquestionable evidence of burial: and our supposed ceremonial altar must therefore be an extraordinary sepulchre.

To prove this it was necessary to lift the sculptured stone, which measured 3.80 metres by 2.20 metres (some 13 by 7 ft.), weighing about 5 tons and constituting one of the most valuable masterpieces of American pre-Hispanic sculpture. The preparations lasted two days in the midst of feverish tension. It was necessary to fell in the forest a hard-wood tree of the kind called in that region "bari," and to cut it into sections of different lengths, lift these along a greasy path to the lorry, convey them by motor to the pyramid, move them by manpower to the temple, lower them by cables through the interior staircase and introduce them through the narrow aperture of the crypt.

The four major sections of the trunk were placed vertically under the corners of the stone and on top of each was placed a railway or motorcar jack. On November 27, at dusk, after a twelve-hour working day, the soul-shaking manoeuvre took place. Every kind of precaution was taken to prevent the stone tipping up or slipping, and, above all, to prevent its suffering any damage. Handled simultaneously and without any jerking, the jacks lifted the stone millimetre by millimetre, and while this was happening slabs were placed underneath it to hold it up. When the jacks reached the limit of their extension, other sections of the tree were inserted and the operation was repeated. A little before midnight the stone was resting intact 0.60 metres above its original level on six robust logs of "bari" and a few days later it was lifted to a height of 1.12 metres.

Once the stone left its seating and began to rise it could be seen that a cavity had been cut out of the enormous block which served it as a base. This cavity was of an unexpected shape, oblong and curvilinear, rather like the silhouette in schematised form of a fish or of the capital letter Omega . . ., closed in its lower part. The cavity was sealed by a highly-polished slab fitting exactly and provided with four perforations, each with a stone plug. On raising the slab which closed it we discovered the mortuary receptacle.

This was not the first time during my career as an archaeologist that a tomb had been discovered, but no occasion has been so impressive as this. In the vermilion-coloured walls and base of the cavity which served as a coffin, the sight of the human remains—complete, although the bones were damaged—covered with jade jewels for the most part, was most impressive. It was possible to judge the form of the body which had been laid in this "tailored" sarcophagus; and the jewels added a certain amount of life, both from the sparkle of the jade and because they were so well "placed" and because their form suggested the volume and contour of the flesh which originally covered the skeleton. It was easy also to imagine the high rank of the personage who could aspire to a mausoleum of such impressive richness.

We were struck by his stature, greater than that of the average Mayan of to-day; and by the fact that his teeth were not filed or provided with incrustations of pyrites or jade, since that practice (like that of artificially deforming the cranium) was usual in individuals of the higher social ranks. The state of destruction of the skull did not allow us to establish precisely whether or not it had been deformed. In the end, we decided that the personage might have been of non-Mayan origin, though it is clear that he ended in being one of the kings of Palenque. The reliefs, which we have still to uncover on the sides of the sarcophagus and which are now hidden under lateral buttresses, may tell us before long something of the personality and identity of the glorious dead.

Even if he had not been buried in the most extraordinary tomb so far discovered in this continent of America, it would still be perfectly possible to assess the importance of this personage from the jewels which he wore—many of them already familiar in Mayan bas-reliefs. As shown in some reliefs, he was wearing a diadem made from tiny discs of jade and his hair was divided into separate strands by means of small jade tubes of appropriate shape; and we discovered a small jade plate of extraordinary quality cut in the shape of the head of Zotz, the vampire god of the underworld, and this may have been a final part of the diadem. Around the neck were visible various threads of a collar composed of jade beads in many forms—spheres, cylinders, tri-lobed beads, floral buds, open flowers, pumpkins, melons, and a snake's head. The ear-plugs were composed of various elements, which together made up a curious flower. From a square jade plate with engraved petals, a tube, also of jade, projected and this ended in a flower-shaped bead; while on the back of the square plate (which carries a hieroglyphic inscription) a circular plug was fitted. All these elements would be united by a thread and it would seem that there hung as a counterpoise to them, behind the broad part of the ear, a marvellous artificial pearl, formed by uniting two perfectly-cut pieces of mother-of-pearl polished and adjusted to give the impression of a pearl of fabulous size (36 mm.). Over the breast lay a pectoral formed of nine concentric rings of twenty-one tubular beads in each. Round each wrist was a bracelet of 200 jade beads, and on each finger of both hands a great ring of jade. We found these still fixed on the phalanges, and one of the rings was carved in the form of a crouching man, with a delicate head of perfect Mayan profile. In the right hand he held a great jade bead of cubical form, and in the left, another, but this one spherical, the two being perhaps symbols of his rank or magical elements for his journey to another world. Near his feet we found another two great jade beads, one of them hollow and provided with two plugs in the shape of flowers. A jade idol of precious workmanship stood near the left foot and is probably a representation of the sun god. Another little figure of the same material must have been sewn above the breech-clout. From the mouth cavity we extracted a beautiful dark jade bead, which, according to the funeral rites of the Mayans, was placed there so that the dead person should have the means to obtain sustenance in the life beyond the tomb. At the moment of burial, the personage wore over the face a magnificent mask made of jade mosaic, the eyes being of shell, with each iris of obsidian, with the pupil marked in black behind. Of the hundreds of fragments, some remained on the face, adhering to the teeth and the forehead, but the greater part were lying on the left side of the head, clearly as the result of the mask's slipping off during the burial. The corpse must have been set in the sarcophagus entirely wrapped in a shroud painted red, and the same cinnabar colour adhered to the bones, the jewels and the bottom of the sarcophagus when the cloth and the flesh decomposed. The mask was fitted directly on the dead man's face, the fragments being stuck in a thin coating of stucco, the remains of which fitted to the human face. Nevertheless, the mask had to be prepared beforehand and may perhaps have been kept on a stucco head. It is perfectly possible that its main traits, realistic as they are, represent more or less those of the actual dead man. After the burial the sarcophagus was closed with its lid and covered with the enormous sculptured stone. Some jewels were thrown upon this—a collar with slate pendants and what was probably a ritual mask made of jade mosaic—and there were placed underneath the coffin various clay vessels, perhaps containing food and drink, and two wonderful human heads modelled in stucco, which had been broken from complete statues. At the closing of the crypt six young persons, perhaps sons and daughters of important persons at Court, were sacrificed to act as companions and servants of the dead man in the other world. In the best-preserved of their skulls could be noted the cranial deformation and the mutilation of the teeth which were customary in the nobility alone. A serpent modelled in lime plaster seems to rise straight out of the sarcophagus and ascend the steps which lead to the threshold of the room. Here it is transformed into a tube, running as far as the flooring of the corridor and after this it leads on to the temple, in the form of an echeloned moulding, hollow and superimposed on the steps. This amounts to a magical union, a conduit for the spirit of the dead man to ascend to the temple in order that the priests might continue to be in contact with his deified being and able to explain his mandates. Our search for an older building under the Temple of the Inscriptions could therefore not lead to the expected result, but in exchange it revealed a tomb whose discovery leads to considerable modification of certain established concepts concerning the function of the American pyramid. It was formerly thought that this was solely a solid base for supporting a temple, unlike the Egyptian pyramids, which are vast mausoleums. Palenque's "Royal Tomb," as it is now popularly called, with a certain intuitive propriety, perhaps—brings us a great deal closer to the Egyptian concept once we grant that the pyramid which hid it, although supporting a temple, was also constructed to serve as a grandiose funeral monument. The monumental quality of this crypt, built by thousands of hands to challenge the centuries and enriched with magnificent reliefs; the sumptuousness of the tomb itself, a colossal monument weighing 20 tons and covered all over with bas-reliefs of stupendous quality; the rich jade finery of the buried personage; all this expense of toil and this magnificence suggest to us the existence in Palenque of a theocratic system similar to that of Egypt, in which the all-powerful priest-king was considered during life or after death to be a real god. This Palencan Royal tomb also leads us to suppose that the attitude towards death of the Mayan "halach uinic" was very close to that of the Pharaohs. The stone which covers the tomb appears to confirm this obsession and synthesises in its reliefs some essentials of the Mayan religion. The presence here, in a sepulchral slab, of motives

Low-relief stone lid of sarcophagus, Temple of Inscriptions

which are repeated in other representations, gives perhaps the key to interpret the famous panels of the Cross and the foliated Cross (in Palenque) and also some of the paintings in the codices. On the stone in question we see a man surrounded by astronomical signs symbolising heaven—the spatial limit of man's earth, and the home of the gods, in which the unchanging course of the stars marks the implacable rhythm of time. Man rests on the earth, represented by a grotesque head with funereal traits, since the earth is a monster devouring all that lives; and if the reclining man seems to be falling backwards, it is because it is his inherent destiny to fall to the earth, the land of the dead. But above the man rises the well-known cruciform motif, which in some representations is a tree, in others the stylised maize-plant, but is always the symbol of life resurgent from the earth, life triumphing over death.

26

Since navigation appears to have played only a minor role in pre-Columbian America and most culture centers were inland, the post-World War II boom in water-borne archaeology has never quite caught on in the New World—except for diving for sunken Spanish galleons—as it did in the Mediterranean. A notable exception is the exploration of the lakes in the lands of Maya colonization. Edward H. Thompson at the Chichen Itzá *cenote* during the years 1904 to 1907 anticipated the modern pastime by half a century. His exploits helped to publicize the Mayas' propensity for casting precious articles and pottery into sacred water holes to propitiate the gods. Other archaeologists were to confirm this custom at the *cenotes* of Dzibilchaltún, at Lake Guija on the Guatemala–El Salvador border, and elsewhere. The Briton J. E. S. Thompson, when reporting on the antiquities of Cobá, expressed his strong belief that the adjacent lagoons would one day yield votive objects in profusion. But so far the Cobá lakes have not been combed.

That the custom of committing treasures to water also prevailed in the highlands of Guatemala was first adumbrated by young Guatemalan sportsmen at Lake Amatitlán. This picturesque natural lake, set among volcanic mountains some seventeen miles south of Guatemala City, is a popular resort area. Benefiting from Jacques-Yves Cousteau's invention of the aqualung, which permitted free diving without cumbersome suits and tubing, frogmen began in 1954 to search the twenty-five square miles of the lake for fishing grounds. A year later, one of them accidentally came across ancient pottery when reconnoitering in a southwestern arm of the lagoon. Within little time the aqualung fraternity had instigated a thorough search of the lake bottom and assembled an impressive collection of artifacts. Though amateurs, they wisely kept notes on the precise locations and depths at which the various objects were found. Each specimen was numbered.

It so happened that in the summer of 1957 there was working in Guatemala Dr. Stephan F. Borhegyi, a Hungarian-trained archaeologist who on coming to the United States after World War II had switched from classic Greek and Roman to pre-Columbian archaeology. By then Borhegyi was no longer a stranger to Guatemalan antiquities. Already in the late 1940's he had investigated and mapped archaeological sites in the Lake Amatitlán area. He even knew of local fishermen every so often coming up with Maya pottery vessels. But like everybody else he had no anticipation of the enormous trove about to be recovered from the lake bottom.

In 1957 Borhegyi was excavating with a group of students from San Carlos University at the well-known Mayan site of Kaminaljuyú just outside Guatemala City. He got wind of the cache brought up from the waters of Lake Amatitlán. Given an opportunity to examine the materials, he was surprised to find that the story of "a small collection" turned out to be one of those rare archaeological understatements. There were several hundred superb, well-preserved Maya pottery vessels and sculptures, including an array of incense burners and offering vessels bearing a variety of unique decorations. Several Maya as well as Toltec gods were represented. Borhegyi was so much taken by these specimens that he held council with his students and thereupon decided to transfer operations to Lake Amatitlán. It was the beginning of a productive partnership between archaeologists and skin divers.

For the rest of the summer and during the consecutive season (1958) Borhegyi and his students set out to map the lake area and specify all the lacustrine sites of deposits: they established some nine of them. Curiously, most of the offerings were found near geysers or hot sulphurous springs, which must once have been held in great awe. It soon became obvious that the finds at any one site were related to each other in style. Possibly they belonged to the same age and originated from the same center. Subtle analysis showed several of the artifacts to date from before the birth of Christ, while others were as recent as the era of the Spanish Conquest. Furthermore, in a neat combination of underwater and dirt archaeology, it was possible to lay free sites of human occupation along the lake bed and correlate them with specific lake assemblages. From nearest locations along the shore, and during distinct periods of Amatitlán Maya history, gifts had been dispatched to the gods of the deep. As a result, Borhegyi wrote a new chapter in Guatemalan archaeology. The shore of Lake Amatitlán, though secondary to the Kaminaljuyú zone, emerged as an important Maya area. Since the highlanders built in adobe rather than stone, few ruins had previously been detected and the past had seemed wiped out for good. Now the archaeological history of Amatitlán could be reconstructed in its continuity of two and a half millennia. Influences traveling from Kaminaljuyú and from as far as Teotihuacán in central Mexico had left their unmistakable imprint on Amatitlán religion and art. Each lake site in turn marked a phase in this long evolution. Borhegyi's account of his researches owes not the least of its fascination to his description of the ingenious methods by which such a record came to be pieced together.

As to the manner in which Maya objects were lodged in the lake, Borhegyi observed that not all were purposely thrown into the water as at the Chichen Itzá *cenote*. Several had no doubt been originally placed near the lake, but were submerged when the waters rose. Still others— such as a number of bowls grouped in an orderly arrangement—must have been presented to the angry fire-spewing gods on flowing lava streams about to enter the water.

Even though no skeletal remains to speak of were discovered, Borhegyi assumes that Maya priests here, too, dispatched human and animal sacrifices into the watery depths. Such likelihood is enhanced by pictorial evidence from the ceramics, which even suggests that in some cases the tearing out of hearts from victims may have preceded their drowning.

On a less gory plane, Borhegyi was amazed to note the tenacity of millennia-old Indian customs in present-day religious adaptations of lake rites.

Dr. Borhegyi's association with Guatemalan antiquities started in 1949 when he became associate professor of anthropology at the capital's university. The Central American republic decorated him in 1951 for his reorganization of the national museum. From 1954 to 1959 he directed the Stovall Museum of the University of Oklahoma and has served in a similar capacity since 1959 at the Milwaukee Public Museum, while holding a professorship at the University of Wisconsin. The results of Borhegyi's work at Lake Amatitlán were to give further stimulus to American underwater archaeology. Borhegyi himself later had occasion to supervise exploration at a number of other Guatemalan lakes.

UNDERWATER ARCHAEOLOGY IN GUATEMALA

Stephan F. Borhegyi

The recovery of archaeological treasures from the murky depths of the sea has, in recent years, become the favorite pastime of amateur skin divers and many archaeologists. With the perfection of the free diving apparatus, commonly known as the aqualung, a new chapter has been added to the romance and mystery of archaeology which makes earth-digging almost prosaic in comparison. Although the sea has long been a storehouse of ancient remains the scientific exploration and excavation of underwater sites goes back only to the beginning of this century. . . .

As early as the middle of the 19th century, travelers to Guatemala frequently mention archaeological specimens found along the shores of Lake Amatitlán. Professor Eduard Seler, the famous German archaeologist, visited the lake in 1896 and described "curious spiked vessels occasionally decorated with maguey-like leaf decorations." He noted that they had been found in the shallow water at the southern shore of the lake, near some hot water springs, where they had probably been thrown in as offerings to the gods. Although the National Museum of Archaeology in Guatemala City also had several of the same type of spiked vessels from the lake area, it was not known until recently what diverse and great amount of archaeological material was hidden at the bottom of the lake.

Since 1954 a group of young Guatemalan aqualung enthusiasts have been exploring the waters of Lake Amatitlán in Guatemala with the object of locating good fishing grounds. In April 1955, one of them, Manfred Töpke, discovered the first archaeological specimen in the southwest corner of the lake. Since that time an amateur group . . . have carried out further explorations and have brought up from the lake bottom more than 400 virtually intact pottery vessels, incense burners, and stone sculptures. . . .

Beautiful Lake Amatitlán, known by its Maya name meaning "under (or near) the Amatle tree," is a popular resort area only 17 miles south of Guatemala City. . . . The lake is seven and one-half miles long, three and a quarter miles wide, and its depth varies from 30 to 131 feet. Lava hills surround the lake, which owes its origin to a volcanic dam, subsequently breached by the Río Michatoya working headward up the

---

From "Underwater Archaeology in Guatemala," *Thirty Third International Congress of Americanists.* San José, Costa Rica: Antonio Lehmann, 1959, Vol. II, pp. 229–40.

Pacific slope. The major inlet, the Río Lobos, has built a large delta into the lake on the north side, and the river has shifted its course so that it now has its outlet close to the extreme right edge of the delta. A great deal of fine silt brought down by the Río Lobos makes the lake rather turbid. . . . The temperature of the lake is between 21 and 25° C. The lake and the village of San Juan Amatitlán are located at an altitude of 4,084 feet, only 826 feet lower than the capital. At its western end is a colony of weekend cottages and two hotels which feature thermal baths, said to be beneficial for arthritis, rheumatism and general health. Sailboats, motorboats and waterskiers are numerous on the lake during weekends. The town of San Juan Amatitlán is much quieter. Due to its presence in the midst of a resort area the town's present day population is composed of about 6,000 permanent residents who are largely "ladinos" of mixed Spanish and Pokomam Indian ancestry.

The first task of our archaeology group was the preparation of accurate maps of the lake with the aid of bathymetric maps and aerial photographs, kindly provided by the Oficina de Cartografía. Once this was accomplished we attempted to locate the exact sites of all underwater discoveries made since 1955. This proved to be a not altogether simple task. Nearly 400 archaeological specimens in various private collections were photographed by Miss Joya Hairs of Guatemala City, described and measured and each piece was catalogued according to its original location beneath the waters of the lake. The collections consisted of literally hundreds of offering bowls, incense burners and covers, ranging in size from a few inches to four and one half feet in height. Many of the censers were of the three-pronged variety and bore unusual designs: cacao trees and pods, papaya fruits and flowers, quetzal birds, jaguar heads, spider monkeys, snakes, lizards, bats and even human skulls— motifs hitherto rare or unknown in the Highland Maya area. Among the gods represented were Tlaloc, the Jaguar god, the Sun god, Eecatl, Xipe Totec, the Death god and beautifully executed human heads peering from jaws and beaks of animals and birds.

Meanwhile we also proceeded with the mapping of the archaeological sites located on the southern shore of the lake. *Contreras* (Site B), the oldest, shows continuous occupation from the beginning to the end of the Maya Formative period (approximately 1000 B.C. to 200 B.C.). None of the five mounds of the site have been examined more than cursorily except for a burial in Mound 2 that was exposed by treasure hunters. *Contreras* lies at or a little above the level of the modern lake, which suggests that this level has not been higher than today for the last two thousand years or more, but more excavation is needed to establish this important point. The Early Classic (300 to 600 A.D.) site of *Mejicanos*

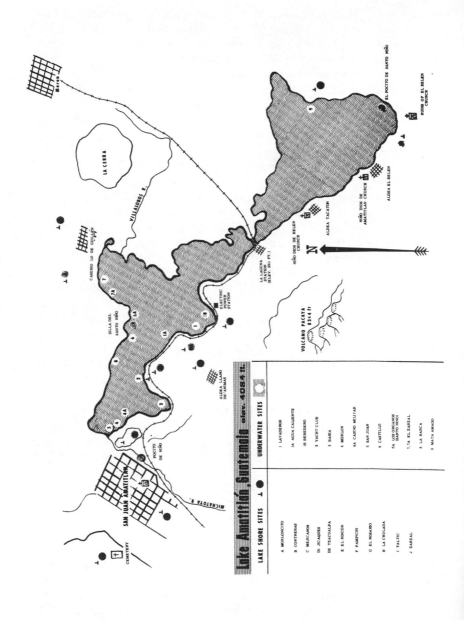

Lake Amatitlán, Guatemala.

LAKE SHORE SITES ⚓ ●

A. MORLONCITO
B. CONTRERAS
C. MEJICANOS
D. JICAQUES
Dʼ TZACUALPA
E. EL RINCON
F. PAMPICHI
G. EL ROBARTO
H. LA CHULADA
I. TALTIC
J. ZARZAL

UNDERWATER SITES

1. LAVADEROS
1A. AGUA CALIENTE
1B. BEBEDERO
2. YACHT CLUB
3. BAÑA
4. MORLON
4A. CAIRO MILITAR
5. SAN JUAN
6. CASTILLO
6A. LOS ORGANOS (SANTO NIÑO)
7, 7A. EL ZARZAL
8. LA BARCA
9. MATA AMADO

(Site C) consisting of four mounds is also at or a little above the lake level while the large (about 25 mounds including 2 ballcourts) Late Classic (600 to 900 A.D.) site of *Amatitlán* (Site A) is on higher ground. Movement to higher, more easily defensible positions, however, was characteristic Maya behavior during periods of disturbance, and does not necessarily imply that the lake level rose. Two additional archaeological sites were located during the summer of 1958. *Contreras Alto* (Site D$_1$) and *Los Jicaques* (Site D$_2$) were discovered on the slopes some 500 feet higher than the previously known site *Contreras* (Site B). Both sites must have been quite extensive with large mounds and excellently cut cyclopean masonry. Although the majority of the pottery collected from these two new sites dates to the Late Pre-Classic and Classic periods, sufficient amounts of Post-Classic red-and-black-on-white (Chinautla polychrome) pottery was found on the surface to indicate the possibility that the lake area was inhabited at the time of the Spanish Conquest (1524 A.D.) and one of the sites might even have been the original location of the long searched for ruins of Zacualpa which were shown on the 1690 map of the noted Guatemalan historian Francisco de Fuentes y Guzmán. Previously, another lake shore site, that of *Amatitlán* (Site A) was thought . . . to be ruins indicated on this early map.

The records of the archaeological specimens uncovered by the amateur divers from the lake indicated a definite correlation between the typology and age of the specimens and the nearest archaeological site on the shore. In order to test this correlation the subsurface lake area near the Early Classic *Mejicanos* site (Site C) on the south shore was re-examined during the Summer of 1958. Student divers from the summer school of the San Carlos University descended several times to depths of 30 to 40 feet and brought up some 80 archaeological specimens. The pieces were predominantly of Early Classic type and seemed to corroborate our theory. Specimens consisted of cylindrical tripods, face-neck jars and several two-chambered incense burners and covers with bow-tie adornments and decorations strongly resembling Early Classic Kaminaljuyú and Teotihuacán styles such as adornos with shell and butterfly symbols, rain drop symbols, and treble scrolls. Many pieces were identical with the sherds collected by us earlier from the surface of the *Mejicanos* site. Some of the small flaring sided pedestal based offering vases were found on the slopes of the lake floor in piles of six or seven, neatly fitted into each other. This, as well as other observations, convinced us that some of the archaeological objects found in the lake were deposited as ceremonial offerings at a time when the water level was probably lower than it is at present.

Another important discovery was made by Mr. James Kitchen, a local petroleum geologist. We were test diving at *Lavaderos* (Site 1A) when Mr. Kitchen surfaced with a rather ordinary looking face-neck jar. This brown-black ware jar with a modeled Tlaloc face on the neck was found 30 feet from the shore at a depth of 20 feet. It was unusually heavy and upon investigation turned out to contain liquid mercury. After further cleaning we also found in the jar fragments of cinnabar, graphite, and nearly 400 of what appeared to be ceremonially smashed fragments of jade ear spools. This is the fourth instance that a vessel, containing liquid mercury, has been found under archaeological conditions in the New World. In all three previous instances . . . offerings also contained, in addition to shell and pearls, jade and cinnabar and were of Early Classic date. The Tlaloc jar with its unusual contents suggests that some of the specimens found under the waters of Lake Amatitlán must have been special offerings to the lake gods and were ceremonially cast into the lake waters.

The 1958 summer's diving brought several fragmentary and complete stone sculptures from the lake waters. At the *Lavaderos* site (Site 1A) in addition to metates and manos a complete stone yoke, some fragments of mushroom stones and fragments of stone sculptures representing seated cross-legged individuals came to light. The similarity of these stone sculptures with the Cotzumalhuapa art style of the south coast of Guatemala was striking. This poses an intriguing chronological problem. All the material discovered in the lake at *Lavaderos* is of Early Classic (300–600) date. The Cotzumalhuapa sculptures have been thought to be of Late Classic date and possibly of non-Maya, Pipil manufacture. . . . The Pipil preference for the representation of speech scrolls, jaguars, spider monkeys, human skulls, intricate flowers and vines, is clearly present on most of the Early Classic specimens recovered by us from the lake. Could it be that the Early Classic Teotihuacán influence from Mexico, felt almost everywhere in the highlands of Guatemala, was actually brought by migrating Pipil groups to the Maya area? Does this also mean that what most archaeologists generally assume to be the Early Classic in the Maya area is but a ceremonial assemblage found only in association with burials and caches within ceremonial precincts? If so, this would suggest that what Middle Americanists have been calling Late Classic material was actually in use during both the Early and Late Classic periods by the common people living nearby and working for the ceremonial precincts. . . .

In reconstructing the ancient history of the lake we are probably safe in assuming that the strange natural phenomena of bubbling sulphurous hot springs (97° C.) and geysers inspired awe in the minds of the pre-Columbian inhabitants. This awe, combined with the fear of the active volcano Pacaya, whose four peaked cone overlooks the lake (elevation

8,344 ft.), could easily have given rise to the belief that the lake was the abode of particularly powerful spirits or gods. The predominance of jaguar features on the incense burners suggests that the Maya rain and water gods, commonly associated with this much feared beast, may have been the recipients of the many ceremonial offerings thrown into the lake. Unlike the *Cenote* of Chichen Itzá, however, the lake has thus far revealed no evidence of human sacrifice. Nevertheless, the presence of human skull features on some of the offering vessels and the sacrificial knife noted in the hands of the applied figures on some of the incense burners leads us to believe that human or animal sacrifices may have constituted part of the ancient lake-ceremonies at Amatitlán. . . .

Symbolic rendering of water lily, after a stucco relief at Palenque

To answer the questions of just how and why such amazing quantity of specimens happened to be at the bottom of the lake calls for an additional bit of theorizing. There seem to be two possible answers. On the southern shore many of the offering bowls were found stacked in piles and in some cases the incense burners were found in groups of four or five, standing erect and occasionally embedded in lava on the lake floor. This may indicate that to placate the angry volcano many of the objects were placed along the shore within the lava flow and were carried by the flow into the lake. Other artifacts, haphazardly strewn over the lake floor, were found so distant from shore and at such a great depth that they must have been thrown deliberately into the lake as ceremonial offerings.

Today Lake Amatitlán still occupies a mystical and religious place in the beliefs of the inhabitants of the region. The seventeenth century stone church on the town plaza of San Juan Amatitlán is the home of an elaborately carved Spanish Colonial wooden figure of the *Santo Niño de Atocha* which has won wide acclaim for its miraculous healing powers. According to old legends, similar magic power was once attributed to a carved stone figure, *"Jefe Dios,"* which stood in pre-Columbian times on the north shore of the lake. One night, sometime during the seventeenth century, so the story goes, there was a great rumbling in the earth accompanied by a severe hailstorm and the stone figure sank beneath the waters of the lake. The following morning devout visitors to the "pagan" shrine found in its place the charming wooden statue of the *Santo Niño*.

Each year on May 3rd, the day of the Festival of the Cross, devout pilgrims from all parts of the Republic of Guatemala come to the Fiesta of Amatitlán. The wooden figure of the *Santo Niño* is taken from the church in a magnificent procession across the lake to the place where legend has its miraculous appearance. Hundreds of gaily-painted boats follow the statue on its journey, and flowers and fruits are thrown into the lake by the pilgrims. Can this colorful Christian festivity at Amatitlán be a survival of ancient Maya lake rituals? . . .

The aqualung discoveries at Lake Amatitlán . . . suggest that natural lakes, as well as *cenotes,* may have been considered sacred abodes for water gods and it is possible that they were venerated by special rituals throughout Mesoamerica in pre-Columbian times. If so, there must be much more archaeological material awaiting recovery by aqualung divers and archaeologists.

27

Writing—the contrivance of symbols for transmission of speech and thought—has been acclaimed as the very touchstone of civilization. If proof were needed of the advanced development of the Mayas, it is demonstrated by their possession of a script and of prodigious records on stelae, walls, tablets, lintels, murals, jades, and ceramics. In this skill the Mayas outranked all other peoples of the New World. The Incas and their predecessors in the Central Andes apparently never outgrew their primitive method of committing information to knotted *quipus*. The Toltecs, Zapotecs, and Aztecs knew how to write and, like the Mayas, produced books on folded animal hide or pounded vegetable fiber, but they never arrived at a standardized system of writing and relied to an excessive degree on pictorialization, which probably made it impossible to lay down a precise rendering of any text. Though the "Olmecs" were perhaps the original inventors of the pebble-shaped (calculiform) Maya characters, and though there exist some affinities between Maya and Zapotec and Mixtec glyphs, the uniformity, refinement, and profusion of the Maya script are unique in Mesoamerica. For all we know, the Mayas alone developed a literate culture. Of them the oft-mentioned Diego de Landa wrote, in the sixteenth century: "These people also made use of certain characters or letters, with which they wrote in their books, their ancient affairs and their sciences, and with these and drawings and with certain signs in these drawings, they understood their affairs and made others understand them and taught them."

Nothing facilitates the task of the archaeologist more than authentic documents left by the same people whom he aims to recover from the abyss of destruction and oblivion. Once the writings can be read, a mute race of a sudden becomes articulate; it enters the mansions of history. Such a miracle has happened with the ancient Egyptians and a host of Near Eastern and Mediterranean peoples of the Old World. Unfortunately, archaeologists cannot claim such spectacular successes with the

Mayas. What makes the failure even more tantalizing is the fact that at least until the blotting out of the Itzá retreat at Tayasal in 1697 there must have been priest-scribes around who knew how to write the ancient hieroglyphs and composed elaborate codices.

Every so often noisy announcements have been made that a key to Maya script has at long last been found and that the remaining codices and inscriptions can now be read. However, such sweeping claims have invariably fallen into dead silence after the first ruffles and flourishes. Even the recent assurance by Russian savants that they have cracked the glyphs with the methods of electronic computers has failed to convince their Western colleagues. The full translations they have promised have not yet appeared.

How can we account for such extraordinary difficulties, considering that much older and once equally perplexing scripts such as Linear B and Hittite hieroglyphics have eventually been deciphered?

For one thing there is the scarcity of hand-written books, which, if we are to believe Landa and his contemporaries, covered a wide range of subjects, including literature and history. In all, only three "codices" have survived the bonfires of Spanish fanatics. Paradoxically, Landa, to whom we owe more of our knowledge of the Mayas than all the other Spanish writers put together, was the chief nemesis of Maya books. To the above-quoted reference from his *Relación de las Cosas de Yucatán* on the nature of Maya documents, he himself added: "We found a great number of books in these characters, and, as they contained nothing in which there was not to be seen superstition and the lies of the devil, we burned them all, which they regretted to an amazing degree and caused them affliction."

Another reason for the frustrations is the complexity of the Maya writing system which apparently consists of various phonetic, ideogrammatic, and pictorial elements—nobody quite knows for certain in what proportion. Hence the unlikelihood that it can ever be reduced to an alphabet or syllabary, or even a fixed number of symbols. In fact there may not be a pat solution or key. In addition one must consider the possibility that few of the texts rendered coherent sentences, but, as in central Mexico, may have served as memory aids which enabled highly trained sages or priests to recall the precise wording or meaning of a statement.

Nevertheless, about one third of all Maya hieroglyphic signs can be read today. These deal almost exclusively with the calendar and astronomical computations. They have been deduced by a number of scholars largely on the basis of Bishop de Landa's account of Maya customs and idolatries, which was rediscovered by the Abbé Brasseur de Bourbourg in

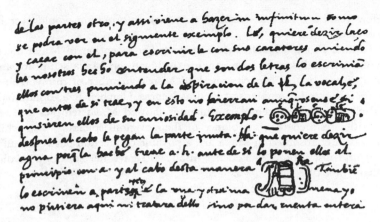

Passage from Bishop Landa's manuscript, with reference to Maya symbols

1863 in a Madrid library. Thanks to Landa we are now quite well oriented on the chronology of the Mayas, their obsession with time, and their astonishing astronomical knowledge. Maya scholars long have argued that, because of this very preoccupation, the extant texts, even if they could be read, would be of kindred astronomical-astrological and religious-ritual content, unlikely to yield any factual or historical data. This has been the verdict of the leading Maya epigraphers of our time, foremost among them Sylvanus G. Morley and J. Eric S. Thompson. In reviewing the Maya inscriptions Morley wrote: "They are in no sense records of personal glorification and self-laudation like the inscriptions of Egypt, Assyria, and Babylonia. They tell no story of kingly conquests, recount no deeds of imperial achievement; they neither praise nor exult, glorify nor aggrandize, indeed they are so utterly impersonal, so completely non-individualistic, that it is even probable that the name glyphs of specific men and women were never recorded upon the Maya monuments."

But then in 1960 Tatiana Proskouriakoff made the astounding announcement that she had been able to find references to actual princes, their wives and children, and dates of birth and accession on the stelae at Piedras Negras in Guatemala. Her new approach to the script seems to have demolished the pessimism of her predecessors; it may be the first great breakthrough in Maya epigraphy since Landa's book was exhumed. J. Eric S. Thompson acclaimed Miss Proskouriakoff's studies of Maya sculpture and her success in relating sculptural motifs to the accompanying hieroglyphic texts. As he says, her researches "opened up a vista of Maya dynasties, particularly at Piedras Negras, and have even given us a peep at the family life of the rulers of those far off days. . . .

A few years ago no one dreamed that such information would ever be recovered."

Tatiana Proskouriakoff, before turning her attention to Maya hieroglyphs, was well known as a ranking authority on Maya sculpture and architecture. In this capacity she had been a member of many United States-sponsored campaigns at Piedras Negras, Chichen Itzá, Bonampak, and elsewhere. Her exemplary drawings showed Maya temples and entire cities restored to a semblance of their original splendor. Yet, while she was fully absorbed in Maya art, a possible connection between sculptures and inscriptions excited her mind, and gave her studies a revolutionary new direction.

THE LORDS OF THE MAYA REALM

Tatiana Proskouriakoff

We Mayanists spend an inordinate amount of time deciphering half obliterated hieroglyphic texts. Often it seems that our results are not worth all that effort; but now and again some minor fact that hardly seems worth mentioning at the time can be used to pry open a chink in the wall of obscurity that surrounds the past, and suddenly we get a new and exciting glimpse of events that have left their traces on the old stones of Maya sites. When, in 1943, J. E. S. Thompson changed the date of Stela 14 of Piedras Negras, Guatemala, from A.D. 800, given it by Morley, to A.D. 761, the correction seemed of purely academic interest. The stela was on loan at the University Museum since 1933, and Satterthwaite, by the use of studio-quality photographs, was able to substantiate the new readings. Epigraphers made a note of them in their notebooks for future reference, and there the matter rested.

Thompson had described the stela and others like it as showing "gods seated in niches formed by the bodies of celestial dragons," and remarked in passing, without ascribing any special importance to the fact, that the correction of the date made Stela 14 the first monument to be erected

"The Lords of the Maya Realm," by Tatiana Proskouriakoff, Carnegie Institution of Washington, in *Expedition*, the Bulletin of the University Museum of the University of Pennsylvania, IV:1 (Autumn 1961), pp. 14–21.

in front of Temple O–13. One day, several years later, while wondering what the niche and celestial dragon motif might mean, I noticed that Stela 33, though it has no niche, presents a similar scene, and realized for the first time that the new reading of Stela 14 made all monuments of this type the first to be erected in a given location. Monuments with other motifs were then set up every five years in the same place until another similar group was started near another temple. Thus there were distinct sets of monuments, each beginning with a "niche" stela. My first thought was that the "niche" motif represented the dedication of a new temple, and that the ladder marked with footsteps ascending to the niche symbolized the rise to the sky of the victim of sacrifice, whose body was sometimes shown at the foot of the ladder. It occurred to me that if I searched the inscriptions for a hieroglyph peculiar to these stelae, I might find the glyphic expression for human sacrifice. What I found instead started an entirely new train of thought and led to surprising conclusions.

True enough, there was a record of a date just prior to the erection-date on each "niche" stela, and this date of some immediately preceding event was always followed by a hieroglyph that Thompson, with one of his delightful flashes of humor, has dubbed "the toothache glyph." Anniversaries of the event were often subsequently recorded, but only on

Two forms of the "toothache" or "accession" glyph

monuments of the same group. What I had not expected to find was that the only dates that any two groups of stelae had in common were some that marked the ends of conventional time periods, and even this happened rarely, though the recorded dates of two contiguous groups invariably overlapped in time. Evidently each group of monuments presents an independent set of records. Moreover, it is not the "toothache glyph" date that is the earliest in each set, but another that is anywhere from twelve to thirty-one years earlier and is always accompanied by the so-called "upended frog glyph." This earlier event could not have had much public importance when it happened since no notation was made of it at the time. It was first recorded after the "toothache glyph" event occurred, and only then began to be celebrated by anniversaries.

Doubtless there are various events in history that are paired in this way, but surely the most common is the birth of some person who in his mature years acquires great prestige or political power. But if the "upended frog" date is a birth date, the fact that it was celebrated for only a limited period suggests that that period was the person's lifetime, and effectively refutes my original notation that the "toothache glyph" expresses the human sacrifice shown on "niche" stelae. More likely, these stelae portray the accession of a new ruler, the "seating on high of the Lord," as the Maya books put it. Subsequent stelae, too, are probably portraits of the lord.

To test this new idea, I calculated the length of time covered by each set of records. There were only three sets whose full span was known, and the figures were 60, 64, and 56 years. These are reasonable lifetimes for rulers who lived at a time when the ordered setting up of monuments suggests tranquil conditions. I was greatly encouraged, feeling that at last I might be on the right track.

"Upended frog" or "birth date" glyph

The next step, of course, was to identify the names of the lords, or at least to make sure that the birth and accession date referred to the same individual. If so, the "upended frog glyph" (birth date), and the "toothache glyph" (accession) of each set of records would be followed by the same glyph, which would differ for every set. This actually proved to be the case, though the name was expressed by three or four glyphs, and sometimes a glyph was omitted or substituted by another. After all, an important lord is bound to have various honorifics and titles. The first glyph was always the same after both dates, and I felt confident that my identification of the name phrases was correct. But did these "names" refer to the sculptured figures?

I was convinced that they did when I examined the texts on Stelae 1 and 2. These stelae are eroded on the front, where the portrait of the lord appears, and on the sides, but on the back each has a complete text and a sculptured figure dressed in a long robe. Many Mayanists had believed that the robe was a priestly garment worn by men, but here both texts record the same birth date followed by the same two name glyphs with a prefix which is clearly a face of a woman, identified by a black (cross-hatched) spot or a lock of hair on the forehead. What is more, on

Stela 3, which shows a small figure seated beside the one in the robe, the text contains a second birth date, thirty-three years later than the first and only three years earlier than the final date on the stela. This later birth date is followed by a different set of name glyphs, though they, too, are prefixed by female faces. How can one reasonably doubt that both robed figures are portraits of the same person, that the person is a woman, and that her little daughter, not yet born when Stela 1 was erected, is shown on Stela 3? The theme of family suggested by this woman and child is quite consistent with the theme of dynasty in which questions of marriage and descent are always involved, but it would be difficult to reconcile it with a theme of Maya religion.

"Name" glyphs of a mother and daughter, depicted on back of Stela 3, Piedras Negras

In retrospect, the idea that Maya texts record history, naming the rulers or lords of the towns, seems so natural that it is strange it has not been thoroughly explored before. The reason is that the only substantial progress made in the decipherment of texts dealt with astronomical and calendrical notations, and these form such a large part of the inscriptions that there appeared to be no room left for historical narrative. The Maya, however, had a conception of history different from ours. Even in colonial times their historical statements were very cryptic and were often. mixed with prophesy, for they believed that every event casts its shadow on the future. Thus, if we accept the "dynastic hypothesis," as it is currently called, we may yet find that the birth date of the lord and his accession date were not inscribed for historical purposes alone, but mainly to provide a base for the prognosis of the fortunes of a given reign. This may explain the emphasis on astronomical data given with the dates. In any case, it is well to remember that the hypothesis is still far from being established to everyone's satisfaction. A great deal remains to be done before a crucial test of it can be made. One of the first tasks will be to study the structure of all the purported "name phrases," so that we can separate proper names from titles, lineage designations, and other epithets applied to the lords and their dependents. The identity of some of the persons or entities mentioned in the texts is still clouded with complications and contradictions, and doubtless will continue to trouble us for some time.

There is one group of hieroglyphs in particular for which I have not found a satisfactory explanation. This group comprises jaguar-glyphs with varying prefixes and super-fixes. Two of the combinations appear to be names of lords who ruled Yaxchilán, a city up-river from Piedras Negras and on the opposite bank. Here, on Lintels 29 and 30, are clearly recorded the birth and accession dates of a certain Bird-Jaguar, who also has additional designations. His accession in A.D. 752 is recorded again on Stela 11, where he is shown wearing a sun-mask before three prisoners. Above him (in the sky?) are two seated figures, a man and a woman, with their names inscribed at the sides. The man's name includes a Shield-Jaguar glyph, and elsewhere appears on earlier Yaxchilán lintels, so that even without having the accession date we may suppose that the Shield-Jaguar is the predecessor and perhaps the progenitor of the Bird-Jaguar lord. So far everything is clear and consistent with our hypothesis.

But on Stela 12, which was apparently erected at the same time as Stela 11, the accession date of the Bird-Jaguar is followed not by its usual expression, but by a variant form and then by an unusually complicated name phrase including a Jaguar glyph preceded by a Bat. There is some possibility that the Bat-Jaguar is named here as the heir-apparent to the Bird-Jaguar lord, or as a co-ruler or high official. What is curious is that his accession date does not appear at Yaxchilán, but at Piedras Negras, where it is incised on the background of Lintel 3, next to a throne on which a chief holds audience before a group of people. The precise date of this accession is uncertain (probably A.D. 757, five years after the accession of the Bird-Jaguar, and seemingly during his reign), and it is not recorded on any of the surviving stelae. The lintel itself was carved after A.D. 782, but the dates recorded on it cover more than thirty years, and it is impossible to say which of the recorded events is shown in the sculpture. The first date recorded falls in A.D. 749, and is stated to be the twenty-year anniversary of the accession of a ruler portrayed on Stela 11 of Piedras Negras, in front of Temple J-3. About twelve years after this accession, a very unusual and striking motif was carved on Stela 10, which stands in the same group. Here the lord is shown seated on a cushion, and behind him is a huge jaguar, reared on hind legs and with one forepaw extended forward over the head of the seated figure. There are no hieroglyphs surviving except those of the currently completed period. What can be the meaning of this obviously symbolic scene? Is the jaguar a god-protector of the lord? Is he a foreign overlord to whom the ruler of the town is subject? Or does he represent a lineage, symbolized by the most powerful animal known to the Maya? Above all, is there any significance in the fact that the accession date of the current ruler is linked with the Bat-Jaguar from Yaxchilán on Lintel 3?

According to Satterthwaite's calculations based on radiocarbon dates, near the beginning of the eighth century, probably even prior to the reign of the Shield-Jaguar at Yaxchilán, the motif of the jaguar-protector was carved on a wooden lintel in Temple I at Tikal. Roughly forty or fifty years later, it was repeated on a lintel of Temple IV, this time with the "protector" in the form of a man, still bearing, however, certain jaguar and sun symbols. The texts of both lintels contain jaguar glyphs, but not as names of the ruling lords. The rulers' names are known from contemporary stelae, and appear on the lintels linked with the jaguar-glyphs in clauses. On the later lintel, the jaguar glyph is prefixed by the sign *Kin* (day or sun), and this same Kin-Jaguar is mentioned also on Stelae 1 and 2 at the newly discovered site of Aguateca, many kilometers south of Tikal. On these stelae, the Kin-Jaguar glyph is part of a name-phrase, but again is apparently not the proper name of the ruler, for it is preceded by another glyph that seems to indicate some sort of relationship between the lord named and the jaguar. On accession of the next lord of Aguateca, in A.D. 741, the Kin-Jaguar is replaced by a turtle-glyph, which is one of the designations of the lords of Piedras Negras. One may note that this is the very year when the jaguar-protector motif was carved at Piedras Negras, but whether this fact has any relevance is not at all clear to me.

So far, I have been unable to untangle the obscure connections between the jaguar glyphs and the "protector" motif. What may be signifi-

Various combinations of the jaguar glyph

cant about them is that all the associated dates seem to belong to that period known as "The Period of Uniformity," when many elements of costume and artistic style, formerly local, became widely dispersed through the Maya area, and when all large cities adopted a uniform lunar count. A. V. Kidder once remarked that only under the pressure of political unification is such agreement among a group of clerics conceivable. Perhaps the ubiquitous jaguars of this period hold some clue to the nature of this unification. Is it possible that the lords of Yaxchilán, a city whose militant battle scenes are unique in Maya sculpture, succeeded in subjecting to their will such great and ancient cities of the Petén as Tikal and Piedras Negras, or is it merely that they incorporated in their proper names the designation of a widespread lineage? Was there some political or military alliance that took the name of the jaguar, with member states denoted by varying prefixes?

Such speculation, unfortunately, is just as likely as not to lead us astray. What is needed now is some new fact: perhaps no more than one clarified date, perhaps an observation of some small detail on the sculptures, or some relation between them that has escaped notice. Sooner or later, someone is bound to come upon this crucial little fact that will solve the enigma of the jaguars, and we can take another step forward in the interpretation of Maya texts.

In the meantime, some scholars hold that it won't be long before the electronic computer will solve all the major problems of glyphic decipherment and put our present efforts to shame. One experiment has already been made in Russia, but its results are not published, and its success is therefore still unknown. Much will depend on the validity of the assumptions concerning the nature of Maya writing on which the programming was based. It is not at all certain that a completely linguistic rendering of hieroglyphic passages is possible, but even if it is, we may still be far from understanding their meaning, for known Maya texts of Colonial date, written in Roman characters, are replete with metaphors and allusions completely incomprehensible to us. I hope that no one, relying on the marvels of modern invention, will be deterred from pursuing the more laborious method of minute simultaneous scrutiny of texts and sculptures, which is the only way we can make sure that any reading proposed in the future does in fact express the intention of the text. Even if our most optimistic hopes are fulfilled, the full understanding of Maya hieroglyphic inscriptions will require many years of effort. However, if it is true that they contain history and narrative, we may expect ultimately to gain a far more intimate knowledge of the social and political aspects of Maya life than, until now, we have dared to anticipate, and it will be exciting to explore various paths by which we might approach this goal.

PART V

UNITED STATES

ESKIMO SNOW HOUSE

LONG HOUSE

PLANK HOUSE

PLANK HOUSE

ESKIMO HOUSE

NORTHWEST
COAST

ARCTIC

NORTHERN

EARTH LODGE

WIGWAM

WIGWAM

EARTH LODGE

LONG HOUSE

PLATEAU

TIPI

NORTHEAST

WICKIUP

PLAINS

WIGWAM

CALIFORNIA

PRAIRIE LODGE

PUEBLO

WICHITA HOUSE

MISSISSIPPI HOUSE

WICKIUP

SOUTHWEST

SOUTHEAST

PRAIRIE MAT-COVERED LODGE

MEXICAN

AZTEC TEMPLE

TIPI

WICHITA GRASS HOUSE

PUEBLO APARTMENT HOUSE

AZTEC TEMPLE

MISSISSIPPI TEMPLE

Cultural areas of North America, with typical houses

28

The deeper white settlers penetrated into the territories later to become the United States of America and Canada, the more they became aware of a profusion of earth mounds scattered all over the Mississippi Valley and beyond, from Manitoba and Ontario into Wyoming, northern New York State and as far south as the Florida Keys. Today's estimate of one hundred thousand earthworks is probably conservative. That these regularly shaped hills were not natural elevations but had been raised by men was no longer doubted once skeletons and skillfully made implements had been retrieved by farmers or curious amateurs. But nobody had any clear idea who the people were who had raised those countless monuments. Nor could they say when they had been built or what religious notions may have inspired them. Most mystifying of all: Where had the people gone when they abandoned these mute memorials to the wilderness? And where had they come from before they developed populous communities presumably superior in crafts and organization to those of the "savage" Indians encountered by the European intruders? Their large-scale building projects must have called for a far from primitive economic and social level, and a high degree of cooperative effort.

From the days of the early Pilgrims onward, the "Mystery of the Mounds" was enshrined in the romance of pre-historic America. As elsewhere in the New World, the traces of a bygone race evoked wild speculations. Usually the mounds were ascribed to one or another of the great civilized nations of the Old World, while more imaginative antiquarians conjured up a primordial indigenous American man. At any rate, the view prevailed for a long time that northern America had been inhabited eons ago by a great vanished race, the so-called Mound Builders, who had unaccountably disappeared from the land even before the advent of the Indians. Allegedly they had a uniform culture, which spread across the better part of the continent east of the Rocky Mountains.

In the course of two centuries of mound exploration, the attempt to

Group of mounds in Arkansas

solve the puzzle was to become something of a case history of endless debate and archaeological frustration. Only with the methods of twentieth-century physical analysis has the veil largely been lifted.

Though standing near the beginning of archaeology in America, one man, Thomas Jefferson, paid little heed to recurrent myths, and foreshadowed the verdict of science by more than a century across generations of spinners of fancy tales. Unlike others before and after him, Jefferson did not confine himself to grandiloquent discourses. Instead, he took to the spade.

Some time during the closing years of the Revolutionary War—about 1780, if not earlier—he singled out and excavated a "barrow" in the Piedmont of Virginia, on the right bank of the Rivanna River just north of where he was to found the University of Virginia. Jefferson's *Notes on the State of Virginia*, written up in 1781 and first presented to the public in 1787, contain a lucid description of this operation—showing an intuitive grasp of stratigraphy (distinction of successive, chronologically differing layers) which has caused a modern authority on excavating technique, Sir Mortimer Wheeler, to call the American statesman "the first scientific digger."

Quite ahead of his time, Jefferson shunned the customary pursuit of precious or curious articles. He dug not for rarities but for information— with the sole purpose of settling an historical or anthropological problem. His procedure was equally advanced. Finding the surface wanting in evidence, he decided on sinking a trial ditch to get at the composition and sequence of the accumulated deposits. However, his achievement as an archaeologist goes beyond technical sophistication. Never neglecting the larger objective, he entered the debate over Indian burial customs and asserted that the excavated mound and others like it were piled up by members of the same Indian race met by the colonists. There is no hint that he considered any of the mounds of the Virginia area of unfathomable age.

From the evidence of his fieldwork, *Notes on the State of Virginia* turns to a broader and more philosophical inquiry. In a generally empirical manner, he discusses theories concerning the peopling of the hemisphere and the possible routes of entrance. Stressing racial similarities between Asiatics and American Indians, he sees again beyond most of his contemporaries, even though he ventures the dubious opinion that the greater diversity of American languages might point to the fact that the people of the Americas are more ancient than their distant kinsmen of Asia. Jefferson's recommendation for the study of aboriginal languages and their interrelations in order to trace Indian origins was nevertheless a fruitful approach, followed in the nineteenth century by a number of scholars. He himself made a start in this direction when he gathered various Indian vocabularies. On one occasion, in 1791, James Madison joined him during a visit to a Long Island village where he took down word lists from three old squaws. Unfortunately these particular notes were later destroyed in a fire, and duties of state kept him from realizing other ambitious plans for the preservation of rapidly disappearing linguistic data. But even as President he maintained his interest in the American natives and their past. Thus, when it came to launching Lewis and Clark on their explorations he charged these men with the task of reporting on anything pertaining to Indians. As late as 1816 he donated his collection of Indian vocabularies to the American Philosophical Society.

While he made the most notable contribution, Jefferson was just one of several American Presidents to take an interest in Indian antiquities. From George Washington to Warren Harding, in or out of office, the country's leaders were eager to see the mystery of the mounds solved. So were such prominent statesmen as Benjamin Franklin and New York's De Witt Clinton. William Henry Harrison, seventh President and a former general of the Indian Wars, examined the large earthworks near Cincinnati in 1793 and later wrote a full-fledged treatise on the subject, *A Discourse on the Aborigines of the Valley of the Ohio* (1838), for the Historical Society of Ohio. This lengthy dissertation was in its day highly esteemed for its literary qualities and scholarship. He subscribed to the theory of great antiquity of the earthworks, which, judging by the return of the forest, he argued, had been deserted for many centuries. Hence his conclusion that the Mound Builders had long ago left the land. And after exiling them from the pleasant valley of the Ohio, he expended much ingenuity to recover the fugitives in other parts. His argument in brief was that they were most likely the ancestors of the Aztecs of Mexico or at least closely connected with them. It is clear that where Jefferson was a sharp, detached, and analytical observer, Harrison, the seasoned military man of log cabin fame, was surprisingly sweeping, theoretical, and rhetorical. He turned away from the physical evidence of the mounds before him to hold forth on the ultimate fate of the enigmatic Mound Builders. The persistent problems of North American archaeology could only be settled by adopting the methods, and still more the spirit, of Thomas Jefferson, pioneer archaeologist.

A VIRGINIAN GENTLEMAN
OPENS AN INDIAN BARROW

Thomas Jefferson

I know of no such thing existing as an Indian monument: for I would not honour with that name arrow points, stone hatchets, stone pipes, and half shapen images. Of labour on the large scale, I think there is no remain as respectable as would be a common ditch for the draining of lands: unless indeed it would be the barrows, of which many are to be found all over this country. These are of different sizes, some of them constructed of earth, and some of loose stones. That they were repositories of the dead, has been obvious to all: but on what particular occasion constructed, was a matter of doubt. Some have thought they covered the bones of those who have fallen in battles fought on the spot of interment. Some ascribed them to the custom, said to prevail among the Indians, of collecting, at certain periods, the bones of all their dead, wheresoever deposited at the time of death. Others again have supposed

---

From *Notes on the State of Virginia* (1801 ed.), pp. 99–104.

them the general sepulchres for towns, conjectured to have been on or near these grounds; and this opinion was supported by the quality of the lands in which they are found (those constructed of earth being generally in the softest and most fertile meadow grounds on river sides) and by a tradition, said to be handed down from the aboriginal Indians, that, when they settled in a town, the first person who died was placed erect, and earth put about him, so as to cover and support him; that when another died, a narrow passage was dug to the first, the second reclined against him, and the cover of earth replaced, and so on. There being one of these in my neighbourhood, I wished to satisfy myself whether any, and which, of these opinions were just. For this purpose I determined to open and examine it thoroughly.

A Virginia mound, nineteenth-century romantic view

It was situated on the low grounds of the Rivanna, about two miles above its principal fork, and opposite to some hills, on which had been an Indian town. It was of a spheroidical form, of about 40 feet diameter at the base, and had been of about twelve feet altitude, though now reduced by the plough to seven and a half, having been under cultivation about a dozen years. Before this it was covered with trees of 12 inches diameter, and round the base was an excavation of five feet depth and width, from whence the earth had been taken of which the hillock was formed.

I first dug superficially in several parts of it, and came to collections of human bones, at different depths, from six inches to three feet below the surface. These were lying in the utmost confusion, some vertical, some oblique, some horizontal, and directed to every point of the compass, entangled, and held together in clusters by the earth. Bones of the most distant parts were found together, as, for instance, the small bones of the foot in the hollow of a scull; many sculls would sometimes be in contact, lying on the face, on the side, on the back, top or bottom, so as, on the whole, to give the idea of bones emptied promiscuously from a bag or basket, and covered over with earth, without any attention to their order. The bones of which the greatest numbers remained, were sculls, jaw bones, teeth, the bones of the arms, thighs, legs, feet and hands. A few ribs remained, some vertebrae of the neck and spine, without their processes, and one instance only of the bone (the os sacrum) which serves as a base to the vertebral column. The sculls were so tender, that they generally fell to pieces on being touched. The other bones were stronger. There were some teeth which were judged to be smaller than those of an adult; a scull, which on a slight view, appeared to be that of an infant, but it fell to pieces on being taken out, so as to prevent satisfactory examination; a rib, and a fragment of the under jaw of a person about half grown; another rib of an infant; and part of the jaw of a child, which had not cut its teeth.

This last furnishing the most decisive proof of the burial of children here, I was particular in my attention to it. It was part of the right half of the under jaw. The processes, by which it was attenuated to the tem-

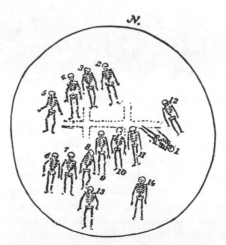

Diagram of burial mound, Tennessee

poral bones, were entire, and the bone itself firm to where it had been broken off, which, as nearly as I could judge, was about the place of the eye-tooth. Its upper edge, wherein would have been the sockets of the teeth, was perfectly smooth. Measuring it with that of an adult, by placing their hinder processes together, its broken end extended to the penultimate grinder of the adult. This bone was white, all the others of a sand colour. The bones of infants being soft, they probably decay sooner, which might be the cause so few were found here.

I proceeded then to make a perpendicular cut through the body of the barrow, that I might examine its internal structure. This passed about three feet from its centre, was opened to the former surface of the earth, and was wide enough for a man to walk through and examine its sides. At the bottom, that is, on the level of the circumjacent plain, I found bones; above these a few stones, brought from a cliff a quarter of a mile off, and from the river one-eighth of a mile off; then a large interval of earth, then a stratum of bones, and so on. At one end of the section were four strata of bones plainly distinguishable; at the other, three; the strata in one part not ranging with those in another. The bones nearest the surface were least decayed. No holes were discovered in any of them, as if made with bullets, arrows, or other weapons. I conjectured that in this barrow might have been a thousand skeletons.—Every one will readily seize the circumstances above related, which militate against the opinion, that it covered the bones only of persons fallen in battle; and against the tradition also, which would make it the common sepulchre of a town, in which the bodies were placed upright, and touching each other. Appearances certainly indicate that it has derived both origin and growth from the accustomary collection of bones, and deposition of them together; that the first collection had been deposited on the common surface of the earth, a few stones put over it, and then a covering of earth, that the second had been laid on this, had covered more or less of it in proportion to the number of bones, and was then also covered with earth; and so on. The following are the particular circumstances which give it this aspect. 1. The number of bones. 2. Their confused position. 3. Their being in different strata. 4. The strata in one part having no correspondence with those in another. 5. The different states of decay in these strata, which seem to indicate a difference in the time of inhumation. 6. The existence of infant bones among them.

But on whatever occasion they may have been made, they are of considerable notoriety among the Indians: for a party passing, about thirty years ago, through the part of the country where this barrow is, went through the woods directly to it, without any instructions or enquiry, and having staid about it some time, with expressions which were constructed to be those of sorrow, they returned to the high road, which they had left about half a dozen miles to pay this visit, and pursued their journey. There is another barrow much resembling this, in the low grounds of the south branch of Shenandoah where it is crossed by the road leading from the Rockfish gap to Staunton. Both of these have within these dozen years, been cleared of their trees, and put under cultivation, are much reduced in their heighth, and spread in width, by the plough, and will probably disappear in time. There is another on a hill in the Blue ridge of mountains, a few miles north of Wood's gap, which is made up of small stones thrown together. This has been opened and found to contain human bones, as the others do. There are also many others in other parts of the country.

Great question has arisen from whence came those aboriginals of America? Discoveries, long ago made, were sufficient to show that the passage from Europe to America was always practicable, even to the im-

Indian village, Virginia, in the 1500's

perfect navigation of ancient times. In going from Norway to Iceland, from Iceland to Groenland, from Groenland to Labrador, the first traject is the widest; and this having been practised from the earliest times of which we have any account of that part of the earth, it is not difficult to suppose that the subsequent trajects may have been sometimes passed. Again, the late discoveries of Captain Cook, coasting from Kamschatka to California, have proved that if the two continents of Asia and America be separated at all, it is only by a narrow strait. So that from this side also, inhabitants may have passed into America: and the resemblance between the Indians of America and the eastern inhabitants of Asia, would induce us to conjecture, that the former are the descendants of the latter, or the latter of the former: excepting indeed the Eskimaux, who, from the same circumstances of resemblance, and from identity of language, must be derived from the Groenlanders, and these probably from some of the northern parts of the old continent. A knowledge of their several languages would be the most certain evidence of their derivation which could be produced. In fact, it is the best proof of the affinity of nations which can ever be referred to. . . .

29

As close as Thomas Jefferson may have come to a rational view of the
problem of the mounds, he saw but a small part of it. He had apparently
no conception of the bewildering proliferation of his continent's man-
made protuberances. The tumuli known to him were on the far edge of
the mound-building zone and of the simplest type. There is no evidence
that, at least at the time of writing the *Notes on the State of Virginia*, he
had as much as heard of the enormous earthworks in the country's West
and South. How else could he have started his observations with the
statement: "I know of no such thing . . . as an Indian monument," only
to follow it up with a derisive note: "there is no remain as respectable as
would be a common ditch for the draining of lands." In this Jefferson
mirrors the skepticism of the European Enlightenment toward the abilities of America's aboriginal race. Like the contemporary Scottish historian
William Robertson, who wrote a popular history of the New World, and
the French *philosophes,* Jefferson discounted the tales of the Conquistadores
reporting magnificent native monuments. The specimens he knew were
only moderately sized, conically shaped burial mounds, which happened
to be of quite modern date. As we now know, those of his native Virginia were erected perhaps as recently as 1600. Jefferson was right in this
respect: the barrows of Virginia could be credited to familiar Indian
tribes and did not belong to remote epochs. But had he seen the far more
imposing and bizarre-looking mounds in the areas beyond the Alleghenies
where his countrymen were just then settling, he might have been as
puzzled as were the host of travelers and amateur antiquarians who were
to describe them in publication after publication.

What people generally called, collectively, "mounds" were actually a
scattering of the most varied structures imaginable, the only common de-
nominator of which was that they were all made from accretions of soil
and were eventually covered by vegetation.

In addition to burial mounds, which themselves varied considerably in dimensions as well as in the number and form of graves, there were, above all, the temple mounds with a square or rectangular base, often consisting of several levels and flattened at the top. Some of these were of tremendous size, like the Cahokia group at East St. Louis, of which the largest truncated pyramid measured about 1,000 by 700 feet and rose to a height of 100 feet. This was the "Monks' Mound," so named because it came to be occupied by a Trappist monastery. The majority of these temple pyramids were built in the lower Mississippi Valley, south of St. Louis toward the Gulf of Mexico, and in the southeastern states of Georgia, Alabama, and Florida.

Even more noteworthy were extensive earthworks laid out to enclose large areas in circles, parallelograms, squares, octagons, or other astoundingly precise geometric patterns. Within these enclosures might also be located burial mounds and ceremonial platforms. It has been surmised that some ridges were thrown up to serve as fortifications or refuge for the people during hostilities with other tribes. Several of the most impressive of such clusters of earthworks have been found in the valleys of southern Ohio, along the Scioto, Muskingum, and Miami rivers, where they have provoked much comment since the late eighteenth century. But what is perhaps the most extensive of all, a number of ramparts stretching for eleven miles, was only discovered in recent years through air and ground observation at Poverty Point, a plantation in Louisiana.

Even beyond these, there could be distinguished still other types, foremost a number of non-geometric mounds, which were particularly common in Wisconsin and which represented a variety of animals: bears,

Earthworks of the Muskingum, Ohio, from an early nineteenth-century engraving

opossums, alligators, turtles, deer, buffalo, eagles, reptiles, and, on rare occasion, even humans.

A view of these many kinds of mounds as creations of one and the same mound-building culture was one of the stumbling blocks in gaining a proper understanding. Yet, decades after Jefferson, men persisted in this thesis. William Henry Harrison, who had studied the enormous earthworks in Ohio, was haunted by the mystery of *one* departed race of giants. So to some degree were even the two young antiquarians—Ephraim George Squier and Edwin Hamilton Davis—who initiated the systematic surveying of the mounds in the 1840's.

Jefferson's painstaking dig on the Rivanna River was just one of those isolated scientific coups of no immediate consequence, which are often launched by a man of genius when a new field of inquiry has barely been called into existence and long before pioneers are past the stammering stage. But the thorough cataloguing of the North American earthworks half a century later under Squier and Davis marks a true beginning and has left an enduring imprint. Their survey, taken up in 1845, resulted in what is the first scientific treatise on American antiquities, an impressive piece of work even when measured against the contemporary literature of European scholars. A Swiss archaeologist called it "as glorious a monument of American science as Bunker Hill is of American bravery." It had the distinction of being selected by the newly founded Smithsonian Institution of Washington as the first volume of their *Contributions to Knowledge*.

In *Ancient Mounds of the Mississippi Valley* (1847), the young New Yorker Squier (then pursuing a journalistic career in Ohio) and the Ohio-born Davis, a physician who had long been interested in the earthworks, purposely eschewed all conjectures ("no hypothesis to combat or sustain") apart from a few general conclusions in the final paragraphs. They gave factual descriptions of the hundreds of mounds they personally investigated in the Ohio and Mississippi valleys, furnishing maps, exact measurements, and reliable data and illustrations of the artifacts they had collected. Here at last were distinguished clearly the different types of mounds, and the point was made that the pyramidal structures of the southern United States, with ramps leading up to once temple-topped terraces, exhibit strong affinities with the ceremonial centers of Mexico and Yucatán. Though their main object was to carry out a topographical survey, Squier and Davis were also successful excavators and brought forth fine examples of the art of the moundbuilders, who had excelled in copper work (some they found dated perhaps from the second millennium B.C.), cutouts from mica, the famous ornate pipes of stone and clay, terra-cotta figurines, carvings of animal and human bone, and the making of jewelry from semi-precious stones and pearls. A few pottery pieces included stirrup-shaped vases much like those from Peru and Tlatilco. (In order to cover their expenses, and unable at that time to interest an American institution, they sold the bulk of their collection to the Blackmore Museum of Salisbury, England.) Squier and Davis were much impressed by the frequency with which conch shells from the Gulf, turquoise from the Southwest, grizzly bear teeth from the Rockies, mica from the Carolinas, copper ore from Lake Superior, and other raw materials had reached remote parts, even if they may have been mistaken when they read into such long-distance trade signs of cultural, or even a kind of political, unity.

North American ceremonial pipe

Not the least merit of their survey is to have preserved records of earthworks which have since been obliterated by cultivation and settlement. Some of the major sites they located had never previously been reported. Foremost among these was the Great Serpent effigy mound of Ohio—which for sheer size, strange shape, enigmatic meaning, and good condition was perhaps the outstanding aboriginal monument in the entire United States. No word of it had spread beyond the vague notions of a few settlers in its then secluded vicinity near Brush Creek in Adams County. Squier and Davis were told during their researches in these parts of a "work of defense with bastions at regular intervals," which induced them to visit the place. "The true character of the work," as they say, "was apparent on first inspection."

Years later, Frederic W. Putnam, a man who was to be in the forefront of Americanists as curator of the Peabody Museum of American Archaeology and Anthropology at Harvard University, made the Serpent

Mound and its surrounding area the target for an extensive campaign of several seasons. For *Century Magazine,* Putnam perceptively recorded his impressions on approaching the mound and his decision to excavate. Like Squier and Davis he cautiously related the effigy to a global serpent cult with striking similarities to earthworks in Scotland and elsewhere. Intrigued by this prehistoric mound, he pleaded for its preservation from the encroachments of expanding agriculture. To this end, he mobilized the good ladies of Boston and effected its purchase by the trustees of the Peabody Museum. The deed was transferred in 1900 to the Archaeological and Historical Society of Ohio, and the land was set aside as a free state park. Putnam's effort on behalf of the sleekly twisting reptile set a precedent happily followed by others.

Since then the immense idol has never ceased to fascinate visitors. Yet its actual significance in the animistic cults of prehistoric Indians remains obscure. One Ohio Baptist minister argued for some years that the site marks the scene of the Fall of Adam and Eve, its obvious purpose being to warn mankind of the ever-present schemes of the Devil. The minister also knew the identity of its builder—God Himself, as borne out by Job XXVI: 13: "By His Spirit, He hath garnished the Heavens; His hand hath formed the crooked serpent."

Frederic W. Putnam (1839–1915) started his scientific career at Salem, Massachusetts, with private studies of fish and birds. Louis Agassiz lured him to Harvard and made him his assistant. Years later, excavations of shell heaps on the New England coast turned Putnam's attention to American man and eventually led him to become the organizer of anthropological collections and university departments at Harvard, New York, and Berkeley. These offices as much as his presidency of the American Association for the Advancement of Science and his direction of the anthropological exhibit at the World's Columbian Exposition in Chicago (1892) made him a tremendous force in American archaeology. He initiated excavations in the United States, Middle America, and elsewhere, and as a professor at Harvard and the University of California he helped to train platoons of fine scholars in pre-Columbian research. Though he personally conducted campaigns in 37 states of the Union, he returned again and again to the Ohio mounds. His meticulous methods of digging and recording set new standards for mound excavation. At the famous Turner Group at Moundsville, Ohio, he made some of the most spectacular discoveries in the field—among them literally "gallons" of precious pearls.

However, even in Putnam's lifetime, the problems connected with the moundbuilders were not fully resolved, though he and his contemporaries made short work of the myth of a vanished superior race and left little doubt that all these works had been erected by the ancestors of modern Indians. Only gradually there came a realization that the many mounds had been raised at different times, just as they could be ascribed to various cultural horizons. The pyramid structures of the south were clearly built under the influence of Mesoamerican civilizations and were of comparatively late date. In fact, construction continued into the early colonial era. This was supported by neglected Spanish accounts, even though Noah Webster and Benjamin Franklin were at one time convinced that the mounds could be attributed to none other than the Conquistadores themselves.

Among the northern mounds, some type sites such as Adena, Hopewell, and Fort Ancient gave names to successive cultures, whose beginnings, according to radio-carbon tests, reached into the first millennium B.C. Hopewell, identified with some of the largest earthworks and finest craftsmanship, apparently already had passed its peak by A.D. 700 when

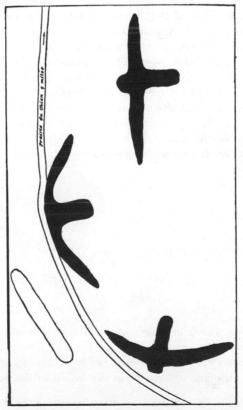

Group of bird-shaped effigy mounds, Wisconsin

the southern temple mounds had just begun to make their appearance.

Even though excavation has brought some understanding, the origin of the custom of building earthworks in North America from about 1000 B.C. onward is still shrouded in darkness. A few scholars trace all forms back to Mexico, while others maintain that such a global phenomenon does not require an outside impulse in order to arise anywhere but rather is due to parallel human responses, which may manifest themselves everywhere and in all ages.

It is of course well known that mounds can be found widely scattered over the Old World from Scotland and Scandinavia to North Africa, the Arabian Peninsula, Siberia and China. A mound was heaped by Achilles over dead Patroclus, we are told in the *Iliad,* and a large tumulus was built to inter the Greeks fallen at Marathon, which twenty-four centuries later helped to locate the battle site. Strewn all across Russia are a multitude of *kurgans.* The Chinese since at least the age of the Chou buried their notables in mounds; the one in which Confucius rests is still standing. Because of the strong resemblance between the earliest burial mounds of North America and those of eastern Asia which preceded them, and because the preparation of the dead for entombment (frequently in stone- or log-lined compartments) was similar in both areas, the possibility cannot be ruled out that mound building was introduced from Asia. This hypothesis gains further strength from the fact that the characteristic pottery of the ancient Woodland Indians of North America bore Old World "cord-marked" decorations and must have entered the New World from Siberia around 2000 B.C. Why should not the tradition of raising mounds have followed pottery?

THE SERPENT MOUND OF OHIO

Frederic W. Putnam

In September 1883, in company with four fellow-archaeologists, I started from Hillsborough, in Highland County, Ohio, on an excursion to several ancient earthworks which we had long wished to see. Our plans were so arranged as to take us first of all to the Serpent Mound,

From "The Serpent Mound, Ohio," *Century Magazine* (n.s. XVII), XXXIX, No. 6 (April 1890), pp. 871–76, 888.

thence to Fort Hill, and down Paint Creek to the Scioto, stopping from day to day to visit the most interesting of the many ancient works along the route.

Approaching the "Serpent Cliff" by fording Brush Creek from the west, our attention was suddenly arrested by the rugged overhanging rocks above our heads, and we knew that we were near the object of our search. Leaving the wagon, we scrambled up the steep hillside, and pushing on through bush and brier were soon following the folds of the great serpent along the hilltop. The most singular sensation of awe and admiration overwhelmed me at this sudden realization of my long-cherished desire, for here before me was the mysterious work of an unknown people, whose seemingly most sacred place we had invaded. Was this a symbol of the old serpent faith, here on the western continent, which from the earliest time in the religions of the East held so many peoples enthralled, and formed so important a factor in the development of succeeding religions?

Reclining on one of the huge folds of this gigantic serpent, as the last rays of the sun, glancing from the distant hilltops, cast their long shadows over the valley, I mused on the probabilities of the past; and there seemed to come to me a picture as of a distant time, of a people with strange customs, and with it came the demand for an interpretation of this mystery. The unknown must become known!

This thought took complete possession of me, and on that same evening arrangements were made with Mr. Lovett, the owner of the land, to have the place cleared of underbrush that we might see the great work in its entirety. By noon of the following day the clearing was roughly made, and the view thus obtained of the serpent and the egg—as the oval work in front of its jaws has been called—led to a still stronger

The Serpent Mound, Ohio

desire to know more, and a resolve to do all in my power to preserve this singular structure, which seemed so strangely transplanted from the mythology of the East.

When Squier and Davis, after their survey in 1846, gave to the world the first account of this earthwork, it was covered with a thick forest, from which many a noble tree has been cut, as indicated by stumps still standing at the time of our visit. Thirteen or fourteen years after their visit a tornado swept its path directly along the serpent hill, and with the exception of a few saplings the forest was laid low. This led to clearing the land, and to the cultivation for a few years of the portion occupied by the serpent. Nature soon covered the scars with a protecting sod, which was followed by a growth of sumach, redbud, and briers.

On my return to the East I took every opportunity of urging the importance of preserving the Serpent Mound, as well as other ancient monuments. In 1885 I again visited the serpent, and finding that its destruction

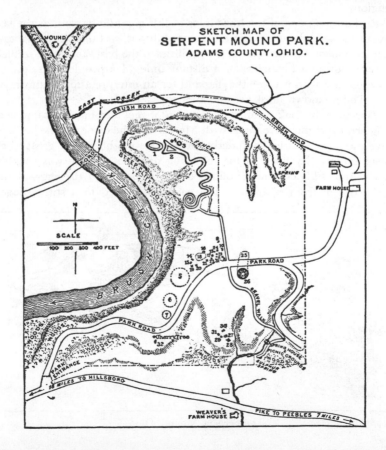

was inevitable unless immediate measures were taken for its preservation, I secured a contract that it should remain intact for a year, and agreed upon a price for its purchase. Returning home I urged anew the importance of its preservation. Yet, although an interest was awakened in the object, I fear it might have come to naught if Miss Alice C. Fletcher, meeting in Newport a few Boston ladies, had not taken the opportunity to appeal to them for assistance in the work which she knew I had so much at heart, and which was, at the same time, so thoroughly in accordance with her own views. Her earnest presentation of the subject had the desired effect. In the winter of 1886 several of Boston's noble and earnest women issued a private circular which had the indorsement of Mr. Francis Parkman and Mr. Martin Brimmer of the Corporation of Harvard University. Subscriptions were solicited to purchase the Serpent Mound, which was to be given in trust to the Peabody Museum for perpetual preservation, and also to enable me to carry on such explorations of the work and its surroundings as might throw light on its origin and purpose. This appeal was cordially met, and in June, 1886, I was provided with nearly $6,000 with which to buy such land as seemed to be required for the purpose in view, and to take steps for the preservation of the serpent, while at the same time I made such explorations as seemed desirable. The trustees of the Museum, of whom the Hon. Robert C. Winthrop has been chairman since Mr. Peabody founded the Museum, in connection with Harvard University, in 1866, accepted this additional trust, and about sixty acres of land were at once purchased in the name of the trustees. Soon after, several acres of land along the new pike leading from Hillsborough to Peebles, the nearest railroad stations, were added to the purchase, and the whole was laid out as the Serpent Mound Park, of which Brush Creek forms the western boundary.

Here for three seasons, living in tents, I have carried on the work of protecting the serpent, exploring its surroundings, and laying out the grounds. . . .

A winding road leads from the pike up the steep hill to the plateau, which it crosses, and then winds down to the little wood of maples, oaks, and other trees in the southeastern corner of the park. Here, on the grassy hillside, under the spreading oaks and maples, is a delightful resort for picnic parties; and here one may find a refreshing draught of clear cold water from the spring bubbling out of the old devonian rocks. Over the spring a substantial house of stone has been built to keep it clean and pure. A little farther along is a sulphur spring, which flows from the rocks on the opposite side of the little ravine, along which runs a brook over a rocky bed.

Following a graveled path winding up the hill from the picnic grove to the plateau, the first point of archaeological interest is reached. This is a conical mound nine feet high and seventy feet in diameter (26). Northwest of this, and not far from the serpent, is an old burial-place which was afterwards the site of a village (8, 19), as shown by the ash beds, the many implements in various stages of manufacture, the many thousand chips of flint and other stones foreign to the locality, and the many potsherds and other objects scattered throughout the dark soil. A small mound (17), about a foot high, west of the path leading from the road to the serpent, and a few stones (10) nearer the path, mark the position of the cemetery, and all about there skeletons have been found in the dark soil or in the clay below it.

On the south side of the park road, on one of the projecting points of the plateau, now marked by several piles of stones (27–31) which were taken from around the graves in the clay below the soil, were graves of the first period of occupation. On the knoll west of this, over which a wild cherry tree now casts its shade, is a low oblong mound (32), a monument over four ancient graves. From this knoll, looking towards the setting sun, there is a grand view of the valley and the hills beyond; and standing on this spot one can readily imagine why it may have been chosen as the burial-place of the honored among a people whose sacred temple was near by.

North of this knoll, on the declivity from the plateau to the cliff, are three circular pits, varying in size; and much of the clay used in building the effigy of the serpent was probably taken from these places.

Following the ridge of the hill northerly to the overhanging rocks, one is forced again to pause and admire the scene before him—the beautiful hill-girt valley with its acres of waving corn; the silvery line of the river with giant sycamores and graceful elms along its banks; and the vistas opening here and there, where the broader and deeper portions of the river are bordered with dark-green undergrowth, brightened by gleams of rich color.

Turning from this view, and ascending the little knoll behind the ledge, eighty feet from the edge of the cliff is the western end of the oval figure (1) in front of the serpent's jaws. This oval is one hundred and twenty feet long and sixty feet in greatest width, measured from the outer edge of the bank, which is about four feet high and eighteen feet across. Near the center of the inclosed area is a small mound of stones, which was formerly much larger, since it was thrown down over fifty years ago by digging under it in search of supposed hidden treasure, the popular belief which has caused the destruction of many an ancient cairn. Many of the stones show signs of fire, and under the cliff are similar burnt stones which were probably taken from the mound years ago; for I have been informed by an old gentleman, who remembered the stone mound as it was in his boyhood, that many stones taken from the mound were thrown over the cliff.

This portion of the hill was either leveled off to the clay before the oval work was made, or there was no black soil upon the hill at that time, as none was used in the construction of the embankment, nor left below it. The same is true of the serpent itself. Careful examination of several sections made through the oval and the serpent, as well as laying bare the edge along both sides of the embankments throughout, have shown that both parts of this earthwork were first outlined upon a smooth surface along the ridge of the hill. In some places, particularly at the western end of the oval, and where the serpent approached the steeper portions of the hill, the base was made with stones, as if to prevent its being washed away by heavy rains. In other places clay, often mixed with ashes, was used in making these outlines; and it is evident that the whole structure was most carefully planned, and thoroughly built of lasting material.

The geological formation of the hill shows first the ledge rock, upon which rests the decayed grayish rock forming the so-called marl of the region, the upper portion of which has by decomposition become a grayish clay. Over this lies the yellow clay of the region, filling in all irregularities, and varying in thickness from one to six feet. Upon this rests the dark soil of recent formation, from five inches to nearly two feet in thickness in different parts of the park. It is necessary to have this formation constantly in mind, as we must, to a certain extent, rely upon it in determining the antiquity of the works and burial-places.

Upon removing the sod within the oval the dark soil in the central portion was found to be nearly a foot in depth, where it must have formed after the oval work was built. How many centuries are required for the formation of a foot of vegetable mold we do not know; but here, on the hard gray clay forming the floor of the oval, was about the same depth of soil as on the level ground near the tail of the serpent, where it has been forming ever since vegetation began to grow upon the spot. The same results were obtained on removing the soil from a triangular space between the serpent's jaws; and that there was about the same amount of soil on the embankments is shown by the fact that the several plowings had not disturbed the underlying clay of which the embankments were constructed. . . .

Nine feet from the eastern end of the oval, and partly inclosing it, is a crescent-shaped bank, seventeen feet wide. From the extremities of this crescent, which are 75 feet apart, begin the jaws of the serpent, formed by banks 17 feet wide and 61 and 56 feet, respectively, in length, measured on the inside from the point of union with the crescent to their point of meeting, 47 feet from the convex or eastern edge of the crescent. We must here notice that the open jaws are shown as if the serpent's head was turned upon its right side, and the crescent embankment seems to have been designed to express this by uniting the open jaws across the mouth, indicated by the triangular space. This design was also carried out by making the northern or upper jaw the longer of the two. The head of the serpent across the point of union of the jaws is thirty feet wide and five feet high. From this point the neck extends eastward more than one hundred feet, with a slight curve to the north. Then begins what may be called the body of the serpent, making a graceful curve to the south, then winding to the east and north, then again to the south, and westward down the declivity of the central portion of the hill, where another graceful convolution is made up the opposite ascent to nearly the same level as the head; here it folds round in another full convolution, and the tail follows with a long stretch to the southwest, terminating in a triple coil.

The end of the tail points across the deep gully in the hillside to the western end of the oval, which is 496 feet distant in an air-line, but 1,348 feet if measured from the western end of the oval to the neck of the serpent, and then along the dorsal ridge to the tip of the tail, thus following all the curves. Measured from the tip of the upper jaw to the end of the tail, the serpent itself is 1,254 feet in length. The average width of the body of the serpent is about twenty feet, and its height along the head and body is from four to five feet. From the beginning of the tail it gradually decreases in width and height until it terminates in a bank about a foot high and nearly two feet wide.

The graceful curves throughout the whole length of this singular effigy give it a strange, lifelike appearance; as if a huge serpent, slowly uncoiling itself and creeping silently and stealthily along the crest of the hill, was about to seize the oval within its extended jaws. Late in the afternoon, when the lights and shades are brought out in strong relief, the effect is indeed strange and weird; and this effect is heightened still more when the full moon lights up the scene, and the stillness is broken only by the "whoo-whoo, hoo-hoo" of the unseen bird of night. . . .

What light is thrown back over one brief period of the past by this study of the Serpent Mound and its surroundings, this singular structure in the midst of many other strange earthworks in the Ohio Valley! If history can now lend its aid and bring out some points with clearness, much will be gained. But it must be critical and trustworthy history, and not the simple patchwork of vague generalities.

Here, on this commanding point of land, in many ways adapted to what we know of the ancient faiths of man, is an imposing structure in the form of a huge serpent guarding an oval inclosure within which is a mound of burnt stones; all essential points in the fulfillment of special religious rites connected with the older faiths, which, so far as we know, had their greatest development in Asia, which is the land, more than any other, that we have reason to consider as the original home of the brachycephali, one of the early peoples of America. Exploration has shown us that this serpent was made many centuries ago, and it is evident that a structure of such magnitude, so carefully planned and executed, was intended for some great purpose deeply affecting the people who made it. Again let me ask, what other than a religious motive could have been sufficient? Assuming this to be the case, we naturally give it the meaning of a religious shrine to which the people came at specified times to worship their gods. It is evident that there was never a very large community living on the plateau near the shrine, and the probability is that it was more a place of habitation in after than in early times. Here, near this sacred shrine, ceremonies of great import have taken place; individuals of importance have been buried in connection with ceremonies of fire, and in two instances, at least, accompanied by the burning of human bodies—possibly human sacrifice, that constant accessory of many ancient faiths. In later times the shrine was still a place of resort, possibly as one held sacred in myths and legends; and finally a few of the scattered bands of the last century made their habitation on the spot, probably without any legendary knowledge or thought of the earlier worshipers at the shrine, overgrown and half hidden by a forest which seventy years ago was of the same character as that on all the hills about.

Now another race has come, and the old shrine, cleared of rubbish, is again held sacred; not for ancient and awful rites, but for the study of future generations, when a wider knowledge of the past in other countries shall lead to a better knowledge of that of our own.

Copper plate, from an Illinois mound

30

To generations of Americans the Southwest of the United States has been Indian country *par excellence.* This is the scenic land, part desert, of terraced mesas covered by firs, pines, piñons, and junipers; of fertile river valleys tributary to the Colorado and the Rio Grande; of arid plains and of weathered rust-colored canyons digitating in intricate webs through broken plateaus. The geological battlefield, in which four states meet, roughly comprises Arizona, New Mexico, southwestern Colorado, and southern Utah. For geographical and anthropological reasons, sections of Nevada, Texas, even Kansas, California, and the Mexican states of Chihuahua and Sonora, are sometimes included. Only in the Southwest survive a few of the compact community settlements or *pueblos* of the Indians, inhabited for centuries before Columbus and continuing, relatively unmodified, into the present. Here live the Zuñi and the Hopi, descendants of the Pueblo group of prehistoric farmers and town builders, and such relative newcomers as the Navajo—members, like the fierce Apache, of the great Athabascan family—who have adopted the peaceful crafts of their Pueblo neighbors.

Some of the most ancient traces of *Homo sapiens* in the hemisphere have been found in the Southwest. Several scholars consider it the "cradle" of pre-Columbian man. Today there is probably no other area in the Americas which has been as thoroughly plowed by the archaeologists, though notice has been taken of its antiquities only since the late nineteenth century. John Lloyd Stephens had to go to Central America to find evidence of pre-Columbian architecture. Apparently he had no inkling of the existence of imposing ruins on what was then the very doorstep of the United States. To his countrymen, American pre-history was tied up with the Mound Builders. The ancients of the Southwest did not raise any earthworks. They built no temple platforms. Yet, unknown to the world at large until the 1870's, they did leave edifices as unusual as any on the globe.

The Conquistadores entered this region following a rumor of the fabulous Seven Cities of Cibola. But, failing to locate any great wealth or splendor, they found little worth reporting. While they noticed scattered pueblos both inhabited and abandoned, for all we know they never penetrated deep into the rugged mesa country. Spanish priests, on their way to the California missions near the Pacific coast, now and then camped in the vicinity of ruins festooned in mountain crags. But they continued on their travels without noticing, or at least reporting, anything startling. By 1848 most of the spectacular mesas and gorges were still unknown and unnamed. At last, in the wake of American acquisition, the Union government sent military and engineering parties into the new territories. From one such reconnaissance, in 1849, a lieutenant of the U.S. Army, one J. H. Simpson, brought back a brief account of sighting from a distance houses which nestled inside cliff caverns. Army officers like Simpson were followed by American prospectors, trappers, herdsmen, and settlers, whose eyes were fixed on making a living in the wilderness. They were too busy dodging live Indians to pay much attention to the traces of dead ones, or to venture, for that matter, into treacherous canyons.

The Mesa Verde, a great mountain block in southwestern Colorado with cliffs dropping a thousand feet to the valleys at the bottom, was then a natural refuge for bands of displaced Utes. All but a few white men kept away from it. Not until 1874 was a white party brave enough to explore the precipitous cliffs and to enter deserted dwellings perched high on ledges of escarpments. In September of that year a local American prospector, who was on amiable terms with the Indians, guided William Henry Jackson, the pioneer photographer of the Western frontier, and his men into the Mancos Canyon.

Four years earlier, in 1870, William Henry Jackson had become associated with Ferdinand V. Hayden, a professor of geology at the University of Pennsylvania, who appeared one day at Jackson's photographic studio in Omaha and persuaded the young Civil War veteran to join his survey of the Yellowstone region. At the time, the Rockies were "as unknown to the outside world as the middle of Tibet"; William Jackson's pictures of the Yellowstone and the Tetons, of high peaks, waterfalls, and hot springs were the first to capture their natural glories. Jackson lived to be ninety-nine, and his tens of thousands of photographs and many paintings brought the Far West to his countrymen as nothing else could have done.

Jackson was for nine seasons a member of the Hayden Survey (later to be called the U.S. Geological and Geographical Survey of the American Territories). In 1874 he had already taken off from Denver with

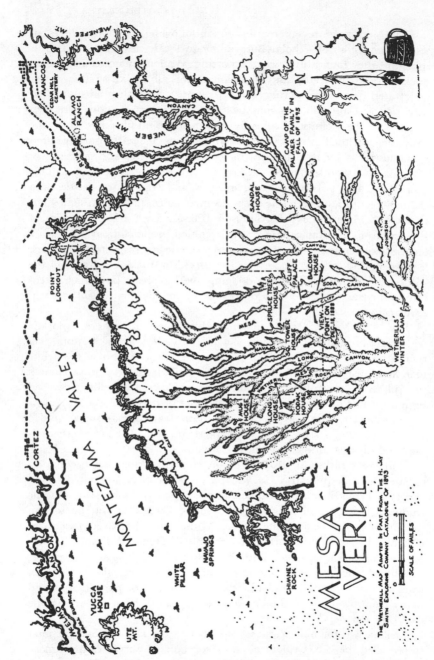

Map of the Mesa Verde, drawn by Frank McNitt

seven members of his photographic division, when he picked up unexpected news of ruins. Without the slightest hesitation, he veered from his previous destination and headed for the Mesa Verde. In his official report to the U.S. Government on "Ancient Ruins in Southwestern Colorado," Jackson described the difficult terrain he came to enter: "Throughout its entire length, the canyon preserves an average width of about 200 yards, sometimes much wider and again narrower. The stream, meandering from side to side, and frequently interrupted by beaver-dams, cuts a deep channel in the friable earth, which characterizes all the valley-lands of this region. The banks upon either one side or the other are perpendicular, so that it was an extremely troublesome matter to cross. Added to the difficulties of getting in and out of the stream was the thick-matted jungle of undergrowth, tall, reedy grass, willows, and thorny bushes, all interlaced and entwined by rough and wiry grapevines. The current is sluggish, and the water tinged with milky translucency, gathered from the soil. The bottom is gravelly, but is covered by a depth of two or three feet with a very soft and miry mud. In every turn were deep pools gouged out, so that the streams seemed to be a succession of them; rifles or bars of sandy gravel intervening, through which the water oozed rather than flowed."

At the upper end of the canyon Jackson's party struck at last an old Indian trail, over which Indians with their horses and goats had just passed. Here and there along the banks they could make out traces of decayed habitations, largely reduced to heaps of debris. More vestiges of former occupation were visible on promontories some fifty feet above the stream. Aside from foundations, no masonry was left, though quantities of broken pottery were strewn around. They found nothing of much significance before shadows lengthened and camp had to be pitched. Where were the rumored prehistoric houses suspended in crevices hundreds of feet above? Had their guide misled them? Gnawing doubts beset the men by the campfire. Did cliff dwellings really exist?

Just as the sun was setting, someone challenged the guide to produce a ruin. The man responded with a hasty movement of his arm pointing toward the radiant top of the mesa. Probably luck rather than knowledge had swung his arm in the right direction. In any case, one of the men thereupon insisted that he could clearly distinguish a two-storied house far up the face of the perpendicular cliff. Though darkness threatened to overtake them, all the men set out at once.

Jackson and his companion Ernest Ingersoll, a correspondent for the *New York Tribune,* and their group thus became the first white men to visit an ancient canyon building. They poked about, and went back next morning to sketch and photograph. Jackson named the place Cliff

House. "The entire construction of this little human eyrie," he remarked, "displayed wonderful perseverance, ingenuity, and some taste."

Upon the party's return to Washington, Professor Hayden took just one glance at the half-dozen photographs Jackson had taken of Cliff House and immediately made up his mind that Jackson should go back, take more pictures, and explore further. The Hayden Survey, hitherto mainly dedicated to the geology and mineralogy of the western and southwestern territories, now added archaeological exploration to its pursuits.

Cliff ruins, drawn by W. H. Jackson

In 1875, and during two more consecutive seasons, Jackson returned to the Southwest and ventured into more forlorn valleys and gorges. At the same time, the Hayden Survey was put under the direction of William H. Holmes, an artist and geologist whose encounter with Southwestern ruins was to make him in years to come one of the country's leading authorities on pre-Columbian America. Holmes tracked down more ruins in the Mancos Canyon, while Jackson went on to scan the defiles of the McElmo, Hovenweep, Montezuma, and Chaco canyons. Between seasons Jackson was busy producing clay models of cliff houses for the Centennial Exposition to be held at Philadelphia. These, in combination with photographic displays, were one of that fair's chief attractions. They drew, as Jackson recalled in his autobiography *Time Exposure*, "almost as many visitors as Dr. Alexander Graham Bell's improbable telephone, and, had a Gallup Poll existed at the time, I am confident that nine persons out of ten would have voted my models the better chance of enduring."

CLIFF DWELLINGS OF THE SOUTHWEST

William Henry Jackson

The other outstanding event of 1874 . . . was the trip to Mesa Verde.

Stopping for few pictures, we covered eighty miles in less than three days, and on August 27 we stood at the head of the Rio Grande opposite Cunningham Pass. Beyond it, and below, was Baker's Park, our next scheduled field.

On our way up the Rio Grande we caught up with three miners driving burros. One of them turned out to be an old friend from Omaha, E. H. Cooper, whom I had known in 1868. We all camped together that night, and when Cooper learned the business that had brought me to his corner of Colorado he suggested that we might wish to visit the cliff ruins not so far from their placer workings on La Plata River. He himself had not seen them; but the big boss was familiar with their exact location and would undoubtedly give us full directions.

Although we had not planned to go beyond Baker's Park, the ruins sounded so exciting that I decided to strike there directly. Numerous cliff dwellings, remnants of a civilization that had died long before the first Spaniards arrived, had already been found in the Southwest; but the ones Cooper described promised to be quite the most magnificent find of all. Even the name of the place was exciting—Mesa Verde, the green tableland.

At the mining camp Cooper introduced us to a slight, bearded man with shoulder-length hair. He was John Moss, chief owner and operating head of the claim, and according to Cooper, "hy-as-ty-ee and high muck-a-muck of the whole La Plata region." Whatever that may have meant, John Moss was affable; and soon he expressed not only a willingness to give directions to the cliff dwellings but to show us the way himself.

On the way Moss interested me very much by his remarks on the Indian situation. The Southern Utes had not been well treated. The boundaries of their reservation had been altered and their best hunting grounds taken from them by prospectors. Promised compensation had not been made, and, in consequence, the Utes were ordering white men —surveyors in particular—to leave the reservation. So far no hostilities had been reported. But Moss was none too sanguine about the future. He himself had no fears; for he had made a private treaty with the re-

Reprinted by permission of G. P. Putnam's Sons from *Time Exposure: The Autobiography of William Henry Jackson* (pp. 228–35). Copyright © 1940 by William Henry Jackson.

gional chiefs. In exchange for some twenty-five square miles of La Plata land he had agreed to pay an annual rental in the form of horses, sheep, and a little cash. It was worth it, he said, to live secure in the friendship of his neighbors. And it was also just and intelligent. Much good blood might have been saved if John Moss's course had always been the rule.

It pleases me to point to another manifestation of John Moss's practical mind. Our host and guide was a candidate for some political office in the new and sparsely settled County of Rio Grande, and since residence requirements were on the sketchy side for this first election, it was an easy matter for my photographic party, including the boys, to help vote him into office. After our ballots had been cast Moss closed the polls, and we were off. That night, September 8, we spent at the ranch of a settler named Merritt in the Mancos Valley, who was associated with the miners in an agricultural experiment. His little log house, with immense stone fireplace, was then the only white man's dwelling west of the Animas River in the entire San Juan Basin.

Mancos Valley, drawn by W. H. Jackson

Late on September 9 we arrived within rifle shot of the ruins. As we were riding through the deepest part of Mancos Canyon with the Mesa Verde eight hundred feet above us, Moss suddenly pointed toward the top of the plateau and said, "There it is."

"I see it," was the instant answer of Steve, the packer; and in a moment all of us had managed to pick out something that looked like a house, with spots suggesting windows and a door, sandwiched between two strata of sandstone almost at the top. Abruptly all of us forgot the day's long ride. Only the top would do, and at once.

For the first 600 feet or so we had a stiff climb but not a difficult one. Then we found ourselves facing a flat, vertical wall rising some 200 feet above the ledge on which we were standing. Fifty feet above our heads, in a shallow cave, was a two-story house. But how to reach it?

At that point everybody but Ingersoll and me decided to leave all problems until morning. We two, however, were determined to look for the way up at once. And it was not wholly the zeal of the inexperienced which pushed us on. Ingersoll was a newspaper man, and I was a photographer. Even in those days men of our callings got their stories.

We made it, too. After Moss and the others had gone down we found an old dead tree which we propped up and used to reach some ancient handholds and footholds cut in the rock. Invisible in the twilight, they served our need, and up we went to the house. It was worth everything I possessed to stand there and to know that, with Ernest Ingersoll, I was surely the first white man who had ever looked down into the canyon from this dwelling in the cliff.

And now I want Ernest Ingersoll to take up the story. When we returned to Denver he sent the full account of our preliminary discoveries to his newspaper, and the *New York Tribune* thus was the first to publish, November 3, 1874, a description of the ruins which subsequent explorations established as the most remarkable in this country.

". . . We came down abundantly satisfied, and next morning carried up our photographic kit and got some superb negatives. There, seven hundred measured feet above the valley, perched on a little ledge only just large enough to hold it, was a two-story house made of finely cut sandstone, each block about 14 by 6 inches, accurately fitted and set in mortar now harder than the stone itself. The floor was the ledge upon which it rested, and the roof the overhanging rock. There were three rooms upon the ground floor, each one 6 by 9 feet, with partition walls of faced stone. Between the stories was originally a wood floor, traces of which still remained, as did also the cedar sticks set in the wall over the windows and door . . . Each of the stories was six feet in height, and all the rooms, upstairs and down, were nicely plastered and painted what now looks a dull brick-red color, with a white band along the floor like a base-board. There was a low doorway from the ledge into the lower story, and another above, showing that the upper chamber was entered from without. The windows were large, square apertures, with no indication of any glazing or shutters. They commanded a view of the whole valley for many miles. Near the house several convenient little niches in the rock were built into better shape, as though they had been used as cupboards or caches; and behind it a semi-circular wall inclosing the angle of the house and cliff formed a water-reservoir holding two and a half hogsheads . . .

Cliff House, drawn by W. H. Jackson

"Searching further in this vicinity we found remains of many houses on the same ledge, and some perfect ones above it quite inaccessible. The rocks also bore some inscriptions—unintelligible hieroglyphics for the most part . . . All these facts were carefully photographed and recorded.

"Leaving here we soon came upon traces of houses in the bottom of the valley in the greatest profusion, nearly all of which were entirely destroyed, and broken pottery everywhere abounded. The majority of the buildings were square, but many round, and one sort of ruin always showed two square buildings with very deep cellars under them and a round tower between them, seemingly for watch and defense . . . Another isolated ruin that attracted our attention particularly consisted of two perfectly circular walls of cut stone, one within the other. The diameter of the inner circle was twenty-two feet and of the outer thirty-three feet. The walls were thick and were perforated apparently by three equidistant doorways. Was this a temple?

". . . A little cave high up from the ground was found, which had been utilized as a homestead by being built full of low houses communicating with one another, some of which were intact and had been appropriated by wild animals. About these dwellings were more hieroglyphics scratched on the wall, and plenty of pottery, but no implements. Further on were similar but rather ruder structures on a rocky bluff, but so strongly were they put together that the tooth of time had found them hard gnawing; and in one instance, while that portion of the cliff upon which a certain house rested had cracked off and fallen away some distance without rolling, the house itself had remained solid and upright. Traces of the trails to many of these dwellings, and the steps cut in the rock, were still visible, and were useful indications of the proximity of buildings otherwise unnoticed.

"We were now getting fairly away from the mountains and approaching the great, sandy, alkaline plains of the San Juan River. Our Valley of the Mancos was gradually widening, but still on either side rose the perpendicular sides of the mesa, composed of horizontal strata of red and white sandstone . . . Imagine East River one thousand or twelve hundred feet deep, the piers and slips on both sides made of red sandstone and extending down to that depth, and yourself at the bottom, gazing up for human habitations far above you . . .

"Keeping close under the mesa on the western side—you never find houses on the eastern cliff of a canyon, where the morning sun, which they adored, could not strike them full with its first beams—one of us espied what he thought to be a house on the face of a particularly high and smooth portion of the precipice . . . Fired with the hope of finding some valuable relics, the Captain (Moss) and Bob started for the top . . . After a while an inarticulate sound floated down to us, and looking up we beheld the Captain, diminished to the size of a cricket . . . He had got where (as it appeared to us below) he could not retreat, and it seemed equally impossible to go ahead.

"There was a moment of suspense, then came a cry that stopped the beating of our hearts as we watched with bated breath a dark object, no larger than a cricket, whirling, spinning, dropping through the awful space. . . .

"The Captain had thrown down his boots.

"He was still there, crawling carefully along, clinging to the wall like a lizard, till finally a broader ledge was reached; and, having the nerve of an athlete, he got safely to the house. He found it perfect, almost semi-circular in shape, of the finest workmanship yet seen . . .

"Photographs and sketches completed, we pushed on, rode twenty miles or more, and camped just over the Utah line, two miles beyond Aztec Springs . . .

"Our next day's march was westerly . . . The road was an interesting one intellectually, but not at all physically—dry, hot, dusty, long and wearisome. We passed a number of quite perfect houses, perched high up on rocky bluffs, and many other remains . . ."

This was the end of our season's work. From the eastern edge of Utah we returned through Baker's Park to Denver, and by the beginning of November I was back in Washington.

Those discoveries of ours attracted considerable attention, of course. But no great official notice was taken for some years. In 1888 local ranchers, brothers named Wetherell, found extensive ruins in canyons that Ingersoll and I had not explored, and with report of new canyons rich in prehistoric dwellings interest was reawakened. But it was not until 1906 that Congress set aside Mesa Verde National Park—50,000 acres studded with the best preserved cliff dwellings to be found anywhere in the world.

31

On a chilly morning in December 1888, Richard Wetherill, eldest son of a Quaker family of ranchers who had recently settled in the Mancos Valley of southern Colorado, was pursuing stray cattle across a northern plateau of the Mesa Verde, accompanied by his cousin Charlie Mason. Their horses had to struggle through deep snow and gnarled coniferous underbrush. Snowflakes danced before their eyes, blotting out the view. Suddenly the trail through the white solitude ended, on a rocky promontory; they dismounted, and clear vision returned. Practically under their feet, a wide chasm opened. The two young men gasped. All at once, Richard cried out in excitement. Directly across the canyon, half a mile away on an enormous opening of the cliff face and crowding it up to its arched brim, was a jagged silhouette of storied houses and of round and square towers—by far the most impressive rock-bound city they had ever beheld.

"Cliff Palace," as Richard Wetherill named the ruins, greatly exceeded in size all the cave settlements sighted by Jackson and Holmes. It remains the largest known, containing some two hundred rooms and twenty-three *kivas* (the strange cylindrical chambers, first thought to be sweat baths, *estufas*, where the men gathered for religious observances). Built eighty feet deep and four hundred feet long into a natural niche at about seven hundred feet above the ground, it was accessible only by ropes and ladders. Its elaborate walled masonry appeared at first glance like an enchanted palace-fortress of a prehistoric lord of the mountains, but undoubtedly belonged to an extensive aboriginal village of farming people built over the years without any definite plan.

Interest in the lost cities of the Southwest, which had faltered since the days of the Hayden Survey, revived with the discovery of Cliff Palace. From then on the name of the Wetherill family was to be associated with the exploration of the region. Mainly due to the Wetherills' efforts, it was at last realized that the vaults of the countless canyons and gullies branching out from the San Juan, the Little Colorado, the Chaco, and other rivers harbored many more aboriginal structures of unexpected grandeur. The Mesa Verde alone, it has been estimated, contains at least five hundred cliff ruins, many never entered by white men, and probably others in forlorn meanders never even seen at all. (Several such structures were located by Earl H. Morris in the 1920's.) Richard Wetherill, on the day after the discovery of Cliff Palace, found the much better preserved "Spruce House," now one of the best known and most accessible of the ruins visited by tourists to Mesa Verde National Park. Everywhere in the Southwest hollows of precipitous cliffs are lined by stone dwellings of varied sizes. The majority are poised at dizzy heights. Those of the Mesa Verde came to be rivaled by Betatakin and Kitsiel in the Navajo Reservation (National Monument) of northern Arizona— the former discovered by Richard Wetherill, the latter by John Wetherill and Byron Cummings. In a class by itself is Montezuma's Castle, a compact over-sized cliff house of five stories, which rests on two limestone ledges above Beaver Creek.

Cliff Palace at once attracted a stream of visitors to the Four Corner region. The wonderland of canyons, desert, candelabra cacti, and petrified forests marked a new archaeological frontier, and the "lost race" of the Cliff Dwellers became as mysterious a presence among the antiquity-minded as the Mound Builders. Though the list is long of the early scholars who came to study the ruins and to probe the questions posed by them, it was Richard Wetherill himself, together with his four brothers and their cousin, who took the lead. Their aged father's Alamo Ranch became an open house for visitors and a center for the exchange of information. The Wetherills acted as a kind of archaeological task force in the Mesa Verde area, locating ruins, guiding the curious, and launching digs of their own. It seems that they owed to their good relations with Ute Indians some hints on remote cliff houses as well as safety of passage during their search.

Yet, it must be admitted, the Wetherills' road to Southwestern archaeology was as tortuous as the crags they had to climb to reach the eyries of prehistoric men. While they were undoubtedly possessed by curiosity and a love of adventure, and had the Quakers' innate reverence for the Indian, they soon learned the material value of cave relics, for which the ever-growing popularity of the Cliff Dwellers and the increasing tourist traffic created a ready market. They also realized a substantial profit from assembling collections of artifacts for several United States museums. Initially, their efforts were carried out at the expense of the sites from which the articles were taken. Some of the dwellings were so thoroughly ransacked that it is no longer possible to guess their

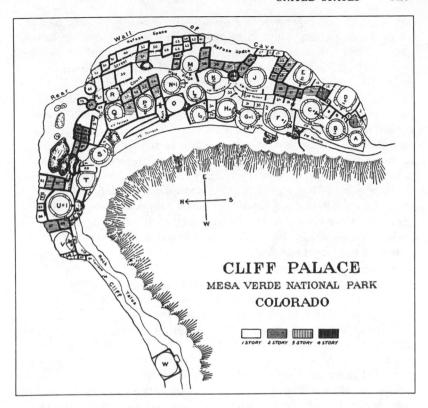

CLIFF PALACE
MESA VERDE NATIONAL PARK
COLORADO

1 STORY   2 STORY   3 STORY   4 STORY

layout or even trace the extent of a settlement. Even more deadly to
the unique remains, however, the demand for ancient ware brought a
good many other men to the scene, who readily used explosives and
caused more destruction than the Wetherills. Such practices were only
stopped when the Mesa Verde and other cliff zones were declared National Parks or Monuments at the beginning of the twentieth century.

To Richard Wetherill goes the credit for seeing beyond the immediate financial attractions of mere collecting. In time, he developed genuine archaeological interests. When the Swedish scientist Baron Gustav
E. A. Nordenskiöld came sightseeing in 1891, Richard persuaded him to
investigate and humbly submitted to the younger man's instructions. The
result was a pioneer work on Southwestern archaeology acknowledging
its debt to Richard, besides offering him an invaluable training course
in sound procedure. Later Richard participated in systematic excavations at the Pueblo Bonito ruins at Chaco Grande and led a number of
expeditions sponsored by the Hyde brothers of New York. During these

operations he laid down exacting methods of work which, as he pledged, "must stand the most rigid inspection . . . we do not want to do it in such a manner that anyone in the future can pick flaws in it."

In 1893 Richard ventured into the Grand Gulch of southern Utah, a territory containing some of the wildest scenery of the canyon and mesa land. It was this unassuming cowboy who, though not the first to explore there, added to the science of American antiquities another chapter in some respects more important than the actual discovery of cliff dwellings. First at Cottonwood Wash and then in the caves of other gullies, he found dried bodies buried several feet below the level of cliff-dweller habitation. These corpses, he noticed, were never accompanied by any traces of pottery, but had with them instead a profusion of baskets. As Wetherill quickly learned, there were neither bows and arrows nor stone axes in evidence anywhere. However, several of the dead had spear points lodged in their bones. Physically, the desiccated mummies were exceptional for their markedly long and narrow heads. To Wetherill they appeared to belong to a different race from the more broad-headed Cliff Dwellers. He tentatively referred to them as "Basket People," but left the honor of baptizing them to his sponsor, Talbot Hyde, who promptly called them "Basket Makers," a name that has stuck.

Richard Wetherill's recognition of a culture horizon in layers lower than those of the Cliff Dwellers and hence of greater age and apparently less development amounted to the first full application of the principle of stratification in Southwestern archaeology. In this he advanced far beyond Jefferson's interpretation of the superimposed strata of a Virginia burial mound. At one stroke Wetherill thus expanded the record of human occupation and introduced the concept of time and succession into what had been an impenetrable darkness of pre-history. Twenty years were to pass before Nels C. Nelson of New York's American Museum of Natural History applied stratigraphic techniques of excavation at the Galisteo Basin of New Mexico, soon to be followed by Alfred V. Kidder's epoch-making campaigns at Pecos which established a coherent framework of Southwestern archaeology. Meanwhile, however, Richard Wetherill's discoveries met with a great deal of skepticism. Kidder himself recalled that in his student days he was warned by a Harvard professor about the "invention" of the Basket Makers, which the professor described as nothing but a fraudulent attempt to raise "the sales value of Wetherill's collection." But when Kidder went out to dig in Arizona in 1914 he was startled to come across the same materials ascribed long ago by Wetherill to the "Basket Makers." Kidder became immediately converted: "Faith was restored and Basket Makers ceased to be a myth after 1914."

Richard Wetherill was a man of the outdoors, of little schooling and hence awkward with the pen. When he was prematurely felled by hostile Navajos in 1910 he was still in the painful process of educating himself. At some time in his future he had hoped "to do something in the way of putting my work in book form." It is on account of this reticence that the work of the Wetherill brothers has rarely received its due. Despite their profound influence, their contributions had to rely on more articulate contemporaries to gain a hearing. Among these interpreters was Dr. T. Mitchell Prudden, an eminent New York professor of medicine, who spent many summer vacations in the Southwest and became deeply attached to the Wetherill family. In an article written for *Harper's Magazine* in 1897 he gave the first printed account of the Basket Makers. This popular summary was written with the active assistance of Richard Wetherill, and for once gives him ample credit for his discoveries.

Theophil Mitchell Prudden (1849–1924) was a long-time member of the Rockefeller Institute who gained an international reputation in the fields of pathology and bacteriology, and pioneered in the use of serum to combat an epidemic of diphtheria in New York City. He also figures in his own right in the archaeology of the Southwestern United States. Repeated visits to the land of the Cliff Dwellers led him to write widely on antiquities and turned a hobby into another specialty. As a natural scientist familiar with geology, he made valuable studies of Western topography, besides furnishing maps of uncharted sections rich in ruined sites. The lean, gentle Eastern professor was revered by the natives as few other white men had been.

Prudden's own studies centered on the smaller surface dwellings of the Pueblos. From his examination of such structures, he established a "unit-type" of Pueblo building, and thereby came to lay, in the words of A. V. Kidder, "the foundation of all subsequent research on the developmental side of southwestern civilization." Earlier, in espousing the Basket Makers, Prudden subscribed to Richard Wetherill's view of an ancient people, racially quite distinct from the Cliff Dwellers who probably massacred them. The tendency today is to see in the Basket Makers—or rather in Basket Maker I–III—earlier stages of the desert culture, which, starting around 300 B.C., reaches (with Pueblo V) right into the present time. The broader skulls of the Cliff Dwellers, as against the earlier dolichocephalic Basket Makers, are held to be attributable in the main to the use of cradle boards which deformed the crana of infants. Though there may have been an occasional influx of other elements—be they migrants or marauders—the Southwest possessed from Basket Maker to Pueblo considerable racial and cultural unity. Anthropologists have given these people the overall name Anasazi, which means "Ancient." Richard Wetherill, quietly absorbed in the past of their ancestors, had been given the same name by his Indian companions.

BASKET MAKERS

T. Mitchell Prudden

The purpose of this paper relates to some recent discoveries in the hot wonderland which lies along the San Juan River and its northern tributaries, mostly in southeastern Utah. It relates to people whom the Spaniards never saw—for the very good reason that they had long been buried safe under the sand before the Old World folks knew how "the other half lived," or even that there was another half. Buried, too, they were in a region into which those intrepid and heroic explorers were never lured by God's service or the color of gold.

But all these red folks, like their surviving types in the pueblos, lived no doubt in sympathetic touch with the spirit of the earth and air and sky; and so, before unveiling the secret which the parched earth has kept so long, I should like to give to the reader a passing glimpse of their deserted land.

As you go over the Rocky Mountains towards the west from Colorado Springs or Pueblo or Trinidad, you come into a region of jumbled ranges interspersed with mountain parks. The Colorado River, sweeping southwestward, has sculptured the wonderful valleys and sublime gorges known as the Grand Cañon. From the east the San Juan River, rising in the San Juan Mountains, and receiving from the north several tributaries, now mostly dry, joins the Colorado in southern Utah. North of the San Juan River, and between its namesake mountains on the east and the Colorado River on the west, lies a triangular region about as large as Massachusetts, Rhode Island, and Connecticut together, and called the Northern San Juan Plateau Country. A few small peaks rise here and there above the plateau, while everywhere great cañons, wild and forbidding, or broad valleys with terraced sides, and lofty buttes or mesas rising gigantic from the bottoms, relieve the general level. The plateau region south of the San Juan River is the home of the Navajos.

There are two or three small villages along the upper reaches of the San Juan River. But for the most part the broad valley, bordered by imposing bluffs, is in summer a hot, bare, stifling stretch of desert, with the sullen, muddy stream sweeping silently through it. Only toward the end the river enters a profound chasm, and roars its way to the Colorado. But one town, Bluff City by name, with some two or three hundred of

From "An Elder Brother to the Cliff-Dweller," *Harper's Monthly*, XCV, No. 565 (June 1897), pp. 56–63 *passim*.

the Chosen, a solitary outpost and oasis of Mormondom, exists, and even thrives in a half-hearted way, as thrift goes in a desert, in the southeastern corner of Utah. This town, ninety miles from the railroad, is the metropolis of the San Juan Valley. A swiftly subsiding gold craze brought many adventurers to the valley a few years ago. But now only a few placer miners are left, struggling here and there against odds, far down the stream, picturesque and pathetic beside their rough sluices and quaint water-wheels.

It is from Bluff that you most conveniently enter the country of which I write, and you see no fixed human habitation, and probably no white man, until you get back, brown, tired, and dusty, to Bluff again. The nearest railroad is at Mancos, in Colorado, and here at the Wetherills' Alamo Ranch one can obtain an outfit and most competent guides, hardy, bright sons of the household, and wise in the lore of the hills, for the rough trip by way of Bluff to the plateau of the northern San Juan district. Access from Bluff to the plateau is mostly by dim and devious Indian trails, which meander along the rough bottoms of the cañons, or clamber toilsomely to the uplands, over whose bare or pine-clad surfaces they stretch tortuously away. Water is scanty at the best, its situation known only to a few, and in dry seasons long and trying marches must often be made to reach the hidden and meagre pools and springs. . . .

The great cañons and their tributary gorges, which have been carved out of the plateau in the past, thousands of feet deep in places, by wind and sand and rain and mighty rivers, are now almost wholly dry, save when a cloud-burst or a storm on the far mountains sends a mad torrent roaring down. But this soon passes, and in a few hours the horseman may be struggling along the parched bottom faint from thirst. . . .

This great desolate plateau, so inaccessible and so far from the usual routes of travel, is rarely visited save by cattle-herders, and is inhabited only by a few renegade Utes, who in summer live in wickieups built of boughs, and cultivate the few moist bottoms in the valleys. Even the best government maps are very faulty, and practically useless for the location of water.

One of the great cañons, about fifty miles long, and in places two thousand feet deep, with sheer cliffs overhanging the narrow winding bottom, and unnamed upon the map, is known to the herders as Grand Gulch. It harbors scores of large and imposing cliff ruins. But for the most part the ruined houses of the Cliff-Dwellers in this region are small and widely scattered. Some are built in shallow caves far up the cliffs; some are under the overhanging rock near the bottom.

Exploration of these ruins and their adjacent graves show that these

Cliff-Dwellers were the same sort of folk as those who once inhabited the Mesa Verde in southwestern Colorado, and the vast region stretching southward from the valley of the San Juan. The stone weapons, pottery, fabrics, etc., are similar, as are the skulls, which are short and flattened behind.

Richard Wetherill and his brothers, of Mancos, Colorado, have made many and fruitful explorations of the cliff dwellings in this region. Part of their collections are now at the American Museum of Natural History in New York, some are in Denver, some in Philadelphia, some are in their possession at Mancos, and some are in private hands elsewhere. Several persons from Bluff have gathered valuable material from these cliff ruins, part of which is in Salt Lake City, part dispersed without record.

But I must hasten to my purpose and speak of a remarkable discovery made by the Wetherills in their work among the cliff ruins, and in the caves of the cañon walls in the northern San Juan country, which has not, so far as I am aware, been yet recorded. . . . Here, much to their surprise, they came upon another set of graves of entirely different construction, and containing relics of what appear to be a different group of people.

These older graves are in the floors of shallow caves. They are egg-shaped holes, in the earth or sand, either stoned at the side, or lined with clay plastered directly upon the sand. The mummies of men, women, and children are found, often two bodies in one grave.

Sandals woven of yucca fibre upon the feet, a breech-cloth of woven cedar bark, strings of rough beads around the neck, about the body a rudely constructed blanket of rabbit fur, enveloped in a yucca cloth, over the head a small flat basket, and a great finely woven basket over all—such was their burial fashion.

The graves never contain pottery, as those of the Cliff-Dwellers are so apt to do, and the skulls of the people are narrow and long, and never flattened at the back. Bone implements, stone spear-heads and arrow-heads, twisted cords of human hair, well-formed cylindrical stone pipes, and baskets filled with seeds and ornaments are found with the bodies.

Spear-points between the ribs, stone arrow-heads in the backbone, a great obsidian spear driven through the hips, crushed skulls and severed limbs—these secrets of the old graves show clearly enough that there were rough times in the cañons now and then, and that these old fellows were proficient in the barbaric art of killing men—the art towards which some of our wind-and-paper patriots would fain have us climb back.

Over these graves the rubbish heaps of the Cliff-Dwellers have in places accumulated to a depth of two feet, showing a long residence

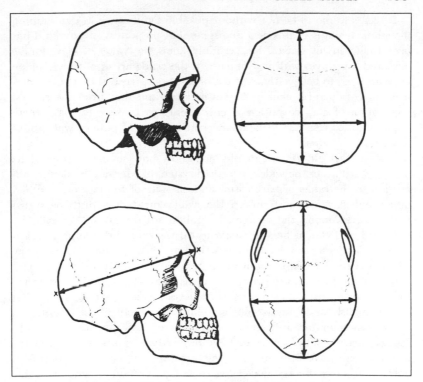

Broad Pueblo and narrower Basket Maker skulls

above the graveyards, of whose existence they may well have been unconscious. In many places great rocks have fallen upon the graves. . . .

There is no evidence that the Basket-Makers ever built in these caves.
While their graves are often found under the cliff dwellings, they also
occur in caves in which the Cliff Men had no houses, and with the earth
level and hard above them. The skull has great significance in the lore
which anthropology gleans here and there the world over out of forgotten graves, and the difference in the form of the skull between the Cliff-
Dwellers and the Basket-Makers would seem—I speak with the reserve
which becomes a poacher upon anthropological preserves—to exclude
their identity.

One need be a student only of the human nature of to-day to conclude that the newly found people were not mere intruders upon the
domain of the Cliff-Dwellers, vanquished and hurriedly buried; for the
solicitous care with which the bodies are furnished for their journey into
"the country which is out of sight" forbids the notion.

It seems to me to be not without possible significance in determining the ethnical status of this new aborigine that no pottery of any kind has been found in his graves. He certainly knew the value of clay, for he plastered his graves with it. Students in the crude art of pottery-making have been led to believe that the use of clay was preceded by the acquirement of considerable skill in basket-making, and that from the earliest application of clay coverings or clay linings to baskets, to make them impervious, or resistant to heat, the manufacture of pottery was gradually evolved.

Now if this old American did not know how to make pottery, he must, according to the widely accepted system of Morgan, be denied admission to the ranks of barbarism, and, in spite of the fact that he had discovered clay and just missed the achievement of a dish, be thrust sternly back among the savages. He might still be saved, however, by the creed of Tylor, if he knew how to till the soil; and though no agricultural implements were buried with him, as they often are with the Cliff-Dwellers, he was thoughtful enough to stow away in his excellent baskets some corn and seeds. So, as far as I can see, while he is damned to savagery by the American doctrine, he is saved to barbarism by that of the Englishman. May we not give him the benefit of the doubt? . . .

The whole matter at present rests just here, until the various furnishings of their burial-places shall have received systematic study, and the country shall have been more widely explored. But one may hazard a guess that these Basket-Makers were nomadic Indians who used the sheltered caves as burial-places before the Cliff-Dwellers settled the country and utilized the rocky shelters for their homes. There must in the old days have been many a fierce encounter up and down the rugged faces of the rocks when the Cliff Men met their foes with stone-tipped arrow, axe, and spear—perhaps over the very spot where the elder folk, now still and crumbling in their unsuspected graves, had fought and lost.

To one who has travelled much in this southwest plateau country, and knows not only just how dry it is, but also just how dry it is not, the residence of these early peoples in small scattered communities along the now remote cañons and valleys is neither surprising nor mysterious. Here were warmth and shelter the year round, and for those who had learned to build were houses half made already by the cave walls of the cliffs.

It does not require very much food for bare subsistence, and a very small patch of corn suffices for a family. While springs and pools are rare, there are a good many places, in valleys apparently dry the summer through, in which the seepage from the back country comes down some sag in the hills and furnishes moisture enough for a crop of corn. The beds of dry streams also, where sand is plenty, are often moist beneath the surface.

In fact, here and there all over the Cliff-Dwellers' country to-day, in stream-beds, mostly dry, or in low places in the bottoms, with no water visible, one comes across groups of Navajos or Utes, camped beside little green patches of corn which seems to be growing out of the driest of sand banks. It is easier for the corn roots than it is for the humans to get enough drinking-water, and the Indians are very clever to-day, as the older fellows doubtless were, in finding the few places here and there in which the deep moisture suffices for a modest crop of corn.

It has been the writer's good fortune, half on knowledge, half on pleasure bent, to journey over this desolate country under the skillful guidance of Al. Wetherill, to delve among the ruins of the cliff dwellings, to search through the opened graves of the Basket-Makers, and so to gain a conception at first hand of the land they lived in, the old folks, and their graves. And it is with Richard Wetherill's permission that I record this interesting discovery of the Basket-Makers which he and his brothers made some time ago. I am eager to do this because the enthusiasm, devotion, and practical knowledge which he has brought to his life work in the cause of American archaeology should find more general appreciation, and in the hope that means may be forth-coming from some quarter for the pursuit, under Wetherill's direction, of this promising research.

Will none of our great universities realize before it is too late that the treasure-house of folk-lore among the Pueblo Indians is crumbling fast, and that these fields of American archaeology in the Southwest are wide and fruitful?

If you have seen the living Indian from his better side, which too often is the side away from the white man, have learned to admire the qualities which so well fit him for his life in the open, and have come to realize—not mayhap without a tinge of wistfulness—how close he stands in every act and purpose and sentiment to the powers above and to the presences about him, you may come to have an esteem, and even a certain dreamy affection, for the silent Cliff-Dweller, so abounding that it shall include, bloody old warrior though he was, this new-found elder brother also.

32

The persistent question "How Old?"—no matter how exasperating—has been an effective challenge to archaeologists. In the absence of written documents, which could provide a chronology for defunct civilizations, it was long deemed nearly hopeless to date prehistoric artifacts in the Americas. History, as it has usually been understood, began in the Western Hemisphere only with the landfall of Columbus. Everything before 1492, since it was believed outside the realm of documentary proof, belonged to eons of obscurity which could be breached by little but conjectures and rough estimates. Though it was recognized that the Mayas had left precise date inscriptions, their calendrical system, and even more the correspondence of such time markings with Old World counts, remained open to debate.

Pre-Columbia continued to be equated with the twilight zone of prehistory. Hence the wild guesses about the American past. Hence the allegations by serious students of the stupendous age of the Tiahuanaco ruins; hence Cummings's excessive claims for the great antiquity of the lava-buried Cuicuilco temple pyramid. The mounds of the American Woodlands were ascribed to a remote era when another mighty non-Indian race of high cultural attainment strode the plains. Notions about the Cliff Dwellers of the Southwest were almost as vague. No one was quite sure how far they were removed from the builders of the great pueblos on the tablelands and their still surviving descendants in the Hopi and Zuñi towns. Were they older or more recent than the Pueblos —or contemporaneous and identical?

And what about the Basket Makers? At least one had here a soupçon of a sequence. Basket Maker implements were invariably deposited in layers lower than those of the Cliff Dwellers, and for this reason had to be of greater antiquity. But such information could at best yield an age relation between the two cultures. Absolute dates were missing. Likewise, the sophisticated method of charting changes of style in local pottery and assigning them to successive periods yielded only a relational time scale. Even when the stratigraphic survey was pushed from a colonial and datable Indian settlement into its pre-Conquest subsoil, as A. V. Kidder did at Pecos, the time spans computed were hypothetical.

Design on a Mesa Verde bowl

Archaeologists might well have despaired of the problem, had it not been for studies begun in the early 1900's by an astronomer in the American Southwest. Though originally lacking any connection with the exploration of the human past, these researches led to an unexpected method of reading time in nature's own annals. Years before the discovery of the carbon-14 disintegration rate in organic matter, and with far greater exactitude, it became possible to date ruins of the Southwest which had been abandoned before the arrival of the Spaniards. At length the Gregorian calendar could be extended backward for hundreds of years to the North American contemporaries of Richard Lionheart, Charlemagne, and Julius Caesar. As a consequence, every major phase of Southwestern culture history can now be charted in terms of the Christian time count.

The very development of the new dating method was closely tied to the physical conditions of the Southwest, where it was invented and where it proved most fruitful.

Andrew Ellicott Douglass (1867–1962), a Harvard-trained astronomer who was for many years director of the Steward Observatory at the University of Arizona, had taken up the study of periodic phenomena connected with solar radiation. In particular, it was his aim to show that there existed a definite relationship between sunspot cycles and the annual growth of tree rings. This assumption, he thought, was warranted by the influence of the sun on rates of rainfall—the latter being the single most important factor in the varying width of tree rings in the arid Southwest. Series of tree rings were to supply him with an accurate chart of solar and pluvial performance through the years.

In order to examine older tree specimens and thereby extend the meteorological record, Douglass looked to archaeologists to supply him with wooden beams from Pueblo ruins. It was at this stage that the American Museum of Natural History and Earl H. Morris entered the picture with pieces of timber collected in the Southwest, in the main from Aztec Ruin and pueblos in northwestern New Mexico. Unwittingly, archaeology, an occasional aide to Douglass's researches, would soon become their principal beneficiary.

Douglass realized that growth was recorded similarly by the great majority of trees in a given area. Characteristic ring patterns resembling each other from tree to tree stood for a specific set of years with their changing incidence of moisture. Ring systems, never repeated in at least 1,200 years, could be associated not only with climatological changes but with definite sequences of years.

However, the full implications to archaeology of "crossdating" wooden pieces and constructing from them a continuous series so that the ruins from which the samples had been taken could be dated took some time to trace. Douglass's own primary interests, after all, lay in solar cycles and the enormous task involved in refining the analysis of tree rings for climatological observations. In addition, there was a gap between the colonial record and the "floating" sequence compounded by Douglass from trees that had been felled in "pre-history." Nevertheless, upon prodding from Dr. Clark Wissler of the American Museum of Natural History, Douglass could prove that the Aztec Ruin (New Mexico) had been built more than twenty years later than Pueblo Bonito, just as both Pueblo centers of the Chaco Grande antedated most of the Cliff Dwellings of the Mesa Verde. These were notable steps up what Douglass later called "a ladder into the past."

Douglass had been able to furnish a complete series of tree rings from the sequoias of the California Sierras, which eventually extended from the present backward for more than 3,000 years (to 1305 B.C.). He could not, however, correlate the California growth patterns with those of the trees of the Southwest. All the same, a method of giving the actual age of a prehistoric ruin was close at hand. The ultimate incentive came from Neil M. Judd, an archaeologist active since 1920 at the Chaco Canyon on behalf of the National Geographic Society.

Judd was engaged in the renewed exploration and partial restoration of Pueblo Bonito, in the excavation of which Richard Wetherill had participated twenty years earlier as a member of the Hyde Expedition. Pueblo Bonito was and remains one of the best-known and biggest of the Pueblo community settlements, a giant D-shaped complex of some 1,600 rooms, far more extensive than any Cliff Dwellings and in fact the largest "apartment house" in the United States until a building project in New York City exceeded it in the late nineteenth century. Logs from Pueblo Bonito, shipped by the Hyde party to the American Museum of Natural History, had already been examined by Douglass.

In December 1922, Neil Judd was at the Carnegie Institution in Washington, D.C., attending a lecture by Douglass on cyclical phenomena. This happened to be his first opportunity to familiarize himself with the analysis of tree rings for the purpose of determining sun-spot influence. When Douglass mentioned as a seemingly minor side effect of his investigations the possibility of giving comparative ages to Southwestern ruins, Judd was instantly seized by a vision of a "succession of annual growth rings leading from living forests back across the broken walls of seventeenth century missions to ruins which surviving Pueblo clans claimed as their ancestral homes." Could it, by chance, be extended to the charred logs of Pueblo Bonito? At this point, Judd confessed, "the very idea of dating prehistoric ruins from their old ceiling beams seemed altogether fantastic."

Judd immediately sought the support of Douglass. He then mobilized the Research Committee of the National Geographic Society. Subsequently, three successive beam-collecting expeditions were launched with the sole objective of computing the age of Pueblo Bonito. That quest was brought to a successful conclusion only in 1929; into it are woven pieces of purple velvet and precious turquoise, protracted conferences with Indian chiefs, and burned ruins covered by drifting sand. Archaeology itself made a vital contribution by guiding the search for used logs to ruins with pottery of an intermediary age for which the tree-ring record had hitherto been missing.

With an absolute date for Pueblo Bonito, and some forty other ruins of the Southwest, came a new science, baptized by Douglass *dendrochronology*, from the Greek words for "tree" and the "counting of time." Douglass became its principal formulator and developer (though it should be mentioned that the method had been vaguely anticipated by Charles Babbage, a British mathematician, in 1838). For many years thereafter, tree-ring profiles were personally checked by him. In time, dendrochronological laboratories were set up at the University of Arizona, the University of New Mexico, Gila Pueblo, and elsewhere. The first course in the new science was given by Douglass at the University of Arizona in 1930.

Tree-ring research has continued at an increased pace since 1934, and has been regularly reported in the *Tree Ring Bulletin*. Several hundred ruins have now been properly dated. While the record stood in 1929 at A.D. 700, it has gradually been extended to 59 B.C., thus making it possible to date even Basket Maker sites.

Dendrochronology has, however, yielded much more than bare dates. From the dates one can deduce a surprising array of details pertaining to stages of construction of a ruin as well as its temporary or permanent abandonment. Influences, development of styles, migrations, settlements, can be made explicit and help to put Pueblo culture into an authentic historical perspective. One all-important detail, a long and catastrophic drought in the second half of the thirteenth century (1276–99), at last was as clearly marked as the Black Death in medieval Europe. There it was, indelibly registered in the chronicle of tree rings. The drought is probably linked to one of the major upheavals of the Four Corner region: the wholesale abandonment of dwellings and the exodus of their inhabitants to other parts of the Southwest. Truly, the "talkative tree rings" had blurted out their secrets.

Though most successful in the Southwest, dendrochronology has also been attempted elsewhere. In the United States much work was carried out in the various mound-building areas, but with rather disappointing results. From 1946 on, Edward Schulman has been devising an independent tree-ring chronology for northeastern Utah, which has been traced to A.D. 397. Comparable work is in progress in the Colorado basin. Equally encouraging were the researches of the late J. Louis Giddings among Eskimo ruins in Alaska. It is of considerable interest that in those subarctic zones temperature rather than rainfall appears to be the principal determinant in the width and pattern of tree rings. Some success with tree-ring analysis has also been reported from Scandinavia and from Turkey, where it was introduced by an American archaeologist, Bryant Bannister, trained in the Southwest. Conceivably other areas, perhaps the undated desert cultures of coastal Peru, might one day prove a rewarding field for dendrochronology.

DATING PUEBLO BONITO

A. E. Douglass

Our study . . . began . . . in an attempt to solve certain astronomical problems related to solar changes and their indirect effects on tree growth. . . . Ancient roof logs, like recently felled pines [foremost the ponderosa

---

From *Dating Pueblo Bonito and Other Ruins of the Southwest.* Courtesy National Geographic Society, Washington, D.C. (Contributed Technical Papers, Pueblo Bonito Series, No. 1, 1935, pp. 7-38 *passim*). See also *Material Culture of Pueblo Bonito; Pueblo del Arroyo, Chaco Canyon, N.M.;* and *Architecture of Pueblo Bonito.* Neil M. Judd, Smithsonian Institution Miscellaneous Collections.

or Arizona (western yellow)], contain a definite and precise succession of annual growth rings any one of which may be nearly identical throughout the Pueblo area and yet given groups of which have not been duplicated closely in a millennium. On examining an old beam the first question is: Do its annual rings include any sequence found also in living trees or in those felled in a known year? Our record of these modern trees reaches back 500 years. If we find in that record the particular sequence sought, our problem is solved at once. We merely count from the latest dated ring back to the group and so ascertain the age of the latter. But rarely do we discover in Pueblo ruins beams so recent in point of time. How then can we extend our known succession of rings back to reach the unknown? The answer is simple: Go to houses that were built two or three centuries ago and seek logs cut at that time. The outer parts of such logs will match the inner parts of our modern 500-year-old trees and the inner rings of the old logs will extend our chronology of known rings farther back into the untrodden and unmeasured past. Logs from still older ruins will carry the line even farther back. Somewhere in this sequence of annual growth rings, if extended far enough, we may expect to find a group of successive rings exactly duplicating a given series taken from almost any prehistoric beam. Thus we date the ruins and at the same time develop a tree-ring calendar extending centuries into the past, a calendar that enables us quickly to learn the age of other ruins that fall within its range. . . .

In 1914 . . . Dr. Clark Wissler of the American Museum of Natural History, New York, offered me specimens of prehistoric wood for general examination. The offer was accepted and in the early part of 1916 a group of seven large sections was received, collected at Dr. Wissler's request in northwestern New Mexico. These specimens gave the first practical part of tree-ring technique: namely, the size and form of specimens and kind of wood. In February 1919, six beam sections recovered by Earl H. Morris during excavations at Aztec were secured and their rings quickly crossdated. In this group a second item of technique was developed: namely, the use of a hypothetical or "floating" chronology, a measure that has become a necessary part of all dating by tree rings. This was the "Relative Dating" (RD), based on a certain large and distinctive annual growth ring which appeared in each of the prehistoric beam sections then in hand. To this outstanding ring I gave the purely hypothetical date "500"; its actual age was not determined until June 1929. The ring before it was called RD 499; the one before that was RD 498, and so on to cover all rings whose definite relation to RD 500 was known. Such a series of numbers served to express the time relation between different ruins, or different parts of a single ruin, whether known in

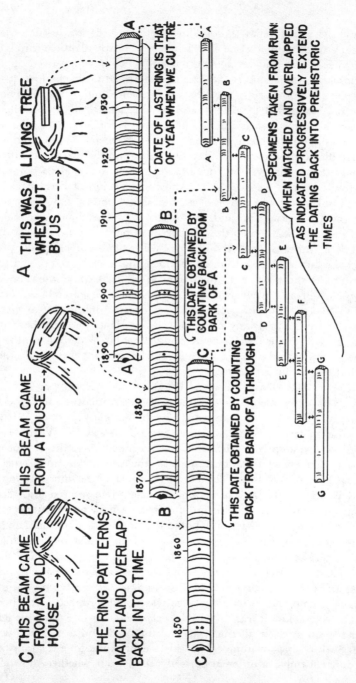

A schematic sketch of the construction of a continuous chronology from "overlapping" wooden specimens

terms of our own calendar or not. Such an assumed date is like "x" in algebra; it is a quantity that, itself unknown, can be built into all our equations of relative age and so used until the final solution comes. . . .

In 1911 the similarity of ring sequences in northern Arizona conifers was noted; it became possible to assign definite dates to individual rings in trees felled a known year. This led at once to realization that the dating of ring groups by their own characters, and quite independently of the time when the tree was cut (first accomplished experimentally in 1904), was a process that could be applied generally over considerable areas. Lumber camps near Flagstaff provided an abundance of material for examination.

In 1915 I obtained my first long sequences of the giant sequoia (*Sequoia gigantea*); three years later their annual growth rings had been counted back to 1300 B.C. Upon securing a definite ring chronology from Aztec Ruin in 1919, I made every effort to find a correspondence between Aztec and the well-dated sequoias, but without success. In spite of this, attempts were made for years to match the Arizona tree records into the long-lived sequoias.

The actual technique of Pueblo dating that later proved successful was first definitely formulated in 1919 . . . but its successful application appeared hopeless on account of the seeming impossibility of getting such great numbers of timbers. . . . [In 1920, the] American Museum supplied the needed link. They sent me nine sections cut from logs obtained in Pueblo Bonito by the Hyde Expedition of 1896–1899. These were promptly crossdated with each other and identified in terms of Aztec log rings. . . . The construction at Aztec was thus proved to have been 40 to 50 years after that at Pueblo Bonito. This agreed exactly with the fainter archeological evidence of the relative age of these two ruins and gave a precision never before dreamed of.

But it did more than that, for it opened the door to a tree-ring calendar of indefinite extent and appealed especially to Mr. Neil M. Judd who was just starting work at Pueblo Bonito for the National Geographic Society and who knew far better than I the marvelous resources in ancient timber possessed by many ruins of the Pueblo area. . . .

[There] developed in Mr. Judd's mind a definite vision of a major dating process that might lead to the actual age of Pueblo Bonito. He believed it possible to obtain a sequence of beam sections from successively older Pueblo villages, beginning with timbers salvaged by the Hopi when they destroyed the Spanish missions in 1680 and which he had seen still in use at Oraibi in 1920. Mr. Judd's conviction took form on hearing evidence I presented at the First Conference on Cycles, in Washington, December 8, 1922. He formulated a plan of procedure, won the approval of the Research Committee . . . , and thus brought about The Society's three beam expeditions. . . .

With confidence in the possibility of dating old ruins the first need was obviously a large number of sections and borings from many places in the Pueblo area. These would show us, it was hoped, where intensive work must be expended to build a complete tree-ring calendar from the present time back to the period of Pueblo Bonito. The Society's first beam expedition set out from Flagstaff in June 1923, under the joint leadership of Mr. J. A. Jeançon of Denver and Dr. O. G. Ricketson, now of the Carnegie Institution of Washington. I accompanied them for the first ten days, during their visit to the Hopi villages, going first to Oraibi which was partly in ruins. . . . In this way I could communicate to them the limited experience already gained in collecting suitable material. . . .

The expedition next went north to the Black Mesa without much result; then east to Chinle where samples were collected that subsequently played a principal part in building a late prehistoric chronology known as Citadel Dating. The expedition visited Zuni, Chaco Canyon, and several pueblos of the Rio Grande Valley, in New Mexico; the Mesa Verde and other districts in southern Colorado. A section from Chinle, Arizona, later gave the first date to White House ruin and the Mesa Verde pieces lengthened my late prehistoric ring sequence. Additional borings obtained in Chaco Canyon placed Kinbiniyol among the several related ruins of Pueblo Bonito age. . . .

An even hundred beam specimens were collected. In this, as in other ways, success was largely due to the tactful approach of Mr. Jeançon, who had lived for a time in the Tewa village of Santa Clara in the Rio Grande Valley, and to the knowledge of southwestern travel previously gained by Dr. Ricketson. One of their most interesting experiences was the conference at Walpi for the purpose of gaining permission to make borings in kiva logs, thus referred to by Mr. Jeançon:

"At Walpi we had a council with the two kiva chiefs who appeared the most interested of all the men with whom we had to deal. I promised them that I would make the necessary medicine to protect them fully against any evil influences that might attempt to injure them. In accordance with this, when we had finished the boring in the beam in the Moen Kiva, I broke up some turquoise and placed it on the end of the plug and after saying some Tewa prayers, I inserted the plug, and they were perfectly satisfied."

At this same conference I promised one of the priests to let him know the age of the log and when his ancestors had cut it, little thinking it would be years before I could fulfill that promise. It was, however, finally done in 1928. The timber was felled near 1500 A.D. and was one of the largest we encountered that unquestionably dated from before arrival of the Spaniards. It gave a superb series of rings back to 1297. In 1929 we were sorry to learn that this rare old beam had been used for firewood, having been replaced by new spruce logs presented to the Indians by the Government. Many another old log, with its wonderful hidden story, perished at that time.

While it was impossible to complete the necessary microscopic work on these hundred specimens for several years, there was a very important, related study which I pursued intermittently as opportunity offered. This was a comparison of living trees over the Pueblo area. We well knew that building a chronology of such length as that visioned would depend on complete success in a wide-spread crossdating. At that time we had found satisfactory resemblance between the pines of Flagstaff and those near Prescott on the west, Grand Canyon on the north, Pine and Cibecue on the south, Aztec and Basin Mountain 250 miles to the northeast. Ancient Aztec had been joined to Pueblo Bonito and other Chaco ruins, but the natural question arose: how generally over the whole area will crossdating be found feasible? If it should not prove possible, then we must proceed cautiously before incurring added expense. The answer to our question could easily be ascertained by further comparisons between modern trees.

The result of these tests was very reassuring. We found the entire Pueblo area bound together in a similarity that was astonishing. . . .

Direct attack on the dating problem was resumed in the spring of 1927. In April, Wupatki rings in the Flagstaff area were identified as late in the main Pueblo Bonito calendar. Then followed the placing of Kinbiniyol and Solomon ruins (northwestern New Mexico) slightly after the main construction time of Pueblo Bonito. It was found also that White House ruin, in Canyon de Chelly, was built in Bonito times.

The seven months ending with January 1928 were occupied with a typical experience in the solution of our general problem that deserves mention. It was the construction of a major section of the tree-ring chronology and its insertion in the general calendar. It resembled a picture puzzle. The picture is not always assembled in steady succession from the first piece to the last. Sometimes a large part is put together on the side and inserted as a whole, filling up some major vacant space. And that is exactly what happened when I added my Citadel Dating sequence to our tree-ring calendar.

There were on hand in the summer of 1927 a hundred Beam Expedition specimens and, in addition, a hundred or so from Wupatki. The Wupatki beams curiously divided themselves into two groups, giving two separate chronologies, which I mentally referred to as the "large beam" sequence and the "small beam" sequence. The former was joined to our Pueblo Bonito series in April 1927. Then the small beam sequence, not to be outdone, reached out to encompass such readings as we had acquired at Citadel Ruin (10 miles north of Wupatki) and Fewkes' Ruin J (two miles beyond).

But the Wupatki small beam sequence did not stop here. It took to itself three beautiful sections from the Tower in Mummy Cave, northeastern Arizona; then added eight or ten similar sections from Mesa Verde, in southwestern Colorado. That does not mean these several ruins were all built at the same time but rather that definite time intervals were found between them. Wupatki came first, then, 40 years later, came the Mesa Verde cliff-dwellings and, 40 to 45 years later still, the Tower of Mummy Cave. The old ceiling beams that provided these readings altogether gave 140 years of excellent rings in unbroken sequence, but they were yet to be identified with Pueblo Bonito or with modern trees.

On the basis of a comparative study of potsherds from the several sites, Mr. Judd assured me that Mummy Cave, Mesa Verde, Wupatki, and Citadel unquestioningly were later, not earlier, than Pueblo Bonito. Thus by the end of July 1927, my "small beam" sequence at Wupatki had expanded into a very considerable, but quite independent, tree-ring record which I assumed to belong somewhere in the large gap between Chaco dating and modern trees. I soon found myself identifying this independent sequence as "CD—Citadel Dating" because it alone included the ring record of the single specimen up to that time found at Citadel Ruin. . . .

Obviously this new chronology, hanging somewhere between Pueblo Bonito times and the twentieth century, must soon join one or the other. The latter possibility seemed most unlikely and attempts to match it with our Bonito records were delayed several months pending examination of new Pueblo Bonito material. These newly acquired pieces were all found to belong in the early Bonito chronology and then, turning once more to my Citadel sequence, I was considerably surprised to note how readily it fitted into its proper place at the later end of the Bonito series. This happened on February 1, 1928, and then, as a second surprise, it appeared the two distinct chronologies, RD and CD, actually overlapped by nearly 40 years. However, this overlap depended chiefly on one single, reliable specimen of Citadel Dating which extended its ring series back into Chaco times. Thus the entire Citadel series at last found its true place in the prehistoric picture. . . .

By February 1, 1928, most of the results which could be obtained from the First Beam Expedition material had been secured. A long, prehistoric sequence had been assembled extending over an interval of 585 years. To this prehistoric tree-ring chronology something like 30 different ruins had contributed, and thus were bound together in a complex of relative dates. Then followed a gap of unknown duration but supposed to be between 50 and 200 years.

At that time my modern tree records extended back from 1929 to 1400, with possible extension to 1300 on some doubtful pieces. A very old tree had been discovered near Flagstaff whose stump showed 640 rings going back to the late 1200's, and actually evidencing a drouth near its center, but its early rings were variable and did not strengthen the chronology before 1400. Therefore every indication pointed to the need for studying early historic material. This could be done at Oraibi, oldest of the Hopi villages.

Oraibi is the only one of the present Hopi towns known to be in its original sixteenth-century location. The others had been moved to their mesa summits after the Pueblo Rebellion of 1680. In 1898, I had visited Oraibi and found a large village with a population of 900. Doors at street level were an innovation and everywhere stone stairways still led from one story to the next; people lived on the lower roofs. Together with perhaps 30 other white guests I saw the Snake Dance in the small, sloping plaza between the Snake and Antelope kivas. These old remembrances came back to mind on my subsequent visits, in 1923, 1926, and especially in 1928. . . .

The first object of The Society's second expedition was to secure samples from a large number of old beams in Oraibi, with the hope some of their inner rings would go beyond the gap and join our prehistoric series. This "gap," it will be recalled, was the unknown interval separating my dated sequence of annual growth rings in pines recently felled in the forests of northern Arizona and a similar, undated, sequence from old ceiling timbers recovered in various Pueblo ruins. The abandoned part of Oraibi offered the most promising place for such search. There houses had been built on the remains of previous houses; beams projected from these old walls and on many of them the unmistakable evidences of stone-ax work indicated great age.

For reasons every anthropologist will readily understand, samples from these old timbers, if obtainable, must be collected by someone living in Oraibi. On recommendation of Dr. Byron Cummings, Professor of Archeology at the University of Arizona, an advanced student in his department, Mr. Lyndon L. Hargrave, was selected for this responsible task. Mr. Hargrave and I spent six days in old Oraibi during March 1928, and after I left, he continued there for five weeks. We went first to the old kivas to examine their ceiling beams. From our initial tests we learned that juniper and cottonwood were practically useless at this stage of the search; that pine and Douglas fir were highly valuable and that dried and weathered logs are hard to distinguish as to kind of wood. We found evidence that the desirable kinds of wood ceased to be used in the village after about 1780. Without doubt all such trees within portable distance had by that time been cut down.

Ruins of Oraibi, a Hopi village in northeastern Arizona

Mr. Hargrave collected over 200 specimens in Oraibi, 65 in Shongopovi, and perhaps a dozen in Walpi and adjacent villages. Since none of these gave promise of supplying the rings that would unite our historic and prehistoric chronologies, it seemed wise to take advantage of the still early season and secure information regarding those villages from which the Hopi people had migrated to their present location. The beams in such villages would perhaps be old enough to supply ring records through the gap. Accordingly Mr. Hargrave, accompanied by Mr. J. W. Hamilton, was sent out to look especially for late Hopi ruins which might contribute further toward solution of our problem.

Early in June he returned to Flagstaff from this circuit trip, bringing some 50 specimens of wood from various ruins and many small bags of potsherds which proved of great use in subsequent plans. For immediate operations, he felt that the Jadito area was the region in which search for gap material should next be made.

In early August Mr. Hargrave returned from another visit to the Jadito area. At Kawaika on the surface near excavations a few years old, he had found fragments of wood that looked like pine. Many of these were decayed and charred, only an inch or two long, yet contained 50 or more clear-cut and sensitive rings. Again and again these rings were recognized as belonging to the years between 1363 and 1425. While practically convinced, I realized that some of the rings were hard to read and, since so much was at stake, I hesitated to accept the testimony of these small fragments. The better treatment we now give decayed wood and charcoal would perhaps have settled the dating at that time. But it then seemed wise to seek additional evidence.

Later that same month we learned Mr. E. H. Morris was about to make some excavations in these regions for the University of Colorado. We suggested that, if consistent with the objects of his expedition, he do his work at Kawaika and thus aid our search for datable wood. He kindly consented to do this and during the early autumn excavated a number of rooms at points indicated by us. No solid wood was encountered, but, from rooms near the location of the fragments above mentioned, additional pieces of badly decayed pine were recovered. These were treated with preservatives and their rings carefully plotted. Finally, in October, a piece of charcoal the size of one's fist was discovered. It proved to be Douglas fir with a perfect set of rings from 1400 to 1468; our other charred scraps extended this building record to 1357 and to 1495. Thus Kawaika received the distinction of being the first prehistoric ruin of the Southwest to be dated accurately by tree-ring methods. . . .

This achievement was accomplished at Kawaika while Hargrave and I were guests of Mr. and Mrs. Morris. It was of course noticed how near the last date, 1495, came to the years of Coronado's famous expedition, 1540 and 1541. We surmised that some of his men must have seen this ruin when actually occupied. . . .

In reviewing the progress made in 1928 it was seen that 52 percent of 830 collected beam samples had been brought into the single sequence of relative dates, covering the classical and late prehistoric periods of Pueblo history. Altogether this gave a floating series 585 years long. Twenty-six large ruins were tied together in this chronological complex. Then came the gap, followed by my modern ring sequence. The latter reached as far back as 1300 in reliable form, but extended weakly to 1260. . . . It was felt at the time that this gap we sought to bridge must represent some great crisis in the history of the Pueblo people. . . .

Without realizing how close was the solution of the age problem of the Pueblos, we formed detailed plans for the season of 1929. First we must concentrate on a very few specially promising ruins with full permission to make such excavations as seemed necessary. This permission was obtained from the Interior Department and covered all the principal ruins which we had previously investigated. Second, with a more exact knowledge of the pottery sequence, we could concentrate on such ruins as showed presence of the transition orange ware which, in a general way, was presumed to correspond to the gap in age. The presence of charcoal formed a third basis of selection.

There was no doubt that timbers of gap age existed in many of the large Jadito ruins. But these covered from 6 to 10 acres each and no one could tell beforehand just where to dig. It might be necessary to go down 10 feet to find beams in good condition. Only small portions of the Jadito ruins could be depended on to have that depth. Beams near the surface would be thoroughly decayed unless preserved in the form of charcoal. Accordingly, a ruin where charcoal was likely to be found would be preferable. This at once turned our attention to known ruins near the pine forests, where firewood was abundant and house fires necessary in winter. Of these, Showlow and Pinedale, 60 miles south of Holbrook, were already familiar to us. Mr. Hargrave had brought back some small sections from Pinedale which seemed to date in late prehistoric times and he reported large pieces of charred pine accompanying a pottery collection held by Mr. Edson Whipple, who owned the Showlow ruin.

The wood reported at this latter site seemed well worth examination as a preliminary to summer activity. Accordingly, in March 1929, Mr. Hargrave and I drove to Showlow just in time to enjoy a heavy snow storm. To our disappointment, the pottery collection and the pine fragments had been sold. A few charred scraps I picked up in the empty storeroom showed very sensitive, but unidentifiable, ring sequences. These demonstrated at once the need for tracing the larger pieces. We found them in possession of Mr. Harold S. Gladwin, Director of the Association for Prehistoric Research in the Southwest (now Gila Pueblo), at Globe, Arizona, who kindly permitted me not only to examine the fragments but to take away for my collections a duplicate ring series.

Two months later, this Showlow series was joined to our prehistoric sequence and extended it some years through and beyond an evident great drouth in late prehistoric times. Tracing the ring sequence through this drouth was difficult and very uncertain.

It was my urgent wish that a group of archeologists should assist in deciding which ruins were likely to provide gap material. The field party finally included Mr. Neil M. Judd, representing the National Geographic

Society, Dr. H. S. Colton, Director of the Museum of Northern Arizona, Mr. Lyndon L. Hargrave, Assistant Director of the same, and the writer. Mr. Hargrave's experience in the preceding year made his help very important to the beam researches contemplated for 1929. At inconvenience to the Museum, his services were kindly lent to our expedition for a period of two months.

The appeal of Showlow and Pinedale was so strong that Mr. Hargrave was left at Showlow on May 28 to begin our search. The point selected for initial excavation was immediately back of Joe Whipple's house, somewhat west of the center of the ruin. Small pieces of charcoal began to appear at once and attempts to date them by the skeleton-plot process promptly followed. A room at the Museum of Northern Arizona was generously placed at our disposal for a laboratory. To speed the work before us, we needed another assistant so that search might go on at a second site. Mr. Emil W. Haury, a student of archeology under Dr. Byron Cummings at the University of Arizona, was selected and sent on to join Mr. Hargrave.

On Saturday, June 22, 1929, Mr. Judd and I drove out from Flagstaff to Showlow. Hargrave and Haury enthusiastically exhibited some newly exposed fragments of charred beams. Rings of the 1300's were quickly recognized; some specimens showed the drouth year 1316 and nearly all were cut near 1380.

Later we were shown a log still in place at the extreme northern edge of the ruin. This lay near a stone wall marking the property line and at a point not before excavated although earth had been taken away for grading purposes. The log was scarcely more than a foot below the surface and, because it appeared very fragile, had been bound thoroughly with string. Its diameter of seven inches made it look like a large beam. However, it broke away from the ground with suspicious ease. We carried it to a nearby shed and there, in the course of handling, it fell apart and disclosed the fact that it was only the remains of a charred shell which had once been the end of a solid log. The wood had decayed entirely except where preserved by its charred state.

I readily identified rings of the fourteenth century; the outside extended to the vicinity of 1380. In a minute microscopic examination of the inner rings the drouth of the late 1200's, beginning in 1276, was very conspicuous. Ring 1270 showed small as always; 1263-4 were very small. Before that, the rings were large except 1258, 1254, 1251, which were very small, and 1247, which was below average.

In consequence of the afternoon devoted to study of this precious old log, my skeleton plot of modern drouth years was extended to 1237. . . .

That night, as Messrs. Judd, Hargrave, and Haury sat with me under

Pueblo Bonito, New Mexico, restored

the brilliance of a gasoline lamp in the little living room of the local hotel, Judd suggested, "Maybe the gap is not very big." I immediately ran my skeleton plot of prehistoric rings along the edge of the newly extended, historic sequence and at once noted a position of coincidence, highly attractive though not perfect because of slight disagreement within the drouth period. However, since most trees were defective at that time, there need be no occasion for surprise if some rings were missing in the decayed and charred fragment before us. After carefully checking this apparent correspondence on the original, as well as on the two plots, the agreement seemed more convincing. But, still with natural hesitation, I preferred to think it over and remarked that, while it looked very encouraging, we would try it again in the morning. . . .

On retiring, I found it possible to produce before the mind's eye vivid pictures of all the rings involved. Every one was passed in review and weighed in the matter of identity between its historic and its prehistoric appearance. There could be no doubt of the identity in date for those rings between 1240 and 1300 in both the prehistoric and the historic specimens. Our "gap" was closed. [Footnote] It was later found that 1283 and 1288 were omitted in almost all trees that lived through the drouth. When these were inserted in the lower skeleton plot of the late prehistoric rings, the agreement shows through the whole length of the overlap.

In this successful conclusion of our work the unexpected feature was that there had been no real gap at all. Rather, our two chronologies already coincided for as much as 25 years, but, owing to the single historic specimen that made this overlap (BE 269) and to the almost universal defects in specimens that lived through the great drouth, it would have been utterly impossible convincingly to join the historic and prehistoric ring sequences without the new material produced by the excavations of the Third Beam Expedition.

Thus the "gap" was due in part to the greatest drouth evidenced in our tree-ring calendar, now continuous from 700 A.D. to 1929. Our surmise of the preceding year that this hiatus represented some great crisis in the history of the Pueblo people was amply confirmed. The break in the continuity of Pueblo history at the time of the drouth was tremendous and far-reaching; how great it was will sometime be an interesting study for an archeologist. The word "gap" still finds frequent place in our vocabulary, but it no longer means an interruption in our ring sequence— rather, it reminds us of a very difficult problem solved at last. . . .

33

"I constrained the mighty river to flow according to my will and led its waters to fertilize lands that before had been barren and without inhabitants." Thus boasted a cuneiform inscription on the tomb of the Assyrian Queen Semiramis in the ninth century B.C. Diverting waters from rivers, distributing and storing it for the cultivation of crops in an arid land, has given life sap to ancient societies from Egypt, Mesopotamia, and the Indus Valley to China. Vast irrigation schemes not only helped to support growing populations in parched deserts, but created surpluses for leisure and cultural pursuits. They also brought about joint efforts of the inhabitants and necessitated large-scale planning and control. Modern historians have learned to talk of the great "hydraulic civilizations" of antiquity, and indeed it may be to irrigation that civilization itself owes its decisive impulse.

Outside Peru, the extent of irrigation among the peoples of the New World has rarely been studied. In Middle America, the absence of major rivers set a limit to the rise of a centralized hydraulic state, but canals and reservoirs were in wide use, particularly in the central highlands of Mexico. However, nothing on the continent can compare with the vast network of prehistoric canals in the valleys of the Salt and Gila rivers of southern Arizona. Here, in a forbidding, drought-ridden country, where little but thorny cactus and sagebrush had grown, prehistoric farmers made hundreds of thousands of acres bloom. Here they cultivated the three Indian staples: corn, beans, and squash. Here they multiplied and prospered. While the sheer physical labor that must have gone into the excavation of miles on miles of deep ditches—aided by little but Stone Age tools and baskets for carrying the soil away—defies computation by the statistic-minded, the engineering skill of these people—their primitive implements notwithstanding—is at least as astonishing. They knew how to prevent seepage through the sand by plastering the canal beds; they impounded dams, and probably used head gates to block the flow. They thought nothing of cutting through three miles of volcanic rock at a depth of up to twenty-five feet. Mormon settlers in 1878 simply took over such an old cut and thereby saved themselves the expense of an estimated $20,000 in pre-inflationary money.

Yet, at the time white settlers from the East filtered into southwestern Arizona, few had any conception of the extensive canal system, even though they utilized sections here and there, which they found serviceable. Badly decayed ditches were filled up, built over, or turned under the plow. That Indians of a thousand years ago should have practiced irrigation was then discounted. Those of their descendants who did, must have picked it up from the Spaniards—who, according to general belief, had been the actual builders of the canals.

When at last archaeologists began to turn their attention to the Indian remains of the area, most of the old waterworks had disappeared. Ironically, the revival of irrigated cultivation, following closely in the footsteps of the prehistoric agriculturists, systematically wiped out their traces. Mammoth reservoirs, named for former U.S. Presidents, covered large tracts and released streams which washed the imprints of the past away. Luckily, a mushrooming modern oasis city on the Salt River, Phoenix, had the good grace to preserve parts of aboriginal canals in its Park of Four Waters.

In the 1920's, Byron Cummings, then director of the Arizona State Museum, mapped a complex of ancient canals along the Gila. Neil M. Judd, a former Utah school teacher who had become one of the Southwest's leading archaeologists, was just completing his campaign at Pueblo Bonito, when he made a preliminary survey of the canals in 1929. He then came to the saddening conclusion that at most ten per cent of the 230 miles of canals charted in 1922 were still in evidence, and those were vanishing fast. "Each succeeding civilization builds on the remains of its predecessors," was his philosophical verdict. This was no occasion for archaeological tears. Instead he hit upon the idea of following the example of the Lindberghs in Yucatán and the Shippee-Johnson expedition in Peru, enlisting aviation for making visible what progress had obliterated. The result—recorded in words and photographs—was an articulate profile of a native American irrigation civilization, which, at least in hydraulic know-how, could vie with ancient Egypt and Mesopotamia.

The aboriginal people who farmed in the Gila and Salt valleys had abandoned their land before a Jesuit missionary discovered the ruined sites. What their name was, why they left, or where they went—we do not know. We are not at all certain what they looked like, since they had the "bad" habit—reprehensible by the necromantic standards of archaeologists—of cremating their dead. (Well preserved mummies found at nearby Ventana Cave may, however, represent their kinsmen.)

It has long been customary to class the vanished aboriginals with the

Pueblos of the cliffs and mesas of the Four Corner region. But intensive study of Southwestern antiquities, while allowing for some underlying traits held in common by all the desert people ("co-tradition"), has undermined the simplistic view of the ancient Southwest as a cultural and racial unity. Considering the physical closeness, some exchange of goods, ideas, or people undoubtedly always took place, although invading hordes of savage hunters and influences traveling from the more advanced southern lands beyond the Rio Grande affected various parts differently. Today we distinguish at least four major cultures or sub-groups, which went their separate ways: the Anasazi (the Pueblos of the Four Corners), the Hohokam, the Mogollon, and the Patayan. The last, tied to northern and western Arizona along the Colorado, are the least known. Both Hohokam and Mogollon, who were isolated by scholars only about 1930, are often held to derive from the food-gathering Cochise Indians of southern Arizona, whose roots go back to 6000 B.C. These two groups were neighbors, with the Mogollon occupying east-central Arizona and southwestern New Mexico, while the Hohokam are identified with the irrigation farmers of south-central Arizona. The term Hohokam is taken from the Pima words for "those who have gone away," which was the stereotype answer local Indians gave to an inquiry about the ancient canal builders. Like "Anasazi," the label is distinctive enough to have caught the fancy of archaeologists.

Hohokam clay figurines

In addition to practicing cremation and large-scale irrigation, the Hohokam differ notably from the Anasazi in many cultural traits from architecture to ceramic technique. Possibly they were the first to receive corn from Mexico. Their primitive figurines of clay are almost indistinguishable from those of Mesoamerica. And they were the only group in the present United States to build ballcourts, some of which measured two hundred yards in length. A rubber ball, no doubt used in their games, was found buried in a vessel. Evidently traded from tropical Mexico, it remains the only surviving specimen anywhere. (Though the Aztecs collected large quantities of rubber balls as tribute, none has ever been recovered on Mexican territory.)

The Hohokam were second to none when it came to ceramic art, and excelled in decorating shells, a favorite material they obtained from the Pacific shore. A tastefully incised conch shell found in Gila Pueblo and dated from around A.D. 1100 has become famous as the first known example of etching, probably by means of an acid extracted from a local cactus. Not before the fifteenth century do Europeans report the use of a similar technique on a coat of armor.

Dating Hohokam ruins and the phases of their culture has proved a tricky business leaving range for considerable disagreement. Some scholars like Emil W. Haury, who excavated extensively in the area during the 1930's, think the Hohokam built an agricultural society as early as 300 B.C., which would put them ahead of some of the people of western and northern Europe. Others move their beginnings up to A.D. 600, but at present a period roughly around the birth of Christ is widely accepted as the onset of their Pioneer or Formative Age.

Tree-ring time counts unfortunately cannot be applied directly to the Hohokam. The extreme aridity of the region does not provide suitable trees: the only igneous materials the people used in their wattle and daub houses were cactus fibers and cottonwood. However, wares from Anasazi sources, now datable, are encountered in Hohokam strata, just as Hohokam goods crop up in Pueblo sites. Thus, by crossdating, dendrochronology has furnished at least a rudimentary outline of Hohokam "history." It is fairly well established that a Pueblo people moved into the Hohokam area around A.D. 1300. Their coming appears to have been entirely peaceful, and they worked side by side with their hosts while maintaining their own individuality. It is due to them that there suddenly appeared the typically multi-storied walled community houses resembling those of the northern mesas. The famous Casa Grande ruins—today a National Monument forty miles southeast of Phoenix—can be attributed to them. About one hundred years later, the newcomers apparently just moved on. It was then also that the entire Hohokam canal system fell into disrepair. What exactly happened, no one can tell, though the usual explanations have been offered by the metaphysicians of cultural decadence. Conceivably it may have been a severe drought, inroads by savage Apache, or perhaps saline saturation of the water. The Hohokam probably abandoned their valleys at that point. But there is the possibility that some Hohokam blood flows in the Pima and Papago of southern Arizona.

In scale and technique, Hohokam irrigation stands comparison with that of the ancient Near East. Its success must have demanded a civic contribution equally great, even if less reluctantly rendered. Undoubtedly its construction and maintenance could have been carried on only in a spirit of social discipline. Yet there is no evidence here of the despotic hydraulic state with its hierarchy and a ruling leisure class of priests and nobles. The surplus did not go to finance monster monuments as in the bloodthirsty theocracies of Mexico. Hohokam houses, lacking utterly in architectural distinction, are all very much alike and do not point to any flagrant social or economic inequalities. The population's skill and energy went above all into the canals which served quite simply the material well-being of everybody alike, rather than the ravenous appetites of personified "spiritual" forces lording it over them. There was, nevertheless, scope for artistic endeavor and for games.

It would be absurd to put Hohokam cultural achievements on a level with those of Egypt or Babylon, or even Teotihuacán, Tikal, and Moche. The Hohokam did not create a civilization in the proper sense: no cities, no writing, no clear-cut division of labor. But then, there are alternatives to civilization and its discontents.

ARIZONA'S PREHISTORIC CANALS

Neil M. Judd

Out in central Arizona, where cotton fields, citrus groves and date palms reach out across endless miles to caress jagged igneous and sandstone buttes, prehistoric peoples once erected a noteworthy civilization upon an agricultural foundation. That ancient civilization is gone now— lost with the desert acres on which it flourished—and few traces remain of the gigantic canals that made its primitive agriculture possible.

But those few traces merit careful preservation. They are all we have left to remind us of that unnamed, aboriginal folk whose engineering achievements rightfully arrest the attention of our mechanical age. For those prehistoric canals—it has been estimated that half a century ago there were no less than 300 miles of them in the Salt River valley alone— were so accurately and efficiently constructed that portions of them, taken over by white settlers of 1870 and thereabouts, are actually in use at the present time. And here is another point we are apt to overlook: Every

"Arizona's Prehistoric Canals, From the Air," by Neil M. Judd. From *Explorations and Fieldwork of the Smithsonian Institution in 1930.* Reprinted by permission of the Smithsonian Institution.

mile of those ancient channels was literally dug by hand, since the Arizona Indians knew nothing either of beasts of burden or metal tools until well on in the seventeenth century.

Following the old canal banks, one occasionally happens upon the fragment of a stone "hoe"—a thin blade of igneous rock, chipped on one side to a cutting edge. With such rude tools, with fractured cobblestones and sharpened sticks, the canal builders hacked and prodded at the hard desert soil. In baskets and blankets, we may safely conjecture, women and children carried the loosened earth out from the excavation. Thus, mile after weary mile, an entire community labored to construct the canals that watered their communal fields.

Nowhere else in the New World has evidence been found of prehistoric irrigation systems comparable to those of central Arizona. They may even have surpassed, both in size and in the number of acres served, those famous systems of the Tigris and Euphrates valleys—irrigation works that watered the seed of native ability and brought forth into full bloom high civilizations that made Mesopotamia known throughout the ancient world.

With prodigious labor, the Peruvians of pre-Spanish times led irrigation ditches along craggy heights of the Andes to their terraced gardens. Among the highlands of Mexico and again in various sections of the southwestern United States, Indian farmers had learned that irrigation was necessary to the successful cultivation of food crops. In November 1694, Padre Eusebio Kino stood before the drab walls of Casa Grande ruin and speculated upon the feasibility of restoring its abandoned, overgrown canals. Five hundred years before Kino was born the inhabitants of Pueblo Bonito, in Chaco Canyon, New Mexico, were capturing the midsummer rains, taming and guiding them onto thirsty fields. But none of these efforts matched the colossal, prehistoric irrigation systems of the Gila and Salt river valleys.

We wanted maps of these latter, hand-made Indian canals. We wanted to know their extent, their position relative to each other, the approximate acreage they once watered. Similar desires on the part of other

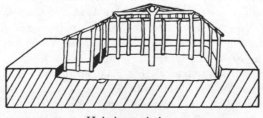

Hohokam pit house

observers had prompted surveys which were not altogether successful for the simple reason that so little is now visible of the ancient ditches. Modern agriculture has been too destructive; it has plowed and planted until the aboriginal farming communities and their works were pretty thoroughly obliterated. From the ground, one's range of vision is too limited; from the air it might be possible to recover data for the maps we had in mind. At least this seemed the most promising, expeditious method when I made a preliminary study of the situation in the autumn of 1929.

So, at the solicitation of United States Senator Carl Hayden, the Smithsonian Institution and the War Department cooperated in an aerial survey of the Salt and Gila river valleys, beginning late in January 1930. Lieutenant Edwin Bobzien and Sergeant R. A. Stockwell, pilot and photographer, respectively, were detailed from the Air Corps unit at Crissy Field, San Francisco, and I was designated Smithsonian representative, to advise with the aviators.

Our small party assembled at Phoenix, blocked out the areas to be photographed and speedily set to work. Smoke and ground haze drew an impenetrable blanket over Salt River valley each morning and evening, thus restricting flying time to a brief two hours at midday when shadows are at a minimum. The longer shadows of early morning and late afternoon would naturally have thrown into greater relief those slight elevations which mark ancient house sites and irrigation ditches.

But, despite handicaps of various sorts, our air survey proceeded about as we had planned it. First of all there was the Gila River valley, from its union with the Rio Salado to the northwestern slopes of the Tortilla Mountains—a far-reaching plain whereon Pima and Papago farmers tilled favored patches of irrigable land long before the advent of missionaries, trappers, Pony Express riders, and other pioneers of a period now all but forgotten.

American settlers trailed into the upper Gila valley during the third quarter of the nineteenth century and drew so heavily upon the available water supply that the Indian farmers below were finally brought to a state of destitution. Government promises of relief were made and remade but a half century passed before the Coolidge Dam was completed and provision thus made to meet the needs of whites and Indians alike. The great reservoir is slowly filling and, 70 miles away, farm lands wait thirstily for the life-giving waters.

With huge, snorting machines that make an Indian's home-made tools seem, by comparison, as nothing at all, 56,000 acres of desert land are being cleared, leveled, and otherwise prepared for irrigation at the rate of 20 acres a day. But the mechanical monsters of the modern engineer are no respecters of prehistoric canals! The latter were being destroyed along with other heritages from the past. Ours was the task of discerning and recording some vestige of those ancient irrigation systems while fleeting opportunity permitted.

Up one side of the Gila and down the other, Lieutenant Bobzien held his blue Douglas observation plane on a fixed course at 10,000 feet elevation while Sergeant Stockwell pointed his camera through a hole in the floor and snapped the shutter with clock-like precision to picture a square mile on each successive negative. Over famed Casa Grande ruins the ship sailed lower in search of those ancient canals seen by Kino and which new cotton fields seem to have erased absolutely. And then back to the Indian gardens that border the meandering Gila from Sacaton to Pima Butte and beyond.

Like strips of Grandmother's quilt those gardens are! Queer, misshapen patches with thin ribbons of dark green running this way and that where lesser irrigation ditches crazy-stitched the variegated scraps together. Yet, hopelessly confused and insignificant as these miniature farms appear from a height of nearly two miles, they played a not unimportant part in the conquest of southern Arizona.

Indian farmers tended those fertile fields for untold generations before Francisco Vásquez de Coronado and his band of resolute adventurers marched gayly northward out of Mexico in 1540 to dig mythical gold from the Seven Cities of Cibola. When Padre Kino came plodding his patient way toward salvation of the Pima and Papago tribes late in the seventeenth century, those funny Indian gardens fed his men and mules. And they supported, too, the westward-bound gold-seekers of '49; the animals and personnel both of the Pony Express and the later stage-coach companies; the U.S. Army units stationed in Arizona before and after the Civil War. Except for those gardens and the Pima and Papago scouts who served so faithfully throughout the protracted Apache campaign, Victorio and Geronimo doubtless would have continued their murderous depredations for still another decade. The peaceful Indian tribes of the Gila valley have well merited, and with interest, the Government-aided irrigation system which once more makes possible the successful cultivation of their Lilliputian farms.

In the Salt River valley, prehistoric peoples also converted cacti-covered wastes into gardens of maize, beans, and squashes. They built, nearby, thick-walled, flat-roofed homes of mud, pressed and patted into layer upon layer. Here, as along the Gila, industrious generations dwelt in peace and plenty, tending their growing plants, digging new ditches, hunting deer among thorny mesquite, until some great, irresistible force came finally to claim possession. What that force really was no one knows today. It may have been a slight diminution in annual rainfall; more likely, it was increasing pressure from nomadic tribes. But, in either case, after a period which none may yet measure, the Indian farmers of the Rio Salado vacated their cultivated fields, abandoned their compact settlements and moved on to other, perhaps less favored localities. Substantial dwellings crumbled into low, spreading mounds; irrigation systems slowly filled with wind-driven sand; the desert crept back to claim its own.

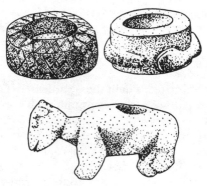

Hohokam stone bowls

Not until the middle nineteenth century did Salt River valley reawaken to such industry as it had known in prehistoric times. Not until 1865, or thereabouts, did hardy pioneers follow in on the dim trails of the beaver trappers and the gold-seekers to select the thorny plains of the Rio Salado as a likely place in which to build their humble homes.

Among these pioneers was one Jack Swilling, somewhat more imaginative than his neighbors, who appears to have been the first to recognize the possibility of local irrigation. Obviously influenced by the nearby prehistoric canals, Swilling started to clear out one of these as a ready means of watering his own fields. And then, in 1867, he organized the company which constructed the first modern canals in Salt River valley.

Remnants of this old "Swilling ditch" and sections of three ancient Indian canals are still visible in "The Park of Four Waters," wisely preserved by the city of Phoenix. Close by stands the ruin of Pueblo Grande, a huge pile of crumbling walls and pale yellow clay, excavation of which was initiated in 1929 by City Archeologist Odd A. Halseth.

Largest surviving example of the communal dwellings which dotted Salt River valley in prehistoric times, Pueblo Grande marks a former center of population from which industrious Indian farmers trudged forth to their daily toil. From the flat roofs of their earth-walled homes those same farmers saluted the rising and setting sun as the father of all living things. For in olden times, no less than today, the sun meant life to dwellers in Salt River valley.

Over on the south side, Pioneer Charles T. Hayden camped one day at the foot of Tempe Butte and watched the swollen river race past. Then he constructed a rude ferry to float his wagons across; remained to transport other early settlers, to build the first local store, walled with mud-plastered willows. More than this, he cleaned out an old Indian canal and drew into it, from the Rio Salado, water with which to turn the wheels of his primitive mill. The new Hayden mill, erected on the same site, is no longer powered by an irrigation ditch but it served, none-theless, as one of our principal landmarks in the recent aerial survey of Salt River valley. . . .

Inquiry elicits the information that there are no fewer than 1,200 miles of these modern watercourses. Most of them measure from 18 to 90 feet wide at the top and average about five feet in depth; sections of them have cost as much as $22,000 a mile to construct. But the prehistoric canal builders, with barefooted helpers instead of caterpillar tractors, with stone hoes as precursors of the steam shovel, unhesitatingly set about the completion of comparable works. I photographed one aboriginal canal north of Mesa that stands today 66 feet wide and 8 feet deep. It led from the Rio Salado far across the valley; as the river cut its channel below the canal floor, the useless ditch was replaced by another which connected with a new intake, farther up stream. Such substitutions were necessitated by altered conditions in prehistoric times no less than today.

Modern irrigation canals and the industry they symbolize have done most to erase from central Arizona former vestiges of that native civilization which once prospered there. The sad ruins of aboriginal homes have been leveled with their neighboring fields; the ditches which once watered those fields have been filled or scraped away. Where Indian farmers eight or ten hundred years ago cultivated gardens of beans, maize and squashes, vast acres of cotton, lettuce and melons are now harvested. Neat orchards of dates and grapefruit flourish where catclaw and mesquite stretched their spiny branches only a generation ago. The diabolical Apache has been tamed if not conquered. Bow-legged cowboys, garbed according to the latest fashion notes from Hollywood, ride herd on eastern "dudes." Attractive dwellings and sumptuous winter resorts, with green lawns and flower-bordered walks have replaced the mud-walled habitations of the ancient folk.

As one looks down from the air upon this Paradise that is Salt River valley today, one is impressed first of all by the orderly habits of mankind. At least there is a semblance of order, from a height of 2,000 feet or more. Long, straight roads on which autos slither away like headless roaches; brown and yellow fields all nicely squared; orange trees that seem as tiny pellets of dark green, patiently arranged, row upon row; little cubed houses, fringed with flat green things.

Reaching across these fields and under these houses, light or dark streaks mark former prehistoric Indian canals which only the aviator may readily detect. Silt deposited in those old ditches shows dark brown against the drab desert soil; pale yellow lines remain where embankments have been smoothed away. Slight differences in vegetation, imperceptible when close at hand, take on color variations that enable one at a considerable height to retrace works which otherwise have been wholly effaced.

The blue Army plane glides down from the clouds and back to port with numbed crew and empty cameras. Camel Back Mountain squats complacently at one side and looks out across the valley where such momentous changes have taken place within memory of men still living. Squaw Peak lifts her unkempt bulk to frown upon this new civilization, as she did upon the old. A setting sun momentarily gilds the giant sahuaro whose long, fingered shadows point eastwardly to rugged mountain ranges whence flow the life-giving waters of the Gila and the Rio Salado.

PART **VI**

EARLIEST AMERICANS

34

Basket Maker, as it turned out, was by no means the oldest Southwesterner. But before he could be credited with a long line of ancestors, American anthropologists and archaeologists had to do a lot of rethinking. What brought the problem of Early Man in America to a head and radically changed all its aspects was a well-placed spear point found in 1927 between the ribs of a fossil bison of an extinct species. It struck the academic quagmire with the force of a guided missile and once more constrained American archaeology into new channels.

The Folsom story had actually had its beginnings some years earlier with a Negro cowboy riding through an arroyo called Dead Horse Gulch, a few miles west of the little town of Folsom in northeastern New Mexico. Noticing bleached bones protruding from a wall of the little valley, some four feet from the top, he was curious enough to dismount and extract a few specimens. His find brought others to the scene. Eventually word reached the Denver Museum of Natural History.

Until the Folsom discovery there had raged for several decades a violent controversy over the existence of ancient man in the New World. Scholars from various camps presented conflicting facts, generously sprinkled with speculation, ardor, and prejudice. Champions of great antiquity were suspected of being muddle-headed dreamers, while their detractors were likely to be accused of undue dogmatism and blindness to blatant evidence.

To be sure, only a few crackpots held that *Homo sapiens* had roamed over the Western Hemisphere nearly as long as over Asia, Africa, and Europe, or that the species could have evolved here (none of the higher apes—apart from long-extinct *Notharctus*—has ever been encountered in the Americas). In the main, the issue hinged on whether the New World had played host to humans as far back as the Pleistocene, the period of the four ice ages (the end of which was then anybody's guess). Definitely not, was the verdict of the physical anthropologists: All the skeletons ever unearthed are essentially those of modern man. Geologists, on the whole, were not as categorical in their pronouncements, since they were used to taking a more generous view of time, but they tended to agree with the palaeontological analysis. Some archaeologists, however, felt that the diversity and complexity of American cultures and languages pointed to an evolution of many millennia. Hence they were more inclined to embrace the antiquity credo. Unfortunately quite a few of them, uncritically enamored of the hoary past, could not hold their own when it came to a scientific evaluation of the data. They were thus an easy target for their debunkers.

Map of Southwestern United States, with early man sites

Announcements of fossilized human bones embedded in geologically old strata had been reported from time to time. One such discovery was made by a Danish naturalist as early as 1842 and as far away as Brazil. Likewise, there were repeated reports of excavations of unusual projectile points associated with the bones of glacial mammals. Yet, by the beginning of the twentieth century the great majority of the scientifically minded put little trust in such claims. Invariably they declared the evidence spurious. Whenever a daring neophyte took the stand for American Ice Age Man, he was treated with scorn. After a while, self-respecting savants who disagreed with the skeptical worthies occupying most of the university chairs in anthropology and influential museum posts learned to keep their heretical views to themselves and left the field to over-enthusiastic amateurs. When it came time to honor Professor F. W. Putnam of Harvard on his seventieth birthday with a *Festschrift* of twenty-five essays on various aspects of American archaeology, the subject of early American man, which Putnam had vigorously pursued for many years, was discreetly omitted by his colleagues. Mark R. Harrington, who, a generation later, took up the cause anew and helped it triumph, recalled the advice given to him by Putnam when as a young man Harrington joined the staff of the American Museum: "If ever you make a find that seems unusually old, just report it—don't interpret it, or you will get into trouble." And Frank H. H. Roberts, Jr., a chief witness of the Folsom discovery who became director of the Smithsonian Bureau of American Ethnology, declared that for some twenty-five years it was nearly fatal to any scholar's advancement to suggest that "he had discovered indications of a respectable antiquity for the Indian."

Today, after the battle for Early Man has been won, hindsight will make his enemies look foolish. Yet it should be granted that the arguments put up by the anti-antiquity faction were pretty solid. They had all the earmarks of superior scientific sophistication. In the light of the then available knowledge of the evolution of modern man and of specific geological and climatological implications, they did make sense. If we consider that even forty years after the Folsom revolution only two finds of incomplete human skeletons from the entire hemisphere are accepted—more or less conclusively—as ancient by all the experts, stubbornness and derision in the face of much flimsy evidence seems appropriate enough.

In the forefront of the "modernists" were William H. Holmes (once himself an eager pursuer of Ice Age Americans) and Aleš Hrdlička, valiantly poised at the glacial land bridge across the Bering Sea and fighting, as has been noted, like Horatio to keep ancient "Indians" from entering the New World. With incisive logic, and to their own satisfaction, they and their followers neatly discredited whatever physical evidence of early man had been submitted to them. For example, they could make the point—quite justly—that allegedly primordial characteristics of human skulls were by no means proof of great age since they could occasionally be found among present-day Indians as well as other races. Crude stone weapons as such need not be ancient either: American natives continued to manufacture them into modern times. Some such lithic tools were simply discards. If human artifacts or burials really occurred in relatively old strata, the skeptics had an infallible counter-argument: intrusion, *i.e.,* a later, secondary deposit into a geologically much older layer. As to extinct animals, there was the real possibility that they might have survived into recent pre-Columbian centuries. Thus, in brief, was cold water

Indians breaking a large stone, after W. Holmes

poured over the irritating "antiquity phantom." The consensus, at least among the physical anthropologists, was that the first Americans had come long after the last ice age, at most two or three thousand years before the beginning of our era. Around 1920 the pendulum had swung way over to the side of the anti-antiquity camp.

It is a token of the general climate of opinion that when in 1926 J. D. Figgins, a palaeontologist of the Colorado Museum of Natural History, informed colleagues of other institutions of his find of man-made weapons with a bison of an extinct species, he failed to gain any endorsement. This taught him a valuable lesson for the consecutive phase of his operations. Indeed, had it not been for his circumspect handling of the Folsom excavations, the now celebrated site—which gave its name to a Palaeo-Indian and to the fine fluted projectiles he shaped—might have received little but a footnote in learned monographs. Figgins saw to it that several experts were summoned to the scene. Among them was Frank H. H. Roberts, Jr., a distinguished anthropologist. In a paper published in 1935 which dealt mainly with his own subsequent Palaeo-Indian researches, Roberts gave a concise account of the truly historic occasion when, under the watchful eyes of fellow scientists, Barnum Brown from the American Museum of Natural History liberated "Folsom Man."

Roberts and his colleagues who were present during the unveiling alerted other archaeologists and anthropologists in the United States to the incontrovertible facts of human association with defunct glacial fauna. Though some of the traditional doubts were raised at first, they died down quickly. Within a few years the reversal in the antiquity debate was complete. Even the high priest of the recency of American man, Aleš Hrdlička, began, at least in private, to talk of human habitation in the New World in terms of 10,000 or more years.

Meanwhile Brown continued excavations of the Folsom site in 1928. He recovered the bones of more than forty bison (of the species *Bison antiquus* or *B. taylori*), among which were scattered seventeen darts. He saw the carcasses as the unmistakable result of slaughter by Indian hunters, perhaps at a lake site. The animals had probably been butchered, even though most of their skeletons remained intact. If any further sign of human presence were needed, Brown could point out that almost all animals lacked their tail bones for the simple reason that they had been skinned and, according to the hallowed custom of hunters everywhere, "the tail goes with the hide."

Even today the age of the Folsom horizon cannot be determined with any degree of precision. Geologists think it likely to overlap with the close of the Pleistocene and the beginning of the Recent, about 9,000 to 10,000 years ago. More extensive material came from Lindenmeier, in northern Colorado, one of the major sites of Folsom artifacts. This was a prehistoric campsite of long occupation, identified by Roberts (who excavated it in 1934) as a veritable prehistoric factory of Folsom points and related flint tools. A charcoal specimen collected there was tested in 1960 for its radio-carbon content and gave an age of 10,780 ± 375 years. The New World was getting older.

THE FOLSOM MISSILE

Frank H. H. Roberts, Jr.

In the summer of 1925 Fred J. Howarth and Carl Schwachheim of Raton, N. Mex., both now deceased, notified Director J. D. Figgins of the Colorado Museum of Natural History, Denver, of a bone deposit which they had found in the bank of an arroyo on the upper sources of

From "A Folsom Complex," by Frank H. H. Roberts, Jr. *Smithsonian Miscellaneous Collections*, Vol. 94, No. 4 (1935). Reprinted by permission of the Smithsonian Institution.

the Cimarron River near the town of Folsom in eastern New Mexico. Samples of bone sent to the museum indicated that the remains were those of an extinct species of bison and of a large deerlike member of the *Cervidae*. Prospects for fossil material were so promising that the Colorado Museum sent a party to the site in the summer of 1926. During the course of the excavations, carried on under the supervision of Frank Figgins [also a member of the Museum staff] and Mr. Schwachheim, parts of two finely chipped projectile points were recovered from the loose dirt at the diggings. Near the place where one of them had been dislodged a small, triangular piece of "flint" was found embedded in the clay surrounding an animal bone. This fragment was left in the block of earth, and when the latter was received in the laboratory at Denver, the dirt was carefully cleaned away from the bit of stone. It appeared to be from the same material as one of the points, and close examination showed that it actually was a part of the point. This evidence seemed unquestionably to demonstrate that here was a definite association between man-made objects and an extinct bison.

Director Figgins was so impressed with the find and was so thoroughly convinced that it was of importance to students of American archeology that he took the points with him that winter when he visited several of the large eastern museums on paleontologic business. In most places his announcement was courteously yet skeptically received. One authority on stone implements marveled at the quality of workmanship that the specimens exhibited and even remarked that they were reminiscent of the finest examples from Western Europe. He was doubtful, though, of the trustworthiness of the association. He thought that it could perhaps be attributed to an accidental mixing of material. Others said that the points had no significance because they could be duplicated in existing collections. At a few museums, notably the American Museum of Natural History, Mr. Figgins was urged to continue the work in the hope that additional evidence could be obtained.

The Colorado Museum again sent a party to Folsom in the summer of 1927 and had the good fortune to find additional points. One of these was noted before it was removed from the matrix, even before it was completely uncovered. Work was stopped immediately on that part of the excavation, and telegrams were dispatched to various museums and institutions inviting them to send representatives to view the point in situ. The writer at that time was attending the first Southwestern Archeological Conference at Pecos, N. Mex., and, upon receiving notice of the find and travel instructions from Washington, proceeded to Folsom. Arriving at the fossil pit, on September 2, he found Director Figgins, several members of the Colorado Museum board, and Dr. Barnum Brown, of the

American Museum of Natural History, New York, on the ground. The point, which became the pattern and furnished the name for the type, had just been uncovered by Dr. Brown. There was no question but that here was the evidence of an authentic association. The point was still embedded in the matrix between two of the ribs of the animal skeleton. In fact it has never been removed from the block, which is now on exhibit in the Colorado Museum at Denver. On returning to Raton, N. Mex., that evening, the writer telegraphed to Dr. A. V. Kidder at Pecos and urged that he visit the site. Dr. Kidder arrived two days later, and he and the writer drove out to the bison quarry. After the whole situation had been carefully studied, it was agreed that the association could not be questioned. Furthermore, it was ascertained that the points were totally different from the ordinary types scattered over that portion of the Southwest.

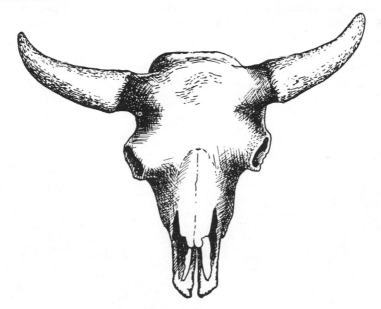

Skull of early American bison

At the meeting of the American Anthropological Association held at Andover, Mass., in December of that year Dr. Barnum Brown and the writer reported on the Folsom finds. There was considerable discussion of the subject and although many agreed that the discoveries were important, there was still a general feeling of doubt. Numerous explanations were offered to show that the points might have gotten into such an association without actually being contemporaneous with the bison remains. Several mentioned that points of that type were numerous in collections from certain mound sites, from village sites in New York State, and elsewhere, and for that reason they could not be very old. Others insisted that, although they accepted the conclusions on the genuineness of the finds, there must be some mistake about the antiquity of the animal remains.

The summer of 1928 saw the American Museum of Natural History and the Colorado Museum cooperating at the Folsom site. The expedition was under the leadership of Dr. Barnum Brown, who was assisted by several graduate students in anthropology. The latter were under the general supervision of Dr. Clark Wissler. Additional points and bison skeletons were found, and telegrams reporting the discoveries were sent to various institutions. This time numerous specialists—archeologists, paleontologists, and geologists—rushed to see the evidence. The consensus of the informal conference held at the site was that this constituted the most important contribution yet made to American archeology. Some of the most skeptical critics of the year before became enthusiastic converts. The Folsom find was accepted as a reliable indication that man was present in the Southwest at an earlier period than was previously supposed.

35

Once raised to respectability, early American man made, in a manner of speaking, great strides. Throughout the Southwest, finds proliferated. Even those discovered prior to the Folsom digs were retrieved from limbo. Mark Raymond Harrington of the Southwest Museum at Los Angeles, who had first visited Gypsum Cave in southern Nevada in 1924, demonstrated that human activities in that area near Boulder Dam, some sixteen miles east of Las Vegas, reached beyond the time when the giant ground sloth became extinct—presumably in the late Ice Age. Harrington's campaigns in that limestone cavern from 1929 onward furnished the second authoritative proof of the contemporaneity of Palaeo-Indians with glacial animals. No longer could anyone doubt that ancient Americans had preyed on a whole menagerie of Tertiary creatures, from mammoths and mastodons to native American horses, camels, and saber-toothed tigers.

Unlike the site of the Folsom massacre of bison, Gypsum Cave with its five connecting chambers had not been just the scene of a brief and ferocious encounter between man and beast, but left a record of consecutive—if perhaps intermittent—human occupation. Basket Maker, whose presence had marked the rock bottom in cliff dwellings, now practically floated on the surface with the modern Paiute. Furthermore, painstaking investigation of various layers of relics in the site not only extended the culture horizon by thousands of years but bridged the gap between the Pueblo and Palaeo-Indian.

Nor was the presence of humans authenticated by stone projectiles, scrapers, and knives alone. Thanks to the preserving graces of the dry cave, there came to the fore actual wooden implements made from the same trees and bushes (elder, buckthorn) that thrive in southern Nevada today. Foremost among these wooden articles were much-sought specimens of the spear thrower (*atlatl*), the primitive but ingenious device for adding momentum to lance propulsion, which in the Americas was never fully supplanted by the very late bow and arrow. Some of the wooden pieces retained traces of paint and feathers with which they had been decorated. Fragments of baskets, though of somewhat doubtful stratigraphy, judging by their strange weave and resemblance to samples later found elsewhere, probably belonged to the oldest cave inhabitants. Spear points of these ancients were of an unknown lozenge-shaped type, thenceforth called Gypsum Cave. In several instances, their convex short base still showed traces of pitch with which they undoubtedly had been fastened to spears. The wooden dart shafts, though of cruder shape than those of the Basket Makers, were probably painted. Gypsum Man, it seemed, lit his dreary precinct with torches made from canes. He kindled fire with wood and dung. In Cavern I a fireplace was laid out eight feet below the modern surface at the lowest level.

The *atlatl* (spear thrower) and its use

The clearest evidences of this early hunter's association with Pleistocene fauna were, of course, the physical remains of animals, many of them deposited in close proximity to human implements. Traces of that kind had been the principal reason Harrington launched a thorough exploration of the cave. Rummaging about the floor, he had come across *atlatls* and wooden dart shafts buried in a thick layer of fibrous dung. This waste deposit appeared to Harrington quite different from that of any present-day animal. By its composition it had to be ascribed to a vegetable eater, and at that, to one of considerable size. Besides, only a prehistoric beast able to make its way into Gypsum Cave by crawling through its opening would qualify. From such clues Harrington shrewdly deduced that the cave must have been a favorite haunt of the giant ground sloth. His hunch was corroborated by the experts he consulted. The final proof came during his full-scale campaign in 1930 when a skull and eventually entire skeletons of the mighty fossil mammal turned up, accompanied by patches of reddish hair and horny claws.

Once again Gypsum Cave's unusual dryness had made it possible to rescue organic materials the age of which had to be counted in millennia. Having such substances meant that, two decades later after the discovery of the disintegration rate of radioactive carbon, an approximate date could be assigned to the artifacts. Samples of sloth dung submitted by Harrington to the Institute for Nuclear Studies of the University of Chicago gave 10,455 ± 340 years for a deposit at a depth of six feet four inches, and 8,527 ± 250 years for a higher one at two feet six inches. These figures were in considerable agreement with the estimate earlier made by geologists who had associated an underlying mineral layer deposited by seeping water with a pluvial period of the late Ice Age.

Mark R. Harrington was a seasoned spelunker when he tackled Gypsum Cave. He had taken up the pursuit as early as 1900, when he excavated Leatherman's Cave near Greenwich, Connecticut. For several seasons he worked in caves of the Ozark Mountains, identifying the Ozark Bluff Dweller culture in Arkansas and Missouri. At another cave in Nevada he had previously extended the Basket Maker horizon to this distant outpost of the Southwest. He made archaeological history at a cave near the southern coast of Cuba, where he traced two prehistoric West Indian cultures. He has written entertainingly of discovering a stone idol during that campaign. The National Speleological Society of the United States named him an honorary member in 1950.

Born at Ann Arbor, Michigan, in 1882, Harrington has done extensive archaeological work all over the United States. In order to study modern North American Indians he has lived among twenty-three tribes. Since 1928 he has been associated with the Southwest Museum as director of research and curator. In several of his later campaigns he investigated outdoor sites for ancient human remains, most notably at Borax Lake, California. Not far from Gypsum Cave, at Tule Springs, Nevada, he found ashbeds, laid open by erosion, which contained animal bones and man-made implements. When in 1954 some of the charcoal from these ashes was tested for its carbon-14 by Dr. W. E. Libby, an age of at least 23,800 years was obtained. This was proclaimed one of the oldest pieces of evidence for early man in America, though it has recently been challenged on the grounds that the verdict of radio-carbon testing may be invalidated by the possibility of contamination of the ancient specimen.

GYPSUM CAVE, NEVADA

Mark R. Harrington

I think it was in Arkansas, years ago, that an obviously frightened Negro approached me as I stood in the door of my tent. "Please, suh," he faltered, twisting his cap in his hands, "Is you-all Gypsums? Does you-all tell fo'tunes?"

Having, since then, spread my tent under many skies I have always regarded myself as a more or less respectable Gypsy, and now that we are encamped at "Gypsum" Cave, near Las Vegas, Nevada, I feel "Gyppier" than ever. However, it was not myself, but Yewas, alias Bertha Parker Pallan, our ambitious niece, who found the first sloth skull in the cave, the skull which Dr. Scherer [Director of the Southwest Museum, Los Angeles] has christened the "Gypsy Sloth," although Dr. Stock insists that it is a *Nothrotherium* [*shastense*]. Bertie is expedition Secretary, but once-in-a-while she steals away to the Cave, trowel in hand, with her miner's light and dust-mask, and she never comes back empty-handed. How she happened to stick her head under one rock in such a position that she could see the skull hidden under another I can't imagine, but she did it.

We knew that the said skull could not possibly belong to any "varmint" that roams the Nevada hills today, so we sent it in to headquarters for examination. And while we were waiting, none too patiently, for a report, we dug away busily in the cave. Goodness knows how many tons of rocks and dirt we had moved, finding only a few small bones, and occasional scattered Indian things, when something happened. Mrs. Myrtle Evans, wife of Oliver Evans, one of the assistants, visited the cave with little Lyman Evans, her nephew. Mrs. Evans makes no claims as an archeologist or paleontologist but she is a Washo Indian and her eyesight is excellent. And it was not the sweating toilers in the trenches that found the second sloth—it was Myrtle Evans and little Lyman.

Tiring of watching the diggers, they had wandered off with their carbide lights to a far end of the cavern, and there they scratched with a trowel beside a rock. And there they found a bone—a section of the backbone of some strange, massively-built beast. When I saw it, something in my heart cried, "Ground-sloth!" and I called Willis and Oliver away from Trail Trench No. 3 to tackle the new place. A few hours later they had uncovered a mass of ground-sloth bones, under the foot of a

From *The Masterkey:* "The 'Gypsy' Sloth," Vol. 3, No. 8 (March–April 1930), pp. 15–16; "The Gypsum Cave Mùrder Case," Vol. 4, No. 2 (June–July 1930), pp. 37–42. Courtesy of Southwest Museum, Los Angeles, California.

rock-slide, some of them very well preserved, a huge claw with its horny covering still intact, and even shreds of hide and bunches of the coarse sandy hair with dark brown shading that had once clothed the great beast. I wired for help. The job looked too big for a mere archeologist to tackle alone.

The North American ground sloth

A few days later a solemn conclave gathered at Camp "So-we-mu" ["Big House on the Hill"] to view the remains of his slothship. Among its members, besides our own Dr. Scherer and myself, were Dr. Chester Stock and Dr. E. L. Furlong of "Cal-Tech," both distinguished paleontologists, and Ex-Governor Scrugham of Nevada, former owner of Gypsum Cave [who had first alerted Harrington to the site].

And we all agreed that in Gypsum Cave, which is a dry one, we have what is probably the best chance in the country to study the long extinct ground-sloth, for its remains seem to be better preserved here than anywhere else. Even Dr. Stock had never seen the hair and claws before. And because we have found in the same cave many things, mostly fragments of weapons, left by the earliest known human inhabitants of the Southwest, the Basket Makers, we agreed that here is probably the best opportunity for paleontologist and archeologist to work together on a single problem, North America's "Earliest Man."

An archeologist is after all a sort of detective, a detective specializing on very cold trails. His business is to trace the foot-steps of a man who lived two or three thousand years ago or more, and make a careful record of his life and habits. . . .

In Gypsum Cave, near Las Vegas, Nevada, we have had a real detective problem, for in this case there was a suspicion of murder. . . .

Here we have the family of old Mr. Ground-sloth living peacefully in an ancient ancestral home. Suddenly their life in the cave came to an end, and we soon found enough of their bones to show that death, not removal, was the cause.

Now, in the same cave we found a lot of things made by Mr. Man, about ninety-five per cent of them weapons, and the suspicion was strong from the beginning that Man had something to do with the demise of the old Sloth family.

It makes no difference that the Sloth family have been deceased ten or maybe twenty thousand years and that the alleged murderer was gathered to his fathers before Egypt or Babylonia, Greece or Rome had pipped the shell. It's our job to gather the evidence in the case and to find out first of all whether Man ever visited the cave in the days of the Sloths, or whether he simply wandered in some thousands of years later.

The next step, of course, would be to actually prove the killing; but if we can show that Mr. Man even met Mr. Sloth, little additional proof is necessary, for Man has always had a very bad reputation for assisting his neighbors, human and otherwise, into the great Hereafter.

After about four months searching for clues, we could say that out of the evidence uncovered, by far the greater part points to the guilt of Mr. Man, or at least to his presence on the ground when the demise of the unfortunate Sloth family took place.

Our cave is a big one, three hundred feet long by a hundred and twenty feet wide, and contains five rooms, in every one of which we uncovered bits of evidence.

It must be remembered, too, that the cave is extremely dry as well as big, which accounts for the fact that the hair, claws, and even bits of the skin of the Sloths remain undecayed after many thousands of years, not to speak of the wooden dart-shafts, strings, and even pieces of baskets left by the human visitors. When we began our digging, the floor of Room 4, which the Sloth family used as a bedroom, was a sight to behold. It reminded one of the accumulated manure in some old stable yard or horse corral—yet Sloths and only Sloths were responsible.

In Room 1, while we have traces of Pueblo Indians near the surface and of the Basket Makers, who are supposed to have lived about 1500 B.C., directly below them, one has to dig down through several layers

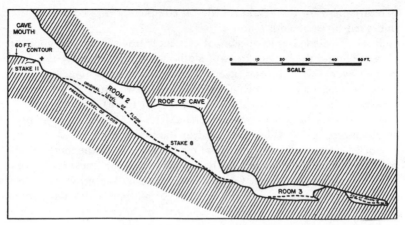

Plan of Gypsum Cave, Nevada

more to a depth of more than eight feet to find any sign of the Sloths. In one layer at that depth, however, we found not alone a considerable amount of Sloth manure (the Sloths were not neat housekeepers) but also some charcoal and a piece of wood that had undoubtedly been shaped by the hand of Man.

In Room 2 the evidence was even better, because here we found *beneath* a deeply buried layer of matted sticks containing sloth manure, and at a depth of from eight to ten feet from the surface, some fragments of painted dart-shafts such as were used by the earliest known human inhabitants of America in hunting and in war,—a piece of evidence very hard indeed to dispute.

Room 3 also had an interesting story to tell, for in the very *bottom* of a rock slide in this room we found some flint points for similar darts and on the *surface* of this same slide a short distance from one of them lay the skull of one of the victims, a full-grown ground-sloth.

Room 4, which is the biggest room in the cave and the one in which we have found more bones of the slain than in any other, yielded a number of bits of evidence, the most important of which was a dart-point imbedded in a layer of partly solidified gypsum between two burnt layers of ground-sloth manure. Less than two feet distant in the same layer lay a sloth arm-bone and not more than five or six feet away in the layer above it were the bones of a slender-limbed little camel, smaller and more delicately formed than any living member of the camel tribe.

In the passage between Room 4 and 5 some other clews appeared, the best of which were a piece of wooden dart-shaft imbedded in a layer just beneath the dung and a collection of sticks burnt on one end, apparently pieces of torches, in a little pit completely capped over with an unbroken layer of sloth manure.

Room 5 yielded only one bit of evidence, but that was a good one. Here we found the bones of a baby sloth at a depth of twenty-two inches capped over with unbroken layers of cave debris and dung. Five inches to the northeast and one inch above them were two small pieces of arrow-cane burnt at both ends (evidently pieces of a torch), and there was no apparent way that these fragments could have reached the vicinity of the bones except by being deposited at the same time. . . .

Such was the list of our principal evidence down to the tenth of May, indicating that Mr. Man was in the vicinity when the last sloth lay down and closed his eyes forever. Of course, we have had negative evidence in abundance, that is to say, any number of sloth remains without any trace of man, and hundreds of fragments of ancient weapons not associated with the sloths at all so far as we could see.

In only a very few instances, however, did we find any really contrary evidence—that is to say, finds of strictly modern objects in apparent connection with the sloth which might cast reflections on the reliability of our other silent witnesses. One of these was a bullet, imbedded several inches deep in ashes resulting from the burning of sloth manure; another was a tin can—a bean-can, I believe, deep in a crevice such as had, in other cases, yielded darts and traces of the sloth.

Such things worried us little, however, because the weight of the bullet would be sufficient to carry it down into the soft ashes from the surface, and the bean-can was probably the special treasure of some recent pack-rat's collection.

Another puzzling find was that of an Indian bean along with a handful of other seeds buried a long way down below the layer of sloth dung in a layer altogether too early for the development of agriculture in America. This would have bothered us and perhaps caused us to doubt some of our other deductions if the seeds had not shown gnawing by mice and had not been found in an open crevice connected with other open crevices through which a mouse could easily find his way in from the present surface and hide away his winter's food supply.

Speaking of crevice finds, we found in a crevice some tiny feathers wrapped with sinew, possibly part of some old hunter's headdress, or part of the decoration of the prayer-sticks (*pahos*) he may have offered to his slain foes. Adjoining them were the well-preserved bones of our very first sloth.

Ignoring all crevice finds, however, we felt that the evidence against Mr. Man was almost strong enough to submit to the "Grand Jury," which, I suspect, should be composed of archeologists and paleontologists. . . .

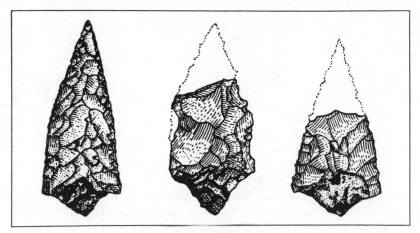

Gypsum points from Gypsum Cave

May 13th, we uncovered one of our best pieces of evidence yet—a wooden foreshaft for a dart imbedded in gypsum, under a four-inch layer of sloth manure, which in turn was capped by a gypsum layer. Part of this gypsum was rather loose, but another part formed a practically continuous crust.

The case looks bad for Mr. Man! It certainly appears now as if he had been hanging round the cave for some time before the Sloth family met their untimely end.

36

When, at a meeting of The New York Academy of Medicine in March 1928, Aleš Hrdlička once more summed up his disbelief in any vestiges of ancient man in the Western Hemisphere, his most persuasive argument was that, had humans lived there during the last glaciation, profuse materials would long ago have been forthcoming from *caves* as they had in Europe. There is, he said, "not one favorable cave or shelter for human habitation in old France, Belgium, Moravia, the foothills of the Pyrenees, and elsewhere, that has not been the place of some ancient man. . . . Wherever ancient man lived, in caves or in open air, he has left not a single implement or what not, as appears in American finds, but large numbers, such large numbers that already they clog some of the museums in Europe. In addition, early man, wherever he lived, lived essentially on the animals of his time . . . and he left their bones as a testimony of his presence. Where are any such things in America? Where are the habitations and refuse accumulations of our old rivers and caves? Where are the implements, the bones of animals upon which these old men have fed? . . . To this day not a single case of anything such as in Europe. Where is the explanation of all this? What is the matter?"

It was Hrdlička's misfortune to have made this statement just as the Folsom find was tipping the scales. At that time, with Gypsum Cave still undiscovered, the few signs of early Americans came from campsites and kills situated in the open. This was indeed puzzling, considering palaeolithic man's penchant for caves. But Hrdlička's plaintive argument, well founded as it seemed, suffered from a regrettable fallacy: it was made *ex silentio*. That is to say, it generalized from the absence or insufficiency of evidence to non-existence. In fact most anthropologists of today will concur with Hrdlička that human life was relatively widespread in palaeolothic Europe, but at the same time they allow for a more sparsely populated North America that inevitably left a scantier, though hardly a blank, record. The early bands of roaming hunters and food gatherers probably never entered the majority of caverns or rock shelters, yet a considerable number of caves have now—unbeknownst to Hrdlička—produced signs of early human occupation. Weapons and the bones of slaughtered animals are no longer in short supply.

Since Hrdlička's day, studies of caves from the Aleutians to Patagonia have tremendously expanded our conception of the earliest Americans. It is no exaggeration to say that their career in the Americas has been reconstructed largely from deposits in caves or rocky recesses. The record includes a nine-thousand-year-old "factory" of woven sandals in Oregon, primitive cobs of domesticated corn from Mexico bearing on the beginning of agriculture, and remains left by what may have been the first migrants to reach the tip of South America.

If caves are prime sites for tracking down palaeolothic vestiges (just as tombs, temples, and palaces are the principal receptacles of more advanced cultures), projectile points serve as the key artifact for identifying early men. They are infallible and ubiquitous testimony of human presence, and characterize a people or a culture. Furthermore, being virtually indestructible, they have come down to us in great quantity.

Projectile points made from flint, quartz, chalcedony, or other stones are known to vary significantly among different peoples. In size, shape, and fashioning they are of an infinite range. No matter how conservative primitive societies tend to be, they will eventually modify and adapt these vital instruments. Hence projectiles are bound to mirror development in time and levels of craftsmanship, as well as responses to a changing environment.

It is really quite amazing how much information can be gleaned from flaked or chipped pieces of stone. Did a new people appear on the scene? Do weapons show affinities with the cultures of other regions or even continents? Did a style persist through several layers of deposits and thus show long duration? With what mode of propulsion was a point associated? Was it geared to the slaughter of particular animals? These and many more questions can be answered by a thorough examination. Above all, the association of spear or dart points with animals of extinct species and with geologically more or less datable strata allows us to arrive at the age, sequence, and spread of palaeolithic cultures. No wonder that arrowheads and the like have become as indispensable to the study of palaeolithic man as pottery has to that of his neolithic descendants. The functions of these two types of durable artifacts in archaeological analysis are really quite similar. Both may equally exasperate the non-specialist, and tables on tables with sketches of stone tips, blades, choppers, or axes are generally considered the ultimate in scientific pedantry. However, once one realizes with what skill those ancient objects may have been produced, how extraordinarily varied, if not ingenious, they are, and how meaningful they have turned out to be in summoning up lost generations of palaeolithic forebears, these minutiae take on a fascination of their own. Vying with the professionals, more than one Sunday archaeologist has taken off in hot pursuit of Indian "arrowheads."

Earliest America has come to be known by its spear points. Its reconstruction started in earnest with the Folsom point. This beautifully flaked stone projectile, with characteristic longitudinal grooves on both sides, compares favorably with the finest pieces from the Old World's Stone Age. Apparently, its peculiar shape was confined to the New World.

Folsom or rather "Generalized Folsom" (Clovis) fluted points were eventually found all over the United States and beyond, from Alaska to Ecuador. But soon other points cropped up. They were quite differently shaped and executed. Gypsum Cave points may have been slightly more recent than Folsom, as were the most delicately worked of all projectiles, the Eden or Yuma, which, though older, surpassed in finish even the neolithic tips from Denmark and Egypt, which they resemble.

Once excavations were stepped up in the Southwest and elsewhere, a whole crop of new names such as Clovis, Lehner, Abilene, Plainview, Scottsbluff, Lerma, and many more were added to the archaeological vocabulary. All of these names designated locales of specific stone industries.

Its much cruder flakes and secondary chipping as well as its occasional occurrence in lower Southwestern layers indicate that Clovis was probably older than traditional Folsom, though it may have remained longer in use elsewhere in the Americas. It was Mark R. Harrington who first observed that Clovis points, for some unexplained reason, happened to be linked in the Southwest to the hunting of Columbian elephants, while the Folsom projectiles had as their chief quarry *Bison antiquus.*

A cave, once again in New Mexico, was to add still another name with its lithic materials: Sandia. Sandia Man made Folsom Man a mere Johnny-come-lately, and easily doubled the span of antiquity of early Americans. Further millennia were thus added to the Palaeo-Indian's American birthright. Though we are today less sanguine about the claim of his discoverer, Frank C. Hibben, that Sandia Man was indeed the earliest of them all and is not likely ever to be superseded, we still lack a serious competitor. He lived probably some twenty to twenty-five thousand years ago, based on the study of geological formations and their connection with climatological phenomena of the Ice Age. Radiocarbon tests seem to confirm this estimate, but doubt has been cast on the reliability of the examined material, elephant ivory.

Located in a limestone ridge of the Sandia Mountains near Albuquerque, New Mexico, Sandia Cave was not as spacious as Gypsum Cave,

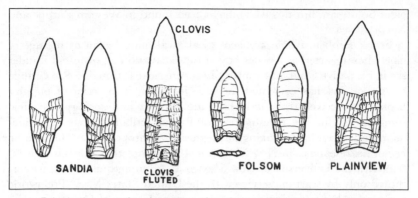

Principal types of early spear points from the American Southwest

nor did it enjoy such long periods of dryness as those which helped to preserve wooden and organic materials at Gypsum. It was so narrow that there is little likelihood that any of the large Tertiary beasts would have sought refuge there. Today it is the crowded abode of pack-rats and bats, which have turned it into a malodorous powderkeg of lung-choking dust. Yet, such drawbacks notwithstanding, it proved literally the answer to an archaeologist's prayer.

Sandia Cave provided in plenitude what Hrdlička had denied American caves: layers studded with cracked bones of horses, camels, mammoths, bison, wolves, and other animals. Ashes and hearths were ineluctable signs that the butchered creatures had been dragged into the cave for high-protein barbecues. Accompanying such debris was an assemblage of all kinds of stone tools and weapons. The stratification of the cave bottom was clear-cut: hard limestone covers, laid down during periods of high precipitation, interleaved between the softer layers of human occupation.

In four campaigns from 1936 onward, Frank C. Hibben and his assistants and students from the University of New Mexico dug at the cave. Hibben could derive considerable satisfaction from finding at last Folsom Man's actual living quarters. But meeting this early American, hitherto considered the continent's oldest inhabitant, on his own home grounds was only a prologue. Once Hibben pierced through a thick layer of reddish ochre (its iron content must have come from a lush growth of fir trees in the cave area), he discovered Sandia Man—or rather Sandia points. The characteristic stone projectiles were unique. Considerably less finished than Folsom or Clovis, they were leaf-shaped with a fairly round base and had an inset or notch on one side for hafting them to a spear. In shape the Sandia points were remarkably like the older Solutrean flint tips which have been found in Western Europe and North Africa.

Frank Hibben, whose archaeological awakening began at the age of nine when he acted as a water boy at the excavation of a Mound Builder site in his native Ohio, has hunted "Lost Americans" from the Rio Grande to Alaska and has presented the case for them in a series of popular books. He received training in both archaeology and zoology—an ideal combination for the investigation of Palaeo-Indian hunters of extinct mammals. Even before taking his degree in anthropology at Harvard he began his researches in New Mexico in 1934. Since that year his association with the University of New Mexico at Albuquerque has been interrupted only by wartime service with the United States Navy. Prehistoric exploration has taken him beyond America to Germany, Czechoslovakia, France, and Yugoslavia and has made him a renowned authority also on the Old World Stone Age. As a hunter of big game he visited South America, Asia, and Africa. After his original discovery of Sandia points, Hibben found similar projectiles at an open site near Lucy, New Mexico, where he excavated during the years 1954 and 1955. As recently as 1966 he reported traces of circular dwellings at a Folsom site along a vanished Lake near Albuquerque. Dating back to about 8000 B.C., evidence of a semi-permanent outdoor settlement of such age in the Americas came as a great surprise. Meanwhile, single-notched Sandia points have been reported from Texas to Saskatchewan and Oregon.

SANDIA MAN

Frank C. Hibben

The human animal has from earliest times been a cave animal. This truth can be demonstrated in a dozen ways in Europe and Asia. Many of the earliest remains of our forefathers have been rooted from the rubble of cave floors. Some of the caverns of Europe were occupied for thousands

From *The Lost Americans*, by Frank C. Hibben. Copyright © 1946 by Frank C. Hibben. Thomas Y. Crowell Company, New York, publishers. [Apollo Edition, 1961, pp. 135–50.]

of years. Generations of human beings cowered in the gloom of these caves and looked out with apprehension into the brightness of an outside world teeming with fearsome animals. Any natural rocky crevice served as a shelter and a protection to our practically defenseless ancestors. Many a weak animal has eked out an existence amid savage and inimical surroundings by spending most of its time in a burrow or a hole.

We are surprised to discover, then, the remains of the early hunters of America in open camp sites. Lindenmeier and Clovis and even the original Folsom quarry were all places along stream banks and around the edges of marshes and ponds. The early American hunters apparently lived unafraid, even where the bison and the pounding herds of mammoth came to water.

This statement becomes even more inexplicable when we remember the bad weather that we have described for those remote times. The chilling winds that whistled down from the glacial ice walls must have made living cold and uncomfortable indeed on the open plains. Even in partially protected valleys the wet and the rain with the attendant cold would have made existence miserable. The Folsom men of course possessed the secret of fire, but even this would mitigate only in a small way the discomfiture of exposure to the elements.

The absence of any indication of habitation or shelters on the open hunting sites deepens the mystery. Even if the homes were lodges made out of brush and sticks of such an ephemeral nature that no trace exists, it still would seem an uncomfortable way for a thin-skinned animal such as man to get along in a glacial climate.

Until 1936 it was common archaeological opinion that early man in the New World was such a hardy creature that he remained close to where the game animals were to be found in abundance, and that an open camp site in the wet grass along a stream was his natural habitat. Then, by accident, we came upon a New World cave man, a primitive hunter that satisfied all our expectations as to how ancient man should act and live. The most remarkable thing was that this primitive proved to be even older than Folsom man himself, whom we had originally thought was the earliest American.

This discovery involved a quiet Sunday afternoon and a student from the University of New Mexico. This particular young man, Kenneth Davis by name, was spending his week end in exploring caves in the vicinity of Albuquerque and collecting such bits of evidence in them as might be of interest to the museum at the University. On this particular occasion, he brought in, on a memorable Monday, a cigar box full of ancient baubles of no especial note. He had garnered from the floor of one of the caverns a few bits of pottery, a piece of deer antler cut with

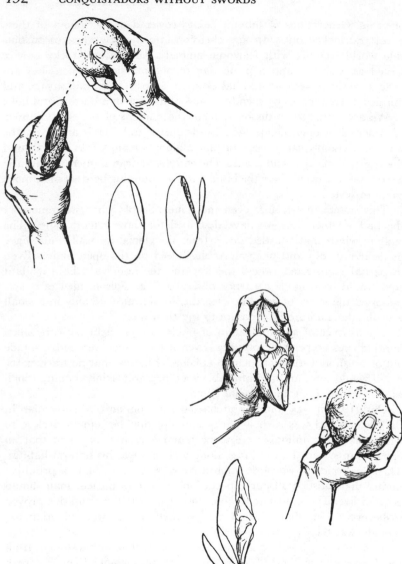

Primitive methods of making stone blades by percussion, after W. Holmes

a knife, and some fragments of woven yucca sandals and basketry. This collection elicited no special interest in itself, as the remains were of the sort usually found in comparatively modern Indian encampments. Apparently some Pueblo Indians of the last few hundred years had used the cave as a stopping place during hunting trips into the mountains. The pottery fragments were of the type familiar to the Pueblos in the Rio Grande Valley. However, the cave had been inhabited, and that in itself was something. Armed with flashlights, candles, cameras, trowels, and notebooks, we set out to check further on this particular cavern.

The cave proved to be one of a group of five, located high in the limestone wall of Las Huertas Canyon in the Sandia Mountain Range just east of Albuquerque. Of the five holes in the limestone cliff in this place, only one is of any size or depth, and even this one cannot be described as pretentious. It was from this one, however, that the odds and ends of old civilization had come. We called the cave Sandia Cave, from the name of the mountains on whose edge it is located.

Sandia Cave may more properly be described as a tunnel leading back into the cliff some 200 yards. Throughout a considerable portion of its length, the debris and dust are piled almost to the roof. Locomotion past these strictured spots may be made only by slithering along on one's stomach. The cave is exceedingly dry and redolent with the characteristic smell of bat guano and pack rat remains. It did not look particularly promising, because of its long slender form and its lack of roominess.

As the scientific party had crawled and groveled almost to the end of the tunnellike passageway, a flight of bats was disturbed from a chimneylike aperture that led upward from one of the galleries. With characteristic squeaks and the rustle of leathery wings, the bats rushed down the narrow passageway for the cave mouth. As they passed, the party involuntarily flinched close to the rocky walls to give them ample room. As they did so, one of the group felt beneath his hand, on a pile of debris, a curved bone. Even in the dark it felt unusual and important.

With some excitement we made our way to the cave mouth, and there, in the light of a New Mexico afternoon, examined our find. It was indeed a bone, but certainly no ordinary one. It was shaped like the curved flat blade of a Turkish dagger. It was a core from the claw of a giant ground sloth—that lumbering animal so typical of late glacial times. It could be nothing else.

This was a find indeed. If ground sloth remains were in the cave, and also human remains, we might find some evidence that men lived there at the same time as the sloths. We might yet find an American cave man. We did.

Even in our preliminary digging near the mouth of the cave we began to find evidences of human occupation. Men and women too had lived in the cave long before Pueblo times. We had stumbled by chance upon a cave that had been long inhabited by humans and in which they had left their remains in the same manner as had their European forebears.

We early found that the mouth of Sandia Cave, as it exists today, was in reality far back from the original entrance to the cavern. During the many thousands of years since the early men had lived there, the face of the cliff had sloughed away many feet, taking with it the original mouth of the cave. At the present day, the Sandia Cave mouth is small and unimposing and rests on a cliff face approached only by a narrow ledge. The evidences that we were finding in the cave apparently had slid down into the tunnellike passage that led off the back of the original occupation cavern. There was left, after all these thousands of years, only the rearmost portion of what had been the ancient Sandia Cave, but even this fragment was not disappointing.

We built ladders up to the entrance to facilitate excavating work, and a safety scaffolding around the mouth to keep enthusiastic students from falling off the cliff. During the last of the four seasons of work on the Sandia Cave, it became necessary to install a special suction apparatus to clear the fine penetrating dust from the cave as the work progressed. Even with the workmen wearing dust masks, this dust—dried and undisturbed for many centuries in the cave—was so fine and permeating that it rose in clouds at the slightest movement of a shovel or trowel. Penetrating into the lungs, the dust produced nausea and a type of dust pneumonia for the unfortunate excavators. But the results were worth even this hazard of cave excavation.

On almost the first day of digging, we discovered that the cave debris was not a simple pile of stuff that had gradually accumulated in the limestone passageway. The rubble and detritus that filled up the cave were made up of several different layers of material. These layers, as we came to know them after several months of excavation, proved to be extremely significant. Actually this stratification gave us as much information as to the early history of the place as the artifacts and implements themselves.

Throughout the cave, and especially thick near the mouth, was a layer of modern accumulation. By *modern*, in this instance, we mean the last several centuries or possibly the last few thousands of years. This modern stuff consisted of dust, blown in by winds of many unrecorded storms, as well as the pack rat and bat accumulation deposited over this same time. Here and there fragments of limestone, fallen from the roof, were mixed with the dust, as records of earth tremors of many years ago. Near the entrance of the cave were a few fragments of Pueblo pottery and an abandoned metate or corn-grinding stone, showing that the

Pueblo Indians of the fourteenth and fifteenth centuries A.D. had occasionally crawled into the cave for a night's shelter. Man's natural penchant for cave shelter has not changed in many thousands of years. Some scientists believe that agoraphobia stems from this human desire to feel protected by walls of rock with an opening only on one side.

In places in the Sandia Cave this modern dust accumulation was 6 feet thick. Toward the rear of the open cave passageway, the dust feathered to only a light coating some inches thick. Throughout the length of the cave, however, the dust could be identified as an accumulation that had occurred since glacial times.

Beneath the dust accumulation of more recent origin, we came upon a hard crust of cave stone. This layer of material was the same as that which forms the stalactites and the stalagmites of the usual limestone grotto. Stalagmitic formations were quite rare in the Sandia Cave. However, typical cave-drip formations had formed on the walls in many places where sheets of stalagmitic stone could be seen. This same material had formed a solid crust over the floor of the cave, as thick and hard as a cement floor. After clearing the dust debris from the topmost layer, it was necessary for us to break through this crust with sledge hammers. We did not mind this arduous labor, however, because the crust served effectively to seal in any more ancient material found below it. It was like opening the lid of a gigantic sardine can, whose contents would give you all the evidence you wanted for the earliest history of the New World.

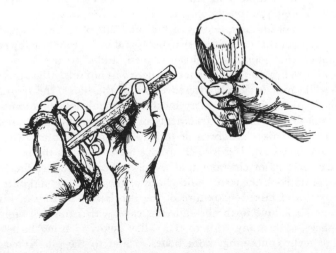

A further step in early stone industry: indirect percussion with a hammer and a punch of wood or bone, after W. Holmes

This travertine crust was only 3 to 6 inches thick in most places and contained no implements or evidences that humans had been there while it was forming. It was, however, one of the most important features of the cave.

We did not need the clouds of penetrating dust to remind us that the Sandia Cave is dry at the present day and had been so for the many centuries that the dust was accumulating. This stalagmitic crust beneath the dust, however, could have been laid down only during a wet period. Such cave formations are formed by percolating waters seeping down through limestone crevices and depositing limestone secretion which the water carries in solution. This liquid limestone may be deposited in the form of iciclelike stalactites and stalagmites, or it may form in sheets of stony material over the cave floor. It formed in this latter way in the Sandia Cave, as the limestone-permeated waters dripped and oozed out over the cave floor and evaporated there. The crust in the Sandia Cave, then, was laid down during wet and dripping times. What could these be but the lush times of the glacial period? Professor Kirk Bryan of Harvard University confirmed this point for us. The crust on the top of our "sardine can" marked the last wet period of the glacial era. What would we find beneath it?

Arduously chipping down with sledge hammers and crowbars into the concretelike mass below the crust, we came upon an ancient cave floor. This habitation level was marked by an accumulation such as the dirty human animal invariably leaves behind wherever he lives. There were fragments of bone, purposely split to extract the marrow, and the teeth of many kinds of animals. Scraps of flint and bits of charcoal were scattered throughout the mass. Stone fragments and dirt, brought in by countless comings and goings of prehistoric men, added to the mass of the layer, for the debris on this ancient cave floor was not solely the accumulation of wild animals. The shattered bones of the horse, the bison, and the camel had not been left there by their original unfortunate owners. No mammoth had brought fragments of his teeth and tusks into the cave. These remains had been left there by men—hunters who had brought the bones and bits into their cave home to gnaw the meat from their surfaces. Bits of charcoal told a story of cave cooking fires, built so long ago to cook the steaks and chops of these Ice Age animals. The very broken and mixed-up nature of the debris told a story of human movement back and forth through the cave with countless nights of lairing there, with many trips to the valley below to bring back other chunks of meat containing more bones to add to the pile. It was the accumulation of centuries.

If we had needed additional evidence that men—American cave men

—had actually lived in the place at this time, there were the flint points. Mingled amidst the bones and rock fragments, scattered just as they had been lost many thousands of years ago, we found several flint spear points on the old cave floor. The percolating lime-permeated water, seeping down through this ancient material during the wet period when the crust was forming, had cemented all the debris into a mass much like friable concrete. The flint points that we found were often glued fast to a rock or bone by the limy water which had seeped down over them for so long. It was extremely difficult to extricate the flint specimens without breaking them, and it was necessary to screen all of the material carefully after it was broken up so that no bit of lime-coated evidence might escape us in the gloom and flickering shadows of the excavating lamps.

As we carefully chipped, with a small dental tool, around the first of the flint points that we encountered, we saw the story clearly. There was the characteristic indented base and the beginning of the channeled grooves up either face of the point—it was a Folsom point. So Folsom man had laired in this cave, had dragged these animal bones into his home, had thrown them back over his shoulder into the darkness.

We found more and more Folsom points, most of them typical and exactly like those from the classic Folsom quarry where Folsom man had first been discovered. We found other points that differed slightly, yet maintained the main Folsom characteristics. There was no doubt that at least some Folsom men had lived as cave men in the Sandia Cave.

In addition to the Folsom spear points, there were flake knives of flint and flat chipped flint blades, probably used for skinning the animals that these hunters killed. There was even one point made out of a fragment of ivory from a mammoth tusk. We found, too, the small fine-pointed gravers which the Folsom people probably used for tatooing themselves. It was a typical Folsom assemblage. There could be no doubt that the same people who hunted Taylor's bison on the edge of the Great Plains had also used the Sandia Mountain fringe as a hunting ground and had stayed in the Sandia Cave during their trips.

If the discovery of a Folsom floor in the Sandia site were its only claim to glory, the cave would not be especially remarkable. As a matter of fact, we would have expected to find Folsom people using caves when they could. However, in the Sandia Cave we dug farther, down below the level of Folsom man, and we found what we had hardly dared to hope for.

Below the half-cemented bones, flint, and debris of the Folsom floor, we dug through a considerable layer of fine yellow ochre. This stuff lay in thin laminated strata, obviously laid down by water at another time when the cave was wet. Although originally deposited in a moist period, the yellow ochre was as dry at the present day as everything else in the cave and rose in penetrating yellow clouds at the slightest disturbance. This noxious stuff gave color to the cave in more ways than one, so much so that we contemplated at one time calling the Sandia Cave, Yellow Ochre Cave.

But the yellow ochre level was not the lowermost level of the cave. Digging still farther down through this soft pigment, we encountered another ancient cave floor with evidences of man. Below the yellow ochre were other fragments of animal bones and flint and evidences of fire. It was another whole level of occupation and it occurred well below the Folsom cave floor.

At first we could see no difference between this lower debris, and the Folsom occupation level. There were bone fragments and teeth of the horse, camel, bison, mammoth, and mastodon. There were also the usual carnivores, the large wolves and cats of Ice Age times. As far as the animals were concerned, the Sandia Cave level, as we came to call this particular one, seemed no different from the Folsom.

As before, the flint points gave us our greatest information. We had come to look upon these flint spearheads that the ancient hunters had made as being extremely indicative of their times. A Folsom man chipped his intricate flint points with exactly the same technique and the same result as had his grandfathers before him. Changes in these weapons were extremely slow.

The flint points that we carefully lifted with the trowel from among the debris of the Sandia Cave floor were totally different from the Folsom. The Sandia points, for so we immediately called them, were rather crudely made. They were roughly chipped in a leaf shape with a notch or shoulder at one side of the rounded base. Though rougher and less skillfully made than the Folsom points, they were nonetheless distinctive, and we recognized at a glance that we were dealing with a different kind of man. These were Sandia Cave men, and they had lived as many thousands of years before Folsom times as it had taken to deposit the yellow ochre that separated their two levels of occupation in the Sandia Cave.

The accumulation and trash of the Sandia Cave level was not cemented like that of the layers above. In this level we traced out fireplaces with small rounded boulders outlining them. There were lenses of charcoal, still intact, where ancient cooking fires had been, and around their blackened borders were the split bones and fragments that showed where men had sat around these same fires and had gnawed the greasy flesh from these same bones and thrown them to one side. We could almost see, in the flickering excavation lights, the Sandia Cave men of so long ago, squatting around these now-dead embers.

Pressure flaking—Stone Age Man's most advanced method of shaping weapons and tools, after W. Holmes

The flint flake knives, the chipped skin scrapers, and the chips and debris of flint workings were mixed among the animal bones in much the same way as on any other cave floor that had been occupied by hunters. Indeed, the Sandia Cave life must have been similar to that of the Folsom. Sandia and Folsom men were both hunters and they had both hunted much the same animals. The weapons that they used were undoubtedly similar, even though the flint points that tipped them differed greatly. The important difference was that the Sandia Cave men had slept in this cave and had hunted in these valleys long before the Folsom men. We had thought the Folsom men to be the first, but now we realized that the Sandia men were obviously the earlier.

The first question asked by any visitor who was enthusiastic enough to crawl into the cave with us was: "But how long before Folsom men did the Sandia men live here?"

Again Professor Bryan helped us. He pointed out that the various levels in the cave represented a succession of wet and dry periods. The dust of the topmost level represented the dryness of recent centuries. The crust that sealed in the ancient occupation was laid down when the cave was wet and dripping. The Folsom debris was accumulated when the cave was comparatively dry or Folsom men could not have used it. The yellow ochre had been deposited below the Folsom floor during a period of wet when the cave actually contained puddles of accumulated water. The Sandia occupation below the others, when the Sandia hunters slept and built fires in the cave, was also a period of dryness. Below the Sandia Cave floor was a layer of white clay and an ancient water channel which indicated again the presence of water in the cave long before even Sandia man had used it.

At first thought, the wet and dry periods of the Sandia Cave might appear to correspond with the four great glacial eras as they have been defined by geologists. Because of a number of difficulties, however, such an explanation did not fit. The time span of both Folsom and Sandia man was not enough, even if we applied our wildest chronology to them. Professor Bryan, logically building up his evidence piece by piece, showed us that the Sandia Cave wet and dry levels must correspond with fluctuations of the last ice sheet that swept down from the Rocky Mountain area. The tongues and protrusions of this tremendous ice mass had advanced and retreated in an oscillating fashion, consuming several thousands of years with each of their minor advances and retreats. This complexity in the glacial age had been demonstrated from geological evidence, especially in the region of Colorado where these various tongues of ice had left piles of gravel and glacial detritus at their farthest point of advance.

Fitting in the Sandia Cave levels to this glacial chronology of advances and retreats, Sandia Cave men were dated at around twenty-five thousand years B.C. Since a few thousand years makes little difference geologically, Professor Bryan calculated an error of as much as 30 per cent in this estimate. When we finally dated the Sandia man by radioactive means, we were astonished to find how accurate this glacial time table was. We are satisfied now that the Sandia people existed on the North American continent well before the Folsom hunters. It seems extremely unlikely that any hunters earlier than the Sandia man existed on these continents or the many excavations would have given some hint of their presence. The Sandia people, then, were almost certainly the first Americans.

37

Across the pages of myth and fantasy, the stampede of the American mammoth has raised clouds of dust, which have obscured its indubitable omnipresence on the continent. In fact, beginning in early colonial times, before its existence was ever suspected, its bones, and those of its elephantine cousins, were found throughout the Americas. Bernal Díaz, companion of Cortés on the road to the Aztec capital, wrote in his chronicle that he was shown enormous bones at Tlaxcala. The natives ascribed them to their huge ancestors, just as Cotton Mather, nearly two hundred years later, was certain that they belonged to the race of giants mentioned in the Bible. Thomas Jefferson, however, thorough rationalist that he was, had no traffic with such pious imputations. In his *Notes on the State of Virginia* he discusses the testimony of the bones and leaves no doubt that they are the remains of a creature akin to, though much larger than, the elephant. Probably they belonged to the mammoth. At the same time, Jefferson took a stand on what has become the crucial issue of the mammoth controversy: Did the Indians have any first-hand knowledge of the tusked pachyderms? Jefferson adopted the extreme position that these animals have never died out (this, he insisted, would be against the Laws of Nature), and would yet be encountered in some unexplored region.

With the opening of the wilderness, only a few diehards continued to uphold the survival of elephants in far-away vales. The controversy drifted rather to the question of whether any tribe of prehistoric New World men could at some time have been contemporaneous with mammoth or mastodon. Most scientists said, definitely, no! The relatively recent arrival of man in the Western Hemisphere precluded the likelihood that he set eyes upon those exemplars of Tertiary megafauna. Yet there were persistent hints in Indian legends of beasts having elephant trunks and other suspicious features. Jefferson put credence in such traditions. Others collected and analyzed the various tales. The references to elephant-like beasts seemed conclusive. It was all very puzzling. But then it was suggested that these accounts were all of colonial origin. Ultimately, so it was claimed, they could be traced to Negro slaves who retained memories of elephants from Africa and passed them on to the Indians. When white men questioned them, the Indians were glad to oblige with elephant stories that might have brought joy to Kipling. Myths in the making were inadvertently instigated by the very people who tried to get behind them.

No sooner had the mammoth been explained away by scholarly scrutiny, than speculation brought him back into circulation. It was proclaimed that America had had its Hannibals—Mongol conquerors from Asia who, in the late thirteenth century, landed on the American coast with a host of elephants and founded the Inca and Aztec empires. As late as 1880 one theorist concluded by little else than speculation that the Mound Builders had domesticated the mammoth in order to construct their earthworks. The attempts of several romantically minded nineteenth-century archaeologists, from Count Waldeck on, to see elephantine likenesses in Maya friezes at Copán and Palenque became something of a cause célèbre. They, too, were discredited by modern savants to whom the elephant resemblance of these sculptures was coincidental. The seemingly proboscidian outgrowths depicted the orifices of either macaws or tapirs—they could not quite decide which. To link New World man with mammoth came to be considered by most as absurd as the battle scenes between hunched Neanderthalers and dinosaurs in Hollywood spectaculars.

And there the matter stood until the Folsom revolution of the 1920's. Now, all of a sudden, man's antiquity in America was extended to the threshold of the Tertiary. To boot, he was shown to be associated with long-vanished creatures. Undoubtedly, puny though he and his weapons were, he had preyed on over-sized pachyderms, just as the Pygmy of Central Africa does to this very day. Conclusive proof of the contemporaneity of mammoth and its human slaughterer gradually came to light. In 1952, Professor Emil W. Haury of the Arizona State Museum excavated actual sites of prehistoric mammoth hunts at Naco near the Arizona–Mexico border. The excavation of an almost intact mammoth with eight fluted Clovis points in its clay-filled hulk was of greatest importance, particularly since it marked the extension of the so-called Llano complex of the elephant-hunting culture of the Southwestern high plains to southern Arizona.

As anticipated by Haury, further materials were to issue from this region. In 1955 Haury himself hit upon a much larger mammoth kill, twelve miles to the northwest, on a ranch owned by Edward F. Lehner (who had first alerted him). Haury found no fewer than nine mammoth skeletons, in addition to several bones from bison, horses, and tapirs. They were accompanied by thirteen more Clovis points together with characteristic "llano" implements of scrapers and knives. The Lehner site, like Naco, included campfires, which yielded invaluable charcoal for carbon-14 tests. However, the data received from these specimens were, if anything, misleading. Examined by various laboratories in Chicago, Michigan, and elsewhere, the Naco carbon gave a reading of 9,250 years, which Haury considers too recent. He tends to agree with the geological analysis of the site by Dr. Ernst Antevs, a Swedish-born scientist long prominent in the age determination of deposits (varves) from receding glacial lakes, which gave an estimate of about 13,000 years. This, however, is a conservative date compared to the 37,000 years assigned by carbon-14 tests to Clovis points from Lewisville, Texas. Even allowing for

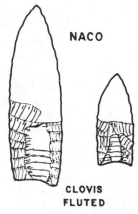

Clovis fluted points from the Naco elephant-kill site in southeastern Arizona

the *genius loci* of the Lone Star State, it is highly questionable whether Clovis points could have been continuously in use during 25,000 years. Obviously, the much heralded dating method of the Atomic Age still suffers serious shortcomings and must be supplemented by other—both more traditional and more recent—techniques.

Emil W. Haury, who gained his first field experience at the excavation of Cuicuilco in 1925, has himself been an active student of dating by tree rings. As we have seen, it was during these studies that, as a young assistant, he helped to furnish a missing link in the dendrochronological chain between the historic and prehistoric past of the Southwestern United States. Though he also explored the land of the Chibchas in Colombia, most of his labors concentrated on the Southwest, particularly on the Hohokam and Mogollon cultures. His investigation of Ventana Cave and its stratigraphy is a milestone. Since 1937 he has headed the department of anthropology at the University of Arizona at Tucson, and he succeeded Byron Cummings as director of the Arizona State Museum in 1938.

Haury's discoveries of animal kills settled forever doubts concerning early human associations with mammoth. Yet, he had to leave many questions unanswered. Nothing definite was known about the time when mammoth, mastodon, and elephant dropped from the American scene, if indeed their disappearance coincided. It has been argued—as Charles Lyell did in the mid-nineteenth century—that American mastodons lingered on into post-glacial millennia, even though they had become extinct in the Old World. There was, for instance, a curious mastodon burial near Quito, Ecuador, which, according to the venerable Max Uhle, was found to be accompanied by an assemblage of allegedly nonintrusive pottery pieces. Such ceramic evidence would make the mastodon a contemporary of at least the formative phases of Andean civilization, and could update its survival by perhaps six to eight thousand years. Conceivably, acceptance of the Quito find might even lead to a revision of our views of the Maya effigies in favor of Waldeck's debunked hypothesis. However, the Ecuadorian site displays incongruities difficult to explain, and must await further examination. Suffice it to say that at present neither geological nor other testimony has convinced scientists that mastodons continued into the post-glacial age.

If the Maya did not depict elephants for the very reason that the beasts were no longer around, are we likely to have any other proof but projectile points and slaughtered bones that Palaeo-Indian hunters met mammoth and his like? Here the answer may well be yes. The affirmative is based on a fragment from the pelvic bone of an elephant which a Mexican archaeologist, Juan Armenita Camacho of the University of Puebla, excavated in 1960 in the desert near Valsequillo, some sixty miles southwest of Mexico City. Into it appear to be scratched in crude outline mammoths or mastodons and, among others, perhaps, a bison and a tapir. The primitive artist worked on the bone while it was still fresh. Estimates of its age based on sound geological analysis run to as high as 30,000 years, which would make this by far the oldest "art work" of the Americas, comparable in age and manner—though hardly in quality—to the Magdalenian carvings on reindeer antlers from western Europe. Did Magdalenians, in pursuit of elephants and mammoths (themselves Old World animals), negotiate the glacial land bridge across Bering Strait?

A MAMMOTH KILL IN ARIZONA

Emil W. Haury

Many of the evidences of America's oldest inhabitants are exposed during Nature's restless rearrangement of the solid matter of the earth's surface. What was once buried is again brought to view. An effective agent in this process is water. Laden with clay, silt or sand, it places a concealing mantle over whatever lies in its course during times of earth-building; in periods of earth-cutting, the same may be exposed. This was the case with the discovery of the Naco mammoth.

Greenbush Creek is a tributary of the San Pedro River, situated about a mile west of Naco, a little Arizona town which straddles the United States–Mexico border some ten miles southwest of Bisbee. This gravel-strewn channel, about 4,500 feet above sea level, is dry during most of the year but at times it becomes a rushing torrent which eats away at the bank. For some fifteen years Fred and Marc Navarrete, father and son who are residents of Naco, have been watching this channel for fossil remains which appeared from time to time. In August 1951, after summer freshets had newly eroded the bank, they noticed that bones appeared in view. This encouraged them to dig in an attempt to salvage what appeared to be part of the skull of a large animal including teeth and tusk. In the course of this work they found near the skull a stone projectile point in an apparently undisturbed context. Additional digging soon revealed the left foreleg, scapula, humerus and ulna. Near the upper margin of the scapula, again in the undisturbed clay, a second projectile point came to light.

At this point the Navarretes realized that the find had great scientific value and they reported it at once to the Arizona State Museum. It is owing to their interest and understanding that this important find was preserved. In the spring of 1952 regular excavation was undertaken.

Excavation entails more than mere removal of objects from the earth. Inevitably there are problems which demand the assistance of a variety of specialists. In this case there was first the physical task of exposing the fragile bones without damage and of determining with certainty that the man-made tools were contemporaneous with the bones. A palae-ontologist was needed, to determine precisely what kind of animal we had found; a geologist's knowledge was vital to the understanding of the age of the discovery. It would also be necessary to save clays for pollen

"A Mammoth Hunt in Arizona," *Archaeology*, VIII:1 (Spring 1955), pp. 51–55.

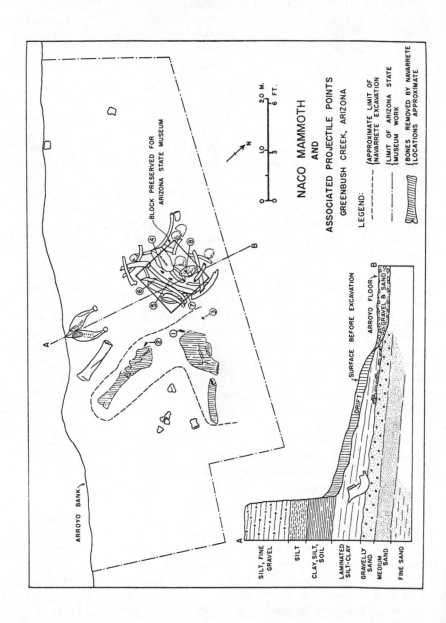

NACO MAMMOTH
AND
ASSOCIATED PROJECTILE POINTS
GREENBUSH CREEK, ARIZONA

LEGEND:

– – – – – {APPROXIMATE LIMIT OF NAVARRETE EXCAVATION}

–·–·– {LIMIT OF ARIZONA STATE MUSEUM WORK}

▨ {BONES REMOVED BY NAVARRETE LOCATIONS APPROXIMATE}

BLOCK PRESERVED FOR ARIZONA STATE MUSEUM

N

0   10   20 M.
0   3   6 FT.

ARROYO BANK

A

SURFACE BEFORE EXCAVATION

DRIFT

ARROYO FLOOR

B

SILT, FINE GRAVEL

SILT

CLAY, SILT, SOIL

LAMINATED SILT-CLAY

GRAVELLY SAND

MEDIUM SAND

FINE SAND

GRAVEL & SAND

analysis as an aid to dating, and charcoal, if present, for Carbon 14 analysis, the newest method for calculating age. Our first move, after learning the location of the bones and the nature of the matrix in which they occurred, was to strip the surrounding area of the covering of silt fallen from the arroyo bank and recently washed in by the creek. This exposed the clay in which the bones were encased and at the same time revealed the extent of the Navarretes' excavation. We could then be sure that we were digging in undisturbed ground. Next came the slow process of removing the clay from around the bones. Gradually the extent of the bone deposit was determined as well as the locality of greatest concentration of ribs and vertebrae, the area most likely to contain other projectile points.

The careful process described above had excellent results, for we discovered eight spear points in all. One was found near the base of the skull, one near the upper margin of the left shoulder blade, five among the ribs and vertebrae and one with position indeterminate.

Although none of the eight points was imbedded in a bone, their positions were such as to leave no doubt that these were the weapons with which the mammoth was killed. Whether the spears were thrust or thrown we shall perhaps never know with certainty, yet the hazards of close-range thrusting at such a formidable creature would suggest that at least the first spears were thrown. Once it had been crippled, the animal could have been dispatched with effective jabs. We reconstruct the story in somewhat this manner: while drinking from a small stream the mammoth was surprised by one or more hunters, who brought it to earth with no less than eight well aimed spears. It fell on the sloping surface of a sand bar in or near the water's edge. The animal was defleshed on the spot and its hind quarters may have been carried away. After decomposition of the tissues remaining after the removal of the meat, some of the bones were displaced. No one bothered to pick up the spear points, which appear to have remained close to the place where they lodged on entering the body.

The exact identification of the animal was determined by careful study of the teeth. Though large, these are not the adult teeth, which were found unerupted in the jaw. This indicates that the animal was comparatively young, between twenty-five and sixty years of age. It is of the species *Mammuthus (Parelephas) columbi,* or Columbian Mammoth.

The spear points, although of various sizes, are all of the Clovis Fluted type, named after Clovis, New Mexico, where the form was first recognized. Similar spearheads have also been recovered among the bones of elephants in Nebraska, Colorado and Texas, which shows that the ancient elephant hunters wandered far afield. Those found at Naco are of two materials: dusky red and brown chert, and a dark gray felsite. The considerable range in the size of the points (5.8 cm. to 11.6 cm.) shows that the largest animals known to ancient hunters were not always hunted with only the largest tips on their spears.

We may visualize the sequence of events leading to the preservation of the bones somewhat as follows: within a few years of the slaughter the stream was dammed and what remained of the carcass then lay in a pond. (That this took place within a few years is indicated by the good preservation of the delicate parts of the bones.) The ponding provided the conditions for the formation of the clays which preserved the bones. Over the years the protective mantle of earth was deepened by successive flooding of the area. It may also be inferred that no one visited the site between the time of the "kill" and the disappearance of the bones under water; else the spear points, some of which must have lain in plain view, would most likely have been carried off.

This and other discoveries have proved that hunters in America killed and feasted upon animals which no longer exist. Exactly when this happened is difficult to determine. The age cannot be based on the kinds of animals killed because as yet we do not know either the exact time or the order of extinction. The climatic history preserved in the earth above the "kill" is, at present, our most reliable and widely used clue. Dr. Ernst Antevs, a leading specialist in this study, has dated the Naco find to a period between 11,000 and 10,000 years ago. Charcoal which was found in the clay near the mammoth bones is also expected to yield information about the date when it has been subjected to Carbon 14 analysis.

The San Pedro Valley has long been known as a fertile source of palaeontological material, and it may be expected to continue to yield information about early man and his way of life.

38

Though scientists took to talking of "Folsom Man" and "Sandia Man" as if they were on fairly intimate terms with them, they had little more to go on than mirages conjured up by syllogisms. All they had been able to verify were peculiarly shaped tools and weapons of considerable antiquity which were obviously man-made. They were even less fortunate than Robinson Crusoe: having detected tracks, they searched in vain for the human perpetrators.

Since the 1920's archaeologists had collected considerable quantities of primitive American artifacts from various parts of the twin continents. The approximate age and geological association of most of the implements could be given with some confidence. They could be assigned to successive phases. They were recognized as mileposts of migration routes and of cultural complexes. Yet, none of the ice-age—or early post-glacial—camping grounds yielded so much as a finger bone of a human infant. Even the sites of mass slaughter of wild beasts failed to furnish bodily fragments of the hunters. Archaeologists emptied cave after cave, finding ample proof of prolonged occupation, but no ancient human skeleton, not even a minute part of one, was forthcoming. They were tantalized by the question of why animal remains—including bones, claws, and fur—should turn up in relative profusion from the frozen muck of the Arctic to the eroded gulches of the desert, while man's mortal substance had so totally vanished.

Such a blank in the archaeological record could give comfort to all the skeptics who considered the evidence of the stone artifacts circumstantial at best. In fact, physical anthropologists like Hrdlička, who long had ignored any corroborative geological data, would accept little but skeletal materials as proof of man's existence in the New World. The case for the Ancient American of 10,000 and more years' birthright was judged to stand or fall by the testimony of human bones. To be sure, a few finds of buried Ice Age man were confidently proclaimed from time to time, but in each instance they were declared to be wanting.

If ever there was a mystery man, it was the elusive early American, who refused to be tracked down by scientists. Apparently nobody had set eyes on him lately. What, if he ever lived, did he look like? Was he Indian? Was he a beetle-browed ungainly Neanderthal?

Standard-bearers of early New World man were in a tight spot to account for the utmost scarcity, if not complete absence, of his skeletal remains. A variety of explanations were advanced, of which one or the other, or a combination of them, probably contains the truth. The principal reason might well be the small scattering of men who roamed the hemisphere in those earliest days, and the consequently small statistical chance that decayed and scattered bones would be encountered in so vast a territory. Another argument touches on possible burial customs: not so much cremation, as simple exposure to elements and beasts, which practically eliminates the possibility that any traces of the dead would be preserved. In addition, the majority of earliest Americans—men, women, and children—undoubtedly met violent deaths and hence were never ceremoniously interred, no matter what the mode of burial then may have been. There is also the strong likelihood that quite a few ancient human bones, uncovered in the modern age by amateurs, farmers, or roadbuilders, were judged to be modern, particularly since, as we now know, they could not have differed markedly from those of present-day Indians. In turn, the debunking of the physical anthropologists did its part to discourage serious investigation.

Considering such adversities, it may seem surprising that the Early American emerged at all. However, cumulative evidence, mainly gathered since the end of World War II, has at last lent substance to him, even if the materials located are few and far between. There is now general agreement that primitive physical features, which physical anthropologists tended to regard as the touchstone, are not a necessary criterion for establishing the glacial origin of a skull or skeleton. Early American belonged fully to our species *Homo sapiens.* His physiognomy would probably blend into a crowd of modern Indians without attracting undue attention.

Ultimately, it is the geologist more than the physical anthropologist who will have to pass judgment. His is the task of establishing the formation and age of the layers in which the buried bones were deposited. Providing that they were not secondarily inserted at a later time and that they are hence geologically contemporaneous, their antiquity can be established. Needless to say, modern methods of age determination such as those based on carbon-14, fluorine absorption, nitrogen content, and the comparative rate of decay of uranium isotopes, are playing an increasing, though supplementary, part. Indeed, it was the combined application of sophisticated post-World War II techniques and sound geological knowledge that made the 1947 discovery of a human skeleton near Tepexpan, some twenty miles north of Mexico City, such an important incident in the search for American ancestors. Not only does Tepexpan Man rank as the first skeleton to be both located and excavated under scientific aegis, "he" was also the first to be widely acknowledged as ancient, even though occasional doubts have been raised since. With Tepexpan Man we move once more south of the United States to lands which were equally hospitable to Palaeo-Indians.

Helmut de Terra, a geologist by training, had a clear notion of where to look when he took up his search at the old shoreline of Lake Texcoco, the once large body of water which in late glacial times may have covered a major part of the Central Valley of Mexico. On previous expeditions he had unearthed in the area a number of primitive stone objects. But what made him focus his interest on the now dry lake bed were, above all, repeated finds of mammoth bones. The Tepexpan Hospital exhibited in the nurses' social room an enormous skull which had been exhumed during construction work. A farmer digging a well in a nearby village freed a whole elephant skeleton: promptly he pulverized it and sold it as fertilizer.

On taking leave of Mexico after his first visit there in 1945, De Terra asked a friend to notify him immediately the next time traces of a fossil pachyderm should show up. The call came less than a year later, with the sensational consequences described below. When setting out for the

Outline map of the Valley of Mexico with ancient lake shores and prominent archaeological sites. Tenochtitlán (Mexico City) is shown on an island linked to the mainland by causeways.

Tepexpan mammoth site, De Terra was already convinced that some of the giant animals had been trapped and massacred by ancient hunters in the marshy fringes of Lake Texcoco. Under such circumstances, he thought, human traces could not be far away. The glacial mammoth hunter must have left a trail. Here by the lakeside he slew his victims and made his camp. Could he himself be buried among the Pleistocene fossils?

Finding the "First Mexican" crowned Helmut de Terra's global search for animal and human fossils. The German-born scientist, who likes to refer to himself as a palaeoanthropologist, had first made a name in the study of Pleistocene geology when, in 1927, the Bremen Museum sent him out on an expedition to Central Asia. After marrying an American girl in 1929 and settling in the United States, he went on campaigns to India for Yale University. His investigations then began to concentrate on palaeontology. In the Vale of Kashmir he dug up a fossil mammoth. With permission of the local authorities, he shipped it to Yale. But then the maharajah had second thoughts and demanded its return. De Terra complied. On his next visit to Kashmir he was not a little surprised to learn that "His Highness had the mammoth in his palace and was using its tusks as coat hangers."

Forays into valleys of bones got De Terra into hot water again later on in Mexico. The police there, seeing him rummaging under a highway bridge, suspected him of planning sabotage and arrested him. Such irritations did not deter him from his investigations, which he continued in both the Old World and the New, except during wartime when he served with the map division of the United States Geographic Board. Right after the war, De Terra decided to make Mexico his special target. His successive campaigns were sponsored by the Viking Foundation of New York. As in his earlier work in Central Asia, he started out with geological analysis, principally of the glacial moraines in and around central Mexico. In post-glacial layers of so-called *caliche* he identified human artifacts of what he named the "Chalco Complex," now generally regarded as one of the earliest pre-ceramic cultures of Mexico.

It was precisely the *caliche,* a limestone sediment laid down up to perhaps 10,000 years ago, which De Terra set up as a kind of dividing line between glacial and post-glacial deposits. From underneath it came the Ice Age fossils, and, at last, Tepexpan Man, ingeniously pinned down by registering irregularities in the subsoil's conductivity of electrical current.

Tepexpan Man, since his dramatic appearance and instant fame, has had his share of ups and downs. Predictably, doubt was raised about his glacial origin. Several anthropologists hinted at an "intrusive burial."

To them the body's contracted position, face down, bespoke of an intentional interment following the customs of North American Indians of a fairly recent age. Unfortunately, methods of excavation left something to be desired and made it difficult to rule out possible intrusion entirely. The racial characteristics of the broad-headed skull occasioned further disagreements. Yet, at present, Tepexpan Man stands restored to glacial dignity. Examination of bones of extinct animals from adjacent sites showed that they possessed a comparable degree of fossilization. More vital still, additional discoveries in 1952 and 1954 at Santa Isabel Iztapan within a few miles of Tepexpan proved once and for all the actual presence of human hunters in the late Pleistocene. In the very same layers in which Tepexpan Man had been found, drainage ditches at Iztapan cut into skeletons of mammoths that demonstrably had been slain and dismembered. Missiles, knives, scrapers, and the like scattered in and around the animal carcasses clinched the case. The stone implements of Iztapan were also of considerable interest because they belonged to types previously associated with complexes ranging from the American Great Plains to Argentina.

As to Tepexpan Man, though his stratigraphy is rarely questioned any more, re-examination of his skull and skeleton has produced new shocks. Like most other bones that aspire to the Early American league, including Minnesota Man ("Minnesota Minnie"), "he" is now thought to have been a woman—apparently the tougher and more longevous sex even palaeontologically speaking. Her age was probably around thirty years. In height, she may have barely exceeded five feet two inches.

Despite additional skeletal finds, Tepexpan Man retains a good claim to the title "First Mexican." Since his appearance, he (or she) had, however, to contend with a few rivals for "First American." Of these by far the best authenticated—and the one unequivocally recognized by all scholars—is Midland Man, taken from a site accidentally hit upon in 1953 on a Texas ranch near Midland. It was meticulously dug from an undisturbed layer which included stone tools and extinct animals. It goes without saying that Midland Man, too, turned out to be a woman.

Helmut de Terra, named adjunct professor of the History of Science at Columbia University in 1959, is now presiding over a research institution in West Germany. He is, like Humboldt, a cosmopolitan German of partly Huguenot extraction, who turned from a narrow interest in geology to ancient man and his culture. He also centered his active scientific work on Asia and the Americas, and made some of his outstanding contributions in Mexico. Nothing was more natural than that De Terra would in time write a biography of Alexander von Humboldt, the scientist and humanist. No one was better equipped.

FOSSIL MAN OF MEXICO

Helmut de Terra

Only three months after my return to the United States there arrived news from Mexico that certainly interested no one more than myself. Near the village of Tepexpan, Arellano, an engineer and geologist, had found the fossil skeleton of an elephant. If this discovery had been made anywhere else, it would not, perhaps, have excited me so much, but Tepexpan seemed to me just the very site where further and most important finds might be possible. It was at Tepexpan that I had recognized ancient beach-formations containing fossils and stone implements. There, also, I had been shown several sites where fossil tusks and bones were to be seen. Before my eyes arose a vision of the ancient lagoon, the volcanic heights, the desiccated lake and, in the distance, the shimmering, silvery waters of Lake Texcoco. It seemed to me that Arellano's discovery confirmed the guess I had made during my first visit, namely that the collection of elephant remains at the site could not have been due to mere chance but that primitive Man himself must have piled up those bones. If the newly-found skeleton could be very carefully exhumed, we might possibly find near it traces of men, and maybe the remains of a fossil man.

The good news could not have reached me at a more opportune moment, for, in any case, I was due to make to a congress of Mexican archaeologists and anthropologists a report on my first investigations. In July 1946, I got to Mexico City and, on the next day after my arrival, Arellano and I went out to Tepexpan.

The site where the elephant bones lay was in a deep and long drainage canal which had been cut some time before, for the purposes of irrigation, parallel to the main automobile highway. During the excavation of this ditch the workmen had lighted upon some huge bones, and the supervising engineer who recognized the importance of the find (I had put a number of questions to him earlier on) had at once advised the Geological Institute of the University of Mexico. Arellano, a member of that Institute, had been entrusted with the work of further clearance of the remains. When he and I got to Tepexpan, the huge skull had already been disengaged. The two tusks, measuring about eight feet long, projected some five feet from the left wall of the trench. The skull itself

From *Man and Mammoth in Mexico,* translated from the German by Alan Houghton Broderick. London: Hutchinson & Co., 1957, pp. 160–71. Original German edition, F. A. Brockhaus, Wiesbaden, 1954.

had lain with the forepart downwards. Near and under it were other portions of the skeleton, ribs and long bones and the gigantic vertebrae in an almost inextricable jumble. The huge skeleton, indeed, seemed to have "fallen to pieces of itself" one might say, but the close examination of the remains and the plan of their disposition made by Arellano, by means of tape-measure and compass, showed that the huge beast had become stuck fast with its forelegs in the bog and, thus rendered helpless, had met its death without being able to extricate itself. On further examination of the bones, it appeared that the skeleton was incomplete. Some back and tail vertebrae as well as the two thigh-bones were missing. As, no doubt, the animal was complete when it came to an end, obviously the missing parts must have been intentionally removed. Since the bones lay in an undisturbed geological site, and were, moreover, covered with a hard limestone, or *caliche* crust, itself underneath layers of earth, there could be no question of clandestine excavation or theft.

The missing bones, then, must have been removed rather soon after the elephant's death. Could these have been carried away by great cats or even vultures, or had some early Mexicans carved off for themselves some titbits from the carcass? If Man had really been at work there then, possibly, we might come across stone implements not so far away. Some confirmation of this possibility was afforded when we examined closely the earth upon which the skull reposed, for eight centimetres under it lay a small artefact. It was a splinter that had been chipped off during the fashioning of an obsidian implement. Nothing could seem more significant than this bit of stone that measured only five millimetres in length (less than a quarter of an inch), but it was enough to lead me to form some provisional conclusions about both the hunters and their quarry. Understandably enough, this very modest piece of evidence was not taken very seriously by my colleagues. If Arellano had discovered a stone arrow-head embedded in between the ribs of the prehistoric pachyderm, then scientific opinion would have been much more favourable to my thesis of Man and Elephant. But six years were to pass before doubts were set at rest by a find that proved that my guess had been accurate enough.

In the same trench we made another discovery, also of an elephant, which some palaeontologists call the *elephas imperator,* the largest of the Ice Age pachyderms. Its remains are not uncommon in strata of the North American middle and late Pleistocene, for this great beast did not (as is shown, for instance, in the sites which occur in the State of Nebraska) survive the middle interstadial of the last Ice Age. The remains we came across at Tepexpan might, then, be those of an animal that lived in the High Valley of Mexico during the last important advance of the continental ice-sheet which was confined to the northern latitudes, that is to say to what are now Canada and the United States.

Altogether, no less than eight different sets of elephant remains were brought to light at various sites in what was once the lagoon of Tepexpan. Obviously a whole herd must have met its end in rather peculiar circumstances. My problem was how to set about to discover, in this elephants' cemetery, the evidences of Man's handiwork, and also, if possible, the bones or skeletons of early men in Mexico. It seemed clear that the search must be undertaken in the clay deposits laid down by the ancient lake, but these were, if only to a slight depth, covered by more recent formations. Earth, humus and pasture-land obviously would offer no clues. So, I came to the conclusion that we must employ the most modern methods to find the skeleton—if indeed it existed. During the 1939–45 war buried mines had been detected by means of a special apparatus; moreover, the geophysicists had developed several techniques for the discovery of veins, lodes and mineral ore. Undoubtedly, then, a geophysicist would be of great help to us.

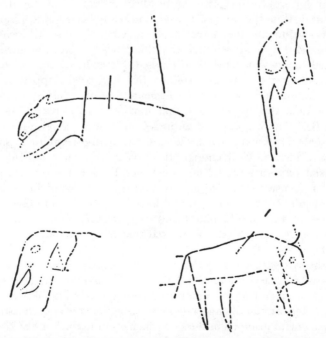

Perhaps the oldest New World "art" work: drawing on an elephant bone found near Puebla (central Mexico) may represent extinct animals of some 30,000 years ago.

So I went back to New York and there consulted Dr. Paul Fejos, the director of the anthropological research institute of the Wenner-Gren Foundation. He mentioned to me the name of a Canadian geophysicist of Swedish origin, Dr. Hans Lundberg of Toronto. He had perfected a number of techniques which had been used in excavations and he seemed to be the very man for my problem. I set before him the geological evidence and persuaded him to undertake a prospection at Tepexpan. A few weeks later his equipment was despatched and in January 1947, I set out once again for Mexico City.

The rumour that I intended to search for elephant bones with a detecting apparatus had already preceded me, but among my colleagues there was no one who thought that the new methods would yield any useful results. Of course, I was quite ready to admit that the whole thing was only an experiment and anyway that it was, as far as I knew, the first attempt to utilize geophysical methods in prehistorical research. Dr. Lundberg himself was not at all certain that his methods would prove to be of much use. Still, the geological conditions were so favourable that we just had to try our luck.

Dr. Lundberg had but twelve days to spare. Other and more materially profitable engagements had to be kept. So I had to make all my preparations in a great hurry. Two days, however, before the date fixed for his arrival in Mexico City, the geophysical equipment had not turned up. We could not imagine where the gear had got to. I therefore took the next plane to the Mexican border and drove in a taxi to the American customs house. There I learned that the cases had, indeed, arrived, but that they could not be released because no export authorization had been received from Washington. Everything, now, depended upon getting the official permit within a matter of two or three hours. Such identification papers as I myself possessed did not seem much to impress the customs officers. However, my obvious excitement and perhaps my powers of persuasion did serve me in good stead and, finally, the cases were handed over to me. I packed the dusty coils of wire and the boxes into a car and ten minutes later was at the Mexican airfield where, in accordance with arrangements I had already made, the aircraft was standing ready to take off at any moment. But the difficulties were by no means over. The Mexican customs demanded an import permit from the general direction of customs. In despair I telephoned for help to the Geological Institute in Mexico City and was promised the necessary official documents for the following day.

In the meantime, with the kind help and assistance of an American geologist, a topographical map of Tepexpan and the surrounding region had been prepared. It was on a sufficiently large scale for us to be able to plot each site in the whole area. This map, plus the geological data I had collected, was the starting point for the geophysical investigation.

When, at last, Dr. Lundberg and his assistants and I could start work, the morning was fine and sunny. The Indians I had hired as workmen stood at the entrance to the village. Manuel, the foreman, took the instruments out of the car. As usual, he emitted a reek of *pulque,* the light alcoholic drink in which the natives hereabouts drown their sorrows. We unrolled the wires and laid down two lengths of three hundred metres each at a distance of about two hundred metres the one from the other. The wires were charged from a simple dry battery and an inductor with a weak alternating current of low frequency. Thanks to the dampness of the soil there was thus created an electric field whose current was conducted through the wires into an amplifier as soon as the holder of the apparatus had connected up the current by means of metal rods stuck in the ground. The amplifier was fitted with two caps that fitted over the ears of the observer. From the amplifier a slight buzzing noise could be heard when the observer stood on a line of voltage. From the careful checking off of these lines, it could be determined if there was any interference in the conductivity of the subsoil, in fact, whether there were, hidden in the subsoil, objects of a higher or a lower degree of conductivity.

As soon as Dr. Lundberg had ascertained the course of the lines showing the same voltage, they were systematically examined. Every five metres listening-posts were set up and each of these was marked on the ground by a wooden peg while the topographer indicated the emplacements of these pegs on a special map.

After a few days the map's surface presented a definite arrangement of lines of similar voltage and it was obvious that these converged in the southern part of the field where, for the first time, irregularities in the lines appeared indicating the altered conductivity of the soil.

In the meantime, geophysicists and some archaeologists had come out from the city to see how our investigations were progressing. Although the method of utilizing linear electrodes had for long been known and employed in successful searches for mineral ore, this new use of electrodes caused a good deal of surprise. One facetious visitor to whom I had handed the headphones maintained that he had heard an air from *Aïda* that a nearby radio station was emitting at full blast. But no one was bold enough to suggest that we might listen in to the trumpeting of Ice Age elephants.

The lines on the map got more and more numerous. Clearly, however, there were three spots where there was obvious interference with the electric current. Only an excavation could determine whether such interference was caused by deposits of bones or by the varied nature of the geological formations.

On the tenth, that was to say the last day of Dr. Lundberg's stay, I plotted out three squares on the surface of that area of the ground where the disturbances were marked upon the map. These rectangular areas were separated from one another by a distance of about twenty metres. In the first spot we struck moist marsh clay but not the hard limestone crust that was so easy to recognize at the site where the elephant remains had been found. The onlookers who were expecting some sensational find at the first dig must have been disappointed enough and some of them, with puzzled faces, began to stroll away. The Indian workmen sat down and refreshed themselves with draughts of *pulque*. Lundberg shared my opinion that it was just the absence of the calcite crust which had allowed of a better conductivity and therefore of irregularities in the lines of voltage. The next day, which was that of Dr. Lundberg's departure, we set about digging in the second of the squares. Nothing was more disappointing to me than the prospect of losing my gifted collaborator at the moment we were making our last attempt to solve the problem.

It was very much more difficult to dig down into the second square than it had been into the first one, for we had now struck a limestone crust so hard that it was the despair of the workmen. But when we had made a pit to the usual depth of something over one metre it was plain that this site also contained no bones. To judge from the stratification revealed by our digging we might reasonably have expected to have encountered bones at a depth of from twenty to forty centimetres (eight to sixteen inches) below the limestone crust.

After luncheon we started on the third square. Our lack of success at the two first excavations seemed to indicate that the conductivity was due rather to differences in the subsoil moisture than to anything else. Such differences, from what we knew of the stratigraphical composition of the site, could be explained satisfactorily enough by the presence or absence of the limestone crust. So, as I took a pick in my hand and began the third dig, my thoughts were directed rather towards geological conditions than to any intrusive objects such as bones.

That afternoon we had only time enough to get down as far as the calcite crust. A dust storm was blowing up and darkened the whole landscape. When the first raindrops began to fall there was no question of any further work that day. So I gave explicit orders to the labourers to do no further digging until my return the next morning. I was trusting enough to imagine that they would do what I had told them.

Early the next day my friend Arellano, my son and I got back to the dig. The workmen were to be paid off, for there was not much chance that the fourth square would be worth while the trouble of digging. Hardly, however, had we caught sight of the first houses in Tepexpan village than we noticed that the workmen were standing about where we had left them the evening before. A rather surprising phenomenon, for we nearly always had to wait some time for them to turn up. From afar Manuel beckoned us to hurry. "There are bones here," he bawled with a beaming face and pointed to our third pit. From its edge we could make out down below a dark, rounded object. For a moment I did not know whether to embrace Manuel or to curse him for having disobeyed orders. The men had gone on working, had bashed through the limestone crust and had reached the lake-clay beneath. The discovery, whatever it was, lay then, under the calcite layer and at approximately the same depth as the elephant remains.

My finger slid over the wet, smooth surface of the rounded object and then caught in a cavity. The ground water had risen during the night and had changed the clay into mud. Arellano helped me to clean the object. It was the top of a human skull. With great care we disengaged the whole of the fossil head and scrambled out of the pit in order to examine our trophy. It was stained a dark colour and was full of slime, the bony substance was hard and, especially in the jaw, rather mineralized, as the technical term has it.

Without further delay we set about the examination of the whole level where the skull had lain. It showed no signs whatever of any disturbance such as would have been apparent if an intentional burial had been practised. The skull had lain at the same level as the elephant bones, which was composed of a sandy loam or clay of the sort we were familiar with from other excavations and especially from the long drainage ditch nearby.

Here, however, the calcite crust was less marked but still sufficiently indicated to be recognizable as the geological dividing line between the old and the more recent of the lacustrine clays. In the lower clay level there were the upright roots of marsh plants which had pushed down from the upper clay stratum to the lower. The shells of small fresh-water snails and the hollow bones of a bird were all that we found in the immediate vicinity of the skull. Soon, however, as we dug out more of the clay we perceived other bones. We left them undisturbed until we could enlist the help of specialists.

The geological evidence was conclusive that the human bones were of great age, they must be as old as the other fossils found in the same level. We had discovered the first man from the late glacial strata of Central America.

Light had been thrown upon the early ages of pre-Columbian history in Mexico. The great scientific importance of the find demanded that we seek the co-operation of Mexican colleagues so I set out at once in the car to bring them to the site of the discovery. Two hours later they arrived, the directors of several scientific institutes, the Mexican archaeologist Pablo Martínez del Rio and Xavier Romero, professor of physical anthropology in the University of Mexico. Shortly after them we had the Press representatives, photographers and camera-men from the Mexican movietone news.

They all stood around the pit, gesticulating and plaguing Arellano and myself with hour-long excited questionings. One Mexican reporter wanted to know the exact year his early ancestor had died, what he had lived on, how old he was at death and why he had such bad teeth. A Polish lady correspondent demanded my whole life-story. The cinema people wanted to film the discovery at once and reconstructed "just as it had happened." Amid all this jostling throng of newspapermen and other visitors it was not easy to keep both one's own head and that of Tepexpan Man. It was only later on that I learned news of the find had made the headlines in the papers of Lima, New York and Stockholm.

This Mexican skull aroused, it is true, more scientific and fewer philosophical questions than did poor Yorick's, but they were scientific questions which could hardly be satisfactorily answered without the rest of the skeleton.

The next day was a Sunday and we prepared to excavate the remaining skeletal material. I asked Professor Xavier Romero to supervise this delicate operation which demanded, if it was to be carried out satisfactorily, much knowledge of the human skeleton. In any case, Romero and Arellano, who were Mexicans, ought to have the honour of themselves extracting from his damp bed the earliest inhabitant yet to be found in their land. On this day, therefore, I confined myself to the role of an interested onlooker who now and then lent a hand when it was needed for cleaning the wet clay off a long bone or a vertebra.

It was soon apparent that the thigh-bones as well as a few of the upper vertebrae and some of the small bones of the hands were missing. It is true that careful search and sifting of the excavated material from the stratum did yield some additional portions of the skeleton but it still remained incomplete. That the thigh-bones were lacking may possibly be explained by the curious position of the skeleton which lay prone, that is to say face downwards. The man had died with his limbs slightly contracted so that the arms had come to lie under the thorax. The position led some of my Mexican colleagues to assume, it must be admitted in error, that we had at Tepexpan evidence for an interment similar to that practised by the ancient Indians. But this theory was obviously untenable since the man had died in the same swampy ground as the elephants, the nearest of whose remains were only some three hundred metres away.

Moreover, the disposition of the Tepexpan Man's bones did not indicate the highly contracted posture usual in Indian burials. It was probably because the body had lain with drawn-up knees and sunk in the marshy soil that the thighs became exposed (possibly owing to water-action) at least long enough to attract vultures or carnivorous mammals.

It was certain that one of the most important aspects of the discovery was that of its relation to the nearby elephant remains: its relation in time and space. This early Mexican, apparently, lost his life when hunting pachyderms and he was probably accompanied by other hunters. Like the elephant he may have perished in one of the shallows that occurred among the deep marshes of the lake's shore. This hypothesis seems to be confirmed by a later discovery at Ixtapan in the immediate neighbourhood of Tepexpan.

Indeed, in March of the year 1952, the Mexican prehistorians Maldonado-Koerdell and Luis Aveleyra found at Ixtapan—about a mile and a half from my site at Tepexpan—and at a comparable depth and in the same geological stratum, the complete skeleton of an elephant with some stone artefacts of which two—spear-heads—lay embedded between the ribs. These spear-heads were, in form and workmanship, somewhat like the implements discovered, associated with bison bones, at Scott's Bluff in the State of Nebraska. The Ixtapan knives and scrapers were of obsidian, a material used by the earliest Mexicans for their artefacts as is proved by the finds made in fossiliferous river-deposits near Teotihuacán.

Pre-Columbian elephants

We were fortunate enough to be able to fix, for the Ixtapan material, a dating of about 9,000 years. I owe this result to the generous financial assistance of the well-known oil geologist, Dr. E. de Golyer, and to the masterly radio-carbon tests carried out by Dr. Laurence Kulp at Columbia University. The Ixtapan specimens were not, as is usual, composed of solid charcoal fragments but of samples of the sediment itself whose very dark colour indicated that it contained organic matter which had become concentrated by chemical action.

The Ixtapan evidence induced me to seek confirmation for my theories about Tepexpan, a confirmation that would, maybe, confound the sceptics who make their voices heard at each discovery of fossil man. Perhaps they might learn how advisable it is not to emit categorical opinion until proofs are forthcoming to support sceptical statements.

Of course, whether Tepexpan Man was contemporary with the hunters of Ixtapan must remain undecided until a radio-carbon dating can be established for my discovery. How actively I concerned myself with this matter of the Tepexpan dating can be seen from an episode during which I once more received the generous help of the *Museo Nacional* in Mexico City. What I wanted to do was to collect a number of the small roots and rootlets which were present in the lake sediment that enclosed the Tepexpan skeleton. This was a most tiresome task and for it the museum assigned no less than eight assistants to help me. These marsh plants, as I have already remarked, had flourished in the layer of soil above the calcite crust and had thrust their roots down through it and into the level of soil below. Here, however, they had escaped the destruction through bacteria, which had almost entirely abolished all traces of them in the upper-soil formation. The radio-carbon dating for these plant remains is more than four thousand years, but does not give us a figure for the skeleton since the plant-roots were intrusive in the skeleton's level, for they grew on soil deposited by a later extension of the lake surface, after the formation of the calcite crust that seals off the level where the bones were found.

An astonishing amount of scientific detective work has been done on the Tepexpan remains. Both an artist and a blood-analysis specialist collaborated with the anthropologists. We may ask, what did the Tepexpan elephant hunter look like? Well, the great age of about 11,000 years which I assigned (on purely geological evidence) to him was enough to induce us to tackle the problem with all the means at our disposal.

From the anatomical evidence we may fix the age of the man as having been between fifty-five and sixty-five at the time of his death. He was of sturdy build, as is indicated, among other things, by the strongly marked bony attachments for the neck muscles. He sorely needed a dentist's care, for his battered teeth were worn right down to the gums, so that, as a matter of fact, the poor fellow would not have been able really to enjoy his elephant steak. A Mexican dentist who took radiograms of the wretched stumps, concluded that the Man of Tepexpan must have suffered acutely from toothache. He may well have been quite intelligent. The brain cavity, for an Indian skull, is rather large and the head itself quite well-proportioned. Its shortness, however, is surprising, insomuch as all the early Amerindians known before the Tepexpan Man, are dolichocephalic, that is long-headed. His head is rather primitive in form, the supraorbital ridges, let us say the eyebrows, are prominent, and the bony ridges at the base of the skull unusually well marked. Yet such anatomical peculiarities need not, from the evolutionary point of view, indicate a being as "primitive" as for instance Cro-Magnon Man and he is completely a *Homo sapiens.* The outstanding cheek-bones and the broad base of the nose in Tepexpan Man point rather to a relationship with those early types of Amerindians whose ancestors came from Asia. Generally speaking, these were, if compared with the *Homo sapiens* of the Old World, more slender in build, and with higher forehead, well-marked eyebrows and delicate articulations. These characteristics are still those of the mass of present-day Indians. When their average height is compared with his, however, the Tepexpan Man (1.72 metres or 5 ft. $8\frac{3}{4}$ in.) can be regarded as relatively tall.

The determination of the Tepexpan Man's blood-group is of interest because it is astounding that the scientific analysis of pulverized human bone fragments can tell us anything at all about blood-groups. In this case, indeed, the experiment was just a sideline undertaken by one of our scientific collaborators.

Of greater general interest was the reconstruction of the Tepexpan head, undertaken, under the close supervision of an anthropologist, by Leo Steppat, the sculptor. To accomplish this reconstitution it was necessary to collect a number of statistical data regarding the thickness of the skin and the soft parts in Indians whose skulls most nearly resemble that of the ancient Mexican. Over thirty different measurements were given to the sculptor, who, working on an exact cast of the skull, applied to it strips of plasticine whose thickness varied according to the statistical data he had received. In this way he obtained a close network of strips which afforded him a reliable basis on which to make his bust. As nothing was known as to the type of hair this was represented by the straight and relatively thick growth such as the Mongoloids usually display. In this way we got the picture of the earliest American man, who in his portrait really does not look his age, nine, or it may be eleven, thousand years.

The skull was first of all taken by plane to the Smithsonian Institution in Washington and then sent back to Mexico where now, after all his adventures, the Tepexpan Man rests in the safekeeping of the *Museo Nacional.*

39

When Helmut de Terra introduced his "First Mexican," most scholars were already prepared to accept the presence of Palaeo-Indians in widely scattered parts of the Western Hemisphere. Folsom Man had been the watershed of opinion. Fluted spear points were serving notice of early men's roving career in the Americas during the glacial dawn. Skeletal finds from Brazil and Peru reported in the nineteenth century, though their authenticity is still in doubt, had sharpened eyes for ancient remains in South America even before the thesis of human antiquity underwent a temporary eclipse.

Assuming that ancient Americans had originally filtered down from the Far North, when did they first cross the isthmian bridge of Panama and penetrate into the southern continent? How far did they venture, and at what time? At which stage did they reach the southern tip of Patagonia in the distant south, unequivocally the end of their hemispheric trek and "literally the bottom of the bag"? To answer the latter question in a plausible manner would be crucial to the entire antiquity problem, since it was tied up with the peopling of the Americas as a whole and might provide a clue to the time it may have taken the earliest migrants to reach the end of their transcontinental journey.

Primitive Indians continue in Patagonia and the adjacent Fuegan islands to this day. They are undoubtedly descendants of prehistoric settlers in this remote area. Charles Darwin more than a hundred years ago, in his diary of the voyage of the *Beagle*, could not help wondering about these people: "Whence have they come? Have they remained in the same state since the creation of the world? What could have tempted, or what change compelled, a tribe of men to leave the fine regions of the north . . . to enter on one of the most inhospitable countries within the limits of the globe? Such and many other reflections must occupy the mind of every one who views one of these poor savages. . . ."

As clearly as Darwin defined the Fuegan problem, it long met with indifference until it occurred to an American archaeologist in the 1930's to reformulate it and follow it up with fieldwork. For Junius Bird, then a young associate of the American Museum of Natural History in New York, it was an opening chapter in his preoccupation with South American roots, leading up to his epochal discoveries in Peru of pre-ceramic horizons and the rise of agriculture. Bird's own archaeological itinerary paralleled the ancient hunters' trail across the continents from ice-bound polar North America to the Antarctic fringes in the southern seas.

Junius Bird was a mere stripling when he struck up an acquaintance with an eminent New York publisher on a commuter train. The man offered him a chance to accompany an expedition to the Arctic. Thus lured from the classrooms of Columbia College, Bird soon thereafter terminated his formal education. Yet, without the conventional academic trimmings, he was to become one of the most respected of American prehistorians, with a fine reputation as a gadfly of flash-in-the-pan excavators and nebulous theoreticians. In 1956 he was awarded the Wenner-Gren (Viking) Foundation medal (designed, incidentally, by Miguel Covarrubias) for outstanding achievement in the field of American archaeology.

Younger son and brother of naturalists, he rummaged the environs of his native Rye, a New York suburb, for Indian relics before he reached the age of ten. As a college freshman, he began active exploration on a voyage to Baffinland, though his shipmates then valued him most for his way with marine engines. On the first voyage he unexpectedly lit upon ruins of the vanished Cape Dorset Eskimo culture, and from then on what he was to call "the Bird luck" never faltered, even when photographing a musk ox which suddenly charged at him, collecting samples of Eskimo body lice for fellow researchers at home, discovering a repository of mummies in the Aleutians, or tracing the farthest point of Eskimo migration in Greenland. Navigating a flimsy oyster boat out of Belize in the Caribbean on his search for prehistoric shell mounds, he braved a hurricane that would have won the respect of Joseph Conrad and Richard Hughes. The American Museum thereupon sent him to South America, which has claimed him ever since. A brief reconnaissance in 1933 was followed (1934–36) by a two-and-a-half-year stay in Patagonia and Tierra del Fuego. Sailing there with his young bride through uncharted bays and inlets on a nineteen-foot sailing boat in one of the world's last outposts, Junius Bird, though he made little ado over it, also performed superior feats of navigation which could stand comparison with Heyerdahl's more publicized Pacific cruise.

Despite the strains of a long campaign and its uninviting and frequently unyielding material, Bird developed an unsentimental appreciation of the southern lands astride Magellan Strait, which were unduly deprecated by Darwin. Near the hemisphere's mainland tip, Bird eventually located caves which had been inhabited by primitive men in association with extinct pre-Columbian horses, cameloids, and ground sloths. From implements in stratified deposits, he identified waves of successive migrations. At last, in a low layer of occupation, he found cremated human bodies as well as charred leftovers from campfires.

With the rough-and-ready methods then at his disposal, the oldest deposits suggested to Bird—with "few degrees better than an outright guess"—a maximum age of 5,400 years. However, later radio-carbon tests and additional excavations have proved that man has lived in the extreme south of the Americas for some 9,000 to 11,000 years. If we consider that migration was hardly a concerted mass movement, but a casual drifting which must have taken several millennia, recent estimates of first human entrance into northern America at least twenty to thirty thousand years ago seem altogether plausible.

The skull bones from the southern caves belong to a decidedly long-headed type which, though not strikingly primitive, is believed to have been characteristic of the earliest migrants to the Americas, possibly showing certain Australoid rather than Mongoloid features. In this they differ from Tepexpan Man and predominantly brachycephalic modern Indians, but resemble skulls excavated in other parts of South America such as Lagoa Santa and Confins in Minas Gerais, Brazil, and Punín and Paltacalco in Ecuador, which appear to be slightly more archaic.

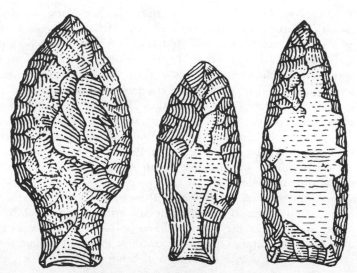

Spear points from Palli Aike cave in Patagonia (Argentina)

Since Bird's campaign in southernmost Chile, excavations at sites in Argentina, Peru, and elsewhere have brought forth cultural materials of comparable age. The resemblances among projectile points from these various deposits are quite striking. But more surprising still is the fact that some of these stone weapons are practically indistinguishable from the Plainview, Angostura, and Lerma types of far-distant North America. Evidently, the peoples and cultures of earliest America—North and South —were much alike. As in the palaeolithic Old World, distances were no obstacle to the spread of common traits. Rather it was agriculture and settled living which came to slow down exchange, thereby promoting isolated developments and increasing discrepancies.

IN CHILEAN CAVES FORLORN

Junius Bird

Columbus, Magellan, Cabot, Parry; start with the Norsemen if you will, list all the explorers you can think of who have added to our knowledge of the Americas, yet you will find few, very few, who have stood where no man stood before. From North Greenland to Cape Horn the land was known to men for many generations. What counts even more, they took with them their women and children and settled most of it.

Who were the real explorers and settlers? When and from where did they come, and how did they live? These are the questions which are bound to grow in your curiosity if you find yourself as did Mrs. Bird and I, during a 1,300-mile journey in a 19-foot sailboat, exploring a little known section of southernmost South America where some of the answers lay literally underfoot.

One wonders how the world was to these early, primitive explorers in farthest South America; whether climatic conditions were different from today and whether they knew animals unlike those of the present. In our searches, for instance, we found traces of the giant ground sloth. This creature has the unique distinction of being perhaps the only pre-

"Before Magellan," *Natural History*, XLI:1 (Jan. 1938), pp. 16–28, 77, 79.

historic animal that has ever been hunted for with firearms, for at least one expedition was led in the hope of discovering the ground sloth alive. Modern man has never seen it and never will, but it left interesting evidence for us of its being known to primitive man at the dawn of recent times, as will be shown later.

Almost everyone has a general knowledge of the early European exploration and settlement of America, and detailed information is available in every library. Yet think how difficult it would be if you had to reconstruct the story several thousand years from now with no written records to refer to. The potsherds, bottle glass, gun flints, and metal objects left would give only a vague story of the people who used them. The significance of the Jamestown ruins or of Columbus' settlement on San Domingo, for instance, would never be known, if indeed you were lucky enough to strike them.

You can therefore see how difficult it is to pick out a spot and say, "This is where the first Americans lived and these are the things they used." All we can really hope for is to determine what types of tools and weapons were used by the first large group to occupy the land, and from them to reconstruct their manner of living, their subsequent migrations and their relations to the people in other parts of the world.

You may ask why we searched in such a remote section. If you look at a map of South America you will notice that it tapers away to nothing. The only access to it, barring sea routes, is from the north. There is no exit. Once a people have traveled that far, they must stop. It is literally the bottom of the bag, but whether the things we found have any relation to the first things thrown into it, only future work will show.

Twenty years ago a book was published in which all the information concerning the people of Tierra del Fuego and the adjacent territory from Magellan's time to the present was summarized and classified. In it the value of future archaeological work there was stressed, but when I first saw it ten years ago in a little secondhand bookshop in lower New York, it was without the slightest thought that I would share in this work.

The first of January, 1933, however, found me alone on the trail over the mountains which lie between Lake Fagnano and the southern shore of Tierra del Fuego. At that latitude, tree line is at an elevation of about 1,500 feet and not far above, there is snow the year round. It is not a difficult trail for one who knows it and is used to traveling with horses, but for a greenhorn to try to take three horses over was asking for trouble. That we got across without being bogged down speaks very well for the horses. The carcass of one horse lying beside the trail with only his head and back showing above the bog and the bleaching bones of others was a sufficient warning of what might happen.

The Beagle Channel country which opens out before one from the top of the pass is a delightful refutation of the popular conception of the Cape Horn region. The summers there will never make one as uncomfortable as in New York, nor will the winters be as cold. It is true that there may be a flurry of snow at what corresponds to mid August but it is not the rule. That the natives used to live the year around with little or no clothing is more a proof of the lack of extreme cold than of their hardiness.

The summer passed all too rapidly but before it was over I had combed through over ten thousand cubic feet of midden refuse, most of it from one of the best middens along the fifty miles of shoreline examined on the north side of Navarino Island. Archaeology loses some of its glamour when the task in hand consists of picking apart a Fuegian midden. The soft mussel shells have disintegrated into a moist mass; specimens are few and far between, a day's work yielding only from two to fifteen, counting every piece of worked bone or stone flake. There is a great deal of duplication, and when one sees the completed collection the first thought may be, "What an unattractive assortment of . . . trash." One wonders how any history can be reconstructed from them; but the story is plainly written.

The first people to reach Navarino and the other islands about Cape Horn were simple folk; more so than the Yaghan Indians Magellan may have met, who are all but extinct today. Their manner of living and their food were almost identical with that of the Yaghans, but their equipment was even more limited. Having available the shell of a giant mussel which could be made into an unusually good knife in a few minutes, they never mastered the technique of pressure-flaking stones into knives or knife points. A few small scraping tools made from stone by percussion flaking, roughly sharpened chopping stones, whetstones, and bola weights, complete the list of the things they made from stone.

Through the centuries following the arrival of the first people there was little alteration in the type or pattern of the things used, then very abruptly we find a change. A new group of people have arrived. They introduce the bow and arrow, pressure-flaked points of stone for arrows, spears and knives, and other items. Even their houses are different: circular pits, 12 to 18 feet across by two to three feet deep, with one entrance instead of two. How to explain the survival of the earlier types of tools and weapons into this period is a matter for conjecture. Perhaps the two groups fused, or it may be that they occupied the region simultaneously. A number of reasons can be suggested, but it will be difficult to prove any one.

We have good evidence that it probably took between 1,500 and 2,000 or more years to build up the numerous and sometimes large middens along Beagle Channel. How these figures are determined is a story by itself, but we must skip it for the present.

Exactly two years after I had my first glimpse of Beagle Channel, my wife and I were at Puerto Montt, Chile, a thousand miles to the north, preparing to launch our 19-foot cutter. We had purchased it there and after installing a small engine and fitting new sails and rigging, were about ready to start south along the coast—just the two of us. We hoped to pick up the trail of the ancestors of our Beagle Channel friends and to follow it down to that region.

When you look at the map and see the maze of islands which lie along the coast between Puerto Montt and Cape Horn, it looks as if it might be the ideal place to go cruising. It is true that there are hundreds of miles of well-protected channels, that the scenery is superb, with mountains rising steeply from the sea to snow crowned summits as high as 12,000 feet with glaciers pouring down their slopes—but it has its drawbacks. The chief one of these is probably the weather. From the Guaitecas Islands down to the Straits of Magellan there is an annual rainfall of 120 inches or more. That would not be so bad if it did not come down in an almost steady, fine drizzle, blotting out the scenery and sun for days and weeks at a time. An Englishman once wrote that the weather of the western channels was "enough to make a man's soul die within him." There is no doubt that he was sincere in saying this for he committed suicide when faced with the prospect of having to spend a few more months there before starting home. But I do not want to give it a worse name than it has, and to prove that its influence is not always so bad I can only say that after five months of it my wife and I stepped ashore from the rather cramped quarters of the *Hesperus* still on good speaking terms.

Along with the excessive rain there is the usually more than excessive wind. It rushes in from an uninterrupted run of 6,000 miles across the Pacific with an exuberant vigor that makes one think that it must love the land to be in such a hurry to get there. Later when we were working on the dry treeless pampa country east of the mountains we decided this wind must be "loco" as it dashes across the plains and off over the Atlantic with an impatience that shows that it has not found what it sought, unless it be the fine haze of dust it carries in its wake.

Another slight drawback to a comfortable cruise is the open character of the coast about the Taitao peninsula and the Gulf of Penas. It is as though the sea challenged a boat to show her worth before allowing her to enter the smooth water of the channels south of the Gulf. The Indians used to portage their canoes and boats over the narrow isthmus of Ofqui and so avoid most of this, but that was impossible for us. Now an open windswept coast is nothing to balk at if one can stand well off and carry on past, but our job was to see as much of it as possible and to search the bays where our friends of the past would have been likely to seek shelter. There were times when we almost wished we had never started.

Two-thirds of this coast is uninhabited save for a few Indians of the Alacaluf tribe and an occasional lighthouse keeper. When we cleared from the little frontier settlement of Puerto Aysen (the last place we could secure gasoline and provisions), we carried sufficient fuel for 600 miles under power alone and four months' provisions, in addition to such incidentals as tools, clothing, cameras, and stove fuel. Anyone used to cruising in a small boat will realize what that meant.

The impossibility of securing more gasoline was a severe handicap. It is pleasant enough to run down a deep, narrow bay or fiord with the wind astern, but another story to beat back out of the same place. Many times we looked wistfully into winding bays and inlets not shown on the existing maps. Even when one knows that men have been there before you, there is an appeal about a place that is still a blank space on our maps which is hard to resist. That we did not always shut our eyes to temptation is indicated by the state of the tanks when we reached the first place in the south where they could be replenished. One was dry, the other held a fifteen minutes' supply, sufficient only to get us clear of a poor anchorage if it were necessary.

If the contents of the Beagle Channel middens are discouraging, those along the western channels are even more so. The ground everywhere is saturated to such an extent that the first move must always be to dig a drainage ditch. This prevents the trench or pit from flooding, but does not check the constant flow which makes hip boots a necessity. The mussel shells here have gone beyond the crumbled stage and become a sticky paste. I can think of no better test for an archaeologist's enthusiasm than to have him work ten hours in the rain on one of those middens. If he is willing to do it again, he merits his title. Four specimens a day represent the average day's collecting, and I have spent a full day in one large midden without finding anything.

When we compare the things found with those from further south, there is no doubt of the connection between the two regions. The most striking difference is the lack of stone tools and weapons. In the older middens of the western channels we find stones used only for sharpening the shell knives and for crude chopping tools or hand axes. At a relatively late date pressure flaking was introduced along with the bow and arrow, but it is not the work of the southern house-pit people.

We had been warned repeatedly against the Indians living between the Gulf of Penas and the Straits of Magellan. They were reputed to be murderers and thieves of the blackest sort; if they did not kill us outright they would at least take our boat and leave us stranded. Part of these tales we attributed to an understandable human desire to put us in the right frame of mind, part to a misunderstanding of the natives' real nature, as the stories improved in direct proportion to the informant's lack of experience. The earliest contacts with whites had been friendly enough but for many generations there have been incidents not calculated to inspire confidence on either side. Natives are living who in the course of their lives have been shot at, and all have probably received the poor end of a bargain when trading skins. Under the circumstances one cannot expect to be greeted as a long lost friend; and when we saw the smoke from one of their camps and crossed over to an island to meet them for the first time, there was a moment when we were almost willing to believe what we had heard.

No one will deny that their looks are against them. Coarse, matted hair, sullen expressions which take but little imagination to construe into looks of hate, and legs dwarfed in comparison with their well formed chests and arms as a result of lives spent entirely in canoes and huts— all these contribute to a poor impression. But face to face with reality one's mental picture fades, the demons become men and women possessed of normal human characters. They have clear ideas of right and wrong, though different perhaps from ours; they may be lazy and indolent but these qualities are not unknown elsewhere. Life makes few demands; there is an abundance of shellfish for food; fuel and drinking water are everywhere, a canoe need be replaced only once every few years, a house can be constructed in a few minutes; they acknowledge no man as chief, hence there are no laws, no taxes, nothing to live for except life itself. It rains all the time, so why not sit by the fire? Having lived with them I do not envy their simple life, no one could; but once they are extinct they will have their champions. Contrary evidence being then lacking, they will doubtless be idealized as creatures to be envied, their life a golden Odyssey.

On our arrival at Magallanes, formerly Punta Arenas, at the completion of the western channel trip, winter was well underway. We had hoped to find some large midden along the Straits where a permanent winter camp could be established, but there are none, on the north shore at least. With no alternative we went further south to Ponsonby Sound

Junius Bird's itinerary in southernmost South America. Solid black line marks voyage by boat; line of dots shows horseback route; dotted line represents travel by auto.

where we had heard of a large rock shelter. This proved an ideal location for winter work, a high cliff protecting and overhanging a large shell mound. With the completion of the excavation there we moved to another shelter I had seen previously on Beagle Channel and later to a third in Yendagaia Bay on the south side of Tierra del Fuego. The results in each case confirmed and added to the information recorded in 1933.

With the coming of spring we returned to Magallanes, bought a twenty-year-old Model T Ford truck and followed the northern shore of the Straits eastward with good success in locating camping places of the Foot Indians. These people lived principally by hunting land animals and differed greatly in physique and culture from the Canoe Indians of the western and southern channels. The "giants," first reported by Magellan, were of this group. It is certain that there were some very tall men among them and that their average was above normal, but the figures given by several authors of between 9 and 12 feet are best explained as travelers' tales, told, as Sir Francis Drake's chronicler puts it, because "they did not think that ever any man would come thither to reprove them, and thereupon might presume the more boldly to lie."

All of this country along the eastern part of the Straits and north into the Argentine is open grassland, good for sheep raising but settled only in the past 50 years. With only a fraction of the rainfall of the forested western coast it is hard to believe that the two regions are so near to each other. Its one unpleasant feature, the strong westerly wind, has worked to our advantage. Because of it the Indians made their camps, when possible, in sheltered places, resulting in concentration of their broken, discarded, or lost belongings where they can more easily be located.

At the close of a successful summer, preparations were made to continue the work on the large island of Chiloé, near Puerto Montt on the west coast. The bulk of our equipment was shipped there by steamer while we were to go in the truck by way of the Atlantic Coast as far as Comodoro Rivadavia, then cross to Puerto Aysen on the Pacific side and continue by boat. Although we did not have a permit to collect or excavate in Argentine territory we wanted to examine a number of private collections which have been made there, and to see some cave paintings near San Julian.

Just before leaving Chilean territory we stopped to look at a cave which we had heard of but had not been able to visit before. Known locally as the Palli Aike Cave, it is near the top of an old volcanic crater ridge but is easily accessible. The interior looked promising: a dry dusty floor about 45 feet long by 25 wide with plenty of headroom. When, after a few days' digging, it became apparent that we had a deposit dating from at least twice as far back as anything we had found previously, our feelings were a curious mixture of pleasure and despair. Without our regular equipment and with only a few days' supplies left, it was impossible to stay longer.

According to the good friend who had been our guide it was questionable how long the track back to Magallanes would be passable. With one assistant it would take at least five weeks to finish the job. More assistants would be impossible without incurring prohibitive expenses. The fine dry dust made the use of masks imperative; a sifter and a wheel barrow would be needed. These and other thoughts came to spoil our pleasure. Moreover we had not even reached the bottom and there was no telling what might be there. Without the record contained in the dust of this old cave our work would be incomplete. It had to be done, somehow.

It was a sad moment when we finally left to continue on through the Argentine, having decided to take a chance on being able to return in the spring. If we had only known how well it would all turn out in the end, how much happier should we have felt.

Auto travel on the Patagonian pampas in winter promises uncertainties and seems to keep those promises. Thanks to the help of the good people along the way we finally made Puerto Aysen, arriving with an intimate knowledge of every other bog hole along many miles of track, as well as a thorough understanding of the value of fencing wire for repairs. No car had crossed the mountains for two months; none other than the old Model T with its high clearance and light weight could have done it.

The coming of spring brought word that the mountain pass was open once more. With dry roads the run south was a contradiction of our previous experience. With a goal in mind the stretches across the high plateaus did seem longer, but Palli Aike hill and cave were still there, just as we had left them.

To give a new assistant training, a smaller cave some twenty odd miles to the west was cleared first. The results were meager. Nearby, beneath the wall of the canyon through which the Rio Chico flows, a place was pointed out where arrow points and flakes lay on the surface. It promised little more than pure exercise, for many tons of stones had piled up against the base of the cliff. The inward slope of the rock suggested a cave but it was choked almost to the top. A little digging showed that it did go on in and that we could work without moving a yard of stone for every foot of dirt.

As barrow after barrow load of dirt and broken bones rattled down the sifter the little things which, added together, tell their story were picked out and laid aside.

The final chapter in the life of the natives was missing, there being no bones of the domestic horse, copper ornaments, trade beads, iron and other signs of contact with whites. Instead there were the finely made, small arrow points of the Ona tribe, known previously only as inhabitants of Tierra del Fuego south of the Straits. With them, a coarser type of arrowpoint proved the presence of another tribe who, though living here the same time as the Onas, had also preceded them.

Then still further down our digging discloses a third type of point used perhaps on spears, perhaps on arrows. It is the type that always marked the bottom during the previous season's work, but in this deepening pit it disappears while the camp refuse still continues. A single spear-point of bone among the usual assortment of scrapers, without a single point of stone, confronts us with a puzzle, and then we are down to what seems to be the bottom. A jumble of lumps and slabs of sandstone cover the floor of the cave; there is nothing to suggest that we should dig further, except one of the simple rules of archaeology which is to dig beyond what seems to be the bottom.

Beneath the sandstone we discover still more bones and among them a type of stone spearpoint new to us. That is gratifying enough, but when we see that the bones are those of horses there comes a most disconcerting feeling.

The domestic horse did not exist in the Americas before the Spanish came, and if these bones should prove to belong to an animal introduced by Europeans, all our conclusions on our previous work were wrong. Though I was willing to swear that 400 years was all too short a time to account for all the material we had uncovered, those horse bones gave us momentarily something of a shock. The only alternative was that they belonged to a prehistoric relative of the common horse. This ancient horse was known to live in South America in times long past, but so far as I knew no one had proved that it still existed when even

The native American horse

the earliest people lived here. Without special training in palaeontology it was not for me to identify these bones, but it was apparent that they were of smaller, stockier animals than those used in Patagonia today. Later examination proved that we had found the first evidence that this ancient horse was hunted and eaten by the early natives of South America.

Further clearing exposed fire pits from which many fragments of burned and charred bones were taken. In one of these was a handful of small bone pellets about the size of peas which could have come from only one animal, the ground sloth.

These pellets are an anatomical oddity; though they had been found in various parts of [the] Argentine in association with fossil sloth remains their exact function remained a mystery until the discovery was made in a huge dry cave about 100 miles west of where we were working of a piece of skin in which were embedded many of these bone nodules. It was then known that they were a sort of "armor" inside the skin. The fragment found was well-preserved and bore bristle-like hairs. With it were the bones and mummified remains of the sloth and a considerable quantity of manure.

The find aroused worldwide attention, and from the fresh appearance of the skin the story started that the animals could still be found in the recesses of the then unexplored mountain forests. A London newspaper even sent out an expedition to capture or kill one. From the presence of some dry grass in the cave it was claimed that the Indians had domesticated the animals and stabled them there; but the evidence does not support this inference. No modern man has ever seen a living ground sloth; and it is quite unlikely that the ancient Indians domesticated it. But our discoveries proved that the animal roamed the country at the same time that some of the ancient natives did.

When we had finished the work at Fell's Cave, for we have named it after the Fell family who own the land and led us to the spot, we had a fairly clear picture of what had happened there. An eddy of the river had undercut the sandstone and formed the cave at a time when the water was about 19 feet above its present level. A floor of sand and clay had been built up and was still new and clean when the people decided that it would make a good home. It had not been used long when a section of the ceiling collapsed. That this happened while it was actually occupied is suggested by articulated sections of a horse skeleton directly beneath the stones, a leg and shoulder at one place, a head and neck at another, and by the perfect tools and weapons on the same level.

For some years after that no one stayed there. With the passing of time, nature began to smooth and level the floor, so again people began to stop there. In the interval the first group or tribe had disappeared together with the horses and sloths. The newcomers had different weapons and lived mainly on foxes and birds. From the work at Palli Aike Cave we learned that their spears were tipped with bone.

The arrival of a third group is suggested by a change from bone points to a new kind made from stone and by the appearance of bolas, a very effective weapon made of a set of two or three stone balls joined by thongs and hurled at birds and larger game. With this the people hunted geese, rhea, and guanaco, an animal of the camel family related to the llama. These had been common in the early days but became rare at the time the horse and sloth were exterminated and it was many years before they returned in sufficient numbers to become the staple food of the people. Then, abruptly as they came, the things belonging to this third group leave the picture, and if we read the signs correctly their right to the land was disputed by a fourth tribe using small, rough arrowpoints. For at another site on the level of the end of the third period, two group burials were found containing the remains of nine men and women and one baby. One of the skulls shows an ugly gaping wound. The absence of weapons of the third type in the subsequent debris tells the result.

Shortly before the beginning of Patagonia's written history, perhaps in Magellan's time, the small arrowpoints of the Ona Indians record their visit to Fell's Cave. If a guest book had been kept there during the years the story could scarcely have been written more plainly.

Later, at Palli Aike, we found the same sequences and by recovering a greater amount of material were able to eliminate some of the questions. That cave had been visited at an early date but the first callers forgot to sign the register and left nothing which would serve to identify them. For a while it was used only by sloths who, dying there, added their bones to the rising floor. Then either the adjoining or a nearby volcano erupted throwing in tons of fine ash and lumps of lava. This leveled and smoothed the floor and was seemingly the renovation needed to attract the local population.

First it was used as a place for the dead. Two adults and one child had been placed in hollows along the wall, covered with grass and brush and cremated. Imbedded in the volcanic ash was a single point of the oldest type found at Fell's hinting that they may have lived in that period. Then the second or bone-point people follow and in their fireplaces are the bones of sloths and horses proving that they had arrived in the south just prior to the complete extinction of those animals. The balance of the record only confirmed what we already knew. . . .

PART VII

NORTHERNMOST AMERICA
(*Eskimo and Viking*)

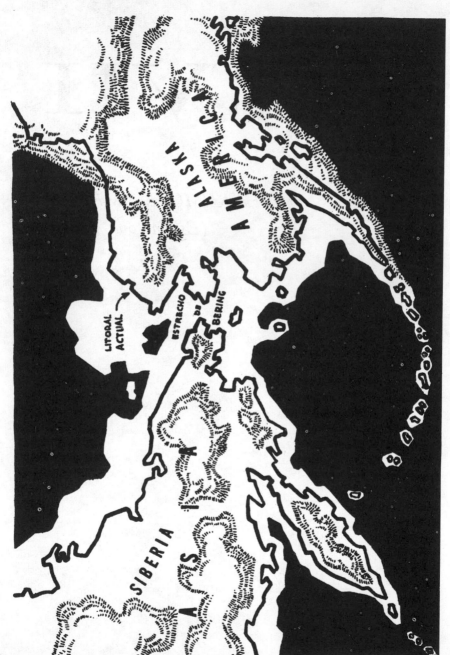

Ice Age land bridge between Siberia and Alaska

40

Any discussion of man's relatively recent age in the Americas presupposes facts and theories about his arriving from elsewhere. No matter how far back one dates his ancestry to the last glacial or even inter-glacial of some 100,000 to 40,000 years ago—American man remains a newcomer. The New World was new also to Columbus's distant predecessors, those nameless wandering bands of hunters who spilled into the virgin lands, some hovering here and there along the icy edges, others venturing down river valleys into fertile basins of moderate climes. Eventually, as we have seen, these earliest Americans found their way into the farthest corners of the hemisphere. At Folsom, in the American Southwest, they killed bison. They lit campfires and massacred elephants in southwestern Arizona. By that time a few of their kinsmen may already have sought refuge in rocky shelters of the Peruvian Andes and Minas Gerais, and in bleak caves of southernmost South America. Waves of migrants, perhaps of different racial types and cultural baggage, followed, dislodging older inhabitants or merging with them. Some Indians and Eskimo may have entered the Americas as recently as 2,000 years ago. How had it all started? Whence had the earliest hunters come?

If primitive hominids never made an appearance in the hemisphere and if ancient Americans were in all respects of our species, it is a matter of sheer logic to look for their origins in the Old World, where modern man had evolved during hundreds of thousands of years. Allowing for occasional, but very late, influences from across the Pacific or even the Atlantic, today there is not the slightest doubt that America was first entered from across Bering Strait where Siberia reaches within little more than fifty miles of Alaska. This thesis is backed by geography, geology, and ethnology—with occasional help from archaeology. The Indians were Asiatics before they became Americans. Their predominantly Mongolian features bear witness to their ancestry.

Not only does the continent of North America face Asia across a narrow, frequently ice-bound channel with the interspersed Diomede Islands as a link, but during the age of glacial advance, Bering Strait was itself dry land. In that era, which lasted until approximately 10,000 years ago, so much water was locked up in land glaciers that, as a consequence, the sea level was lowered by as much as 330 feet below the present coastline. The shallow strait was then a land bridge. Geologists believe that there rose a vast Siberian-Alaskan territory—the so-called Chukchi province—measuring up to 1,000 miles in width. Low humidity and precipitation made Chukchi province, as well as various great Alaskan and Canadian valleys (Yukon, Fraser, Mackenzie), and also parts of Siberia, ice-free for long periods. Man's migration route from Asia must have passed through these more or less hospitable areas where he could gather food and pitch camp.

According to recent theories of a circumpolar Eurasian-American culture zone, most of the men stayed in the northern land where they met with familiar conditions, and only a trickle were unwittingly diverted southward. The peopling of America was never a large-scale or a directed movement; the popular concept of long lines of shivering hordes of Asiatics doggedly trailing the sun to balmier latitudes is quite implausible. What guided these New Americans were not astronomic insights or the lure of Florida sunshine, but food, and above all animals. Ancient Americans pursued such Old World mammals as mammoth and bison across northern Siberia into Chukchi province and Alaska. If anything it was these beasts who first discovered the land route and led the way. Conceivably, there was also an occasional backlash of Indians from America to Asia, just as New World animals like horses and camels made the crossing in the reverse direction.

Any search for the origins and itinerary of First Americans in the Western Hemisphere must touch on northernmost America and its surviving aboriginal inhabitants, the Eskimo. Here in the Arctic, the drama began. At what approximate date, at which sites, and by what kind of men, we still do not know for certain. Were these men related to the Eskimo—and who, anyway, are the Eskimo?

The archaeology of these northlands has rarely drawn the attention it deserves. One main reason is, of course, the difficulty of the terrain, where much of the evidence may be buried deep under ice sheets, hidden in frozen muck, or washed away by ocean tides. One practicing archaeologist has tartly remarked, referring to the obstacles encountered in northwestern America and northeastern Asia, regions to which we look for answers to some of the crucial problems of American antiquity: "While it is very simple to plot migration routes while sitting in an office and looking at a map, the problem assumes new dimensions when one is in the field in this northern country. It takes only a fraction of a second to draw a line half an inch long on a map. However, if that line represents a non-existent path through a hundred miles of muskeg, the situation becomes extraordinarily complicated if one attempts to follow it in person."

Before World War I, hardly any excavation had been undertaken. A big step forward was the Fifth Thule Expedition (1921–24), led by ethnologist-explorer Knud Rasmussen. Therkel Mathiassen (the archaeologist in charge), Kaj Birket-Smith, Peter Freuchen, and Rasmussen traced the ruins of an ancient Eskimo culture from the Greenland site of Thule to Canada's Hudson Bay and then across to Alaska, positing possible roots in Asia. Rasmussen had thus discovered a prehistoric people who, despite their small number, had—like the modern Eskimo—stretched halfway across the diminishing northern latitudes of the globe.

Knud (Johan Victor) Rasmussen (1879–1933) was admirably suited to initiate systematic archaeological work in the Arctic. A Dane, he was born in southwestern Greenland, where his father served as a pastor. His maternal ancestry was part Eskimo. The boy spoke Eskimo before he mastered Danish. For Denmark, which gained virtual control of the vast sub-Arctic island more than two hundred years ago, the study of Greenland's native Eskimo population had long been a subject of national interest. Rasmussen not only continued the tradition, he brought to it an innate sympathy and familiarity with the Eskimo mentality. From childhood he had listened to Eskimo legends and tales. His imagination had been overpowered by rumors of Polar Eskimo in far northern Greenland, who persisted in their paganism and whom he pledged to visit one day. When he became a student at the University of Copenhagen, he quite naturally concentrated on ethnology. In the successive explorations which kept him in Greenland during most of his mature years, he also collected valuable cartographic, geological, and botanical data. On one occasion, he located a large meteorite in the icy wastes. On another he discovered the records left by Admiral Peary in a cave on Greenland's coast, and returned them to the United States. Together with Peter Freuchen, he organized at Cape York in northern Greenland a station called Thule, designed to serve as a commercial and scientific base. However, the spiritual life of the Eskimo people as exemplified in their rich oral traditions claimed his enduring interest. His early publications in that field came to the notice of such scholars as L. Lévy-Bruhl in France and Franz Boas in the United States. It was Boas who noted the close similarity of the Greenland legends and those current in the Hudson Bay area of Canada.

Rasmussen himself had long looked to America for the origin of the

Eskimo race. Greenland alone, he knew, could not furnish all the clues to the Eskimo riddle. He had to cross Davis Strait to Baffin Island and Labrador to investigate the origins and migrations of Eskimo tribes. Apart from studying the living Eskimo of America, he resolved to search for ancient and abandoned settlements, particularly around Hudson Bay. When Knud Rasmussen first set foot in sub-Arctic Canada and met native people, he talked to them in his own Eskimo language. In a sense, it was a homecoming for this descendant of Viking and Eskimo.

On June 18, 1921, he and his companions sailed on the *Bele* from Copenhagen, on what was to be Rasmussen's most important campaign, the three-year Fifth Thule Expedition. Its results, ranging from topographical to zoological and linguistic observations, were to fill twelve volumes. Rasmussen traversed the continent to the very doorstep of the Far East, making the longest dogsledge journey on record. On the way he studied the folklore of many tribes, while Mathiassen and Birket-Smith continued the investigation of material remains in the "Barren Grounds" near Hudson Bay.

Rasmussen and Mathiassen at first believed that they had come close to uncovering the earliest Eskimo culture, which, like that of their modern successors, had a remarkable degree of uniformity from the Pacific to the North Atlantic. While they were not far off in their estimate of the age of the Thule culture and its original focus, subsequent research has established it as rather the latest stratum of Eskimo pre-history. Eskimo homogeneity, it seems, is, in itself, of recent date, hastened by acculturation and actual return of eastern tribes to the Northwest. The Thule phase was preceded by a variety of far more specialized cultures of greater artistic richness and subtlety. Eskimo pre-history thus turns out to be of considerable antiquity. Its oldest manifestations are now attributed to the Denbigh Flint Complex of about 2000 to 3000 B.C., first identified by Louis Giddings at Norton Sound in 1948. Even at that early stage Greenland had apparently been drawn into the Eskimo orbit. As to the actual cultural and ethnic roots of the Eskimo, the evidence from Siberia, an area less explored than sub-Arctic America, is becoming more persuasive through the work carried out there by Soviet scientists. Most scholars agree that Eskimo characteristics from Denbigh on are essentially Asiatic rather than American. Paradoxically the Eskimo represent some of the oldest traditions in America, though belonging to one of the youngest pre-Columbian groups. Their industries to this day show Magdalenian, if not Mousterian, traits of the European Stone Age. No wonder that some imaginative ethnologists have turned them into original Frenchmen who millennia ago, somehow or other, had found their way across the Atlantic. However, in a more sober light, the Eskimo testify to the survival of a marginal people whose rate of cultural change has been slowed down by their environment. This phenomenon has been called "Arctic retardation."

Despite their antiquated features, the Eskimo have so far shed little light on the first people to come into America. The Denbigh Complex, which may well mark Eskimo beginnings, is still recent in comparison to the Palaeo-Indian artifacts recovered elsewhere, including those from farthest Patagonia. There remains a gap between the Eskimo and earliest Americans.

Archaeologists are still hopeful that Arctic America will one day furnish conclusive proof of the first arrivals and their paths, but so far the material has been disappointing. Primitive choppers, scrapers, and bone points, reminiscent of the Old World Palaeolithic, have been collected from time to time. But they come from unstratified locations and hence cannot be dated. Some of the artifacts, such as those reported from the frozen muck in association with extinct mammals or those unearthed on the campus of the University of Alaska, are undoubtedly pre-Eskimo, as may well be the Folsom-like points Hibben found in 1941 at Chinitna Bay on the Alaskan coast. Unfortunately it has not been possible to ascribe to any of them a greater age than to the spear points or flint industries of the American Southwest, which some of them resemble and from which, indeed—instead of having preceded them—they may have been derived.

THE TUNITS OF HUDSON BAY

Knud J. V. Rasmussen

I had halted to thaw my frozen cheeks when a sound and a sudden movement among the dogs made me start.

There could be no mistake as to the sound—it was a shot. I glanced round along the way we had come, fancying for a moment that it might be the party behind signalling for assistance; but I saw them coming along in fine style. Then I turned to look ahead.

I had often imagined the first meeting with the Eskimos of the American Continent, and wondered what it would be like. With a calmness that surprised myself, I realized that it had come.

Three or four miles ahead a line of black objects stood out against the ice of the fjord. I got out my glass; it might, after all, be only a reef of rock. But the glass showed plainly: a whole line of sledges with their teams, halted to watch the traveller approaching from the South. One man detached himself from the party and came running across the ice in a direction that would bring him athwart my course. Evidently, they intended to stop me, whether I would or no. From time to time, a shot was fired by the party with the sledges.

Whether the shots fired and the messenger hurrying toward me with his harpoon were evidence or not of hostile intent, I did not stop to think. These were the men I had come so far to seek from Denmark and from my familiar haunts in Greenland. Without waiting for my companions to come up, I sprang to the sledge, and urged on the dogs, pointing out the runner as one would a quarry in the chase. The beasts made straight for him, tearing along at top speed. When we came up with him, their excitement increased; his clothes were of unfamiliar cut, the very smell of him was strange to them; and his antics in endeavoring to avoid their twelve gaping maws only made them worse.

"Stand still!" I cried; and, taking a flying leap out among the dogs, embraced the stranger after the Eskimo fashion. At this evidence of friendship the animals were quiet in a moment, and sneaked off shamefacedly behind the sledge.

I had yelled at the dogs in the language of the Greenland Eskimo. And, from the expression of the stranger's face, in a flash I realized that he had understood what I said.

He was a tall, well-built fellow, with face and hair covered with rime, and large, gleaming white teeth showing, as he stood smiling and gasping, still breathless with exertion and excitement. It had all come about in a moment—and here we were!

As soon as my comrades behind had come within hail, we moved on toward the party ahead, who had been watching us all·the time. Our new friend informed me that his name was Papik and that he had come from the neighborhood of Lyon Inlet—the next large inlet to the north of our recently established headquarters camp on Danish Island. There was not time for much talk, before we came up with the others; and I was anxious this time to check the dogs before they became too excited. As we approached, the men came out to meet us, the women and children remaining with the sledges.

These men, then, were the Akilinermiut—the "men from behind the Great Sea," of whom I had heard in my earliest youth in Greenland, when I first began to study the Eskimo legends. The meeting could hardly be more effectively staged; a whole caravan of them suddenly appearing out of the desert of ice, men, women, and children, dressed up in their fantastic costumes, like living illustrations of the Greenland stories of the famous "inland-dwellers." They were clad throughout in caribou skin; the fine short haired animals shot in the early autumn. The women wore great fur hoods and long, flapping "coat-tails" falling down over the breeches back and front. The curious dress of the men was as if designed especially for running; cut short in front, but with a long tail out behind. All was so unlike the fashions I had previously met with that I felt myself transported to another age; an age of legends of the past, yet with abundant promise for the future, so far as my own task of comparing the various tribes of Eskimos was concerned. I was delighted to find that the difference in language was so slight that we had not the least difficulty in understanding one another. Indeed, they took us at first for tribesmen of kindred race from somewhere up in Baffin Island.

So far as I thought they would understand, I explained our purposes to my new friends. The white men, Peter Freuchen and myself, were part of a larger party who had come out of the white man's country to study all the tribes of the Eskimo—how they lived, what language they talked, how they hunted, how they amused themselves, what things they feared, and believed about the future life—every manner of thing. We were going to buy and carry back to our own country souvenirs of the daily life of the Eskimo, in order that the white man might better understand, from these objects, the different way the people of the northern ice country had to live. And we were going to make maps and pictures of parts of this country in which no white man had ever been.

I introduced, then, my Eskimo companion (Bosun), a man from Greenland who was almost as strange to the Akilinermiut as I. He had come along to hunt and to drive sledges, and do other work for the white man, while we gave our time to these studies.

My new friends were greatly pleased and impressed. They had just set out for their autumn camp up country at the back of Lyon Inlet, taking with them all their worldly goods. Being, however, like Eskimos generally, creatures of the moment, they at once abandoned the journey on meeting us, and we decided to set off all together for some big snowdrifts close at hand, where we could build snow huts and celebrate the meeting. . . .

I returned to headquarters on Danish Island full of excitement over the promise of my first reconnoitring expedition. Contact with these shore tribes convinced me that farther back, in the "Barren Grounds" of the American Continent I should find people still more interesting, and that our expedition would be able not only to bear to the world the first intimate picture of the life of a little known people, but also to produce evidence of the origin and migrations of all the Eskimo tribes.

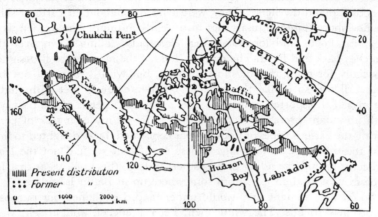

Distribution of the Eskimo across northern North America and Greenland. Dotted areas are no longer occupied.

The key to these mysteries would be found in hitherto unexplored ruins of former civilizations on the shores adjacent to the Barren Grounds, and in the present-day customs of isolated aborigines who were themselves strangers alike to the white man and to the Greenland Eskimos I knew so well.

The "Barren Grounds," as they have long been called, are great tracts of bare, untimbered land between Hudson Bay and the Arctic Coast. Though forming part of the great continent of America, they are among the most isolated and inaccessible portions of the globe. It is for this reason that the most primitive and uncivilized tribes are still to be found there. Despite the zeal with which hunters and traders ever seek to penetrate into unknown regions, the natural obstacles here have hitherto proved an effective barrier, and the territory is known only in the barest outline. On the north, there are the ramifications of the Arctic Ocean, permanently filled with ice, to bar the way. On the south, and to some extent also on the west, lie great trackless forests, where travelling is slow and difficult, the only practicable route being along the little known rivers. Only from Hudson Bay has the east coast of the Barren Grounds been accessible for modern forms of transport. And even here the waters are so hampered with ice that they are reckoned to be navigable for only two or three months a year. These natural obstacles, however, which have kept others away, were all to our advantage, because they have kept the tribes of Eskimos I intended to visit uncontaminated by white civilization, imprisoned within their swampy tundras, unaltered in all their primitive character.

We were now able to plan our first year's work in these regions. Near our headquarters we found a few old cairns and rough stone shelters built by the Eskimos of earlier days for the purpose of hunting caribou with bow and arrow. We were convinced that the excavation of these ruins would be well worth while. The natives we had now met explained that these ruins originated with a mysterious race of "giants," called Tunit. . . .

At noon on the 3rd of April we came up with the icebound vessel *Fort Chesterfield* at Berthie Harbor, a little to the north of Wager Bay. . . .

A little village of immigrant Netsilik natives had sprung up . . . and I took the opportunity of paying them a visit. The oldest inhabitant was an aged veteran from the region of the North Pole, named Manilaq. He had been a great fighter in his day, but was now reduced to resting on his laurels. He lived in a big snow hut with his children and grandchildren, who still regarded him with great respect, treating him indeed, as if he were their chief. He was an excellent story-teller, and always sure of a large audience. Unfortunately, I had not time myself to draw upon his stock of folk lore and personal recollections. It was essential to my plans that we should get as far on into the Barren Grounds as possible while the winter lasted. I hoped, however, to have an opportunity of meeting the old fellow later. As it turned out, this was not to be. A little while after we had left, he committed suicide, in the presence of his family, preferring to move to the eternal hunting grounds rather than live on growing feebler under the burden of days.

The time passed rapidly now, and our sole object was to get on as far as possible. We took short cuts wherever we could, though travelling overland was always an anxious business, unaccustomed as we were at first to the use of this delicate ice-shoeing. Thus we cut across the flat country from Berthie Harbor due west down to Wager Inlet; the mouth of the great fjord here is never frozen over, owing to the strength of the current. From here we came up on land again, and at last, on the 10th of April, reached Roe's Welcome, at a bay called Iterdlak. We could now follow the coast right down to Chesterfield, and though the country itself was very monotonous, there was plenty to interest us here. Every time we rounded a headland we came upon the ruins of some old settlement, which were eagerly investigated. They were not the work of the present population, but of some earlier inhabitants, evidently of a high degree of culture and well up in stone architecture. The ruins consisted of fallen house walls, store-chambers, and tent rings—all of stone—with frameworks for kayaks and umiaks, such as one finds in Greenland, where the boats are set up to keep the skins from being eaten by the dogs. There was evidence of abundant hunting by sea, in the form of numerous bones scattered about wherever the ground lay free from snow. Meat cellars were also frequently found, and to judge from their size, there should have been no lack of food. Every little headland was fenced in by stone cairns placed so close together that they looked from a distance like human beings assembled to bid us welcome. They were set out along definite lines across the ground, and had once been decked with fluttering rags of skin on top, serving to scare the caribou when driven down to the coast, where the hunters lay in wait in their kayaks, ready to spear them as soon as they took to the water.

All these ruins were the work of the "Tunit"; and from all that we could see, this highly developed coastal race with their kayaks and umiaks, must have been identical with the Eskimos that came into Greenland from these regions a thousand years ago. Both Miteq and Arnaruluk felt thoroughly at home in these surroundings. Much of what they had met with among the living natives of the present day was strange to them, but these relics of the dead from a bygone age were such as they knew from their own everyday life at home. . . .

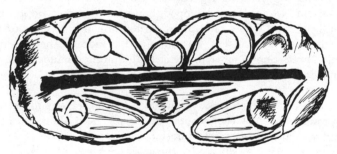

Eskimo snow goggles

There are no written sources for the early history of the Eskimo people; it is to the spade that we must turn if we would learn something of their life in ages past. We have to dig and delve among the ruins of their dwellings, in the kitchen middens of their settlements, for proof of how they lived and hunted, how they were housed and clad. It is often a laborious task, but not less interesting on that account. And it was one of the principal tasks of the Fifth Thule Expedition to investigate, by means of archaeological excavations, the history and development of the Eskimo people, and their migrations into Greenland. Our work in this field has brought to light some six or seven thousand items which afford a good idea as to the mode of life prevailing among the Central Eskimos here in those distant ages.

Naujan lies on the northern shore of Repulse Bay, a little to the east of the trading station. The name, which means "the place of the young seamews," is taken from a steep bird cliff on the banks of a small lake. From the lake, a valley runs down towards the shore, where it opens out into a bay, and it is in this valley, just south of the lake, that the great settlement of Naujan existed in ancient times.

The Eskimos of the present day in these regions use only snow huts in winter; it was the more surprising therefore to come upon remains of quite a different type of house. We found at Naujan a whole little township of these houses, constructed of stone, turf, and the bones of whales. They were built so as to be partly underground and must have been far more substantial and warm, though less hygienic perhaps, than the light, cool, healthy snow huts of today. Various features placed it beyond question that at the time when these houses were built, the land must have lain some ten metres lower than it does now; and this, too, explains why the settlement was found at some distance from what is now the beach, instead of practically on it as is customary. Similarly, in confirmation of our theory, we found, on a little island near by, a pair of kayak stands—pillars of stone on which the skin kayaks are laid to be out of reach of the dogs—some 15 metres up from sea; actually, of course, they would have been built at the water's edge, to save hauling up and down.

The houses themselves had fallen to pieces long since, and the remains were scattered, weatherworn and overgrown with grass and moss to such an extent that our excavations gave but a poor idea of their original appearance. The implements and objects found among the ruins, however, gave an excellent view of the culture of the period from which they were derived. The materials comprised bone, walrus tusk and caribou antler, flint, slate and soapstone, whalebone, some wood, and occasionally metal, this last in the form of cold hammered copper (probably obtained by barter from the Eskimos of the west), with a single fragment of meteoric iron forming the point of a harpoon.

It is of course impossible to mention more than a very few of the finds here; often, too, the most insignificant objects to all outward seeming prove most important from the scientific point of view. Among our most valuable finds, for instance, were three odd broken fragments of rough earthenware vessels. These are only known to exist among the Alaskan Eskimos, and the finding of them here was of importance; few, however, would have attached any value to those three dirty scraps of pottery.

And now as to the age of this Naujan material. We may at once assert that nothing was found which could suggest any intercourse with Europeans. There were no glass beads—which are ordinarily the first thing the Eskimos procure, and always found in their villages—and the only fragment of iron found was of meteoric origin. This at once carries us back 300 years. Beyond this, we have only the alteration in the level of the land to fall back upon. It takes a considerable period, of course, for the land to rise ten metres, but there is no definite standard by which to measure the lapse of time involved. In the north of Sweden, for instance, the land rises 1 metre in a hundred years; allowing the same rate of progress here, this would give us an age of 1,000 years—but this is, of course, mere guesswork.

As to the people who lived here in those days, they were beyond doubt genuine Eskimos; they lived on the shore in regular winter dwellings, drove dog sledges, and hunted whale, seal and walrus, besides bear and caribou; they trapped foxes, and caught salmon. They had at any rate no lack of meat, to judge from the enormous quantities of bones, which indeed, almost smothered the remains of the houses themselves. If we ask the present inhabitants of these regions, the Aivilik, as to the folk who dwelt in these now ruined houses, they will say, it was the Tunit. These Tunit were a race of big, strong men who lived in permanent dwellings and hunted whale and walrus; the men wore bearskin breeches and the women long sealskin boots just like the Polar Eskimos of today. When the Aivilik settled on the coast, the Tunit moved away to the northward; only on the inaccessible Southampton Island did a party remain, and the Sadlermiut, who died out here in 1903, were the last descendants of the Tunit in the country. Thus the Aivilik tradition, and it agrees in all essentials with the results of our investigations.

For on comparing these Tunit of ancient Naujan with the present inhabitants, we find a great difference between them. The Naujan Eskimos lived on the shore, hunted the whale, and built their houses from the skeletons. The Aivilik live in snow huts, and spend most of the year hunting caribou up in the interior. Many of the implements and utensils in use among the Naujan folk, such as the bola, the bird dart, and earthenware vessels, are unknown among the Aivilik; the latter, on the other hand, have others unknown to the ancients, such as combs, big ladles made of musk ox horn, and toggles for dog harness. And on examining the types of implement in use among the two peoples, many distinct points of difference are found.

Where did the Naujan Eskimos come from, and what became of them?

It soon becomes apparent that they link up in two directions across the Eskimo region; with Alaska on the one hand and Greenland on the other. At Thule, in northern Greenland, a find has been made, the oldest of any extant from the whole of Greenland, which points to precisely the same type of culture as that which we found at Naujan; and we have therefore called it the Thule type. Similar finds have been made both in west and north Greenland, and the Polar Eskimos of the present day are very much like these Thule folk in many respects. The Greenland Eskimos, then, must have passed through these central regions at a time when they were still inhabited by the Thule folk.

Eskimo harpoon head made from walrus ivory

Looking now to the westward, we find in Alaska a race of big men, who hunt the whale, live in permanent dwellings on the coast, use the bola, make earthenware, and have almost the same types of implements generally as those we found at Naujan; old finds from Alaska also exhibit even more marked resemblance to the Naujan type. The Thule folk, then, must have come from Alaska, this is beyond question. They spread in a mighty wave from west to east, reaching right across to Greenland. At some time now far distant there was a more or less uniform type of culture prevailing throughout the whole of the Eskimo region; that which we now call the Thule type; then, in the central districts, an advance took place of people from the interior represented by the present-day Central Eskimo: the Aivilik, Netsilik, Copper Eskimos and Baffinlanders. These people, with their culture based on snow huts and caribou hunting, made their way down to the coast, where their mode of life was gradually adapted to some extent, so as to include the hunting of marine animals, while the ancient Thule culture disappeared from the central regions where now only the numerous ruins of stone and bone houses remain as evidence of the culture of earlier times. Thus too we have an explanation of many otherwise inexplicable similarities between the two topographical extremities of Eskimo culture—Alaska and Greenland—features found in the extreme east and in the extreme west, but lacking in the central region.

41

Rasmussen and Mathiassen on the Fifth Thule Expedition barely laid the foundation of Arctic archaeology. Few of the mysteries of the Eskimo past had been solved. Vast areas of prehistoric settlements or migrations in the Far North had yet to be sifted. Search for a primitive Eskimo culture, from which Thule and more modern manifestations may have sprung, would have to concentrate on that part of Alaska which is closest to Siberia, since it was presumably there that the human story in the New World had its beginnings.

However, the next chapter in the exploration of Eskimo antiquity was opened without taking to the field. This happened in 1925, just a few months after the termination of the Thule Expedition. In that year a New Zealand-born anthropologist, Diamond Jenness of the National Museum of Canada at Ottawa, described, from delicately carved, deeply patinated ivory objects in the Museum's collection, another and older Eskimo culture, the Dorset. The culture's prime sites were eventually traced to Cape Dorset on Hudson Strait and several islands in the Bay. Later it was found that the Dorset Eskimo had spread far and wide into Newfoundland and eastern Greenland, but had most likely originated at the Pacific. At many sites they had preceded the Tunits of the Thule culture by several centuries—though the more conspicuous Thule houses built from stone and whalebone were liable to hide the subterranean homes of the Dorset from sight. Meanwhile, in 1926, Jenness had also started archaeological investigations of his own at Bering Strait. On the Diomede Islands—half way between Siberia and Alaska—and at Cape Prince of Wales, he dug up harpoon heads that proved conclusively the presence of Thule remains at this American gateway. At the same time he identified the all-important Old Bering Sea tradition, which, he maintained, went back at least two thousand years and had a central role in the development of other Eskimo cultures. (This has been enhanced by subsequent researches.) Aleš Hrdlička, independently, had come across similar evidence.

The Arctic materials which had been brought forth in the wake of the Thule Expedition served to establish a succession and interdependence of cultures in extreme North America and Greenland. All of them were, despite considerable variations, unmistakably Eskimo. They spoke of a long continuity of those northern hunters' way of life and craftsmanship. In the light of such knowledge, one excavation made at the edge of the continent came as a real jolt. It entailed the discovery of an entirely unknown culture, older by far than the Toltec, Aztec, or Inca, but aesthetically as exciting. And it was centered at what, at least in size, amounted to nothing less than an "Arctic metropolis." To this day it is considered the largest archaeological site in the Arctic. Its people knew the use of iron a thousand and more years before Columbus.

When Knud Rasmussen at the end of his sleigh journey in 1923 reached Point Hope, a peninsula in northwestern Alaska pointing like an arrow toward Siberia, he noticed ruins near Tigara (Eskimo for "index finger"), a modern native village. The actual site was scattered on a long, off-shore sand spit about 125 miles north of the Arctic Circle and 200 miles north of Bering Strait. The land itself was treeless and nearly barren, except in the brief summer when grass and flowers sprouted everywhere. Tigara had only some 250 inhabitants. A Christian mission church was near by. Judging by the ruins, which Rasmussen had already described as the most extensive of the Arctic, the place must once have supported a much larger population. It attracted the interest of three young archaeologists, one from Denmark and two Americans from the University of Alaska, who decided to pool their knowledge of Eskimo antiquity and dig at the Alaskan outpost in 1939.

Two of them were Helge Larsen, a curator of the Danish National Museum at Copenhagen, and Froelich G. Rainey, a professor of anthropology also associated with the American Museum of Natural History in New York. They were later joined by J. Louis Giddings, Jr., who at the time was mainly concerned with determining the age of wooden articles by the analysis of tree rings. In years to come, all three were to be in the forefront of studies of the prehistoric American Arctic. Louis Giddings, in particular, until his accidental death in 1963, made notable contributions in extending the Eskimo horizon and in introducing new concepts of dating at successive beach levels of the Arctic shoreline. Larsen, now chief curator of the Danish National Museum, served as guest professor at American universities in between repeated returns to the Arctic. He also dug in Mexico. Froelich Rainey later (1947) became director of the University Museum of the University of Pennsylvania. There he has been taking a leading part in adapting electronic devices to archaeological fieldwork. Rainey spent two additional seasons at Point Hope, from 1939

Map of arctic region of northwestern Alaska, showing Point Hope

to 1941. The three campaigns were sponsored by the Danish National Museum, the University of Alaska, and the American Museum of Natural History.

Helge Larsen, in a popular article contributed to a Scandinavian-American review, from which the following excerpt is taken, gave a preliminary account of their original campaign. He and his colleagues ran into rivalry from native diggers, whose apprehensions were finally overcome. Initial excavation of surface ruins brought no surprises. The ancient Eskimo who had occupied the place resembled in essence their modern brethren. But late in the summer Larsen and Giddings stumbled upon rectangular depressions in the soil. Digging into these, they uncovered artifacts of an altogether different style. With only three weeks left until the end of the season, when a coastal sloop was to take them back to modern civilization, the three men feverishly gathered thousands of strange objects with designs elaborate beyond anything they had been led to expect. They opened nine buried houses, but knew that these formed only a small part of a large town, which had not yet given up all its treasures. Already they were wondering whether Ipiutak, as they named it, could be fitted into the Eskimo tradition. Was it at all Eskimo?

The following year they planned to resume excavation. But war had broken out in Europe, Denmark fell to the Germans, and Larsen was detained in Copenhagen. (He later managed to escape with his family to the United States and to join Rainey at the American Museum of Natural History in the examination and publication of the Ipiutak material.) Nevertheless, as early as January 1940, Rainey returned alone to Tigara in the midst of the excruciating Arctic winter with its howling gales and 30-below temperatures. His explicit purpose was to share the rigors of life of the Eskimo in order to familiarize himself with their customs and, from a study of the living, to acquire possible clues to the long-gone. Joining the Eskimo on their hunts, Rainey came to respect their advanced skill in adjusting to harsh and limited conditions. He was strengthened in his opinion that no primitives could have devised such adroit techniques. Here was a gifted race in superb control of its environment.

In the spring, Rainey continued digging at Ipiutak with the aid of a graduate student from the University of Alaska. Only now did the dimensions of the prehistoric town stand out clearly. Once again, a phenomenon in the soil came to the explorers' assistance.

It was June and the grass and moss were turning green. But on the house plots vegetation was more vigorous and, besides, retained a yellow tinge from dead grass. Before Rainey's eyes was practically a "blueprint" of Ipiutak as it ran for nearly a mile east to west in orderly rows of some 800 houses, along five "avenues" where Larsen had seen only four. According to a conservative estimate the town must have included some 4,000 to 5,000 inhabitants—more in fact than what was then the population of Fairbanks, Alaska's leading city. Surprisingly, Tigara natives had no tradition relating to the early center, aside from vague notions about a ghost man with ivory eyes, who did his mischief at night and with whose presence they scared their children.

It was this ghost man who was conjured up when Rainey started his search for the prehistoric cemetery. A local Eskimo with the unlikely name of Moses had fallen into a pit near the ruins and found himself in the eerie company of human bones and motley funerary goods. Report of this alerted Rainey to the potential wealth of burials. Yet with the exception of Moses's pit, the graveyard eluded him for some time. Test dig after test dig proved vain. At last he mobilized forty Eskimo men, women, and children, who, oblivious of drenching rain, produced in one day seven tombs. By the end of the summer Rainey had cleared sixty-five of the characteristically log-chambered graves. In them he found deposits even richer than those extracted from the houses. Some objects were of a refinement without precedent in the Arctic, intricately decorated with fanciful designs. Native helpers were simply aghast when Rainey extricated several richly ornamented skulls inlaid with eyes of ivory having pupils of jet. Evidently the dead men's eyes had been gouged out before interment and replaced with imitations, not unlike those in the famous "Aztec" skull at the British Museum, or in the skull Alfonso Caso later found in Tomb 7 at Monte Albán. Noses were stuffed with ivory plugs in the shape of bird heads, also equipped with ivory eyes. One skeleton of an adult male appeared to hold that of a child in its embrace.

Apart from more or less familiar articles like arrowheads, needles, and other common utensils of ivory, bone, and antler, which were all of superior artistry, the graves were furnished with ingeniously wrought and engraved pieces of walrus ivory. Nobody could tell the function of these twisted forms. Nothing of their kind had ever been encountered in pre-Columbian America. Rainey thought for a while that some of the swivel-like objects might have served as dog harnesses. While without parallel in aboriginal North America, spiral motifs were, however, known from the Ainu of northern Japan and the ancient people of the Amur region in Siberia. Polynesians used spiral patterns in their tattoos. Judging from Asiatic analogies, the old ivory carvings may have been insignia of shamans, worn as attachments to their garments.

Its close connections with Asia were almost immediately evident to the discoverers of Ipiutak. There were the log-covered burials, decorative

Swivel-shaped object from Ipiutak

artistry, and extraordinary flint tools which more than hinted at sources from northern Eurasia. Specific animal motifs, such as those of griffins and bears, recalled Scytho-Siberian art. Metal implements (the ore was probably Asiatic) linked Ipiutak with the East Asiatic iron age. Rainey and Larsen tended to think that the people of Ipiutak had themselves migrated from Siberia—perhaps from the Ob and Yenisei—and they made a strong case for Old World affinities when stressing that northern Alaska is geographically closer to the advanced civilizations of Manchuria and even northern China than it is to those of Mexico and Central America.

The Ipiutak people lacked such typical Eskimo equipment as sleds, blubber lamps, pottery, and bone drills. Harpoons were a rare item. Thus the conclusion seemed warranted that they were basically an inland people, conceivably of a more temperate zone, who had not yet fully adapted to the life of marine (particularly whale) hunters and fishermen. The very absence of basic Eskimo utensils, among so populous a group in Arctic America at a relatively early period, convinced Rainey that Ipiutak had preceded all known Eskimo cultures. Even the Old Bering Sea culture, which some exemplars of Ipiutak definitely resemble, was presumably derived from it.

Rainey's early views, shared also by Larsen, of the place of Ipiutak in the larger Arctic culture history carried conviction in the light of then available knowledge, though they reflect the inevitable bias induced by sudden and unique discoveries. Henry B. Collins, another prominent American Eskimo scholar, has severely criticized them, while granting that Ipiutak remains by and large a puzzle. He maintained the priority of Old Bering Sea (with its oldest Okvik phase), a thesis that has now been amply confirmed by radio-carbon dating. Besides, the related "Near-Ipiutak"—first traced by Giddings at Iyatayet at Norton Sound in 1949 and by Larsen at Kuskokwim Bay at Bering Sea in 1951—though apparently older than Ipiutak proper, includes all the essential Eskimo elements. As to the Ipiutak flint industry, it may well stem from the Denbigh Complex, and only via that American station from the Eurasian Neolithic. Indications are that Ipiutak was not just transferred as a sealed culture package from Asia. The "Arctic metropolis" rather testifies to an advanced stage of the intertwining of Asiatic styles with local Arctic-American developments.

Ipiutak may never be fully explained. Like Eskimo archaeology in general it has failed to supply pertinent material on man's first entry into the American North. But through the work of Rainey, Larsen, and Giddings it helped anthropologists and archaeologists to focus their attention on Asia for final answers to New World origins.

However, Ipiutak is more than an index finger to the Old World. The sheer dimensions of the settlement, and its fanciful industries, rank it among the archaeological highspots of the Americas. Appropriately, the U.S. government has set it aside as a National Monument to protect it from vandals and amateur diggers.

IPIUTAK, ALASKAN METROPOLIS

Helge Larsen

Scientists from all over the world assembled in Copenhagen in the summer of 1938 for the Second International Congress of Anthropological and Ethnological Sciences. As usual in such meetings, the important thing was to meet colleagues and discuss problems with them rather than to listen to the lectures. The friendships formed and the informal talks between men of similar interests may lead to important results far beyond the formal program. In this way the Congress in Copenhagen became the direct cause of a cooperation between Danish and American scientists. . . .

Among the distinguished delegates to the Congress was Professor Froelich G. Rainey from the University of Alaska, an energetic young scientist who has devoted himself to the study of Eskimo history and has carried on excavations on the site of old settlements on St. Lawrence Island in the Bering Sea. Inasmuch as I had made similar excavations in Greenland, it was natural that Rainey and I found each other and that we should talk Eskimo archeology early and late. We discussed the possibilities of cooperation between our institutions, the University of Alaska and the National Museum in Copenhagen, in joint expeditions. We thought the Danish knowledge of the eastern and the American knowledge of the western Eskimo territory might be mutually helpful. As the most likely place to start this work we considered northern Alaska, where we might expect to find remains not only of western Eskimo culture, but

From "Point Hope Expedition," *American Scandinavian Review*, XXVIII:3 (1940), pp. 210–22 *passim*.

also of the forms prevalent farther east, as we know them, for instance, from Greenland. . . .

During the spring of 1939 we made all preparations. Tools for digging and instruments for measuring were packed and sent ahead to Seattle. Funds had been raised, and at last, on May 24, all was clear and I could embark on the *Batory* which was to carry me to New York. From there we went by rail to Seattle and by ship to Valdez in Alaska. There Professor Rainey and his wife met me, having driven down from College, the university town.

The drive from Valdez to Fairbanks along the 276 miles of the Richardson Highway, was an experience. Here in two days we saw every phase of Alaska's grandiose scenery. We passed deep canyons with rushing mountain torrents, high peaks, and snowfields that glittered in the brilliant sunshine. We drove hour after hour through dark pine and spruce forests where the bear slunk along the edge of the road, and across endless swampy plains where the moose crashed his way through the scrub forest.

In Fairbanks the expedition was increased by a third member, Mr. Louis Giddings, who is also a member of the faculty of the University of Alaska. . . .

To get from Fairbanks to Point Hope at that time of the year could only be done in one way, namely by air, and we therefore chartered a small hydroplane which carried us to our destination in eight hours. The Eskimo name for Point Hope is Tigara, that is, an index finger, and one could hardly find a better name for the long peninsula, curved at the end, which runs out a distance of fifteen miles into the Arctic Ocean a little north of the Polar Circle. The outer part of the peninsula consists of low banks lying side by side on the coast like great rolling waves that had suddenly stiffened. They are made up of sand and gravel covered by a thick green carpet of grass in which, during the short Arctic summer, millions of flowers form patterns in clear, brilliant colors.

The place has been as attractive to Eskimos as it was to us, not however on account of the beautiful flowers, but because of the easy access to the sea with its wealth of whales, walruses, and seals, and because of the excellent building ground which the well-drained banks afford. Eskimos have had their homes here probably for thousands of years, and at times in numbers greater than at any other place in the Arctic regions. The many ruins of winter houses which lie far out on the tip of the point indicate a period of great expansion and seem to have been built during the last two hundred years. We found only 70 or 80 ruins, but fifteen years earlier Knud Rasmussen had counted 126. Some have evidently been washed away by the sea which every year carries off large pieces of land. How long this destruction had been going on we do not know, and we could only guess how large the settlement had originally been. That there had been a settlement of unusual dimensions according to Eskimo conditions seems evident, and probably Knud Rasmussen's tentative estimate of 2,000 inhabitants is not too large.

The greatest expansion of Point Hope coincided with the boom period of whaling. Old men still relate with pride how hundreds of Eskimos from the south and from the north would settle at Point Hope between April and June in order to take part in the hunting of the monsters of the deep. We can easily imagine the life and bustle on that low point of land. Crew after crew in their little boats of skin would set out to sea for the dangerous and exciting chase which demanded expert knowledge and presence of mind in every single man from the captain of the boat to the common oarsman. A single clumsy movement would be enough to frighten the whale and allow it to escape, or a blow of its mighty tail might splinter the frail craft and send the entire crew to the bottom. When, after many efforts, the harpoon was firmly lodged in the flesh of the colossus, and the long line with its huge bladders of sealskin filled with air had been cast out in order to delay the whale, then the nerve-racking pursuit of the wounded animal began, and lasted until the mortal wound could be given it. No wonder that this dangerous chase required not only human effort, but also the aid of higher powers. Innumerable tabus and other regulations had to be observed by the hunters and their families in order to insure a fortunate catch. There is surely no other place in the world where the whale has dominated the mental and material life of the people as it did at Point Hope. Even the most insignificant act was regulated by law, and woe to him who broke the law! . . .

To maintain law and order [nowadays,] a committee of seven members is elected every year, one of them acting as mayor. They settle all little quarrels and decide matters that concern the community as a whole. It was natural, therefore, that our expedition, as soon as we arrived at Point Hope, applied to this committee and explained what we proposed to do. We were kindly received and asked to come again. Meanwhile the committee would take the matter up with the rest of the people. The next day we met in the store where quite a number of men had assembled. We again explained the purpose of our visit. They declared that they quite understood our object, and we supposed that all was settled. That, however, was not the case. An hour later we were again called to the store, and then the sentiment of the meeting was not nearly so favorable as it had been before. The storekeeper, who acted as interpreter, informed us that the people had agreed to refuse us permission to dig. The reason was curious. It was said that we would interfere with the business of the natives.

During the summer when the seals disappeared from the coast, many of the men exchanged the rifle for the spade and worked as amateur archeologists. In the old ruins they found a great many antiques which they could sell to traders or to the crews on the coast guard cutters, thereby making a neat little sum. We not only meant to conduct excavations on a large scale, but we might compete with them in the market. Our explanation that we had no intention of selling what we found was not accepted. Antiques in their opinion had only value as objects for sale.

Carved ivory piece from Ipiutak, use unknown

The same was true of the ethnographic articles which I purchased for the National Museum and which included everything they used, such as tools, furniture, weapons, and clothing. It surprised them very much that I preferred old things to new, for, as they rightly reasoned, new things must surely fetch more money than old. That the objects were to be exhibited in a museum they either could not or would not understand. In the course of the summer I had many proofs of their interest in my purchases and in the use they thought I intended to make of them. Some thought I meant to fit out an Arctic expedition with them, others that I meant to give them to my family, since there were women's and children's costumes among them, but the subtlest solution of the problem was given me by a young man the very last day I was at Point Hope. "Mr. Larsen, I know what you are going to use all those old things for that you have been buying here." "Well, then tell me." "When you come down to the States you are going to make a movie about Eskimos and it is for that movie you are going to use the costumes and the other things." He was very much surprised when I burst out laughing at his clever idea, but I could not help thinking of how the beauties of Hollywood would like to put on the greasy and smelly boots, trousers, and jackets which had just been taken off by their owners, and had not even been deloused. The idea had probably come to him because a part of Peter Freuchen's film *Eskimo* had been taken at Point Hope.

For a while the outlook for our little expedition was rather dubious, but fortunately Peter Kunuknorak was able to lay the suspicions of the people, and all ended in an era of good feeling. Both parties had every reason to be satisfied with the decision. We were allowed to dig as much as we pleased, and the natives earned good money, partly by helping us in our work, and partly by selling us meat, fish, and furs.

Unfortunately, the account of their activity as amateur archeologists proved only too true, and judging from the results, they must have carried on this traffic for many years. The entire site of the settlement had been dug through from one end to the other. There was not a single ruin that had been left untouched. After long search we found at last a few places where we could make trial excavations. Luckily the settlement was only a few hundred years old, so the loss was not great, for we were really in search of much older things.

But where could we find this older material?

At Jabbertown, about five miles farther in on the peninsula, there were some ruins. We decided to investigate them and we soon found that they were a good deal older than those we had hitherto examined. We dug out a very curious house buried under a layer of earth with no fewer than seven very narrow rooms radiating from the center like the spokes of a wheel. How human beings had been able to live in these narrow rooms was more than we could understand. But the house was very carefully built with fine board floors and walls made of heavy logs supported by strong poles. In this house we found hundreds of implements of all kinds, weapons, tools, furniture, articles not unlike those we knew from earlier excavations in eastern Canada and Greenland. Giddings was busy taking samples of the wood, the date of which he believed he could fix at about 1200. In spite of the length of time that had passed, this culture is not very different from that which has obtained down to our day.

The Jabbertown house was interesting, but by no means sensational. The sensation came one day when we were on our way home from Jabbertown to Point Hope. It was late in the afternoon. The sun was low in the heavens and threw long shadows across the green grass. We were just passing the buildings of the Mission station about a mile from the settlement, when we noticed some faint depressions in the ground which seemed to lie between low banks. There were several of about the same size, quadrangular, and all covered with lush vegetation. They might be natural, but they might also—we simply did not dare to think of what they might be; but we agreed to investigate the phenomenon the following day. The first thing we did was to put people to work digging trial excavations in several of the depressions, and it was not long before we had proof that they were not natural, but made by man. We found articles fashioned by human hands, and when we began to dig out the depressions, they proved to be the sites of square houses which, in the course of time, had crumbled and been filled with sand and gravel.

When we had realized this, we could suddenly perceive that there were a great many of these depressions, and when we began to count them we found that there were several hundred of them lying side by side in four long rows—from First Avenue to Fourth Avenue, we called it. To find an unknown settlement of such huge dimensions was a sensation in itself, and it was all the more thrilling when we gradually realized that the articles we found were very different from other Eskimo implements. There were many types which we had never seen at all, and which we were unable to identify. There was no doubt, however, that these articles

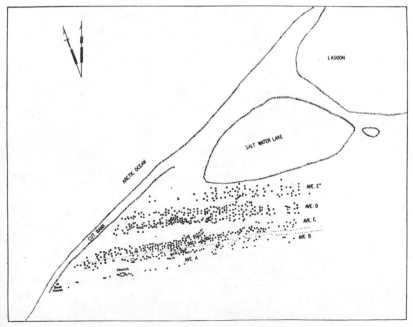

Preliminary plan of Ipiutak ruins

belonged to a hitherto unknown form of culture, most likely Eskimo, but very ancient and very remarkable. Wherever we dug, whether at one end or the other, we always found the same kind of articles. The houses must therefore all have been inhabited at about the same time. They all belonged to the same culture—the Ipiutak Culture we called it after the place where we had found it. . . .

We have before us a tremendous task in attempting, with the aid of the thousands of articles we found in the sunken houses, to reconstruct life as it was lived at Point Hope in that period. What we could do the first summer was but little. We can say we found the treasure trove, lifted the lid slightly, and took some samples home, but by far the greater part of the treasure lies there awaiting us.

42

Even without the "Vinland Map," the appearance of which in the 1960's was greeted with fanfare quite out of proportion to its historical importance, no serious scholar in recent years has questioned the landfall of Vikings in the New World about A.D. 1000. (Nevertheless the popular press every so often will proclaim it as a novelty, particularly when Columbus Day is approaching and one can count on raising Latin blood pressure.) Better than this more or less conventional map—which, if at all authentic, smacks of medieval images of legendary isles and which was drawn long after the event by a Central European, who apparently lacked any first-hand knowledge—we have written records such as the contemporary account by a German churchman, Adam of Bremen, who in the eleventh century took note of the newly discovered western lands. And then there are the Icelandic sagas, which may not be straight history, but have factual basis beyond argument, despite certain contradictions inherent in their poetic medium and oral transmission.

What matters in the issue of Norse discoveries is not whether those fierce blond-bearded sea rovers ever made it across the North Atlantic, but whether we can obtain specific details of their exploits. Unfortunately, the descriptions given in the sagas shed only a dim glow on the different phases of this American adventure. There is much uncertainty on how to interpret the sagas' vague references to geographic features and vegetation in the new lands. The exact locations of Vinland, Markland, Helluland, Straumfjord, and Hóp, mentioned as way stations by the Icelandic bards, remain pretty much in doubt. Until very recently, when the Norwegian explorer Helge Ingstad excavated a site in Newfoundland which is definitely Viking—and possibly represents a camp of Leif Ericson himself—it has been impossible to produce genuine Viking objects from American soil to pin down and corroborate the literary or documentary testimony.

For the past hundred years, United States and Scandinavian printing presses have poured forth an endless stream of articles, reports, and books about the Vikings in America. Few of these are of any lasting value. If anything, they overstated their case and helped to underline a partisanship among Viking champions that verged on a cult.

Anxious devotees of Norse pioneering have long busied themselves in procuring physical traces of Viking handiwork on the American continent. What they put forth ranges from the plausible to the absurd. Admittedly, some of the material has commanded the cautious approval of a few neutral bystanders. The famous Kensington Stone from far inland in Minnesota, dug up—strange as it may seem—in the past century on the farm of a Scandinavian immigrant, convinced many of its genuineness. But it has now been unmasked as a fake. The Newport Tower of Rhode Island, another subject of several learned monographs, and once a chief buttress of the Viking supporters, is most likely a sixteenth-century English watchtower. The proof of mooring stones on the Atlantic seaboard, used to tie Viking long ships, is flimsy at best. Some of the undoubtedly medieval Scandinavian weapons which turn up here and there, probably represent family heirlooms or collectors' items brought over not too long ago. As to curious iron halberds from the Midwest, which one Norwegian expert dated from about 1500—a date which was not exactly helpful to either camp—they were eventually identified as tobacco cutters, commissioned by the American Tobacco Company from a Springfield, Ohio, ironworks to advertise "Battle Axe Plug Tobacco."

Over the years Viking archaeology on the American continent has thus met with endless frustrations. No incontrovertibly Norse monument or object was forthcoming. The lack of physical evidence by no means weakened the likelihood of medieval landings, but it did reflect the rather incidental and haphazard nature of these enterprises which, for all we know, left no impact on pre-Columbian American developments.

However, the westward adventure of the Vikings does not depend only on spurious material from Minnesota or New England to be illuminated by archaeology. There was also Greenland, geographically a part of the New World (just as its natives were a New World people). Across Davis Strait the globe's largest island is separated from the American mainland by less than 200 miles, and actually approaches Ellesmere Island in Canada's north within twelve miles, a narrow stretch that can easily be walked over in the long winters. Once the Vikings had arrived in Greenland, their reaching the American continent proper was, of course, only a matter of time. In fact, it took little more than a year, once Eric the Red had set up a settlement in Greenland (if we are to give precedence to Bjarni Herjulfson over Eric's son Leif—as, incidentally, even the "Vinland Map" does). Navigation between Greenland and America was shorter and easier than between Greenland and Norway, the mother country. If there is any element of surprise in the Viking story it is not at all that Norsemen "discovered" America, but rather that their contacts were so tenuous. However, there are indications that the Norse settlers of Greenland trafficked with the western lands for several centuries. Shipments of timber from Markland are reported as late as 1347. Hence, we should return Rasmussen's visit and look first to the archaeological record of Greenland in order to reconstruct the westward trail of the Vikings.

Norse ship, from the Bayeux tapestry

Sources on the Viking discovery—made accidentally by the Norwegian Gunnbjorn around A.D. 900—and the peopling of Greenland are more copious than those on Vinland, but they too depend largely on Icelandic sagas and are far from satisfactory. As an outpost of Western Christendom which continued from the days of Eric the Red's colonization in the late tenth century through a long decline into the fifteenth century, Greenland was not entirely ignored in Europe. Starting in the twelfth century, the Roman Church sent its bishops there. The first of them embarked for Vinland, but was never heard of again. As late as 1492, Pope Alexander VI brooded in a letter over his distant flock in Greenland, residing, as he put it, "at the end of the world." By that time, the last Norsemen on the island had probably died.

There has been considerable speculation about the fate of those settlers. It was once generally assumed that they "went over" to the Eskimo and were absorbed by them. However, the Danish scholar Poul Nørlund, who for years carried out extensive excavations of Viking settlements in Greenland, believes that mainly climatic deterioration, the drying up of the northern trade, and inbreeding led to the settlers' gradual decadence until they were completely wiped out by natural death and Eskimo massacre. Ironically, the Vikings vanished from the scene just as the voyages of exploration were re-opening sea routes and awakening new interest in Greenland and the lands beyond.

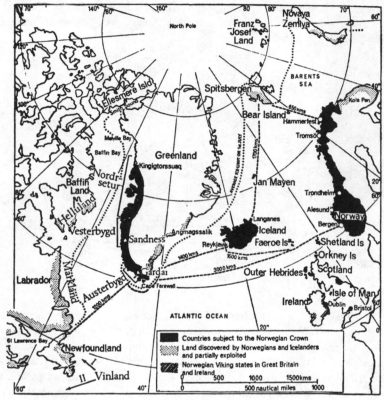

Map showing Viking footholds in the North Atlantic

Poul Norlund (1888–1951), a former director of the National Museum of Denmark, excavated in Greenland during the 1920's, concentrating on the area of the so-called East Settlement near the present-day center of Julianehaab. Here the bulk of the Norse pioneers, several thousand of them, had settled. Nørlund's first campaign, in 1921, explored the farming village of Herjolfsnes and came up with amazingly varied and well-preserved articles bearing not just on the life of a remote European colony in the northern wastes, but on the everyday life of common medieval folk in general. The clothes he found in graves allowed him to date the deposits from the fourteenth and fifteenth centuries. Undoubtedly, they belonged to a late phase before Greenland life began its rapid disintegration. Buried in Arctic soil, the clothing had been frozen, and thus has come down to us almost intact—virtually the only extant specimens of vestments of ordinary folk of the Middle Ages. Just as scraps from the deserts of Africa have pointed up unexpected aspects of imperial Roman history, so the sub-Arctic muck of a glaciated island in the Western Hemisphere has filled gaps in our knowledge of the European Middle Ages—from fashions and utensils to farming methods. This is one of the uncanny results of archaeology, that a dig far from the main scene of world events may unlock a door to the lost past. Greenland antiquities have therefore assumed considerable significance to European medieval studies. Above all, as Nørlund underlined, archaeological research on the Greenland coast furnished a sound basis for describing the Viking achievement in that rugged western land. To him, Nørlund confessed, the testimony of the spade spoke as eloquently as any sagas, besides giving the truth unadorned. It was also bound to enhance the epic role of the Norsemen in the New World. It may yet guide scholars to related materials left by the Viking in American soil.

The truth as such was spectacular enough. It led to Eric the Red's own farm at Brattahlid, excavated during Nørlund's final campaigns in Greenland. From Brattahlid the rest of Greenland had been colonized. There, on his father's farm, lived Leif Ericson after bringing Christianity to Greenland and returning from his voyage to Vinland. Nørlund's operations at Brattahlid, by the way, were greatly assisted by air reconnaissance and photographing, carried out by the air section of Rasmussen's Seventh Thule Expedition.

Between Herjolfsnes and Brattahlid lay many other sites for Danish excavators to probe. Nine Christian churches in the East Settlement and three in the West Settlement were rediscovered; they were found to resemble the architecture of Scotland, rather than of Iceland or Norway as one might have expected. None of Nørlund's other campaigns, however, compared with the one in 1926 when he located the old episcopal seat at Gardar, across from Brattahlid on a land tongue between two fjords. Gardar had probably been laid out in the first half of the twelfth century. It came to include a cathedral, fittingly dedicated to St. Nicholas, patron saint of mariners. Nørlund excavated its ruins, as well as the bishop's residence and a mighty festal hall that could hold several hundred people for ecclesiastical and secular occasions. It seemed to reverberate with the raucous celebrations described in the sagas. There, too, the *Althing*, the settlers' parliamentary body, may have congregated annually.

A highpoint of the campaign was the discovery of a bishop's burial at the east end of the cathedral. Within the bishop's grasp was his staff, a superb piece of craftsmanship with a crook carved from walrus ivory. Subsequent analysis of the crozier made it likely that it had been fashioned around 1200 in Iceland. Though Nørlund at first would not venture any guess as to the bishop's identity, he later came to the conclusion that the cleric was Jon Smyrill, who is known to have died in 1209. Conceivably the crozier had been given to him by his friend the bishop of Iceland. We may even surmise the artist's name, since the then bishop of Iceland had in his employ a woman sculptor, Margharet, who was famed for her skill in fashioning ivory. While the bishop's staff is now a cherished exhibit in the Danish National Museum, the bishop's body, after it had been examined in Copenhagen, was returned to Greenland and reburied at its original site in an iron casket. A gravestone was raised to carry inscriptions in Danish and Eskimo.

Poul Nørlund, member of a prominent family of Danish intellectuals and a brother-in-law of the physicist Niels Bohr, was trained in medieval and ancient history. He was a long-time curator of the Danish National Museum and became its director in 1938. Aside from his pioneering work in Greenland, he excavated medieval military installations at Trelleborg. In several later studies he turned to the history of Danish painting and church architecture.

Nørlund's researches in Greenland were continued under the aegis of the Danish National Museum by his associate Aage Roussell and then by C. L. Veback, who led his own first expedition in 1939. During excavations in the West Settlement facing Baffin Island, objects were recovered of unmistakably American origin, that the Vikings had apparently taken back from one of their visits to the neighboring continent. Veback returned to Greenland after the war, and took a special interest in the elucidation of its medieval agriculture. Among his notable postwar discoveries was a large Benedictine nunnery. One cannot help marveling at these devout manifestations of Christianity carried overseas to a bleak land at a time when the faith had barely penetrated beyond the Oder and the Vistula.

Greenland, though outside Europe, is archaeologically perhaps of greater relevance to the Old World than to the New. Yet, only a narrow and pedantic concept of American territorial confines can afford to overlook its antiquities—be they Eskimo or Viking. Like Easter Island, but physically much closer, it is tied to the Western Hemisphere for geographic, if not ethnic, reasons. Those two islands, far outposts though they are in the South Pacific and the North Atlantic, point to the center of one of the persistent problems of New World pre-history: transoceanic contacts. It so happens that they also involve two of the greatest seafaring races of the pre-Columbian world, the Norsemen and the Polynesian "Vikings of the Sunrise."

THE BISHOP'S SEE OF ANCIENT GREENLAND

Poul Nørlund

In the western European countries, which suffered from the Viking invasions of long ago, people are often amused and occasionally perhaps amazed at the unblushing pride which we Scandinavians take in our wild and savage forefathers. For truth to tell, the majority of them, whenever they appeared, brought trouble or even disaster to peaceful folks. But a few figures stand out from the bloody horde, not because of a greater chivalry or humanity, but because, in addition to the romantic ferocity of their history, there was also about them a certain cultural air of a particularly magnificent kind.

Such a figure, standing head and shoulders above the rest, was Eric the Red, the discoverer and colonizer of Greenland. Of his grim character we have more than sufficient evidence. For manslaughter in his youth he left Norway with his father and set out for Iceland. For a second homicide he was sentenced in Iceland to banishment from his adopted country. As an outcast he set out once more upon a voyage of discovery across the dangerous western ocean, and found here—hidden behind the drifting polar ice-belt—the smiling Greenland fjords, which offered to frugal peasants conditions equally as good as those in many parts of Iceland or northern Norway. He was not one of those discoverers who were satisfied by merely seeing a country once, and then leaving for ever what they had found. He brought settlers from Iceland and established in Greenland quite a little "kingdom" of his own, which continued for nearly five hundred years (approximately A.D. 1000–1500) as a distant outpost of European civilization, first as an independent republic, and later as a feudal state under Norway.

"The Bishop's See of Ancient Greenland," *Discovery*, IX (1928), pp. 305–9. Reprinted by courtesy of *Science Journal* (now incorporating *Discovery*).

About the time when the southern Europeans discovered America, however, these Norsemen lost touch with Europe, and after the lapse of some time they must have perished. The population died out, the houses collapsed, and grass and willow undergrowth covered the ruins. Eskimo tribes settled on the points and promontories, but inside the fjords, where the Norsemen lived, everything became silent and still. For centuries all human life stagnated, and a wanderer visiting these parts might well walk for days without finding any signs of life, other than a frightened, nervously cackling grouse or an eagle circling in unfathomable silence over his head.

Ruins of a Norse church in Greenland

The remains of Norse habitations are still to be discovered almost everywhere in these parts. It sometimes happens that traces of a path are found, leading straight up to the ruins of a stone house. This path was made by the peasants walking for centuries along it upon their daily journeys to and from the well, the pond, or the landing stage, and even the ages that have elapsed since then have not succeeded in effacing it entirely. The grass upon it is shorter and thicker and of another colour. The ruins are well hidden by the undergrowth, and they are easily missed upon a first search; the surest signpost is usually found in the fresh green of a former midden, gleaming brightly from the brown grey moors.

In fact, in the firths of southern Greenland, where all human activity now has been dead for centuries, there is hardly a spot which the old-time peasants did not try to turn to account. Every valley had its farm, every hill slope its sheep fold. Even the smallest rocky islet, and tracts of land stretching right in under the fringe of the inland ice were utilized. The country was really "fully inhabited," as they put it in the old reports. Thus there is an example of the culture of the Middle Ages hidden away here in South Greenland, more undisturbed than would be possible to find almost anywhere else in Europe, an exceptionally fascinating field of research for archaeologists. . . .

It might perhaps be assumed that necessarily a poor and primitive form of culture must be found in these distant places, with hardly anything of interest to the general cultural history of Europe. But this assumption has proved somewhat erroneous. During our expedition to Herjolfsness in 1921 we had found a large number of dresses of the Middle Ages, which might possibly be called poor, in that they were woven of simple wool, as well as the Greenland women were able to weave them, but which in their cut and style are faithful copies of the European fashions of that time. The hoods (chaperons) with the long tail hanging from the back of the head, or the long ample skirts, which with but little difference were used by both sexes, are almost the only everyday dresses of the European Middle Ages now extant, and if only for this reason, therefore, are naturally of considerable interest.

Our finds at Herjolfsness gave us some insight into the tragic end of these Norsemen, for anthropologists have been able to read from the skeletons found that they were those of a population greatly degenerated by intermarriage and malnutrition. There is something very touching about the fate that met these brave and long suffering colonists, who, after being left entirely by themselves, slowly perished, either of actual hunger or by the arrows of the Eskimo natives. But in spite of their tragic end, it is important to recall the prosperous times which these colonies also enjoyed; and to throw some light on this period, we turned our attentions during our latest expedition to the old see of the Greenland bishops at Gardar (now Igaliko). . . .

Our first impression, on arriving there, was one of great disappointment. Where were the many ruins, which we had heard about from former visitors? We saw now only huts of the usual type used by modern Greenlanders. Alas! we soon found the explanation; the beautiful, regular stones of which the huts were built, had all been taken from the old ruins. For 150 years the inhabitants have been pilfering stone from the Norsemen's houses, and now every part of the low walls standing above ground level has disappeared. Some of the Eskimo huts certainly looked a little peculiar. There were, for example, a couple of outhouses for winter fodder for the domestic animals, of which the roof consisted of a single enormous block of stone, some five tons in weight. Now this is not the sort of work that the modern Greenlander would care to tackle, as everyone knows who has had anything to do with him. It was then discovered that these outhouses originally had formed the entrance portals of Norse dwelling houses. The roof was simply the top stone of the portal, and the Greenlanders had merely added a wall at either end of the passage to make what, to their ideas, was an easily made and roomy tool-and-provision shed. A better example of the difference between now and then—between the natives of small stature and the virile brawny fellows who lived there in the Middle Ages—could hardly be found than that of an old porch which originally connected two rooms in a cowshed now forming a whole house for the modern Eskimo.

During the summer we excavated a large number of ruins, as fortunately the natives had been unable to remove the foundation stones. It was a surprisingly comprehensive and ambitious lay-out when we remember how far away from civilization it all was. The cathedral, the first building to be cleared, must not, of course, be compared with those in Europe or even in Scandinavia, for in comparison it dwindles into a mere country church. After all, it is possible in that way to make almost anything appear small. The one thing to do is to find the right measure, and here we find one ready to hand. Iceland was the mother country of the Greenland colonists, and thus in the Saga island we find the best measure with which to appraise properly what we find in Greenland. It is seen, surprising as it may be, that the old Greenland parish churches, or "peasant" churches, which have been excavated during the last generation, are considerably *larger* than their Icelandic equivalents. And, from what we know, the bishops' churches in Iceland during the Middle Ages seem to have been in no way larger or better than that in Greenland, although the two Icelandic bishops were the spiritual heads of over 330 churches.

So it was with the bishop's "palace"—the actual dwelling used by the bishop and his retainers. We found it, after careful search, hidden away in the Greenlanders' turnip field, where the former walls served as the foundation of the stone walls now dividing one small allotment from the next. Each single room thus forms a separate little field all to itself. Of these rooms I will mention only the reception hall, where great festivals were held on such occasions as the gathering for the annual parliamentary meetings, which took place upon the Gardar plain, and for the important church celebrations, especially that of Christmas. Christmas even from heathen times was celebrated as a solstitial festival, for in mid-winter the sun rises above the mountains for a couple of hours only, and the festival marked the date from which the days were about to lengthen again.

The bishop's reception hall measured 16.7 by 7.8 metres, or about 130 square metres. This is quite a respectable room even to our ideas. . . .

Of the extent of the farming upon the bishop's land we may also draw

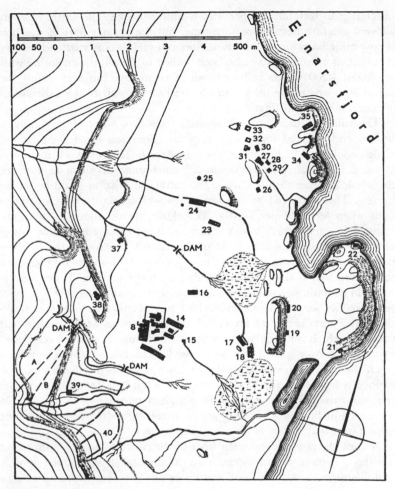

Map of the bishop's see of Gardar, Eastern Settlement, Greenland. The bishop's residence (8) is adjoined by the cathedral to the north.

our own conclusions from the ruins, and we are bound to admit that it must have been considerable. Besides a number of small sheds for sheep and goats, horses and pigs, there were two cowsheds, the largest being 75 metres long, and the two together being large enough to house several hundred cows! We must assume that these sheds were not built bigger than circumstances required; but it is certainly puzzling to discover whence was procured the winter fodder to feed all these animals. There was certainly an enclosed home field (tun) of about forty acres, which in relation to Icelandic proportions is no mean size. The cattle were not allowed to graze here in summer time, but the greater part of this field is now quite barren and the whole does not yield many cartloads of hay. A couple of meadows have also been walled in. In all, the enclosing walls are about 1,200 metres in length, all of them low, but very strong, being at least one metre thick and obviously the result of the expenditure of much labour and time.

The ruins on the Gardar Plain tell their own story plainly enough, broken and uncared for though they be. They tell us of a strong and virile people, full of life and energy and ready for any work that came to hand. The bishop's farmhands did not lounge about at a loose end the whole summer through, while the cattle out grazing could be tended by few. This is proved by the numerous walrus' skulls, which came to light wherever we began to dig. The skulls are reminders of the great summer journeys which took the hunters often hundreds of miles away, northwards along the west coast of Greenland, or around the southern point to the dangerous ice-bound east coast, seeking for the big sea creatures from which they procured valuable trade articles. These were so much in demand in Europe that European merchants were even tempted to make the journey to Greenland to buy them. Soft furs and heavy skins were obtained, and above all the white tusks of the walrus and narwhale which were sold all over northern Europe as ivory. Even Peter's Pence to the Pope were then paid by the Greenlanders in walrus tusk. . . .

Of the bishops themselves little is known beyond their names, and occasionally from historical records the dates when they came out and when they returned home. It was therefore a great satisfaction to us when we succeeded in finding a bishop's grave in the cathedral. It was the most important event of the summer's research work.

Among the pebbles under the floor of the North Chapel we discovered one day a little piece of bone with an ornamental design carved upon it, and it aroused a definite hope among us all. For over two days excavations were carried on extremely slowly and carefully; it was important that nothing should be destroyed or damaged. From hour to hour the carved piece gradually emerged, until it began at length to take a curved shape. We knew then that it really was the spiral curve of a bishop's staff which we had found, carved in walrus tusk, the most valuable material in the country. When the surrounding debris was finally removed and the crook lay there in all its gleaming dark-brown beauty, with its characteristic carvings, we could not but feel a certain reverent awe. For the first time a work of art had been brought to light from the old Norse ruins in Greenland.

The further uncovering of the fragile skeleton to which the staff had belonged was hardly less difficult. The exciting question was whether the bishop's ring was also preserved. Sure enough, it encircled still the ring finger of his right hand, where it had been placed by the Norwegian archbishop at his solemn consecration at Trondhjem Cathedral. Both the gold ring and the carvings on the staff indicate the time as about 1200, but just at the beginning of the thirteenth century several bishops followed one another quickly in succession, so it would be difficult to say with any degree of certainty who it was that lay buried here. He must remain anonymous as "the Bishop of Greenland 700 years ago," and so will we reverence his memory. Far too many of his clerical brethren left for home again after only a short time in office, or did not even venture to come out at all! Conditions were naturally not exactly inviting for a spoilt prelate, but here was one of them who had remained with his congregation.

The Gardar bishop's staff, of carved walrus ivory

The bishopric and the trade interests were the only two links which bound Greenland to European civilization. Thus was forged a fine chain which reached right down to Rome. The bishops travelled all the way down there after their appointment, and so even the Pope himself received some knowledge of the conditions existing in this his most distant diocese. It was, however, a limited understanding which was acquired, for example, in 1270 the northern countries received a flat refusal to their application to be allowed to use a substitute for grape wine and wheat flour for altar wine and oblations. At the Papal Court they appeared unable to grasp the fact that both Iceland and Greenland lay so far away that sheer necessity made them tolerate substitutes if the Sacrament was to be given at all.

In 1377 the last bishop who resided in Greenland died. For yet another 150 years the Popes continued to appoint new bishops of Gardar, but they were only titular bishops, who never visited Greenland nor attempted to do so. It was one of the great faults of the Catholic Church at that time, that such abuses could take place. But the evident reluctance of the bishops is one of the first evidences of the critical condition of the Norsemen in Greenland; just as their presence out there had been the strongest expression of the importance of the settlement. . . .

Index